HISTORY OF ILLINOIS,

FROM

1778 TO 1833;

AND

LIFE AND TIMES

OF

NINIAN EDWARDS.

BY HIS SON,

NINIAN W. EDWARDS.

SPRINGFIELD:

PUBLISHED BY THE ILLINOIS STATE JOURNAL COMPANY.

1870.

PREFACE.

When I commenced this work, it was to comply with the request of the Chicago Historical Society to prepare, for publication, a memoir of the late Governor NINIAN EDWARDS. To this request was added a desire of my brothers to have a copy of his speeches, messages, and his extensive correspondence with many of the most eminent men of the country. Whilst I had no doubt that it would add much to the interest of the work, as simply a memoir of Governor Edwards, to make him the corresponding center, around which all the important historical facts may be grouped, yet, as such a course would have been very difficult and embarrassing to me, I have concluded to make it more comprehensive by including, also, a history of the County, Territory and State of Illinois, from the year 1778 to the time of his death, in 1833. Satisfied that such a work would be of great interest, and of the highest importance for the historical facts it would contain, and that the character of the materials I had collected, with the numerous papers in my possession, were accurate and of great value, I submitted my manuscript to the Chicago Historical Society, for their examination and approval, and expressed the desire that some one more competent should take my materials and rewrite the work. It was referred to a committee consisting of the Hon. M. Skinner and Hon. I. N. Arnold, with the Secretary, and in their report (which explains the character and object of the work) the following resolutions were, at a regular meeting of the Society, unanimously adopted:

"WHEREAS Ninian W. Edwards, Esq., has submitted to this Society, for their examination and approval, a manuscript memoir, entitled 'A Memoir of the Life and Times of the Hon. Ninian Edwards, first Governor of the Illinois Territory,' and the same has been examined with attention and care by a committee duly appointed for that purpose;

"*Resolved*, That this Society express their cordial and high estimation of the laborious, faithful and judicious manner in which Mr. Edwards has executed the work now submitted, and that, in their opinion—in the importance of the particular subjects treated by him, the full and authentic character of the materials collected by him for their illustration, with the numerous and extended details recovered by him and now first brought to the public attention—the work, viewed as a *History of Illinois*, may be regarded as in several respects the most important contribution yet made to the history of this State.

"*Resolved*, That the collected correspondence of the late Gov. Edwards, accompanying the above named memoir—including numerous letters from William Wirt, John C. Calhoun, J. McLean, and other statesmen of eminent standing in the United States, hitherto unpublished—possess a high national interest, as connected with important events and movements in the history of our Federal Government, and are well worthy of publication, while adding in a material degree to the public estimation of Mr. Edwards' work.

"*Resolved*, That the Society's thanks are due and be returned to Mr. Edwards, for the patriotic zeal and filial devotion with which he has engaged in this just tribute of honorable commemoration to the late Gov. Edwards, who, from his long-continued public service of the State of Illinois—both in the councils of the State and the Nation—merits an honored place in the esteem and gratitude of the people of this State."

In communicating the above to me, the Secretary says he "has the pleasure to state, that at the meeting at which the above was adopted, the warmest interest was expressed by gentlemen in the progress and desired success of the work—for whose satisfactory completion and successful issue the most cordial wishes were indulged;" and adds, "I may be allowed to state my individual impression of the very great value of the epitome of our early legislation, which will have a high degree of interest to strangers and be a desirable acquisition to our own citizens. Even as regards the sketch of the early history of the Territory, from the time of its organization by Virginia as a county, it appears to me a natural introduction to the main work, viewed, as you regard it, in the light of a historical sketch of the Territory and State, rather than a personal memoir."

Another motive I have in its publication is, to correct the misrepresentation of Gov. Edwards' real sentiments on the subjects of slavery, the public lands, and other important measures.

NINIAN W. EDWARDS.

SPRINGFIELD, ILLINOIS, 1870.

PRELIMINARY CHAPTER.

Organization of Illinois as a County of Virginia—Letter of Instructions from Governor Patrick Henry to John Todd—Cession to the General Government—Action of Congress—Ordinance of 1787: *its general provisions.*

The territory of Illinois was organized into a county, by the Legislature of Virginia, on the 12th of December, 1778, and John Todd was appointed Lieutenant-Commandant thereof, by Patrick Henry, then Governor of the State of Virginia. The following is a literal copy of the letter of appointment and instructions to John Todd from Governor Henry:

WILLIAMSBURGH, *Dec.* 12, 1778.

To MR. JOHN TODD, ESQ.

By virtue of the act of General Assembly which establishes the county of Illinois, you are appointed County Lieutenant-Commandant there, and for the general tenor of your conduct I refer you to the law.

The grand objects which are disclosed to your countrymen will prove beneficial, or otherwise, according to the nature and abilities of those who are called to direct the affairs of that remote country. The present crisis, rendered so favourable by the good disposition of the French and Indians, may be improved to great purposes; but if, unhappily, it should be lost, a return of the same attachment to us may never happen. Considering, therefore, that costly prejudices are so hard to wear out, you will take care to cultivate and conciliate the affections of the French and Indians.

Although great reliance is placed on your prudence in managing the people you are to reside among, yet, considering you as unacquainted in some degree with their genius, usages and manners, as well as the geography of the country, I recommend it to you to advise with the most intelligent and upright persons who may fall in your way, and to give particular attention to Col. Clark and his corps, to whom the State has great obligations. You are to coöperate with him on any military undertaking, when necessary, and to give the military every aid which the circumstances of the people will admit of. The inhabitants of Illinois must not expect settled peace and safety while their and our enemies have footing at Detroit and can intercept or stop the trade of the Mississippi. If the English have not the strength or courage to come to war against us themselves, their practice has been and will be to have the savages commit murder and depredations. Illinois must expect to pay these a large price for her freedom, unless the English can be expelled from Detroit. The means for effecting this will not perhaps be in your or Col. Clark's power, but the French inhabiting the neighbourhood of that place, it is presumed, may be brought to see it done with indifference, or perhaps join in the enterprise with pleasure. This is but conjecture.

When you are on the spot, you and Col. Clark may discover the fallacy or reality of the former appearances. Defense, only, is to be the object of the latter, or a good prospect of it. I hope the French and Indians at your disposal will show a zeal for the affairs equal to the benefit to be derived from establishing liberty and permanent peace.

One great good expected from holding the Illinois is to overaw the Indians from warring on the settlers on this side of the Ohio. A close attention to the disposition, character and movement of the hostile tribes is therefore necessary. The French and militia of Illinois, by being placed on the back of them, may inflict timely chastisement on those enemies whose towns are an easy prey in absence of their warriors. You perceive, by these hints, that something in the military line will be expected from you. So far as the occasion calls for the assistance of the people composing the militia, it will be necessary to coöperate with the troops sent from here, and I know of no better general directions to give than this: that you consider yourself as the head of the civil department, and as such having command of the military until ordered out by the civil authority, and to act in conjunction with them.

You are, on all occasions, to inculcate on the people the value of liberty, and the difference between the state of free citizens of this Commonwealth and that slavery to which the Illinois was destined. A free and equal representation may be expected by them in a little time, together with all the improvement in jurisprudence and police which the other parts of the State enjoy.

It is necessary, for the happiness, increase and prosperity of that country, that the grievances that obstruct those blessings be known, in order to their removal. Let it therefore be your care to obtain information on that subject, that proper plans may be formed for the general utility. Let it be your constant attention to see that the inhabitants have justice administered to them for any injury received from the troops. The omission of this may be fatal. Col. Clark has instructions on this head, and will, I doubt not, exert himself to quell all licentious practice of the soldiers, which, if unrestrained, will produce the most baneful effect. You will also discountenance and punish every attempt to violate the property of the Indians, particularly on their land. Our enemies have alarmed them much on that score, but I hope from your prudence and justice that there will be no grounds of complaint on that subject. You will embrace every opportunity to manifest the high regard and friendly sentiments of this Commonwealth towards all the subjects of his Catholic Majesty, for whose safety, prosperity and advantage you will give every possible advantage. You will make a tender of the friendship and services of your people to the Spanish Commandant near Kaskaskia, and cultivate the strictest connection with him and his people. The detail of your duty in the civil department I need not give; its best direction will be found in your innate love of justice, and zeal to be useful to your fellow-men. Act according to the best of your judgment in cases where these instructions are silent and the laws have not otherwise directed. Discretion is given to you from the necessity of the case, for your great distance from Government will not permit you to wait for orders in many cases of great importance. In your negotiations with the Indians confine the stipulation, as much as possible, to the single object of obtaining peace from them. Touch not the subject of lands or boundaries till particular orders are received. When necessity requires it presents may be made, but be as frugal in that matter as possible, and let them know that goods at present is scarce with us, but we expect soon to trade freely with all the world, and they shall not want when we can get them.

The matters given you in charge being singular in their nature and weighty in their consequences to the people immediately concerned, and to the whole State, they require the fullest exertion of your ability and unwearied diligence.

From matters of general concern you must turn, occasionally, to others of less consequence. Mr. Roseblove's wife and family must not suffer for want of that property of which they were bereft by our troops. It is to be restored to them, if possible; if this can not be done, the public must support them.

I think it proper for you to send me an express once in the month, with a general account of affairs with you and any particulars you wish to communicate.

It is in contemplation to appoint an agent to manage trade on public accounts, to supply Illinois and the Indians with goods. If such an appointment takes place, you will give it any possible aid. The people with you should not intermit their endeavors to procure supplies on the expectation of this, and you may act accordingly.

(Signed) P. HENRY.

Illinois continued to form a part of the State of Virginia until the year 1784, when the country, being a part of the Northwestern Territory, was ceded by the State of Virginia to the United States. Immediately on the execution of the deed of cession the General Government proceeded to establish a form of government for the settlers in the territories thus ceded. The whole subject was referred to a committee, of which Mr. Jefferson was chairman. The report of the committee, after being somewhat modified, was finally adopted by the passage of resolutions and ordinances for the government of the territories that had been or might be ceded to the United States, for the establishment of both temporary and permanent governments by the settlers, and for the admission of the new states thus formed into the Union. It was provided, among other things, that the settlers, either on their own petition or by act of Congress, should receive authority to create a temporary form of government, and that when there should be twenty thousand free inhabitants within the limits of any territory, they should have authority to call a convention to establish a permanent constitution and government for themselves, without any other limitation except the following:

1st. That they should forever remain a part of the confederacy of the United States of America.

2d. That they should be subject to the articles of confederation and the acts and ordinances of Congress like the original States.

3d. That they should not interfere with the disposal of the soil by Congress.

4th. That they should be subject to pay their proportion of the Federal debt, present and prospective.

5th. That they should impose no tax upon lands the property of the United States.

6th. That their respective governments should be republican.

7th. That the lands of non-residents should not be taxed higher than those of residents.

8th. That any State, having adopted a constitution and having as many free inhabitants as the least numerous of the thirteen original States, might be admitted into the Union on an equal footing with the original States.

The report of the committee contained the following clause: "That after the year 1800, of the Christian era, there shall be neither slavery nor involuntary servitude in any of the said States, otherwise than in the punishment of crimes, whereof the party shall have been duly convicted to have been personally guilty." But, on a motion by Mr. Spaight of North Carolina, which was seconded by Mr. Read of South Carolina, it was decided that the above clause should not stand as a part of the report of the committee, and it was struck out because it failed to receive the support of a majority of all the States. The following States voted for retaining the clause: New Hampshire, Massachusetts, Rhode Island, Connecticut, New York, New Jersey and Pennsylvania. Maryland, Virginia and South Carolina voted to strike it out; North Carolina was divided; one State lost its vote by having only one delegate present; Delaware and Georgia were not represented. Mr. Jefferson voted in favor of the clause, and his two colleagues voted against it.

This proviso was renewed by Rufus King, in 1785, as a condition upon which the State of Massachusetts would cede her territory. It was referred to a committee by a vote of eight States, but it does not appear that the committee reported it back, and Massachusetts ceded her territory without such condition.

The government of this country, as thus established, continued until the passage of the ordinance of 1787, for the government of the Northwestern Territory, of which Illinois formed a part. After the division of the Northwest Territory, Illinois became one of the counties of the Territory of Indiana, from which it was separated by an act of Congress in the year 1809. At the time of its separation from the Territory of Indiana, it was divided into two counties—the counties of St. Clair and Randolph.

That the resolutions of 1784 were considered in force and gave authority to the people to organize a government under them, is evident from the fact that they were recognized by the ordinance of 1787 in the following words: "Be it ordained by the authority aforesaid, that the resolutions of the 23d of April, one thousand seven hundred and eighty-four, relative to the subject of this ordinance, be and the same is hereby repealed and declared null and void."

Under the ordinance of 1787 the Governor and Judges, or a majority of them, had power to adopt and publish in the district such laws of the original States as were necessary, and best suited to the circumstances of the

Territory, subject to be disapproved by Congress; but when the General Assembly was organized, the Legislature had authority to alter them as they should think fit. The Governor had the power to appoint and commission all the militia officers below the rank of General officers, and, previous to the organization of the General Assembly, the Governor had the appointment of such magistrates and other civil officers, in each county and township, as he might think necessary for the preservation of the peace and good order in the same. After the organization of the General Assembly, the powers and duties of the magistrates and other civil officers were to be regulated and defined by the Assembly; but all magistrates and other civil officers whose appointments were not provided for by Congress, were to be appointed by the Governor even after the organization of the General Assembly. The Governor had also the power to lay out parts of the Territory, in which the Indian title was extinguished, into townships and counties.

Another article of the ordinance provided that so soon as there should be five thousand free male inhabitants of full age, upon giving proof thereof to the Governor they should have authority to elect representatives to the General Assembly.

To be eligible as representative, the ordinance required that a person should have been a citizen of the United States for three years and a resident of the district, or a resident of the district for three years; and, in either case, that he should hold in his right, in fee simple, two hundred acres of land within his district.

To qualify a person to vote, it was necessary for him to hold fifty acres of land in the district and to have been a citizen of one of the States and a resident in the district, or the like freehold and two years residence in the district.

The General Assembly consisted of a Council, House of Representatives and the Governor, but no law could be passed without the approval of the Governor. The right to elect a delegate in Congress devolved on the Council and House of Representatives, in joint session.

The above are some of the leading provisions of the ordinance of 1787.

On the 2d of May, 1812, Congress passed a law authorizing the admission of the Territory into the second grade of territorial government. This act extended the right of suffrage so as to authorize any free white male person of twenty-one years of age, and who shall have paid a territorial or county tax previous to any general election, and be at the time of the election a resident of the district, and who shall have resided one year in the Territory previous to the election, to vote for representatives and members of the Council and a delegate in Congress.

So much of the ordinance of 1787 as had required that there should be five thousand free white male inhabitants in the Territory, had also been repealed.

I find the draft of the memorial to Congress, praying for the admission of the Territory into the second grade, and the extension of the right of suffrage, among the papers of Gov. Edwards, and in his hand-writing.

By an examination of the ordinance of 1787 it appears, from the following provision, that under the second grade of government the Legislature had unlimited power of legislation, unless restrained in the exercise thereof by the articles in the ordinance: "The Governor and Judges, or a majority of them, shall adopt and publish in the district such laws of the original States, criminal and civil, as may be necessary, and best suited to the circumstances of the district, and report them to Congress from time to time; which laws shall be in force in the district until the organization of the General Assembly therein, unless disapproved by Congress; *but afterwards the Legislature shall have authority to alter them as they shall think fit.*" From this provision it appears that only the laws which might be adopted by the Governor and Judges were subject to the disapprobation of Congress; that such laws were required to be reported to Congress not, as has generally been supposed, for their approbation, but they were to be in force until they were "disapproved" by Congress. 2d. That after the organization of the General Assembly, the Legislature should "have authority to alter the laws as they shall think fit," without being required to report them to Congress.

On the 8th of May, 1792, Congress passed another law "respecting the government of the territories of the United States, northwest and south of the River Ohio."

The first section of this law provided that the laws of the territory northwest of the Ohio, that had been or hereafter may be enacted by the Governor and Judges, shall be printed, under the direction of the Secretary of State, and that two hundred copies thereof, together with ten sets of the laws of the United States, shall be distributed among the inhabitants for their information; and that a like number of the laws of the United States shall be delivered to the Governor and Judges of the territory southwest of the Ohio River.

Section two authorized the Governor and Judges of the territory northwest of the River Ohio to repeal the "laws by them made whenever the same may be found improper."

Section three provides that the official duties of the secretaries of the said territories shall be under the control of the laws of the territories.

Section four authorized any one of the supreme or superior judges, in the absence of the other judges, to hold court.

Section five directed the Secretary of State to provide seals for the public officers in the said territories.

On the 17th of August, 1789, a law was also passed by Congress, in order to adapt the provisions of the ordinance of 1787 to the constitution of the United States. By this act the secretary of the territories, in case of the death, removal, resignation or necessary absence of the Governor, was required to execute all the powers and perform all the duties of the Governor during the vacancy occasioned by the removal, resignation or necessary absence of the Governor.

The sixth article of the ordinance provided that there shall be neither slavery nor involuntary servitude in the said territory, otherwise than for the punishment of crimes, whereof the party shall have been duly convicted.

Having deemed it necessary to give a history of the different forms of government under which the people of the Territory lived, I now proceed to give a sketch of the life of Ninian Edwards, who filled such a prominent place in the political history of both Territorial and State governments.

CHAPTER I.

Genealogy of Gov. Edwards—His Birth and Early Education—His Removal to Kentucky—Dissipated Habits—Election to the Legislature—Becomes a Lawyer and enters upon a Lucrative Practice—Is advanced to the Bench—Becomes Chief Justice of Kentucky—His Political Views—His Marriage—Speech as Presidential Elector in 1804—*Speech as a Candidate for Congress*, 1806—*Charge to the Grand Jury—His Relations with Mr. Clay.*

Benjamin Edwards, the father of Ninian Edwards, was the son of Hayden Edwards, of Stafford county, Virginia, who married Penelope Sandford, by whom he had four sons and several daughters. They removed to Kentucky before the close of the last century, where they lived honorable, virtuous and Christian lives, and each died at about the age of ninety years. They were raised in connection with the English branch of the Episcopal Church of Virginia, but afterwards became members of the Baptist Church.

The following obituary notice of the Hon Benjamin Edwards, their son, and father of Ninian Edwards, was written and published by the late Hon. William Wirt:

Died on the 13th November, 1826, at his residence in Elkton, Todd county, Kentucky, Benjamin Edwards, in the 74th year of his age, and the 56th of his Christian life. His venerable consort, Mrs. Martha Edwards, after a union of more than fifty years, preceded him to the grave about three months before. They both resigned this world with that perfect composure and full assurance of future happiness, which religion can inspire, and left behind them a numerous and respectable family of children and their descendants, to imitate their virtues and to deplore their loss.

Mr. Edwards was a native of Stafford county, in Virginia; and before he came of age, he intermarried with Margaret, the daughter of Ninian Beall, of Montgomery county, Maryland, and resided, for nearly twenty-five years, on his farm of Mount Pleasant, about nine miles above the court house of that county. His pursuits were those of agriculture and merchandize, which he conducted with industry and irreproachable integrity.

He had not the advantage of a classical education, but nature had given him a mind of extraordinary force and comprehension, and a moral character of uncommon elevation and energy. He was one of nature's great men; and she had stamped this character most strikingly on his countenance and person. He was large and well formed; his countenance strongly marked with intelligence and benevolence; his step and movements uncommonly dignified and commanding; and in his whole action three was an easy, unaffected gracefulness, which proclaimed the gentleman and the man of feeling, in a manner not to be mistaken. Though his manners were highly prepossessing, conciliatory and kind, yet such was the dignity that surrounded him, and the respect with which he impressed all who approached him, that no man dreampt of using an irreverent liberty, or indulging in a thoughtless levity in his presence. His colloquial powers were unrivalled in any company in which the writer of this article ever saw him. He had a manly and melodious voice, a natural fluency and eloquence that never hesitated, the most striking originality and vigor of thought, the aptest and happiest illustrations drawn from the objects of nature around him, and an accuracy and integrity of judgment, which have never been surpassed, on the objects that called for his decision. He had supplied the deficiencies of youthful education by careful reading, and had acquired a correct style, which was yet marked with the native strength and originality of his thoughts, and he conversed with great power, even on the subjects of literature, taste and science; and many have been the flippant scholars and collegians, who, after the interchange of a few remarks, have felt themselves rebuked by his superior mind, and learned to listen with instinctive reverence and delight.

He made himself an excellent historian, both in ancient and modern history; and to his children and their young companions, (of whom the writer was one,) with whom he always took pleasure in conversing, he was one of the most instructive companions whom the kindness of Providence could have sent them. Though always pious, there was nothing austere, obtrusive or revolting in his religion; and in his domestic circle he would often indulge himself with great playfulness, and with the most successful humor; yet no occasion was ever lost in instilling into them pure and honorable and lofty sentiments and principles, and kindling in them the flame of patriotic and virtuous emulation, holding up to them, with great eloquence, the example of ancient patriots, orators, and statesmen, with which he was so much enamored, as if he were still in his youth.

He rose to considerable distinction before he left Maryland, which was about thirty years ago. He represented the county of Montgomery for several years in the State Legislature; was a member of the State Convention which ratified the Federal Constitution; and, afterwards, a member of Congress for the district in which he lived. Though nature had made him an orator of high order, he was restrained, by his unconquerable diffidence, from hazarding himself often in public debate. He spoke but rarely, and then on local subjects, when forced forward by a high sense of duty; yet on one of these occasions, in the Assembly of Maryland, with so much force did he strike the House, that the late Samuel Chase, and several others of the most competent judges of eloquence in that body, crossed the floor of the House, to congratulate him, and to assure him that it rested with himself to become one of the most distinguished speakers of the age. But he was restrained, by diffidence, from profiting by this suggestion, and a man who may be justly pronounced to have been one of nature's happiest efforts, has now passed away, to be forgotten by the world. Never will he be forgotten by the grateful heart from which this humble tribute flows; nor that excellent woman, who was the fit and happy counterpart of so extraordinary a man. They were both an honor to their species, ornaments to the church to which they belonged, and are now amongst the spirits of the blessed, who surround the Throne on High.

WILLIAM WIRT.

He removed from Maryland to Kentucky in the year 1800. Ninian Edwards, of Illinois, was their eldest son. He was born in Montgomery county, Maryland, in March, 1775. His domestic training was well fitted to give his mind strength, firmness and honorable principles, and a good foundation was laid for the elevated character to which he afterwards atttained.

His education in early youth was in company and partly under the tuition of the Hon. William Wirt, whom his father patronized. Mr. Wirt was the eldest by two years and four months, but they were not merely companions in their studies, nor was the relation exactly that of tutor and pupil. They became devotedly attached to each other, and the foundation was laid for the friendship and brotherly affection that lasted during life. At the period this intimacy commenced Mr. Wirt was at the age of fifteen, and he survived Mr. Edwards six months, wanting two days.

Mr. Wirt had been instructed in the Latin and Greek classics by Rev. James Hunt, an Episcopal clergyman, who taught a select school in Montgomery county for a period, and when that school closed he was received into the family of Mr. Edwards, nominally as private tutor for his son, where he remained twenty months. This arrangement was an act of kindness and beneficence on the part of Mr. Edwards to aid Mr. Wirt in his education, without the restraint that charity imposes.

The studies of young Edwards were further prosecuted under the tuition of Rev. Mr. Hunt, at Montgomery court house, from whence he was sent to Dickinson College, at Carlisle, Pa., then under the presidency of the Rev. Charles Nesbit, D.D.

After leaving college he commenced, with several others, the study of law. It was required of the law class that they should read, for one-half of the time, history; but young Edwards having, under the instruction of his father, become a good historian, devoted the portion of time required for that study to the reading of medicine, and so thorough was his knowledge of that science, that he became, where he was known, almost as eminent in that department of science as he was in the law. Before finishing the study of law, he removed to Nelson county, in the State of Kentucky, where he had gone, under the direction of his father, to open a farm for him, and to purchase homes and locate lands for his brothers and sisters.

Nature here had lavished her gifts with wanton wildness. The character of society was then unformed. Frivolty and dissipation prevailed over the glowing feelings and volatile temper of youth; and the examples of age and experience were not such as were calculated to ward off the temptation. His father furnished him with ample means for his immediate support, and he had all the prospective advantages of a new and growing country.

Thus sent forth upon the theatre of a new world, surrounded by companions whose pleasures and pursuits were in sensual indulgencies, it is not surprising that this inexperienced youth, with natural talents above the ordinary level, and the foundation laid for a virtuous and solid education, should have given away to excesses and indiscretions, till the hopes of his friends and his own aspirations of rising to distinction in any honorable profession, had withered.

I should do injustice to the ingenuous principles of his nature, were I to pass over silently these two or three years of his early life. I have heard him allude to it with those feelings with which an individual narrates his sudden and unexpected deliverance from the most imminent peril.

Amidst the dissipation that surrounded him, and in the toils of which he seemed effectually caught, it is gratifying to remark, that he retained a nice sense of honor, and that the truths of revealed religion, in which he had been educated, had not lost their hold upon his mind.

During this period he was professedly engaged in legal studies. Such habits, then, did not prevent his election to the Legislature of Kentucky, as the Representative of Nelson county, before he had quite attained the age of twenty-one years; and so well did he discharge the duties in that station, that he was reelected in the subsequent year, by an almost unanimous vote. In 1798 he was licensed to practice law, and the following year was admitted to the courts of Tennessee.

About this time he left Nelson county for Russelville, in Logan county, broke away from his dissolute companions, commenced a reformation, and devoted himself to severe and laborious study. He had previously squandered his patrimonial inheritance, impaired his health, and dissipated the hopes of his friends and parents. But from this period he was able to resolve successfully. He soon rose so rapidly in his profession, that he was not only considered one of the most eminent lawyers of that or any other country, but, in the short space of only four years' practice, he amassed a large fortune. He evinced, at a very early period, no ordinary power, with habits of regular and unremitting industry.

He practiced extensively in the courts of Kentucky and West Tennessee, and soon displayed talents and legal knowledge of a high order. And let it be noticed that he was not drifting along the current of his profession without competitors. At that period some of the brightest talents of Kentucky and Tennessee were at the bar, fired with the ardor of youthful aspirants—and it was no easy task for a young lawyer, with such competitors as Clay, Grundy, Rowan, Bibb, Boyle, J. H. Davis and others, around him—yet among such competitors he was not excelled; and after the short space of four years' practice, he filled, in succession, the offices of Presiding Judge of the General Court, Circuit Judge, fourth Judge of the Court of Appeals, and Chief Justice of Kentucky, before he was 32 years of age.

As early as 1799, in a reply to a letter from his father, who wished to know something of his political creed, he says: "Suffice it to say, on this head, I am a warm friend to the Union, and have a sufficient confidence in the constituted authorities, that when they determine it necessary and expedient to adopt any particular measure, so far as my efforts in society can go I will endeavor to support them, and shall always be willing to rally to the standard of my country. I do approve most of the measures of the administration—still I cannot consent to be a blind adherent to them all. Yet, I shall always be an enemy to any other than a constitutional appeal, in any case. I have been one of the most active friends of government since the rupture with France. I was active because I thought the situation of my country rendered it my duty to be so, and I have the satisfaction of believing that my efforts were not lost. The political fervor has entirely subsided among us. I have entirely withdrawn myself from politics, and am directing my whole attention to the law, in which I have succeeded beyond my most sanguine expectations, and I find myself handsomely requited thereby. I have the reputation, at least, of being at the head of the bar, in the district in which I practice, and I know that the profits of my practice are greater than those of any other. I am relieving myself fast from a variety of embarrassments, in which dissipation had involved me, and am so far satisfied wlth my own conduct, that I am under no apprehension that you will ever again hear, that I am 'a young man of fine talents, but extremely dissipated.' On account of my health, I shall decline the practice of law, provided I can obtain an appointment in the judiciary, of which I have no doubt, upon the first vacancy. The salary is too low, being only £180, and nothing but indisposition could induce me to accept it." In this letter, after stating the amendments which had been made to the Constitution of Kentucky, he says: "I am not astonished that the convention has made the constitution worse instead of better; for what more could be expected of a set of men, the most of whom were ignorant of the principles of human nature, ignorant of the principles of civil society, and still more so of the science of government? It is impossible that such men can entertain just conceptions of the principles of government; neither can they devise the most eligible mode of concentrating power, for the benefit of society. As well might we expect the uneducated to develop and elucidate the most abstract principles in the science of philosophy, physic or jurisprudence, as that they could compile a constitution, originating, distributing and restraining, in the most judicious manner, the power necessary to the purposes of civil government and the complete organization of a populous community. It was attempted, in the convention, to subvert the present judiciary system, by abolishing district courts and courts of quarter sessions, and establishing, in lieu of them, circuit courts; and in the first attempt, there was a decided majority in favor of it. This, evidently, would have been flagrantly improper, for no regulation in civil society ought to be more particularly adapted to the political state of that society, than the judiciary system—and at no period ought the political state of a society to be more maturely considered than when the rules of society are forming such a system. That the present system is best adapted to the situation of our country, there is, in my opinion, no doubt. But suppose it is admitted, on all hands, that the circuit system was the best—the convention, in my opinion, had nothing to do with that or any other. The only power they ought to have exercised was, to declare that the judiciary should be forever separate, distinct, and independent of the legislative and executive departments; in what manner the judges should be elected, how long and upon what conditions they should hold their office, how removed and how vacancies should be filled; but the division of that power ought to be intrusted to the Legislature, which is the proper body to define its ramifications. That is certainly the best judicial system from which justice can be most completely dispensed at the least expense; but how a system is to be made to attain that end the combined experience of mankind has not determined. While society is in a state of progression, and has not attained its utmost perfection, it would be unwise to adopt too permanent a system, by incorporating it in our constitution, and thereby precluding ourselves from the advantages of future experience; for suppose the system the convention might adopt should prove very defective, to what a situation would we then be reduced? To the necessity of choosing one of two evils: either that of submitting to the inconveniences growing out of such a judiciary system, or the calling of a convention. This circumstance ought to have been sufficient to have convinced all thinking men that the convention had nothing to do with it, but that, (as I have before observed,) the organization of this branch of power ought to be intrusted to the Legislature, that it might be improved whenever experience and observation should point out the necessity, and might undergo different modifications, without producing any sensible inconvenience; whereas, if the convention had undertaken to modify this branch of power, no amendment could have been made, except through the medium of another convention. This would introduce too frequent changes in the constitution, for however the idea of the immutability of compacts, by which communities agree to support any system of government, may be exploded, and justly too, it is my opinion that too frequent changes in the constitution of a state is among the greatest of evils, for it unhinges government, relaxes the springs, begets incertitude in its operations, and creates a political chaos in society."

A very short time after the date of this letter, his anticipations were realized by receiving the appointment of Judge.

Having already alluded to his rapid promotion in the judicial department of government, it cannot be doubted that this promotion was the result of the able and satisfactory manner in which he had discharged the duties in that department of the government.

In 1802 he received a commission of major, from Gov. Garrard, to command a battallion of Kentucky militia, and the next year, 1803, he was appointed judge of the circuit in which he resided. The same year he made a visit to his native land and to his father's domicil. Here he formed that most interesting connection, which frequently determines a man's character and prospects in future life. The choice of his affections, the endeared companion of his future days, the mother of his children, and at the time of his death his disconsolate widow, was Miss Elvira Lane, from a respectable family in the vicinity of his father's residence, and who returned with him the same season to Kentucky.

His official duties were discharged with ability, and met the general approbation of the people. So strong a hold upon the confidence of the people had he taken, that in 1806 he was promoted to the station of fourth Judge of the Court of Appeals, and in two years after, to the responsible and dignified station of Chief Justice of the State. The Rev. J. M. Peck, speaking of him, says: "I have conversed with many persons who knew him in all these judicial stations, and have not found one to complain of remissness in duty. All concur in giving him an uncommon character for the correctness of his judicial decisions, consistency of his course, and unwearied industry. Evidently he possessed, in a high degree, the confidence of the people. Hundreds of people who knew him as a judge, have visited him for legal advice, since his residence in Illinois, which was gratuitously bestowed. They had great confidence in the extent of his legal knowledge, honesty of purpose, and correctness of judgment."

In 1804, whilst he was a judge, he was chosen as one of the electors for President and Vice-President of the United States. The following is an extract from one of his speeches during that canvass:

Fellow-Citizens:

Believing that it is expected that I shall say something to you on the subject of the approaching election, for electors, I beg leave to solicit your attention. You will soon be called upon to exercise your right of suffrage by designating the persons upon whom you wish to confide this all-important right of representing you upon one of the most important occasions that can arise under our government. The propriety and necessity of exercising the right of voting, must be obvious to every reflecting mind. By negligence and inattention to its exercise, the people lose the proper sense of its advantages and inestimable importance; and although the occasional neglect of it, abstractly considered, might produce no dangerous consequences, it begets a habit of inattention, which perfectly destroys that vigilance and strict inquiry so essential in every republican government, and may, in process of time, produce that degree of supineness from which it will be impossible to arouse you but by the dreadful storm that destroys you. These suggestions are by no means fanciful or visionary. The faithful page of history affords too many melancholy evidences of the truth of them. You now feel yourselves secure from danger; so probably did all the republics that have hitherto existed. At some period of their government they felt as secure as you now do; yet those governments, if history is to be credited, sooner or later eventuated in despotism, and from the want of proper attention to the representative principle and a frequent recurrence to its first or fundamental principles. It is true there is no analogy between our government and the ancient republics. They lacked the representative, as applied to all its branches; but it will be the same thing if we, possessing the principle of representation in so eminent a degree in our constitutions, do not preserve it in its full vigor, which can only be done by the most zealous regard and undeviating attention to our right of voting. Our glorious revolution, which, under a beneficent providence, ended in the establishment of the rights of men, and made us a free and happy people, has recognized the people as the source of all power. To the people is assigned the right of raising and putting down our rulers, not with the violence of an infuriated mob, but with the mild and equitable decision of an enlightened judgment. Ours is, I believe, the first fair and full trial of the representative system, and it has so far, at least, triumphed over prejudice and opposition. On this foundation our government rests, and while it is preserved in its full and constitutional vigor, in vain may the tempests of a corrupt world beat against it. It is a rock against which the most violent billows, rushing with the utmost impetuosity, may dash in vain, and must fall impotent at its base. Its strength and durability will only be the more conspicuous by the troubled and unstable state of all that surronnd it. These are considerations which I submit to you, my fellow citizens, to show you the propriety of every man's voting when the constitution and laws of our country require it. They are so far made on general principles, but our peculiar local situation may furnish reasons that ought to be no less operative with you.

After dwelling at length on the measures more immediately relating to the interests of the people of the West, he proceeded as follows:

Should I meet with your approbation, and that of my fellow citizens of the district, I pledge myself to you that I shall vote for Mr. Jefferson as President, and Mr. Clinton as Vice-President. The experience of almost four years has evidently demonstrated how much Mr. Jefferson is worthy of the confidence the people have reposed in him. Not a single friend has deserted his cause, while many of his former enemies have honorably acknowledged their mistake, and have been the most zealous supporters of his administration. In vain have his enemies scrutinized all his public measures, with a hope of finding some dangerous omission. In vain have they attempted to throw odium on his private life, finding his public character unexceptionable. All their efforts to wound his fair fame with the most malignant shafts of calumny, have ended in showing how much he is beloved by his grateful countrymen. His intelligence, virtue and patriotism have irradiated and purified the public councils, dispelled the mist of delusion, and restored liberty to her full vigor and pristine benignity. In vain then may his enemies employ every method in their power to destroy the confidence of the people in his administration.

He succeeded in this election, and had the honor of casting the vote of his district for Mr. Jefferson.

In 1806 he was a candidate for Congress, against the celebrated Matthew Lyon, but, on being promoted to the Court of Appeals, he declined before the election.

That the reader may understand and properly appreciate the character of the man who was selected by Mr. Madison to be the Governor of Illinois, I give extracts from a speech in this contest with Matthew Lyon:

Let us, by all means and at all times, endeavor to preserve, in the utmost purity, the advantages which we enjoy over other republics, and to transmit liberty unimpaired, as the best legacy to a grateful posterity, in the same manner, if not more perfect, than we have received it from our glorious ancestors. That we may enjoy the advantages and security I have mentioned as being peculiar to our form of government, will be fruitless, unless we use the means of preserving them. This advantage evidently consists in the perfection of the principle of free representation. It is from the people, then, that representation immediately flows by the mode of election. While, then, the people are in the habit of cultivating public virtue, of preserving the purity of elections, we need not fear corruption in the government. The power and virtue of the people can only be exercised in elections, as far as relates to government. Elections, therefore, must be considered as the test of public virtue; it is the vital principle of free government; it is the corner-stone of the mighty fabric we have reared. If, then, the public sentiment should not be correctly exercised—if the respective merits and demerits of the candidates who solicit your favor are not duly considered, without regard to anything but the public good—if elections become corrupted—the source is polluted; the different branches of government must partake of that pollution; the whole will become contaminated and liberty will be jeopardized.

That you should only be guided by the merits of the candidates who solicit your favor must be obvious to every thinking and dispassionate mind. It will be the duty of your representative to protect you in the enjoyment of private property and personal security, liberty and public tranquillity. Who does not consider these as momentous questions? Is there a man among you who, if he were going to law for the paltry sum of one hundred dollars, would not select an attorney to manage his business whom he considered the most capable of serving him, provided he could confide in his integrity? And if this is the case where only a little property is involved, how much more should it be the case where your absolute and relative rights as citizens, and your liberty—Heaven's best gifts—are concerned? It is not the question whether you like this or that man better; but it is upon whom it is your interest to confide your trust. The people in every district, in making their selection of a person to serve them, should be as cautious as if he was the only man upon whom their interest and welfare depended; for it surely can not be considered safe to be inattentive in this respect, upon a supposition that if your representative is not calculated to advance and secure your interest and protect your rights against all invasion, from what quarter soever they may proceed, that still there may be some one from some other quarter who can and will do it. If this disposition should be manifested by you, the same principles that have operated on you may operate on a majority of the different districts throughout the United States, and this inattention might become universal. Should this be the case, this problematical character may not then be found, but some one might probably be found of ingenuity, strategem and address sufficient to successfully assail your best and dearest rights. At all events it is best to be on the safest side.

Again, he said:

That the success of our government depends upon the purity of election, is self-evident. Our greatest patriots, our best and wisest men, have proved incontestably that such is their belief. * * * If, therefore, you do not discountenance those who are disposed to practice this corruption (treating at elections)—if you do not withhold from such men your confidence, and teach them that it is their interest to act otherwise in order to gain your approbation—instead of inspiring the minds of your fellow-citizens with a laudable and patriotic ambition to serve their country and excel in virtue, you cherish their vices by rewarding them; you establish a school of vice and depravity in our country tending to contaminate not only the present but succeeding generations; you foster in your bosoms the deadly adder which sooner or later will sting you to death. The deadly poison will insinuate itself in the heart of society, and from thence diffuse itself throughout all parts of it. Let it be conceded that you are willing to see the practice of "treating" for an election once introduced among us, and what will be the consequence? The precedent, once established, will become less and less objectionable by becoming more familiar to you; it will finally become fashionable, and ultimately necessary to success. I ask you, then, where is your boasted equality? Where is the fair and open field in which talents and merit may successfully exert themselves and receive their just reward? It will vanish forever, or only remain like a dream upon the mind. All distinctions will then be confined to the rich, for they alone will be able to meet the expenses of an election. A man in moderate circumstances, be his talents ever so great, will not be able to contend with his more wealthy competitor, and we shall find ourself completely under the dominion of an aristocracy, while we are only amused with the name of a free government. He who has paid the least attention to the current of events, or histories of other countries, may be satisfied that unless this most formidable enemy to freedom, corruption, is successfully repelled by the virtue and wisdom of the people, in his first attempt to invade us, he will rise in his strength, like a mighty torrent, and tear down everything before him. * * * For the sake of guarding against the evils that have befallen them—for the sake of public virtue—the people should discourage this practice in any shape in which it can make its appearance. * * * The candidate who practices this corruption would not do so unless he thinks that it would benefit his election. How, then, is it to promote his election, unless he supposes that more people will vote for him in consequence of his whisky than would otherwise do so. Does he not, then, attempt to buy their votes? Certainly; for he buys the whisky, and this he gives for the purpose of getting votes, and all he receives in consequence of it are as much bought as if, instead of the whisky, he has paid the value of it in money. Whether he succeeds or not, it must be evident to all thinking men that this is his object. * * Would he give it unless he thought it would gain him votes? and is there anything that ought to fill the minds of enlightened and independent freemen with more indignation than the supposition that their minds were to be influenced in this way? Can a man insult them more than to show that he conceives them so mean and mercenary; and can you suppose that a man is not influenced by other motives than the public good, when he endeavors to succeed in his election by purchasing it—in other words, by bribery and corruption?

This is the only view which I am capable of taking of the subject, and I hope my observations will be received as a sufficient apology for my not falling into this too common practice. I cannot but feel too great respect for my fellow-citizens to show that I conceived them capable of being either directly or indirectly corrupted; and if I did conceive them so, I cannot reconcile it to my conscience either to practice it upon any one or violate the spirit of that constitution which I am sworn to support. I love national liberty; I esteem the practice of which I am speaking as the most formidable engine of attacking it; and if we ever do lose our liberties, I will venture to predict that it will only be effected by destroying the purity of election. No man is fonder of the approbation of his fellow-citizens than I am. My disposition and habits have always led me to cultivate their friendship. I esteem it a most distinguished honor and a most valuable and desirable acquisition. I am anxious to attain the honor of serving my country; I have endeavored to qualify myself for it. But I am not disposed to attain this honor, by any other than the most honorable means. I can never sacrifice my integrity, my ideas of propriety or my independence to procure it. I do most sincerely wish your approbation, but I only wish it upon proper principles. The best criterion for judging the character of a man is by his acts.

Governor Edwards, from the time he was nineteen years of age until he was twenty-one or twenty-two, led a dissolute life; he indulged in dissipation and gambling to an extent which alarmed his friends. He therefore knew well the effects and consequences to individuals and society from the practice of such habits, which were so prevalent in a new country. Having, therefore, determined to reform himself, he was equally zealous, on all proper occasions, in exerting himself to promote good morals and public virtue. With a view of showing the opinion of our early legislators on the subject of gambling, profane swearing and Sabbath-breaking, as well as to show his efforts to check those habits and practices having a tendency destructive to the mind and morals of the people as well as the government, and also to show his high regard for religion and its importance in a national point of view, I give his opinions, as expressed in his charge to the grand jury in Kentucky, in 1803, as follows:

I consider vagrants and gamblers as objects particularly meriting your notice and reprehension. Such persons, in general, having no estates of their own, and who are too indolent to use means to get a support, you may rely upon it are ready to employ all manner of unjust, nefarious and unlawful means of acquiring money, and the necessity of subsisting in some way disposes them for committing all kinds of misdemeanors, from which must spring a school of vice in the bosom of your country which will not fail to spread its infection and corrupt the manners of your fellow-citizens. These are consequences of a general nature, in which the public are interested, but it would be a very easy matter for you to extend your views to the immediate pictures of distress—to those who feel the effects of the conduct of such men as I have mentioned—I mean to their wives and children, reduced to penury, and struggling, naked and comfortless, with their adverse fortunes, in a world not much disposed to ameliorate their cruel destiny, and in many instances depending upon the uncertain and precarious fortune of gratuitous subsistence from their neighbors. Experience and observation must have convinced you that such cases are not only very probable, but actually do exist. The desperate lives of vagrants and gamblers have a natural tendency, besides shedding around in the circles of their association the baneful contagion of evil example, no less destructive to the mind and morals than the most virulent and raging pestilence to the body; but they produce and bring down upon the families the most complicated misfortunes, the con templation of which shock the mind of sensibility and make humanity shudder to think of. Whose heart is so adamantine that can behold, without sympathy, a poor desolate woman, with a house full of helpless children, forsaken by her husband, the natural protector of herself and children. She is left to her hard fate without means of subsistence, in an open cabin not sufficient to shelter her and her helpless children from the inclemency of the weather, and in the midst of disease and bodily affliction tormented with the cruel reflection of her undeserved misfortunes; her heart swollen, ready to burst its vital springs asunder at the miseries of her family, and nature almost sinking under the weight of anxiety to relieve their wants, which nature constrains them to vindicate, but which she is unable to relieve. This, I am inclined to believe, is not a hypothetical case; my information is that such a case does exist. It is your duty to inquire into such cases, and I hope these suggestions will superinduce extraordinary efforts on your part to bring the offenders to trial. The prevention of higher crimes is effected by a strict attention to the exercise of the most important duties with which you, as a grand inquest, are invested, by suffering no individual who comes within the description of gamblers and vagrants to escape your notice. They will then not multiply from impunity. A few examples may dissipate those pests of society who infest our peace and the public repose.

Drunkenness is also another offense properly coming within your jurisdiction, and I fear the frequency of it, instead of impressing your minds with the importance of applying to those who commit it the legal correction, has almost obliterated the proper sense of the impropriety and danger of this most degrading and beastly vice, for my own observation convinces me that a number of such cases exist. The few presentments for the number of offenses of this kind that are committed cannot fail to impress my mind with the idea that jurors have not hitherto duly appreciated the power they ought to exercise on such occasions. The laws of the State expressly prohibit it, which ought to be a sufficient consideration with the jury to induce them to bestow on it the most particular attention; but I am astonished that this offense should pass with such impunity, and should by law be so inadequately punished, particularly on public occasions, when I consider the nature of it, and reflect upon the train of evil consequences it produces. The mind of man, distempered and intoxicated with liquor, renders him fit for the commission of the most savage deeds—it brutalizes him; it causes the profligate to extend the sphere of his licentious indulgence; it frequently brings into action the most turbulent passions the human mind is capable of entertaining; it demoralizes a man, and for the time being destroys every virtue he ever possessed; it frequently dissolves the tender ties that unite society. If it has such a tendency among mankind whose minds are humanized by the highest degree of civilization, what can we expect from its practice in a frontier settlement, where there has scarcely been time to tame the wild and refractory by exhibiting to them the efficiency of the law. Who does not recollect that he has witnessed an immense group of evils resulting immediately from this vice. Let any man who cannot rely upon his own observation, as a test of its dangerous consequences, examine the faithful page of history, and I promise him that he will find in consequence of it many horrid deeds committed. But, laying out of view the high and important crimes it sometimes produces, I ask what are its almost universal tendencies? It certainly incites the mind to every species of mischief; to profane swearing; it produces assaults and batteries, affrays, routs and riots, etc., and begets an entire contempt for the laws and legal authorities. It is evident, by attending to this branch of your jurisdiction, by making examples of guilty persons, you will lessen the number of offenses which require to be presented by you by removing and extirpating, as it were, the cause that produces them. I will venture to assert, that one-half of the offenses against the penal laws, usually presented by grand jurors, would not have been committed were it not for intoxication. You will, by this means, greatly benefit the people who are guilty of this vice, as you will save them from those excesses to which it may hurry them, and the expenses, fines and forfeitures necessarily attending thereou, and thereby prevent them from injuring their constitutions, exhausting their pecuniary resources, and thereby distressing their innocent families. What constitutes drunkenness is a matter of fact, of which you are the proper judge; but for my part I have no idea that, to give you cognizance of such cases, it should appear that a man was so drunk that he could neither talk, walk or stand, for I really think that although such cases ought never to be overlooked by a grand jury, that that is the most harmless intoxication which prevents a man from insulting or injuring another or disturbing the public repose; but I am clearly of the opinion that although a man may walk and talk as well as another, yet, if his mind is distempered, his natural and common reason and discretion impaired by liquor, if it tends to render him more dangerous and less peaceable than in his sober moments, I should be inclined to think he ought to be presented. He, in fact, in such a situation, is dangerous because he has the disposition and the power of disturbing the peace, and his example is equally pernicious to society, if not more so, than he who can not move.

Profane swearing and cursing, Sabbath-breaking and blasphemy are also offenses to which I beg leave to call your attention. Though trivial, as they are thought by some, and so very leniently punished by our laws, they are very severely denounced by that law by which we must at last be judged. Since both the municipal laws of the land and the law of God prohibit these offenses, I trust that they will meet with the proper attention from a grand jury who have obligated themselves to discharge their duties by a solemn appeal to Heaven. Our laws do not assume the right of controlling men's consciences; but they very wisely restrain mankind from open abuses of sacred things, from profanity, blasphemy, etc., which are not necessary to the enjoyment of any religion that ever has or ever will exist, but which must be not only incompatible and uncongenial with any religion or any system of ethics or morality. Thus far our laws go; not to shackle the opinions of mankind, but to restrain them from the commission of acts which every reflecting mind must consider highly improper; and I hope that the detestable poison of infidelity has not so far insinuated itself into the minds of this grand jury, as to lead it away by the cant reasoning of those who are inimical to religion of every kind, from bestowing the proper attention to these objects of their jurisdiction. These observations, I hope, are a sufficient answer to the objections which have frequently been made to these laws, upon the ground of unconstitutionality. But it could be easily demonstrated, that it is to the interest of the Commonwealth to cherish a love for religion, and those cannot be very deserving citizens who make it their business to depreciate its influence: for in the first place it is the foundation upon which the fabric of our jurisprudence rests. What becomes of an obligation of an oath, if you destroy the idea of a state of future rewards and punishments? Where is the check to sordid avarice, domineering over the great host of evil passions? Gentlemen may theorize in their closets as long as time lasts upon the light of reason and its influence to govern mankind, but they will never succeed in any practical system. They should reflect before they attempt to undermine the fabric of future hopes. They ought to weigh well the consequences of success to society in general. They should pause to consider whether, if nine-tenths of the world are not restrained from the commission of high offenses neither by the fear of the penalties of municipal laws, nor future punishments, under their present opinions, how much more likely would they be governed by the light of reason, especially when it is considered, as it must be conceded, that they do not possess, independent of the fear of present and future punishment, light of reason sufficient to satisfy them that they act wrong, both as it relates to themselves and society. As, then, it is evident that all those checks, with this fantastic light of reason, are insufficient to control the passions of lawless and evil-minded men, it is paradoxical and absurd to contend that it is to the interest of society to destroy any one of those necessary checks, and it will be recollected that the laws are designed to govern men of the aforesaid description—from all which considerations I infer that as the particular tendency of blasphemy, profanity, etc., is to destroy the influence of religion and morality on the minds of our fellow citizens, that they ought for that reason to be punished. What is the proper religion I shall not pretend to say, nor is it my province; to determine; but that some religion is necessary is evident from the history of past events. Any religion is better than none at all, if there is the least credit to be given to sacred or profane history. The last, I presume, is an authority that infidels are not disposed to question; and society is interested in the support of religion. We find from history that the Assyrian Empire, that of the Medes and Persians, Grecian and Roman, all flourished whilst they adhered to their religion and scrupulously practiced reverence and piety toward their gods; but as impiety and wickedness gained ground, they began gradually to decline and ultimately sunk into total destruction. Who can read the history of the proud, superb, and unequaled cities of Babylon and Jerusalem, without seeing the evidences of God's wrath and chastisements for their wickedness in their signal destruction; and if Jerusalem itself experienced those visitations of the Almighty wrath in consequence of its wickedness, how shall we hope to escape whilst we tolerate profanity and impiety, and thereby permit their influence to extend to the rising generation, accumulating as it rolls on to the greatest magnitude, and that, too, at a time when we have just experienced greater dispensations of goodness and happiness than any other nation has enjoyed? In the dark ages of antiquity, impiety was looked upon as the greatest offense; they would not tolerate the least want of reverence for their supposed dieties, but severely punished supposed offenses against them. Shall we, possessing the light of revelation, permit an open irreverence and open opposition to the only true God? I hope not. It may be asked, why may not men be left, in such cases, to their conscience and to their future destinies? Because they would carry along with them the same fate for others whom they corrupt. We cannot consent that they shall blight and destroy our fairest hopes by contaminating, by their evil example, our children. Knowing that mankind is generally more disposed to embrace error than truth, to adopt vice than virtue, and knowing the fascinating influence of example, the law will not permit these persons to transfuse their poison into the breasts of others. These observations do not exclusively apply to profane swearing, Sabbath-breaking and blasphemy, they equally apply to other objects of your jurisdiction.

That Mr. Edwards was a very distinguished lawyer and able jurist no one can doubt, after reading his opinions whilst he was one of the judges of the highest court of the State of Kentucky; and to estimate, properly, his reputation as a lawyer and jurist, it must be borne in mind that he was selected to fill his judicial stations from the bar, composed at that time of some of the most eminent lawyers in the United States. Judge Bibb so highly appreciated his talents as a lawyer and judge, as to say that he knew of no one who could write a more able opinion, and in so short time, as Judge Edwards. The great secret of his success was owing to his powerful intellect and to his energy and untiring industry.

At a very early period he was selected by Mr. Clay to attend to important legal business for his father-in-law, Col. Hart, and in one of the letters from Mr. Clay to him, dated in July, 1800, Mr. C., after finishing what he had to say in relation to Mr. Hart's business, says:

I am happy to hear that we are anxious for the election of the same President. It is now almost certainly ascertained that Mr. Jefferson will be elected. The election of representatives in New York has been in his favor, and he will, it is affirmed, certainly get every vote in that State. You have, no doubt, heard that Pickering is dismissed and McHenry resigned; the violent friends of the administration seem to be quitting public service. Harper is no longer a candidate, and Sedgwick, the speaker, has also declined offering.

Permit me to inform you that as Mr. Thurston declines offering for the clerkship of the Senate, I shall, amongst many others, be a candidate for that office. Having lived in the clerk's office of the High Court of Chancery of Virginia, and acted sometimes as the amanuensis of the Chancellor, I have been induced to believe that I can discharge the duties of that office. Should you have it in your power to render me any service, and think me deserving it, I will be much obliged to you for the favor.

I am, dear sir, you most obedient,

HENRY CLAY.

CHAPTER II.

Organization of the Territory of Illinois—Appointment of Mr. Edwards as Governor—His arrival at Kaskaskia—Address of the Citizens of Randolph county, and Gov. Edwards' Reply—Superintendent of the U. S. Salines—His Appointment of Territorial Officers—Mr. Crittenden's appointment as Attorney-General of the Territory.

In February, 1809, provision was made by Congress for the organization of the Territory of Illinois, to take effect by the first of March. The duties and responsibilities of a territorial Governor, at that time, were peculiarly arduous and weighty. Judge Boyle, one of the associate judges of the Court of Appeals, of which Ninian Edwards was then Chief Justice, received this appointment, but declined accepting it. To this important station the Chief Justice was appointed by President Madison. This commission bears date the 24th of April, 1809. The Territory was duly organized by the Secretary, Nathaniel Pope, on the 28th of the same month.

Gov. Edwards arrived in June, and on the 11th of that month took the oath of office and entered upon the administration of the government.

The following are among the letters of recommendation to his appointment to the office of Governor:

KENTUCKY (FRANKFORT), 10*th April*, 1809.

To the President:

DEAR SIR—Mr. Boyle having accepted the office of Judge of the Court of Appeals of this State, I presume it will become necessary immediately to appoint a Governor of the Illinois Territory in his stead. N. Edwards, Esq., Chief Justice of our Court of Appeals, is desirous of filling this vacancy, and it is with pleasure that I bestow my suffrage on his recommendation. The honorable appointments which this gentleman has held (first as a judge of our Superior Court, and then promoted to his present station,) evince how highly he is estimated amongst us. In them he has acquitted himself with great ability and general satisfaction, nor can a doubt exist of his entire fitness for the office in question.

I am, sir, your most obedient,

HENRY CLAY.

In a letter of the same date, to the Hon. Robt. Smith, Mr. Clay speaks of him thus: "His political principles accord with those of the Republican party. His good understanding, weight of character and conciliatory manners give him very fair pretensions to the office alluded to. Should further information be desired in relation to him, I have no doubt that the whole representation from the State, when consulted, would concur in ascribing to him every qualification for the office in question."

The following tabular statement contains a list of the officers appointed by the Federal Government for the Territory of Illinois, from 1809 to 1818, inclusive:

Officers.	Office.	Date of Commission.
John Boyle	Governor (declined)	March 7, 1809
Ninian Edwards	Governor	" 7, "
Nathaniel Pope	Secretary	" 7, "
Alexander Stuart	Judge	" 7, "
Obadiah Jones	"	" 7, "
Jesse B. Thomas	"	" 7, "
Stanley Griswold	"	" 16, 1810.
John Caldwell	Receiver of Public Moneys	April 2, 1812.
Thomas Sloo	Commissioner Public Land Claims	" 2, "
Ninian Edwards	Governor	Novem'r 12, 1812.
Nathaniel Pope	Secretary	June 1, 1813.
William Sprigg	Judge	July 9, 1813.
William Mears	Attorney	August 1, 1813.
Philip Fouke	Marshal	" 1, "
Shadrick Bond	Receiver of Public Moneys	October 3, 1814.
Ninian Edwards	Governor	January 16, 1816.
Thomas Towles	Judge	" 16, "
William Rector	Surveyor Public Lands	April 29, 1816.
Benjamin Stevenson	Receiver Public Moneys	" 29, "
John McKee	Register Land Office	" 30, "
Joseph Philips	Secretary	Decem'r 16, 1816.
Augustus Chouteau	Indian Commissioner	Febr'y 19, 1818.
Richard Graham	Judge	April 20, 1818.

On his arrival in Kaskaskia, to enter upon the discharge of his duties, Gov. Edwards received the following address from the citizens of Randolph county:

Kaskaskia, *June*, 1809.

To His Excellency Ninian Edwards,

Governor and Commander-in-Chief of the Illinois Territory:

We, the undersigned, citizens of the county of Randolph, in the said Territory, beg leave to address you, on your arrival at the seat of government to assume the important duties of the high station to which your country has called you, from the honorable one which you held in the State of Kentucky. While, on this happy occasion, we greatly acknowledge the justice of the United States in granting the prayers of our reiterated petitions for the division of the Territory, permit us, sir, to congratulate you on that event, and to assure you that we entertain the highest sense of your merits and character, and appreciate the prosperity and happiness which we flatter ourselves will result to the citizens at large from your administration. Presuming that you may be in some degree unacquainted with the feelings and sentiments of the citizens at this important crisis, we cannot forbear to express our hopes that you will take into consideration that the majority, whose incessant exertions effectuated a division of the territory, have a claim on your excellency for the calumnies, indignities and other enormities which those who opposed that measure never ceased to heap upon the friends and advocates of the present system of our government.

In announcing these truths, while we deplore that the gentleman who was elected to Congress, and ultimately succeeded in obtaining justice for us, was hung in effigy at Vincennes, by the opposers of the division, and that one of the warmest friends and ablest advocates of the measure was assassinated at Kaskaskia, in consequence of their machinations, we derive great consolation from a firm belief that your excellency will gratify the virtuous majority, to whose patriotic exertions the citizens are indebted for a government of their choice, and your excellency your high station, with that honorable indemnity which is in your gift, and which would be considered by them as a remuneration for all those indignities and a pledge of their future support to your administration.

Having been informed that your excellency is vested with authority to inquire into the conduct of the land office of the district of Kaskaskia, we conceive it necessary, as a precautionary measure for the security of our titles, that all the books and papers in the office should be sealed up until the determination of the inquiry and a new board shall be organized.

In tendering you assurances of our highest respect and sincere attachment, we beg leave to express a hope that you will shortly bring your respectable family to our charming country, to make a permanent residence in the Territory, where we hope your administration may be long and popular.

(ANSWER.)

Gentlemen:

Your approbation of my appointment, and the friendly reception with which I am honored by you, while they cannot fail to elicit from me the expression of my gratitude and respect, they will, at the same time, inspire me with the strongest desire to merit a continuance of your friendship and support. In the administration of this government my first object is to do right, by a faithful discharge of the important duties with which I am intrusted; my next object will be to render the most general satisfaction—and I presume, with the enlightened citizens of Illinois, the latter will be most effectually secured by a strict observance of the former. On subjects of a political nature, it is not to be expected that mankind will ever perfectly agree, in all cases, and it is highly probable that on some occasions I may think differently from a portion of my fellow-citizens. Should this be the case, though I shall maintain my own opinions with firmness and moderation, I shall always take great pleasure in treating with the utmost respect the opinions of those who may disagree with me, recollecting that the fallibility of my own nature should suggest to me the best apology for the errors of others.

In the present state of society, and in the infancy of this government, I cannot expect to please everybody. On the threshold I am met by a crowd of difficulties, which I fear it will be impossible successfully to surmount. In this situation I only ask for that liberal indulgence which one honest man ought to extend to another. This I hope for; but should I be disappointed, I know that I cannot be deprived of the consolation of having endeavored honestly and independently to do my duty. To protect the equal rights of all (and not a part only) of the citizens of this Territory, is the object of the government; and it is designed not only for the benefit of those who are now residents, but also for all those who may choose to become so.

An office is a trust, deposited in the hands of the individual, who holds it not for his individual benefit and advantage, but for the public good; and in all appointments by me the public interest, and not a system of favoritism, shall be my governing principle. A partisan I can not and will not be. Had I been such heretofore, and an actual resident of this country during those contentions with which it has been convulsed, and which I deplore as much as any man, I should think the feelings of the man ought to be lost in those of the officer, whose duty it should be to consider himself as the guardian and protector of the equal rights of his fellow-citizens, that therefore, as such, he should have no friend to serve, no enemy to punish.

My powers with regard to the land commissioners are totally inadequate to the object of your request.

To promote the happiness of the people and the prosperity of this country will always engage my most earnest exertions.

With your country I am highly pleased—I agree with you that it is a charming country; and as soon as it is possible, I shall endeavor to bring my family to it.

Accept my thanks for your polite attention to me, and be assured that your expression of friendship in your address is most sincerely reciprocated by me.

Should this answer not be as full or explicit as you expected, the few moments you allowed me must be my apology.

N. EDWARDS.

At the time of his appointment to the office of Governor, he also received the appointment of Superintendent of the United States saline. As Superintendent it was his duty to make all the contracts for leasing the salt works, to collect the rent, and to provide for the shipment and sale of the salt which was delivered to the government in lieu of a cash rent. The following conditions were required to be inserted in the leases:

1st. The quantity of salt to be made annually, by the lessees, was not to be less than 120,000 bushels of salt, and as much more as the Superintendent might think practicable and might be proposed by the lessee; and, in order that this condition should be complied with, a penalty of one bushel for each bushel falling short of the quantity was exacted, to secure which there was to be a constant deposit of salt in the hands of the agent of the United States.

2d. The maximum price of salt to be fixed at not less than 80 cts. nor more than one dollar per bushel, leaving it between those limits, at the discretion of the Superintendent.

3d. A rent to be paid quarterly, in salt, equal to the difference between what is judged a fair price for the lessees to sell at, and the maximum price fixed by the lease; but to be calculated only on 120,000 bushels a year, whether the quantity actually made exceeds or falls short of that number. It was also stipulated that the salt paid to the United States should not be sold at a price less than that fixed by the lease, except by common consent the price should be lowered—in which case the rent was to be diminished in the same proportion.

4th. Conditions must be introduced to effectually prevent the waste of timber and to encourage the use of coal; to encourage which the Superintendent was authorized, at his discretion, to diminish the rent.

5th. It is left discretionary with the Superintendent to let the whole saline to one or more companies.

6th. No lessee should be concerned, either directly or indirectly, with any other salt works.

The above instructions were given by Mr. Gallatin, then Secretary of the Treasury, in the year 1809.

During the first three years of his administration of the territorial government, from the year 1809 to 1812, he had the power to make new counties and the appointment of all the offices; and yet, in all cases, he adopted as a rule, which was invariably adhered to, to allow the people of each county, by an informal vote, to select their own officers, both civil and military.

The following is taken from a publication, made by him, on the subject of the appointment of the militia officers of the Territory:

GENTLEMEN:—I regret very much the necessity which has hitherto rendered my visit to this county, at an earlier period, impracticable. For a considerable length of time immediately previous to my appointment to the office with which I am now honored, I was engaged in the most arduous duties attached to the one which I lately held, in the State of Kentucky. On the notification of my present appointment I delayed repairing to my new station no longer than about ten days, which time was actually spent in deciding and disposing of such causes as had previously been argued in the Court of Appeals, and which could not have been decided, without me, but at very great inconvenience to the litigant parties, and a delay highly injurious to the public interest. Such imperious calls of public duty I could not feel myself at liberty to resist; and whilst I yielded to them exclusively, the short time of my delay, my private concerns were totally overlooked and neglected. These considerations rendered my return to Kentucky at as early a period as possible so indispensable, and the business of the Territory required my presence so much, at the seat of government, that I found no time to devote to a visit to this country.

Independent of the pleasure which I would have felt in an opportunity of cultivating the acquaintance and friendship of those whose most important interests are confided to my care and guardianship, I doubt not but it might have been useful to myself, and satisfactory to my fellow citizens, by enabling me to develop to them the principles on which I mean to administer the government, and the motives by which I have been and shall continue to be governed. The interval of my absence from the Territory has increased the difficulty, but it has not destroyed my hopes of convincing my fellow-citizens that their good—the peace, and tranquillity, and happiness, and prosperity of the Territory—are the objects of my most ardent wishes.

The human mind is oftentimes the victim of prejudice. The utmost perfection of human nature is not entirely free from its influence. The best of men are sometimes subject to its dominion. And when mankind, instead of checking its approaches and guarding against its progress, admit its entrance by opening to it every portal and avenue of the heart, and invite its residence by cherishing it, the best, the noblest affections of the mind are superceded by dislikes, hatred and jealousies almost as injurious to those by whom they are entertained as to those against whom they are directed. And while I am very ready to admit that I may have erred in some instances—as I pretend to no exemption from the fallibility of human nature, and know too well my own liability to err—yet I think it highly probable that some portion of prejudice must have intermingled itself in the judgment which some of my fellow-citizens may have passed on my official acts, and, if so, that prejudice has become the more obstinate by being more matured, and consequently will be the more difficult to remove. But this is a difficulty at which I am neither startled nor appalled. The experience of thirteen years, every day of which I have been engaged in public service, in various stations, has convinced me that on the candor, the good sense and justice of the people I can always confide. I never mean to pay my court to demagogues. I will never admit that one, two, three or more persons shall exercise the right and claim the privilege of giving life, shape, motion and effect to public opinion, where I am concerned. My appeal shall always be to the people; and at the same time that I most firmly declare that I never will yield to mere popular clamor, resulting from popular delusion artfully produced, I take a pride in declaring that I would take as much pleasure in explaining my conduct to the humblest individual in the government, with a view to satisfy him, as I would to the highest personage, the most exalted character or the most influential man in it.

Deriving the portion of public patronage with which I have been honored from no high birth or noble ancestry, but being wholly indebted for it to those principles of liberty and equality, those fundamental rights of man, that have been secured by our glorious revolution and free constitution, by which every man of merit may be rewarded, whatever may be his situation in life, I cannot but venerate and respect those principles; and while I consider myself, as a citizen, inferior to no man whom God has ever made, I feel no superiority to any other honest, well-behaved man, however humble his station in life may be.

I am not ignorant of the facility with which the best actions of a man's life may be perverted, misconstrued and distorted by malicious interpretations; nor am I ignorant of the ease with which public sentiment may be corrupted and public prejudices excited; nor am I to be deterred by them. I have often experienced the inconveniences of them; for I have, in the course of my political life, met with as much opposition as any man whatever. But hitherto I have, in no instance, ever failed to overcome it; for in nothing that I have attempted in the political way have I ever experienced a personal disappointment; and in all my elections by the people, the least majority I ever had was upwards of three hundred votes. My dependence has always been upon the people. They may be wrong sometimes, but my political creed is that they will get right; and my firm belief is that the best means of securing their lasting and permanent approbation is a firm and independent course, even if they should not entirely concur; for there is a native magnamimity in the souls of freemen, which leads them to admire a man who is nobly wrong much more than one who is meanly right.

Gentlemen, I will close these general remarks with one more observation. I never will shrink from opposition, even if I should fall under it, for I would far rather fall nobly than rise meanly; but I never will court opposition—I will avoid it as long as possible. I will spare no pains to satisfy any dispassionate man, who is willing to be convinced, that my motives at least are pure, if he will with common frankness give me the opportunity to do so.

The particular object that I had in view, at the present time, was to give some elucidations of and explain the reasons that had lead me to adopt the plan to which I had resorted for the purpose of organizing the militia of this Territory, and I had expected to confine my address exclusively to those gentlemen who have recently been elected by the people as officers, having only requested them to meet me on this occasion. I calculated that I could not only convince them that my motives had been pure, but that my conduct had been correct, and that they, returning to the various sections of the county where they reside, would have it in their power to disseminate correct information upon the subject among their neighbors. That other citizens, however, do me the honor to attend and hear me, is to me a source of additional felicitation. I solicit all of you to lay aside your prejudices, if you have any, and yield to the dictates of your own judgment, dispassionately exercised.

That my plan is perfect I shall not contend; perfection is the lot of no man. No human institution that ever existed is free from imperfections of some kind, arising either from the incompetency of the human judgment that conceived and planned it, or the frailties, weaknesses or wickedness of those on whom it is designed to operate. This renders it quite easy to find fault, but very often as difficult to furnish a better substitute; and I will venture to say that no plan that has ever been suggested to me is either more correct in principle or better calculated to give general satisfaction. It is not enough to say it has its evils, it produces some discontents, unless you could point out some plan that would have been free from these exceptions.

The peculiar situation of this Territory would have presented difficulties almost insurmountable by a man acquainted with every citizen; they must be proportionately greater to a man like myself, a total stranger to almost every one—destitute of information, and unable to act without it; embarrassed by representations diametrically opposite to each other proceeding from sources apparently equally respectable.

Unfortunately the Territory had been divided into violent parties. Political controversies had degenerated into personal animosities of the most rancorous and vindictive nature. The combination of political dissentions and private hatred had convulsed the whole society, and exhibited a scene of mutual struggle to put down those who were opposed to each other. In this state of things, so much to be deprecated by dispassionate men, I found the Territory, when I came to it; and I determined to risk the whole combined opposition of both parties rather than yield myself up to the control or enlist under the banners of either. I regretted those dissensions as much as any man could do, and I was anxious to see them hastened into oblivion, because I did believe, and still do believe, that they are not only injurious to the happiness, but in a high degree destructive to the prosperity and the best interest of the Territory. They are also, to a great extent, inconsistent with the liberal and enlarged sentiments of true republicans; for show me the man who cannot tolerate free opinion, or who has so little charity as to believe that every man who differs with him on political subjects must be a knave, and I will show you a man who is fit only to reside in the atmosphere of tyranny. If my neighbor disagrees with me in matter of opinion, I ought not and I would not dogmatically arrogate to myself such perfeet infallibility as making my own judgment the standard to denounce him a fool or a knave. And if my conviction of the correctness of my own judgment was irresistible, to me, I should regret that he was incompetent to take my view of the subject, but it would be most uncharitable indeed to attribute his error to him as a crime. Much less should I suppose that any man, merely for differing with me in opinion, should be shut out from an equal participation in those republican institutions that are introduced for the common good of all. Such a principle is inconsistent with republicanism, which permits to every free man the full enjoyment of his opinions and the liberty of expressing them; but in vain would you allow him such liberty if you annex so severe a punishment to the exercise of it.

—5

To use a homely comparison, this would indeed be presenting the wolf in sheep's clothing. It would be monarchy or aristocracy nicknamed republicanism As to diversity of opinion we ought to expect it, and meet it with the most charitable indulgences; for who is there that has not experienced the fluctuations of his own judgment? Who, that will extend his view throughout the circle of his acquantance, has not seen many men, in whom he has equal confidence, differing in opinion upon the plainest points in politics, in law, in religion, in science of every kind, and even in plain matter of fact? These considerations should teach us not to be either too dogmatical or uncharitable.

They were most conclusive with me in resisting one plan of administration that was warmly pressed on me. That was to appoint none to office, under any circumstances, who had ever opposed the division of the Territory. This proposition was so repugnant to the dictates of my judgment, and to my sense of propriety and justice, that, if my political salvation had depended on it, I would not have adopted it. Yet I hope that, in refusing it, I have showed as much decent respect for the opinion of others as I possibly could do without surrendering my own.

The next plan pressed on me was to reappoint all the old officers. But this itself had its objections; and it would have imposed obligations on me which no Governor ought to be required to discharge. If I had appointed gentlemen to offices merely because they had before filled them, at the same time that I gave them the benefit of their old stations, justice would most imperiously require that I should have subjected them to the inconveniences of them; as, for example, if one of those persons, while in the exercise of his former office, or during his tenure of it, had committed an offense cognizable by a court of inquiry or court martial, surely I ought not to have rendered him intangible to a proper inquiry, or to secure to him impunity by issuing to him a commission of posterior date, whereby no such court of inquiry or court martial could be instituted with competent power either to investigate his conduct or to remove him from office. The difficulty, therefore, could only be obviated by substituting myself in the place of such court, and I do verily believe, if I had consented to undertake this arduous, this unpleasant and unprecedented labor, I should not have been able to have performed it by this time, if I may judge from the disposition manifested to exhibit charges.

To have adopted this plan without making such inquiries would have been unjust and impolitic; to have made the inquiries would have been oppressive to myself and I doubt not, in some instances, very unsatisfactory to my fellow-citizens.

If I had adopted the plan as my governing rule, I should have been like a mere machine, deriving my force and effect from borrowed impulse—all discrimination, all discretion, all selection, would have been perfectly prostrated.

If I had adopted the plan partially, it would have been impossible to have given general satisfaction, or to have avoided the imputation of having adopted a mere system of favoritism, which would have kept up the excitement and agitation of the public mind. Besides, my opinion is that offices are created for the benefit of the people and not the occupants, and no person can properly claim one unless he merits it, and the public interest be advanced by him. This is not the doctrine of venal courts or monarchical and aristocratical governments, where offices are given as bribes, and pensions and sinecures and titles of nobility are given as the wages of corruption, the more successfully to enable the government to invade the rights of the people; but just so much as said principles are beneficial to other governments, they are detrimental to and inconsistent with the genius and spirit of ours.

The government of Indiana had been dissolved, by which all the inhabitants of this Territory were reduced to a perfect equality; and it seemed to me that the dictates of justice, as well as sound policy, required that equality should not be destroyed by the recognition of any presumptive pretensions, nor by any save only those resulting from personal merit. Many persons probably, who were not in office, might be more meritorious than some who held offices, and all ought to have had a fair chance for promotion.

Revolving all these considerations and reflections in my own mind, I determined, without such a suggestion from any person on earth, to adopt my own plan, which was that the companies should elect the company officers and that those should elect the field officers. And here I pass over in silence, without animadversion and without the least resentment, insinuations that I had adopted this plan to favor this and that man. Time will convince you all that such suspicions are totally unfounded; and if I can only demonstrate my course is intrinsically correct, I am not very solicitous with regard to the motives that may be attributed to me.

Either of the other plans that have been mentioned would have been satisfactory to the party by whom it was proposed, but not so to the adverse party. Both parties claimed the majority of the people. On this they predicated their claims on me; and without admitting the propriety of such claim, in those cases, my plan gives to both parties the opportunity of succeeding upon their own ground. I could not select proper characters for officers without information, for I knew none of them. I did not choose to depend upon the information of the leaders here, or the leaders there, for this would have thrown me into the bosom of one party or the other—which I was determined to avoid. I therefore chose to make my appeal to the people, by the most practicable expedient that suggested itself to my mind.

By my plan those officers who were meritorious would be most likely to suceeed; those who were not so could have no cause for complaint. Good republicans ought to submit to the majority, and no man of sensibility would wish to lead to bloody conflict, in defense of their country, men who had not confidence in him; and it is to be hoped that an empty title or the plumage and garnature of a soldier, in time of peace, could not induce any man to disregard those nice and delicate notions of propriety which he would have in time of danger. I am not afraid to consult the people; and I do believe if in any case of militia appointments it is proper to consider their wishes it is in an exposed Territory like this, where the danger of invasion renders confidence in and attachment to officers so indispensible to the service.

If I could have returned earlier to the Territory it is probable that, in some cases, I might have directed new elections. The season is now too far advanced—the weather too likely to be inclement; and I do not consider myself authorized to call out the people in those months in which, by law, they cannot de compelled to muster. A longer delay in the militia business would be injurious, and therefore I must accept the returns of elections that have been made as the best expression of public sentiment which it is in my power to acquire.

Among the first appointments of Gov. Edwards was that of John J. Crittenden, late Senator in Congress from Kentucky, to the office of Attorney General of the Territory. Mr. Crittenden accepted the office, but in a very short time resigned, and his brother, Thomas, was appointed in his place. The following is his letter of resignation:

RUSSELVILLE, *Feb.* 24, 1810.

DEAR GOVERNOR:

I have inclosed you my resignation of the office of Attorney General, with which you were good enough to honor me. I know not how to excuse myself for such conduct. You will call me fickle and capricious, and perhaps you will think me ungrateful. The first epithets I do not think I deserve—the third I know I do not. I feel towards you all possible gratitude. I am bound to you by all that can bind the most susceptible heart to the most generous of benefactors. I trust that my destinies will, sometime or other, afford me an opportunity of convincing you of all this. Whenever I can serve you, I entreat that you will let me know it. I beg that you will command me. If you do not, I shall consider myself slighted. My heart feels no wish more ardently than that of serving you. But, let me put an end to these assurances; I could fill a volume. Capt. Butler is hurrying me. I want to see you much. I want you to sign my justification. I want to lay my whole heart and soul before you, to tell you all my reasons and feelings upon this subject. I beg you will always consider me among the number of your best and most devoted friends.

JOHN J. CRITTENDEN.

His Excellency N. EDWARDS, *United States Saline.*

CHAPTER III.

Indian Depredations and Massacres — Movements of Captain Levering — Indian Council at Peoria — Speech of Gov. Edwards — Reply of Gomo, etc.—Peoria in 1812.

In 1810, a series of massacres and depredations were committed by the Indians of Illinois Territory, upon citizens living in Louisiana Territory, which led to a long correspondence between the Governor of Louisiana Territory and Gov. Edwards. The most daring of these was committed at Portage du Sioux, on July 19th, and created great excitement at the time. It appears, from the correspondence which it occasioned, that on the night in question a party of Sacs stole from William T. Cole, Cornelius Gooch and James Moredough a number of horses and other articles. They were immediately pursued by Stephen Cole, James Moredough, W. T. Cole and Sarshal Brown, who came up with the band on the next day. They were first seen across a prairie, four or five miles ahead. Finding themselves discovered the Indians kept changing their course, which prevented their pursuers from overtaking them. In their rapid march, however, the Indians left behind them a quantity of their plunder, consisting of a valuable pack-saddle, seven or eight deer-skins, two sides of leather, and some dried venison—the property of Mr. Brown—which was recovered. Night coming on, and their horses becoming very fatigued, the pursuers concluded to follow no further, and pitched their camp near a small branch, arranging that the next day they should continue on to the house of Victor Lagotiere, where they would leave the recovered property, and get him (who was known to have great influence with the Indian tribes) to intercede for the recovery of the horses. But about two o'clock in the morning, while sleeping around their watch-fire, they were fired upon by the Indians and four of the party, consisting of C. Gooch, Abraham Patten, W. T. Cole and Sarshal Brown, instantly killed. Stephen Cole was wounded in two places and also tomahawked, but he recovered from his wounds. It was not, however, till the 22d that he and James Moredough (the other survivor, who escaped by hiding in the thicket) were able to get back to the settlement and give the news of the massacre. On the next day a party started back and recovered the bodies of the murdered men, but all the horses, blankets, guns, ammunition, etc., belonging to them, were taken by the

Indians. On the 23d of July, about three leagues below Mr. Lagotiere's, two Indians of the Pottawottamie tribe were seen, by a man named Morris Blondeau, lying in the woods, hungry and without fire, having a number of horses in their possession, but upon their representing that they were just returning from a Buffalo hunt, nothing was thought of the circumstance and they escaped. The proof being ample that the massacre was committed by the Pottawottamies, a requisition was made by the Governor of Louisiana Territory, upon Gov. Edwards, to deliver them up for punishment.

On the 24th of July, 1811, Capt. Samuel Levering was honored with a commission from Gov. Edwards to proceed to the tribes on the Illinois River and demand of them the authors of the murders which had been committed, and the property that had been stolen by the Indians in the Louisiana and Illinois Territories, during the preceding two summers. Capt. Levering departed on that day, from Kaskaskia, and arrived at Mr. Jarrot's, in the village of Cahokia, on the next day, at 11 o'clock, P. M. Capt. Ebert had engaged a part of the crew for the boat, and on the 25th of July, the boat having been furnished by Gov. Clark with the necessary equipments, provisions, etc., they left in the boat for Peoria, with the crew, consisting of Capt. Levering, Capt. Hebert, Henry Swearingen, N. Rector, a Frenchman, that passed for an interpreter, but was intended for a spy, a Pottawottamie Indian, named Wish-ha, and eight oarsmen, each of whom was armed with a gun. The names of the boatmen were Pierre St. John, Pierre La Parche, Joseph Trotier, Francis Pensoneau, Louis Bevanno, Thomas Hull (*alias* Woods), Pierre Vœdre, and Joseph Grammason—all of whom signed the articles of agreement as boatmen and soldiers for the expedition.

On the 28th July, they arrived at Portage du Sioux, where they met Capt. Whiteside with his men, who had just arrived from the blockhouse, near the mouth of the Illinois River. Capt. Whiteside informed them that he and his party had fired, a few days previously, on the Sacs, whose chief was by the name of Quas-qua-me, as they were ascending the river, with the intention of a summons "to bring them to," but that the Indians, not understanding such a salutation, and supposing it to be an act of hostility, returned the fire—whereupon his party, with a good aim, fired four shots.

On the morning of the 29th of July, they arrived at Prairie Marcot, about nineteen miles above the mouth of the Illinois River, where Lieut. John Campbell was stationed with seventeen men. Lieut. Campbell informed them that he had, a few days ago, taken a scout, and had seen path-tracks of fifteen Indians.

Nothing of special importance occurred until their arrival at Peoria, on the 3d of August, where they met Mr. Forsythe, the Indian agent, who informed Capt. Levering that he had delivered to Gomo Gov. Clark's letter to him, in relation to the murderers, and that Gomo replied as though he was disposed to surrender the offenders; that one man could not fight and contend with fifty; that his will was ineffectual and in opposition to that which generally prevailed among the Indians.

On the 4th of August, Jacques Mettie, of Peoria, informed Capt. Levering that one of the Indians who committed the murder on Shoal creek was a Pottawottamie, by the name of Nom-bo-itt, and that he was at that time in a village on Yellow creek, whose chief is named Mat-cho-quis, about ninety leagues from Peoria; and that another, also of the same nation, by the name of Me-nac-queth, was at Latourt, or White Pigeon, on the road leading to Detroit, about twelve leagues from St. Joseph; and the third one of the party that murdered Cox is named Es-ca-puck-he-ah, or Green, who was twelve or fifteen miles beyond White Pigeon, toward Detroit—probably at the apple orchard on the Kick-kal-le-ma-seau.

Mr. Fournier, who had been sent to Gomo's village to apprise him of the arrival of Capt. Levering with a letter to him, from Gov. Edwards, reported that an Indian had arrived in advance of him, and had informed Gomo that the party consisted of fifty armed men, and that, notwithstanding his representations to the contrary, Gomo would not come without fourteen armed warriors with him.

On the morning of August 5th, a United States flag was seen at Gomo's lodge, a quarter of a mile above, on the lake. On Gomo's receiving a message, he came to the quarters of Capt. Levering, who delivered to him the letter from Gov. Edwards. Gomo replied that he would immediately return to his village, and would, on the following morning, prepare his young men, and send them to call the chiefs to the council. He gave the names of the following Pottawottamie chiefs: Neng-ke-sapt, or Fire Medals, at Elkhart, near Fort Wayne; Topenny-boy, on the River St. Joseph; Mo-quan-go, on the Qui-que-que River; Wi-ne-magne, or Cat Fish, on the Wabash River. He said that Marpock and his principal chiefs had gone to Detroit, and probably would not return until the fall. The chiefs of the towns on Fox River resided at Milwaukee; Little Chief, on River Au Sable, or Sand River; Masseno, or Gomo, about seven leagues above Peoria; Black Bird, chief of the Ottawas, on the River Au Sable. Gomo declared his willingness to do all in his power to render justice and to satisfy the Americans.

There was an Indian with Gomo, by the name of Me-che-ke-noph, or Bittern, a half Fulsowine and half Pottawottamie, who said that the murderers of Price were five brothers, of the Fulsowines, whose names he gave.

Capt. Levering furnished Gomo with tobacco, as a message to the chiefs, and he then left for his village.

There was, at first, a difference of opinion in relation to the policy of the measures to be adopted by the council of Indians. One party were of opinion that it would be policy to send a mission to those chiefs who afforded shelter to the murderers, make a demand of them, and surrender them to the Americans. Another party were opposed to making any attempt to deliver up the offenders, but proposed to collect much of the stolen property and take it in, with representations that the offenders could not be found. It was said that Gomo would advocate the first measure, but he abhorred the pusillanimous appearance of attempting that which he could not accomplish. He was heard to say that if he presented himself to the chiefs and demanded the surrender of the murderers, they would say to him that he was a chief on the Illinois River, and that he had better attend to his own tribe.

The most prevalent policy—supposed to be that recommended by the English—was to send Little Chief, who was a "talkative fellow," to make representations and assurances that would answer their present purposes; and that, as other outrages had passed with naught but a frown or two, this would likewise soon blow over.

Capt. Levering was of the opinion, in order that a mission should have its desired effect, and make a serious impression on the Indians, and induce them to deliver up the offenders and stolen property, that it should be a joint one, from the Territories of Michigan, Indiana, Illinois and Louisiana, to convene at Chicago, where the chiefs from the north side of the Lake, as well as those from the Territories, could attend. None of the chiefs could then say, "it is not my business; I am not called upon; it does not concern me."

The party proceeded the next day, and arrived at a village of Indians about seven leagues up the Illinois River. Being dark, the hands—saying they were not hired to work at night—refused to go further. Capt. Levering engaged two Indians to take him and Mr. Fournier in a canoe, about four miles higher up the river to a creek, from which place they were conducted, through a moist and thicketty bottom, to Gomo's village, where they arrived about eleven o'clock, and disturbed Gomo and the Indians from their sleep. They were invited into a lodge—a bark building, 25 by 50 feet inside, tenanting about thirty persons. There were scaffolds, from 6 to 7 feet long, 6 feet wide and 5 feet high, extending all around the building, on which the Indians sat and sleep—stretching themselves from the weatherboarding to the center. Capt. Levering and Mr. Fournier were invited to mount those next to the ones occupied by Gomo and his family. Although it was very late, a dish of food, made of new corn, was brought in by Gomo's wife, and, whilst they were eating, Gomo smoked his pipe. The men generally left their sleeping places, squatted around two fires in the center of the building, "in all the solemnity of profound smoking." This appears, says Capt. Levering, to be an etiquette due to strangers.

Capt. Levering states that the Indians believed that the Americans were their enemies and would constantly intrude on them. This, together with their natural ambition to have it to say, as they do in their drunken frolics, "I am a man: who can gain-say it? I have killed an Osage! I have killed a white!" leads them to outrage; and frequent escapes from punishment leads them to suppose that the whites are supine and indolent.

On the next morning, accompanied by Gomo and another chief, they returned to Peoria. On the next day, Capt. Levering introduced the conversation by saying to Gomo that he wished a private talk with him, which he hoped would be useful; that he would not then speak the words of our father who sent him; that they were more interesting, and particularly concerned all the nation, and that he was reserving them for the council of chiefs who would be convened in a few days.

Gomo replied that he was rejoiced that he had been sent on this errand, and wished that the chiefs could attend and hear for themselves our father's words; for no communication which he or any other Indian might make would be believed. They would, he said, call him *sugar-mouth*, and charge him with being excited by fear or moved by treachery.

For that reason, Capt. Levering wished the presence of as many chiefs and leading characters, from as many villages, as could be collected, that none should be left in a state of ignorance that might and probably would be the means of involving the whole nation in a war. He stated to Gomo that our Great Father desired that peace and friendship should exist between the red and the white man, yet one chief might and could, from want of the proper information, frustrate all these blessings; that it was important for the Indians all to know that, although the whites wished peace and friendship, some of the Indians had committed outrages, which, if not satisfactorily explained and atoned for, would end in their destruction. His father, before sending him, had advised with their fathers on the west of the Mississippi and on the east of the Wabash, and he now spoke agreeably to their united deliberations. Although our fathers did not resent the first injury, it was only through a disposition of forbearance, hoping that it was an act of some unruly individual, which the chiefs would correct; for the whites can not conceive that individuals among the Indians can continue to perpetrate outrages without the countenance and encouragement of the chiefs. They believe that the chiefs can restrain their people from the commission of acts which will be injurious to their nation. The most forbearing, the greatest patience may become fatigued and worn out. Though friendship, on our part, should be abundant as the waters of a great river, yet, interrupt it till you choke it and it will be converted into a flood of destruction, and in its course it could not discriminate the innocent from the guilty—while any good man would lament the sufferings of the innocent.

Gomo wished that all the chiefs could attend and hear the words of their father, and expressed a wish that Capt. Levering should also tell them the words he had spoken. He said that he would send for them, although he thought it probable that the chiefs of the St. Joseph and Qui-que-que Rivers, and Yellow Creek were absent from their homes, for there were a number of runners from the British among them, with talks and messages, which was probably the occasion of Marpock, and many Indians from this and other towns, traveling lately towards Canada. In order to lengthen the conversation Capt. Levering continued, as follows: "At about my age past, the British and the Americans had a seven years' war. Washington, the man that handed you the papers which you showed to me before leaving your village, was our Great Father, that had conducted our warriors to the war. He is now dead, but we love him, for he was a good and brave man and fought for our rights against the unreasonable pretensions of the British. They would not allow us to be full men, able to manage our own affairs; but, under Washington, we fought them for seven years. They were worsted, and asked for peace. We love peace and happiness; and Washington became our Great Father. But, ever since, the British cannot be our generous friends; they are jealous of our growing strength, yet they know that in case of war they cannot stand before us, and they are continually striving to get the Indians into trouble with us, in order to resent their enmities. They offer the Indians protection while they are unable to protect themselves. If they could protect themselves, they would wage open war on us. If they could have beaten us my lifetime ago, they would have done it, and Washington, who gave you those papers, would have been hung. But they were conquered, and Gen. Washington, eighteen years ago, made a treaty with the Indians, declaring that we will be friends to the Indians; and they made a law that if an American should kill an Indian, that it should be the duty of every Governor of our different States and Territories to catch that man and put him to death; and that if any one should settle on any of your lands he should pay one thousand dollars and be imprisoned for twelve months. Such are the papers which that great and good man put into your hands, and which you have shown to me. All of our fathers, ever since, would treat you as children. They would also remain at peace with the British; but for our kindness they must at least treat us with justice—not insult us, not murder our people, nor steal our horses."

Gomo's elder brother spoke of a time when the British put the Indians in the front of the battle. Gomo said he saw Washington in Philadelphia, when they made the treaty of 1793. That there were two of the horses in the possession of his tribe, and a third in his own possession, which he had bought—saying, that at the time of the purchase he did not know that it had been stolen. He said that they should be delivered up.

On the 8th of August, 1811, Capt. Levering delivered, at the Governor's request, two commissions—one to Thomas Forsyth, as justice of the peace for the town of Peoria, and the other to John Baptiste Dupond, as captain in and for the same place—both of whom took the oath of office.

Mr. Dupond said the Indians would expect him, now that he was a chief, to give them some meat and tobacco, and that some unpleasantly disposed persons would instigate the Indians to worry him, and that he hoped the Governor would notice such; that he did not wish to accept the commission, but that as there were unfavorable reports of the place, he was willing to let it be known that there is a person well disposed to the government.

On the 15th of August, Miche Pah-ka-en-na, the Kickapoo chief, and eleven of his warriors, arrived, and called on Capt. Levering, who told the chief that as he was the only chief he had seen whom our father knew to be friendly with his white children, he was particularly pleased to see him. He gave them some refreshments, and the chief remarked that he had always heard that our father was kind and good, and he was happy to see an evidence of it in his sons, and more particularly as some of his young men were present to witness the friendly disposition. Capt. Levering told him that their father and his greater chiefs were all known to their white children; some knew them personally. That he knew some of them through the papers, some from the word of mouth, and they all desired to live in friendship with their red children.

On the same day Gomo, Little Chief, and others, waited on Capt. Levering. Little Chief said that he had come to hear the words of his father, and he hoped that they would be all told to them as they were written. Forsyth replied, with much warmth, that if they apprehended any deficiency, they must get another interpreter. Little Chief said if they had come to his village, he would have furnished them with a cabin and plenty to eat; and, as he had come to hear the words of his father, he wished to know where he should go. Capt. Levering replied that the white men were aggrieved and had sent him to talk with the Indians; that he was a sojourner and a stranger among them, but as he had invited them to Peoria, he would furnish them with a house, but being in a strange place and unprovided, he could not give them the kind and quality of provisions equal to his wishes. Little Chief then showed him a paper and asked him what it was. Capt. Levering informed him that it was a pass from Capt. Heald, of Chicago, dated July 11, 1811, stating that Little Chief, a Pottawottamie, was on his way to St. Louis; as a further protection he gave him a flag. The chief replied that he had given him a piece of coarse cloth; and said that he was in the habit of speaking loud, but that when they came to the council they must not mind it. Capt. Levering replied that their white brethren used different kinds of cloth for different purposes; the kind put into the flag was the best to flow in the wind, being light; and when it was made into a flag their white brethren respected it and would hurt no one under it; he carried it to war, and before he would loose it, a good soldier would loose his life. The loudness of your voice will make no difference, if you only talk of the business of the nation. In the evening, about dusk, Capt. Levering walked up the bank of the river, intending, if a suitable occasion should offer, to deliver his address to the Indians. He observed the flag on the fence, flying, with the Union down; and Mr. Fournier standing near, he requested him to tell the Indians that they had hoisted their colors wrong, for the stars should be upward. The Indian that Fournier addressed himself to replied that he knew it, but it was not he that had put it so. Capt. Levering walked on a few steps, and seeing Little Chief coming out of the gate, he walked back a few steps, carelessly, and desired Fournier to say to Little Chief that the flag was hoisted wrong; that the stars should be above. Little Chief replied that he knew it; he was not an American—he was an Indian. Some person must have made it in the night, for it had large stitches and the sewing was very coarse.

Capt. Levering prepared the following address, to be delivered to the Indians on the next morning:

Brothers, Chiefs, and Warriors :

On yesterday I told you how much we respect the flag of the United States; that, through an act of friendship, one has been given to some one of you to guard you in safety to St. Louis. The hoisting of the flag of the United States with the stars downward is considered as degrading the flag, and an insult to the United States, and our white enemies, whenever they take one from us, hoist it with the intention of insulting the government of the United States; nor can the circumstance be less insulting when it is done by the Indians, after they are duly acquainted with the mode and etiquette.

My father, a part of that Government, feels himself aggrieved in his children, by some persons from this quarter; yet, being unwilling to use hasty measures, that are apt to injure the innocent with the guilty, and hoping to find you disposed to be friendly, has sent me to talk with you—yet I can not nor will not while you are insulting the government. You must turn your flag and have it placed properly, or I will immediately leave here without delivering our father's talk.

At a very early hour on the next morning, the Indians had raised the flag *Union up*.

Being informed, on the morning of the 16th of August, that the Indians were ready and on their way to the council room, Capt. Levering invited the inhabitants of Peoria to attend, and, accompanied by Mr. Forsyth, Mr. Rector, Mr. Swearingen and Captain Hebert, met the Indians in the council room. He then proceeded to address the Indians as follows:

Brothers, Chiefs, Warriors:

The weather is cloudy. In the region south and west of this you will see none moving—all having drawn towards their cabins, in apprehension of a storm. But our father, who presides over the tribes between the Mississippi and Wabash, being a good man, has sent me to invite you under this shelter to smoke a pipe in profound meditation—having our ears open to the voice of the Great Spirit, and our hearts disposed to obey its dictates—to see whether all may not subside, be calm, fair and cheerful. But first let us smoke a pipe, and then attend to the talk of our father.

The following is Governor Edwards' address to the Pottawottamies, delivered in council at Peoria, on the 15th of August, 1811:

ILLINOIS TERRITORY, *July* 21, 1811.

To the Chiefs and Warriors of the tribes of Pottawottamies, residing on the Illinois River and its waters, in the Territory of Illinois.

My Children, you are now met together, by my desire, on a very important occasion. You are now to be asked to do an act of justice. Should you refuse, it may once more involve the red and white brethren in all the horrors of bloody war. On the other hand, if you should perform what justice itself calls for, it will brighten the chain of friendship, which has for a long time united the red people with their white brethren of the United States.

My Children, ever since Wayne's treaty, our Great Father, the President of the United States, has faithfully fulfilled all his treaties with you. He has endeavored to make his red and white children live as one great family, loving and obliging one another, and he has always strictly forbidden his white children from doing any harm to their red brethren.

My Children, for a long time the bloody tomahawk and scalping-knife have been buried. The sun of peace has shone upon us, blessing us with his light and giving gladness to our hearts. The red people have enjoyed their forests and pursued their game in peace; and the white people have cultivated the earth without fear. But, my children, these bright prospects are darkened. A storm seems to be gathering which threatens destruction, unless it should be dissipated by that justice which you, as good men, ought to render.

My Children, while we trusted to treaties with you—while we believed our red brethren to be friendly—some of our people, fearing no danger, have been plundered of their property and deprived of their lives by some of your bad men.

My Children, last year a perogue was cut loose on the Mississippi and a considerable quantity of goods was taken out of it, and carried off, by some of your people. A great many horses have been stolen from this Territory, both during the last and the present year, many of which have certainly been carried off by some of your people. Other horses have been stolen from the neighborhood of St. Charles, in Louisiana. I demand satisfaction for these outrages.

My Children, on the 19th day of July, last year, in the district of St. Charles, and Territory of Louisiana, a party of Pottawottamies stole several horses. On the next day they were pursued by the white people, who lost their trail and quit the pursuit. On that night those Pottawottamies fell upon those white men, in their camp, killed four of them, wounded a fifth, and carried off several horses and other property. Among those Indians were Cat Fish, O-hic-ka-ja-mis and Mis-pead-na-mis. I demand that these bad men, and all others who were of the party, together with the property they stole, shall be delivered up to Capt. Levering and his party, or that you yourselves shall deliver them and the property to me.

My Children, on the 2d day of last June, on Shoal creek, in St. Clair county, in this Territory, three of your bad men went to the house of a Mr. Cox, plundered his property, took two guns, two mares and colts, and a stud horse, barbarously killed his son, and took his daughter a prisoner. A few days after this outrage, near the Mississippi, in the same county and Territory, others of your bad men killed a man by the name of Price, and wounded another by the name of Ellis. I demand that these bad men, together with all the property they took off, shall be delivered to Capt. Levering, or that you shall deliver them and the property to me.

My Children, the blood of those innocent men who have been wounded and murdered cries aloud to the Great Spirit for vengeance. The hearts of their relations and brethren bleed with sorrow. The fire of revenge flames in their hearts, and they thirst for blood.

My Children, I have found it almost impossible to prevent the white people from rushing to your towns, to destroy your corn, burn your property, take your women and children prisoners, and murder your warriors. But I told them that those who have done the mischief were bad men; that you would disapprove their conduct, and deliver them to me as enemies both to you and your white brethren. I commanded your white brethren not to raise the tomahawk or go to war with you, and they obeyed me.

My Children, now open your ears to hear my words, and let them sink deep into your hearts. If you wish for peace with us, you must do us justice. If you disapprove those murders and other outrages that have been committed, you must deliver up the offenders; for if you harbor among you such deadly enemies to us, you cannot be our friends, and you ought not to expect our friendship.

My Children, Gov. Harrison demanded some of those bad men, when they were within his Territory, and they fled to the Illinois River and took up shelter among you. I now demand them, and you must not say they are fled elsewhere. They murdered our people—they are our enemies—and if you have protected them, and they belong to your bands, you must find them and deliver them up, or we must consider you as approving their horrid deeds and as being our enemies.

My Children, liars and bad advisers are among you; they profess to be your friends, and they deceive you; they have their interest in view, and care not what becomes of you, if they can succeed in their designs. Avoid such people.

My Children, you can remember when such men persuaded you to make war upon your white brethren of the United States. They promised you great assistance, but they left you to fight your own battles, and you found it necessary to sue for peace. At that time you were stronger that you now are; the woods were then full of game of all kinds; large numbers of you could collect together and traverse the country without fear of wanting meat. But this cannot now be done.

My Children, when we were at war with you, we were then weak; we have now grown strong—have everything necessary for war, and are your near neighbors. Our Great Father's dominions extend over vast countries, bounded by the great waters; his great towns and cities are hardly to be counted; and his white children are thick and numerous like the stars of the sky.

My Children, your Great Father, the President of the United States, has nothing to fear from wars, but he wishes to be at peace with you, because he loves you and wishes to make you happy. You ought to try to merit his kindness and avoid his resentment.

My Children, your Great Father asks nothing but justice from you. Suffer not bad advisers to pursuade you to refuse it. In kindness, none can exceed him; but if you should be determined to treat him and his white children as enemies, storms and hurricanes, and the thunder and lightning of heaven, cannot be more terrible than will be his resentment.

My Children, Capt. Samuel Levering will deliver you this talk; he is authorized, by me, to demand of you the property that has been stolen, and those bad men who committed the murders, and all who were of the party. You will confer with Capt. Levering, and come to as speedy a determination as possible.

My Children, let justice be done, let all cause of quarrel be removed, and let us live like brothers.

Your affectionate father,

NINIAN EDWARDS.

The council again met, on the 16th of August, to receive the answer of the Pottawottamies. Gomo spoke as follows:

We have listened well to your information, and hope that you will give the same attention to our words.

I am very glad that you have come among us, and that you have delivered the words of the Governor to all the chiefs and warriors in hearing. I intended to have gone to see the Governor, but it is much better as it has occurred, that he has sent his talk here.

You see the color of our skin. The Great Spirit, when he made and disposed of man, placed the red skins in this land, and those who wear hats on the other side of the big waters. When the Great Spirit placed us on this ground, we knew of nothing but what was furnished to us by nature; we made use of our stone axes, stone knives and earthen vessels, and clothed ourselves from the skins of the beasts of the forest. Yet, we were contented! When the French first made large canoes, they crossed the wide waters to this country, and on first seeing the red people they were rejoiced. They told us that we must consider ourselves as the children of the French, and they would be our father; the country was a good one, and they would change goods for skins.

Formerly we all lived in one large village. In that village there was only one chief, and all things went on well; but since our intercourse with the whites, there are almost as many chiefs as we have young men.

At the time of the taking of the Canadas, when the British and the French were fighting for the same country, the Indians were solicited to take part in that war—since which time there have been among us a number of foolish young men. The whites ought to have staid on the other side of the waters, and not to have troubled us on this side. If we are fools, the whites are the cause of it. From the commencement of their wars, they used many persuasions with the Indians; they made them presents of merchandise, in order to get them to join and assist in their battles—since which time there have always been fools among us, and the whites are blameable for it.

The British asked the Indians to assist them in their wars with the Americans, telling us that if we allowed the Americans to remain upon our lands, they would in time take the whole country, and we would then have no place to go to. Some of the Indians did join the British, but all did not; some of this nation, in particular, did not join them. The British persisted in urging upon us that if we did not assist them in driving the Americans from our lands, our wives and children would be miserable for the remainder of our days. In the course of that war, the American General Clark came to Kaskaskia, and sent for the chiefs on this river to meet him there. We attended, and he desired us to remain still and quiet in our own villages, saying that the Americans were able, of themselves, to fight the British.

You Americans generally speak sensibly and plainly. At the treaty of Greenville, Gen. Wayne spoke to us in the same sensible and clear manner.

I have listened with attention to you both. At the treaty of Greenville, General Wayne told us that the tomahawk must be buried, and even thrown into the great lake; and should any white man murder an Indian, he should be delivered up to the Indians; and we, on our part, should deliver up the red men, who murdered a white person, to the Americans.

A Pottawottamie Indian, by the name of Turkey-foot, killed Americans, for which he was demanded of us: and although he was a great warrior, we killed him ourselves in satisfaction for his murders.

Some of the Kickapoos killed an American. They were demanded, were given up, and were tied up with ropes around their necks for the murders. This was not what the chief who made the demand promised, as they were put to death in another manner. Our custom is to tie up a dog in that way, when we make a sacrifice.

Now, listen to me well, in what I have to say to you. The red skins have delivered up their offenders.

Sometime ago one of our young men was drunk, at St. Louis, and was killed by an American. At another time some person stole a horse near Cahokia. The citizens of the village followed the trail, met an innocent Kickapoo, on his way to Kaskaskia, and killed him. Last fall, on the other side, and not far from Fort Wayne, a Wyandot Indian set fire to a prairie; a settler came out and inquired of him how he came to set fire. The Indian answered that he was hunting. The settler struck the Indian and continued to beat him, till they were parted, when another settler shot the Indian. This summer a Chippeway Indian, at Detroit, was looking at a gun; it went off, accidently, and shot an American. The Chippeway was demanded, delivered up, and executed. Is this the way that Gen. Wayne exhibits his charity to the red skins? Whenever an instance of this kind happens, it is usual for the red skins to regard it as an accident.

You Americans think that all the mischiefs that are committed are known to the chiefs, and immediately call on them for the surrender of the offenders. We know nothing of them; our business is to hunt, in order to feed our women and children.

It is generally supposed that we red skins are always in the wrong. If we kill a hog, we are called fools or bad men; the same, or worse, is said of us if we kill an horned animal; yet, you do not take into consideration the fact that while the whites are hunting along our rivers, killing our deer and bears, that we do not speak ill of them.

When the French came to Niagara, Detroit, Mackinaw and Chicago, they built no forts or garrisons, nor did the English, who came after them; but when the Americans came, all was changed. They build forts and garrisons and blockade wherever they go. From these facts we infer that they intend to make war upon us.

Whenever the United States make the Indians presents, they afterwards say that we must give them such a tract of land; and after a good many presents they then ask a larger piece. This is the way we have been served. This is the way of extending to us charity.

Formerly, when the French were here, they made us large presents; so have the English; but the Americans, in giving their presents, have always asked a piece of land in return. Such has been the treatment of the Americans.

If the whites had kept on the other side of the waters, these accidents could not have happened; we could not have crossed the wide waters to have killed them there; but they have come here and turned the Indians in confusion. If an Indian goes into their village, like a dog he is hunted, and threatened with death.

The ideas of the Pottawottamies, Ottaways and Chippeways are, that we wish to live peaceable and quiet with all mankind, and attend to our hunting and other pursuits, that we may be able to provide for the wants of our women and children. But there remains a lurking dissatisfaction in the breasts and minds of some of our young men. This has occasioned the late mischiefs, which, at the time, were unknown to the chiefs and warriors of the nation. I am surprised at such threatenings to the chiefs and warriors, (old people,) who are inclined entirely for peace.

The desire of the chiefs and warriors is to plant corn and pursue the deer. Do you think it possible for us to deliver the murderers here to-day?

Think you, my friends, what would be the consequence in case of a war between the Americans and the Indians. In times past, when some of us were engaged in it, many women were left in a distressful condition. Should war now take place the distress would be, in comparison, much more general.

This is all I have to say on the part of myself and the warriors of my village. I thank you for your patient attention to my words.

After Gomo had finished, he laughingly said that we have had long talks; will not a little whisky enable us to sleep? Capt. Levering understood him by lulling their fears.

On the next day, being the 17th of August, Little Chief spoke as follows:

Listen to me, my friends, if you wish to know the ideas and sentiments of the chiefs and warriors here present to-day. Give the same attention to my words that I did to those of yesterday.

At the conclusion of the American and Indian wars the Americans asked us to remain at peace and in quietness. I and my warriors have always observed the advice.

One of the promises of the Americans to the Indians, at that time, was that whenever murders should be committed on either side, the murderers should be delivered up to the opposite party. We have delivered up offenders; the Americans have delivered none.

The intention of the Pottawottamies, Ottaways and Chippeways has been to remain peaceable and quiet, as they always have done, and still wish to do; and when that is observed, there will be nothing to fear on either part, as you will see to-day.

At the peace of Greenville, it was agreed on both sides to deliver up all the prisoners; I myself ran from town to town gathering all; and Gen. Wayne said, "now all is completed and hereafter we will see which of us (red or white) will first take up the tomahawk. It shall now be buried." But from your talk of yesterday you threaten to make war against us; to cut off our women and children.

You astonish us with your talk. When you do us harm, nothing is done; but when we do anything, you immediately tie us up by the neck; sometime ago we brought in a number of Osages, prisoners of war; you demanded them, and we delivered them up. There is no recompense for us.

You may observe the ideas of the chiefs and warriors of the Illinois River. Listen to their talk and see whether it is not right. We wish that the Governor at Kaskaskia may hear our words.

You see how we live—our women and children. Do not, my friends, suppose that we are accomplices with murderers. Take courage and let us live in peace and quietness, as we have heretofore done. You said that we, our wives and children, should live in peace. You hear what the chiefs in council say; they cannot interfere in the demand you have made. They cannot interfere in any bad business of the kind.

You see the situation of the Pottawottamies, Chippeways and Ottaways to-day. The Shawnee Prophet, the man who talks with the Father of Light, blames us for not listening to him. You do the same. We are like a bird in a bush, beset, and not knowing which way to fly for safety—whether to the right or to the left. If our young men behave ill to-day, you may blame the Shawnee Prophet for it.

The chiefs are reproached by the young men generally. They say to us, you give your hand to the Americans to-day, and in future they will knock you in the head. This is the occasion of their late unruly behavior.

Remember what you told us on yesterday. Among other sayings, you threatened to kill our women and children. Do not think that those young men that committed the murders belong to this place. They came from the village of the Shawnee Prophet. All the mischiefs that have been done have been committed through the influence of the Shawnee Prophet, and I declare this to you for the truth.

Behold the Shawnee Prophet, that man who talks with the Great Spirit, and teaches the Indians to pray and look to God! But as for us, we do not believe him. We wish to chase our deer, and live in peace with the Americans.

Ever since the Shawnee Prophet has been on the Wabash River he has been jealous of the chiefs and warriors of this river. He suspects that we give information and a favorable ear to the Americans, and says that the Americans will act like traitors to us.

For my part I suspect no wrong. I do not listen to the bad advice of the Prophet.

Our great chiefs of the Pottawottamies, Chippeways and Ottaways command us to observe the alliance between us and the Americans, that we and our children may live in peace and comfort. These are the reasons for our not listening to the Shawnee Prophet.

My dear friends do not believe us accomplices in the mischiefs recently committed; we wish peace.

Observe the chiefs and warriors in council. We think of nothing but to live in peace and quietness. We would have been very much surprised if the Americans had come and made war on us, feeling ourselves perfectly innocent of these offenses.

We think nothing of what is past, as we are innocent. These are also the sentiments of the Kickapoos; and we, the chiefs of the several tribes now in council, join our hands together and hold them as fast as I now hold the wampum in my hand.

See, my friends, how matters stand to-day. If you wish for war with us, it lies altogether with yourselves. It is better to avoid it if possible.

If the Americans should commence war with us, we would have to fight in our own defense. The chiefs are of opinion that it is best to remain at peace.

I have finished, my friends. Perhaps you take us for little children. We whip our children, but men will defend themselves.

For myself I am indifferent. It would be the same with me to raise or bury the tomahawk. I can but die at last

Observe, my friends: since our peace with the Americans we have been and still are a poor people. We have not even a piece of ribbon to tie our speech. I have finished.

After Little Chief had concluded, Capt. Levering spoke as follows :

Brothers, Chiefs and Warriors:

I have listened with close attention to your words, and I shall be careful to convey them to our father. It is for him to say what shall be done. But, being among you, with my ears and eyes open to things that could not be known to the distance of my father's cabin, I think that he will not disapprove of my speaking to you in my own words, for I shall hold fast to his mind. I discover that you harbor a number of incorrect opinions, that render you dissatisfied with your white brethren; and I am really so far your friend, that in case I saw you and my white brethren about rushing each other into destruction through want of light, if I was able I would inform you of it. But if I thought you were acting with your eyes open, you might abide the consequences; I should not push myself in the way.

As you have spoken on many subjects, I wish to have time to look over them, and I also wish to put my words on paper, that I may show them to my father at Kaskaskia. I shall hope to meet you here again in the morning.

After the council adjourned, the chiefs, in behalf of their respective nations, offered him the hand of friendship.

On the next morning Capt. Levering continued his address, as follows:

Brothers, you have offered me your hands of friendship. If there was not something sincere within, to give your offer a cordial reception, I should not have requested this opportunity of speaking to you.

The brave and generous chief can show himself in his village at all times, and that, too, with his head loftily erect! Honesty, still prouder, can traverse the globe naked, and that through the glare of day.

Our father's minds and words to the Indians being as pure as sterling silver, they have no fear nor objection to their sons talking to them, so that their words are open and as clear as your native fountains; yet they wish you to be careful about listening to every one.

Red men never injured me or my relations, and having grown up far from their paths, I can have no prejudices or resentments against them; and as all men, both red and white, understand how to estimate honesty, I may say that I have no inducement to deceive you. The very nature of my errand must assure you that the welfare of my white brethren commands that I shall speak the truth. I shall be no false prophet. I am not endeavoring to be a chief among you. No generous man would be offended with the free, open, decent candor of another, even though it should come from an enemy. Now, brethren, listen to the facts—all the white people can tell whether I lie, for we have it down in black and white, and the most of them can read.

The first white people that came across the wide waters, and settled on this side of them, were Spaniards, and they settled on islands further distant than the mouth of the Mississippi. These people, seeing flattering hopes in the West, gave the news, and encouraged many people to come over from many nations, residing on the other side of the great waters. The English were the first to settle on any part of the land on this side of the mouth of the Mississippi, and all around the east and north to the end of walking. After them came the French, who settled on the other end of Canada. Then came the Dutch, on another part of the large shores; and many people came from numerous nations, on the other side of the waters, that perhaps you never heard of. The Americans were formerly the British; our forefathers were British; the British King owned us as his children, and we obeyed him like dutiful children.

When he made war against the French in Canada, we went with his young men to fight his battles; and we were proud to be and remain his children, until about forty years ago, when he began to ask things of us that were unreasonable. Although we had at all times regarded him as our father—believing that he had a right to ask it of us, we, as dutiful children, gave him money and warriors, and both he and his big council acknowledged that his American children had done more than their duty. But in course of time he and his council thought that we were growing too rich; that riches would give us the desire of leaving them, and that we would become a nation of full strength. To prevent this they endeavored to take our money from us without asking, and that, too, whether we were willing or not; just as though your chiefs should hamstring your young men, through fear of their leaving them. This is exactly the case, for we never refused his requests; but when he began to draw by force large quantities of honey from a small poor tree, we complained, but our complaints found a deaf ear. We preferred nakedness, cold, hunger, and all the horrors of war, to such degradation. We fought him for seven years, under poverty and hardship. The Indians did not know how much we were injured, or they would not have increased our hardships. But, under Washington—a man now dead, yet we delight in remembering him, for he was good and brave—our warriors fought our battles and led us to well earned victory. The English asked for peace, and acknowledged us to be a separate nation.

This was the beginning of the American nation, when we chose Washington, our victorious chief, to be our Great Father. Since then, the British cannot be our generous friends, although they dare not come to open war with us. As a chief once said to me, "they tell half lie, half truth—firing a gun into our canoe, and saying it was a mistake!" They set the Indians on us to resent their own enmities, and for the purpose of engrossing all the profit of the Indian trade.

Can you not see, brothers, that the British offer you protection, when, in case of open war, they cannot stand in Canada? when they cannot protect themselves? If I had sucked the same breasts with your chiefs and warriors, I would tell you this.

Now, brothers, attend, and you will begin to learn that your complaints against the Americans are founded in error.

Was it the present Americans that crossed the water to your land? We were then British, and governed by a British King, whom we had to fight as an enemy to our rights and welfare. The English settled here some two hundred and ten years ago; the present American nation is not of my age; and our Government and Great Father, in their disposition, are as different from the British King as the summer from the winter day. The present Americans were nowise instrumental in crossing the ocean; the first coming of their forefathers was owing to the British King, who rules his sons far more imperiously than you suspect. If wanted, they must go and fight, and cannot say nay. Even, then, although we were British, and under their King, we, like you, found ourselves here, and from necessity we must be near neighbors. It is, therefore, our interest to cultivate friendship, unless we intend to destroy each other.

I must have proven to you, by this time, that your prejudices to the Americans, at least in one instance, are unfounded. I could, in a little time, make it appear that nearly all of your supposed grievances are owing to a misunderstanding of our nation. If this is true, you will find it agreeable as well as our interest to nourish and water the friendship of the red and white men.

Although our father constructs forts outside the settlements of his white children, he does not, as you seem to think, act differently from the French or the British.

I have seen and have heard of forts all along the British line in Canada. I have seen other forts along the lakes, and elsewhere, that were built by the French; and let me tell you, chiefs and warriors, that the most of the forts in this country were built by the British and French. When we have the Spaniards on one side of us, and the British on the other, in forts, and they are endeavoring to make our red brethren discontented with us, is it not advisable for us to keep up and garrison those forts that came to us by the chance of war? Does the garrison at Chicago, Detroit, Defiance, Ft. Wayne, or that at the mouth of the Missouri, or any other within your knowledge, come out to war on the Indians? Those forts are intended and are kept up merely to protect our friends; and to suppose that they presage or threaten war, when they have never committed any, is rather an overstrained idea.

You say that the whites first led the Indians to acts of outrage, by inviting them to join in war against the whites; and, consequently, the white people are to blame for the bad practice among the Indians! But, I ask, have the Americans ever solicited the Indians to join them in war against the British? or, against any nation? I answer, no. Our forefathers, even while we were yet fighting to become a nation, advised the Indians to lay on their skins at home, raise corn and kill deer, but not to engage in war on either side; and such has been the advice of our fathers to the Indians ever since. It is true that some Indians, since then, have offered to join us, and certainly you would not object to our receiving and taking sides in favor of our friends.

Your ideas of the treaty of Greenville are alike inaccurate. You suppose that our fathers promised that all murderers, on either side, should be delivered up to the opposite party. That cannot be the case; for our laws would not allow our Great Father, or Gen. Wayne with him, to make such a stipulation in a treaty. All offenders against our laws must be tried by our laws and by a jury of twelve of our citizens. This is the way an Indian would be tried under our laws, and in the same manner would a white man be tried for killing an Indian. I know this to be true (although you have said that there is no recompense for an Indian) that when I left Kaskaskia there was a man in jail, fastened with irons by the wrist, for having abused an Indian; and this was done by order of the Governor, because he thought it just. The treaty of Greenville requires of each of our Governors to catch a murderer of an Indian, and to have him tried for murder, and if found guilty, to see that he was hung.

In answer to your complaint in the case of an Indian that was killed in St. Louis, I must tell you more of our laws, and you will learn that the whites equal the red men in their conceptions of justice. I cannot hinder the belief that somebody told you wrong in the case of the Indian at Detroit; but I know something of this at St. Louis. Whenever a man makes an attempt to kill another, a third party coming up may kill the first to save the life of the second; and our laws do say that the third was right in so doing—for the act of the first makes the supposition strong that he was an unruly and bad man; the second might have been a good man, and his life should be saved. All this is like the case in St. Louis. The Indian was drunk, flourishing his tomahawk, and threatening to kill. Judge Meigs (a chief), without weapons, stepped up to the Indian for the purpose of persuading him to be quiet; the Indian drew his tomahawk on the Judge, and the young man, coming up and seeing him in danger, killed the Indian to save the Judge's life. Judge Meigs told me this. He is now Governor of Ohio.

You must not think, from my words, that I am unfriendly to the Spanish, French or English. They are my brothers, and they, as well as we, are here from like circumstances. They, as well as others, who have come from over the waters, are equally under the same care and protection of our Great Father.

Let us acquaint ourselves with times past, and with things that do not immediately concern us, with the view of improving our minds and dispositions, and not strain our brain to find out causes of discontent and quarrel. Let us consider and find out what will promote our mutual benefit and harmony.

You have looked more to the threatenings of our father's words than to the justice of them. Let us think of them for a while; and, in turning to them, I would not, now, or at any other time, make them appear worse against you than the plain talk of truth, and neither of us, I hope, are so far worse than children as to be frightened at facts. It is true, as our father also tells you, that the head chief of all our tribes would, like the sun, bestow his genial blessings on all—the weak and the strong—on the mole-hill as well as the mountain; and even when his goodness should be obstructed, he is yet mild and forbearing for a season, hoping that a sense of right and wrong will correct and restore the evil; but when he finds that forbearance and kindness fail—like the sun, when fogs and poisons threaten, the fire of his justice will dissipate and destroy the evil. Before I left our father's cabin with his words for you, a runner of his had returned from our father and chief on the west of the Mississippi, and one from our father to the east of the Wabash, and our father knew that their minds and determinations were in unison with his, and also with that of our Great Father of all the tribes. Our father told you of the murder of five whites and of the horses that were stolen at the same time, between the Mississippi and Missouri rivers; this summer one has been murdered on one of the creeks that empties into the Kaskaskia, and an attempt was made to carry off a woman; since then, one has been wounded and another murdered near the Piasa rock, on the Mississippi; and I myself have heard of thirty-three horses having been stolen by the Indians, during this summer.

Little Chief said: "My friend, I request you, now, to take the names of the chiefs and warriors, that you may show to your father in Kaskaskia how ready we have been to attend to his words."

On the 18th of August, the Sac chief, Little Sturgeon, called on Capt. Levering, who explained to him the circumstance and cause of Capt. Whiteside having fired on some of his nation on the Mississippi.

The council assembled again; and after Capt. Levering had given his advice, Gomo said:

We have listened with patient attention, and I hope that the great Master of Light was noticing it. When the Master of Light made man, he endowed those who wore hats with every gift, art and knowledge. The red skins, as you see, live in lodges and on the wilds of nature.

The council then adjourned. Gomo delivered up two of the horses, and Little Chief agreed to deliver to Capt. Heald, at Chicago, two more; and Gomo said he would endeavor to have them all returned as soon as they could be found.

The chiefs told Capt. Levering that the murderers of the Coles party were two Indians by the name of Esh-can-ten-e-mane and O-kat-che-cum-mich, and that they were both at a village about twenty miles on this side of the Prophet's village. After the departure of the chiefs, Little Chief returned and said that he wished to tell Captain Levering, in private, that the murderers of the Coles party could be taken without any trouble, by inviting them, among others, to a meeting at Fort Wayne next fall, when, their names being known, the commandant could seize them.

For the purpose of having another talk with the Indians, Gov. Edwards, in March, 1812, issued the following instructions to Capt. Hebert:

"Capt. Edward Hebert is hereby authorized by me to ascend the Illinois River as far as he can, with a view to deliver a friendly talk to the Indians of said river, and also to request the traders of every description to withdraw till our affairs with the Indians have a more settled and favorable appearance. I wish the request made in the most delicate manner; but I also desire that the traders shall know that they need not expect any indulgences, if they should not instantly comply."

NINIAN EDWARDS, *Governor*,
Superintendent of Indian affairs in and over Illinois Territory.

To GOMO, *Chief of the Pottawottamies on Illinois River:*

MY SON—Captain Hebert not long ago told me that you were desirous to come to see me. If you wish to come, you shall be conducted in safety. We never deceived any Indians who came to see us upon our invitation. I do not believe you ever heard of such treachery from any of your Great Father's officers.

It is my wish to preserve peace, to save the women and children, and to prevent the earth from being stained with blood. If this is your wish, also, I want to see you, and you can come with Capt. Hebert. I will send you back safely.

If you are for peace, we are ready to give you our hands. If you are for war, we are ready for you.

I am not surprised that some of your young men are foolish and wish to go to war. But you are old enough to know the folly of it. You are too old to be deceived by the English. They pretend to be your friends, but their object is to get you to fight their battles, and they care not what becomes of you afterwards.

We wish you to attend to your own business. We do not want you to fight for us. We can whip the English ourselves.

The English tell you of the power of their King. They tell you he can conquer us. You ought not to believe them. They told you the same story in the American war; but you know they did not tell you the truth. We were then like little children, but we whipped them then; and if they thought they were now able to fight us, why should they want to get your assistance?

Call together your old men, who have had experience in war and who have felt its bad consequences, and let them advise the foolish.

You have traveled to some of the large cities of your Great Father, and ought to have some knowledge of his strength. You cannot think to conquer him. You have everything to lose and nothing to gain by a war with us.

If the English do not behave themselves we will take Canada, and drive them out of America. You will have no one, then, to help you.

My son, now remember my words. If you and the British will go to war with us, we shall immediately take Montreal and Upper Canada. We will never suffer a

British trader to go among you again. We will call home all our own traders and carry war into your own country. Consider how you are to live without any trade, when you are at the same time harrassed with war.

Your young men may not believe these things, but you are old enough to know that they will come to pass. Why will you bring such evils upon yourselves? We do not wish to afflict you unless you raise the tomahawk. When you do this, you will not get peace as soon as you will want it. For if your Great Father, the President of the United States, is obliged, by your bad conduct, to go to war with you, depend upon it he will strike such a blow as will prevent the red people from ever wishing to go to war with us again.

Council held at Cahokia, April 16, 1812, between Ninian Edwards, Governor of the Illinois Territory, and the chiefs and warriors of the following nations, to-wit:

Of the *Pottawottamies*—Gomo, Pepper, White Hair, Little Sauk, Great Speaker, Yellow Son, Snake, Mankai, Bull, Ieman, Neck-kee-ness-kee-sheck, Ignace, Powtawamie Prophet, Pamousa, Ish-kee-bee, Toad, Man-wess, Pipe Bird, Cut Branch, The South Wind, and The Black Bird.

Of the *Kickapoos*—Little Deer, and Blue Eyes (representative of Pamawattan), Sun Fish, Blind-of-an-eye, Otter, Mak-kak, Yellow Lips, Dog Bird, and Black Seed.

Of the *Ottaways*—Mittitasse (representative of The Blackbird,) Keeska-gon, and Malsh-wa-she-wai.

Of the *Chippeways*—The White Dog.

Gov. Edwards addressed them as follows:

Chiefs and Warriors of the Pottawottamies, Kickapoos, Chippeways, and Ottaways:

My desire to preserve peace and friendship, if possible, between the red and white people, induced me to send for you; and I am glad you have come to see me, according to my request, because it shows a desire on your part, as well as mine, to keep the tomahawk buried.

My Children, your Great Father, the President of the United States, has given many proofs of his love for the red flesh, and the red skins will always find him a kind protector so long as they act with pure hearts. He loves both his red and white children, and does not wish either to do hurt to the other.

My Children, for a long time the bloody tomahawk and scalping-knife have been buried. The red people enjoyed their forests and pursued their game in peace; and the white people cultivated the earth without fear. We were all then happy, and your Great Father was glad to see it. For some time past, a storm has appeared to be gathering. Injuries have been done, anger has been produced, and war has appeared to be almost unavoidable.

My Children, that great deceiver, the Shawnee Prophet, has been hired by the British to tell you falsehoods and to cause you to raise the tomahawk against your white brother. He pretended to hold talks with the Great Spirit, to impose upon the weak and foolish. He promised many things. He promised his followers victory at the battle of Tippecanoe; but the American chief, Gov. Harrison, proved that he was a liar.

My Children, before the Shawnee Prophet began to work with a bad heart, you were all happy; but he has distracted the red skins and their happiness is gone.

My Children, those who listened to the Shawnee Prophet have gained nothing but misery; many of them were wounded, and others lost their lives and left their friends to mourn over their folly.

My Children, the British have had other bad birds flying among you. I am not surprised that some of your young men should have been deceived by them. But there are some of you great chiefs who are old warriors, and wise enough to know them better. Some of you know the horrors and folly of war well enough to wish to avoid it.

My Children, you can remember when the British advised the red skins to make war upon their white brethren of the United States. They then promised you great assistance; but they deceived you and left you to fight your own battles, and you found it necessary to sue for peace. At that time you were stronger than you are now; the woods were then full of game of all kinds; large numbers of you could collect together and travel through the country without fear of wanting provisions. But this cannot now be done.

My Children, when the red and white people were formerly at war, we were then weak; we are now grown strong—have everything necessary for war, and are your near neighbors. Our Great Father's dominions extend over vast countries, bounded by the great waters; his towns and cities are hard to be counted, and his white children are as thick and numerous as the stars of the sky.

My Children, your Great Father has nothing to fear from war with you, for if it were possible for the red skins to conquer one army, he could soon have another ten times as strong to oppose you. But he does not wish for war. You have nothing to hope from it, and you can have peace if you will do justice and comply with your treaty.

My Children, we are about to engage in a war with the British. I wish you to see how different our conduct is from theirs. We do not wish you to take any part with us in the war; we do not wish you to fight for us, because we know we are able to whip them without your help; when we were as little children we fought, conquered them, and took the whole United States away from them; and if we fight them again, we shall whip them and take the Canadas away from them. For this purpose our Great Father now has an army of 185,000 men.

My Children, the British pretend to be your friends, but their object is to get you to fight their battles; and they care not what becomes of you afterwards. They tell you of the power of their King over the great lake. They say to you that he can conquer us, but they know this is not true. If they thought they were able to fight us, why are they so anxious to get you to assist them?

My Children, the British would now load you with presents, if you would engage in the war, but remember these presents would last you but a little while and would cost you very dear; for if you join them in the war against us, remember now my words: We shall take Montreal and all Upper Canada. British traders and English goods will never be suffered to go among you again. Our own traders will all be recalled. War will be waged against you. Your country will be taken and strong garrisons will be built in order to retain it. Consider how you are to live without any trade, when, at the same time, you will be so harassed with war, that you can hunt nowhere with safety.

My Children, your young men may not believe these things, but your old warriors and brave chiefs have sense enough to know they will come to pass. I tell you

—8

these things because I am so much your friend, that I do not wish you to bring those evils upon yourselves, your wives and helpless children.

My Children, we do not wish to afflict you unless you raise the tomahawk. When you do this you may not get peace as soon as you may want it: for if your Great Father, the President of the United States, is obliged, by your bad conduct, to go to war with you, he will strike such a blow as will be sufficient to prevent the red people from ever going to war with us again.

My Children, remember it is easy to get into war, but hard to get out of it again with advantage,

My Children, I am satisfied that many of you have too much sense to listen to all the Prophet's lies, and hate him in your hearts, because he deceived your friends and has brought trouble on you all. But some of your people have listened to him, or other bad advisers, and they have done us injuries which cannot be overlooked.

My Children, guilty as the Prophet has been, he has not done all the mischief; others have done mischief, hoping they would escape punishment by laying the blame upon him; but this must not be suffered. While some of your tribes have been professing peace, your men have been committing depredations upon us. This cannot be suffered; unless such bad men shall be given up for punishment, the tribe must be answerable for their conduct. Your Great Father has been waiting to see if justice would be done in those cases by yourselves, and this has led you into an error; for you suppose that because he has not made war upon you to revenge himself, that he does not mean to have satisfaction, and you do not seem to think yourself bound to deliver up such bad men; but even protect them, knowing their guilt, and they are encouraged to do more mischief. If this conduct should be suffered, our people might be murdered every day, and we never could get satisfaction—because we could not distinguish the guilty from the innocent.

My Children, while we trusted to treaties with you—while we believed our red brethren to be friendly—some of our people on this side and some on the other side of the Mississippi, fearing no danger, have been plundered of their property and deprived of their lives by some of your bad men; many horses have been stolen, for which no satisfaction has been made, although it was promised. On the 19th day of July, 1810, four men were killed and a fifth wounded, in the district of St. Charles, in Louisiana. On the 2d June, last year, three of your bad men went to the house of a Mr. Cox, in this country, plundered him of a great deal of property, barbarously killed his son, and took his daughter a prisoner. A few days afterwards another party killed a man by the name of Price, and wounded another by the name of Ellis, in this country also, and near the Mississippi.

My Children, these were great outrages, but I used my exertions to prevent the people from rising to revenge themselves; and I sent Capt. Levering to you to demand of you to give up the offenders, as you had bound yourselves, by treaty, to do. You did not deliver them up, yet you say that you wish to be governed by the treaty, and still you will not comply with it.

My Children, when I demanded those bad men, by Capt. Levering, you professed not to know where they were; and still you said you could not deliver them up. Since that time I have found out that some of them were actually with you—that they are positively of your party, and have resided near Peoria ever since.

My Children, you stated that the chiefs did not know, when mischief was done, who of their party committed it. We know enough of your customs to satisfy us that such things are seldom concealed among you. But this, if true, was no excuse for failing to deliver those you knew to be guilty.

My Children, you complained that we never delivered up our men to you when they did mischief. We are not bound to do so by the treaty; we punish our men when we can prove them to be guilty, just as we would punish the red people for the same offenses. But you have failed to give up the late offenders for us to punish them, nor have you punished them yourselves, though you know them to be guilty.

My Children, when I sent Capt. Levering to you with my talk, I was sorry to find, in the answer I received, statements so much like those which the Prophet is in the habit of expressing. You attempted to draw a contrast between the people of the United States and French and British; you then said the French and British never built forts, but that the Americans did so. This is not true. When the British first made great canoes and crossed the great lake, they always built forts; and so did the French. There are the remains of old forts everywhere near the great lake; both the French and English built forts at Pittsburgh, on the Ohio. You see those works at St. Louis. There is also a fort, called Fort Chartres, between this place and Kaskaskia. There are forts in Canada and many other places that were built by the British and French.

My Children, you also said to Capt. Levering that when the French and British made presents to the Indians, they never asked any land; but that the Americans never made you any presents, except they asked first for a little land and then for a great deal.

My Children, there is indeed a difference between us and the French and British, in this respect. We never take your land without paying you for it. They claimed all your land and took it whenever they wanted it, without paying you anything. They did not acknowledge that you had any land, and they have transferred it all to us, without paying any regard to your claim.

My Children, when the British first crossed the great lake, the red people owned all the land to the great water. The British took it all from you, and never paid anything. The red people also owned Canada; but that has been taken from them, and you have never heard that the Indians received anything for all the lands that the British now hold there, nor did you ever hear that the French paid for the land they held on this or the other side of the Mississippi River.

My Children, we never want to buy your land, or take it from you, unless you wish to sell it, and then we will give you the price that you ask for it. You cannot show that we ever took a foot of your land, since we got clear of the King of England, without paying for it, and we are not answerable for the sins of the British King; for we all know that he is not a good man, and that he did great injustice to the red people, by taking their land without paying for it, although he now pretends to be their friend, because he wishes them to fight for him. I hope, therefore, I shall hear no more upon this subject.

My Children, you told Capt. Levering that if we did not have peace with you, it would be our fault. This is not true; we only ask justice of you. If you do justice, we wish for peace; but we cannot consent that the land shall be stained with the blood of our innocent brethren, without some satisfaction being given. Peace, upon such terms, is worse than war.

My Children, the blood of these innocent persons who have been wounded and murdered cries aloud to the Great Spirit for vengeance. The hearts of their relations and brethren bleed with sorrow, and they thirst for revenge.

My Children, now open your ears to hear my words, and let them sink deep into your hearts. If you wish for peace with us, you must do us justice. If you disapprove those murders and other outrages that have been committed, you must deliver up the offenders, or punish them yourselves; for if you harbor among you such deadly enemies to us, you cannot be our friends, and you ought not to expect our friendship.

My Children, you can choose peace or war upon proper terms. If you choose peace and will do justice, it will rejoice the heart of your Great Father and the hearts of all your white brethren.

My Children, if you or any other red people should be for war, we shall be ready for you. I have an army coming on for the defense of my people. It will soon be at this place, and if any more murders should be committed upon our people, I shall take revenge. You must not let any such bad men come from among you, and you must not harbor among you bad men of other tribes, knowing that they have injured us.

My Children, it now appears that the Winnebagoes are about to make war upon us, and it is probable that other red people will also do mischief, hoping that it will be laid upon the Winnebagoes; but I shall be upon my watch to detect and punish all such.

My Children, there has lately been much mischief done. I have strong reason to believe that others, besides the Winnebagoes, have been concerned, and that some of you have knowledge of it. If you are friends I expect you will tell us all you know.

My Children, let justice be done, let all cause of complaint be removed, and let us again live like brothers.

My Children, we do not want your land. We have more land already than we can use, and I shall neither propose to buy it, nor does your Great Father, or myself, wish to take a foot of it from you. Those who tell you to the contrary tell you lies and wish to deceive.

My Children, shut your ears against all evil counsellors and comply with your treaty, and you shall still be treated as friends and brothers.

METTETASSE rose and said: This is the one (pointing to GOMO) who is to answer your speech of yesterday, in the name of us all—Pottawottamies, Kickapoos, Chippeways and Ottaways.

THE PEPPER—My Father, my brother here, the oldest chief, will answer you. We have all heard your speech of yesterday, and we will all hear his answer to you; and, when the council is over, we all desire to go home.

THE LITTLE DEER—My Father, I am of the village of the Great Lick. I speak in the name of Blue Eyes, the representative of Pamawatam. I give you my hand, and wish to be peaceable. You might have heard talk of me, and I am well known by all these Indians here, and it is well known to them all that I never listened to the Prophet; and I am the first chief who, after the battle of Tippecanoe, went to Gov. Harrison with my flag.

My Father, my chiefs and warriors are here, who all know me to be a peaceable Indian. My village is small. This man (meaning GOMO) will speak to you, and we will all agree to what he will say.

My Father, the people of my village are now anxious for my return, to hear the result of this council.

My Father, we have reflected on your speech of yesterday, and we have consulted together. GOMO will answer in the name of us all. We wish to cross over so soon as the council is over.

GOMO'S ANSWER.

My Father, you have heard what my war chiefs have said. I will speak to you as the Great Spirit inspires me.

My Father, in this manner the Great Spirit has taught me to speak by giving me a pipe and tobacco, therein to make my father smoke.

My Father, this is the pipe we have smoked together. I smoked out of it in coming down to see you.

My Father, all the chiefs that I left at home hold their pipes in their hands, to smoke with us on our return.

My Father, we always kept fast hold of the pipe of peace. That pipe will remain with you; and although it remains with you, it is still in our hands.

My Father, while you are smoking that pipe, your children smoke also with you.

My Father, when the Great Spirit created us, he gave us the pipe of peace. The wampum we wear was made by our white brothers.

My Father, the manner in which I present you the pipe is our way and was transmitted to us by our ancestors, and we now know you hold it.

My Father, all that you said yesterday was well said, and I assure you it has sunk deep into my heart, and it is from the bottom of my heart that I will speak.

My Father, if I came here, it was to hear your words, and therefore I thank you for what you did say.

My Father, I am not to make a council of myself, and when my chiefs tell me what to say, I do so. Therefore, what I now say is from them all.

My Father, I now show you I obeyed your orders. I intended to go and quarrel with the Prophet, but I have put that off because you sent for me.

My Father, what has scared all our towns and villages is that affair that happened on the Wabash.

My Father, we have reflected considerably since yesterday. It is neither you nor I that made this earth, and the Great Spirit is angry, and we do not know what he will do.

My Father, by what I see to-day, probably our Great Spirit is angry, and wants us to return to ourselves and live in peace. What I now say is from the bottom of my heart.

My Father, you see many children have sold their lands. The Great Spirit did not give them the land to sell. Perhaps that is the cause why the Great Spirit is angry.

My Father, you have often been deceived. A chief will come and sell land. Can a chief sell land? I am a chief, but I am poor and worthy of pity, and I want to live in peace on our land.

My Father, if there could be found among us one chief who had influence enough to deliver a murderer, I would be happy to see such a chief.

My Father, you probably think I am a great chief. I am not! I cannot control my young men as I please.

My Father, I am a red skin; I am not a great chief. I am a chief whilst my young men are growing, but when they become grown I am no more master of them.

My Father, the Great Spirit created us all. We have not the same power that you have. You have troops and laws. When a man does ill, you have him taken and punished; but this we cannot do.

My Father, I could very easily secure or kill the murderers you mention; but unless the whole of my chiefs and young men are consenting, I would be killed.

My Father, concerning the murderers, we will consult all together, and we will then know what we will do.

My Father, I have not forgotten Gen. Wayne's counsel, and I have always tried to follow it and to live in peace.

My Father, at the time the red skins were fighting, I was not among them. I was then traveling through the States, and went to Washington City to see our Great Father, and I was led to several sea-ports in America.

My Father, when Turkey-foot came here and killed your white children, you desired he should be killed. We got together and consulted among ourselves, and we killed him.

My Father, the Kickapoos were those that killed your children on the Missouri. You demanded the murderers. Here is the Blue Eyes present who brought them in.

My Father, it is impossible for us to bring in murderers. They are too much dispersed and too far off.

My Father, here is my oldest brother (Gen. Clark), that I saw two years ago, who told me to live in peace, which I have always done.

My Father, in our treaty we are bound to deliver up murderers. I am not the only chief who could not deliver up murderers.

My Father, at the Miami village a Pottawottamie was killed by an American. We never demanded the murderer, but the factor there covered our dead brother by giving us goods.

My Father, I have heard the good advice of your speech. I never listen to any evil birds. I am for living in peace, and I will return to my people and rehearse them your speech.

My Father, at the time the British and Americans fought, in the last war, we never meddled in it. We used to come down here and follow the advice of a chief who was then here.

My Father, I have already said to you we never meddled in the British battles; and, therefore, do you think we would now join them? No, never!

My Father, no one can say I ever went to the English factories, or ever got a blanket from the English. When I wanted a blanket, I would buy one from our trader.

My Father, I must tell you the truth. I went to see them two years ago, and when I got there the Indians, on seeing me, said, "here comes an American!" and it was with difficulty that I got home without starving.

My Father, a father, when he wants his children to do well, instructs them. You did so yesterday, and I was well pleased.

My Father, you asked me to tell you what was going on in our towns. I cannot now say, for I have been a long time absent, in our sugar camps. When I return home, I will be able to learn.

My Father, I will state what I learnt last fall.

My Father, when Mainpock went to war, he had one of his young men killed, who was an Ottawa, and related to another old man; and this old man sent his son to the English. He said, "my father has sent for goods." And they told him he must be very sorry for the loss of his son.

My Father, the British then told him, "why do you go to war against the Osages? Go against the Americans; they are close."

My Father, when his son returned the old man answered the British agent, telling him to fight his own battles, as he was determined to live in peace.

My Father, do you think we would join the English? We remember, when you beat them, they left us in the lurch, and we had to fly. Certainly we will not join them again.

My Father, we have friends among us who often tell us not to join the English—that they will again forsake us; therefore we remain in peace.

My Father, I do not speak for all the Indian nations; I speak for those here.

My Father, you will easily know those who will assist the English; it cannot be kept hid.

My Father, sometimes it makes me reflect, when I consider on the promises you made us not to leave us in misery.

My Father, you told us, when you spoke to the Black Bird, that our fires would always be kept up clear, and that we should not suffer. This has not been kept.

My Father, my chiefs have gone among the nations and received prisoners, and returned them.

My Father, I never tried to sell land to get goods to cover us. I always got my covering from my hunt.

My Father, I am not of those men who go and see their father to sell land. I go and see my father to hear his words.

My Father, my desire is that our land remain as clear as this blue ribbon.

My Father, you see I have brought you our wives and children, to show you how ragged they are.

My Father, I thought of asking you to place a factory in our town of Peoria, but on account of the Winnebagoes, who are roving about, should any be killed, we might be blamed; therefore I will not, at present, ask for one.

My Father, if it was your wish to send us goods, we would wish the factor to be a man who has resided and does reside with us.

My Father, I have been asked to go and see our Great Father. The voyage is so long that I would wish to remain at home in peace.

My Father, you sent for us and we came down, and were fired at. We wish you had a fort at the entrance of the Illinois River, at which, in coming down, we might stop.

My Father, when a garrison will be there we will come and see you oftener, and feel better protected.

My Father, we are four nations here. Whatever the English may do, you may rest assured none of us will join them.

My Father, I am at the other end of Peoria Lake. It is there where we will reside, and remain at peace in hunting to support our families.

My Father, we intend to meet and draw near to one another, with the intention of living together in peace.

My Father, I have not much sense, but when you shall send any of your young men into our towns, they shall not be afraid for it.

My Father, when you sent us Capt. Levering, he was received and well treated by all our people.

My Father, it is all I have to say. I hope the Great Spirit will assist me in complying with what I have said.

GOV. EDWARDS' REPLY.

My Children, I will speak to you in a plain and short manner, and I wish my words to sink deep into your hearts.

My Children, if any of your white brethren had gone among you and committed murders and robberies, your Great Father never would have forgiven them for it, but they would have been punished as soon as their guilt could be proved.

My Children, your Great Father cannot forgive those who have murdered his white children and taken their property. Your Great Father's children would no longer love him if he were to suffer such things to pass unpunished.

My Children, your Great Father now asks you to do nothing for him but what he would do for you, in the same circumstances.

My Children, you objected to give up those bad men to be hung, like dogs, as you call it, and I now agree to permit you to kill them yourselves; and, if you will consent to do it, I will send a man with you to see it done, and we shall then have peace.

My Children, you do not acknowledge that any of the murderers are of your party, except those who killed Cox and took his sister prisoner. What you say may be true, and I now only demand that you shall deliver to me or that you shall kill those murderers that you acknowledge are of your party.

My Children, these three murderers that I now demand are Pottawottamies, and I call upon you, great chiefs and brave warriors of the Pottawottamies, to comply with your treaty and deliver up these bad men, or kill them yourselves.

My Children, I want to see if you will do that justice which you acknowledge is in your power, and then I shall believe you tell the truth when you say you wish for peace; and you shall be treated as good and dutiful children of your Great Father.

My Children, you say our people are not always punished when they do you injury, but we always punish them, if we can find them out; and you have no excuse for not punishing those who have lived among you and whom you know to be guilty.

My Children, you say these bad men are gone to the Prophet. This I know is not true—for one of them you left near Peoria, with a sore foot, and they have lived within three leagues of Peoria for a long time.

My Children, it is no excuse for you to say that these men are gone to the Prophet, because they were with you when I demanded them of you last year, and you have had it in your power to deliver them up for a long time.

My Children, you cannot suppose that we are people who can suffer our brethren to be murdered without having revenge. When we demand the murderers of you, you say they are gone to the Prophet. When Gov. Harrison demanded them of the Prophet, he said they were gone to you. You cannot suppose us such fools as to be put off this way.

My Children, suppose some of our bad men were to go and kill your warriors, and you could prove the fact! You find them to be the children of the American chief, Gov. Harrison. You go to him and demand that they should be punished. He tells you they are gone to Gov. Edwards. You then come to me. I tell you they are gone to Gov. Howard. You go to him. He tells you they are gone to Gov. Harrison!—by which you could get no satisfaction. You would think we were trying to make fools of you. And we now think the same thing of you! You would want revenge, and so do we want revenge; and we will have it.

My Children, think of these things. One day or other you will be sorry that you did not listen to my advice, and you will then be convinced that I was your friend.

My Children, I have heard your words, and I am sure there are good men among you, and wish we could be friends. It may be a hard case for you to punish your bad men; but you must remember it is a hard case for us to have our children and brothers murdered without revenge. If you will do us justice by punishing your murderers, and be friendly with us as brothers, you shall be protected against white people and red people also. The Great Spirit made us all, and loves us. I wish to take you to my heart and cover you with my wing. We do not want to buy your land, but we will not give up what we have bought. You sold the lands, or your fathers did, and you have no right to keep the pay and the land too. If twenty of your men murders a hundred of our people, what are we to do? We cannot find them and you will not punish them; what are we to do? You surely do not expect that we will let our people be murdered, without revenge. If you will not give up your bad men who kill us, we must kill as many of yours—and then we may kill the innocent, which we do not wish to do.

GOMO'S REPLY TO THE GOVERNOR'S SECOND SPEECH.

My Father, we are happy to hear what you have said, for we have come down here for that purpose.

My Father, what you have recommended me to do, I will do.

My Father, we came here to hear your words; the chiefs and warriors have all heard you. You will hear what I have done when I get home.

My Father, this is all I have to say to you. We will pay attention to your words.

PEORIA IN 1812.

Sometime in the fall of 1812, Capt. Thos. E. Craig was ordered by Gov. Edwards to go to Peoria, and take prisoners those persons who were there for the purpose of assisting the savages to murder our frontier settlers. Capt. Craig was successful in the expedition and returned to Camp Russell on the 16th of November, 1812, bringing a number of the inhabitants of Peoria as prisoners, together with a considerable quantity of different kinds of property. The prisoners were taken to St. Louis and discharged.

Gov. Coles, in his report to the Secretary of the Treasury in relation to claims to lots in the village of Peoria, Illinois, refers to that place thus:

The village of Peoria is situated on the north-west shore of Lake Peoria, about one and a half miles above the lower extremity or outlet of the lake. This village had been inhabited by the French previous to the recollection of any of the present generation. About the year 1778, the first house was built, in what was then called La ville de Maillet—afterwards the new village of Peoria—and of late the place has been known by the name of Fort Clark. The situation being preferred in consequence of the water being better, and its being thought more healthy, the inhabitants gradually deserted the old village, and, by the year 1796 or 1797, had entirely abandoned it and removed to the new village.

The inhabitants of Peoria consisted generally of Indian traders, hunters and voyagers, and had formed a link of connection between the French residing on the waters of the great lakes and the Mississippi River. From that happy facility of adapting themselves to their situation and associates, for which the French are so remarkable, the inhabitants of Peoria lived generally in harmony with their savage neighbors. It would seem, however, that about the year 1781, they were induced to abandon their

—9

village from the apprehension of Indian hostility; but soon after the peace of 1783 they again returned to it, and continued to reside there until the autumn of 1812, when they were forcibly removed from it and the place destroyed by a Capt. Craig, of the Illinois militia, on the ground, it was said, that he and his company were fired on in the night, while at anchor in the boats, before the village, by the Indians, with whom the inhabitants were suspected, by Craig, to be too intimate and friendly. The inhabitants of Peoria, it would appear, and from all I can learn, settled there without any grant or permission from the authority of any government; that the only title they had to the land was derived from possession.

It appears, from this report of Gov. Coles, that the following persons were driven from Peoria in 1812, by Capt. Craig: Thomas Forsyth, Jacques Mette, P. Larasier, (*alias* Chamberlain,) Antoine Le Claire, Michael Lacroix, Francis Racine, Sr., Francis Racine, Jr., Felix Fontaine, Hypolite Maillet, Francis Bauche, the heirs of Charles La Belle, Antoine La Pance, Antoine Barboune, and Louis Pencenneau. In the above list is not included the women and children. From other authentic sources I am inclined to believe that the number of inhabitants then in Peoria was between two and three hundred. It was not settled again for many years, and the following account is given of it in a letter from Gen. Joseph Street, of March 30, 1827:

The whole county, as now cut down, contains about thirty or forty men, and in its best state the whole docket does not exhibit thirty cases. There is nothing doing on land and still less on the water, if such comparison is admissible. The harbor and town site are the best, I presume, in all the western country; but not one sail enlivens the monotonous prospect or one oar dips into the "dark blue waves" of the fairy lake from one year's end to the other—if you will except the ferry boat, with now and then the canoe of a few miserable savages in quest of a dram.

After describing the country on both sides of the river, he continues:

This is the country, and a view of the resources and present prospects has been hinted at and partially detailed. Upon this view, what is your opinion, my friend? What should I do here or how could I do? It is true there is no prospect of getting bread for my numerous family, but there is great reason to believe they would not long want food at such a place. I could have gotten the county clerkship, but the recorder and judge of probate's offices, Dixon, has determined to hold. The other two are not worth $50 per annum—no, not $30. I cannot possibly go there. The clerkship of Peoria is worth nothing; the place, at present, has no attraction for me.

As Gov. Edwards' term of office expired by law, he was subsequently reappointed in 1812, and again in 1815, and continued to fill the executive chair until the organization of the State Government. For nearly four years, in the early period of his administration, no Territorial Legislature existed. The laws were made and administered by the Goveror and Judges. The Governor had power to authorize the formation of a Territorial Legislature whenever *he* judged the interests of the country required it; but, in accordance with those principles to which he was always devoted, he chose to be guided by a deliberate expression of the will of the people. Accordingly, in March, 1812, he issued a proclamation for an election to be held in the different settlements, to ascertain whether a majority were in favor of a Legislative Government. Such being the decision of the people, as expressed at the polls, he issued another proclamation, dated September 14, 1812, ordering an election to be held on the 8th, 9th and 10th of October, and authorized the people to choose one delegate to Congress, and members for the two houses of the Territorial Legislature; and, at the same time, made provision for the organization of Madison, Gallatin and Johnson counties. Two counties—St. Clair and Randolph—had been organized under the jurisdiction of the Northwestern Territory.

Here we ought to return and contemplate the situation of the Territory of Illinois, at the period of his appointment as Governor. Its population, much divided by habits, and even by language and national peculiarities—untried in the art of government—numbering less than nine thousand souls, and these residing in a few French villages or scattered through a few feeble American settlements. The Indians occupied by far the greater portion of the Territory, greatly outnumbering the whites, and meditating hostilities on the whole line of frontier settlements. After putting the machinery of the new government into operation, his penetrating mind perceived the necessity of learning the numbers, strength, position, resources and intentions of the Indian tribes in the interior. Accordingly he employed, at different times, trusty persons of the French population, acquainted with the Indian character, languages and habits, and who could safely penetrate the Indian country and gain the desired information.

Thousands of the citizens of this now flourishing State, who have known and highly appreciated his services in more conspicuous stations of public life, have little knowledge, probably, of his unremitting vigilance, quick penetration of danger and timely application of means to prevent attack, during the period immediately preceding the war, and while the artful and talented chieftain, Tecumseh, was striving to effect a combination of all the tribes, from Canada to the Floridas, preparatory to an attack upon the frontier territories. For several years the correspondence of Gov. Edwards with the War Department, and other authorities, was voluminous, and does honor to his talents as a writer, his patriotism and his sagacity.

No one can read this correspondence, now on file in the office of the Secretary of State, without being convinced of his sleepless vigilance and his ardent devotion to the welfare of the people of that trying period. No father ever felt more acutely for the preservation of his children, when exposed to danger, than did Gov. Edwards for the safety of these frontiers.

In the year 1812, having, by the utmost vigilance and industry—for which he was distinguished—penetrated the designs of the Indians, and clearly foreseeing the imminent danger which threatened the Illinois Territory—finding it entirely abandoned to its fate, by the officer to whom its defense had been intrusted, and believing its overthrow inevitable without a vigorous effort to defend it—he determined, at the risk of his private fortune, (which would have been sacrificed had not his conduct been approved by the General Government) to undertake its defense. Without any instructions to justify it, and, during the most important crisis, without any commission—his old one having expired and no new one having been received—he marched, at the head of a considerable body of volunteers raised by him for the special occasion, with whose assistance he successfully repelled the attacks of the savages and carried the war into their own country.

Mr. Lanman, in his Biographical Sketches, says that "before Congress had adopted any measures on the subject of volunteer rangers, he organized companies, supplied them with arms, built stockade forts, and established a line of posts from the mouth of the Missouri to the Wabash River. He was thus prepared for defense; and, during the Indian wars on the frontier, was most devoted to his country's service."

I need not repeat how much the success of these measures depended upon the fidelity, confidence and patriotism of the people. I only advert to it to show that the people regarded him as wise in planning and energetic in executing these measures for the protection of their families and defense of their country, and most cheerfully yielded him their united support. Nor does it comport with the present occasion for me to name those patriotic citizens that, with him, shared the hardships and responsibilities of that day of trial in subordinate posts of honor and authority.

While embodying and forming the citizens into the ranks of military service of defense, and while it was somewhat doubtful whether the measure would so far meet with the approbation of the General Government as to procure a remuneration of their expenses, the Commander-in-chief hesitated not to assure them that if the Government failed to provide for their services, no one should suffer while his own ample fortune could supply their necessities.

In the campaign of 1812, it became necessary to remove or disperse the hostile Indians from the regions of Mackinaw and Peoria. Aid was expected from Gen. Hopkins, who had marched from Kentucky with a considerable force of volunteers, and who was instructed to form a junction with the rangers and volunteers of Illinois, under the command of Gov. Edwards. Though Gen. Hopkins penetrated a considerable distance into the prairies west of the Wabash, he never arrived at the point of the contemplated attack. A boat loaded with provisions, fortified and manned with a small company, under the command of Capt. Craig, was dispatched up the river to wait at Peoria for the relief of the army.

All the U. S. rangers and mounted volunteers who could be spared for this enterprise were only about three hundred and fifty. After organizing at Camp Russell, near where Edwardsville now stands, and each man furnishing himself with provisions for twenty or thirty days, which he carried on his horse, the Governor, with this small force, took up the line of his march through the prairies into the heart of the Indian country, one hundred and sixty miles distant. I have not time to recount the hardships and sufferings of this campaign. In one particular its object was defeated—in not meeting with Gen. Hopkins and his volunteers; but the bravery, skill and success on the part of the Illinois rangers and volunteers, under the guidance of their able commander, were not less conspicuous. They broke up the Indian towns on the Kickapoo, Mackinaw, and the bluffs near the head of Peoria Lake, destroyed their crops, killed a number, took some prisoners, and returned in safety with one man mortally and three others slightly wounded.

Gov. Edwards was faithfully devoted to his country's service in laborious and watchful days and pensive and sleepless nights. Was there danger in the field, he was the first to meet it; was there toil, hardship and anxiety, he was the first to feel it. The soldiers looked to him with reverence, confidence and respect, for he was their companion and friend. The rights of his fellow-citizens were sacred to him, and they loved and admired him as their protector.

The following letter to the Secretary of War contains an official account of the expedition to Peoria:

ELVIRADE, RANDOLPH CO.,
ILLINOIS TERRITORY, *Nov.* 18, 1812.

To the HON. WM. EUSTIS,
Secretary of War, Washington City.

SIR: Of the perils to which this Territory has been exposed, during this year, I need add nothing to my former communication; but I beg leave to trouble you with a sketch of my military operations.

In the early part of the season, and until the month of August, my measures were entirely of a defensive and precautionary character—having kept a few companies of mounted riflemen ranging across the Territory in such a manner as to cover our frontier, their line of march being sometimes three and never less than one day's journey in advance of our settlements.

While this plan afforded the best practicable means of obtaining timely notice of the approach of a large body of Indians, I thought that small parties, from whom I apprehended at that time the most danger, seeing our line of ranging so far beyond the settlements, would naturally be afraid to cross it, lest their trail should be discovered and they be cut off. And as there were so many points in the Territory equally accessible to them, I preferred this disposition of my small force to that of collecting it together at any one place; and my success has exceeded my most sanguine calculations—not having lost a single life, on as dangerous and exposed a frontier as any in the United States.

In the latter part of August, being convinced that a large body of Indians intended to attack us, and Col. Russell, who had arrived only a short time before with one company of rangers, being called off with them to Vincennes, I immediately determined to collect and organize the most efficient force in my power, to take the command of it myself, and defend the Territory to the last extremity. Many circumstances induced me to believe that the meditated attack would be made on that part of our frontier which lies between the Mississippi and Kaskaskia Rivers—under which conviction (which subsequent events proved to be well founded) I established and supported several forts, at convenient distances on a line from one river to the other, and as near to the centre of that line as a due regard to other circumstances, which were entitled to weight, would admit of. I built a large strong fort, at which I collected my principal force—it being a point from which I could most conveniently aid or relieve every other part that might be attacked.

Whilst the small body of infantry I had in service were relied on for the defense of these forts, between four and five hundred mounted riflemen were kept almost constantly ranging in the country between us and the enemy. But scarcely were these measures put into operation, before I ascertained the very day on which the Indians proposed to assemble at Peoria for the purpose of coming down upon us, the route they intended to take, and the objects they had in view; and I collected together, with as much dispatch as possible, all my mounted men, with the intention of setting out on an expedition against them—so planned as to fall in their rear and surprise them, from which I did anticipate the most glorious result; and I am well convinced I would not have been disappointed, for they had taken such extraordinary precautions to prevent their intentions being discovered, that they themselves entertained no doubt that they had succeeded. But with every effort in my power to accomplish my object, I was forced most reluctantly to abandon it, merely because the contractor failed to supply the necessary rations.

It then became necessary to meet the danger in some other way; and calculating rather upon desultory attacks from the enemy, than a united one, I endeavored to have them opposed at every avenue through which they would be most likely to invade us—for which purpose I detached one company up the Illinois River, in a well fortified boat, armed with muskets, blunderbusses and swivel.

The mounted riflemen I sent out in separate detachments to different parts of the same river, with orders to keep up a constant communication with each other, and to act either separately or together, as circumstances might require.

All these detachments, except one, soon fell in with Indian trails, gave chase to the Indians for several days in succession, and would certainly have overtaken them, had they not been retarded by the heavy rains that fell about that time. Finally those Indians, after having stolen seven horses and wounded two men, in an unsuccessful attack they made on one of our forts, were completely repulsed, and returned about the last of September to their own villages. Of their number various accounts have been given. All, however, agree that it was considerable, and I am pursuaded that there is not one well informed man in this county who does not now believe that if timely preparations had not been made to resist them on the frontier that I occupied, the consequences would heve been melancholy and distressing. As the least of them, had only a few families been killed, others would have removed, and terror would have pervaded and depopulated this Territory.

When I found that the Indians had retired from our frontier I began to prepare for an expedition against them, being fully convinced that I could so regulate it as to surprise them in their villages at the head of Peoria Lake. At this time I calculated on no assistance or forces whatever, beyond what I had raised in the Territory; but after every preparation was made, and the day of our departure fixed on, I received a letter from Col. Russell, proposing to me an expedition somewhat similar, and promising to come on before the day I had appointed for marching He accordingly arrived, with a part of two companies of rangers, consisting of fifty privates and their officers, and tendered me his services, which I gladly accepted by appointing him second in command—well knowing and duly appreciating his great experience in Indian warfare and his merits as a military officer.

Through him I also learnt that Gen. Hopkins was to march to Peoria with at least two thousand mounted volunteers, and would arrive at that place about the time I expected to be at the head of Peoria Lake.

In consequence of this latter information, as an addition to my original plan I sent one company of volunteers, with two boats, to Peoria—one of them being well fortified and the other carrying as much provisions as I could collect, and the necessary tools to enable Gen. Hopkins to build a fort at that place, provided he chose to do so, or, otherwise, to build it myself under cover of his army, whilst it was marching, as he proposed it should do, up the Illinois River.

On the 18th of October, having made arrangements for the defense of the frontier in my absence, and leaving a force which, under existing circumstances, I deemed adequate to that object, I commenced my march with about four hundred mounted volunteers. On our way we burnt two Kickapoo villages, on the saline fork of Sangamon River—till which time I had permitted it to be understood that I intended to march to Peoria and cross the Illinois at that place. But as my plan was entirely a different one, I then thought it advisable to call a council of officers and unfold to them my real views and intentions, in which, they all concurring, we marched with uncommon rapidity to a large village at the head of Peoria Lake, inhabited by Kickapoos and Miamies. It was situated at the foot of a hill, which terminates the low grounds of the Illinois River at that place and runs many miles parallel with it. In front of this village the bottom, which is three miles wide, is so flat, wet and marshy, as to be almost utterly impassable to man or horse. Unfortunately our guides, instead of leading us down the hill at the village, as I had expected, led us into the bottom about three-quarters of a mile below it, and thereby deranged a plan of attack which I had at first contemplated. As we approached the town the Indians were seen running out of it in considerable numbers, and for some time I thought they were forming to give us battle. With the centre of my little army I was marching in a direct course towards them, the right wing being ordered to gain their flank on the right of us, whilst the left was directed to cut off their retreat to the river. But in a short time I discovered them, some on horseback, others on foot, all running as fast they could in a course at right angles from that which I was pursuing, towards a point of woods in which I expected they intended to form. I immediately changed my course, ordered and lead on a general charge upon them, and would have succeeded in cutting off their retreat had it not been for the unsoundness of the ground over which we had to run. We, however, rushed upon them with such impetuosity that they were forced to scatter and take refuge in the swamp, in which those who were on horseback left their horses so completely mired that they could not move. A part was pursued through the swamp to the river, where several were killed and the town of Chequeneboc, (a Pottawottamie chief, who headed the party that came down to attack us,) together with all the pro visions and other property it contained, was burnt. Another party was pursued into the swamp in a different direction; several were killed, but finally they rallied at that point in such numbers that those who pursued them were forced to retreat. I then sent in a reinforcement, which induced the Indians entirely to give ground. The pursuit and fight over, we returned to the village, which, with a great quantity of provisions and other valuable Indian property, we burnt and otherwise destroyed. We brought off with us about eighty head of horses and four prisoners, having killed, according to the Indian accounts, frequently given, between twenty-four and thirty Indians, without the loss of a single man, and having only one wounded; which, in my opinion, was entirely owing to the charge that was made upon the enemy, as they were run so hard that when they attempted to form they were out of breath, and could not shoot with sufficient accuracy.

Not meeting with nor hearing from Hopkins, and knowing that my force was too weak and our horses too much fatigued to attempt anything further, I detached a party the next day to Peoria to leave directions for the Captain who commanded the boats to return, as speedily as possible. This party burnt another village that had been lately built within half a mile of Peoria, by the Miamies; and we all returned to my headquarters, at Camp Russell, after a tour of thirteen days only.

The conduct of both the men and officers under my command was highly honorable to themselves and useful to our country. They were uniformly obedient to my orders, appeared sincerely desirous of giving me every assistance in their power, and in the attack upon the Indians they displayed a gallantry and intrepidity that could not be surpassed.

You will clearly perceive, from the nature of my arrangements and plans of operation, that they have been actively employed in the most arduous duties, and I hope they will soon receive the reward that is due to their services.

The boats did not return till the 15th inst., which has delayed this communication to this time.

I have the honor to be,

Very respectfully, sir,

Your most obedient servant,

NINIAN EDWARDS.

CHAPTER IV.

Termination of the War with the Indians—Gov. Edwards' Speech to the Officers and Soldiers of the Army—Reply of the Army—Address of the Governor to the Legislature—Reply to his Message by the Legislature.

Gov. Edwards' address to the late detachment of militia from St. Clair county, Illinois Territory, on discharging them from service:

Gentlemen, Officers and Soldiers :

In discharging you from the military toils in which I have participated with you for more than two months past, I should do equal injustice to my own feelings and to your just deserts were I not to express to you the gratitude I feel for the services you have rendered and the assistance you have afforded me in defending this Territory against the extraordinary perils with which it has been threatened.

Fortified by a consciousness of having discharged my own duty and served my country with effect, and honored by repeated public and private declarations of confidence in me by those who have had the best opportunity of judging my conduct, I might bid defiance to all the silly tales, dastardly insinuations or wicked misrepresentations which folly, malice, ambition or interest have invented to injure me, or I might content myself with challenging the most scrutinizing and implacable personal or political enemy to point out a solitary case in which I have not forseen every emergency that has presented itself, and been prepared with the best means within my power to meet it.

This course I should probably adopt, were it not that the injuries meditated against me have been attended with the severest privations and sacrifices, on the part of the good people whose interest and safety have been confided to my care; but this being the case, I shall at some future and no distant period exhibit such a history of the transactions of this year (illustrated by a chart and geographical notes) as will prove that I have faithfully discharged my duty both to the General Government and to the people of the Territory, who will find that if any peculiar hardships have been imposed upon them, no blame whatever can attach to me.

Ignorant, indeed, must that man be of the geography, history and situation of this country, of the residence and number of savages, and of their habits, who can suppose that any part of the frontier has been in a more dangerous situation than ours.

The greatest body of Indians in America reside on the Mississippi, and the water courses that empty into it above St. Louis and Cahokia—thus having a facility of invading us by water, which all past experience and recent facts prove they uniformly prefer, for ease, safety and expedition.

Our thin and dispersed population, with the extent of our frontier, presented many points to the attack, to which those blood-thirsty savages were invited by the fair prospect they had of doing the greatest injury to us with the least possible danger to

—10

tbemselves. Besides, notwithstanding all the noise and bustle that was made about Indian depredations, in the course of last year, ours was the only frontier that was actually attacked. A knowledge of these facts rendered me indefatigable in my exertions to defend my fellow-citizens, and to explore every source of information that was accessible to me, for the purpose of ascertaining the disposition of the Indians towards us.

Upon some of you devolved the execution of all my defensive operations, and I reflect with peculiar pleasure that, whenever my plans have been explained, they have met the most unqualified approbation of those who had to execute them, that they uniformly inspired with confidence those who were most exposed to danger, and, above all, that they have been crowned with such success that not a life has yet been lost on as exposed a frontier as any that belongs to the United States.

My diligence in ascertaining the disposition of the Indians and the machinations of their allies, have not been less successful—as my communications to the government, together with facts which have subsequently developed themselves, incontestably prove.

Ever since the battle of Tippecanoe I have uniformly maintained the opinion (probably with more zeal than discretion) that nothing short of the most vigorous offensive operations against the Indians could procure us peace with them. Hostility, engendered by British influence, had rallied them against us, and as our difficulties with England seemed to increase, I never could see any reasonable ground to hope that that influence would be withdrawn or that it would be less efficient than it had hitherto been—more especially as the savages constantly failed or refused to surrender a single murderer or to do any other act of justice that would argue their return to a friendly disposition towards us. And I feel sincere regret at finding that all my predictions on this subject have been completely fulfilled.

Many suggestions which I had the honor to make, no doubt, at the time were thought to be very visionary; but time has proved that they were well founded.

The intrigues of Dickson with the Sioux and Chippeways—the important fact that the British had sent immense quantities of Indian goods to Fort St. Joseph, by way of the Ottawa River, for the purpose of aiding those intrigues and of counteracting any bad consequences that might otherwise result to them from the loss of Malden—the dispatches that were sent by Innis of Ambersburg to Dickson, informing him of the intention of the British to capture Mackinac, and the contemplated attack on Chicago—were all communicated by me.

At length I obtained and transmitted to the War Department, documents which proved the existence not only of a most formidable hostile confederacy, but the very points which it proposed to attack. Copies of them were forwarded to the Governor of Kentucky, whose opinion upon them, as well as that of Governors Howard and Harrison, perfectly corresponded with my own, as their letters to me will show.

These documents completely proved the danger with which our part of the frontier was threatened; they were duly appreciated by the Hon. Secretary of War, who expressly (predicating his instructions upon the information I had communicated) directed Gov. Harrison and myself to confer with each other, empowered us to call upon the Governor of Kentucky for assistance, and instructed him to furnish it.

In pursuance of the authority given me, I lost not a moment in asking the Governor of Kentucky for a regiment of infantry. It was promptly promised me by Gov. Scott. The promise was renewed by his successor, Gov. Shelby. The newspapers of Kentucky announced that a regiment had been sent to my aid. Gov. Harrison, who happened to be at Frankfort about that time, requested also that it should be sent, and in subsequent letters, which have been published, he renewed the same with an additional requisition. But what has been the result? Not a man has yet arrived. And at a time when we had most cause to apprehend danger, even Col. Russell, who was here with about fifty Kentucky rangers, under the authority given him by the President, was called off with them to Vincennes, leaving us to shift for ourselves, without the aid of a single man who had not been raised in the Territory, whilst a force consisting of thousands was accumulating in Indiana Territory, which has double our population, and which certainly (to say the least that could be expected) was not in greater danger, whilst its proximity to Kentucky furnished a facility for obtaining aid upon any sudden emergency, which, from the remoteness of our situation, was unattainable by us.

Upon these facts I wish to make no comments—my object being more to free myself from blame than to fix it upon any other person. Any *ecclairecissements* that may be due to the government, to the public or to the gentlemen interested, I leave wholly to themselves.

I must, however, acknowledge that the reliance I placed in the promises of assistance that were made me, was very near proving destructive to the Territory, by throwing me off of my guard and preventing me from calling into service and organizing such a force as was found indispensably necessary to repel the hostile invasion, which shortly thereafter actually took place.

On the receipt of Col. Russell's letter, announcing to me his orders to repair to Vincennes, I instantly determined to call out one-half of the militia and put myself at their head. I had every difficulty to encounter. Without a cent of money to pay the militia for their services last year or for months of past services in the present year, or for any future services, and without a sufficiency of arms, ammunition or other munitions of war, your patriotism, however, seconded my exertions, freed me from the necessity of an extensive draft, and enabled me, in a very short period, to organize the force to which this country is indebted for its salvation.

It was about the first of September that I took the field with you. You will remember that I then informed you that in the light of that moon a furious attempt would be made to invade our northern frontier—that I endeavored to stimulate you to exert yourselves to make the necessary preparations to resist it; and everything happened precisely as I had predicted. Nothing, I believe, was omitted, on my part, which it was possible for me to do.

For some time previous to the invasion, the Indians had made use of every precaution to prevent their intentions being discovered. Notwithstanding which, I knew the very day they assembled at Peoria for the purpose of coming down upon us, and you know that I planned an expedition to fall in their rear, which would have been successfully executed had I not been (much to my mortification) greatly disappointed by the contractor, who failed to furnish the necessary rations.

We have, however, great cause to acknowledge the goodness of Heaven and to felicitate ourselves upon the events that have taken place.

Your bravery has enabled me to repel hostile invasion and to wage war upon the enemy in their own country, with as much success and effect as has ever been accomplished by the same numbers since the first settlements of the Western country.

Your intrepidity and patriotism have been equally honorable to yourselves and useful to your country, and should events render it necessary for me again to take command, I sincerely pray that I may again have your aid.

Gentlemen, for the partiality and personal attachment which the whole of you, (without an exception to my knowledge,) have manifested towards me—for your public as well as private professions of confidence in me—for the unexampled harmony and good order that has been observed—I beg you to accept the sincerest thanks of a grateful heart, and in returning to the bosom of your families, to recollect that you carry with you my most unfeigned wishes for your happiness and prosperity.

NINIAN EDWARDS.

November 10, 1812.

The following is the reply of the officers of the militia to Gov. Edwards' address:

HEADQUARTERS, CAMP RUSSELL, *Nov.* 10, 1812.

To His Excellency, GOVERNOR EDWARDS:

SIR—Our opinion as to the danger our Territory has been exposed to is exactly like yours, and we are free to declare that in our estimation you have greatly increased your claims upon the gratitude of the country for the wise measures which you adopted for our relief. We have witnessed your having anticipated and disappointed the views of our enemies. We have always found you well informed concerning them, and, as the danger increased, we were happy to see you disregarding the hardships of camp life and forsaking a comfortable home, ready at the post of greatest danger to place yourself at our head. We have seen you undergo the fatigues of a successful expedition into the Indian country. We have witnessed your coolness, deliberation and promptitude in the hour of peril, and should we again be called into service, we shall be as happy to be commanded by you as you will be to command us. We sincerely believe that it is owing to the measures which you put into operation that this country has not been deserted and desolated. These are facts recorded in the hearts of your fellow-citizens, which speak for themselves, and which must render harmless all misrepresentations of your enemies—if you have any. The sacrifices of the brave men whom you have commanded have been great. Some of them have been in service since last spring; none of them have received any pay, and many of them, we well know, are in great want of it. We hope no exertion in your power will be wanting to procure them just compensation, and we think that you might, with propriety, urge the distinguished services which they have lately performed as an inducement to pay them as soon as possible. We take the liberty of soliciting your approbation to the publication of your address this day, to us, together with this answer, and we offer you our best wishes for your success and prosperity through life.

Signed in behalf of the officers, at their request, by

WILLIAM WHITESIDE,
LT. C. C. I. M.,
Chairman.

JAS. B. MOORE,
Clerk.

It appears from a letter which Gov. Edwards received from Gov. Shelby, dated March 2, 1812, that the latter expressed his conviction that the troops ordered from Kentucky "had been prevented from reaching the Territory by dishonorable steps." But the dangers, difficulties and embarrassments resulting from this disappointment were averted by the indefatigable exertion of Gov. Edwards. Gov. Shelby says, in this letter, that Gov. Edwards is entitled to the honor of having planned and the glory of executing so successfully this expedition to Peoria.

Gov. Edwards, in alluding to this expedition in a letter to Gov. Shelby, dated December 20, 1812, says that "some attempts have been made to deprive me of the honor which you say my exertions entitle me to, by giving to Gen. Hopkins the credit of planning it, and to Col. Russell the glory of executing it. Although I cannot feel indifferent to the injustice done me, nothing can provoke me to withhold from Col. Russell the just tribute of applause to which his conduct, under my own view, has entitled him. I acknowledge myself indebted to him for many and great obligations. To me his assistance was important. Distinguished as he is for his bravery and good conduct, nothing that I can say can add new lustre to his reputation, and one of the first wishes of my heart is that his country may appreciate his merits as highly as I do, because I am sure it would, at the same time, eventuate in advantage to the public and do justice to an individual.

"It is, however, a duty which I owe to myself, to declare most explicitly, that my expedition was planned by myself; that it originally depended, in no respect, upon Gen. Hopkins or Col. Russell; that I had prepared for it and had appointed a day for marching, previous to my hearing from either of them.

"Disappointed in all the assistance that had been promised me, menaced by formidable combinations of Indians, and seeing no measures adopted which were calculated to afford security to the frontier, I felt the necessity of turning out as Commander-in-Chief of my own militia, nearly one-third of whom became volunteers under me; and after having encountered the greatest difficulties, and having successfully defended the Territory under such circumstances, it was hardly to be presumed that I would have relinquished the command of my own volunteers to any one.

"I knew my legitimate powers as Governor of the Territory, and I determined to maintain them, so far as related to my own militia, at all hazards, as the means of affording that protection to my fellow-citizens which they had a right to expect from me, and for which they looked in vain elsewhere. I have not disappointed *their expectations;* and I feel amply rewarded by the testimonies of approbation with which I have been honored by the people and the Legislature of this Territory, and by the brave officers and soldiers whom I lately commanded, which, added to a consciousness of having discharged my duty and a conviction that facts cannot always be perverted, renders me fearless of all attempts to do me injustice."

This correspondence was published in the St. Louis Gazette, and other papers, immediately after the expedition had returned; and had there been any truth in the reports that it had been either planned by Gen. Hopkins or executed by Col. Russell, the published correspondence, in which Gov. Edwards claims to himself the exclusive credit, would have been answered.

Again, it appears, from Gov. Edwards' official report of this expedition, to the Secretary of War, that on Col. Russell's arriving at the camp, a few days previous to their march, with about fifty men under his command, Gov. Edwards accepted their services and appointed the Colonel second in command.

MESSAGE OF GOV. EDWARDS.

Fellow-Citizens of the Legislative Council, and of the House of Representatives :

The communications of the plenipotentiaries of the United States, charged with negotiating peace with Great Britain, which have been recently communicated by the President to Congress, by declaring the conditions upon which alone our enemy is disposed to put an end to the existing hostilities, evince the insincerity of those declarations which accompanied his invitation to treat at Gottenburg, account for the motives which, on his part, so long delayed a meeting of the negotiators, and leave us no other ground to hope for a speedy return to the blessings of peace but by the employment of the utmost resources of the nation in a vigorous prosecution of the war. Infatuated by his success in Europe, forgetful of the mutability of all human things, and yielding to his jealousy of our growing commercial prosperity, to his thirst of universal monopoly and to his unprincipled ambition, which have equally distinguished him in peace and in war, the enemy has not only openly and officially avowed but has particularly demonstrated his disregard of the laws and usages of civilized warfare; and whilst he stands disgraced, and must eventually be execrated by the civilized world for this gothic and vandalic destruction of the public edifices at the city of Washington, and his wanton robberies and devastation of private property on the Atlantic waters, he has unblushingly acknowledged his alliance and identified himself with those ruthless savages whose maraudings and indiscriminate slaughters of men, women and children, both before and since the declaration of war, have been so often repeated and so severely felt and deeply deplored on the frontiers of our unfortunate territories.

Mortified that the charm of his invincibility on the ocean has been dissolved, by the superior skill and bravery of our valiant naval heroes, and calculating highly upon the immense disposable force which the late unparalleled events in Europe have placed at his command, he seeks a base, unmanly revenge; hopes to regain his lost fame, and by his barbarous warfare to spread universal dismay and terror throughout our land; dreams of naught but victories, and, assuming the tone of a conquerer, arrogantly demands a surrender to himself of part of the State of Massachusetts, a considerable portion of our Northwestern frontier, a stipulation on the part of the American Government not to maintain or construct any fortification within a limited distance of the shores of any of the lakes, from Ontario to Superior, both inclusive, nor to maintain or control any armed vessels upon those lakes, nor in the rivers which empty themselves into the same; and for his Indian allies. in consideration of their meritorious services in plundering our property, conflagrating our habitations, massacring our prisoners, and with inexorable ferocity murdering and mangling the bodies of peaceable citizens, innocent infants and helpless females, as a *sine qua non* of any treaty, that they shall be included in the pacification, and that, as incident thereto, the boundaries of their territories should be permanently established and its integrity guaranteed—proposing, as the basis of such boundary, the lines of the Greenville treaty, which would include in the proposed cession the whole of this Territory, a few spots only excepted, a great portion of other lands for which we have paid the Indians a valuable consideration, and a large extent of territory besides, which, in the treaty of 1803, he himself solemnly acknowledged to be a part of the United States, thus evidently manifesting his intention to monopolize the fur trade. to increase his influence with the savages, to perpetuate his disgraceful alliances, and to secure to himself additional facilities of annoying and desolating our frontier at his pleasure, whilst he seeks to protect himself against the consequences of his ambitious views and nefarious conduct, by interposing an extensive barrier between our Western settlements and his American provinces, and by obtaining the right to erect and maintain naval and military establishments on and near to the lines which he proposes shall separate them.

Conduct like this, to which history scarcely furnishes a parallel since the eruption of the northern hive of barbarians into the Roman empire—presumptuous and arrogant, overlooking the old and introducing new subjects of controversy—demanding the most important and unprecedented concessions, instead of tendering reparation for the wrongs and injustice which forced our Government into the declaration of war against him—prove the fallacy of all calculations upon his justice, moderation and magnanimity; portray in the strongest colors the most implacable hostility towards us, and unfold his ambitious views against the prosperity and independence of our country,

Such circumstances appeal loudly to the pride and patriotism of every true Amercan. They admonish us to abstain from all party disputes among ourselves, and will doubtless unite and animate the whole American people (who proudly identify themselves with the Government of their choice) in courageous and patriotic efforts to resist the relentless tyrant who seeks to overwhelm us; for it cannot be imagined that the sons of America are yet so degenerate as not only to be willing to submit to the wrongs and oppressions which were practised upon us by Great Britain, previous to the war, but also to reward both her and her savage allies for their subsequent shocking and disgraceful barbarities by yielding to the humiliating concessions that are demanded of us, and thereby offering inducements to the future repetition of similar enormities.

Great and powerful as the enemy is, he will find obstacles and difficulties in carrying on the war at such a distance from Europe, against a people determined to be free and to maintain the honor and independence of their country, which, notwithstanding the lessons of experience that he might have derived from our glorious Revolution, his inflated vanity has not permitted him to anticipate. No doubt, from the nature of his demands and the tone he has assumed, he flattered himself that, with the immense armaments which he has detached to our coast, and the armies he organized on our frontier, he would be able in a single campaign to reduce us to unconditional submission; but, so far, he has been most mortifyingly disappointed, without anything to console him or to remunerate him for his vast expenditure, but success in the *honorable* employment of stealing negroes, plundering and devastating private property, ruining individuals, robbing Alexandria, and destroying, at the city of Washington, models of taste and monuments of art which are held sacred and are protected by all civilized nations. On the other hand, while our success in the South and at Baltimore have been equally glorious to us and disgraceful to him, the brilliant achievements of our arms on the Niagara frontier, at Plattsburg, and on Lake Champlain, begin to develop our resources for war, demonstrate the superiority of freemen, fighting for their just rights, over the boasted mercenary legions of Lord Wellington, and, with the increasing unanimity of our fellow-citizens, afford us a happy presage of our future victories, which, with the blessing of the Divine Being, who has hitherto so signally protected us, will produce the total discomfiture of the enemy and his final expulsion from the American continent, or reduce him to the necessity of tendering peace upon just and honorable terms.

With regard to our relations with the Indians, and the consequences that were expected to flow from them, much diversity of opinion has heretofore unfortunately prevailed. Mine has, however, on former occasions, been freely and unreservedly communicated to you and the public, and the bloody scenes which some of you have lately witnessed, and the rest have heard of, afford lasting and mournful evidences of its general correctness, and have, I believe, resulted in a universal conviction that nothing less than the most energetic and efficient exertions on our part can maintain the tranquillity and safety of our frontier.

Incapable of properly appreciating the liberal and philanthrophic views of our Government in regard to them, and influenced by the traditionary accounts among themselves of our having expelled their forefathers from their favorite abodes, the savages possess an hereditary hatred of us, which, with the intrigues and machinations of British agents, and their own jealousies and inquietude, arising from our increasing population and the constant approximation of our settlements to their villages and hunting grounds, so predisposes them to war with us, as to render it easier at all times, when they can be flattered with the least prospect of success, to engage them in alliances and open hostilities against us, from which nothing hitherto has or hereafter can restrain them, as every man who possesses any practical knowledge of them well knows, but the powerful influence of fear alone. Instead, therefore, of confiding in professions on their part, which have so uniformly been insincere and perfidious, or relying upon temporizing expedients that have hitherto proved to be fallacious and inefficient, we ought to indulge in no calculations of peace with them, except such as are predicated upon the degree of fear with which our measures may be calculated to inspire them, and these, to succeed, ought to be such as to be produce an immediate and direct and not merely consequential and future pressure upon them. As to the future and remote consequences, they either do not think of them at all, or always hope to elude them. It is indeed greatly to be feared that we shall not shortly realize the sanguine hopes that have been entertained of reducing them to submission by cutting off their intercourse with the British.

This plan has been pursued ever since the commencement of the war. Partial, but important, interruptions of that intercourse have certainly been produced, and yet we have found the hostile confederacy constantly increasing, and no one now doubts that it is greater and more formidable than it has been at any former period.

Although custom and habit have rendered the British trade a convenience to some of the savages, many of them who are now arrayed against us have but partially enjoyed it, and none of them are so absolutely dependent upon it as we are apt to imagine—of which we have full proof in the wretched independence of some of the more Western tribes; and, in the recent instances of our present Miami prisoners, who, though long accustomed to such trade, have, nevertheless, existed for the last two years without it, living in the meantime upon the beasts of the forest and clothing themselves and their families with their skins.

Like other nations in a state of barbarism their real wants are few and simple; and to supply these and at the same time to wage war, nothing is indispensably nenessary to them but ammunition and arms. Of the former they want powder only, having themselves inexhaustable stores of lead, and in the last three years the enemy has supplied them with a very considerable number of the latter. Admitting, however, the ultimate practicability of succeeding in destroying the intercourse that has been mentioned, still we could not hope for any immediate advantages from it, for the enemy must have been destitute of foresight or regardless of precaution, and the most positive information supported by much concurrent testimony cannot have the shadow of truth to support it, if, to provide against such an event, he has not accumulated, at points convenient for distribution, supplies abundantly sufficient to last his allies for a considerable time yet to come. His means of doing so have been ample, for, independent of other channels that have been accessible to him, the communication by way of Grand River has constantly remained uninterrupted; and, although you have seen the impracticability of the navigation of that river announced, in a late official communication, yet we know, and the history of the fur trade will prove, that, for mere commercial purposes only, it has long been annually frequented, and that immense quantities of goods have been and continue to be transported through that very channel.

But, supposing the British actually deprived of the means of furnishing future supplies, and their present stock exhausted—we are not now and cannot shortly be prepared to substitute with any of our own, and consequently have neither the means of conciliating nor any inducements to offer the Indians, sufficient to prevail over the double motives of hatred to us and partiality to our enemy: whilst the emissaries of the latter, by their exclusive associations with them, would be able to alleviate any particular pressure upon them by inspiring them with the hopes that its duration would be of short continuance, and at all events could easily satisfy them that they would have nothing better to hope for by shifting sides and uniting with us.

It is, however, very doubtful whether anything, short of the complete conquest of the Canadas, can enable us to prevent the intercourse between those Provinces and the Indians. We may, indeed, subject it to inconvenience by closing up some of their ordinary commercial avenues; but on a frontier of such vast extent, and through the uninhabited regions contiguous thereto, there are a variety of other channels of communication, which, though it might be unprofitable to pursue them in a time of peace, do nevertheless furnish sufficient facilities of transportation for the purposes of war, and that, too, without subjecting it to greater increase of difficulties and expense than we ourselves, on some occasions, had to encounter. And knowing, as we do, the obstacles which the British surmount, in time of peace, in sending their goods between three and four thousand miles into the northwestern parts of America, through numerous lakes and rivers, intercepted by more than two hundred rapids and one hundred and thirty additional portages, along which both the goods and canoes have to be carried on men's backs, and knowing, also, that ever since the commencement of the war goods have been packed on horses from Montreal to the southern parts of Lake Michigan, we ought to begin to profit by the errors of our past calculations, and should not rely too certainly upon the inability of the enemy to furnish the few articles which of themselves are sufficient to enable him to retain his influence with and command the services of the savages. For even if we could succeed in totally obstructing his communication with them from Canada, it is an incontrovertible fact that goods can be furnished them on the Mississippi, from Hudson's Bay, by way of the Red River of Lake Winnepeg, with less expense and greater facility than they have hitherto been carried from Montreal to many parts of the Northwest. And if there be any reality in the supposed alliance, or any intended concert of operation between the enemy and the Spanish North American provinces, it will doubtless greatly enlarge the sphere of his influence and increase his means of preserving it. Seeing how tenacious of the interests of his allies he has appeared to be, in the *sine qua non* which he tendered to our Commissioners at Ghent, we cannot reasonably doubt that he will avail himself of all possible means of commanding their further assistance; and the recent disasters on our own particular frontier are most unhappily but too well calculated to give success to his efforts.

The frequent and unpunished incursions of the Indians, which have been too successful in spreading death and desolation in their train; the defeat of our forces and the surrender of the fort at Prairie du Chien; two subsequent successive repulses at Rock River; the late extraordinary evacuation and destruction, by our own troops, of Fort Johnson, and the total abandonment of the respectable settlements of Shoal and Sugar Creeks, leaving property to a great amount in the power of the savages—are events which betray our weakness and can hardly fail to invigorate their hopes and invite their future enterprises; while the accounts they will receive of the causes of the rupture of our negotiations for peace will tend equally to increase their hostilities to us and to strengthen their confidence in their ally. Many of them have lately taken off the mask, which has been too successful in paralyzing the energies of our government and in postponing the punishment due to their perfidy and atrocities; and I hazard nothing in saying, that, from their proximity to us, thousands of them could reach St. Louis or Cahokia from their own homes in five or six days.

Under these inauspicious circumstances, and having lost the services of a very valuable officer, by his untimely death, it is very fortunate for the territories that their future defense is confided to the gallant Col. Russell, who, schooled in our Revolution, being one of the distinguished heroes of King's Mountain, and having probably seen more Indian fighting than any officer now in America, possesses all the ardor and enterprise, corrected by the experience of age, and, with his knowledge of the geography of the Indian country, needs only the aid of a competent force to act with energy and efficiency; and indeed, disastrous as I think must be the final issue of relying on the protracted measures of mere defense—producing an annual expenditure to a great amount, without gaining an inch of ground or a single advantage of the enemy—I nevertheless have no doubt that with a well appointed force of 2,000 infantry, a proper proportion of artillery, and 1,000 mounted riflemen, the war upon our frontier, and with it the necessity of any further disbursements on our account, could be terminated in three months. And as there fortunately happens to be no contrariety of opinion to prevent or retard the adoption of such a measure (all those with the best means of information concurring, now, in the absolute necessity for it), it is to be hoped a change so advisable with a view to public economy, and which would at the same time so happily conduce to the safety and prosperity of these exposed territories, will not long be delayed.

In the meantime, every dictate of prudence recommends the amendment of our militia system, so as to render it better adapted to the present conjuncture, to free it from unnecessary delays in its operation, and to secure, by more certain and adequate punishments, prompt obedience to such requisitions as emergencies may from time to time require. Although this Territory has exhibited examples of patriotism that have rarely been equaled and never surpassed—having, in the last five years, brought into service a body of volunteers nearly equal in number to one-half of the aggregate amount of its militia, and this year having tendered a number considerably exceeding that proportion—yet, there are individuals who, regardless of their obligation to participate with their fellow-citizens in the necessary defense of their country, have constantly failed and refused to perform any duty whatever, and whose obedience the existing laws have been found inadequate to command. And as all men under similar circumstances, who receive equal protection from Government, owe to it the same obligations, and upon the vital principles of equality are bound to the performance of similar duties, the laws which with us are designed to govern all should be as competent to enforce the obedience of the perverse and refractory as that of dutiful and virtuous citizens. And to add to their efficiency in the cases alluded to, by insuring their speedy and prompt execution, it would be advisable to provide that whenever a draft shall be ordered in any regiment, a court martial shall be convened therein, with power to hear and determine upon all excuses for exemption from service and to inflict, in cases of delinquency, the fines prescribed by law—which it seems just and reasonable should be sufficient at least to obtain the services of a substitute for him who, without reasonable excuse, shall have failed or refused to perform his term of duty.

It may, however, be expedient (making proper exceptions in favor of those conscientiously scrupulous of bearing arms) to subject any person whose services shall be required, and who shall have legal notice thereof, to the same coercion and penalties, in every respect whatever, as if he had been actually mustered into service, unless he shall in due time furnish a substitute, or be able to procure a certificate from such a court martial as I have mentioned that he has exhibited an excuse deemed sufficient for his exemption.

Instructed, from their infancy, in the most artful means of inflicting the greatest injury upon their enemy with the least possible danger to themselves, and regardless of the shame of a retreat, the savages usually make their incursions so suddenly, and conduct them with such secrecy and caution, as to be able to surprise and ravage our settlements or murder our fellow-citizens before we are notified of their approach—after which they retreat with such celerity as generally to escape with impunity. I, therefore, feel it my duty to recommend the temporary organization, in each regiment, of a corps of mounted riflemen, as the only species of force calculated to afford protection against those desultory attacks of which the savages are so fond, and from which our extensive frontier, detached settlements and numerous vulnerable points are greatly exposed.

In consequence of the effects resulting from opening the Land Office of the United States in this Territory, a revision of our revenue laws has become necessary, and it is to be hoped that you will be able to devise a more just and equal system of taxation and to lessen the public burden upon our fellow-citizens, to which the pressure of the war upon and the peculiar difficulties to which it has subjected them offer the most powerful inducements.

I cannot, however, refrain from expressing my decided opinion that the salary of $100, allowed the Attorney General, at the last session of the Legislature, for attending to important duties required of him throughout the whole Territory and in the courts of every county therein, is not only insufficient but is not proportionate to allowances for other purposes. Experience evinces that much of the good effects to be expected from our penal laws depends upon the talents and integrity of our Prosecuting Attorney. The compensation, therefore, ought to be such as, under all circumstances, would be deemed reasonably sufficient to command the services of one who is not only willing but able to perform, with advantage to the public, the duties of that station. The gentleman who has for some time past discharged these duties, with equal zeal and ability, in the early part of the year resigned his commission, in consequence of the inadequacy of the compensation, but was prevailed upon to re-accept it, under the expectation that the Legislature might bestow on the subject that reconsideration which I have felt it my duty to invite.

Other subjects, on which, owing to my long continued and existing ill-health, I have not heretofore been able to bestow the necessary attention, must be reserved for future special recommendation. In the meantime I beg leave to assure you of my readiness to afford you every facility to the discharge of your duties, and of my sincere desire to coöperate cordially with you in all measures calculated to promote the public good.

NINIAN EDWARDS.

REPLY TO HIS MESSAGE BY THE TERRITORIAL LEGISLATURE.

KASKASKIA, *Dec.* 2, 1812.

To His Excellency NINIAN EDWARDS:

SIR—The House of Representatives, being much gratified with the communication which you have made, would disguise their feelings and do injustice to those of their constituents, were they not to express their approbation of the measures you have pursued to protect our frontiers and secure to us the advantages which nature evidently designed for us.

This protection, secured by your means, announces to us the interest which the General Government takes in our welfare. It commands our attachment to the present administration, while we are fully penetrated with the conviction that the most beneficial results have been produced by the instrumentality of a public servant who, we believe, has been influenced by a desire to promote the public welfare and happiness. The objects that he has recommended shall engage our earliest attention. We wish you may long continue to enjoy the confidence of your country, and with it health and happiness.

The above address, being engrossed, was read a second time, and unanimously concurred in and signed by the Speaker; and it was therefore ordered that Messrs. Jones and Short be appointed to carry said address and present it to the Governor.

CHAPTER V.

Message of Gov. Edwards in reference to the Territorial Judiciary System.

The Legislature, at its session of 1814, passed "An act to establish a Supreme Court for Illinois Territory," which, in many material points, changed the judiciary system adopted upon the organization of the Territory. Much discussion arose as to the power of the Legislature, under the ordinance, to pass the act, and strong doubts were expressed, in high quarters, as to its validity. The Judges of the Territory were requested by the Legislature to state their opinion, in writing, on the merits of the new law, and they took emphatic ground against it. They argued, that, as the United States Government, in pursuance of the terms of the ordinance, had established a general court, and had reserved the right of appointing judges to conduct it, that the Territorial Legislature, which is an inferior authority, had no power to change or modify it. They said, "it would have been futile in Congress to establish a court, leaving the power in other hands to establish a tribunal superior to it, which would be to annul it;" that "the court established by the ordinance cannot be subject to the revision or control of any tribunal established by the Territorial Legislature; and an appeal from the same court to the same is a solecism which we do not suppose to be the intention of this bill." "Neither," said the judges, "are we prepared to admit that the general court can be so localized as to be reduced entirely to a county, though supreme within the county." That "it was a question, whether a court can exercise a part of its jurisdiction and forbear the rest, according to circumstances, and as a regard to public convenience and the due administration of the law might require." The Judges went on to argue the invalidity of the law at considerable length. Their argument was signed by Judges J. B. Thomas and William Sprigg. Judge Griswold was absent, and did not attach his name to their opinion.

In reply to their objections, Gov. Edwards, by request of the Legislature, prepared an answer, which was also submitted and spread at large upon the journals. It notices, fully, the arguments adduced by the Judges, and is as follows:

ANSWER OF GOV. EDWARDS TO THE OPINION OF THE JUDGES.

Fellow-Citizens of the Legislative Council and House of Representatives :

On Wednesday last, I received, for my approbation and signature, a bill, entitled "An act establishing a Supreme Court for Illinois Territory." On the succeeding Saturday evening, a joint committee from your honorable body presented a letter from the honorable Judges Thomas and Sprigg, addressed to the Legislature of Illinois, and at the same time a joint resolution of your two houses, among other things requesting my opinion, in writing, upon the objections to the passage of the aforesaid bill contained in said letter.

Although I had long known, from the presentments of grand juries, composed of some of the most respectable persons in our country, and from a variety of other sources, that a change in the judiciary system, by abolishing the Court of Common Pleas and transferring their duties to the Supreme Judges, had been determined upon by the people, and although I had, immediately after the commencement of your session, ascertained your determination to carry some such plan into execution, yet I can most truly declare that on no occasion have I attempted to influence a solitary individual to such a determination; and never, until I have been informed by the members of your honorable body that Judges Thomas and Sprigg were willing to execute such a law as the present bill contemplates, had I the least agency in it whatever.

I am not, however, insensible of the weight of responsibility which this case, under all its circumstances, seems to be likely to devolve upon me, as a component part of the Legislature and Executive. As the case really appears to be, I shall not hesitate to comply with your request, in which, while I must use the freedom necessary to investigation, I hope to observe all the decorum and respect which is so justly due to the occasion, and sincerely do I regret that my indisposition renders me so illy qualified to do justice to the subject.

The language of the Judges in the conclusion of their address, their acknowledgment of the independence of the three coördinate departments of this government, and the inference thence deduced that each ought to confine itself within the proper sphere of its legitimate authority, would warrant me in concluding, if, indeed, their words were not otherwise sufficiently explicit, that their objections to the passage of the bill in question are predicated on the want of power only in the Legislature; and in that point of view I shall proceed to consider them.

In their first objection, they state that "if this were merely a bill to change the style of the general court, we should deem it objectionable in principle and inconvenient in practice." But to me it is inconceivable how a change merely nominal, and in no wise substantive, could be supposed to violate principle. The appellation of a court may sometimes be very absurd, but it can never add to nor diminish the powers with which it is invested. In some of the States, courts, organized like some of your courts of common pleas, and possessing similar jurisdiction, are called quarter sessions, county courts, or circuit courts; and if you, believing one of the latter appellations to be more appropriate, were to adopt it, instead of the present style of the court of common pleas, without further alteration, it would certainly be no more objectionable on principle, according to my comprehension of the terms, than if you were to call a son "John" in preference to "Thomas."

Declaring, however, as the Judges do, "that the ordinance, the laws of Congress and their commissions point out the court that is to be constituted by them," their objection to the style given by the present bill seems to be the more extraordinary and unsubstantial, since it is evidently more conformable to those authorities than any others, and is in no respect inconsistent with any exposition that has ever been given to either—inasmuch as the ordinance and their commissions are silent as to any epithet of distinction, while the law of Congress explicitly terms them "Supreme Judges," and the laws of the Northwestern Territory of Indiana and of this Territory all concur in defining the court of which their honors speak to be a "Supreme Court," thereby rendering any additional style superfluous, or at least unnecessary.

Speaking of their court as established by a higher authority than that of our Legislature, they say that it has always borne the style of the "General Court." A correction of this error, or explanation of this statement, would not be deemed necessary, but for the purpose of showing the real origin of the style of which they appear so tenacious, and the authority by which it was created. It certainly derived its existence only from a law of the Northwestern Territory; and I believe the doctrine that one Legislature can assume such omnipotent power as to endow a subsequent one with equal authority, in such cases as the present, if it ever existed, has long since exploded. No such question can, however, arise in this case, because a law of Congress, amendatory to the ordinance, vested the Governor and Judges with a power of repealing any of the laws which they had adopted; and the ordinance expressly declares that after the organization of the General Assembly within the Territory, "the Legislature shall have authority to alter the laws adopted by the Governor and Judges, as they shall think fit." There cannot, therefore, be any doubt but the Governor and the Judges had the right to repeal the law alluded to, or that the Legislature that succeeded them had authority to alter or modify it; and if the law itself had been repealed, I presume it will not be conceived that the style of the court, which was wholly dependent upon it, would not have ceased to exist.

If, then, the powers of this Legislature are not inferior to those of that which existed in the Northwestern Territory, can there be a doubt of your power to repeal any of your laws? And if you were to repeal all the laws in relation to the general court, what, then, would be the style of that court which their honors say has been established by a higher authority than this Legislature?

Their next objections are, that the bill contemplates two grades of courts, and that the supreme court cannot be localized to counties, though supreme therein. In support of these objections, great reliance seems to be placed on the ordinance, which they say has established the court of which they are members; and although they allow it is defective and not sufficiently minute in its details, yet they say it has received, on certain points, a "practical construction, which we are not disposed to innovate ourselves nor to sanction those innovations which cannot be reconciled with either the received or true construction of that instrument." And as they also declare they consider the bill in question eminently calculated to introduce into the Territory a state of confusion and anarchy, it seems to be important to show (if it can be done) that those fatal consequences, so much to be deprecated, will result more from an innovation on the practical exposition that has, on certain points, been given to the ordinance, and a departure from it hitherto received a worse construction, on the part of the Judges, than from any such act or disposition on the part of the Legislature.

This I shall attempt to show by a brief review of some of the leading features of the bill in question, and by a reference to the ordinance and to the practice under it.

The present bill was certainly planned in a spirit of conciliation, and with a view to render the duties assigned to the Judges as light and as little oppressive as possible—contemplating that each of them should have a circuit of two counties only, in each of which he should hold two courts in the year; and that, for the purpose of revising or correcting any erroneous decision that might take place, that they or a majority of them should attend at the seat of government, as they are now required by law to do. But, being aware that some objections might be made to the different grades of courts, and believing that the same court might be required to hold its sessions at different times and places, they have put it in the power of the Judges to act as though it were one court, only, by all acting together, or to divide the duties among themselves and to act separately—either of which, it appears from the words of the bill, would meet the wishes and fulfill the intentions of the Legislature. But, considered in either point of view, it seems to be thought by them a violation of the ordinance—the words of which, as far as they are applicable to the case, are that "there shall be appointed a court, to consist of three judges, who shall have a common law jurisdiction," but how, when or where that jurisdiction is to be exercised is not pointed out, and therefore it is subject to the modification and direction of the Territorial Legislature. If this were not the case, and the clause above recited were to be construed according to the nice technical rules of law, it would, rom there being no limitation prescribed, oblige the Judges to take cognizance of all cases at common law, however inconsiderable the amount, and it would follow that no other tribunal could be constituted by you with concurrent jurisdiction in any of those cases, for it is a well established maxim in law that "*selectio unius est exclusio alterius.*"

It is, however, evident to me that Congress intended merely to appoint and pay the Judges, leaving it to the Territorial tribunal to adopt or form such a judiciary system as they might conceive to be most conducive to the public good. For if Congress had intended to perfect the establishment and organization of the court, it is fairly to be presumed they would have been more explicit on that subject. And this construction is the more rational, because the next succeeding clause seems to be well calculated to supply the manifest deficiency by making it "the duty of the Governor and Judges, or a majority of them, to adopt such laws from the original States as might be necessary, and best suited to the circumstances of the Territory."

Many of the States had judiciary systems equally as liable to the objection of the Judges as the one under consideration, and several of them had such as were analagous to it. Could not the Governor and Judges have adopted any of them? Suppose they could have obtained the system of Pennsylvania, the General Court system of Kentucky, or that of the Superior Court of Tennessee or Georgia, all of which possess features very much resembling the present bill: could they not have adopted one of these? And if they had thought it the best suited to the circumstances of the Territory, would it not have been their duty to have adopted it in preference to any other? Of this there can be no doubt, and most certainly it would not have been improper in the Judges, or a violation of the ordinance, for them to have executed any law which it was or might have been their duty to adopt; and the authority of the Legislature to alter, as they "think fit," any adopted law, demonstrates that your power is not less than theirs was.

This is also the "practical exposition" and the received construction of the ordinance, on this very point. For we find that the Governor and Judges of the Northwestern Territory actually adopted the law of Pennsylvania, by which the Judges were bound to hold the general court in two different counties, circuit courts in counties, and courts of oyer and terminer or jail delivery. The laws thus adopted were required to be submitted to Congress for their approbation, and though the same system, with different but not very material modifications, has existed for many years, it does not appear to have been ever disapproved by that body; but we find them expressly recognizing the circuit courts, by providing specifically for the expenses of the Judges in attending them.

The laws of Indiana, in force when this Territory was erected into a separate government, and when our first Judges were commissioned, required them to attend the general court and circuit courts in counties, and courts of oyer and terminer. The construction given to the ordinance, in both the territories of which we have formed an integral part, was certainly acquiesced in by the Governor and Judges of this Territory, as is evident from their official acts; for in the year 1809 they organized a general court, to sit in Kaskaskia, and courts of common pleas, to be holden by the Judges, with a separate clerk to each court. In the same year it was deemed advisable to change the system. The common pleas was abolished, and the general court was required to be held twice a year in the counties of Randolph and St. Clair, which were all that then existed, and the jurisdiction of the court in each county was limited to the bounds thereof. In these measures Judge Thomas concurred, and indeed, at the respective times of their adoption, I knew of no dissenting voice.

Under a law of Congress organizing the government of the Missouri Territory, recognizing three Superior Judges, appointed by the President and Senate of the United States, as explicitly as our ordinance does, the Legislature of that Territory, without any greater powers in that respect than you possess, have required the superior court to be held in every county within each of which its jurisdiction is localized, and the Judges, or a majority of them, have decided that the law is valid and have determined to execute it.

Without referring to analagous cases in some of the States, I trust I have said enough to convince you that, on the points which I have so far endeavored to investigate, you are not "justly chargeable with innovating the practical exposition or received construction" of the ordinance; and it will doubtless be to you a source of felicitation that the Judges have declared that they themselves have no disposition to make such innovations.

They also say, that "an appeal from the same court to the same, is a solecism." But if this measure can justly be considered beneficial (without which it is to be presumed you would not have adopted it), I believe it will be very difficult for them to establish that it is an infraction of the ordinance. Any system which gives to any court original and final jurisdiction, is neither perfect nor very usual; but, owing to the peculiar circumstances of the Territory, it may be found impracticable to establish any other. It, therefore, becomes prudent to guard, as far as possible, against the defects that are inherent in such a system. These in part consist of hasty decisions, sometimes given from necessity, after a jury is sworn, and at other times without due deliberation or a sufficient opportunity of consulting authorities upon the subject; and, to obviate any ill consequences that might otherwise result therefrom, it has been deemed advisable to declare that the Judges, upon the application of a party who supposes himself aggrieved, shall, according to the forms prescribed by law, revise their own judgments; and I believe there are few judges who will not admit that these decisions would be much more likely to be correct, upon a review of them at a fixed place favorable to the production of the greatest number of books and to the ablest investigation, and where they would be free from all the embarrassments attendant upon jury trials. These are considerations that strongly recommend the measure. No appeal can be allowed but in those cases in which it at present exists. By compelling the party complaining to preserve the ordinary forms, you subject him to the costs and damages prescribed by laws, sufficient to correct a mere litigious disposition; and in no instance can a plaintiff be longer delayed than under existing regulations. As, then, the measure promises some substantial good, at least, and is productive of no injury, its being denominated a "solecism" ought not to be sufficient to prevent its adoption. And, indeed, it is as reconcilable to common sense as systems that have been sanctioned by legislatures of the greatest intelligence; for there are some at least that require the same judges to constitute circuit and supreme courts, in the latter of which they can sit in judgment and give the casting voice in decisions they have made in the former. Nor is the provision in this bill as novel as it seems to be supposed, for we find, by the laws of Georgia, a power is specially given to the supreme court to correct its own errors; and a party dissatisfied with a verdict of a jury may, as a matter of right, enter his appeal in the clerk's office at any time within the four days after the adjournment of the court.

The objection appears to be more to form than substance, for there has probably never been a court that has not, in one way or another, revised its own decisions. This power the Judges at present possess. Its exercise, however, depends on their own discretion, and if the Legislature think it best to regulate it by fixed rules, or that it is more consistent with justice to give to their fellow-citizens, as a matter of right, that which the Judges may equally grant or refuse them, as a mere matter of discretion, it cannot, in any manner that I can conceive of, possibly violate any clause in the ordinance—which is all that I attempt to prove. If, however, the two grades of courts exist, as their honors suppose, and they are not disposed to innovate the "practical exposition" of the ordinance, or its "received construction," the objection will not be found to exist.

Their last objection is to the appointment of a plurality of clerks, or of one for each county in which the court is directed to be held; and, in support of this objection, they say, "if the ordinance established more than one clerk to the same court, why have not several been appointed heretofore? If no such office was established by that instrument, whence the authority to fill it?"

If their honors mean to prove, by these interrogatories, that the Legislature cannot create more than one clerkship, because the ordinance has established but one, I would ask if the same reason will not prove that you cannot establish any court whatever with common law jurisdiction. In the one case they say the ordinance, though silent, has, by necessary implication, established a clerkship. In the other it has explicitly declared that there shall be a court, with common law jurisdiction. Whence, then, is the authority, according to their reasoning, to establish another one? There are no express restrictions upon you in either case. If, then, you have the power to constitute a court of common pleas, to lessen and divide the duties of the court established by the ordinance, have you not equal authority to create an additional clerkship, to lessen and divide the duties of the one also established by the same instrument? Provided you should consider the measure necessary and best suited to the circumstances of the Territory, upon principle it is perfectly immaterial how you divide the duties of the latter—whether you make them equal or unequal—for the argument of their honors is, that you cannot establish an additional clerkship under any modification whatever, because the office is ministerial; and if the clerk cannot do all the business himself, he may employ as many deputies as he chooses. They allege that "not only the very nature of the court and the constitution of every other Territorial tribunal and of the Federal judiciary in general, but all courts in the United States, unless very particularly constituted, demonstrates their construction to be the true one." It is, I think, very probable, that, in many of the cases alluded to, there may be but one clerk to each court; but this is rather an evidence that one has been considered sufficient, than proof of the want of legislative power to create more. Those cases, however, carry with them no authority, unless they can be shown to be analagous in their circumstances to the present bill. I think I have already proved that the true as well as received construction of the ordinance would have authorized the adoption of the judiciary system of North Carolina, which requires the superior court to be held twice a year in every county in the State, and that you have the right to require the Judges to hold the court at more places than one. Instances, therefore, where a court is held at one place only, can never be considered as applicable to the present case; because, in the former, there is neither the same reason nor necessity for having two more clerks. But in Georgia and Ohio, there is a clerk to the supreme court in every county. In Tennessee, the superior court was and I believe still is held at three different places, and has separate clerks at each. Similar regulations exist, as I am informed, in other States; and in Missouri Territory, where the superior court is established by a law of Congress, and where the objection now under consideration would apply with equal or greater force, there has been established a separate clerkship to that in each county, under regulations precisely similar to those contained in the present bill. The hitherto received construction of the ordinance in this Territory was, that a plurality of clerkships could be created; for in this opinion the three Judges who constituted the court, previous to the appointment of Judge Sprigg, all concurred, upon several repeated arguments at differen t times and places, as a journal now in my possession will show. And, indeed, it was with some surprise that I found Judge Thomas referring to the case of the court at Cahokia, as in that very case he not only wished to establish a separate clerkship, but often maintained the opinion that it could be legally done, and that the Governor and Judges, though vested with power to legislate *sub modo* only, and limited to the adoption of laws, were competent to do it, even without being able to find such a law in any State. Thus it appears that the power to adopt laws from any of the States, and not from particular ones only, presupposes the authority of the Legislature to alter them as they shall think fit; and thus other powers enumerated in the ordinance, at its received construction, as far as it can be ascertained, all combine to prove that yours is the correct construction of that instrument, and that you have power to create a plurality of clerkships, if they are necessary and best suited to the circumstances of the Territory. That they are so, seems as capable of demonstration as any proposition in Euclid. Suppose the inferior courts had not been established, as is now contemplated, whilst this was a part of the Northwestern Territory—what monstrous oppressions must have been produced, by obliging the people to have gone to the office of a single clerk for a writ to redress the most outrageous grievance! How inconvenient and expensive would it even now be to compel all our fellow-citizens to come to the seat of government, for every species of process; and how much more so might it have been, if the war had not prevented the settlements of Prairie du Chien, Green Bay and other places from extending themselves.

The convenience of the people and cheap and speedy administration of justice are the principle objects, in requiring the court to hold its sessions in the different counties. The same considerations, or a part of them, at least, render it as obviously proper and necessary that it should be separate clerk's offices. But though these are no more contemplated by the ordinance than separate clerks, yet their honors say the duties of them might be performed by deputies, as was done when the general court was held at Cahokia and Kaskaskia, and had a separate office at each place. But is this either just in itself or expedient in regard to the public? It is evident that no one clerk could execute the duties of the office in all the counties, and surely he ought not to be paid for labor wholly performed by another; nor is it to be presumed that he could make a more judicious selection than the constituted authorities, or that he could, for a part of the profits only, employ persons as well qualified and as deserving of trust as those who could be engaged for the undivided emoluments of the office.

In concluding my remarks, I beg leave to remind you that, as you witnessed the severe indisposition that now afflicts me, and which has preyed upon me for several months, I flatter myself that your liberality will make the proper allowances for the many imperfections that are but too obvious in this attempted investigation.

NINIAN EDWARDS.

December 12, 1814.

In view of the whole matter, the Legislature adopted resolutions for transmitting the contemplated act, together with the letter of the Judges and the answer thereto of Gov. Edwards, to Congress, accompanied by an address "requesting the passage of a law declaring the aforesaid enactment valid, or to pass some law more explanatory of the relative duties and powers of the Judges aforesaid and of this Legislature, in order to remove any future or existing difficulties that may arise between the Judges and the Legislature." Congress accordingly, on the 3d of March, 1815, passed "An act regulating and defining the duties of the United States Judges for the Territory of Illinois."

CHAPTER VI.

The Indian Tribes and Villages of the Western Territory — Treaties with the Indians— Gov. Edwards' views on the Indian Trade and U. S. Saline adopted by the General Government.

With a view of being acquainted with the country, the Indian villages and the respective forces of different Indian tribes, Gov. Edwards employed agents to ascertain the different routes of travel to and from the lakes, the location of the villages and the number of warriors belonging to each tribe, and such other information as might be useful during the year.

From notes furnished to him, and the maps on which are designated the rivers, villages and routes from Mackinaw to St. Louis, in the year 1812, I find the following:

Michilimakanac is an island, situated between Lakes Huron and Michigan. From Mackanac to the main land on the north side of Lake Michigan it is six miles to a place called Point St. Ignace; from Point St. Ignace to Point de Chêne, or Oak Point, the distance is six miles; from Point de Chène to the Poussette Island it is fifteen miles. These islands are situated about one mile from the shore, in very shallow water. From the Poussette Islands it is fifteen miles to a small river, called by the Indians Min-a-coquin; from Min-a-coquin River it is fifteen miles to a point called Patterson's Point, at which place it is very rocky, the water is very shallow, and the navigation is very dangerous when the wind is high. Mr. John Hays, a very intelligent person, with whom I am well acquainted, says that it was called Patterson's Point from the fact that a Mr. Charles Patterson, one of the principal members of the Northwest Fur Company, with all his crew, perished there in a bark canoe, about the year 1788. Mr. Hays says he passed through there soon afterwards, and that he was well acquainted with Mr. Patterson.

From Patterson's Point to Soucheware (an Indian name) it is fifteen miles. At this place there is a most excellent harbor, situated behind a rock; it is very difficult to enter in high winds, and it is an excellent place to catch white-fish. From Soucheware it is fifteen miles to a very handsome river called Manesty; a few miles up this river there was a small Indian village of Chippeways. From the River Manesty it is nine miles to Point de Ecoise, or Bark Point. From thence to Detour it is twenty-one miles, from which place cross over to the south side of the lake, leaving a large bay or bend, called the Bay de Knocke, on the north, about one hundred miles from Green Bay; a number of Indians—Ottaways, Chippeways and Wild-oats—resided in this bay. From Isle Detour it is three miles to Isle Broulès, or Burnt Island; from thence it is six miles to Isle Vert, or Green Island; from thence to Isle de Pou, or Pottawottamie Island, it is six miles; from Pottawottamie Island to Petite Etraite, or Little Strait, it is nine miles; at this place there is a village of two lodges of Chippeways. From thence to Port des Mort, or Death's Door, (the mainland on the south side of the lake), it is six miles; this place was called Death's Door on account of a number of Indians, in their canoes, having been drowned there; it is a very high, rocky and dangerous place in high winds, and is about one hundred and sixty miles from Chicago. From Death's Door to Isle de Raccio, an island in form of a circle, it is twenty-one miles, at which place there is an entrance for boats in which no winds whatever can molest them, as there is a very large basin for a harbor; this island is about one and a half miles from the shore. From thence it is three miles to two small islands, near the shore, called by the Indians Nicola-Kechis, on which there is a village of two lodges of Chippeways. From Nichola-Kechis it is twenty-one miles to Bay de Tourgeon, or Sturgeon Bay, where there is a village of three lodges of Chippeways; this bay is very deep. From this bay to Red River it is twenty-one miles. From Red River to Cape de Pouant, or Winnebago Cape, (a very high and handsome place, and where there was formerly a Winnebago village,) the distance is fifteen miles. From Winnebago Cape to Point au Sable, or Sandy Point, a bay where a few Wild-oats live, it is three miles—from which point cross over to the entrance of Green Bay, a distance of six miles. From Green Bay to Minne-Wakey, on the route to Chicago, it is one hundred and fifty miles. From Minne-Wakey (at and near which there are a number of Pottawottamies, Ottaways and Chippeways) it is ninety miles to Chicago; the country around Green Bay is very beautiful, the land is excellent, and it is settled on each side of the river (which empties into the bay) by Canadians and some Americans; there are here about forty houses, and the inhabitants are mostly all farmers; the north side is the most settled; there is an excellent grist mill and distillery, and there is also, near this place, a large village of the Wild-oats, situated on the north side, who have always been very friendly. Three miles from Green Bay is Rapide de Pere, where there is a grist mill. Six miles from Rapide de Pere is Petite Kakalin Rapids, where there is a village of six lodges of Wild-oats. Nine miles from this place is the Grand Kakalin Rapids and portage, where there is a small village of Wild-oats. Six miles from the Grand Kakalin Rapids is the small falls of the Petite Calumi. Six miles from Petite Calumi is the Grand Calumi and the portage, where the falls are much more considerable. Nine miles from Grand Calumi is the Rapids de Pouant, at the head of the entrance of Lake de Pouant, where there is a village of about seven lodges of Ponants; this village, though now reduced to seven lodges, formerly contained as many as thirty. Lake Pouant is about twenty-one miles long and about four or five miles wide; at the end of this lake is the entrance to Fox River of the Wisconsin, at which place Mr. Hays says he has seen a very large village of Pouants, but at that time (1812) there was not one lodge. From the mouth of Fox River it is nine miles to Bute de Morte, or Death's Hill—so called in consequence of a number of Indians having been killed there, a number of years ago, by the French; on the north side of the river at this place the Wild-oats have a village. From Death's Hill it is three miles to the Rivier des Loup, or Wolf River. From this river it is fifteen miles to Wakan, formerly a village of Winnebagoes, but now abandoned. From Wakan it is fifteen miles to Tounere Jannof, or Yellow Thunder. From Yellow Thunder it is fifteen miles to Le Plane, a remarkable place for encampment. From Le Plane to Mak-kan, a small river, on which there was formerly a Winnebago village, it is fifteen miles. From Mak-kan to Lake A-pock-way, where there is a village of two or three lodges, but where once there was a very large village, it is fifteen miles; this lake is nine miles long. From thence to Buffalo Lake it is fifteen miles; this lake is nine miles across. From Buffalo Lake to Little Rock it is fifteen miles. From Little Rock to the Forks it is fifteen miles. From the Forks it is fifteen miles to the Wisconsin portage; the length of the portage is two and a-half miles; at the portage there is a village of Winnebagoes, of three lodges, at which place a Frenchman lives who carries over the goods, boats, etc., with wagons; it is about three hundred and sixty miles from Lake Michigan to the Wisconsin River. From the portage of Wisconsin it is about one hundred and twenty miles to a village of Winnebagoes, of ten lodges, about sixty miles from its mouth, where it empties into the Mississippi River; there is nothing remarkable in the Wisconsin River except the big turn on the north side, about ninety miles from the mouth and the same distance from the portage. From the mouth of the Wisconsin it is six miles to Prairie du Chien, and twenty-one to Village La Porte, a village of ten lodges of Foxes. From Village La Porte to Turkey River it is nine miles; on this river there are about fifteen lodges of Foxes. From Turkey River to Village Batard, consisting of about eight lodges of Foxes, it is fifteen miles. From Village Batard to Little Prairie, a village of three lodges of Foxes, it is nine miles. From Little Prairie to Petite Makoketè, where there are six lodges of Foxes, it is nine miles. From Petite Makoketè to Old Mines it is nine miles. From Old Mines to New or Spanish Mines it is six miles; near this place there is a village of Foxes, up a small river. From Spanish Mines to Death's Head it is fifteen miles; this is the place where Hunt's men were killed. From Spanish Mines to the River Sussenneway, opposite Death's Head, it is also fifteen miles. From the River Sussenneway to Fever River, on both of which rivers there are excellent lead mines, it is three miles. From Fever River to Village Chaniere, containing ten lodges of Foxes, it is nine miles. From Chaniere to Grand Makoketé it is six miles. From thence to Apple River it is six miles. From thence to La Prairie de Frappeau it is fifteen miles. From thence to Potato Prairie it is fifteen miles. From thence to Che-che-qui-me-nanque, formerly an Indian village, it is about nine miles. From thence to Marais de Angè it is nine miles. From thence to Pecesuisenany, formerly an Indian village, it is nine miles. From thence to the Rapids of Rock River it is nine miles; these rapids are about eighteen miles in length; at the foot of them there are about thirty lodges, having formerly for their chief Peau Blanc, or White Skins, but at present his brother, Mohawk, is their chief. From this village to Rock River it is three miles, and about one and half miles up Rock River, on the south side, there is a very extensive village of Sacs, of nearly two hundred lodges; up this river, also, about twenty or thirty miles from the mouth, there is a considerable Winnebago village. From Rock River to Grand Muscatine it is thirty miles. From thence to Iowa River it is thirty miles. From Iowa River to Skunk River it is sixty miles. From thence to Horse-shoe it is twelve miles. From Horse-shoe to to Fort Madison it is nine miles. From thence to the head of Rapids des Moine it is nine miles; these Rapids are eighteen miles long. From the foot of the Rapids to the River des Moine it is about three miles. From thence to Fox River it is six miles. From Fox River to River Wacanda it is twenty-one miles. From thence to Prairie Wacanda it is three miles. From thence to Bay Boston it is nine miles. From thence to L'eau Froide, or Fabian River, it is eighteen miles. From Fabian River to Two Rivers it is three miles, to Prairie Joffreon. From thence to Bay Charl it is fifteen miles. From thence to Petite Glaze it is twelve miles. From Petite Glaze to Fort Mason it is two miles. From thence to Salt River it is twenty-seven miles. From Salt River to River Denoyer it is three miles. From River Denoyer to Buffalo River it is three miles. From Buffalo River to River Callumè it is four and half miles; it was near this river that O'Neal's family were killed. From Callumè to Fort Boucher it is six miles. From Fort Boucher to Dog Island it is six miles. From thence to Bell's Point it is twenty-four miles. From Bell's Point to Cape au Grey it is fifteen miles. From Cape au Grey to Cuiver River it is three miles. From thence to La Peruque, a small French village, it is six miles. From La Peruque to the River Dedain it is six miles. From thence to the Illinois River it is six miles. From thence to Portage de Sioux it is nine miles. From Portage de Sioux to the Missouri River it is six miles. From thence to St. Louis it is eighteen miles. From St. Louis to Cahokia it is four miles.

The *Pottawottamies*, on the Illinois River, are divided into three bands, to-wit: that of Gomo, consisting of about 150 men; they reside at the end of Peoria Lake about seven leagues from Peoria. The Pepper's band at Sand River, about two leagues below the Quinqueque, consisting of about 200 men of different nations—as Pottawottamies, Chippeways and Ottaways; Letourneau and Mettetasse are of this band. Sand River is fifty leagues above Peoria and twenty leagues below Lake Michigan. Mainpoc's band resides seven leagues up the Quinqueque (now called the Kankakee), and consists of about fifty men. The remaining Pottawottamies live on the River St. Joseph, on which there are three or four villages. On the Fox River, which empties into the Illinois River at the Charboniere, or Coal-pit, about thirty-five leagues above Peoria, is another band of Pottawottamies, Chippeways and Ottaways, having for their leader Wa-bee-saux. This river takes its source from Mil-waa-kee. In this band there are only about 30 men.

The *Kee kaa-poos* are divided into three bands: Pamawatans, consisting of about 100 men, exclusive of those at the Prophet's, are now making their village on Peoria Lake, three leagues from Peoria. The Little Deer has also abandoned their great village, and is now forming his village opposite to Gomo's. His band consists of about 70 men. Of this band there are also about 50 men, and the same number of Pottawottamies with the Prophet. At the Little Makina, a river on the south side of the Illinois River, is a band, headed by no particular chief, but generally by warriors. Le Bourse Sulky is generally regarded as the main chief. This tribe consists of Kees, Chippeways, Ottaways and Pous, and number about 60.

At the camping place of Chicago, three leagues from the lake, is a village of about 30 men, of Pottawottamies, Chippeways and Ottaways, having for their chief Co-wa-bee-may.

The distance from Peoria to the Rock River on the Mississippi, is about twenty leagues by land, and can be traveled in two days on foot and in one on horseback. The country is mostly prairie and very fine open woodland. Opposite to the River Vermilion, which is nearly thirty leagues above Peoria, by cutting across the land, one would reach Rock River near Milwaakee. The whole country between the Illinois and Mississippi Rivers is a fine open country, easy to travel through, chiefly prairie, but high land. The Winnebago village on Rock River is about thirty or forty leagues from the mouth and within one day's march of their old village on the Lake Ap Quay, in the Fox River, that comes from Green Bay. The distance from the Winnebago River to Milwaakee can be traveled in one and half days.

Leaving Chicago to go to Makina, on the south side of Lake Michigan, the first river you reach is the Little Calumick, about five leagues from Chicago. There is on this river a village consisting of about one hundred men, of Pous, Chippeways and Ottaways. Old Camp-pignan is their chief. He has a burnt hand and broken nose. It was reported this spring that he was killed, on his way from Niagara to Detroit. Man-mon-qai, who was his second, will probably be their next chief.

About ten leagues up the St. Joseph, a river about thirty leagues from Chicago, there is a village of about 10 men, of Pottawottamies, with no particular chief to head them. On the Terre-coupee, a small river that empties into the St. Joseph, there is a village of 100 men, of Pous, headed by Mock-kua gon, about ten leagues on a straight line from the lake and about thirty leagues by land, to Chicago. The roads from this place to the lake and to Chicago are very fine, and pass through an open country.

There is another village on the St. Joseph, about forty leagues above the mouth, of Pottawottamies, the number of whom is not known. This village is situated at the entrance of a small river called La Reviere Pirette, or Speckled River. The chief of this band is named Mon-neck-quai-bee.

On the Stagheart, a small river, which also empties into the St. Joseph, there is a village of Pous, the number of whom is not known. Their chief is Nån-quee-sai.

At the entrance of the Keck-kaa-ne ma-zo River into the lake, about fifteen leagues north of the St. Joseph, there is a small village of 7 or 8 men, without any chief and about twenty five leagues up the river there is a village of Pous and Ottaways, of about 60 or 70 men. Their chief is unknown.

On the Grand River, ten leagues beyond the Keck-kaa-ne-ma-zo, there are four villages of Ottaways, containing in all about 200 men. The first village is about three leagues, the second about fifteen, the third about twenty-five, and the fourth about forty leagues from the entrance, on a small river called Riviere de Plaines. This grand river extends very nearly to Detroit.

Four leagues beyond the Grand River is the Mash-kee-gon, on which there are two villages of Ottaways—the first about fifteen and the second about thirty leagues from the mouth. The chief of the first is Peck-kwa-nai, or Smoke; of the second, Wampum.

Four leagues beyond the Wash-kee-gon is White River, one league beyond which, on the bluffs, is a village called the Bluffs of Ottawa, of about 70 or 80 men, whose chief is not known. Twelve leagues beyond the White River is the River Pere Marquette, on which there is a small village of Ottaways, chief unknown.

NAMES OF THE RIVERS EMPTYING INTO THE ILLINOIS RIVER.

The first river, in going up the Illinois River, is the Fouchai River, on the south side and about six miles from the mouth of the Illinois River. The River Ma-ka-pinn is two miles above the Fouchai and on the same side of the Illinois. On the south side and three leagues above is the Lionoise. On the same side and two leagues above is La Pomme, or Apple River. On the north side and two leagues above Apple River is River Chabot. Mouse River, on the south side, is three leagues higher, and from this river it is one day's march to the Mississippi. Two and a half leagues higher, on the north side, is Blue River. Two leagues above Blue River, on the north side, is Pierre a la Fleche, or Arrowstone River. On the south side, two leagues above Pierre a la Fleche, is Negro River. Mauvaise-terre River is one and half leagues higher. Labellansine, on the south side, is four leagues above. Mine River, on the north side, is two leagues above, and from this river it is one and half day's march to the Mississippi. Four leagues above, on the north side, is La Riviere a Bordelle, or Brothel River. On the south side, one and half leagues above, is Sain-quee-mon River. This river extends to Wecas, near Vincennes, and on its branches were formerly Kee-ka-poo villages. On the south side, about ten leagues above the Sain-quee-mon, is the River Meequen, which keeps a direct line with the Illinois River for a long distance. Little Shwaa-yan, on the north side, is three leagues higher. Shee-shee-quen on the north side isfour leagues higher. Little Makina is five leagues higher, on the south side; the Kickapoos have a village here. The river is four leagues higher on the north side and one league below Peoria. Lake Peoria is seven leagues long, at the end of which is Gomo's village and a river called Moran's River. Little Deer's village is opposite to Gomo's. Eight leagues higher is Corbeau River, or Blackbird River, on the south side. Bureau River is six leagues higher, on the north side. Vermillion River, on the south side, is nine leagues higher. Fox River, on the north side, is four leagues higher. River Massan is about nine leagues higher, on the south side. From here we can get to the Wabash, through a fine open country. Sand River, on the north side, is three leagues higher. One and a half leagues higher is the forks of the Quin-que-que. On the south side at this place the Illinois loses its name, and is called from here Chicago River, to the lake, a distance of about twenty leagues. On the north side of Lake Michigan, about thirty leagues from Chicago, is River Mill-waa-kee, where may be found villages of Pottawottamies and Nolles-awanes. At the Sauk River, on the same side, is a village of Ottaways and Chippeways, and from this river it is but twelve miles to Green Bay.

The description of the several routes, villages, tribes and country is taken from notes and maps furnished to Gov. Edwards, in 1812, by Mr. John Hays and Mr. John Hay, both of whom filled important offices and were intelligent Frenchmen. The latter was, for many years, clerk of all the courts, and judge of probate of the county of St. Clair, in the State of Illinois. I extract the following from a letter of John Hays to Gov. Edwards, of August 20, 1812:

The route from Montreal to Michilimakanac, by the Grand River, is called 900 miles, the most difficult route perhaps in the world. There are 36 carrying places, where all the goods are carried on men's backs over these portages, and in most of those places the bark canoes are likewise carried on men's shoulders. There are also 36 places where half canoe loads are carried, owing to the great rapids. The canoe starts half loaded and deposits the half load at a certain place, and then returns for the other half load. No boats of any kind can ascend this river—only bark canoes which carry seventy pieces, weighing one hundred pounds each; every man carries two of those pieces over each carrying place. The canoes are navigated by ten or eleven men, with paddles. By this route all the merchandise from Montreal is carried to the Grand Portage, Nippegand Arthateaska, and all the other wintering places on Lake Superior, and the peltries return by the same route. A few years past all the merchandise from Montreal to Mackanac was taken by the same route. The fort St. Joseph is about seventeen leagues from Mackanac. Goods may be brought from St. Joseph along the main land and by the Island of Mackanac. Those brought the last fall into the Mississippi, by Mr. Dickson and others, were brought by this route.

The following description of Prairie du Chien is taken from a letter of N. Boilvine to the Secretary of War, of the 2d of February, 1811:

Prairie du Chien is an old Indian town, which was sold by the Indians to the Canadian traders about thirty years ago, where they have ever since taken their merchandise, from which place it was sent in various directions. The Indians also sold to them, at the same time, a tract of land measuring six leagues up and down the river and six leagues back of it—the village between thirty and forty houses, and the tract just mentioned about thirty-two families—so that the whole settlement contains about 100 families. These men are generally French Canadians, most of whom have married Indian wives; very few white females are to be found in the settlement. These people attend to the cultivation of their land, which is extremely fertile; they raise considerable quantity of surplus produce, particularly wheat and corn; they annually dispose of eighty thousand pounds of flour to the traders and Indians, besides a great quantity of meal, and the quantity of produce would be greatly increased if a suitable demand existed for it. Such is the beauty of the climate, that the country begins to attract the attention of settlers. A variety of fruit trees have lately been planted and promise to grow well. Prairie du Chien is surrounded by numerous Indians, who wholly depend on it for their supplies. Great danger, both to individuals and the Government, is to be apprehended from the Canadian traders, who endeavor to incite the Indians against us, partly to monopolize their trade, and partly to secure their friendship in case a war should break out between us and England. They are continually making large presents to the Indians.

The United States, by the adoption of one simple measure, can secure this trade and put an end to the intercourse between the Canadian traders and the Indians. Prairie du Chien, from its central position, is well calculated for a garrison and factory. It affords health, plenty of fine timber and good water. The Indians have turned their attention to the manufacture of lead, from a mine about 60 miles below Prairie du Chien. During the last season they exchanged four hundred thousand pounds of that article for goods. They might be prevailed upon to open more mines, as the profits from the manufacture of lead are much greater than from the laborious pursuit of peltries. A few tools will be necessary for them, and perhaps a blacksmith to repair them. As soon as the Indians turn their attention to lead, the Canadian traders, who have no use for that article, in the way of commerce, would abandon the country. The factory ought to be well supplied with goods to be exchanged for lead. This trade would be more valuable to the United States than peltries, as lead is not a perishable article and is easily transported, whereas peltries are bulky and large quantities are annually spoiled before they reach market.

After the war, and in connection with Gov. Clark and Col. A. Choteau of St. Louis, Gov. Edwards was appointed by the General Government to hold a treaty with the Indian tribes that had been concerned in the war. This treaty was of vital importance to the future interests of Illinois and Missouri, and no small portion of its advantages may be attributed to the forecast of Gov. Edwards. In one of his communications to the Legislature, he thus refers to one of the objects he had in making this treaty:

In 1816 a tract of land bounded by Lake Michigan, including Chicago, and extending to the Illinois River, was obtained from the Indians, for the purpose of opening a canal communication between the lake and river. Having been one of the Commissioners who treated for this land, I personally know that the Indians were induced to believe that the opening of the canal would be very advantageous to them, and that, under authorized expectations that this would be done, they ceded the land for a trifle. Good faith, therefore, towards these Indians, as well as the concurring interest of the State and of the Union, seems to require that the execution of this truly national object should not be unnecessarily delayed; and nothing is more reasonable than that the expenses should be defrayed out of the proceeds of the very property which was so ceded for the express purpose of having it done.

The replies to his communications, both from the Territorial Legislature and the Chiefs of the Departments at Washington, show in what high estimation his opinions in relation to the Indians, the salines, and his public services, were held. His intimate knowledge of the character of the Indian tribes enabled him, when requested by the General Government, to give important advice in the adoption of measures relative to our intercourse and trade with them; and in every instance, without an exception, his views were adopted by the Government. Wm. H. Crawford, who was Secretary of War in 1816, refers to Gov. Edwards' views on the subject of the Indian trade in a highly complimentary manner. He says, "his view of the subject, as well as several other important ideas, are more fully developed in the communication of Gov. Edwards;" and in a letter to Gov. Edwards, he says, "the Department has the fullest confidence in the rectitude with which your superintendence has been exercised." The same may be said of the views entertained and the opinions communicated by him in relation to the U. S. saline and lead mines, as will appear from his extensive correspondence on those subjects.

"Owing to his knowledge and experience with the Indian character and affairs," he was called upon by Mr. Calhoun, Secretary of War in 1818, for his views in relation to the Indian trade, and for his ideas, also, on the "relative merits of the system as it then was or with the improvements of which it was susceptible, and the one proposed to be substituted by Congress."

In the year 1817, he received a letter from a very distinguished gentleman, stating that his friends in Washington City were urging his appointment as Secretary of the War Department. The editor of the "National Register," in Washington, and one of the most influential papers of the city of Baltimore, also presented his claims for that office.

CHAPTER VII.

Organization of the State Government and Gov. Edwards' election to United States Senate—Speech on the Public Land Question—United States Mineral Land—The Illinois Question—Letter of Mr. Wirt in reference to his Retiring from Public Life—Mr. Calhoun's Letters in reference to his Advancement—Graduation of the Price of the Government Lands.

The State Government was organized in 1818, by the election of Shadrack Bond, Governor, and Pierre Menard, Lieut. Governor. Elias K. Kane, who was afterwards elected Senator in Congress, was appointed Secretary of State, and Daniel P. Cook was elected the first Attorney General of the State. Gov. Bond had been a delegate in Congress from the Territory from 1811 to 1815, at which time he was appointed Receiver of the Land Office, which office he held at the time of his election as Governor of the State. He had made himself deservedly very.popular by his efforts in Congress to secure the payment of the troops during war, and for his support of the measures having for their object the protection of our frontier settlements.

Gov. Edwards and Jesse B. Thomas were chosen by the Legislature to represent them in the Senate of the United States. .In this conspicuous station, and one of the highest to which an American citizen can aspire, while the great and complicated interests of the whole country came under his eye, Gov. Edwards relaxed not his accustomed vigilance for the rights and interests of his more immediate constituents.

During the time he was Senator in Congress, no one had a higher standing as a debater or statesman. His policy in relation to the Indian trade, the management of the lead mines and the U. S. salt works, had been previously adopted by the General Government. Among the first of his speeches delivered in the U. S. Senate was one on the subject of the admission of the State of Missouri into the Union. Though from a free State, and opposed to slavery, and especially to its introduction into his own State, he ably contended for the right of the people of each State to have such a constitution and institutions as they might adopt for themselves, provided their form of government was republican and not in violation of the constitution of the United States. His speech, on a resolution of Senator Lloyd of Maryland, proposing to give to each of the old States, for the purpose of education, a portion of the public lands equal to the amount granted for the same purpose to the new States, contains, among other things, an able exposition of the powers of the General Government on the subject of appropriating the lands or funds of the Government for mere local purposes. It places the right of the new States to the land, for those purposes, on the ground which was afterwards adopted: that the land appropriated for such objects would tend to enhance the value of the remainder, and bring into market a vast quantity so much earlier, that the Government would actually gain by the appropriation to the new States. On the publication of this speech, Mr. Edwards received the following letter from Mr. Blair, who was a member of Congress:

April 12, 1822.

Mr. Blair's most kind respects to Gov. Edwards of Illinois, and begs leave to present his best thanks for the speech (in pamphlet form) on the resolution proposing to give the old States lands for the purposes of education, &c.

At the same time he cannot refrain from assuring Mr. E. that this very *able* speech has probably saved him from giving an erroneous vote. Mr. B. had thought it *reasonable* that the old States should participate in the benefit of the public lands equally with the new States, without considering that the school donations of land were made to the new States as a bonus for settling in a wilderness, &c. Mr. B. also begs leave to assure Mr. E. that, in his opinion, this speech is equally creditable to the head and to the heart. While it breathes the purest spirit of philanthrophy and benevolence, it, in point of reasoning, "leaves no stone unturned."

I have also before me a letter from Hon. John Crowell, a member of Congress from North Carolina, dated April 27, 1822, in which he says that "Gov. Branch, of that State, has read your speech on the Maryland proposition, and says you have changed his opinion, and that your arguments are unanswerable." The following extract from that speech shows how well he understood, at this early day, the questions in relation to the powers which respectively belonged to the General and State Governments:

The appropriation which we are asked to make is avowed to be for a mere State purpose. The question then is, can the resources of this nation be thus applied? In discussing this subject, I may, I presume, safely premise that the powers, duties and objects of the Federal and State Governments are separate and distinct, and the prosperity and happiness of this nation depend upon the fidelity and wisdom with which those governments, respectively, discharge their appropriate functions. Each government has, for those important purposes, and as necessary thereto, its own particular resources, which cannot be yielded up or misapplied, without impairing its capacity to fulfil the objects of its institution; for nothing could be more nugatory than a grant of powers without the means of executing them. But, sir, whether the national domain has been acquired by conquest, cessions from particular states, purchases from foreign powers, one thing is undeniable—it has, doubtless, been acquired by and exclusively belongs to the Confederation or Union. It must, therefore, be considered as National and not State property, and, by fair inference, is applicable only to National and not State objects. It is true that it is a common fund in which all the States are interested. So, sir, is the revenue and every other species of property belonging to the United States; in relation to all of which the interest of the States is precisely the same. Being a common fund, applicable to the use and support of the General Government, the States can enjoy the benefits of it only in its just and ligitimate application to National purposes. I hold, therefore, that no State can rightfully claim, and, of course, to none can be granted the separate and distinct use and enjoyment of the property or funds of the nation, in consequence of a right to a common participation therein.

In this speech he further argues that Congress, having bound themselves, by solemn compact, to dispose of those lands for the use and benefit of the Union, "and for no other use or purpose whatsoever," cannot withdraw any part from the use of the Union; that it was an acquisition in their Federal character, in which character only could the States participate in the benefits of it; that, with the same propriety, the common funds of the nation may be appropriated to objects to which the powers of Federal legislation are not pretended to extend, and that if the States have no right to the separate and distinct use and enjoyment of the common property and funds of the nation, the Congress has no power to confer such a right over them; that Congress could have no pretence of power to enforce the application; and that Congress has no more right to grant away the funds of the nation than the powers of the Government. This argument is conclusive against the power to appropriate the funds of the nation to internal improvements, except for works of national character, or to divide the proceeds of the public lands among the States. But the grants to the State lose all their character as donations, because the increased value of the reserved alternate sections will increase the national fund.

The "National Intelligencer" thus alludes to this speech: "We omit several articles to-day for the purpose of presenting entire, in one paper, the speech of Mr. Edwards of Illinois, in the Senate of the United States, delivered at the last session of Congress, on the proposition to grant to the old States portions of the public lands for the purposes of education. Circumstances, which it is unnecessary to mention, have interfered to prevent an earlier publication of this speech, which, though it is in opposition to the policy we ourselves deem wise and have uniformly advocated, we must confess is an argument of great ability, and so strong as to be calculated to weaken in some degree the confidence of those who have been most zealous and conscientious in maintaining the opposite doctrine."

Not only the people of Illinois, but those of all the United States, are indebted to him for having defeated a policy which, had it prevailed, would have resulted in a division of the public lands, or the proceeds arising from their sale, among all the States of the Union, which would have prevented those grants of land within their limits to the new States, for the purpose of internal improvements. It would have also prevented the reduction of the price, and consequently retarded their settlement. It was conceded by all parties, at Washington, that the efforts of Gov. Edwards on this occasion defeated the passage of those resolutions. His policy in relation to the public lands was, to facilitate every one in acquiring a home. In a speech which he delivered as early as 1806, in Kentucky, he said: "My wish was that every man might have an opportunity of procuring a freehold of his own; that there might be as few tenants as possible. I have always considered tenants too subject to the influence of their landlords, and landlords in general so much disposed to abuse that influence as to render it dangerous and highly inimical to republicanism. With these views I have zealously persevered in exerting the small portion of influence I possessed to ameliorate the situation of the citizens of the district, and to promote the general prosperity of the State."

In his message to the Legislature, in 1826, he says the course of policy adopted by the General Government "is so restrictive of natural rights, and at the same time so unexampled, that it is only to be justified by urgent necessity, and should no longer be pursued after that necessity has ceased to operate. Acknowledged authorities on the law of nature recognize to all men a natural right, according to the beneficent intentions of the Creator of the world, to a portion of the land which He has made for their benefit; and although this right, like all others, may be modified by the institutions of civil society, yet, these should conform, as far as possible, to natural rights. It would seem that no government, holding immense tracts of waste and unappropriated lands, can, without acting contrary to Divine intention and will, refuse to permit its own citizens to occupy a reasonable portion of these lands, but for a price which many thousands of them are unable to pay. Why, then, should this policy be continued? Justice, sound policy, the beneficent intentions of the Creator of the world—who made the land for the common benefit of all mankind, and conferred upon every human being a right to a portion of it—will forbid it. The system, therefore, sooner or later, must and will be abandoned."

These were not, however, the only grievances which he pointed out and used his efforts to have remedied. There were other measures assumed, by the General Government, in relation to the public lands, which threatened to undermine the foundations of the sovereignty and independence of the States, and to subvert both our civil and political liberties. Declining to sell, the United States claimed and exercised the power of leasing out the whole of the mineral lands of the State, thereby establishing the relation of landlord and tenant between the United States and the citizens of the State, and introducing a population among us dependent upon themselves, and at that time numerous enough to decide all our general elections and to control our most important municipal affairs. At the session of

Congress in 1829 a bill was pending, in the House of Representatives, "to authorize the President of the United States to appoint a Superintendent and Receiver at the Fever River Lead Mines, and for other purposes," which, among other things, required those officers to report to the President "such alterations in the manner of governing and leasing said mines as may to them appear necessary for the better security of the interest of the Government," and empowered the President to prescribe such rules and regulations for the government of said officers and mines, leasing and surveying the mineral grounds, licensing smelters, and for preserving the property of the United States, as to him may appear necessary and proper. Gov. Edwards, in calling the attention of the Legislature to this subject, said, "this project, by the concentration of so much power in the hands of any one man, violates all the acknowledged principles of well regulated liberty, and had not its parallel in the United States, nor even in Great Britain since their emancipation from the misrule of the Stuarts; that, divided as we had been upon the great question of slavery, its exercise might have given the population of the mineral country a decided preponderance to the one side or the other; and that, with such means at the command of the General Government, there was nothing to prevent its deciding for us any other great question of national or state policy, upon which an ordinary division of public opinion prevailed. A further exercise of this power (he said) might subject our property, liberties and lives to the uncontrolled domination of the mere dependents and tenants at will of a government that never was intended to have any agency in our local affairs." He called upon the Legislature to prevent its exercise by their timely interposition; for, said he, "there is the same authority to lease the whole as a part of the public domain within the limits of the State."

I give further extracts from his messages to the State Legislature on the subject of the public lands, as follows:

Adverse to our interest and welfare as has been the policy which the General Government has long pursued in relation to the public lands, there has been nothing so well calculated to awaken our apprehension as certain principles which it has recently avowed and acted upon. Seriously injured by a system which prohibits settlement and cultivation without previous purchase—refusing to sell, but upon terms far more exorbitant than have ever been demanded by any State in the Union, or any of the powers of Europe that have held land on this continent, and which exacts the same price for lands, good, bad and indifferent—we have, year after year, implored Congress to discontinue the grievances thus produced, by granting small donations out of the vast public domain, to poor but meritorious and useful citizens who are unable to buy; and by reducing the price, and apportioning it to the quality of the land. Reasonable as were these petitions, they have, however, not only been utterly fruitless, but an aggravation of the evils, already so severely felt, is seriously threatened. A high functionary of the Government, sensible of the magnitude of the interests at

—14

stake, but unappalled by it, in an elaborate and eloquent official report to Congress, at the last session, in glowing colors, depicts even the present poor encouragement afforded to the settlement and cultivation of the public lands as an evil to the nation, and, with uncalculating intrepidity, powerfully urges the means of lessening "its absorbing force."

In this report, the Secretary of the Treasury says: "It cannot be overlooked that the prices at which fertile bodies of land may be bought of the Government, under this system, operate as a perpetual allurement to their purchase. It has served, and still serves to draw, in an annual stream, the inhabitants of a majority of the States, including amongst them, at this day, a portion, not small, of the Western States, into the settlement of fresh lands lying still farther and farther off. If the population of these States, not yet redundant in fact, though appearing to be so under this legislative excitement to emigrate, remained fixed in more instances, as it probably would by extending the motives to manufacturing labor, it is believed the nation at large would gain in two ways: First, by the more rapid accumulation of capital; and next, by the gradual reduction of the excess of agricultural population over that engaged in other vocations." Referring to the public domain itself, he remarks, that "its very possession is conceived to furnish paramount inducements, under all views, for quickening, by fresh legislative countenance, manufacturing labor throughout other parts of the Union. It is a power to be turned to the account of manifold and transcendant blessings, rather than reposed upon for aggrandizing too exclusively the interest of agriculture, fundamental as that must ever be in the State. Agriculture itself would be essentially benefited; the price of lands, in all the existing States, would soon become enhanced, as well as the produce from them, by a policy that would, in anywise, tend to render portions of the present population more stationary, by supplying new and adequate motives to their becoming so. And, as it is, the laws that have legally, in effect, throughout a long course of time, superinduced disinclinations to manufacturing labor, by their overpowering calls to rural labor in the mode of selling off the public domain, the claim of further legal protection to the former kind of labor, at this day, seems to wear an aspect of justice, no less than of expediency."

Without stopping to contest the wisdom and necessity of legislative enactments to check a great and acknowledged excess of agricultural labor, in a free and enlightened country, where every one is left to pursue his own interests, consult his own inclination, and choose his own vocation, or to inquire how agriculture could be "essentially benefited" by increasing the price of lands, or manufactures advanced by enhancing the value of the products of agriculture—and without denying the advantages of a wise and judicious division of labor, properly and fairly effected—I may be permitted to say, that it seems to me a new discovery that, in a nation abounding with vast regions of waste lands of unparalleled fertility, any vocation is better calculated to increase its capital or promote its welfare than agriculture, or that, under such circumstances, legislative discountenance should ever be interposed to bind or check it, for the sake of promoting any other interest. This is believed to be an assumption, which is contradicted by all the records of experience and observation, and the policy which the Secretary predicates upon it, and which Congress seems to have adopted, is as clearly inconsistent with the universally acknowledged and most solemn obligations of a nation. Vattel declares the cultivation of the earth to be the natural employment of man. In pages 91, 92 and 129, he says: "Of all the arts, tillage or agriculture is doubtless the most useful and necessary. It is the nursing father of the State. The cultivation of the earth causes it to produce an infinite increase; it forms the surest resource and the most solid funds of rich commerce for the people who enjoy a happy climate."

"This affair, then, deserves the utmost attention of the Government. The sovereign ought to neglect no means of rendering the land under his obedience as well cultivated as possible."

"The government ought carefully to avoid everything capable of discouraging the husbandman, or of diverting him from the labors of agriculture."

"The cultivation of the soil is not only to be recommended by government on account of the advantages that flow from it, but from its being an obligation imposed by nature on mankind. The whole earth is appointed for the nourishment of its inhabitants; but it would be incapable of doing it, was it uncultivated."

Referring to desert places not necessary as such to the safety of a nation, and which it is unable to cultivate, he says: "It is equally agreeable to the dictates of humanity and to the particular advantages of the State, to give these desert places to strangers who are able to clear the land and render it valuable. The beneficence of the State thus turns to its own advantage; it acquires new subjects, and augments its riches and powers. This is the practice in America. The English have carried their settlements in the new world to a degree of power which has considerably increased that of the nation. Thus the King of Prussia also endeavors to repeople his States, laid waste by the calamities of ancient wars."

The title of this nation to the public domain is primarily derived from these principles, and must forever remain subject to the obligations they impose. America, when first discovered by the European nations, was inhabited by a people thinly scattered over its surface, who neither would nor could cultivate it, and who consequently could not lawfully claim the whole of it; and hence those under whom the nation claims, as against the aborigines, lawfully took possession and acquired title. Admitting, then, the public lands belong to the United States, is not the government thereof bound, by the eternal principles of justice, and by a just regard to the laws of nature, which is the Divine will, not only to permit, but to encourage the settlement and cultivation of those lands, wherever it can do so without endangering the general welfare? And, if the dictates of humanity imposes on any nation an obligation, as is said by the author above quoted, to give desert places "to strangers who are able to clear the land and to render it valuable," how can a government like ours, so emphatically relying for its support upon the virtue and affections of the people, and professing to be actuated by sentiments of justice and philanthropy, refuse a similar boon to a poor and dependent, but faithful and useful citizen? All civilized nations acknowledge the justice of the principles I have quoted. Virtuous and enlightened ones recognize, and, as far as circumstances admit, respect the obligations they impose. The monarchies of Europe which have held territory on this continent, have conformed to them with a beneficence and liberality which does them honor, and is particularly worthy of the imitation of this nation, since no little of its present wealth, and power, and prosperity is justly attributable to that source. Why, it may be asked, should not the Government of the United States be as liberal in this respect as those of Great Britain, France or Spain, which it has succeeded? Is it that the public lands, having been obtained by the common efforts of all the States, should be disposed of for their common benefit, and therefore cannot be rightfully transferred for the encouragement of agriculture? Were not those very lands originally obtained by the common efforts of those nations? How then did their governments acquire the right to give them away for the encouragement of agriculture? And why were they not equally bound to exact for them the highest price in cash that could be obtained for the benefit of their respective nations? A monarch has no more right to disregard the interest and welfare of his nation, than the constituted authorities of a republic. It was not without incurring vast expenses and sacrifice of much property and many valuable things, that those nations discovered and possessed themselves of their respective domains on this continent. Nor did any of them escape the necessity of bloody and expensive wars to maintain them. And if the acquisition of our public domain from Great Britain, by the common blood and treasure of the nation, marks such a right of property in it as prohibits the Government of the United States from disposing of it, but for pecuniary considerations, it would seem that nothing could have more imperiously imposed a similar restriction upon the government of that nation, than the immense expenditure of her blood and treasure, not only in numerous conflicts with the natives, but in her ever memorable war of '56, with France, to maintain and preserve it.

The people of Virginia sufficiently participated in the cost of the very lands in question, to impose an obligation on the Government of the State, not less than that of the Union, to dispose of them for the common benefit of all her citizens: yet Great Britain and Virginia never thought themselves restricted from the right of giving desert places even to strangers who were able to clear the land, and render it valuable; nor absolved from the duty of employing all means of rendering the land under their obedience as well cultivated as possible, and of avoiding everything capable of discouraging the husbandman, or of diverting him from the labors of agriculture. No nation but our own, however it may have acquired its public domain, whether by discovery, concessions, purchases, or conquests, has ever avowed or acted upon such principles in regard to it. None could do so without neglecting its duties to itself, violating its obligations to others, and disregarding the intention and will of the Divine Creator and Governor of the Universe. The whole world, physical and moral, is governed by laws. Nations as well as individuals are subject to established rules of conduct. The former owe the same respect and obedience to the law of nature, that the latter do to any lawfully prescribed rule of civil action. In its application to nations, it is emphatically termed the necessary law of nations, because they are all obliged to conform to the precepts it prescribes. And, indeed, so deep and solid, so sacred and eternal, are its foundations, that they have neither the right to change it, nor dispense with the duties it enjoins. So far from countenancing the restricted obligations that have been supposed, it expressly declares that the sovereign ought not even "to allow either communities or private persons to acquire large tracts of land in order to leave it uncultivated;" that "every nation is obliged, by the law of nature, to cultivate the ground that has fallen to its share;" that nations who, by retaining an idle life, "usurp more extensive territories than they would have occasion for, were they to use honest labor, have no reason to complain if other nations, more laborious and too closely confined, come to possess a part;" and that "no nation can lawfully appropriate to itself a too disproportioned extensive country, and reduce other nations to want subsistence and a place of abode."

Great Britain acquired and held the lands in question subject to those obligations, and not only apportioned the price of them to their qualities and descriptions, and granted them on terms calculated to invite population, but actually made settlement, cultivation and other improvements, conditions of her grants. France and Spain did the same with their Territories, so long as they remained in their possession. This practice still prevails in the Canadas, Mexico, and all the South American Governments. Virginia, under whom the United States claim, followed the example of Great Britain, and consulting both her power and her duty, made sales at a very moderate price, and liberally granted pure donations to actual settlers.

Had, then, the right of property of the United States in that part of the public domain which is included within this State, been derived from its acquisition, at their joint expense, not only in treasure but in blood, it is evident from the law of nature, and the immutable laws and universal practices of nations, that it should have been held subject to all those rights, obligations and duties, in the same manner as if it had been in the hands of any other nation in the world. But this assumption of the derivation of title is not less contradicted by reiterated admissions and acknowledgments, and various solemn official acts of the Union, than repugnant to the deliberate and well defined agreement under which all the States united their common efforts for independence; for the Articles of Confederation not only affirmed the right of every State to all the lands within its limits, but expressly declared that "no State shall be deprived of Territory for the benefit of the United States." Virginia, therefore, acquired as much right, and the United States as little, by the issue of that glorious contest, to those lands, as to the capital of the State itself. The title of the United States was, therefore, exclusively derived from the cession so liberally and magnanimously made by Virginia. In making it, she could not exempt those lands from any conditions to which they were subjected by the law of nature in her own hands, nor absolve the United States from any obligations or duties which their tenure so imposed upon herself. Nations have no more right than individuals to violate the law of nature; and all treaties, conventions, customs, and practices, contrary to the precepts it prescribes, or that are such as it forbids, are unlawful and invalid. Virginia, therefore, could neither have required, authorized, nor justified, any policy contrary to the law of nature, which has for its object the advancement of the welfare of the original States, at the expense of that of the new ones, by encouraging manufactures to raise the price of public lands in the former, and prevent settlement and cultivation in the latter. Nor does her cession afford the least countenance to doctrines so extraordinary, or objects so inconsistent with the equal rights of the new States. On the contrary, it clearly prohibits them; for while it absolutely requires that the lands shall be disposed of, this policy is calculated to prevent and defeat that very disposition of them which was contemplated by both parties. Admit, as has been too long contemplated, that this stipulation means that they should be sold for the highest price that can possibly be got for them in cash; still it is doubtless a stipulation that binds the United States to sell them. Would not, then, any plan, deliberately adopted with a view to lessen the inducements to agricultural labor, and to prevent purchases, involve such a palpable violation of good faith as no nation ought to be guilty of?

The stipulation for the division of the territory into distinct States, and for their admission into the Union on an equal footing with the original States, would seem to forbid everything on the part of either of the contracting parties calculated to retard or defeat these objects, and evidently contemplated, if it did not absolutely require, all usual and ordinary inducements to settlement and cultivation as means of their accomplishment within a reasonable period.

The stipulation that the lands should be disposed of for the common benefit of all the States, imposed no other obligation, except in so far as it prohibited their being retained in a waste and uncultivated state, than would have existed without it; for had they been acquired by conquest, or in any other way, they could not rightfully have been disposed of, but for the common benefit of the whole nation.

As the citizens of Virginia had the same right to participate in all the advantages of these lands, while they remained in her hands, that the State had, after their transfer to the Union, it is not to be presumed that she either wished or intended, by this stipulation, to restrict the United States in the right to dispose of them in the same manner, and upon the same terms, which she herself had done, since she could not have done so, without an acknowledgment of having committed injustice to her own citizens. Nor is there anything in the whole history of her conduct, from that day to this, to warrant the belief that she ever would have consented that their settlement and cultivation should be discountenanced by legislative enactments, for the sake of promoting domestic manufactures. However allowable or expedient such a policy may be in regard to the Territories of the United States, nothing could be more unreasonable and unjust than its application to that part of the public domain which lies within the new States. The admission of the State into the Union ought to conclude all question as to the expediency or duty of permitting, if not encouraging, settlements co-extensive with its limits. Yet even these, it appears, are to be discountenanced and checked, upon theoretical calculations of increasing the capital of the nation by some more prolific means than agriculture, which are known to have utterly failed in the most distinguished, if not the only, experiment that has been made upon them by any enlightened nation. Nothing could be supposed capable of producing "a more rapid accumulation of capital" than the rich and inexhaustable mines of Spain and her colonies, yet though the most fertile, she has become, by encouraging the manufacture of bullion and coin, and by neglecting agriculture, the poorest country in Europe.

It is not intended by these remarks to make any complaint, individually, against the distinguished gentleman who has been named, and for whose talents, integrity, and patriotism, the highest respect is entertained ; nor will it be denied that the present administration of the General Government have fully equalled, if not exceeded, any of their predecessors in the manifestation of a friendly disposition towards our interests. The views disclosed by the remarks that have been quoted from the Secretary's Report, are only alarming from an abundance of concurring proof, afforded by other acts of the Government, that they are not individual, but common to a majority of the nation, and from a just apprehension, thence arising, that they will continue to influence the Government. And even in this point of view, though the experience of their deleterious effects warns us of our duty to use all reasonable means of averting them, or at least of mitigating their severity, it should not betray us into a hasty and uncharitable conclusion that our brethren of other States have been influenced by a deliberate wish or intention to oppress us, or withhold from us any just right. Bound by our honor, duty, and interest, to cherish the utmost cordiality, in all our social and political relations and intercourse with them, the imputation of dishonorable motives would be discreditable to ourselves, and equally betray a want of confidence in the intrinsic merits of our cause. Great allowances are due to a habit of thinking in regard to those lands, which has been so naturally produced by the peculiar circumstances under which they were obtained, and the correctness of which, in its present application to them, has probably never been sufficiently inquired into, investigated, and tested by principle.

When these lands were originally acquired by the United States, they were without the limits of all of them, and all having then precisely the same interest, they were at liberty to dispose of them in any manner whatever that might be thought most to their advantage—since there was no other State to object whose welfare could be checked, or whose sovereignty, freedom, independence or jurisdiction could be violated or impaired by any disposition of which they were susceptible. The old States appear still to think that the admission of the new ones into the Union, which contain within their limits considerable portions of the public domain, confers no rights that create any restriction or impose any new duties or obligations in reference to the original power and objects of disposing of those parts of the domain. We think differently. The Government appears to think itself under no obligation to encourage their settlement and cultivation ; that, it is only bound to sell them for the payment of the public debt; that, in reference to every other object, it may or may not dispose of them, as the particular interest of a majority of the States may seem to require. On the contrary, we contend that our admission into the Union involved an obligation on the part of the Government to permit, if not encourage, the settlement and cultivation, upon reasonable terms, of all lands within our limits. And while we should treat the opinions of our brethren throughout every part of the Union with the utmost deference, we should be wanting in duty to ourselves by forbearing, temperately, firmly, and perseveringly, to insist that these, and all other questions, growing out of our federal relation to the Government, should be decided, not arbitrarily, but upon principle. It is not to be supposed that the Government will not, ultimately, yield to the combined authority of the laws of nature, and of nations, and of the Federal constitution ; and if the rights for which we contend cannot be sustained upon principles which they all recognize, we ought to submit, and doubtless will do so cheerfully.

It is contended, on our part, that the Government of the Union is bound, from its nature and objects, as far as its authority legitimately extends, to act upon national principles ; to look to the general welfare of the whole Union as a unit ; to explore and cultivate every resource of general wealth, power and happiness ; to extend the blessings of freedom and independence to all its citizens in whatever part of its territory they may reside ; to fulfil all the obligations imposed upon it by the laws of nature and of nations ; to provide for its own interests, and leave the States to manage theirs ; to respect the just claims of every State without regard to any consequences that are not of Federal cognizance ; and to do injustice to none, with a view to promote the interest of others.

If these principles be correct, and they are believed to be undeniable, it follows that the duties they enjoin cannot be neglected or disregarded, to the injury of any State, without violating the essential principles of the Union, and furnishing just cause of complaint. As they necessarily exclude all jurisdiction of the particular interests of all the States, the Government has no authority to provide for or act upon them—no right to be influenced by them. And hence it is no legitimate consideration, that any warranted encouragement to the settlement and cultivation of lands in the new States, might "draw, in an annual stream," inhabitants from the old ones Suppose it should do so, no right is violated ; such emigrants generally better their condition, increase their property, render the public lands more valuable, augment the resources and power of the Union, and still continue as much its citizens as before their emigration. Is, then, the Government to withhold from its own free citizens means of pursuing their interest and happiness, to which they are justly entitled, and to forego such benefits to the nation, merely to afford to certain States a protection which they have no right to claim, and which it has as little right to grant. This would indeed be to descend from the elevated objects of its institution, and to degrade itself into a mere guardian of the particular interests of States, and this, too, in direct opposition to those most sacredly committed to its charge.

It would be still less justifiable, and more impolitic and cruel, to withhold such rights from its citizens, and forego such benefits to itself, with a view "to enhance the price of lands" in the old States, since this would be to favor a particular class of citizens only, and would tend to render the multitudes who are without lands, less able to acquire them, and thus make the rich richer, and the poor poorer.

As, however, the measures recommended by the Secretary, with a view to these results, have been adopted by Congress, "our gravest attention may, on this account, be but the more wisely summoned to the consideration of correlative duties, which the existence of such a system, in the heart of the State, imposes." And with this view, let us, with a due consideration "of the magnitude of the interests at stake," and with an "earnest desire to arrive at correct opinions," endeavor to ascertain what right the United States have to the public lands within the limits of this State.

In considering this question, the nature of the Federal and State governments, and their relation to each other and to the people of the United States, should be constantly kept in view. Sovereignty, with all its attributes, being an essential and inherent right of the people, which they may either retain in their own hands or confide to agents, and governments deriving their existence from the will of the people only, it follows that no government can rightfully claim or exercise any powers whatever but such as have been granted it. The Federal and State governments, as essential parts of a great system, and with distinct power which marks the limits of their respective duties, having therefore been instituted by the people, for their common security and welfare, they both derive all their authority to act from the same source, and consequently must, from the nature of things, be, within the respective limits assigned them, as independent of the control of each other, as though they were distinct independent nations—as power which is not inherent, but depends on delegation, can no more exceed the authority given in political than civil affairs. Both are agents, and but agents, of the people, with separate functions equally important and essential to the common safety and happiness. Each possesses the sovereign authority within its own sphere, and none whatever out of it. Neither, therefore, can transcend the limits prescribed for it, nor invade the province of the other, without being guilty of an usurpation, which it would not be less criminal to acquiesce in than to perpetrate. And it should not be forgotten that a State has an equal right with the United States to judge of all such matters—right which, though it should be exercised with great moderation and discretion, can never be surrendered without endangering our liberties. The Constitution of the United States is, at the same time, the evidence of the terms on which they agreed to form their present union, and the instrument by which it was effected; and as it contains the only grants of power to the Federal Government, so it must decide all questions of Federal rights. It might be sufficient to rely upon general principles, and its specific and limited objects, as declared in the Constitution, to show that the Federal Government has no powers but those that have been granted to it. This, however, happily, is not left to construction, for the jealous caution of the States, not content with an enumeration of the powers actually granted, but with a determination to prevent, by securing all others of every description in other hands, the possibility of its acquiring any more, insisted on and carried the following amendment to the Constitution, viz: "The powers not delegated to the United States by the Constitution, nor prohibited by it to the States, are reserved to the States, respectively, or to the people."

As, then, every State in the Union, however it may have got there, may, within its own limits, exercise all the powers of sovereignty that have not been delegated to the United States by the Constitution, nor prohibited by it to itself, so the United States can neither possess nor exercise the powers of sovereignty over nineteen-twentieths of the territory within the limits of a sovereign and independent State, (as is attempted in this) without being able to show the delegation of such powers to themselves and their prohibition to the State. These must be shown by the Constitution alone—for that being the fundamental law, all the powers of the State and Federal Governments combined are incompetent to change it. All bargains, agreements, compacts or treaties, to abridge the powers thus secured by the Constitution to every State, or to lessen the restriction imposed by it upon those of the United States, are therefore perfect nullities. Nor are they less opposed to the spirit than to the letter of the Constitution. It evidently contemplates a union of co-ordinate, sovereign and independent States, in which each yields and retains precisely the same powers, and in authorizing the admission into the Union of new States, could not have intended that they should be admitted upon any other than terms of perfect equality—since nothing could have been more averse to the principles of the Union, or dangerous to the liberties of the States, than to have permitted the Government of the United States to acquire an undue influence, by peopling at pleasure its immense domain, dividing it into nominal States, introducing into the Union a host of dependent communities, and overruling the original States by those who were not their equals. Nor could the equilibrium of powers, thus established between the State and Federal governments, be altered or destroyed in any other way, without changing the nature of the Union and violating the Constitution. If, then, it does not permit the admission of new States into the Union but upon terms of equality, as to every natural, political and fundamental right, with the old ones, it follows that no bargain, whatever its consideration, or by whomsoever made, can so far change this great fundamental law as to reduce them to a condition of inferiority. The admission of a State into the Union imposes duties as well as confers rights. At the same time that it secures to the new States an equality of powers with the original States, it imposes upon them the same restrictions, obligations and duties, and therefore the Federal Government can no more increase the powers to which the Constitution has restricted it, by a bargain with a new than with an old State; for, as no old State could confer upon that Government any part of the powers "reserved to the States respectively" by the Constitution, so a new State is equally bound to withhold, retain and exercise all its powers. And if the Government of the United States can make no bargain with a State in the Union for a part of its sovereign rights, it can make no such bargain with a State out of the Union, to be executed after its admission into it; for the moment of admission terminates the power of the Government to enforce and the ability of the State to fulfil it, as no State, all of whose officers are sworn to support the Constitution, could permit the Federal Government to usurp and exercise, within its limits, any of the powers of sovereignty not only not delegated but prohibited by that sacred instrument. All bargains, therefore, with the people of a Territory, or other communities, not authorized by the Constitution, or restrictive of the equal rights of a sovereign and independent member of the Union, are, after admission, not only voidable, like civil contracts made during infancy, but absolutely null and void as being incompatible with and repugnant to the fundamental law. Had this State, then, been simply admitted into the Union without any declaration of its equality, the United States could have had no more power to hold lands within its limits than within those of any other State in the Union, and could only then hold them for the same purposes.

Its equality, however, has not been left to encounter the dangers of construction, for on the 3d December, 1818, Congress adopted a resolution, declaratory of its admission into the Union, in the following words:

"*Resolved by the Senate and House of Representatives of the United States of America, in Congress assembled*, That the State of Illinois shall be one and is hereby declared to be one of the United States of America, and admitted into the Union on an equal footing with the original States in all respects whatever."

Human language does not admit of terms more comprehensive or better adapted to include and secure to the State every right, privilege, power and exemption that could be claimed, in any respect whatever, by an original State, since "equal footing in all respects whatever" necessarily excludes inequality in any respect whatever. And this being an act for the release of the people from the thraldom of a Territorial Government, and investing them with all the rights of free citizens, in pursuance of both the letter and spirit of the Constitution, it is entitled, like all statutes made for the public good, to the most liberal and enlarged interpretation. And hence the preamble to this resolution has no controlling or restraining influence upon it, and ought to be discarded from all consideration in the investigation of this subject.

It is a general rule of construction, that where any doubt arises on the words of an enacting part of a statute, the preamble may be resorted to to explain it; but if it be expressed in clear and unambiguous terms, the preamble cannot control it. Referring to the rule of construing statutes by their preamble, it is declared by the highest legal authority "that this rule must not be carried so far as to restrain the general words of an enacting clause, by the particular words of the preamble—and that the general enacting words of a statute are not to be restrained by any words introductory to the enacting words." (6 Wilson's Ba. Abr. 380—1.) If such be the rules in regard to a common act of legislation, which may affect only the civil rights of an individual, they are much more essential and important, and cannot be less applicable to a great national act, affecting the entire natural, and political, and fundamental rights of a whole community.

If, however, the preamble to this resolution were not inefficient on this account, there are other considerations that should render it utterly so. The constitution having determined the powers that accrue to a State on admission into the Union, they can neither be increased nor diminished by any subordinate instrument or authority, and, therefore, as no declaration of the terms of admission could increase the powers of a State, so no preamble to an act of admission can restrict or diminish them. As, then, this preamble could not invalidate or repeal the Constitution of the United States, its reference to that of the State, as having been formed in pursuance of the law of Congress and in conformity with the ordinance of '87, should not be considered as a recognition of them, any further than they are consistent with the Constitution of the United States, and, at all events, can give no validity to such parts of them as are repugnant to that paramount authority.

It seems pretty evident, therefore, that this State should be considered as having, in fact, been admitted into the Union on "an equal footing with the original States in all respects whatever," and this having been done by Congress, must, thenceforward, operate as a release of the State from all obligations to the United States, inconsistent with its new political condition. It would not, however, be on an equal footing with the original States in a very important respect, if the United States could hold more lands, or hold them for different purposes, within its limits, than theirs, since this would be to subject it to a danger from which they have very prudently exempted themselves. But vastly different and unequal, indeed, would be the footing on which it would be placed, if, while the United States cannot, without the consent of those States, exercise any jurisdiction over or hold one foot of land, for any purpose whatever, within their limits, and even, with their consent, can hold no more than may be necessary "for the erection of forts, magazines, arsenals, dockyards and other needful buildings," they may hold and exercise sovereignty over nineteen-twentieths of all the lands within this State, not only without its consent, but in direct opposition to its wishes. But let us see what power has been delegated to Congress in this respect.

By the eighth section of the first article of the Constitution of the United States, it is declared that Congress shall have power "to exercise exclusive legislation in all cases whatsoever, over such district (not exceeding ten miles square) as may, by cession of particular States and the acceptance of Congress, become the seat of government of the United States, and to exercise like authority over all places purchased, by the consent of the Legislature of the State in which the same shall be, for the erection of forts, magazines, arsenals, dockyards, and other needful buildings."

Now, this being the only delegation of power to the United States, in respect to the acquisition of lands within a State, or in respect to the exercise of sovereignty over lands so situated, it could only authorize the acquisition of the one or the exercise of the other, in the cases specified and for the objects declared—even if the amendment of the Constitution, before noticed, had not expressly reserved all powers not granted; for as no such rights could exist without delegated authority to acquire them, they can exist only to the extent of the authority conferred.

And hence it seems clear, that as the United States cannot acquire or hold any lands in an original State, even with its consent, except such as may be necessary "for the erection of forts, magazines, arsenals, dockyards, and other needful buildings," they can hold no more in this State. For, besides its declared equality, it is not less evident from the spirit than the letter of the Constitution, that it is entitled to be on an equal footing, in this particular respect, with each and all of the original States; since, whatever may have been the pecuniary considerations which imposed this restriction upon the power of the United States, they can scarcely be considered less necessary or applicable to a new than to an old State—to a young and feeble, than to an old and powerful member of the Union.

But even for those purposes, the United States never having obtained "the consent of the Legislature of the State," are not, at present, authorized to hold lands within its limits; for as the right to do so has been made to depend upon such consent, it cannot exist without it. And here I do not deem it important to insist upon the distinction between a Territorial Legislature or Convention, and the Legislature of a State, further than as it obviously shows that the Constitution requiring the consent of the Legislature of the State, must have contemplated the consent of a State after its admission into the Union as a member thereof. Indeed, it would seem impossible to doubt that this was the intention, whatever phraseology had been used. For, till admission into the Union, this State was but a Territory of the United States, without any right to object to their acquiring or holding lands wherever they pleased, and whose consent or refusal was equally indifferent. It was only by first becoming a member of the Union and thereby acquiring the right of refusing, that its consent, as a State, in any case, could be obligatory upon itself or of the slightest advantage to others. Till its admission into the Union it had no right as a State, under the Constitution, and consequently no competency to act in that character. It was then, for the first time, that it became a party to the compact or contract of union, and from thenceforward, being bound by its provisions, became entitled to all its benefits without any offset in consequence of or reference to anything which it might have previously done in a different character or during its political minority. It cannot, therefore, be said that this State, whatever the dependent people of the late Territory may have done, has ever consented, in the meaning of the Constitution, that the United States should hold lands within its limits, for any purpose whatever. It will hardly be contended that they may, notwithstanding the section of the Constitution above quoted, purchase, without the consent of the Legislature of this State, lands lying within it, "for the erection of forts, magazines, arsenals, dockyards, and other needful buildings;" and if they cannot, without such consent, acquire and hold a small quantity of land for purposes so legitimate and so essential to the common preservation and general welfare, it would, indeed, be a singular anomaly, if they could, against its will, hold millions and millions of acres within the State, for almost every other conceivable purpose. It is therefore contended that, in both these respects, they being necessarily included in "all respects whatever," this State has been admitted into the Union "on an equal footing with the original States."

We will now endeavor, briefly, to consider this subject in reference to the cession made by Virginia—and the terms on which it was accepted by Congress.

On the 10th of October, 1780, the old Congress adopted the following resolution, viz: "*Resolved*, That the unappropriated lands that may be ceded or relinquished to the United States by any particular State, pursuant to the recommendation of Congress, on the sixth day of September last, shall be disposed of for the common benefit of the United States, and be settled and formed into distinct republican States, which shall become members of the Union, and have the same rights of sovereignty, freedom, and independence, as the original States, &c."

Thus invited by Congress and influenced by elevated sentiments of patriotism and magnanimity, Virginia, on the 1st of March, 1784, ceded to the United States the lands in question, on the following, among other terms and conditions, not necessary here to be noticed:

1st. "That the Territory so ceded shall be laid out and formed into States, containing, &c., and that the States so formed shall be distinct republican States, and admitted members of the Federal Union, having the same rights of sovereignty, freedom, and independence as the other States."

2d. "That the French and Canadian inhabitants, and other settlers of the Kaskaskias, St. Vincents and the neighboring villages, who have professed themselves citizens of Virginia, shall have their possessions and titles confirmed to them, and be protected in the enjoyment of their rights and liberties."

3d. And "that the lands so ceded shall be considered as a common fund for the use and benefit of such of the United States as have become or shall become members of the Confederation or Federal alliance of the said States, Virginia inclusive, according to their usual respective proportions in the general charge and expenditure, and shall be faithfully and *bona fide* disposed of for that purpose and for no other use or purpose whatever."

Upon these terms the cession was accepted by Congress; and thus was a compact formed, in relation to the rights of Virginia, the United States, and the then inhabitants of the ceded Territory, obligatory upon the two former by express agreement, and upon the latter by tacit consent. For, as a people transferred by the sovereign authority of a country are not obliged to submit to the new sovereign, but are entitled to the privileges of selling their lands, and removing with their other property elsewhere, so their declining to exercise that privilege implies their consent to the transfer, makes them parties to the compact, and entitles them to the benefit of all its provisions in their favor. There were, then, three parties to this compact. The moment it became obligatory upon them, each acquired vested rights by it, and no alteration, enlargement or diminution of its terms or conditions could, afterwards, be made but by common consent. The inhabitants of the Territory were, at that time, not less numerous, and, it is believed, were much more so than at the period of the establishment of the temporary government for the "Territory of Illinois." It was those inhabitants that were entitled to the benefits of this compact; and, being so entitled, they cannot, in reason or justice, be considered as losing a particle of their rights, or as coming under any new obligations, in consequence of a constructive agreement with future emigrants, resulting from a supposed acquiescence in any law or ordinance of Congress, not warranted by the terms of the original compact.

Admitting, for argument's sake, the power of Congress to impose conditions upon the settlement of the public lands, still, none could be bound by them, but those who, by settling after they were prescribed, might be presumed to have consented to them; and consequently, they could not impair the vested rights of those who had previously settled under an entirely different state of things.

The inhabitants of the territory, on the 1st of March, 1784, and their descendants, having, therefore, acquired rights by the compact then made, cannot have lost or forfeited them by any implied or even expressed consent of others. Nor could Congress make any agreement with future emigrants or settlers, inconsistent with the rights thus secured or provided for. And hence subsequent settlers, as well as the inhabitants of 1784, are entitled to every political right which that compact authorizes, and are equally free from all restrictions repugnant thereto, since these could not be insisted on, or enforced, without a violation of the political rights of those who had never consented, and were not bound to submit to them. And therefore, all restrictions or limitations prescribed by the ordinance of 1787, not authorized by the compact, ought to be wholly disregarded.

Although none but the civil rights of the inhabitants of 1784 are specially named and provided for, they are not the less entitled, on that account, to every political right and privilege contemplated by the compact; for, had those rights been wholly omitted, and nothing affecting these people included but the single political right of admission into the Union, at a future day, on the terms proposed, it might, indeed, have lessened their motives for submitting to the new sovereign, but not their right of free acceptance or rejection, nor the obligations imposed upon the government by their consent to remain and submit to its authority, on the terms submitted to their decision. They, therefore, had an unqualified right, which the consent of no other persons in the world could impair, to admission into the Union on an equal footing with the original States, and unrestricted by any conditions or limitations to which they themselves had not given their free assent.

If it be said that the stipulation in favor of the new States, as above contended for, is repugnant to that for disposing of the lands for the common benefit of the United States, let it be conceded—and what does it prove? Why, nothing more than that the latter is repugnant to the former also. And which should a great and magnanimous nation prefer? The one involves the most important natural and political rights of millions of freemen, and the peace and harmony of the whole Union. The other presents a mere question of dollars and cents. The former offers no violation to the spirit or letter of the Constitution, and is calculated to maintain and strengthen the vital principles of the Union, which, like gravitation in the material world, are intended to confine the State and Federal Governments in their respective spheres. The latter is calculated to sap the foundations of the present system of government, destroying the equilibrium of powers, established by the Constitution, between the State and Federal authorities; and by bringing into the Union dependent States, liable to undue influence, and fit instruments in the hands of the latter for increasing its powers, and usurping the rights of the States. The surrender of the public lands to the States in which they lie, for the purpose of promoting their settlement and cultivation, though possibly not the most profitable mode of disposing of them, would, nevertheless, be a disposition of them for the common benefit of the nation; since, as has been already shown, this would be a means of multiplying its commercial resources and augmenting its power, and, therefore, would not, in fact, amount to a violation of the compact. On the other hand, to deny the new States a perfect equality with the old ones, would equally violate the letter of the compact, and the fundamental principles of the Government. It cannot, then, be doubtful which ought to be preferred.

But whatever difficulties ingenuity, or the love of property, may suggest, the case itself presents none. Neither party has a right to insist upon one of these stipulations, to the exclusion of the other. Both were clearly within the intentions of the contracting parties, and equally derive all obligatory force from their will. They should, therefore, according to an established rule of construction, which has never been questioned by any enlightened individual, receive such an interpretation as to render them consistent with each other. And this can only be done by limiting the dominion of the United States over those lands, or the power of disposing of them, to all that period of time preceding the admission of the State into the Union; in other words, to its political minority. And this would, from the very nature of things, seem to be the case, had simple admission been provided for, without any express agreement as to its terms, or the rights to be conferred by it. But seeing that it is expressly declared, that the new States shall be "admitted members of the Federal Union, having the same rights of sovereignty, freedom and independence, as the other States," it is difficult to conceive any plausible ground to contend that an undefined discretionary power of disposing of the lands, and which has been exercised with great latitude, authorizes a restriction of these States to inferior or fewer rights of sovereignty, freedom and independence, than those of the original States.

As, then, this State is clearly entitled, by the compact, to this equality of rights, with the original States, it can only be necessary to show that their complete and exclusive dominion over all public lands within their limits, is a right of their sovereignty, freedom and independence, to entitle this State to the same right to all the public lands within its limits. For this purpose, then, let us inquire a little into the nature and objects of those rights. And here it may not be altogether useless to notice a strange misconception, which has regarded the stipulation embracing them as securing the civil rights of the people of the late Territory and present State, when, in fact, they are only political rights, which, instead of affording the supposed protection, include as well the power of destroying as protecting civil rights. Being applicable only to communities, and not to individuals, they will be considered in that point of view exclusively.

The sovereignty of a State includes the right to exercise supreme and exclusive control over all lands within it. The freedom of a State is the right to do whatever may be done by any nation, and particularly, includes the right to dispose of all public lands within its limits, according to its own will and pleasure. The independence of a State includes an exemption from all control by any other State or Nation over its will, or action, within its own territory. Now, just so much and so many of these rights as any of the States of the Union possess, this State is entitled to, by express agreement. How, then, did Virginia acquire her right to the very lands in question? She never bought, or paid a cent for them; cannot be said to have obtained them by conquest; and had no other title to them than such as resulted from her sovereignty, freedom and independence. The right of any State or Nation to the public lands that lie within it, is not only a right of independence, but is inseparable from it; for complete independence cannot exist without it. And this right is always the same, by whatsoever means independence may have been effected.

But let us hear Vattel on the subject. He says, "the whole space over which a nation extends its government, is the seat of its jurisdiction, and called its territory." (p. 157.)

"Everything susceptible of property is considered as belonging to the nation that possesses the country, and as forming the entire mass of its wealth." (p. 168.)

"The right which belongs to the society, or to the sovereign, of disposing, in case of necessity, and for the public safety, of all the wealth contained in the State, is called the eminent domain" (p. 171.) "which is nothing but the domain of the body of the nation, or of the sovereign who represents it; (and) is everywhere considered inseparable from the sovereignty." (p. 226.)

"The general domain of the nation over the lands it inhabits is naturally connected with the empire. Thus we have already observed that in possessing a country, the nation is presumed to possess at the same time its government. We shall here proceed farther, and show the natural connection of these two rights in an independent nation. How should it govern itself, at its pleasure, in the country it inhabits, if it cannot truly and absolutely dispose of it? And how shall it have full and absolute dominion of the place, in which it has no command? Another's sovereignty, and the right it comprehends, must take away its freedom of disposal." (p. 226.)

"Sovereignty is that public authority which commands in civil society, and directs what each is to perform to obtain the ends of its institution. It is solely established for the safety and advantage of society. (p. 69.) Every sovereignty, properly so called, is in its nature one and indivisible." (p. 83.)

"The empire united to the domain establishes the jurisdiction of the nation in its territories, or the country that belongs to it. It is that, or its sovereign, who is to exercise justice in all the places under his obedience, to take cognizance of the crimes committed, and the differences that arise in the country." (p. 226)

"Every nation that governs itself, without any dependence on foreign power, is a sovereign State. To give a nation a right to make an immediate figure in this grand society (of nations) it is sufficient if it be really sovereign and independent, that is, it must govern itself by its own authority and laws." (p. 58.)

It would be a waste of time to attempt to enlarge upon these clear and well defined rights of a sovereign and independent State. The several States of the Union would possess them absolutely and unconditionally, but for the grant of a part of them to the United States. They should, therefore, be considered as retaining all that they have not so parted with. They have, however, an additional security for their enjoyment, in an expressed exclusion of the United States from all interference with them. Besides the right of this State to the equality contended for, upon those general principles, the express agreement that it should have the same rights of sovereignty, freedom and independence, with other States, will not admit of a doubt that it is entitled to hold the same relation to the United States; to be equally independent of their control; to have the same exclusive jurisdiction, the same right to govern itself, and the same freedom of disposing of the public lands within its limits. For, if it have not these, what rights of sovereignty, freedom and independence has it? And how are they to be ascertained?

Having thus endeavored to show, from the Constitution of the United States, the resolution of admission into the Union, the compact with Virginia, and the laws of nations, that this State is entitled to all the public lands within its limits, I proceed to notice the only section of the Constitution of the United States that is supposed to afford the least countenance to their claim to or authority over these lands. This is the third section of the fourth article, and is in the following words:

"Congress shall have power to dispose of and make all needful rules and regulations respecting the territory, or other property belonging to the United States; and nothing in this Constitution shall be so construed as to prejudice any claims of the United States or of any particular State."

It might be a sufficient answer to every argument that has been or can be predicated upon this section, to show, that one of the most enlightened tribunals in this or any other country has, on mature consideration, decided that it has no application to the case in question, but that it "is clearly adapted to the territorial rights of the United States, beyond the limits or boundaries of any of the States, and to their chattel interests." (17 Johnson's Reports, 223.)

But, if I have been fortunate enough to establish my positions, it follows, that Congress, by admitting the State into the Union, have released the claim of the United States to all lands that lie within it, as effectually as could have been done by any deed of release or conveyance whatever; and, consequently, that nothing is left for this section to operate upon.

It has been shown, that the whole space over which the Government of the State is extended, is technically called and legally considered its territory and the seat of its jurisdiction; consequently no part of this space can be the territory of the United States—since, as the right of the one necessarily excludes that of the other, it cannot belong to both at the same time. And therefore, as everything else in this section relates to mere chattels, it has no relevancy to the present question—the right of the United States to hold lands, with jurisdiction over them, within the limits of a sovereign and independent State.

Involving no question as to the means of acquiring, or the right to hold, territory anywhere, but assuming the right, the power thus granted simply authorizes Congress to dispose of and make all needful rules and regulations concerning territory to which the United States are entitled. Although it neither decides nor affords any means of ascertaining what shall be so considered, it may, nevertheless, assist to demonstrate, that the United States have no right to claim, as their own, any part of the Territory of this State, for as this power applies to all territory of the United States, without exception, none can be claimed as such that is not as subject to its operation as any other. Whatever, therefore, terminates the power of Congress over any territory of the United States, must, at the same time, divest them of all right to it. This section has been long and uniformly considered as authorizing, and even rendering necessary, the establishment of Territorial Governments. If, then, the United States have the right to the territory they claim in this

State, Congress have a correspondent power to exercise the rights of sovereignty, and to establish a Territorial Government, co-extensive with it. And thus, instead of that equality with our sister States, with which we had flattered ourselves, we should be reduced to the twentieth part of a State, with little detatched spots of sovereignty, to be ascertained only by going to the Land Offices, and hunting for the quarter and half quarter sections of lands represented on the plats, with the letter "P" marked on them. As domain and empire are inseparable, so if the territory in question belongs to the United States, they have the exclusive right to govern it, and if they have not this right, the territory cannot belong to them. Both rights must concur, or neither can exist. If this be not the case, what powers of sovereignty may not the United States exercise over this domain? Where is the limit? And to what principle is it referable? "The full domain is necessarily a proper and exclusive right." (Vattel 225) "Sovereignty gives the empire, or right of commanding in all places of the country belonging to the nation." (Vattel 172.) As this is, in its nature, an exclusive right, it cannot belong to the United States and to this State, at one and the same time. If it belong to them, they cannot confer it upon us. If we are entitled to it, we cannot surrender it to them; for, it is not less true in political than civil laws, that delegated powers cannot be transferred. "Every true sovereignty is unalienable in its own nature." (Vattel 87.) Georgia did not, as has been said, alienate any part of her sovereignty to the United States; she did what it belongs to a sovereign and independent nation to do: she disposed of a part of her territory, and lessened her boundaries, but, as a State, remained as sovereign and independent as ever. And this is the only way by which Congress can acquire a right to exercise any of the powers of sovereignty over the domain which lies within this State. We must exclude it from our boundaries, and limit them to the spots designated by the letter "P."

If these positions be correct, and they are supported by the highest authorities, they cannot be deliberately and duly considered, without presenting, in fearful array, consequences of vast importance in relation to the past, to every well informed, intelligent and reflecting mind. Every future advance upon the principles that have hitherto prevailed, will increase and aggravate them; and however much present power may be disposed to overlook or disregard them, the sagacious politician will perceive that the time is rapidly advancing which will give a new tone to public sentiment in regard to such matters; and that right, whatever it may be, will ultimately be too vigorously and powerfully insisted on, to be safely resisted. But without looking to the past, for I shall not be the first to bring the subjects alluded to into view, let us inquire a little more particularly into the powers which Congress may exercise, if the United States still hold "all right, title and claim, as well of soil as jurisdiction," to the public lands within this State. In this case, Congress has the power to deprive us of the poor privileges of feeding our flocks and hunting upon their lands, and of fishing and fowling upon their waters; to erect highways, bridges, and causeways, exact heavy tolls for passing over them, and restrain us from passing any other way; to build mills, and demand what toll they please, or to prevent their erection altogether; to establish and regulate manufactories; to erect public granaries, regulate the price of provisions, monopolize the market, and manage everything with a mercantile spirit; to prevent the settlement and cultivation of their lands, or rent them at pleasure; to exempt their tenants from taxation, militia duty, serving on juries, working on the roads, and all other responsibility to our laws; and, in short, to extend their exclusive authority over all persons and things within their limits, and in certain cases, by virtue of incidental powers, even into our little spots of sovereignty.

If they have not all these powers they have none, in virtue of the right of jurisdiction. The exercise of one is, therefore, a claim to all, and a claim to that demands a dispassionate and respectful, but fearless and scrutinizing investigation. Such a monstrous anomaly could not have been intended by the enlightened statesmen and venerated patriots to whom we are indebted for our present system of government; nor is it to be readily believed that they have subjected us to it. And such would seem to be the opinion of the Supreme Court of New York, who, in a very celebrated case, uses the following impressive language: "We regard it as a fundamental principle, that the rights of sovereignty are never to be taken away by implication. We are of opinion that the right of exclusive legislation within the territorial limits of any State can be acquired by the United States only in the mode pointed out in the Constitution: by purchase, by consent of the Legislature of the State in which the same shall be, for the erection of forts, magazines, arsenals, dockyards, and other needful buildings."

It is not denied that one state or nation may hold lands within the territories of another, and this is presumed to be the case with some of the States of this Union; but lands so held are subject to the jurisdiction and all the rights of eminent domain that belong to the State in which they lie, and, therefore, may be appropriated to public use or taxed as the lands of an individual. Nor can they be even exempted from taxation, but in virtue of such stipulations as Congress has no power to enter into. According to Vattel, "the useful domain, or the domain reduced to the rights that may belong to a particular person in the State, may be separated from the Empire—and nothing prevents the possibility of its belonging to a nation, in the places that are not under its obedience. Thus many sovereigns have fiefs and other properties in the lands of another prince—they therefore possess them in the manner of individuals." If, then, the United States could possess lands within the limits of any State, they would be subject to its sovereignty, not theirs. But as the Constitution does not permit them to hold land so situated, for any other purpose than the erection of forts, magazines, arsenals, dockyards, and other needful buildings, they cannot hold the lands in question, even in the manner of individuals. And if they could, they would be subject to taxation. Nor is there anything in our compact with them to prevent it, particularly if, as the law books say, the expression of one thing is the exclusion of another. The only stipulation in this compact that has any reference to that matter, is in the following words: "That every and each tract of land sold by the United States, from and after the first day of January, 1819, shall remain exempt from any tax laid by order or under any authority of the State, whether for State, county or township, or any other purpose whatever, for the term of five years, from and after the day of sale; and further, that the bounty lands granted or hereafter to be granted for military services during the late war shall, while they continue to be held by the patentees or their heirs, remain exempt, as aforesaid, from all taxes for the term of three years, from and after the date of the patents respectively, and that all lands belonging to citizens of the United States, residing without the said State, shall never be taxed higher than lands belonging to persons residing therein."

The exemptions thus provided for, apply, not to lands of the United States, but to such only as shall have ceased to be their property; and if the domain actually belong to them, there would be nothing inconsistent in taxing it while in their hands, and exempting it from taxation for a limited period afterwards—for, while the latter might afford encouragement to purchase, the former would not be less efficient in producing a willingness to sell, and thus, coöperating, they might be amongst the most effectual means of promoting the settlement and cultivation of vast bodies of fertile lands, that now lie waste and useless. But though the power of taxation is one of the unquestionable rights of sovereignty, freedom and independence which belong to the State, and which Congress has no power to control, it is not to be believed that the State would ever exercise unjustly, even for the purpose of producing results so desirable. But I forbear to press this subject, from a perfect conviction that the United States have neither the right of soil nor of jurisdiction to the lands in question, nor to any part of them, but that they all belong to the State.

* * The surrender of the lands to the States in which they lie is the only means of effectually quieting the public mind. In this event the States would doubtless grant liberal donations to actual settlers, dispose of the balance on moderate terms, and appropriate the proceeds thereof to the making of internal improvements; and thus, the beneficence of the nation would be turned to its own advantage by providing for and rendering most useful to itself its own poor citizens, facilitating intercourse between its various parts, strengthening the cords of union, and increasing its resources and power. * * Upon the whole subject of the public lands, it seems desirable that the General Assembly should transmit to Congress a respectful memorial, representing their views of the right of the State to those lands, and asking their surrender upon equitable terms. Whatever strict legal right might give us, yet I do not think we ought to wish to obtain those lands but upon the principle of assuming the obligations of the United States to the Indians and paying all the lands have cost. * * I honestly believe the State is entitled to all the public lands within its limits. My former message and this address, taken together, show my reasons for entertaining that opinion. I may be wrong; and shall always treat the opinion of others, who differ with me, with all the respect that becomes a gentleman.

The Legislature almost unanimously sustained him in their memorial to Congress on the subject. Gov. Edwards was not, however, the first to assert this right. Gen. Smyth, an eminent statesman of Virginia, in a speech delivered in Congress, in 1823, asks, "is it certain that admitting a new State into the Union, on an equal footing, in all respects, with the original States, would not vest in the State the domain? Would it not operate like an acknowledgment of a colony?"

In May, 1826, Mr. Tazewell, Senator of Virginia, offered the following resolution:

Resolved, That it is expedient for the United States to cede and surrender to the several States within whose limits the same may be situated, all the right, title and interest of the United States to any lands lying and being within the boundaries of such States, respectively, upon such terms and conditions as may be consistent with the due observance of the public faith and with the general interest of the United States.

And in 1828, he (Mr. T.) proposed that the lands "remaining unsold after having been offered at twenty-five cents per acre, shall be ceded to the State in which the same may lie, to be applied by the Legislature thereof in support of education and the internal improvement of the State."

General Jackson, in his message in 1833, recommended the reduction of the price of the public lands, and that the lands remaining unsold after having been offered for sale for a certain number of years, "shall be abandoned to the States, and the machinery of our land system entirely withdrawn." The State of Indiana, through her Legislature, also instructed her Senators in Congress to assert her right to the lands within her limits. A Senator from Michigan, and also a Senator from Arkansas, as late as in 1841, asserted the same right to the lands within the limits of their respective States; and Mr. Clay, in his speech (in 1842) on the preemption bill, says that Mr. Calhoun's bill to cede away, "without any just or certain equivalent, more than a billion of acres of public land" to the States in which the lands were situated, received the vote of seventeen Senators.

It will be seen that the discussion of this question by Gov. Edwards, notwithstanding the statement of Gov. Ford that the claim was asserted without any confidence in its validity, has resulted in securing to the new States large grants of lands for internal improvements, and a surrender of the refuse—the swamp lands—to the States in which they were situated.

Whilst making a speech on the Missouri question, in consequence of a very sore throat he was unable to proceed with his remarks—on which occasion he received a complimentary note from Mr. Randolph, in which he expressed great regret at his inability to finish his speech, which, from the commencement, promised to do him so much credit. He had a very important agency in bringing about the compromise which resulted in terminating the controversy in regard to the admission of Missouri into the Union. Although the proviso which passed was proposed by Jesse B. Thomas, his colleague in the Senate, it was the result of a conference of public men, before whom it was introduced by Senator Edwards in the form in which it finally passed.

The following is a sketch of the remarks made by him on the bill for the admission of Missouri into the Union:

MR. PRESIDENT: Having long been out of the habit of public speaking, and finding myself unable to command that composure of mind and self-possession which are so essential to the investigation of a subject as important as the one now under consideration, I should leave the discussion of it to gentlemen who are infinitely more competent to do justice to it, were it not that my silence might seem to sanction the imputation of an honorable gentleman who has thought proper to express the opinion, that, by my vote of Friday last, which I thought it my duty to give, I had abandoned the interest of the non slave-holding States of the West.

If such a suggestion be well founded, nothing can be more certain than that I have not been misled by personal considerations; for, my permanent residence and the most of my property being in one of those States, and holding a seat in this house by the kind partiality of the citizens thereof, which I have also often experienced on other occasions, and for which no one could be more thankful, I should be unjust to myself, ungrateful to them, and equally regardless of the dictates of interest and duty, were I not anxiously disposed to promote the best interest of the State which I have the honor in part to represent.

Were I to consult my popularity only, I well know that it would be much easier to swim with, than to resist, the present popular current, which threatens to overwhelm all opposition, and to deluge the non slave-holding States of the West, with what I consider, with all due deference to the opinions of other gentlemen, political heresies, replete with mischiefs calculated to impair their present as well as future prosperity and happiness.

Sir, I love popularity so well, that I would gladly retain it by the utmost devotion to the interests of my constituents; but I would far rather surrender all pretensions to it, than preserve it at the expense of my conscience. I respect public sentiment as much as any man, and should at all times derive the sincerest gratification from being able to discharge the trust confided to me, in strict conformity with the wishes of those whom I have the honor to represent—but never can I consent to shelter myself even from the tempest and hurricane of popular excitement, by a violation of that Constitution which I, as well as the gentlemen from New Hampshire, (Mr. Morrill,) have solemnly sworn to support. But more of this by and by.

Were an attempt made to introduce slavery into the non slave-holding States of the West, then, indeed, might there be just cause of alarm; and I can assure gentlemen that there is no man who would oppose such a proposition with more determined zeal than myself. But, taking for granted what I shall presently endeavor to prove, that neither the slave-holding States nor any of us who oppose the proposed restriction upon Missouri, are influenced by a desire to increase slavery in the United States, and that the proposed restriction is not necessary to prevent, nor its omission calculated to augment the importation of fresh slaves, it is inconceivable to me how the interest of the non slave-holding States of the West can be compromised by the admission of domestic slaves into Missouri, more than to permit them to remain in the States where they now are; for, if that portion of political power which, under the Constitution, arises from the slavery that now exists, is to be deprecated and dreaded at all, surely it cannot be worse for us, in the hands of those whose identity of interest with ourselves affords additional security against its influence being exerted to our disadvantage. As yet, we have had no cause to regret that a portion of such power has been transferred from some of the Southern States to Kentucky and Tennessee, whose sympathies, friendship and assistance have never been withheld from us in the hour of need. Our experience, therefore, furnishes nothing to cause us to dread the influence of a similar transfer of power to Missouri.

For my part, considering every part of the Western country identified in interest, and that its domestic improvements, commercial prosperity, and political influence, cannot fail to be promoted by every increase of population, it does appear to me to be the interest of every State in the West, that fair and equal inducements to emigration thither should be afforded to the citizens of every section of the Union, whether slave-holding or non slave-holding. But, in opposition to this very obvious policy, with an extent of territory greatly beyond the demands of every description of emigrants, and affording infinitely more than sufficient accommodation for all, without any necessity for collisions of interest, feelings, or prejudices, between them, we are called upon to check the emigration of our Southern brethren, by those who dread our growth, and would gladly put an entire stop to emigration from every other quarter. And thus are we invited to let lay waste and uninhabited an immense frontier of our country, rather than permit it to be occupied by our Southern brethren, who certainly would not be less our friends by becoming our neighbors.

There are other considerations of vital importance to the Union in general, and to the Western country in particular, which I purposely forbear to press, because I do not wish to excite any unpleasant feelings, am anxious to cherish harmony, and most ardently hope that some compromise may take place which will satisfy the reasonable wishes of all parties.

Mr. President, in attempting to discuss the present proposition, it is not my purpose to advocate slavery in any shape, or to deny that, in its mildest form, it is equally inconsistent with the inherent rights of man, and repugnant to every principle of humanity and philanthropy. On the contrary, I rejoice most sincerely, that an increasing sense of its moral injustice and turpitude, and the happy prevalence of more enlightened and magnanimous views throughout every part of our common country, as well as in various other parts of the civilized world, are eliciting the most zealous efforts not only to prevent its extension, but to ameliorate its present condition, which, with the blessing of Divine Providence, I trust will, in due season, eventuate in its final extermination.

The present subject of discussion surely is not the expediency of increasing slavery in the United States by importations from Africa or elsewhere—nor is it a question of slavery or freedom—and it does not appear to me to be consistent with candor, to attempt to give to it the imposing and delusive aspect of either. And how much soever such an artifice may be resorted to in other places, for the purpose of rendering popular feelings and prejudices subservient to political views, I felicitate myself in the firm conviction that such unworthy motives can receive no countenance from this honorable body, and that every member of the Senate would disdain to impute to others sentiments which he does not believe them to entertain.

Were it, in fact, a question whether the further introduction of slavery into the United States, by importation from abroad, should be permitted, the universal abhorrence in which a practice so disgraceful to humanity is held by all classes of our fellow-citizens, and the cordial coöperation of gentlemen from every section of the Union, particularly at the last session of Congress, in measures to prohibit it, forbid the belief that such a measure could find one advocate or friend in this house; nor can there be a doubt that we would all cheerfully unite in such further legitimate means as experience may demonstrate to be necessary to render such prohibition complete and effectual, which I have no doubt is perfectly praticable.

All of us, therefore, entertaining the same abhorrence and repugnance to the further introduction and increase of slavery, the only point of difference between us relates to the slaves that are now amongst us; and as it is conceded, on all sides, that Congress possesses no power to abolish the slavery that now exists, it follows that the question of slavery or freedom is not involved in the present proposition, and that an opposition to the restriction that is attempted to be imposed upon the sovereignty and independence of a State, may well exist without any predilection for slavery—for should our opposition prevail, the new State, notwithstanding, like all others in this Union, would be left perfectly free to abolish slavery, and I am very ready to admit that she would consult her best interest by doing so.

I have, Mr. President, viewed, with feelings of the deepest regret, attempts that have been made to excite local and sectional jealousies, particularly against the slaveholding States, upon this subject, in their nature but too well calculated to sap the foundation of that spirit of conciliation which produced this great confederacy, and to interrupt that social harmony and mutual friendship and confidence, which are so essential to maintain and strengthen the bonds of our union.

Experience teaches us that it is much more easy to produce popular discontent, than to limit its operation and influence to the first exciting causes; and if the proposed restriction upon Missouri is to be carried by arraying popular prejudices in hostility to one principle of compromise, that contributed, in no small degree, to produce our present happy Union, is it not to be feared that it may be difficult to limit that hostility by anything short of the power to assail that principle with success? And if an inequality in the apportionment of representatives in the other branch of the National Legislature, with a correspondent obligation to pay direct taxes in proportion thereto, is to be rendered obnoxious to our fellow-citizens, what security is there that the representation in this house, which, without any such correspondent obligation and without regard to numbers, reduces the largest States in this Union to a level with the smallest, will share a better fate?

I confess, sir, that, while I cannot perceive that the present subject of deliberation furnishes any adequate motives for those attempts at popular excitement, I cannot contemplate them without being penetrated with the most awful apprehensions for the fate of that fair fabric of our freedom which has hitherto been not more our boast than the admiration of the civilized world. Upon what ground, sir, are those jealousies of our brethren of the slave-holding States predicated? Take, for example, if you please, the case of Virginia, the largest of those States. Does she wish the extension of slavery? Let her known conduct decide.

While yet a colony of Great Britain she distinguished herself preeminently by a noble, magnanimous and persevering stand against it, and enumerated its toleration in the list of grievances, of which she so forcibly and eloquently complained against the mother country. True to the principles she professed, she was the first State in the Union to set the example of efficient opposition to a traffic in human flesh, so disgraceful to our country and so abhorrent to the principles for which we ourselves contended, by passing a law to prohibit it, by severe penalties, as early as the year 1778, in which she has steadfastly persevered from that time to the present day; nor has she ever, on any occasion, been less prompt in assisting to interpose the shield of Federal authority to protect the devoted sons of Africa from such ruthless oppression.

Having thus, by the most unequivocal acts, so demonstrated the sincerity of her professions upon this subject, as to extort the highest commendation from the most distinguished advocates of the proposed restriction, and deploring, as she must do, the evils of slavery, what reason have we to suppose that she is now disposed to relinquish those principles and abandon a policy, which, to her honor, she has, for such a series of years, pursued with inflexible perseverence, and the wisdom of which is daily more and more developed? No, sir, depend upon it, Virginia knows too well what she owes to her own character, ever to descend from the proud preeminence which she has acquired upon this subject.

The rest of the slave-holding States have also given such proofs of their decided hostility to the further introduction of slavery among us, as to leave no ground for even the affectation of incredulity upon the subject.

As then those States, equally with ourselves, are opposed to the further increase of slavery in the United States, so, with them as with us, the only subject of controversy which the proposed restriction presents, relates exclusively to the slaves that are now among them. And can they have any motives for opposing that restriction which are not truly national and strictly compatible with the principles of our confederation? If they had heretofore desired to increase their political power, and aggrandize themselves upon the basis of a slave population, would they themselves have voluntarily inhibited the importation of slaves, and united in every means which the wisdom of the national councils has yet been able to devise, for its prevention? Were they now even tenacious of that portion of political power which they derive from the slavery that exists among them, would they be the advocates of a measure calculated to diminish that power, by its tendency to abstract from them and transfer to a different and distant section of the Union a large portion of their slaves? And let it be remembered that to impute to them a desire merely to diminish the number of their slaves, is to admit the most conclusive evidence of their opposition to the increase of slavery, which is the point I have endeavored to maintain.

So far, therefore, from those States being actuated by the motives which, for particular purposes, have been attributed to them, it must be evident that the principles for which they contend are calculated not only to diminish the power of their respective States, but to promote the abolition of slavery itself—for in proportion as you permit the slaves now among us be disbursed, so do you diminish their relative numbers to the white population in any one State, and to that extent, at least, increase their chances of emancipation, as is evinced by the experience of Massachusetts, New York, Pennsylvania, New Jersey, Delaware, &c., and which is also conceded by the supposition that the prohibition of the further admission of slaves into Missouri would be favorable to the emancipation of those who are now there, which seems to be a favorite sentiment with a gentleman (Mr. King of New York) of preeminent talents, who has distinguished himself by his zealous and able support of the proposed restriction, and who admits that a disposition more favorable to emancipation is gaining ground in the States where slavery exists, that the disproportionate increase of free people of color can be accounted for upon no other supposition, and that whatever would tend to provide more satisfactorily for the comfort and morals of emancipated slaves, would increase the practice of emancipation—to all which I yield the most hearty concurrence.

It cannot, however, be denied that the difficulties and dangers attendant upon emancipation, in any State, must be in proportion to the number of slaves therein; and it is well known that several of the States have considered emancipation so incompatible with their domestic safety and tranquillity, as to feel the necessity of absolutely prohibiting it, which is a policy that it is not presumable they will abandon. While, therefore, confining the slaves to those States is calculated to render their bondage perpetual, it must be acknowledged that their dispersion into different sections of the Union would remove many of the most important objections to emancipation, at the same time that it would increase the means of providing more satisfactorily for the comfort and morals of those unhappy beings, and would cherish (by rendering more availing) that increasing disposition to emancipation which imparts so much consolation to every true philanthropist.

The honorable gentleman from New Hampshire (Mr. Morrill), whose eloquent denunciations of slavery we heard on yesterday, and who portrayed its evils and injustice in the most appalling colors, supports the proposed restriction on the ground that, if those unhappy victims of oppression were permitted to be carried to Missouri, their natural increase would be greater—in consequence, I suppose, of the amelioration of their condition and the multiplication of their comforts. But, without pretending to analyze that species of philanthropy which would seek to terminate oppression by the destruction of the oppressed—or that bleeds for suffering humanity, and yet recoils at any alleviation of such sufferings—I beg leave to express my doubts whether there are any known facts that will justify the gentleman's hypothesis itself.

It is readily admitted that the condition of the slaves in the West would be improved; but at a time when, as all sides admit, the influence of our free institutions and the progress of public sentiment, have contributed, in an eminent degree, to mitigate the rigors of slavery in all parts of our country where it exists, it is hardly to be presumed that the difference of the treatment of slaves in the Western and Atlantic States would be such as to produce any material difference in their natural increase. Not only would the obvious interest of the Atlantic slave-holders forbid the practice of that severe and cruel treatment that would be necessary to produce such a result, but the abundance of subsistence which every part of our country affords, and the well established fact that slaves increase faster than the white population, in slave-holding States, or free people of color anywhere, altogether negative such a supposition. Nor is it better supported by any calculation upon the relative increase of slave population in the Atlantic or Western States, which makes due allowances for the effects of emigration upon the latter. But were it otherwise, as it is fully demonstrated, by undeniable documents, that free people of color do not increase by pro-creation as fast as slaves, and as the dispersion of the latter over a greater surface would, under existing circumstances, multiply their chances of freedom, it is but reasonable to suppose that, upon the whole, it would not only tend eventually to diminish slavery, but to check the increase of our black population generally.

But, sir, the honorable gentleman from Massachusetts (Mr. Mellen), who has just resumed his seat, assuming the ground that wherever a market for domestic slaves exists, the introduction of foreign slaves cannot be prevented, has contended that, if the proposed restriction should not prevail, African slaves will be introduced into Missouri. In support of which, great reliance has been placed upon a few cases, much magnified however, of their unlawful introduction into certain parts of our country, which were principally, if not exclusively, attributable to causes merely temporary.

In opposition to the conclusions he has drawn from a special case, we may with propriety recur to facts and experience better calculated to test the correctness of his general proposition. It will not, I presume, be denied, that as good a market for domestic slaves as is ever likely to recur has existed in Delaware, Maryland, Virginia, North Carolina, etc., where the facilities of introducing foreign slaves are as great as could be desired; and yet, it is believed that the experience of those States furnishes nothing to justify the inferences that have been so confidently insisted upon, or, at most, nothing more than a mere apology for such inferences.

Cases, however, more analogous in all their circumstances to that of Missouri, as far as experience can be relied upon, are ample refutation of the argument I am endeavoring to combat. Slavery has never been prohibited in Kentucky or Tennessee, where slaves have been in constant demand; and yet, although I have lived many years in the former, and have long been intimately acquainted with both, I have never heard of the introduction of a single African into either, contrary to law, and hence I think it fair to infer that either the practice has never prevailed in those States, or that the instances of it have been so rare as rather to demonstrate the efficiency of the law to prohibit it, than to justify the apprehensions which the honorable gentleman seems to entertain.

There are Western States, in the proximity of Missouri, nearer, however, to the ocean, and possessing equal facilities, at least, for the introduction of foreign slaves. And if, with a constant market for slaves, offering the most seducing temptations to avarice and cupidity, either very few or no violations of the law, upon that subject, have heretofore occurred in those States, is it reasonable to suppose or does any gentlemen really believe that the proposed restriction would materially affect the number of Africans that, by possibility, may be smuggled into the United States?

It cannot be denied that public sentiment has been progressive upon this subject. It is admitted by the friends of the restriction upon Missouri that the evils of slavery have been so constantly unfolding themselves, as to cause it to be more and more deplored, even in the States where it exists, and that an abhorrence of the practice is gaining ground in every part of our own country; and hence I should infer that we have more reason to hope for a diminution of the evil than cause to dread its increase, even if the prohibition of the importation of slaves were left to depend upon the law that existed previous to the last session of Congress. But seeing that nearly all Europe, animated by more just and enlightened views and generous feelings, is endeavoring to extirpate that nefarious traffic, and, having imparted additional energies to our own laws for the same purpose, I flatter myself that, with the additional aid of public sentiment in favor of those measures, the danger of introducing Africans into Missouri is not less than it has been in relation to Kentucky and Tennessee, but that it is wholly chimerical and visionary.

Upon this view of the subject it does appear to me that we, who on the present occasion are the advocates of State rights, cannot, with any kind of fairness, be charged with either a desire to increase slavery or with any predilection for that which exists. And if the proposed restriction is not necessary to prevent the importation of foreign slaves, it follows that the admission of slavery into Missouri is neither calculated to abridge the power of the non slave-holding States, nor to increase that inequality in the apportionment of representation which depends upon our slave population; for whether those slaves be in Georgia or Missouri they must be included in the apportionment of representation, and whatever power they might confer upon Missouri would be just so much abstracted from the States whence they came. And as an inequality of representation thus produced must necessarily prevail so long as the Constitution remains unaltered, I am constrained to believe that the transfer of a portion of that advantage to Missouri would be as harmless, at least to the non slave-holding States of the West, as to let it remain consolidated, with all its influence, on this side of the Alleghany. And, indeed, although I should greatly regret to see the State which I have the honor in part to represent participate in it, yet it does appear to me that the more it is divided (without increasing it) among those States that wish to receive it, the less will be its evils and the greater the facility and certainty of controlling any sinister influence which it might produce.

Mr. Edwards remarked, that, having endeavored so far to strip the subject of the artifices with which it had most dexterously been clothed, he would next proceed to submit to the Senate the reasons which induced him to believe that the proposed restriction could not be imposed upon Missouri without a violation of the Constitution. He had, however, made but a few remarks upon this branch of the subject, when he observed that he found speaking so painful, in consequence of a very sore throat, with which he had for some time past been afflicted, that it was impossible for him, at that time, to proceed; and expressing a wish to have the indulgence of the Senate to be heard on a future day, he resumed his seat.

In the year 1821 he spoke of retiring from public life, but was dissuaded from doing so by the advice of Mr. Wirt and others of his friends. Mr. Wirt wrote to him as follows, on this subject: "With regard to your determination to retire from public life, I should consider myself a traitor in friendship, if I do not say, in spite of your injunction to the contrary, that I consider you as standing in your own light, in coming to that resolution, and as committing suicide. No man, who has been for so short a time in Congress, has more hopeful or brilliant prospects than you have. This is only a shadow that flits across your path—why should you mistake it for eternal night? If you are right in your view of things, the rectitude of that view will ere long appear, and your political sun will break out with redoubled lustre. Were I constituted for public life as I believe you to be (with the exception, I fear, of a little too much sensibility), neither the machinations of enemies nor the mistakes of friends should lead me to devote myself to voluntary obscurity. Consult your wise and excellent father and let him decide—by whom I would rather be directed, after he knows the whole ground, than by a whole battalion of congressmen."

Mr. Calhoun, in a letter dated in 1823, speaks of Gov. Edwards as follows: "Believing that you possess qualities which are well calculated to advance the interest and honor of the country, on a foreign mission, I would be highly gratified if the most important of all the appointments of that kind connected with this continent should be conferred on you. I must, at the same time, express my belief, that few men are more important, at this moment, as connected with our domestic politics."

In a letter of the same year, Mr. Calhoun says: "You see there is a new Post Master General. I hope the appointment will give satisfaction. I did not fail to bring up your name for consideration, and I thought, as between you and Judge McLean, I could take no active part—believing you both to be highly qualified; I would certainly have been not less gratified with your appointment than his. I believe that the scale was principally turned by the apprehension that the precarious state of your health might prevent you from bestowing that incessant labor and attention which the extensive duties and the greatly disordered state of the Department render indispensable. You may be assured that there is no one whose advancement would give me more sincere pleasure than yourself. I believe there is no one whose zeal and abilities give a stronger claim on the administration."

Throughout the whole period of his public life, and wherever he resided, he was in favor of facilitating to every man the means of acquiring a freehold, and of extending the right of suffrage and citizenship to every free white inhabitant. His correspondence with the Hon. J. J. Crittenden and others, from Kentucky, shows that no one was more active and used greater exertions to reduce the price of public lands to the early settlers of Kentucky. No one spoke more in Congress in favor of the reduction of the price of lands belonging to the General Government; and the journals of Congress show that he proposed the lowest price that had ever been previously suggested in either branch of that body. But when it was proposed to accompany the reduction of the price by requiring the entire payment to be made in cash, and abolishing the credit system, which had previously allowed the poor man to pay for the land in annual installments, he was opposed to this measure, because it would have retarded instead of facilitating to the actual settler the means of acquiring a home.

As early as Feb. 18, 1819, he offered a number of amendments to the bill making further provisions for the sale of public land—the first of which proposed to graduate the price, according to the supposed ability of the different descriptions of purchasers, by reducing it to fifty cents an acre to the purchasers of not more than eighty acres, seventy-five cents an acre for any quantity not exceeding a quarter section, and one dollar an acre for any quantity not exceeding one section. The second proposed particular indulgencies to actual settlers. The third proposed to reduce the price in all cases to one dollar; and that failing, to reduce the price to one dollar and twenty-five cents.

As early as 1820, in a communication to his constituents, he says: "At the last session of Congress it was my ardent wish that the minimum price should not exceed one dollar per acre, and my best talents were zealously exerted, on different occasions, to procure such indulgencies for actual settlers, as would have accommodated the poorest of them, and thereby have invited emigration to the State and promoted the settlement and improvement thereof. These objects failing, I wished the credit system to remain, and to reduce the price to one dollar an acre, in cash—believing, that while speculators would have no inducement to purchase on credit, that system might have afforded some accommodation to a portion of our fellow-citizens who, owing to the present unparalleled scarcity of money, might be unable to purchase upon any other terms.

In relation to appointments to offices, he believed that the Senators and Representatives of the State were the proper persons to recommend to office within the State, and proposed in a letter to Mr. Crawford, then Secretary of the Treasury (in 1821), that two of the persons to be nominated for the land offices created by the act of the last session of Congress should be selected by him and two by Judge Thomas, the other Senator. Mr. Crawford replied to him, that the proposition was deemed by the President inadmissible, as it would in fact be a transfer of the right of nomination, vested by the Constitution in the President, to the Senators of the State. Mr. Edwards, in his answer, said: "It cannot be supposed that I wished to transfer the right of nomination to the Senators. If I recollect rightly, I called upon you and suggested the proposition as one that I thought calculated to give satisfaction, and I did believe from our conversation that you thought favorably of it—limited, however, by a just regard to the right of nomination vested in the President, which no one was more disposed to respect than myself, as was clearly to be inferred from my remarks; for upon your suggesting such limitation, so far from intimating a wish that the right of nomination should be surrendered to the Senators, I expressly declared that I did not wish any one, in relation to any recommendation of mine, to relinquish the right of making objections to any nomination, and that I would not myself relinquish any such right in relation to nominations made upon the recommendation of others. It was well understood, however, that two parties existed in Illinois. I presume the administration did not wish to identify itself with either; and knowing that suitable persons could be selected from both sides for the offices in question, I did not doubt that the distribution which I proposed could be made without any violation or surrender of power on the part of the President, while it was the best calculated to give that general satisfaction which, next to a conscientious discharge of his duties, the history of his life proves has been and still is the first object of his wishes. * * So far from intending that the President should transfer the right of nomination to the Senators of the State, I never intended to propose that he should confine his nominations exclusively to their separate or united recommendations."

Mr. Wirt, in a letter to Mr. Edwards, dated January 11, 1821, says: "I am very sure that the President has the most sincere regard for you. I do not understand, however, that he feels himself *bound* by the recommendation of the Senators of the State in which the office is to be filled, even where the Senators concur. In such a case he has great respect to their opinion, but he considers himself at perfect liberty to put a different character in nomination, without giving just cause of offense to them. The constitutional act of nominating is *his;* he ought to be free, therefore, to nominate whom he pleases. Were *he bound* even by the joint recommendation of the Senators, the nomination would cease to be the act of the President: it would in fact be that of the Senators—while, by the Constitution, the responsibility would still rest on the President. You cannot but admit the correctness of this view of the subject; and I am told that the practice of the Senators is in strict conformity with it: they wait till the President calls on them to express their opinion, and retire, respectfully, from any further interference with the nomination, but with full liberty to exercise their rights, in their turn, as Senators, when the nomination is sent in and they have to vote on its confirmation. The President asks no sacrifice of the rights of Senators in opposing and rejecting his nominations;. and why should they seek to narrow his freedom in making his nominations? * * There is, indeed, another course which he may take, and which I think he ought to take: which is, to nominate no person whom either Senator declares unworthy of the office, if he can find a deserving man in the State free from such objection—unless, indeed, the objection itself is destroyed by being discovered to proceed from a personal feeling, or weakened by flowing from the animosity of local factions."

CHAPTER VIII.

Gov. Edwards' appointment as Minister to Mexico—His Controversy with Mr. Crawford—Letters from Judge McLean, Mr. Adams, Mr. Ingham, Mr. Calhoun, Mr. Wirt, and others, in reference to it—False Charges of Col. Benton—Gov. Edwards' Resignation—Etc.

In alluding to his controversy with Mr. Crawford, it is not the object nor desire of the writer to say anything that would have the tendency to affect the reputation of either Mr. Crawford or Gen. Noble, whose testimony he proposes to investigate. Mr. Edwards stated, in his argument before the Committee, that he did not put in issue, by anything he had said in his vindication, the Secretary's "intentions" in regard to those several acts—(meaning the charges and specifications referred to in his memorial.) He said, in a public communication, that he disclaimed any other construction of them than the most innocent of which they were susceptible.

In 1824, he received the appointment of Minister to Mexico, from Mr. Monroe, which appointment was nearly unanimously confirmed by the Senate. On its confirmation, Gen. Jackson, then a member of the Senate, wrote him a note congratulating him on that event.

Soon after this, and on the eve of his departure on his mission, the Secretary of the Treasury, William H. Crawford, sent a communication to Congress, in which he alluded to Mr. Edwards in the following language:

The Hon. Mr. Edwards, late a Senator of Illinois, having stated on his examination before a Committee of the House, on the 13th February, 1823, that the late Receiver of Public Moneys at Edwardsville had, on his advice and in his presence, written a letter to the Secretary, inclosing a copy of the publication which Mr. Edwards represents himself to have made sometime in the year 1819, announcing his intention of retiring from the Directorship of the Bank at Edwardsville, and that he had advised the Receiver to withhold his deposits from the Bank until he could receive a letter from the Secretary directing him to continue his deposits, the Secretary deems it proper to state that no such letter from the Receiver is to be found on the files of the Department; that the officers employed in it have no recollection of the receipt of such a letter; and that, on an examination of the records of the Department, it appears that no answer to any such letter, directing the Receiver to continue the deposits, was ever written to him by the Secretary of the Treasury.

The Secretary of the Treasury, in his reply to the address of Mr. Edwards, says, as "he had no recollection of the communication to which (Mr. Edwards') testimony referred, he considered himself bound to state the fact;" and adds, the terms in which the communication was made "will show that no disrespect towards him was intended." Any one, however, who will read carefully the communication of the Secretary, cannot fail to perceive that it had the tendency to create the impression that it was intended as an attack on the evidence of Mr. Edwards. It thus appears, from his own statement, that the Secretary did not intend to show any disrespect to Mr. Edwards, and, also, that Mr. Edwards did not put in issue, by any thing he had said, "the Secretary's intentions" in regard to the charges and specifications in his memorial.

Mr. Edwards' veracity having, as he supposed, been thus questioned, he sent a memorial to Congress, in which he preferred certain charges against Mr. Crawford—among which was one in relation to this letter; and for the proof of the charges he referred entirely to documentary evidence; but the Committee to whom these charges were referred thought it important to examine Mr. Edwards as a witness. In the course of the investigation, with a view to impeaching the credit of Mr. Edwards, Gen. Noble was introduced as a witness to prove that he had denied the authorship of certain publications over the signature of "A. B," which Mr. Edwards had avowed himself the author of in his memorial to Congress.

Taken entirely by surprise, by this testimony, Mr. Edwards introduced a number of witnesses to prove that Gen. Noble was mistaken. For the purpose of vindicating himself from those charges and insinuations, by the advice of his friends he voluntarily tendered his resignation of the office of Minister to Mexico, so as to afford him an opportunity of collecting further testimony, and also for the purpose, after making his defense, to appeal to the people of his own State to sustain him.

Besides his reply to Gen. Noble's testimony, which he published in 1825, it may not be improper for me to give the additional evidence; but before doing so, it may be proper to state that the only charge against the Secretary, and on which he gave any testimony in which his veracity was questioned, was the one in relation to the letter of Benjamin Stephenson, the Receiver at Edwardsville. That there was no cause to question his statement in reference to this letter, is evident, from the report of the Committee, in which they say: "In regard to the contested letter of Benjamin Stephenson, of the 12th October, 1819, the Committee see no cause to change the opinion which was entertained and which they intended to express in their former report: that although the letter was written, as stated by Mr. Edwards in his testimony, there was no evidence that Mr. Stephenson communicated or transmitted it to the Secretary of the Treasury."

The following is taken from Mr Edwards' address, in the year 1825:

As the charges against the Secretary of the Treasury were too well founded to admit of a fair and full investigation, it was deemed prudent by those who dreaded their application to divert the course of scrutiny from his conduct to my character, and for this purpose the testimony of the Hon. Mr. Noble was introduced. This operation, it was hoped, would not only weaken the force of my allegations, which, resting on public documents, had the united support of reason and record, but would serve to screen the vulnerable reputation of Mr. Crawford, by drawing off the fire of public curiosity and censure. The stratagem was not only old, but successful; for the proceeding of the Committee was both loose and summary, and as the testimony of the witness, in its application to myself, referred to matters of which I was totally unconscious, it was not in my power to foresee or to withstand its force.

That the proceeding of the Committee was loose is sufficiently evident from their having forced me to testify to facts not embraced in the charges submitted to them, and which, as they themselves declared, were not material to the investigation—thus, without reason, extending the surface of my testimony, thereby impairing its force and augmenting its liability to question, without the countervailing result of presenting more points of weakness in the conduct of Mr. Crawford. In so far, therefore, as the testimony transcended the limits of the charges, the investigation was a trial of me and not of Mr. Crawford. And this injurious irregularity was increased; for while my general reputation was not impeached, the latitude allowed in the examination of Mr. Noble admitted attacks on special points of my character which I could not have apprehended, was of course unprepared for, and which, as they derived all their energy from the surprise they effected, were the more formidable in consequence of their being false.

That their proceeding was also summary arose, probably, from the impatience of members, natural after a long and laborious session, and is proved by their failure to summon several witnesses whose attendance I had formally required, while their most distinguished member was personally active in procuring the appearance of Mr. Noble.

The scheme for diverting the public attention and the weight of the scrutiny from Mr. Crawford to myself, and thus frustrating the object of Congress in raising the Committee, having been determined on, a position was speedily taken in the remote and debatable ground of the "A. B." publications. The first movement was an attempt to prove that I had denied the authorship of these papers in order to secure the appointment of Minister to Mexico—a proceeding which would have been disgraceful to me, but which, even if proved, it is difficult to imagine could have altered the meaning of the public documents, affected in the smallest degree the official responsibility of the Treasurer, lightened the fiscal losses of the Republic, imparted fairness and precision to her financial operations, or appeased the offended dignity of her laws.

It was urged, accordingly, that I had actually secured the appointment by making the denial, although it was known that of the twenty-seven Senators who voted for it, all except Mr. Noble (my *avowed* friend) were political adversaries of Mr. Crawford, and of course would have been not the less friendly to me on account of my opposition to him. This effort, originating in injustice, terminated in abortion; and the marvelous memory of Mr. Noble was relied on to prove that although I did not secure the appointment by disavowing the publication, yet that I endeavored to do so—a charge which, had it been sustained, would have been equally injurious to my moral character, more discreditable to my understanding, but as little illustrative of Mr. Crawford's conduct.

Upon the testimony of Mr. Noble, therefore, it becomes my duty to exercise the right of self-defense, a right in which all the stronger virtues take root, and to demonstrate that it is neither consistent with facts, nor even consistent with itself; and that the disastrous effect it had upon my reputation resulted, not from its truth or veri-similitude, but from the super-sensibility of the public mind, prepared and heated by party contention, "to trifles light as air," when sanctioned, as Mr. Noble's testimony was, by the authority of forms and office, and adapted to particular modes of popular feeling.

As a preliminary to its refutation, it may be fitly observed that if Mr. Noble's testimony be not good against himself, it cannot be operative against another person, and if it be good against himself it proves that he has violated all those principles of honor which forbid the breach of private confidence, and that voluntarily.

It is not my province to designate his motives. He, himself, has declared that his active support of my nomination was blamed by his political friends. That when my address was afterwards presented to the house, it was urged upon him as practical demonstration of his impolicy, with so much force as to require an expiatory sacrifice of friendship and honor, it is more easy to believe than proper to assert. Even if this be the case, he has made ample atonement; for I am free to confess that the peculiar circumstances in which his testimony placed me compelled me, from respect to myself, my friends and my country, to resign an appointment which the combined strength of his friends, in fair opposition, could not, as they well knew, have prevented my receiving.

In regard to that view of his testimony which proposes to consider it extrinsically, a difference presents itself, between the conduct imputed to me by Mr. Noble and that which it is known I pursued, that weighs strongly against its accuracy.

Had I so recently and emphatically denied my authorship of the "A. B." publications, is it reasonable to suppose that I would have been so inconsiderate as to avow it in my address—especially as I was under no strong inducement thus to ruin my reputation? Such a naked and unnecessary adsurdity can hardly be credited of any man, unless we disregard the admitted influence of self-love, and violate those habits of judgment by which we trace the operations of moral causes and form conceptions of individual character. To believe it of any man would be difficult, but to believe it of one who, in an uninterrupted course of public service of twenty-seven or eight years, had constantly been honored with the distinguished approbation of every people whose public servant he had been—who, in the patriotic and enlightened State of Kentucky, had served several sessions in its Legislature, and successively filled the unsolicited stations of a Circuit Judge, a Judge of the General Court, fourth Judge of the Court of Appeals, and Chief Justice of the State, before he had attained his thirty-second year—who had administered the government of a Territory between nine and ten years, with entire satisfaction to two administrations, and at the termination of this service had been elected, almost unanimously, a Senator of Congress by the State which sprung out of the Territory of which he had so long been the Governor, and who was considered by the President, by the Senate and by the Hon. Mr. Noble, himself, qualified both as to principle and capacity for the highest appointment —is impossible!

Again—had I designed, as he insinuates, to carry this denial through him to the members of the Senate, is it credible that I should neither have requested him to mention it, nor ever after inquired of him if he had done so? If the first incident happened, the second succeeded by necessary connection, and yet Mr. Noble confesses [see his testimony] that the latter did not take place. Or, is it possible that after I had thus imposed upon him, by making him consider me "as speaking as an honest man," while I was uttering a falsehood, he should not of his own accord have communicated my earnest and voluntary denial to a single individual on whom it was calculated to operate either in advancement of me or in justification of himself. Moreover, if it be insisted that I made the denial in question, it must be admitted that I made it for some object, and the object imputed is the only one possible; yet it is incredible that I should never have expressed my denial to any Senator but Mr. Noble, himself, who had previously taken a zealous part in my support, and was known to have discharged the very act of favor which it must have been the only possible object of denial to induce him to undertake.

Another circumstance, which would be sufficient to discredit a story of much greater plausibility than Mr. Noble's, is my sickness and extreme debility at the time in which he lays its foundation. He swears that, in the conversation in which I disavowed to him the authorship of the "A. B." publications, that it took place "in *his own room* and on the evening of the day on which he called up my nomination in the Senate." But his memory is evidently false both as to time and place—for the fact is (as the testimony before the Committee shows) I was too sick on the evening of that day to leave *my bed*, much less to be in his room, which was separated from mine by considerable distance and by the intervention of several flights of stairs; and I was too feeble, in any situation, to make the ample and lively gesticulations which he describes in his testimony, or to toss my feet, in the athletic restlessness of ease, "high upon the jambs," as he has frequently asserted, perhaps to corroborate his oath, in familiar conversation.

It is known to a multitude of gentlemen that I had been confined to my bed, without being able to dress or be dressed, for several successive weeks previous to that, toward the end of which Mr. Noble came to reside at Mrs. Queen's. In the course of it, though feeble and exhausted, I had, contrary to the caution of my friends, ventured to ride as far as the capitol in a carriage, and to take some gentle exercise on foot—to which it is most probable my severe relapse was attributable. The insinuation that my illness, tedious and severe as it was, was simulated, is too illiberal for notice, and, as it was witnessed by a number of respectable individuals, too contemptible for refutation. It can only be important to show that, on the day of the alleged conversation (Tuesday, the 24th, or Thursday, 26th February), and for a number of tedious and painful days thereafter, I was in no condition to visit Mr. Noble in his room, or to hold the conversation, or to exhibit the gestures he represents.

Mrs. Queen, the lady with whom Mr. Noble and myself boarded, and a witness before the Committee, being asked by me what she knows concerning my sickness at her house, after my removal into the back building—that is after the 21st February, when I gave up the front room to Mr. Noble—how long I continued sick, and how long it was after Mr. Noble's coming that I became so ill as to be confined to my room, says, upon oath, "I know that you were very sick while you lodged in that room—so ill that the servant was obliged to sit up with you every night;" and, also, that "it was Tuesday or Wednesday you became so sick as to be confined to your room;" and further, that she "does not recollect having seen Gov. Edwards at the table after Monday, the 23d."

Mr. H. W. Queen (another witness), a young gentleman who is the son of the aforesaid Eliza, and who had the best opportunity of knowing the occurrences of the family, upon being interrogated by me, testified as follows: "I am under the impression that you became confined to your room on a Tuesday. I remember your being at breakfast Monday morning, previous. I do not recollect your being out of your room after Tuesday, until you recovered." Upon being asked by Mr. Forsyth, in behalf of Mr. Crawford, "what enables you to fix with so much certainty on Monday and Tuesday?" answers, "Gen. Noble came on Saturday; was not at breakfast on Sunday, and came to breakfast, for the first time, on Monday, in company with Gov. Edwards."

Mr. Asa Hough (another witness), after testifying that he recollected having seen me at Mrs. Queen's after I "occupied the back room," that is after the 21st of February, declares, "you was sick in bed; I cannot remember the precise day; it was sometime towards the latter end of February; I recollect that you was so much indisposed, that I did not communicate the business for which I had come; I called again, sometime afterwards, but, learning that you were still confined to your room, I did not go in."

Mr. J. Mason, Jr., a witness on the part of Mr. Crawford, says he "visited me shortly after my nomination, and shortly after I occupied the back room, and that he then thought me quite ill."

Mrs. A. Lindsay, another boarder at Mrs. Queen's, "thinks I continued confined to my room about a fortnight, and does not recollect seeing me at table after Monday, the 23d of February."

The Hon. Jeremiah Nelson, another boarder, says he "lodged at Mrs. Queen's when Mr. Noble came there, and I removed to a room in the back building; that he understood, from several members of the family, that Gov. Edwards was very sick; and that he visited me in my room more than a week afterwards, and found me still so."

All this testimony was given before the Committee, and represents my condition as certainly very unfit to square with the oath of Mr. Noble. I have since, however, received statements which, though not sanctioned by the solemnity of an oath, have all the force of truth, and render it indisputable that his testimony is not to be relied on, and that he has done me the greatest possible injustice.

The high character and reputation of George M. Bibb, Esq., one of the most eminent lawyers of Kentucky, formerly a Judge of the Court of Appeals of that State, a Senator in Congress, etc., is known throughout the Union. This gentleman was well informed in relation to certain subjects, which rendered me solicitous for an interview with the Hon. Rufus King of New York, on Saturday evening, the 21st of February. Not being able to go out and see Mr. King, (as appears by my letter to him of that date, which he has returned to me with his own indorsement thereon,) and being desirous to have the benefit of what Mr. Bibb knew on the same subject, I wrote to him on the following Monday morning, requesting him to make the explanations relating to it to Mr. King. The following is an extract of a letter to me, from Mr. Bibb, in reply to mine calling his recollection to the above transactions:

"Frankfort, *August* 2, 1824.

"*My Good Friend:*

"When I arrived in Washington City, in February last, you were at Mrs. Queen's, occupying the front room on the first floor. I visited you there several times whilst you were sick and confined to your room. You afterwards removed to the back part of the building, where I visited you frequently; you were sick most generally in bed, but sometimes sat up. The time when you removed to the back room of Mrs. Queen's I cannot state; I recollect, while your nomination was pending in the Senate, unacted upon, you were confined to your room in the back apartment. I had a conversation with Mr. King, of the Senate, on the subject of an anonymous publication against you some twenty years ago, in Kentucky, which publication I understood was dug out of the grave and used, or attempted to be used, to your prejudice. I waited on you at your own room, the same day or the next, and informed you of the conversation; found you sick and confined to your chamber. This was whilst your nomination was pending. Your note to me on the subject of the anonymous publication is not preserved; by that I could have ascertained the date; my memory cannot retain dates. I arrived in Washington early in February. You were sick and confined to your room when I arrived. I left the city in the latter part of March. I have no recollection to have seen you out of your own apartment during my stay in the city. I visited you frequently, because of your sickness, and because the presence and conversation of your acquaintances seemed to cheer your spirits."

It will be seen, by reference to Mr. Noble's testimony, he asserts that previous to my alleged conversation with him in *his own room*, I had been informed *of his having called up my nomination in the Senate*. This information was communicated to me by Hon. G. Moore of Alabama, one of my mess at Mrs. Queen's. The following extract of a letter will show that my confinement to my bed had commenced before I received this *information*, and, taken in connection with the foregoing testimony, must satisfy every unprejudiced mind that I could neither have been in Mr. Noble's room, as he swears, on that evening, nor "for six or eight days thereafter":

"As to your indisposition—having made it my business to call to see you every night and morning, I know I cannot be mistaken. It is also in my recollection, on that or the day in the evening of which I informed you Gen. Noble had moved to take up your nomination, I was informed you had experienced a very severe shake of the ague, and when I gave you this information, you were confined to your bed, and appeared much exhausted, and continued confined and very much weakened and debilitated, I think, for six or eight days, and perhaps more."

In addition to this, I submit the following affidavit of a young gentleman, of perfect truth and respectability, which is positive as to my being sick in bed on Tuesday, the 24th February, and for several successive days afterwards:

"Frederick Hewitt, of Madison county, and State of Illinois, and lately a cadet in the military academy at West Point, deposes and says, that he arrived in the city of Washington from West Point, and put up at Brown's Hotel, on the 24th February last; that being particularly desirous to see and converse with Gov. Edwards, he called, for that purpose, at Mrs. Queen's boarding house, on the same day and within a very short time after his arrival, and found him to all appearances *very sick*, in bed, in a room in the back building of the said boarding house; that Gov. Edwards complained considerably—said he was too sick for conversation at that time, and requested deponent to call again in the evening: upon which deponent took his leave, and returned again after candle-light, and found the Governor still in bed, and a gentleman in the room with him, whom Gov. Edwards called 'Judge,' but deponent does not recollect that he heard the gentleman's name, or, if he did, he has forgotten it.

"This deponent remained in the city till the evening of the 28th of February, and called every day, and sometimes twice a day or more, to see the Governor, who continued sick during the whole of that time, and on the last mentioned day took physic in deponent's presence.

"On deponent's taking leave of Gov. Edwards, on the 28th of February, aforesaid, he expressed a great unwillingness that his situation should be known to his family, and earnestly requested deponent (who had to pass through Edwardsville, where they resided,) not to mention his sickness in the neighborhood, lest it should get to their ears.

(Signed,) "FREDERICK HEWITT,
"District of Columbia, Washington county, etc."

[On the 23d day of September, 1824, Frederick Hewitt personally appeared before the subscriber, a Justice of the Peace for the county aforesaid, and made oath, in due form of law, that the facts stated and set forth in the aforesaid affidavit are true.

WM. HEWITT, *Justice Peace.*]

Independently of the incoherences of his testimony, Mr. Noble himself furnishes the means of establishing the fact and time of my confinement, and the impossibility of his statements being true. He admitted, on the day that the witnesses who testified on this subject before the Committee were examined, and has since reiterated, that I was "*very sick*," and that he, himself, brought a letter from Mr. King to me, "*in my room.*" Fortunately this letter has been preserved. It is dated "Senate Chamber, Tuesday, 24th February, 1824," the earliest possible period at which the alleged conversation could have taken place—inasmuch as Mr. Noble states it to have occurred after he moved to take up my nomination, and the journals of the Senate show that he could not have made the motion at any time before that day. This letter is as follows:

"SENATE CHAMBER, *February* 24, 1824.

"*Dear Sir:*

"The nomination was read this morning, and upon the suggestion of a member that an absent Senator was understood to be prepared to submit to the consideration of the Senate, objections to the confirmation of the appointment to Mexico, and to afford an opportunity of this being done, I moved to postpone the nomination till to-morrow, when the absent Senator expects to be able to attend. It was intimated that it was desirable that some intimation of the nature of the objection should be given, in order that inquiries could be seasonably made by the friends of the candidate. Nothing particular was intimated, though it was understood that Col. Benton is the Senator who is to offer objections. Yours, truly,

"RUFUS KING.

"HON. NINIAN EDWARDS, *of the U. S. Senate.*"

Not having been present, I cannot say with *absolute certainty* whether Mr. Noble *moved to take up my nomination* on the 24th or the 26th of February, (for it appears, from the journals of the Senate, it was taken up on both of those days,) or, consequently, whether the imputed conversation, which he brings within the same day of the motion, is alleged to have occurred on one or the other of those days. All the indications, and his own expressions, however, point to the first, and, by linking his charge with that day, force it into direct conflict with *all* the testimony, formal and informal, above referred to. Give him, however, the utmost possible advantage, and extend the time of the imputed conversation to the 26th, the force of evidence against his oath is still but too formidable.

Mrs. Queen swears that "two or three days after Mr. Noble came to her house, (Feb. 21) I became so ill as to make it necessary for a servant to sit up with me every night, and continued confined to my room about two weeks." Mrs. Lindsay, that "I continued confined to my room about a fortnight." The Hon. Mr. Moore declares that I was confined to my bed the evening of the day on which the motion for taking up my nomination was made in the Senate, and continued confined "six or eight days and perhaps more."

Mr. Hewitt swears I was sick in bed on the 24th, and continued so *until* the 28th, whereon he took leave of me; and if it were necessary to superadd evidence to the same fact, the following letter from Mr. King of New York, to a friend of mine, dated 22d June, 1824, would supply it: "Enclosed I send you two letters from Mr. Edwards to me, dated the 21st and 27th February—the former being subsequent to a note from me to him, from the Senate, respecting his nomination; the latter, as I conjecture, the day after my visit, when I found him in bed in the back part of the house where he lodged." The accuracy of Mr. King's recollection is established by the tenor of my letter alluded to the 27th, the genuineness of which he can vouch for. It contains these words: "I gave you, *yesterday*, a brief sketch of my impressions in regard to, etc. It is, however, a long time since I have seen or even thought of that letter; and sick as I am with a severe attack of fever, that confines me to my bed," etc.

Plain, fair and strict as I intend *this* examination of the testimony of Mr. Noble to be, I will not affect to conceal my conviction that the arguments and exposition already bestowed on it, have completed its discredit. Charity may forgive, but credulity itself can never believe it; yet the chain of proof against it is still longer, and acquires strength as it extends. Among the *memorabilia* of that imputed conversation, he swears I mentioned "that I was about to be attacked in the Senate of the United States, for the purpose of defeating my nomination; that party and political spirit was now high; that I understood that charges would be exhibited against me, and that it had been so declared in the Senate Chamber; that he remarked to me that I well knew, according to the rules of that body, while on executive business, secrecy was required; that he was not at liberty to mention any occurrences or the remarks of a single member, excepting so far as related to himself; that I then replied that I was informed *almost every day* of the transactions and *remarks of individuals* when *my nomination was called up*." *Almost every day* when my nomination was called up! Astonishing! One would suppose from this statement, and indeed (being given without any comment or surprise) it is equivalent to a direct affirmation on his part, that my nomination had, at that time, been *repeatedly called up in the Senate*, and that different members had as frequently made remarks in relation to it, of which the rules of that body interdicted the disclosure; yet let any one consult the journals of the Senate, and compare the facts with the tenure of this affirmation. I was nominated on Wednesday, the 18th February; my nomination was read on that and the succeeding day, as a matter of course, and *subsilentio;* it was called up for the first time on the 24th, the very day on the evening of which Mr. Noble brought me Mr. King's letter, and when he found me, as he himself declares, *very sick in my own room;* the second time on the 26th, the day on which Mr. King visited and found me, as he himself states, sick in bed—and was confirmed on the 4th March, following. Every member of the Senate who was present, except Mr. Noble, will bear me out in the assertion, that no *transactions* or *remarks* of which the rules of that body forbid the disclosure, which could be likely to excite my curiosity or to require his forbearance, could have taken place prior to the 24th February; nor was anything ever afterwards alleged in that body against the nomination, if Mr. Noble himself is to be believed, for he, himself, says, "the fact turned out that there was no opposition."

It was confirmed without opposition, twenty-seven members rising in its favor, and none against it. It is, therefore, not only improbable, but hideously incredible, that the very first day, or even the second, on which a motion was made to take up my nomination, when it is certain an intimation of future opposition was all that had occurred and of course the most that could have transpired, I should have assured Mr.

Noble "that I was informed almost every day (thereby implying several if not many days) *of the transactions and remarks of individuals, when my nomination was called up.*" Believe who can—it is a rule of evidence, founded in reason and justified by philosophy, that when a number of witnesses, testifying to the same fact, contradict each other, the whole amount of their testimony is diminished in proportion to the degree of mutual destruction which their opposite assertions effect; but the destruction of testimony goes much further when a single witness either contradicts himself or encumbers his oath with strong improbabilities and inconsistencies that cannot be reconciled. Both these infirmities are so marked in Mr. Noble's testimony, by the examination already made, that it is hardly worth while to notice the dire contrast between the state of mind ascribed to me by him, and that which, about the same time, Mr. Seaton swears I manifested.

According to Mr. Noble I deprecated opposition, and aimed at conciliating Mr. Crawford's friends. According to Mr. Seaton, one of his warmest friends, I was regardless of opposition and confident of success. Both accounts can hardly be true, and that Mr. Seaton's is most probable, the following extract of my letter to Mr. King of New York, of the 21st February, affords convincing proof: "That I shall meet all the opposition you allude to, I know just as well as that it will be utterly unavailing. I speak advisedly when I say it cannot succeed unless my friends are absent when the vote is taken." Another pertinent fact stated in my address to Mr. Noble, in the summer of 1824, which he has tacitly admitted by his answer and cannot deny, is, that the reason I alleged for being willing to give up to him the front room at Mrs. Queen's, which, for several successive sessions, I had occupied, and which, it is well known, I preferred, was, that I expected, in consequence of my nomination, to remain so short a time in the city, that it was no object with me to retain it, and it was upon that ground, on the 21st February, he himself predicated his application to me for it. This circumstance, though trivial in itself, is not unimportant in connection with others already referred to, which afford not only probability but proof, that at the time of the alleged conversation, I could not have apprehended serious opposition or been in such a state of mind as to make the declarations imputed to me by Mr. Noble, so obviously inconsistent, as they certainly were, with the uniform and undisguised tenor of my conduct towards Mr. Crawford for years before—the more especially, as not a single step had been taken in the Senate on my nomination, after I came to board at Mrs. Queen's, until the day in the evening of which he brought me Mr. King's letter in my own room, when, as he admits, *I was very sick*, and from which time the foregoing testimony incontestably proves, I was confined with severe indisposition until after my nomination was confirmed. I need hardly here repeat my notice of another defect in the testimony of Mr. Noble. It was generally understood, I believe, after my address to the House of Representatives was presented, that Mr. Noble and Mr. Elkins were to swear to the same facts and to corroborate each others testimony. Accordingly Mr. Elkins declared, on his oath, that he had seen an article in the "Richmond Enquirer," in which it was stated that Ninian Edwards, of "A. B. plot" memory, had been nominated by the President as Minister to Mexico, an incident which, he says, led to the conversation with me, out of which his evidence grew, and which, he asserts, happened *during the pendency of my nomination before the Senate.*

And Mr. Noble says, upon his oath, "I saw an article in the 'Richmond Enquirer,' stating that Ninian Edwards, the author of 'A. B.,' or of 'A. B. plot' memory, (I do not recollect which) had been so nominated. The paper I saw at the boarding house of Mrs. Queen, and, I think, *in the hands of Mr. Elkins.*"

It is, perhaps, not to be wondered at, and, in truth, it ought to have been expected, that as Mr. Noble's testimony differed from that of all the witnesses whose testimony appeared consistent and accurate, it should exactly agree with that of a witness who certainly swore to the existence of *that which was not.* I have procured a file of the "Enquirer," and find, after a careful examination, no such article as Mr. Elkins swears he saw, or as Mr. Noble swears he saw, and saw, he thinks, in *the hands of Mr. Elkins.* Such an article, or one in the least like it, I defy either of these witnesses to show in that paper, *during the time my nomination was pending before the Senate*, or at any time after Mr. Noble came to Mrs. Queen's It is surely *possible* that I may have uttered, and that Mr. Noble may have listened to, many absurd, and, indeed, many politic remarks; for the friends of Mr. Crawford (who, with an invention superior to Shakspeare's, attribute to him the utmost wisdom and integrity, while they admit that he repeatedly violated the laws and disregarded the resolutions of Congress, and make me both Roderigo and Iago) assign to me the capacity of a sage and at the same time impute to me the conduct of a fool. Mr. Noble goes so far as to make me a prophet; he says, upon oath, that I told him I never had any fear of not *being nominated*, except for a short time when Pennsylvania seemed disposed to support Calhoun for the Presidency: then I had some apprehension of Dallas' success; but the moment that State gave up Calhoun I had no longer any doubts, as Dallas, I knew, would soon be out of the question. Let us compare the dates of the events here alluded to, and it will be found that Mr. Noble has rendered it morally impossible for any rational being to believe him. Pennsylvania "gave up Mr. Calhoun" on the 4th March, 1824, when the delegates met in convention, at Harrisburg—the very day on which my nomination was *confirmed*, and fifteen days *after* it had been *made* to the Senate. To have told Mr. Noble what he swears I did tell him on the 24th February, it was necessary for me to foresee and assume the fact that Pennsylvania had then done what she did not do for eight or ten days afterwards, and to conceive Mr. Noble himself capable of an equal degree of prescience. Until the mind can be brought to believe that the effect is previous to the cause, no one can credit Mr. Noble. His cruel anachronism is not mended by the referring to the giving up of Mr. Calhoun, by Pennsylvania, to Mr. Dallas' movement in Philadelphia, for that happened on the 18th February—the day my nomination was made. It could not, of course, have been known to me (unless by second sight) and was not known at Washington, as the editor of the "National Intelligencer" can testify, until several days after the nomination had been made, and could not possibly have any influence in removing my apprehensions of "Mr. Dallas' success"—which the nomination itself must have already quieted.

His testimony in regard to the indecent observations, imputed to me, respecting the President of the United States, is equally false and equally incredible. The slanders against that distinguished patriot to which it presupposes an allusion, had not been agitated when I left Washington, nor had any attempt then been made to implicate Mr. Calhoun in my contest, nor had Mr. Hay replied to Mr. Lowne. This mass of incongruity I might heap still higher. I might show, from the absurdity of the remarks alleged, respecting the currency of Illinois and Indiana, in the testimony of Mr. Noble, that no person so well informed on that subject as I necessarily was could have made them, and that they likewise imply a foreknowledge on my part of facts—but I feel for the taste and patience of the reader. In justice to Mr. Noble, however, one observation must be added. It is that, from the peculiar nature of his testimony, it is less disgraceful to him to prove it to be false, than to admit it to be true. Such wide and shocking departures from truth, as he appears to have made, do not necessarily suppose the grossest moral turpitude; they may be imputed to a frail imagination, to a feeble judgment, a confused perception, a faithless memory, a flexible character. Politically operated on, as Mr. Noble was, it is possible that he may have been, in some degree, innocent of the great injustice his testimony has done me. But the utmost degree of charitable latitude cannot save his character from abhorrence, if it be conceded that he has sworn the truth. Unfortunate man! The conviction that he swore falsely is all that can rescue him from infamy. Not to mention the breach of private confidence it implies, nor the readiness to turn against an absent friend which it manifests (for he even professed his friendship for me after my return to Washington), the detestable disclosures relating to the President and the late Col. Lane, which he declares he received from me, amount to damning proof that, as a Senator of the United States, he supported with zeal and activity my nomination, when he knew it had been extorted from the President by corrupt influence. If I told Mr. Noble, as he substantially declares I did tell him, that I knew from Col. Lane (my relation and a member of the President's family) that he, the President, had induced or permitted Col. Lane to mis-spend the public money, and that I calculated, confidently, on receiving an important appointment in consequence of the hold which my knowledge of this fraud gave me on Mr. Monroe's prudence, would it not have been equivalent to information from one Senator to another, that the President of the United States, in nominating a Minister to Mexico, had been operated upon by corrupt influence, that the Commissioner of the Public Buildings had been his instrument or accomplice in defrauding the public, that I, myself, the person so flagitiously promoted, and privy to the profligacy by which my nomination had been effected, was profiting by corruption, which, as a man, it became me to abhor, and, as a Senator, it was my duty to denounce? And does not it fix on Mr. Noble the crime of having concealed this information, of having failed to expose the infamy of the parties concerned, to defend the dignity of the Senate, or to vindicate the rights and property of his constituents? Was it not his duty, as soon as I gave him the information, to lay it before the House of Representatives, to have the President impeached and me summoned as a witness? Instead of this he declares that he considered me "as speaking as an honest man," vehemently disavowed, on the part of Mr. Crawford's friends, anything so illiberal as opposition to my appointment, and warmly supported it himself. How can he justify such conduct to the distinguished gentleman whose pretensions were confided to him, or to the flourishing State whose sovereignty he represented, and whose trust he himself swears he betrayed?

The principal object we have, in the publication of many of the letters to him, is for the purpose of showing that after his resignation as Minister to Mexico, and the investigation of the charges against Mr. Crawford, he was held in high estimation by the most distinguished and purest patriots of the country. Amongst his most devoted friends were Judge McLean, Mr. Adams, Samuel D. Ingham, (Secretary of the Treasury under General Jackson's administration,) Mr. Calhoun, Hon. Gabriel Moore of Alabama, William Wirt, and John J. Crittenden, and they continued so up to the time of his death. In the year 1825, which was a year after the termination of the controversy with Mr. Crawford, and before Governor Edwards' election as Governor of the State, Judge McLean, in a very long letter, commences by saying: "Having a few minutes leisure, I do not know how

I can employ it more pleasantly to myself than by communicating to you the aspect of our political affairs; for I am persuaded it will not be wholly uninteresting to you," etc. In another letter, referring to the election for Governor of Illinois, he says: "From the certainty of your success in the approaching election I derive sincere pleasure; it will be a triumph to yourself and your friends. I believe almost all of that virulence of feeling which was so generally evinced by the caucus party against you, has disappeared, and to a considerable extent has been succeeded by feelings of a very different nature." In another letter, dated in November, 1826, Judge McLean says: "I do not believe that you and I will differ widely in this matter; it would be strange indeed, after looking to past scenes, if we should. * * Had your letter been received before I reappointed ......, I should, as I have always done, have appointed the person you name. I felt sincere regret that I had made the appointment before the reception of your letter. For your success in the late election (although your competitor was an old and, I believe, a sincere friend of mine) I felt a deep interest. It has been often referred to, by me, as a triumphant refutation of the scandles which had been so extensively circulated against you."

In a conversation between Mr. Clay and Mr. Wirt, it will be seen, from a letter of Mr. Wirt as late as 1831, that Mr. Clay says that "the sentiments expressed by Gov. Edwards do honor to his own heart, and I cannot but hope that he may lend his powerful aid and support, at this crisis, to the cause which the most enlightened men throughout the community consider as the cause of our country." Mr. Wirt adds that his motive for mentioning it is "the pleasure I derived from the light in which he views you." In a letter from Mr. Wirt, dated in November, 1826, he says: "Your friends (and I among the foremost) have rejoiced at the recent proof of respect which you have received from your State; it must have been balm to your feelings, as it was to ours;" and in a still later letter he says, "I am much rejoiced, in common with your other friends, at the honorable demonstration you have received of the confidence of your State, so bravely and nobly won."

In a letter from President Adams to Gov. Edwards, dated Aug. 22, 1827, Mr. Adams says: "Your recommendation for the appointment of a sub-agent at Peoria will, in the event of a vacancy in that office, receive the deliberate consideration to which it is entitled, and a disposition altogether friendly to him as recommended by you. And your opinion in regard to any appointment of the General Government, in the State of Illinois, will be always acceptable to me, whenever you may incline to communicate to me. Accept my friendly and respectful salutations."

Mr. Wirt, in a letter dated after the report of the Committee, says: "Very many, whose good opinions are most desirable, think you are right, notwithstanding the report of the Committee: nay, many think you supported by that report to the full extent of all your charges. * * You say that your resignation has exposed you to imputations, etc. The opinion I expressed to Mr. Cook, as to your resignation, was that of every friend of yours with whom I conversed. I learned, from Mr. Cook, himself, that it was also the opinion of Mr. Adams (and, I think, Mr. Calhoun), expressed to him; and I know it was the opinion of Mr. Southard. Indeed, I did not hear one dissenting voice—Mr. Cook, himself, concurred in it;—the opinion being that, with reference to yourself alone, resignation was the only dignified, the only proper course: so that, if the opinion was wrong, it was one in which I erred in company with some of the ablest men in the country, and with all your best friends. It is only because you place your resignation on my single opinion, that I have referred to the concurrent and unanimous opinions of all who wished you well—some of whom were much better qualified by experience, than myself, to estimate the effect of political movements."

The Hon. S. D. Ingham, Secretary of the Treasury under Gen. Jackson's administration, in his letter dated the 20th of July, 1824, says: "I duly received your favor of the 16th, and the same mail brought the report of the Committee, which is the first view I have had of your whole defense. Upon all the charges and specifications you have made out your case completely. I would not dwell on Noble's testimony; you have already given it the proper answer. Those who believe him will consider it no unusual *finesse* among politicians, and it will have much less effect than you suppose. I think Mr. Webster must have winced under your exposition of his expert on the uncurrent funds."

The Hon. Gabriel Moore, in his letter of Aug. 8th, 1824, in reference to Gen. Noble's testimony, says: "Nothing of a similar nature ever astonished me more than the general character of the testimony given before the Committee by Gen. Noble, and particularly that part which has relation to the authorship of the 'A. B.' publications; not only because I know that, among the members, it was generally if not universally understood and believed that you were the author, but because I had some conversation with Gen. Noble, pending your nomination, in relation to this subject, in which, a reference having been made to the authorship as forming some objection to the confirmation of your nomination, by some of the friends of Mr. Crawford, I am clearly and decidedly of opinion that on this occasion I was authorized, from the general tenor of Mr. Noble's remarks, to infer that whether you were the author or not would have, or had, produced no influence on his mind."

Mr. Moore was at that time a member of the House of Representatives, but was afterwards a Senator in Congress and Governor of Alabama.

Judge William Kelly, another Senator of Congress, in a letter dated Aug. 23d, 1825, says: "I called several times while he [Gov. Edwards] occupied the latter room [the back room], and recollect to have seen a gentleman there who was from West Point, as I understood, and bound to Illinois—but cannot fix the precise date of the transaction; but I well recollect that the Governor was so unwell, at the time, as to be confined to his room as he alleged, and his appearance seemed to require it. This was his condition for several days previous to the confirmation of his nomination. On account of his indisposition, I called frequently—perhaps every time I was in the neighborhood of his residence. I recollect conversing with him on the subject of the postponement of the nomination on account of its being stated that an absent Senator had, perhaps, objections that he would like to make, and inquired if it could be the 'A. B.' affair that formed the objection; to which he replied that he could not say or conjecture the ground or nature of the objection, unless it should be the 'A. B.' affair or a newspaper controversy that had occurred in the West some years before, neither of which he considered ought to form any ground of objection. I recollect conversing with him on the subject of his being the author of the 'A. B.' letters, and he did not pretend to deny the fact to me. So far from it, he told me, upon one occasion, that he had prepared another document of considerable length, of the same tenor."

The above statement of Judge Kelly corroborates the statement of Mr. Hewitt, whose affidavit we have given; and the correspondence in another portion of this work shows that the fact that Gov. Edwards was the author of the 'A. B.' publications was known, not only to his friends, but to the members of Congress generally. Is it probable, then, that he would have denied it to Gen. Noble, who had previously taken a zealous part in his support, without asking him to communicate this denial to others on whom it was expected to have some influence? nor that he should not have inquired of him if he had done so? Is it probable that he would have made this denial for the purpose of securing the confirmation of his nomination, and thus run the risk of exposure and the loss of the support among those who so generally had understood, from him, that he was the author—and especially as the majority of the Senators were political opponents of Mr. Crawford? Or is it reasonable that he should have made those articles a part of the address, if he had so recently denied their authorship?

The following letter, from President Monroe, shows that no such denial had ever been made for any such purpose:

OAK HILL, *April* 30, 1826.

SIR: In reply to your letter of the 23d, requesting to be informed whether Gov. Edwards declared to me, before his nomination as Minister to Mexico, that he was not the author of the publications signed "A. B."—on which declaration, it is said, that his nomination was founded—I feel it due to candor to assure you that he never made to me any such declaration, and that his nomination was not influenced in the slightest degree by any considerations but that the quarter of the Union in which he resided had claims to an appointment, and that he was believed to be as well qualified for the office as any other person in that quarter who had been brought to the view of the Executive.

With great respect and esteem,

I am your obedient servant,

JAMES MONROE.

In another letter, to Mr. Cook, on the same subject, dated April 27, 1826, President Monroe requests Mr. Cook to assure Mr. Edwards "of his good wishes for his welfare and happiness."

From the letter of his resignation, a copy of which is among the papers in the possession of the writer, and from the allusions and opinions referred to in Mr. Wirt's letter, respecting the propriety of his resignation, there can be no doubt that it was voluntary on his part, and not required by the President. That such is the fact is also evident from a letter of Mr. Ingham, in which he says, "I am not sure that you have done right by resigning."

Notwithstanding Mr. Clay was of opinion that he "was not liable to pay the out-fit and salary he had received," in which opinion he also believed the administration concurred with him, yet he accounted to the Government for all he had received, except for the time he had held the office and the losses he had sustained in making his preparations to leave on his mission. Mr. Clay said, "if it were my case, I would not return one cent of the amount."

The following is an extract from a letter to Gov. Edwards, dated Oct. 8, 1828, from the Hon. Hugh Nelson, who was a member of Congress from Virginia for fourteen years, and afterwards Minister to Spain:

I wrote to you just before I sailed for Spain, and hope you received my letter, because, having received from you a most kind and affectionate letter, just before my departure, I should regret that an appearance should have been afforded to the presumption that I was regardless of your friendship. I have never participated in the persecution against you, which was started about that time, and have always believed you an upright, honest statesman and politician, and have thought you perfectly right in that affair in which the C—— faction bottomed their efforts to hunt you down. I always said, too, that your talents would enable you to rise against the whole host.

Before Mr. Cook presented Mr. Edwards' memorial to Congress, he says that he submitted it to some of his friends, and states, in his letter in reference to it, that Mr. Adams' friends, Mr. Houston, and all the Tennessee delegation except Mr. Cocke, would stand by Gov. Edwards.

The object in referring to the causes which led to his resignation, and to the settlement of his account with the Government, is for the purpose of proving the falsity of the charges made by Col. Benton and published in his "Debates," and also in his "Thirty Years in the Senate," that, in consequence of the report of the Committee, Mr. Edwards was required by the President to resign and to return his out-fit and quarter's salary. Col. Benton is not satisfied with giving a garbled extract from the testimony, but takes it upon himself to assert as a fact what the accounts in the Treasury Department prove to be untrue; for the records of the Treasury Department show that in the settlement, which he voluntarily proposed, and which was accepted by the Department, he was allowed not only his salary, for the time he had held the office, but also the loss he had sustained in consequence of his resignation. After the Committee had published their report, and of course after the testimony of Gen. Noble had been given, in consequence of its being stated in one of the public journals, in Washington City, that directions were given, by a member of a committee appointed to make arrangements for the celebration of the Fourth of July, not to receive the subscription of Ninian Edwards to the dinner, all the members of the Cabinet, with the exception of Mr. Crawford, who were in Washington, refused to participate in the celebration—as will appear from the following correspondence:

[From the Washington Republican, of Saturday afternoon.]

WASHINGTON, 3*d July*, 1824.

To Messrs. T. Carbery and Jos. Gales, Jr.:

GENTLEMEN: Upon a printed invitation signed by you, we have subscribed our names, for attendance at a dinner at Mr. Williamson's hotel, on the 5th inst., in celebration of the anniversary of our national independence. We find it stated, in one of the public journals of this morning, that one of the members of the committee of arrangements has called at the places where the subscription papers for the dinner has been deposited, and, in the name of the committee, has directed, that if Mr. Ninian Edwards should apply there to join in this celebration of the festival, his subscription should not be admitted.

Our attendance at the dinner, after this notice, would justly be considered as equivalent to an assent, on our part, to this exclusion.

The character and conduct of Mr. Edwards being before the nation, upon the report of the committee of the House of Representatives, yet to be acted upon by the House, we should consider it incompatible with our duties as public servants, as well as with the principles of common justice, to participate in an act which we think would, in no event, be justifiable before a final decision *upon the investigation.* We request you, therefore, to consider this as notice that we have withdrawn our subscriptions for attendance at the dinner.

We are, very respectfully, gentlemen,

Your obedient servants,

JOHN QUINCY ADAMS,
J. C. CALHOUN,
JOHN McLEAN.

The Secretary of the Navy and the Attorney General, not having expected to be in the city, have not subscribed to the dinner. We are authorized to say, that if the Attorney General had received a similar invitation, and had subscribed, he would now have joined in the above letter.

[From the Washington Gazette, of Saturday evening.]

We are authorized and requested, by the committee of arrangements for the celebration of the anniversary of independence, to say, that the publication in the "National Journal" of this morning was unauthorized by them, or any one of them, and that nothing will be wanting, on their part, to make the public dinner on the occasion a national festival, divested of all reference to party politics.

Messrs. Van Ness, Carbery and Gales constituted the committee of arrangement.

[From the National Journal.]

WASHINGTON CITY, 3*d July*, 1824.

To Hon. John Quincy Adams, J. C. Calhoun and John McLean:

GENTLEMEN: The committee of arrangements for celebrating the approaching anniversary of American independence have instructed us to say, that they regret the withdrawal of your subscriptions to the anniversary dinner, and the more so as that withdrawal seems to have been induced by a misconception of the motives which governed the committee in the course they deemed advisable to pursue in the case of Mr. Edwards.

We have the honor to be, with great respect,

Your obedient servants,

THOMAS CARBERY, *Chairman.*

JOSEPH GALES, Jr., *Secretary.*

WASHINGTON, 5*th July*, 1824.

To Thomas Carbery, Chairman, and Joseph Gales, Jr., Secretary of the Committee of Arrangements, for Celebrating the Anniversary of American Independence:

GENTLEMEN: We have had the honor of receiving your letter of the 3d instant, and request you to present to the committee the assurance that we cordially regret the incident which has deprived us of the pleasure we had promised ourselves in uniting with them and the rest of our fellow-citizens, subscribers to the anniversary dinner, at the social board, on the day peculiarly devoted to generous and patriotic feelings. We wish you to add, with the tender of our respect, that the determination to withdraw our names from the subscription was taken from the conviction of our own duty, without inquiring into the *motives* of the committee, or reference to them.

We are, with great respect, gentlemen,

Your very humble and obedient servants,

JOHN QUINCY ADAMS,
J. C. CALHOUN,
JOHN MCLEAN.

The report of the Committee was never acted upon by the House of Representatives. Acquitting Mr. Edwards of the charge against which he had defended himself, and containing no allegation against him, he could not complain, and especially as the Committee had been unable to detect a single inaccuracy in any of the facts he had alleged against Mr. Crawford. Mr. Crawford had no motive to demand any further investigation, as he could not hope to obtain a report more favorable to himself. The charges against him were:

First—That he has mismanaged the national fund.

Second—That he has received a large amount of uncurrent notes from certain banks, in part discharge of their debts due to the United States, contrary to the resolution of Congress in 1816.

Third—That, being called on by a resolution of the House of Representatives to state the amount of uncurrent notes which he received from these banks, he has misstated it—making it less than it really was.

Fourth—That he has, in his report to the House, misrepresented the obligations of those banks, or some one of them, at least, and predicated thereon an indefensible excuse for his conduct in receiving those uncurrent notes.

Fifth—That he has acted illegally, in a variety of instances, by making and continuing deposits of public money in certain local banks, without making report thereof to Congress, according to law.

Sixth—That he has, in several instances, withheld information and letters called for by the House, and which it was his duty to have communicated.

In regard to the second charge, the report of the Committee shows, "That although the Banks of Tombeckbee and Edwardsville were liable to account for such deposits as cash, if the construction which the Committee gives to their contracts be correct, yet, that both the Secretary and the Banks express a different opinion as to the meaning of those contracts, and that the Secretary, in receiving fifteen thousand dollars from the one and twenty thousand dollars from the other of those Banks, appears to have acted according to what he supposed to be the rights of the parties, and with a proper regard to the interest of the United States, under the circumstances which then existed."

In regard to the third charge, "That no intentional misstatement has been made to the House of uncurrent bills received from the Banks, although a sum of two hundred and eight dollars of such bills were omitted through mistake."

In regard to the fourth, "That although the Secretary may have misconstrued the effects of some of the contracts with the Banks to the extent before mentioned, the Committee finds no ground for the charge that he has misrepresented them, inasmuch as the contracts themselves were submitted, with his report, to the House."

In regard to the fifth, "That the Secretary did omit to communicate to Congress the reasons which led him to direct the deposit of public moneys in the three local Banks of Chilicothe, Cincinnati, and Louisville, where the Bank of the United States had branches; but there is no reason for supposing that any concealment was intended or that the omission was occasioned by design."

In regard to the sixth, "That in some instances papers called for, by resolution of the House, have not been communicated with other papers sent in answer to such calls, but that these omissions have happened either from accident, or from a belief that the papers so omitted were immaterial or not called for; and that there is no evidence that any document or information had been withheld from improper motives."

That in regard to the contested letter of Benjamin Stephenson, "Although the letter was written, as stated by Mr. Edwards in his testimony, there was no evidence that Mr. Stephenson communicated or transmitted it to the Secretary of the Treasury."

With regard to the first charge, the Committee content themselves with saying, that, in their opinion, "nothing has been proved to impeach the integrity of the Secretary, or to bring into doubt the general correctness and ability of his administration of the public finances."

If the reader will bear in mind that in making the charges Mr. Edwards stated, in his memorial, that he "disclaimed any other construction of them than the most innocent of which they were susceptible," and that, in pointing out palpable omissions or neglect to lay before the House letters which ought to have been communicated, and that various misstatements had been officially made, he "attributed them to nothing more than forgetfulness, inattention, inadvertence, or some erroneous but innocent views of the subject," it will be seen that the report of the Committee fully sustains him in all his statements, but excuses the Secretary because he acted according to what he *supposed* to be his duty, had made no intentional misstatements, had misconstrued the effect of some of the contracts, and, in his omissions to make important communications and papers that were called for by Congress, no concealment was intended or occasioned by design, or any information withheld from improper motives.

Mr. Edwards, in writing the articles over the signature of "A. B." against Mr. Crawford, claimed that he had the right, wisely guaranteed to every freeman of the Union, of investigating the official conduct of a public officer. Mr. Crawford had been a prominent candidate for the Presidency, for some time previous to the commencement of their publication, and was subsequently nominated for that office, to succeed President Monroe, by the Republican members of Congress, in caucus. In one of Mr. Wirt's letters to Gov. Edwards, dated January 4, 1820, he says: "You may remember that four years ago, when Mr. Monroe was presented to the public for the Presidency, Mr. Crawford was extremely pressed to oppose him. I was in Washington, by chance, at the time mentioned, and I remember that it was extremely dubious whether Mr. Crawford would not have a majority in the caucus of Congress; but he withdrew from the opposition, and I remember he gave great disgust to many of his friends by doing so. He withdrew, too, with the declaration that Mr. M. had the best title to the office." The caucus system had become very unpopular, and the friends of General Jackson, Mr. Adams and Mr. Clay were rallied against Mr. Crawford, and the result was that, for the first time, the candidate thus nominated was defeated.

CHAPTER IX.

Laws of the Territory and State, from 1809 *to* 1830.

THE JUDICIARY SYSTEM.

On the organization of the Territorial Government, the Governor and Judges adopted the laws which were in force in 1809 in the Indiana Territory. Among these acts was one entitled "An act organizing courts of common pleas." This act established a court of record in each county, to be styled the court of common pleas, consisting of three judges (any two of whom shall form a quorum), to be appointed by the Governor. The jurisdiction of said court extended to all crimes and misdemeanors, committed within their respective counties, the punishment whereof did not extend to life, limb, imprisonment for more than one year, a forfeiture of goods and chattels, or lands and tenements, and to all pleas of assize, scire facias, replevins, and to all manner of pleas, suits, actions and causes, real, personal and mixed.

The said judges, and each of them, had power, in and out of court, to take all manner of recognizances; and all recognizances for the peace, behavior, or for appearance, were to be certified to the proper court. All fines and amercements taxed by the court of common pleas were required to be yearly estreated by the clerks of said courts into the general court, to the intent that process may be awarded to the sheriff of the proper county for levying such of their fines and amercements as shall be unpaid to the uses for which they were appropriated.

The fines that were levied by the court of common pleas went to the county, and those that were assessed by the general court went to the territory.

Appeals and writs of error were allowed from the judgment in said court under the restrictions and regulations of the law regulating the practice of the general court.

When the defendant had no property in the county, or could not be found in it, the plaintiff, by making an affidavit that the defendant lies hid or skulks, or hath property in another county in the territory, can require the court to issue execution to the sheriff of the county where the defendant was or where his property could be found.

The clerk of said court held his appointment from the Governor, during good behavior.

The judges, or any of them, had power to send writs to other counties to take persons who were indicted in any courts, and also to issue subpœnas for witnesses to other counties.

This law remained in force until Dec. 19, 1814, when the Legislature passed an act abolishing the court of common pleas, and created courts to be called county courts, to consist of three judges, (who shall be conservators of the peace, any two of whom shall form a quorum,) to be appointed by the Governor. This act conferred on the judges and court the same jurisdiction that the judges and court of common pleas had a right to exercise, except that the jurisdiction for the trial of causes, both civil and criminal, was taken away from the county courts.

The judges were required to hold three terms annually, in each county, and were entitled to receive two dollars for every day they shall sit—to be paid out of the county levy. They were authorized to take every species of recognizance, and, on proper affidavit, to order bail in civil cases.

By a supplemental act, passed Dec. 24, 1814, the county courts and the judges thereof had a right to exercise, and were invested with all the jurisdiction, and were required to perform all the duties, heretofore vested in or required of the courts of common pleas or the judges thereof, except such as had been transferred to the supreme court or the judges thereof. Another act passed, on Sept. 17, 1807, which made it the duty of the presiding judge of the several courts of common pleas in the territory, and of the first judge of the general court, to examine the respective clerks' books and see what fines were due thereon to the territory or county, and to report those due to the territory to the Auditor, who was required to report the same to the Legislature. For failure to pay the fines, the act directed the Attorney-General to obtain judgment by motion against the defaulting clerks.

THE GENERAL COURT.

By an act, passed Dec. 10, 1813, regulating the general court, it was required that there should be holden and kept, at the seat of government, a supreme court of record, to be styled the "General Court." This court had jurisdiction of all causes, matters and things, and also to hear and determine all manner of pleas, plaints and causes which might be removed from any of the inferior courts by appeal or writ of error, as well all pleas in the United States as in all pleas real, personal and mixed, and thereupon to reverse or affirm the judgments; and, also, to examine, correct and punish the contempts, omissions, etc., of any justice of the peace, sheriff, coroner, clerk or other officers, within their respective counties. It had exclusive original jurisdiction of the higher criminal offenses, and of all cases in equity where the value of the matter in controversy exceeded the sum of one hundred dollars. It had power to award process for the collection of such fines as were estreated into the general court, and the judges thereof had the power to issue writs of certiorari, writs of habeas corpus, injunction, and writs of error, and remedial and other writs and process, returnable to their court and grantable by said judges.

The grand jurors sworn before the county courts were required to inquire into offenses cognizable by either the county court or general court, and, in special cases, the judges of the general court had power to direct the sheriff to summon a grand jury for offenses exclusively cognizable in the general court. In cases of a criminal kind, except for offenses in violation of the laws of the United States, the trials were to be had in the counties in which the offenses were committed.

By this act it was provided that, in cases taken to the general court by appeal or writ, the court should take cognizance only of errors in law.

By a subsequent act, passed Dec. 13, 1814, the general court was superseded by the establishment of a supreme court, consisting of the same judges, who were required, in addition to the jurisdiction conferred upon them, to hold circuit courts. As circuit courts they had jurisdiction, in each county, over all persons therein, and in all causes, matters or things at common law or in chancery, arising in each of said counties, except in cases where the debt or amount shall be under twenty dollars; and, also, in all cases of treasons, felonies, misdemeanors, and other crimes; and, also, in all cases against public debtors, sheriffs, clerks, and collectors of public money. This court was also invested with all the powers and the common law jurisdiction, whether of a civil or criminal nature, previously vested in the several courts of common pleas or county courts.

It was also required, by this act, that all suits should be tried in the counties in which they originated, unless in cases specially provided for; and in all cases, except where, in cases of conviction; the offender was punishable with death or burning in the hand, one of the judges might constitute the court. This act was amended, but not materially, in 1817, except the reorganization of the territory into circuits.

JUSTICES OF THE PEACE.

By an act, which passed Sept. 17, 1807, it was provided that a sufficient number of justices of the peace should be appointed for each county, by the Governor. Besides the usual power to cause to be arrested all persons charged with violating the criminal laws of the territory, and to take all manner of recognizances, they had power to hear and determine, according to the course of the common law, petit crimes and misdemeanors, wherein the punishment shall be by fine, only, and not exceeding three dollars, and to assess and tax the costs; and, also, to require sureties for the good behavior of idle, vagrant and disorderly characters, swindlers and gamblers, as well as of dangerous and disorderly persons. They had, also, jurisdiction in cases of debt or other demand, except in actions of debt on bonds for the performance of covenants, actions of replevin, or upon any real contract, actions of trespass upon the case, for trover and conversion, or slander, or actions of trespass *in et amis*, or actions wherein the title of lands shall in anywise come in question; and suit might be commenced in the township either where the debt or cause of action was contracted or arose, where the plaintiff resided, or where the defendant might be found. This latter provision was repealed by an act which passed in 1808, after which no suit could be commenced except in the township where the debt was contracted or cause of action arose, or where the defendant resided or might be found.

In 1814, it was further provided that they should have jurisdiction in all cases wherein the demand should not exceed twenty dollars—which amount was afterwards increased, by an act passed in 1817, to forty dollars. This latter act also required that, where the demand should exceed twenty dollars, either party should have the right to a trial by jury; and that, for the trial of such causes, the justice should hold his court monthly—to which court he should issue his *venire* to the constable, directing him to summon twelve good and lawful men to try all such suits before him.

CRIMINAL LAWS OF THE TERRITORY.

By an act of the Indiana Territory, in force in the Territory of Illinois in 1809, murder and treason were punished with death by hanging; and persons guilty of manslaughter, as the common law had previously punished.

It was declared that persons convicted of burglary should be whipped with not exceeding thirty-nine stripes, and should find sureties for good behavior for a term not exceeding three years; and upon default of sureties should be committed to jail for a term not exceeding three years, or until sentence be performed, and should also be fined in triple value of the articles stolen—one-third of such fine for the use of the territory and the other two-thirds to be paid to the party injured. If the defendant committed or attempted to commit any personal abuse, force or violence, or was armed with any dangerous weapon or weapons, so as to clearly indicate a violent intention, he forfeited all his estate and was subject to be committed to jail for a term not exceeding forty years; and if the death of any innocent person should ensue from any burglarious act, it was declared to be murder. Robbery was punished in the same manner as burglary.

Persons guilty of plots and unlawful assemblies were punished by being fined in the sum of sixteen dollars, and were required to find surety for their good behavior for the space of six months; and persons found guilty of obstructing any authorized persons in attempting to cause rioters or unlawful assemblies to disperse, were liable to be fined in a sum not exceeding three hundred dollars, or to be whipped with not exceeding thirty-nine lashes, and were also required to give surety for their good behavior.

Perjury and subornation of perjury were punished by a fine not exceeding sixty dollars, or by whipping with not exceeding thirty-nine stripes; and persons found guilty of those offenses were required to be set in the pillory for a space not exceeding two hours, and were ever after incapable of holding any office, or giving testimony, or being a juror.

Larceny was punished, for the first offense, by requiring the offender to restore to the owner the thing stolen and to pay to him the value thereof, or two-fold the value thereof if the thing stolen was not returned, and also by a fine not exceeding two-fold the value of the thing stolen or be whipped with not exceeding thirty-one stripes, at the discretion of the court. Upon a second conviction it was provided that restitution and payment shall be made to the owner as aforesaid, and the offender shall be whipped with not exceeding thirty-nine stripes, and in like manner upon every succeeding conviction; and in case such convict shall not have property wherewith to satisfy the sentence of the court, it shall be lawful for the sheriff, by direction of the court, to bind such person to labor, for any term not exceeding seven years, to any suitable person who will discharge such sentence.

For the offense of forgery it was enacted that every person, found guilty thereof, shall be fined in double the sum he shall thereby have defrauded or attempted to defraud another—one-half of which should be paid to the party injured or intended to be injured; and shall, moreover, forever after be rendered incapable of giving testimony, being a juror or holding any office, and shall be set in the pillory not exceeding the space of three hours.

Usurpation of office was punished by a fine of not exceeding one hundred dollars.

Assault and battery was punished by a fine of not exceeding one hundred dollars, and the court might also require the offender to enter into recognizance with surety for the peace and good behavior, for a term not exceeding one year.

All bonds, bills, deeds of sale, gifts, grants, or other conveyances, made with intent to deceive or defraud creditors, were declared to be null and void, and the person so offending was required to be fined in a sum not exceeding three hundred dollars and to pay double damages to the injured party.

For disobedience of children or servants to their parents or masters, upon complaint made, it was lawful for a justice of the peace to send the offender to jail or the house of correction, there to rêmain until he or she should humble himself to the parents' or master's satisfaction; and if any child or servant assaulted or struck his parent or master, two or more justices of the peace, upon conviction thereof, might cause the offender to be whipped with not exceeding ten stripes.

Persons obtaining goods by fraudulent pretences were subject to the same punishment as in cases of larceny.

Arson was punished with death by hanging.

Horsestealing was punished, for the first offense, by requiring the offender to pay the owner the value of the animal, and to receive not less than fifty nor more than two hundred stripes, and to stand committed to jail until such value, with the costs of prosecution, were paid. Upon the second conviction the offender had to suffer the pains of death.

For stealing a hog, shoat or pig, or marking the same with the intent of stealing, the offender was subject to pay a fine of not less than fifty nor more than one hundred dollars, and also receive on his bare back any number of lashes not exceeding thirty-nine nor less than twenty-five.

For altering and defacing marks and brands the offender was required to pay the sum of five dollars, over and above the value of the animal whose mark or brand was altered, and was also punished by whipping with forty lashes, well laid on, on his bare back; and for the second offense to pay the fine aforesaid, to stand in the pillory for two hours, and be branded in the left hand, with a red-hot iron, with the letter T.

To prevent killing cattle or hogs in the woods, the offender was required to show within three days the head and ears of such hog, and the hide with the ears on of such cattle as he may have killed, to a magistrate or two freeholders, under the penalty of ten dollars. Every person was required to mark or brand his hogs, cattle, etc., and to record the same with the clerk of the county court.

Maiming or disfiguring was punished by fine and imprisonment.

Rape was punished with death.

Sodomy was punished by fine, imprisonment, and by whipping with not less than one hundred nor more than five hundred stripes on the bare back.

Bigamy was punished by whipping on the bare back with not less than one hundred nor more than three hundred stripes, and by a fine of not less than one hundred nor more than five hundred dollars, to and for the use of the party injured, and imprisonment of not less than six nor more than twelve months, and disqualification for giving testimony or holding office.

For forcibly taking away any female, for the purpose of marrying her against her consent, the offender was declared guilty of felony. Stealing and marrying females under 14 years of age, was punished by fine and imprisonment.

Persons who were unable to pay their fines were required to be hired or sold, to any person who would pay the fine and costs, for such term as the court might think reasonable; and if the delinquent should abscond from the service of his master, he was liable, on conviction before a justice of the peace, to be whipped with thirty-nine lashes, and required to serve two days for every one so lost.

By an act for the prevention of vice and immorality, it was provided—

1. That any person found reveling, fighting or quarreling, doing or performing any worldly employment or business whatever (with some exception in favor of ferrymen) on the first day of the week, or who shall use or practice any unlawful game, sport or diversion, or shall be found hunting or shooting on said day, shall forfeit for every such offense a sum not exceeding two dollars nor less than fifty cents, to be levied by distress; and in case the fine could not be collected in that way, he was required to work on the highways for two days.

2. Any person, of the age of sixteen years and upwards, found guilty of profanely cursing, damning or swearing by the name of God, Christ Jesus or the Holy Ghost, was punished in like manner with Sabbath-breakers.

3. Swearing and disorderly behavior before a court of justice was punished with a fine of not less than five nor more than fifty dollars; before a judge, justice of the peace, or congregation assembled for Divine worship, with a fine of not less than three nor more than ten dollars.

4. Any person, of the age of sixteen years and upwards, found in the public highways, or in any public house of entertainment, intoxicated by drinking spirituous, vinous or other strong liquors, and making or exciting any noise, contention or disturbance, was imprisoned in the county jail for a term not exceeding forty-eight hours.

For a violation of the preceding sections, any judge or justice of the peace might proceed to try the offender in a summary way, and on failure to pay the fine and costs the judge or justice sentenced the offender to work on the public highways.

Cock-fighting, gambling or running horses in the public highways were punished by fine, and justices of the peace had jurisdiction over such offenses.

Keeping E. O. tables or other devices, in any place whatever, except in private houses for amusement in their families, was punished by a fine of fifty dollars.

Securities and contracts entered into for gaming were declared void, and money lost at gaming might be recovered back within thirty days.

If a person sent a challenge to fight or box at fisticuffs, or if, with intent to bring on a match at boxing, by words or gesture any person should provoke others to commit an affray, whether an affray ensues or not, the offender was fined in a sum not exceeding five dollars nor less than one dollar.

Duelling was punished. For sending, accepting or delivering a challenge to fight a duel, or consenting to be a second in any intended duel, the offender was subject to a fine or imprisonment.

Tearing down or defacing publications set up by authority, the offender was subject to be fined, and for failure to pay the fine was set in the pillory for three hours.

Lotteries were prohibited by requiring a forfeiture of the whole sum proposed to be raised or gained thereby.

Vagrants, and persons suspected of getting their support by gaming, were required to be hired out for a term not exceeding nine months; and if no person would hire the offender, or take him only by furnishing such diet and clothes as were necessary during his servitude, the vagrant was punished by whipping with not exceeding thirty-nine lashes.

In 1810, a law passed to suppress duelling, by enacting that if any person should be killed in a duel, the offender, his aiders, abetters and counselors, being connected thereof, should be guilty of murder; and for challenging or accepting a challenge to fight a duel, the offender was declared incapable of holding or being elected to any post of profit, trust or emolument under the government of the territory; and every person receiving any appointment to any office, either civil or military, in the territory, was required to take such an oath as is prescribed in our present State Constitution on the same subject. It was also declared, in this law, that persons leaving the territory for the purpose of eluding this law, should be punished in the same manner as if the offense had been committed in the territory.

The laws of the territory were very rigid in relation to the collection of debts. All the debtor's property, both personal and real, could be sold under execution; and if the land did not sell for want of bidders, the plaintiff had the right, at his option, to take it at its appraised value by twelve men. If there was not sufficient property, the body of the debtor could be taken and committed to the county jail, or to the prison bounds by giving security that he would not depart therefrom. Prison bounds were required to be laid off by the county courts, by metes and bounds, so as not to extend in any direction more than two hundred yards from the jail.

The laws for the collection of rents, and for the recovery of the possession of land, have not been materially changed by our present laws from what they were under the territorial government. Under the laws of the terrritory, property taken on the premises, let by execution, was liable to be applied, first, to the payment of the rent due; and no property except such as might be found on the premises, unless the tenant had clandestinely removed the same, could be taken by distress.

The law regulating elections provided that if any candidate, or other person for him, should attempt to obtain votes by bribery, or treating with meat or drink, the person so offending should be incapable of holding a seat in either branch of the Legislature for the space of two years next thereafter.

The road laws require that the supervisors should hire and employ a sufficient number of laborers to work upon, open and amend, clear and repair the roads in their township, and to take care that the same should be effectually opened, cleared and amended or repaired.

All male persons, of the age of twenty-one years and not exceeding fifty, who had resided for thirty days in any township, were liable to work for any number of days not exceeding twelve in each year.

The entire jurisdiction over ferries and roads was given to the county courts; and if the court thought a bridge to be of public utility, but too expensive to be borne by the district, they might make an allowance, for the purpose of building such bridge, out of the county treasury. Specific directions were given in the law for the opening and altering of private and public highways, and the mode pointed out for the assessment and payment of damages caused by roads passing through improvements.

Laws were passed at a very early period, similar to those now in force, in relation to the support of the poor; for the payment for improvements on lands claimed by persons who were evicted from land which they claimed by a title deduced from the record of some public office, without notice of any adverse claim; for the partition of land and assignment of dower; concerning the militia; and the regulation of grist mills and millers.

In 1814, an act passed to promote retaliation upon hostile Indians. It provided that if any Indians should make an incursion to our settlements, with hostile intentions, and shall commit any murder or depredation, and any citizen or ranger shall pursue and take prisoner or kill any Indian that may have so offended, such person shall be entitled to a reward of fifty dollars for each Indian so taken or killed; and rangers or other persons, engaged at the time in the defense of the frontier, shall be entitled to receive twenty-five dollars for every Indian so taken or killed. If any party of citizens, having first obtained permission of the commanding officer, should go into the territory of any hostile Indians, they shall be entitled to one hundred dollars for every warrior, squaw or child that may be taken prisoner or killed.

A law was also passed at this session prohibiting, under very severe penalties, any person from selling liquor or giving liquor to the Kaskaskia Indians, or trading without license with said Indians, and providing that if the offender was a negro slave or servant, should be punished with whipping on his bare back, unless the owner of such slave or servant, or some other person for him, should pay for each offense the sum of twenty dollars. A law had previously passed on the same subject, prohibiting the sale of intoxicating liquors to other Indians.

COUNTY LEVIES.

For the purpose of raising a county revenue by the county court, the following rate of taxation was prescribed by law:

On each horse, mare, mule or ass, of three years old and upwards, a sum not exceeding fifty cents.

On neat cattle, of three years old and upwards, a sum not exceeding ten cents per head.

On every stud horse of the above age, a sum not exceeding the rate for which he stands at the season.

On every bond-servant or slave, between the ages of sixteen and forty years, except such as the county court may exempt for infirmities, a sum not exceeding one dollar.

On every able-bodied single man, of the age of twenty-one years and upwards, who shall not have taxable property to the amount of two hundred dollars, a sum not exceeding one dollar nor less than fifty cents.

Town lots, out lots, houses in town, and mansion houses in the country, which shall be valued at two hundred dollars and upwards, wind and water mills, a sum not exceeding thirty cents on each hundred dollars of their appraised value.

On ferries, a sum not exceeding ten dollars for each year.

For the sale of any merchandize, other than the produce or manufacture of the territory, the owner had to procure a license from the sheriff, for which he was taxed at the rate of fifteen dollars per annum for each store. Two persons were appointed in each township to value the property required to be appraised.

To defray the expenses of the territorial government, a tax was levied and collected on land—which was divided into three classes:

On lands of the first class, which included all lands situated in the Wabash, Ohio and Mississippi river bottoms, the rate of taxation was one dollar on every hundred acres.

Lands of the second class included all the uplands, and were taxed at the rate of seventy-five cents on each one hundred acres; and all unlocated confirmed claims were taxed at the rate of thirty-seven and a half cents per hundred acres.

The sheriff was also required to collect from each owner of a billiard table an annual tax of forty dollars.

A list showing the amount of tax due by each person, and also one showing the amount of tax collected by the collector of each tax-payer in his county, were required to be posted up at the door of the clerk's office, in order that each individual might know the amount of his tax, and also whether the same had been paid by the collector.

The entire jurisdiction in relation to the settlement of the estate of deceased persons, the appointment of guardians, etc., was conferred on the county court; but the clerks might take proof of bills and testaments and grant letters testamentary and administration, subject to be repealed by the court.

In 1816 an act passed, amendatory of the "act to encourage the killing of wolves," under which act, as amended, any person was entitled to two dollars for every wolf he killed.

At this session an act passed to prevent attorneys-at-law, residing in the State of Indiana, from practicing in any of the courts of the territory. The reason for the passage is given in the preamble, as follows: "Whereas, by a law now in force in the State of Indiana, persons who do not reside therein are not permitted to practice in the courts of the said State; and whereas that restriction is illiberal, unjust, and contrary to those principles of liberality and reciprocity by which each and every state or territory should be governed; therefore," etc. The law was to continue in force until the laws of the State of Indiana, referred to, should be repealed, and no longer.

At this session no laws of a general nature passed, with the exception heretofore alluded to in relation to the division of the territory into circuits; a law for the incorporation of the Bank of Illinois; and a law making it the duty of the county court to appoint a Commissioner in each township to assess the property therein, abolishing the office of county treasurer, and requiring the sheriff to collect the revenue and to pay out the same on the order of the county court.

The Bank of Illinois was a private institution, was located at Shawneetown, and was so well managed that neither the Government nor any one else lost by it.

In consequence of the scarcity of gold and silver coin, the Legislature also passed, at this session, laws postponing the collection of debts unless the debtor would receive the bank-notes of any of the chartered Banks of

Cincinnati and Chilicothe, in the State of Ohio, and of any of the Banks of the States of Tennessee and Kentucky, and of the Banks of Vincennes, of Missouri, of St. Louis, and of Illinois.

At the next session of the Legislature, commencing in December, 1817, acts were passed incorporating companies for improving the navigation of the Little Wabash River; an act to incorporate medical societies, for the purpose of regulating the practice of physic and surgery in the territory, (under which act no person was permitted to practice medicine or surgery, without obtaining a diploma or license from this society); acts authorizing the erection of mill-dams and a fishery on the Kaskaskia River; an act directing the mode of perpetuating testimony; an act declaring the Big Muddy a navigable stream; acts incorporating the Banks of Edwardsville and Kaskaskia, and the town of Kaskaskia; an act incorporating the stockholders of the Illinois Navigation Company; and an act incorporating the City and Bank of Cairo.

The following is the preamble to the act incorporating the Illinois Navigation Company: "Whereas Henry Bechtle and his associates, citizens of the United States of America, and proprietors of the town of America, in the county of Johnson, and territory of Illinois, purpose to improve the navigation of the waters near the mouth of the Ohio River, in said territory, by cutting canals, erecting locks, and other works, as to them shall seem necessary. And whereas it is proper and advisable to encourage so laudable an undertaking. Therefore—Be it enacted," etc.

This act conferred upon said company authority to cut any canal from the Mississippi to or near the said town of America, on the Ohio River, and erect such locks and otherwise improve as to them shall seem advisable and necessary to complete the objects of said corporation, to build wharves and to collect tolls under certain restrictions, etc.

The following is taken from the preamble of the act to incorporate the City and Bank of Cairo: "And whereas the said proprietors represent that there is, in their opinion, no position in the whole of the extent of these Western States better calculated, as it respects commercial advantages and local supply, for a great and important city, than that afforded by the junction of these two great highways—the Mississippi and Ohio Rivers; but that nature, having denied to the extreme point formed by their union a sufficient degree of elevation to protect the improvements made thereon from the ordinary inundations of the adjacent waters, such elevation is to be found only upon the tract above mentioned (the present site of Cairo), so that improvements made and located thereon may be deemed perfectly and absolutely secure from all such ordinary inundations, and liable to injury only from the concurrence of unusually high and simultaneous inundations in both of said rivers—an event which is alleged but rarely happens, and the injurious consequences of which it is considered practicable, by proper embankments, wholly and effectually and permanently to obviate. And whereas there is no doubt but a city, erected at or as near as is practicable to the junction of the Ohio and Mississippi Rivers—provided it be thus secured by sufficient embankments, or in such other way as experience may prove most efficacious for that purpose, from every such extraordinary inundation—must necessarily became a place of vast consequence to the prosperity of this growing Territory, and in fact to that of the greater part of the inhabitants of these Western States. And whereas the above-named persons are desirous of erecting such city, under the sanction and patronage of the Legislature of this Territory, and also of providing for the security and prosperity of the same, and to that end propose to appropriate the one-third of all the moneys arising from the sale and disposition of the lots into which the same may be surveyed, as a fund for the construction and preservation of such dykes, levees and other embankments as may be necessary to render the same perfectly secure—and also, if such fund shall be deemed sufficient thereto, for the erection of public edifices and such other improvements in the said city as may be from time to time considered expedient and practicable, and to appropriate the other two-thirds parts of the said purchase moneys to the operation of banking. And whereas, etc.—Be it enacted," etc.

The proprietors of said city were John G. Comyges, Thomas H. Harris, Charles Slade (who was afterwards a member of Congress from the State), Governor Bond, Michael Jones, Warren Brown, Edward Humphries, and Charles W. Hunter. It was provided that there should be not less than two thousand lots, each lot being not less than sixty-six by one hundred and twenty feet, and the streets to be not less than eighty feet wide, and to run as nearly as may be at right angles to each other; and that the price of the lots should be fixed and limited at one hundred and fifty dollars each, and that the moneys arising from the sale thereof should be appropriated as follows: Two-thirds parts thereof—that is to say, the sum of one hundred dollars on each and every lot—shall constitute the capital stock of the Bank, which capital stock should be divided into twice as many shares as there were lots, one of which shares should belong to the purchasers of the lots in proportion of one share to each lot, and the remaining shares to the proprietors; and that the remaining one-third part of the purchase money should constitute a fund, to be exclusively appropriated to the security and improvement of said city.

By the practice act any one could, by himself or agent, sue out a writ, by filing with the clerk a declaration, or petition, or other statement, in writing, containing the true nature of his, her or their demand or complaint, accompanied with a copy of such writing or account.

It was also provided, in 1812, that an action on the case might be brought for any fraud whatsoever, and that the plaintiff in any such suit might file written interrogatories, which the defendant was bound to answer, in writing, at the time of filing his plea; and the defendant, in all cases wherein he suggested fraud in the demand of the plaintiff, had also the right to file in like manner written interrogatories, which the plaintiff was required to answer and file with his replication.

No appeal could be taken from an inferior court to the supreme court, unless the judgment or decree was final, and amounted, exclusive of costs, to fifty dollars, or relate to a franchise or freehold.

In 1818, a law passed for the establishment of circuit courts, dividing the State into two circuits, and conferring upon the courts all the jurisdiction which had previously been conferred on the supreme or general court, with the exception of its appellate jurisdiction.

The county court system was also changed, by conferring all its jurisdiction on a court consisting of all the magistrates of the county, any three of whom could constitute a quorum to do business.

A very important act, in relation to the sale of real estate, also passed at this session, and the adoption of its principles are well worthy of the consideration of our legislators of the present time; and so thoroughly convinced am I of the justice and importance of its provisions, that I can not pass it by without further notice. I am convinced that if such a law had been in force, it would have saved much litigation. It provided that whenever the sheriff shall levy upon lands of the defendant, and any other person should claim the same, it should be the duty of the sheriff to return the execution to the next circuit court, in order that there might be a fair trial of the right of property. This act also provided for the sale of the equitable interest of the defendant in lands purchased from the United States, and on which part of the purchase money was still due.

The principle might be extended so as to allow an injunction against the sale of property in cases where it is now denied, because a party may have his remedy at law after a void sale. At the first session of the Legislature after the admission of the State into the Union, the Legislature re-adopted, with but few exceptions, the acts at that time in force, adapting them to the provisions of the State Constitution; and, as a system, the laws thus modified continued, with but few alterations, until the time which I propose to close the result of my investigations. The judiciary system in all its ramifications was not changed in its organization or details. The supreme judges were elected in the manner pointed out in the Constitution, and the judges were required to discharge the duty of holding circuit courts in their respective circuits. The revenue laws were changed so as to provide that the lands of non-residents and two-thirds of the tax on lands of residents, together with the tax on bank-stock, should be paid into the state treasury, and that the one-third of the tax on lands of residents should be paid into the county treasury.

Lands, without regard to their locality, were divided into three classes. Those of the first class were valued at $4 per acre; of the second class, at $3 per acre; and those of the third class, at $2 per acre. Before the expiration of Gov. Edwards' term as Governor of the State, all the taxes of the residents' lands were paid into the county treasury, and the State government was supported from the revenue derived from the property of non-residents.

In the years 1819 and 1821, a number of acts passed for the incorporation of academies and towns, and lotteries were authorized for the purpose of raising funds to drain the bottom lands, and the improvement of the navigation of the rivers. Besides a general law for the incorporation of towns, a law passed in 1821 including in one charter such as desired special provisions not contained in the general act.

Soon after the adoption of the Constitution, Commissioners were appointed to select a site for the State government. They selected the site on which Vandalia was located, and the seat of government was removed in 1819. The land belonged to the State, and lots were sold, the proceeds of which were applied to the erection of the public buildings.

At the session of 1822, a law was passed authorizing the Governor to appoint Commissioners, to act in conjunction with Commissioners on the part of the State of Indiana, to report on the practicability and expediency of improving the navigation of the Wabash River, from the point where the eastern boundary of the State leaves the river to its junction with the Ohio River. An act also passed, at this session, entitled "An act to provide for the improvement of the Internal Navigation of this State," appointing Emanuel J. West, Erastus Brown, Theophilus W. Smith, Thomas Sloo, Jr., and Samuel Alexander, Commissioners, to consider, devise and adopt such measures as may be requisite to effect the communication, by canal and locks, between the navigable waters of the Illinois River and Lake Michigan, to determine the most eligible route for the canal, to cause all necessary surveys and levels to be taken, and accurate maps, field books and drafts thereof to be made, and to adopt and recommend plans for the construction of the canal, to make estimates of the expense, and to make a full report of all their proceedings to the next General Assembly. This act, which passed February 14th, 1823, also appropriated six thousand dollars to defray the expenses of the Commission. It was also made the duty of the Commissioners to recommend to the Governors of Ohio and Indiana and the Legislatures of those States, the importance of adopting measures to connect the waters of the Wabash and Maumee Rivers. The importance of these great works had, at a very early period, engaged the attention of all our prominent men. Gov. Bond and Gov. Coles had both urged their importance in their several messages to the Legislature. Congress had, about this time, passed an act granting the right of way over the public lands for its construction, but no measures were taken by the State for its commencement, until after the report of the Commissioners was laid before the Legislature.

At the subsequent session of the Legislature a law was passed, on January 17, 1825, incorporating the "Illinois and Michigan Canal Association," with full powers for the construction of the Canal. It was also provided, in the 7th section of the charter, that "all cessions, grants and transfers made or that may hereafter be made, by the Government of the United States, for the purpose of promoting the completion of the canal, shall pass and vest in said corporation." Owing to the passage of this law, the State came very near losing the benefit of a grant of lands from Congress; and Mr. Cook, who was then our only member of Congress, not only found it necessary to address a long communication on the subject to his constituents, but he deemed it of importance to return to the State and use his influence with the members of the Legislature to have the law, making this grant to a company, repealed. He contended that as nothing had been done under the act of incorporation, there was no vested right which would prevent its repeal. The corporators afterwards voluntarily surrendered their charter and the act was repealed.

It is remarkable that our members of Congress found it necessary to have a law repealed making a similar grant of whatever public lands Congress might grant to the State, for the purpose of making the Illinois Central Railroad, to a company consisting of D. B. Holbrook & Co., who had obtained a charter for the construction of the Central railroad. This obstacle to the passage of an act of Congress, making a grant of lands to the State, having been removed, and the Commissioners having reported the practicability and expediency of the work, the Legislature, at its special session in 1826, adopted the following memorial to Congress:

The memorial of the General Assembly of the State of Illinois respectfully represents: That the construction of a canal, uniting the waters of Lake Michigan with the Illinois River, will form an important addition to the great connecting links in the chain of internal navigation, which will effectually secure the indissoluble union of the confederate members of this great and powerful Republic. By the completion of this great and valuable work, the connection between the North and South, the East and the West, would be strengthened by the ties of commercial intercourse and social neighborhood, and the union of the States bid defiance to internal commotion, sectional jealousy, and foreign invasion. All the States of the Union would then feel the most powerful motives to resist every attempt at dissolution. To effect so great and desirable an object your memorialists believe to be of sufficient importance to engage the attention and awaken the munificent patronage of a Government whose principle of action is the promotion of the general welfare. Your memorialists are sensibly alive to the spirit of improvement, that manifests itself in almost every section of our extensive country, and would fain lend a helping hand in so great and good a cause; their situation, however, forbids their doing much, without the aid of the Federal Government—into whose treasury almost all the funds, whether brought hither by immigrants, or earned by the industry of their citizens, are paid, for the purchase of the public lands. While this state of things shall continue, and the money thus paid into the treasury of the Union is taken out of our State, our people will not be able to engage in the glorious work of improving our common country. Ought the people of this State stand by, with folded arms, and behold the great work of internal improvement progress in other States, without making an effort to improve their own condition, and at the same time advance the interest of our beloved country? A condition thus paralyzed is at war, not only with our interests, but with the best feelings of our hearts. Did this State possess the public domain lying within its bounds, as is the case with the older members of this confederacy, your memorialists would not appear before your honorable body to solicit aid in this important work. If, as your memorialists believe, the construction of the canal would be highly beneficial to the Union at large—if the receipts into the treasury of the United States would be augmented by the increased sales of the public lands, and if the interests of the State would be also advanced thereby, is it unreasonable to apply to a paternal government for assistance in the promotion of such beneficial ends? It is unnecessary for your memorialists to enlarge on the great advantages of this canal to the Union, in the facilities to be afforded in the event of a war either with the Indian tribes inhabiting our frontier, or the British nation. Your honorable body is aware that this State is situated on the borders of an Indian country, filled with numerous and powerful tribes of the sons of the forest. If our country should be again engaged in war, the saving of expense in the transportation of the munitions of war would alone defray the expense of the contemplated canal, and justify the United States in making a liberal appropriation for its construction. Your memorialists do not, however, ask your honorable body to appropriate money out of the treasury to aid them in this work. They only ask for a tract of land, through which the contemplated canal may pass, and which for a series of years will be wholly unproductive to the Government, unless the canal shall be commenced under auspices favorable to its construction—in which event all the land in its vicinity would immediately become available to the United States. Your memorialists sincerely believe that a liberal appropriation of land for this object would, even in a pecuniary point of view, be of immense importance to the treasury of the Union. The public lands in the vicinity would not only sell, but at a considerable advance of the minimum price. Should this opinion be correct, (and does not experience justify it?) the United States would be gainer by the proposed donation to the State. Your memorialists further state, that, at their last session, they passed an act of incorporation, upon very liberal terms, authorizing a company to construct the projected canal; but the remoteness of the country from the residence of capitalists has prevented them from engaging in the work. At their present session your memorialists have repealed the charter, and their only hope of soon beginning the work depends upon the liberality of your honorable body. Your memorialists have caused the route to be explored, and estimates to be made of the probable expense of the work, from which it appears that the cost of constructing the canal will not be less than $600,000, and may possibly amount to $700,000. To the end, therefore, that your memorialists may be enabled to commence and complete this great work, we pray your honorable body to grant to this State the respective townships of land through which the contemplated canal may pass—the avails of which to be appropriated exclusively to the construction of said canal, upon such terms and conditions as to your honorable body may seem proper.

Gov. Edwards, in one of his communications to the Legislature of Illinois, says: "In 1816, a tract of land bounded on Lake Michigan, including Chicago, and extending to the Illinois River, was obtained from the Indians, for the purpose of opening a canal communication between the lake and the river. Having been one of the Commissioners who treated for this land, I personally know that the Indians were induced to believe that the opening of the canal would be very advantageous to them, and that, under authorized expectations that this would be done, they ceded the land for a trifle. Good faith, therefore, towards these Indians, as well as the concurring interest of the State and of the Union, seems to require that the execution of this truly national object should not be unnecessarily delayed, and nothing is more reasonable than that the expense should be defrayed out of the proceeds of the very property which was so ceded for the express purpose of having it done."

In 1817, Major Long made a report on the subject of a canal to connect the waters of Lake Michigan with the Illinois River, which was printed by order of Congress. [See Vol. 2, No 17, of the Reports of the session of —— Congress.] He says: "A canal, uniting the waters of the Illinois River with those of Lake Michigan, may be considered the first in importance of any in this quarter of the country, and at the same time the construction would be attended with very little expense compared with the magnitude of the object."

It will be seen from the same document that another favorable report was made by Richard Graham and Chief Justice Phillips, of the State of Illinois. Mr. Calhoun, the Secretary of War, recommended, in 1819, in a report to Congress, the attention of the Government to this point as being important in a military point of view. [See Vol. 4, Pub. Doc., 2d session, 15th Congress.]

In 1820, a law was passed by Congress, authorizing the State to open a canal through the public lands. The State appointed Commissioners to explore the route and prepare the necessary surveys and estimates, preparatory to its execution, but being unable, out of its own resources, to defray the expense of the undertaking, it was abandoned until some time after Congress made the grant of land for the purpose of its construction.

In 1825, a committee of Congress reported in its favor, and among other reasons urged "that, in a political point of view, its importance will be found not less imposing than in either of those in which it has already been viewed. In uniting and drawing together the interests of the remote extremities of the Eastern, the Southern, and the Western sections of our

Union, no work of the same magnitude, it is believed, can be more effectual. The geographical position of Illinois and Missouri—the two States particularly interested in it—is such, that they will, under the advantages of this communication, have a common and almost equal interest in preserving their connection with the North and the South. Their trade will ultimately flow through the lakes and the Mississippi, and the advantages of a choice of market will be so important to them, that they must ever be unwilling to surrender it. By a reference to the map of our country, it will be seen that these States will have it in their power at all times, in the event, should it unfortunately ever occur, of any internal commotion, to command the waters of the Ohio and Mississippi. From their commanding position, therefore, as well as from their capacity to sustain a dense, and it must mainly be a free population, they will always hold the balance of power in deciding every effort that may be made to separate the West from either or both of the great geographical divisions of the Union; and, if from no other cause, their interests will direct their exertion of that power in favor of the Union. Nor is the interest of these States in preserving a free outlet for their commerce, both through the lake and the Mississippi—the latter of which opens to them the New Orleans, the West India and South American markets—stronger than must be that of the North and South in being united with them."

Daniel P. Cook was the author of this report.

Gov. Edwards, in a letter in 1825, to Mr. Clay, thus alludes to the canal: "A favorite object, and indeed, a political hobby, that supercedes all others, in this State and Missouri, is a canal to connect Lake Michigan and the Illinois River. Nothing could sustain the administration or its friends in these two States so effectually as its countenancing this measure. Connecting the waters of Lake Erie and the Wabash, is also a desirable object in a part of the State of Indiana. Ohio is executing a similar project. Now, do I venture too far that it might be very judicious in the President, without descending to any particular case, to introduce in his message to Congress some sentiment favorable to the connection of our great lakes with the Atlantic and Western waters? This might probably satisfy the friends of these different projects. I know it would contribute greatly to the support of the administration."

In an address of Mr. Cook to the people of the State of Illinois, dated October 28th, 1825, he says: "But this is a work in which the nation is interested and which the General Government should, therefore, aid in executing. As a ligament to bind the Union together, no work of the same magnitude can be more useful. Occupying, as Illinois and Missouri do, a central position in the great semi-circle of States on the North and West, and commanding, as they do, the commerce of the three great rivers of the West, the Ohio, Mississippi and Missouri, they may well be called the keystone of the widely projected arch. From New York to Louisiana, following the frontier curve of that portion of the Union, in the event of any political commotion or attempt at separation, the influence of these States would, ere long, be sensibly felt, and would even decide the contest. And their interest will be so happily balanced, by their desire for a free outlet through both the Mississippi and the lakes, that so long as commercial advantage continues to influence the policy of the States, they must and will decide against disunion. The friends of the Union, therefore, have a strong interest in this communication."

Among other inducements to assist in this work, Mr. Cook urged that there was no position combining greater advantages for an extensive National Armory than at the rapids, either on the Illinois or Fox Rivers—both points being within a few miles of the place where the canal must have its southern termination. "In the midst of exhaustless beds of stone coal, and surrounded by a country of almost unparalleled fertility as well as great salubrity, with a water-power adequate to all necessary purposes in the manufacture of arms, as well as fabrics for domestic purposes, I believe those points are destined to become the seat of as extensive manufacturing establishments as any in the whole Western country. And from their local position, with a view to convenience in distributing arms and clothing to a large portion of our frontier posts, no place can be more desirable for such establishments."

Congress, on the 2d of March, 1827, made the grant of lands to the State "for the purpose of aiding her in opening a canal to connect the waters of the Illinois River with those of Lake Michigan," and the Legislature passed a law, on the 22d of January, 1829, for the appointment of three Commissioners, whose duty it was "to consider, devise and adopt such measures as may be required to facilitate and effect" the construction of the canal. It was made their duty to fix the route of the canal; to select the alternate sections of land granted to the State by Congress; to cause the surveys and levels to be taken, and accurate drafts, field-books and maps thereof to be made; and as soon as they could command sufficient funds, and should deem it expedient, to commence the work. They had power to lay out towns, and to dispose of the lands and lots upon the same terms and conditions as the lands of the United States were sold, and it was provided that the Commissioners might sue and be sued in the name of "The Board of Commissioners of the Illinois and Michigan Canal," with full power "to enter, take and use any lands, waters and streams necessary for the prosecution of the work." The canal was required to be forty feet in width at the summit water-line, twenty-eight feet wide at the bottom, and of sufficient depth to contain at least four feet of water, and so constructed as to insure a safe and convenient navigation for boats of at least seventy-five feet long, thirteen feet six inches wide, and drawing three feet of water. Although this act was subsequently amended, and that too before any sales of any consequence had been made, as in express terms to reserve the right of the State, in all sales of lands, to take, "free from any cost, charge or liability whatever," any stone, timber, ground, water, or other material, necessary for the construction of the canal, and although Congress had expressly granted to the State the right of way, thousands of dollars were claimed and paid as damages for what was so expressly reserved.

Dr. Gershom Jayne of Springfield, Edmund Roberts, then of Kaskaskia, and Charles Dunn of Pope county, but who was afterwards one of the United States Judges in Wisconsin, were the first Commissioners. They selected the lands, surveyed the route of the canal, laid out the principal towns, and performed every other act that was necessary for the commencement of this great and important work—the history of which I profess to be familiar with from its commencement up to the present time; but, having only intended to bring down the history of the legislation of the State to the close of Gov. Edwards' administration, I must reserve many important facts for some future occasion.

On the 27th March, 1819, an act passed for the incorporation of the subscribers to the State Bank of Illinois. The law was repealed, and another act passed in 1821 establishing the State Bank of Illinois—the capital stock of which was not to exceed the sum of five hundred thousand dollars, to be owned exclusively by the State. The notes or bills of the bank provided, on their face, for interest at the rate of two per centum per annum, and loans were made chiefly on real estate security, at the rate of six per cent. interest. The only fund for the redemption of the bank notes was the land, town lots, and other property belonging to the State, and the funds and the resources which then or thereafter might become payable to the State. The directors were to be appointed by the Legislature. For a more particular history of this bank—which in a very short time exploded, involving in its winding up a great loss to the State—the reader is referred to Gov. Edwards' speeches and messages to the Legislature. The law was declared to be in violation of the Constitution of the United States, which prohibited a State from the emission of bills of credit, and many of the debtors took advantage of this decision to avoid the payment of their just debts. For further information in relation to the finances of the State from that time until the year 1830, the reader is also referred to the communications from Gov. Edwards.

Resolutions were passed at this session requesting our Senators and Representatives in Congress to use their exertions to have the national road extended from Wheeling through the seats of government of Ohio, Indiana and Illinois; thence to St. Charles on the nearest and best route. And, also, to use their exertions to secure a grant of land, for the opening and improving the same, to the extent of the unappropriated sections through which the road would pass.

At the subsequent session resolutions passed approving of the proposed amendment to the Constitution of the United States, by the State of Pennsylvania, "that Congress should pass no law to incorporate any bank or moneyed institution, except within the District of Columbia;" of the proposed amendment by Vermont in favor of single districts for the election of members of Congress and electors of President; and, also, a resolution asking the State of Kentucky to grant to the State concurrent jurisdiction on the River Ohio.

By the seventh section of an act supplemental to the act establishing the State Bank, Auditor's warrants were made receivable in payment of bank debts. These warrants having been issued for three times the amount for which they were paid out, bank debtors could get off by the payment of one-third of their debts, and the other two thirds were of course taken from the pockets of the people, who had nothing to do with the bank. For the purpose of relieving bank debtors, an act was also passed declaring that no other real or personal estate should, in a proceeding to foreclose the mortgage, be liable to satisfy a debt secured by mortgage, but the mortgaged premises. Previous to the passage of this law, in such cases a general judgment was rendered, and if the mortgaged premises were not sufficient to satisfy the debt, execution could he issued and any other property sold for the payment of the balance; and it does seem to me that there cannot be any good reason, especially in cases where there has been personal service, in requiring the expense of an additional suit in such cases.

In consequence of the depreciation of the paper of the State Bank, in which the State officers received their salaries, an act was passed, at the session of 1822, authorizing the Auditor to issue his warrant in their favor for a sum, to each, not exceeding fifty per centum upon their established salaries; and the appropriation bill appropriated, to be paid to the Speakers of the House and Senate, the sum of nine dollars per day, and to each member such sum as he should designate, by writing the same on a piece of paper, he was willing to receive per day for his services, not exceeding seven dollars per day. No other measures of importance were passed at this session, except resolutions declaring: 1. That the appropriations made by Congress to certain States, in the South and West, of lands lying within said States, for the purposes of education, were made for National and not for State purposes. 2. That the public lands do not form a fund out of which appropriations may be made, for the use of schools, to any State other than such wherein said lands lie and are offered for sale, except upon a good and valuable consideration given therefor. 3. That it would be derogatory to State sovereignty, and tend to disturb the harmony and peace of the Union, to give one State jurisdiction over or a right of property to lands lying within another State, without the consent of the State in which the same might lie.

In February, 1823, an act passed for the election, by the Legislature, of a judge of probate in each county, and conferring upon the judges the same jurisdiction, in their respective counties, as the judges had who were elected under the act which had previously passed for the establishment of courts of probate.

At the regular session in December, 1822, the circuit court system was established, but it was repealed at the next session, and the supreme judges continued to discharge the duties of holding circuit courts, except in one circuit in the military district, of which the Hon. R. M. Young was elected judge.

In January, 1825, the revenue law was so amended as to authorize the lands of residents to be sold by the Auditor for taxes. Residents were required to pay their taxes annually, while for some reason non-residents were not compelled to pay their's oftener than once in two years. The lands in the military district were to be sold in January, 1826, and every two years thereafter; and those belonging to non-residents, in other portions of the State, were to be sold in January, 1827, and every two years thereafter.

The salt springs within the State, and the lands which had been reserved for the same, were granted to the State on its admission into the Union, on the condition, however, that the State should never sell nor lease the same for a longer period than ten years.

The U. S. Government had realized a considerable sum, annually, from leasing the salt works in Gallatin county, and it also appears, from the reports of the State Treasurer, that the State had also derived a considerable amount of revenue from the same source.

An act was passed, in 1827, appointing Commissioners to dispose of thirty thousand acres of the least valuable of the salt lands, provided that Congress would consent to their sale; and also, to designate, at each situation suitable for water-works, within the reserve, twelve acres of land, and so much of the ripple and water-course and the banks thereof as may be necessary for the erection of dams and water-works—to be constructed so as to promote, but not obstruct, the navigation of the Saline creek. The proceeds arising from the sale of the site for the water-works were to be applied to the improvement of the navigation of the Saline creek, the improvement of the road across the Maple swamp between Equality and Carlyle, and to the erection of a bridge across Eagle creek on the road from

Equality to Ford's ferry, on the Ohio River. One-half the proceeds arising from the sale of the thirty thousand acres were appropriated for the erection of a penitentiary at Alton, one-fourth to improve the navigation of the Saline creek, the improvement of the road across the Maple swamp and the erection of the bridge across Eagle creek, and one-fourth to improve the navigation of the Little Wabash River by canaling around Robinson's mill-dam, in White county, and to remove other obstructions in said river—provided, that neither of the two last appropriations should exceed five thousand dollars.

By the same act Shadrach Bond, William P. McKee and Gershom Jayne were appointed Commissioners to select a site for a penitentiary, on the Mississippi, at or near Alton.

Provision was also made for selling ten thousand acres of the Vermilion saline reserve, and to apply the proceeds to the improvement of the navigation of the Great Wabash River. Appropriations were also made, out of the proceeds from the sale of these lands, to the improvement of the Big Muddy River, and the building of a bridge in Pope county.

At the subsequent session additional appropriations were made, out of the same proceeds, for local purposes in a number of other counties in the State, among which one thousand dollars was for the improvement of the Sangamon River, and two thousand dollars for the improvement of the Kaskaskia River.

Congress, in the meantime, had assented to the sale by the State.

CHAPTER X.

Slavery—Gov. Edwards' Views on the Slavery Question—The Attempt to Introduce Slavery into the State—Education—Proprietors of Upper Alton the first to establish Free Schools—State Laws on the subject of Schools—Gov. Edwards' Speeches during his Canvass for Governor of the State.

Notwithstanding the sixth article of the ordinance of 1787 provided, that "there shall be neither slavery nor involuntary servitude in the said territory, otherwise than for the punishment of crimes, whereof the party shall have been duly convicted," an act was passed by the Legislature of the Indiana territory, on September 17, 1807, which was continued in force in the Illinois territory, authorizing the owner of any negroes above the age of fifteen years to bring them into the State, and to have them bound to service for such number of years as might be agreed upon between the negro and his master. The master was required to take his negro before the clerk of the court of common pleas, and to have him indentured and registered within thirty days after bringing him into the State; and if the negro would not consent, sixty days more was allowed the master to take him back into any State where slavery was allowed.

By another section of this law any person could bring negroes under the age of fifteen years, and hold them to service or labor—the males until they arrived at the age of thirty-five, and females until they arrived at the age of thirty-two years.

It was also provided, by this law, that the children, born in this territory, of a parent of color owing service by indenture, shall serve the master or mistress—the male until the age of thirty years, and the female until the age of twenty-eight years.

Another act was passed, in 1814, providing that slaves might, with the consent of their masters, voluntarily hire themselves within the territory, for any term not exceeding twelve months; and that his continuance in the territory according to such hiring should not operate in any way whatever to injure the right of property in the master in and to the services of such slave.

This last act was accompanied by the following preamble: "Whereas the erection of mills and other valuable improvements in this territory cannot be made from the want of laborers; and whereas, also, experience has proved that the manufacture of salt, in particular, at the United States saline, cannot be successfully carried on by white laborers; and it being the interests of every description of inhabitants to afford every facility to the most extensive manufacture of that article, so necessary to them all—as the most natural means of obtaining a certainty of the necessary supplies thereof, at the lowest prices," etc.

On the 20th December, 1813, an act also passed to prevent the migration of free negroes into the territory. This act provided that if any such negro should not leave the territory after fifteen days' notice, he should be whipped on his bare back not exceeding thirty-nine nor less than twenty-five stripes.

It was also provided that free negroes, then in the territory, should register themselves and their children with the clerk of the county court, on the failure of which they were subjected to severe penalties.

There was another class of colored persons who were held and recognized as slaves, both under the Territorial and State governments, until 1847. These were held by the French and others, previous to the adoption of the ordinance of 1787, and the following are the reasons for contending that such persons and their posterity were bound to perpetual servitude:

1. It was contended that, under the Governments of France, England and Virginia, slavery was permitted; that the then inhabitants of the country lawfully acquired and held slaves; and that each of the governments, in surrendering the rights of the soil and jurisdiction of the country, respectively, made ample provision for the protection of the inhabitants in the enjoyment of all their property, of which slaves constituted a large and valued portion.

2. After the conquest of the country by Gen. George R. Clark, the jurisdiction of Virginia was, by act of their Assembly, extended over it, and afforded as much protection to this description of property as any other, until the first of March, 1784, at which time Virginia ceded its right to the soil and jurisdiction of the country to the United States, upon the following, among other conditions, viz: that the French and Canadian inhabitants and other settlers, etc., "should have their possessions and titles confirmed to them, and be protected in the enjoyment of their rights, and of which rights that to hold their slaves was as perfect, according to all existing laws, as to hold any other species of property."

3. By the ordinance of Congress, passed the 23d of December, 1784, the existence of slavery within the ceded territory is impliedly acknowledged by the repeated mention of *free* males of full age being entitled to certain privileges therein mentioned; and this ordinance, so far from imposing

any restriction as to slavery, actually gave to the free male settlers the right "to adopt the laws of any one of the original States," and of course to sanction slavery (if it had not previously existed) as far as it was then sanctioned by the laws of any State in the Union. In this situation things continued under the Government of the United States until the 13th day of July, 1787, a period of about three years, when the last ordinance was passed.

4. As slavery existed under the Governments of France, England and Virginia, if not expressly authorized by Congress, until the last mentioned period, the right to this species of property was as perfect within the ceded territory as in "any one of the original States," and for any violation of this right, the settlers, up to that period, were as much entitled to an action of *detinue*, or for damages, as if they had resided in "any one of the original States."

5. Congress, in 1784, and 1785, had refused to prohibit slavery in the territories.

6. Slaves, therefore, were property, and to hold them as such was a legal right, secured by the existing laws, with adequate remedy for its privation at the date and for three years after the compact between Virginia and the United States, and of course was among those rights which, according to one of the express conditions of the deed of cession, the United States became bound to protect the French and Canadian inhabitants and other settlers "in the free enjoyment of"—a condition which Congress, even, with far less limited powers, could not violate.

7. But Congress has not violated this condition by the ordinance of 1787, and if not, all the rights, of whatever character they may be, which previously existed, are unaffected by that instrument. Independently of the phrases "free males of full age," so frequently used in it, and so clearly implying a knowledge of the existence of other males of full age, who were not free, it cannot be supposed and no lawyer will assume that Congress was ignorant of the fact that slaves were lawfully held by the settlers of the ceded territory at the date of the ordinance, and that, being so held, they were emphatically property.

Taking it, then, for granted that Congress understood the state of the facts on which they were legislating, and the evident meaning of their own language, it will be seen that, instead of violating any of the conditions in relation to the inhabitants of the ceded territory, to which the United States had bound themselves, that body intended faithfully to fulfil them. The very first section of the ordinance embraces all the property, both real and personal, (not excepting and of course including slaves which those inhabitants possessed) and prescribes the manner in which both descriptions might be disposed of—thereby recognizing not only the right to hold, but to dispose of the very property in question.

Besides other recognitions of the rights of those inhabitants, and with a view to protect them in the enjoyment thereof, according both to the obligations of the compact and the principles of justice, it is expressly declared in the first of the articles—made unalterable except by common consent—that no man shall be deprived of his property, but by the judgment of his peers or the law of the land; and that it shall not be taken away from him, even for the common preservation, without full compensation being made for the same. Slaves were, at that time, property, to which the ordinance referred, and on which it must be considered as intended to operate as much as upon any other property whatever, since no discrimination was made. As, then, this property has neither been taken away, nor paid for, in the manner prescribed by the article last referred to, all right to it that ever existed must still remain.

What, then, is the meaning of the article which declares that "there shall be neither slavery nor involuntary servitude" in the said territory? Presuming that it is an acknowledged rule of construing all laws, that effect shall, if possible, be given to every part thereof—a rule which more emphatically applies to constitutions, or other written instruments, intended to prescribe the general principles on which government is to be administered—it would seem that the article should receive a construction consistent with those previously noticed, and, particularly, since it cannot be supposed that the United States in Congress assembled intended to violate the compact, or to do themselves or to permit others to do that which they declared should not be done. Adopting this rule of construction the conclusion is irresistible, that while Congress intended to protect the inhabitants of the territory in the enjoyment of their rights to their slaves, they equally intended to prevent the increase of slavery without violating the vested rights of any individual whatever. And this would be the case even if the last article referred to were to be taken without its context. It is, however, by considering it in this point of view, as an isolated sentence, that so much misapprehension has prevailed in regard to it. It should be taken in connection with the preamble, which equally applies to all and each of the six articles, and shows conclusively that its operation was intended to be prospective and not retrospective—to prevent a failure, and not to destroy a previous sanction—to guard against the further introduction of slavery, and not to object to that which then existed—to prevent future authorized requisitions of slave property, and not, without a moment's notice or any equivalent whatever, to take away from the inhabitants of the country that which they had lawfully acquired.

Taking this article with so much of the preamble as applies to the question, it would be substantially as follows: To fix and establish those principles as the basis of all laws which forever hereafter shall be formed in the said Territory, it is hereby ordained and declared that the following article shall be considered as an article of compact between the original States and the people in the said Territory, and forever remain unalterable unless by common consent, to-wit: "There shall be neither slavery nor involuntary servitude in the said Territory."

Here it is plainly declared that the object of the article in question was to establish the basis of laws thereafter to be formed in the said Territory. Taking into consideration that this ordinance was designed to enable the people thereof to legislate for themselves, under prescribed limitations, this article can only be considered as a restriction upon the legislative power of the people, and not as an act of legislation by Congress, operating upon and destroying vested rights for the protection of which they had pledged the faith of the nation. Believing that Congress has never freed a slave, and never even intended to legislate on the subject further than to prescribe limits to the power of the local Legislature, and the latter having done nothing to change the common law principle of *partus sequitur ventrem*, it is in full force, and the posterity of those born since the ordinance were subject to its operation.

It is evident that the people of the Territory and the Territorial Legislature considered that there were slaves legally held under the ordinance and deed of cession from Virginia, from the fact that by the revenue laws of the Territory provision was made for the taxation of slaves and servants; and although the laws adopted by the Governor and Council, recognizing the right to hold these slaves, were passed subject to be disapproved by Congress, the very fact that they were not disapproved implies that Congress also recognized this right. That they were so regarded by the framers of the first State Constitution must be conceded, from the language which they used in the following provision: "Neither slavery nor involuntary servitude shall *hereafter* be introduced into this State."

If this article had not been intended to operate prospectively, the words "hereafter introduced" would have been omitted, but being inserted in the article, they imply that slavery existed at that time in the Territory; and that such was the case, the first Legislature which met after the adoption of the Constitution proved, by passing laws for the taxation and punishment of slaves, as well as indentured servants.

The above were some of the arguments which were urged by those who believed that the French, and settlers previous to the date of the ordinance of 1787, were entitled to hold their slaves. The Constitution of the State recognized the right to hold indentured servants, and also provided that the children of such, who might be born after the adoption of the Constitution, should serve—the males until they arrive to thirty-five years of age, and the females until they arrive at thirty-two years of age. The supreme court of the State, however, in the year 1846, decided against the right to hold those persons as slaves; and since that time the State of Illinois has been freed from the evils of slavery.

I cannot imagine how Gov. Ford could have committed so great a mistake in ranking Gov. Edwards among those who were in favor of making this a slave State. His sentiments on that subject were well known, for no one individual in the State had been so active in his opposition to the introduction of slavery. In a message to the Territorial Legislature, in the year 1817, returning a bill entitled "An act to repeal so much of an act entitled 'an act concerning the introduction of negroes and mulattoes into this Territory,'" he says: "I am no advocate for slavery; and if it depended upon my vote alone, it should never be admitted into any State or Territory not already cursed with so great an evil. I have no objection to the repeal which I suppose was intended, but there being no such law as that which is described in the preamble and referred to in the enacting clause of the bill which has been referred to me for my approval, the proposed repeal would be a mere nullity, and with every possible aid of legal construction and intendment would leave in full force the act of 1812." The above bill was intended to repeal so much of an act as authorized negroes to be brought into the Territory for the purpose of being indentured, to the passage of which Gov. Edwards says he would "have no objection."

During the winter of 1819–20, a plan was formed at Washington City for the establishment of a press at Edwardsville, for the purpose of advocating slavery. General Joseph Sheet, who was to have been the editor, spent the winter at Washington City, for the purpose of making the necessary arrangements; and it was believed, from the fact that he at that time held one of the most lucrative offices in the State, which he would have been compelled to relinquish on his removal to Edwardsville, that nothing less than "a very formidable combination could have afforded him sufficient inducements to make the sacrifice." The following communication from Gov. Edwards will more fully develop their plans:

To Messrs. Blackwell & Berry,
Editors of the Illinois Intelligencer.

Gentlemen: Mr. Kane having publicly insinuated, if not explicitly declared, that I had some agency in the editorial remarks which appeared in the "Edwardsville Spectator" of the 11th inst., upon the subject of a real or supposed plan to introduce slavery into this State—and having also declared himself "well convinced" that no such measure was ever "thought of"—I beg leave to assure the public that all and every suggestion that I advised or even wished the publication of those remarks, or that I ever saw a line or letter of them till they were published, or that any of the statements contained therein originated with me, are utterly destitute of even the shadow of truth to support them. And in repelling such foul and malicious imputations, I am happy to have it in my power to afford Mr. Kane himself ample proof of their injustice, and to place him in a situation to feel compelled, if he is disposed to preserve even the semblance of regard for truth or honor, to acquit me—or otherwise, by failing to retract his own gross slander, when deprived of every pretext for persevering in it, to give a public manifestation of that disingenuousness which for years past has characterized his conduct towards me. And for that purpose, besides other gentlemen of this place and St. Louis, to whose testimony I might appeal, I refer him to Dr. Todd, Edward Coles, Esq., Major Theophilus W. Smith, Joseph Conway, Esq., Mr. McKenney, Major Winchester, Mr. May and Mr. Watkins, of this place, and to Mr. Hart and Col. Riddick, of St. Louis, for proof that statements had been made and were believed, weeks before my return from Congress, that a *new press* was to be established at this place, with the *avowed object* and *design* of advocating the *introduction of slavery into this State*, and that it was to be edited by the gentleman who is mentioned in the editorial article above referred to as having been selected for that purpose

Various as are the sources of these reports, it can be most satisfactorily proven, and no one will deny, that they did not originate with any person friendly to Mr. Cook, or disposed to support his election.

Some of the gentlemen referred to can testify that a change of our Constitution in regard to slavery has at least been "thought of" pretty seriously; and knowing as much as I do upon the subject, in relation to certain individuals who are intimate with and support Mr. Kane, I am truly surprised that he should know so little as to believe that the change spoken of had "never been thought of."

I have, however, written testimony in my possession, which at present I do not feel at liberty to publish, but which I will cheerfully show to Mr. Kane, that will prove to his satisfaction that "a change or modification of our Constitution, in relation to slavery," has recently been contemplated, and that there are some men of intelligence, and well acquainted with our situation, who "think the period not remote when the slave side of the question will be the most popular in this State." But for further exculpation of myself I refer to the annexed extract of a letter to myself, from a gentleman of first respectability, in St. Louis, who was at the city of Washington during the discussion of the Missouri question, but left there before its determination, and who was and I believe still is decidedly hostile to Mr. Cook. This letter, however, was procured for a very different purpose, and I regret that Mr. Kane's ungenerous attack upon me has rendered it necessary for me to use it on the present occasion, or to make any remarks whatever upon the subject.

NINIAN EDWARDS.

EDWARDSVILLE, *July* 24, 1820.

[EXTRACT.]

ST. LOUIS, *June* 27, 1820.

I recollect of frequently hearing it said, and perhaps while in Washington may have made the remark *myself*, that it "would be doing nothing more than justice to Illinois (as its citizens were so violently opposed to Missouri, as a State, without restriction) to create a reaction by engaging your side of the river in a contest at home, which would prevent them from so *particularly interesting themselves in our concerns;* and that, to effect this, it would only be necessary to establish a press at Edwardsville that would admit and favor a free discussion of the advantages that would result to the State by admitting slavery," believing that a large proportion of the State was inhabited by emigrants from the Southern States, who would be favorable to such a state of things.

I also understood that a gentleman, highly distinguished on former occasions for his editorial talents, might be prevailed on to establish a press in Edwardsville, and if so, from his sentiments on the subject of slavery (which was then debating at large in Congress) he would most certainly advocate such a course. I afterwards understood that the gentleman alluded to did intend to visit Edwardsville, preparatory to such a step, *but I never understood that you had any knowledge of it, or in any way countenanced it.*

In his special message to the Legislature, at the session of 1826–7, may be found the following paragraph:

As there is some reason to believe that the loans, referred to in my last message as having been made to Thomas J. McGuire, Emanuel J. West and Theophilus W. Smith, were somewhat connected with the establishment of a press at Edwardsville, which was intended to promote the introduction of slavery into this State, they probably merit particular notice. I have been informed, by authority which is presumed to be unquestionable, that Mr. Kinney, the president of the bank, obtained his loan to reimburse Mr. Kinney; that Mr. West gave his bond of indemnity to Mr. McGuire, and Mr. Smith is known to have been the editor of the paper.

Besides the documentary evidence of Gov. Edwards' sentiments on this subject, it is well known to Judge Lockwood, Wm. H. Brown of Chicago, George Churchill, Hooper Warren, and many others, that he was never associated in politics with the gentleman alluded to by Gov. Ford. At this very time Mr. Cook, his son-in-law, was the candidate of the anti-Convention party, against Gov. Bond.

In his speech in the Senate of the United States, on the bill for the admission of Missouri into the Union, he said: "Were an attempt made to introduce slavery into the non-slaveholding States of the West, then, indeed, might there be just cause of alarm, and I can assure gentlemen that there is no man who would oppose such a proposition with more determined zeal than myself......In attempting to discuss the present proposition, it is not my purpose to advocate slavery in any shape, or to deny that, in its mildest form, it is equally inconsistent with the inherent rights of man, and repugnant to every principle of humanity and philanthropy. On the contrary, I rejoice most sincerely that an increasing sense of its moral injustice and turpitude, and the happy prevalence of more enlightened and magnanimous views throughout every part of our common country, as well as in various other parts of the civilized world, are eliciting the most zealous efforts not only to prevent its *extension*, but to ameliorate its present condition, which, with the blessing of Divine Providence, *I trust will*, in due season, *eventuate in its final extermination.*"

At a still later period, in a letter to the Postmaster General, dated Aug. 20, 1829, in which he complains that superior mail facilities have been granted in the State of Missouri to those afforded to the people of Illinois, he says: "Collisions on such subjects are as unpleasant to me as to any other man, but I have never seen the day that I would not risk any personal consequences rather than submit to have the affairs of my own State controlled by members of Congress from other States, or to see it degraded and overlooked as though it were an inferior. Though older in every respect, and superior in the number of its free population and the extent of agricultural improvements and productions, to Missouri, the interest, convenience and accommodation of the latter have of late years been so much more favorably regarded by the Government, that certain magnates of St. Louis, who are in the habit of speaking of us, reproachfully, as 'the free State,' seem to consider us unworthy, on that account, of the equal regard of the Government, and hope, by their influence with the present administration, to impress upon us the stamp of degradation."

After alluding to other conspicuous instances of the preference to Missouri over this State, he says: "It would be easy to demonstrate that better and more eligible locations for the troops at Jefferson Barracks, and for the arsenal near St. Louis, than the sites of either, might have been had in the vicinities of Alton and Kaskaskia, and had we not been the 'free State,' they would doubtless have been preferred. We claim an equality of rights with the citizens of Missouri, and this nothing shall induce me to relinquish—for great is the debt of gratitude which I owe to the people of this State; and they have never been seen to shrink when their rights and interests have been called into question, and, with the permission of Divine Providence, they never shall."

Again, he says: "I can conceive of no reason for this preference, unless it be supposed that because the pecple of Missouri have negroes, to work for them, they are to be considered as gentle-folks, entitled to higher consideration and superior privileges to us plain 'free State' folks, who have to work for ourselves."

Although this letter was written while he was Governor of the State, yet it was not in his official character. It nevertheless portrayed, in such striking colors, the partial and injurious nature of the contemplated changes in the mail routes, for the purpose of accommodating the State of Missouri at our expense, as to secure to the State its just rights.

Although opposed to the introduction of slavery in Illinois, he believed that Congress had no authority to pass the ordinance of 1787, and that it was unconstitutional and void. His opinions on this subject were as follows:

At the time Virginia made her cession, there was a numerous and wealthy population within our limits, all citizens of Virginia, owing to her allegiance and entitled to her protection, and whom, therefore, she had no more right to dismember from the State, and transfer to another Government, than she would have to transfer the citizens of her counties of Loudon and Fairfax. Vattell, a distinguished writer on the "Laws of Nations," says: "A nation ought to preserve itself. It ought to preserve all its members. It cannot abandon them; and it is under an obligation to them of maintaining them in the rank of members of the nation. It has not, then, a right to traffic with their rank and liberty, on account of any advantages it may promise itself from such a negotiation. They are united to the society to be its members. They acknowledge the authority of the state to promote, in concert, their common welfare and safety, and not to be at its disposal, like a farm or an herd of cattle. But the nation may lawfully abandon them, in a case of extreme necessity; and it has a right to cut them off from the body, if the public safety requires it. But this province or city, thus abandoned and dismembered from the state, is not obliged to receive the new master attempted to be given to them. The people, being separated from the society of which they were members, resume all their rights; and if it is possible for them to defend their liberty against him who would subject them to his authority, they may lawfully resist him." (Pages 177-8.)

It was doubtless from the obligations which these universally acknowledged principles imposed, as well as from other benevolent and political considerations, that Virginia so particularly stipulated that we should be admitted into the Union, not shorn of a single attribute of sovereignty, not humiliated by dependence, not degraded by inferiority, nor deprived of any right which we should have enjoyed, in common with herself, had no dismemberment taken place—but with the very same *rights of sovereignty, freedom and independence* as the original States.

Though the people so dismembered and transferred were not bound to submit to the new sovereign, yet they might do so; and the moment they yielded *an express or tacit consent* to the compact of cession, they became parties to it, and acquired vested rights to all and everything stipulated in their favor, of which they can no more be deprived than the people of Louisiana of the rights secured to them by the treaty with France, which ceded that country to the United States. Their consent, also, subjected them to all authority which, as a consequence of the terms of cession, could be lawfully exercised over them, and no more. It warranted no usurpation. In giving it, they must be presumed to have taken into view the powers both of the government that transferred, and that which received them; and in submitting to a government of specified and limited powers, they subjected themselves to no undelegated authority. When, then, had the United States a right to govern them? Never, till their admission into the confederation; and then only as a member thereof. Why so? Because no such power was delegated to them by the articles of confederation; and these restricted their authority to the powers expressly granted. How, then, were they governed? Cut off from Virginia, and owing no other allegiance to the United States than they had previously owed as citizens of Virginia, they had a right to govern themselves, and were in the meantime entitled, by the terms of the cession, to the same protection from the United States as Virginia herself. As citizens of Virginia, which the cession acknowledges they were, they had vested rights and privileges. By what authority, then, could the Legislature of Virginia disfranchise them? By that of their State Constitution? But this was intended to secure those rights and privileges; and all who had submitted to its authority were entitled to its protection. How, then, could the United States do it? Under the articles of confederation? But these gave no such authority, and were intended to protect the rights of all and every citizen of each State in the confederation, so far as they had cognizance of them. If this monstrous power of degrading any portion of the citizens of a free, sovereign and independent State to colonial thraldom, without their consent, or any other act of theirs to justify it, may be exercised over a population of fifteen or twenty thousand, why may it not be extended to one-half or any other number of the citizens of any State in the Union? The principle is the same, however few or many its victims.

The powers of the United States are far greater and more national under the present Constitution than they were under the confederation; yet, it will not be pretended that they could govern the District of Columbia, though ceded to them by the States of Maryland and Virginia, but for that clause in the Constitution that specially authorized them to do so. The Legislature of Virginia could not, with the consent of every State in the Union, without an amendment of the Constitution, transfer the county of Fairfax, which adjoins the district, to the United States, and subject the citizens of that county to their authority; nor could the United States, with all their enlarged powers, receive such a transfer. What, then, gave the Legislature of Virginia greater power over her citizens in the organized county of Illinois than it now has over those of the county of Fairfax? And how, then, did the transfer of the former give to the United States more power to govern them than a transfer of the latter would now give? A delegation of power for such purposes was as necessary then as now, and none having been granted, the ordinance of 1787 was, therefore, as to us, unauthorized, unconstitutional and void.

Whatever the people of Virginia might have done in their sovereign capacity, it is contended that their Legislature had no right to dismember the State, and curtail its jurisdiction. And why? Because no such power had been delegated to them by the Constitution of the State, and it could be derived from no other source. Their's was the power of legislating for the whole State, as it then stood, and was intended to be exercised by them and their successors forever. For what end? For the preservation and security of the whole territory, and all its inhabitants. To suppose, then, that they could transfer any part of the State, or its jurisdiction, is to admit their power to annihilate rights as effectually secured to their successors as to themselves, and to destroy the whole ends and objects of their own institution—for if they could dismember a part, they might have transferred the whole; and as to the question of power, might as well have surrendered it to the King of Spain, who, about that time, was very anxious to obtain a part of the United States. As well, it might be contended, that the Legislature of a State, the Constitution of which establishes the boundaries thereof, could change the territorial limits, as to maintain that the Legislature of Virginia could have made this transfer of a portion of her territory. What right, then, it may be asked, had the Legislature of Virginia to cede that portion of the territory which is now included within the District of Columbia? The question is easily answered. It was derived from the Constitution of the United States, and its ratification by the Convention of the State; and the admitted necessity of a clear delegation of power to authorize that cession is, of itself, a good argument to show that nothing less than such authority could authorize any other. As it is agreed, on all sides, that Virginia cannot now transfer to the United States an acre of her territory, except for certain purposes specified in the Constitution, it is for those who contend that the cession under consideration was not a perfect nullity, to show that her Legislature had greater power to dismember the State than at present.

As to the right of the United States to hold, dispose of and govern the territory, and to enact the ordinance of 1787, they all depend upon the powers delegated by the articles of confederation, and involve the question whether that feeble Confederation, which was limited to powers expressly granted, among which these were not included, could do more than the present powerful National Union, with all its train of incidental powers. It is admitted that the United States cannot now, even with the consent of every State in the Union, purchase or hold a foot of land within any State, except in the few cases permitted by the Constitution, and this merely because no such power has been delegated to them; and that they could neither dispose of any part of the public domain, nor make any rules or regulations concerning it, but for the powers that have been specially delegated to them for these purposes. How, then, could they do all these things under the confederation which granted no such powers, and the second article of which prohibited them from exercising any *sover-*

eignty, power, jurisdiction or right which was not therein expressly delegated to them? It would seem that every candid mind must admit that the exercise of these powers by the Confederation was not only unauthorized, but expressly forbidden. It follows, then, that the United States acquired neither the territory, nor the jurisdiction over it, by the cession of Virginia. To whom, then, it may be asked, did the right of jurisdiction belong? Like all countries abandoned by their owners, it was subject only to the laws of nature and of nations, and belonged to the people that possessed it. They owed allegiance to no other state or nation than Virginia, and were entitled to her protection; and as they could not transfer the right of protection, so, neither, could she transfer the right of allegiance. When, therefore, they were formally abandoned by the only government that had any claim to their obedience, they were of course independent. It was upon this very principle that the Swiss declared their independence, and maintained it, with all the rights of domain and empire, against the Emperor of Germany. "The country of Zug, attacked by the Swiss in 1352, sent for succor to the Duke of Austria, its sovereign; but that Prince, being employed in talking of his birds, when the deputies appeared before him, would scarcely condescend to hear them; upon which this people, thus abandoned, entered into the Helvetic confederacy," (Vattell, 155) and were rightfully lost to their former sovereign forever, by his failure to afford them that support which, from the reciprocal obligation of allegiance and protection, they were entitled to.

Well, then, if neither Virginia nor the United States had any right to govern these people, and the ordinance of 1787 was void as an act of the Congress of Confederation, have they gone all this time without any government at all? Certainly not. They have been constantly governed, and under the ordinance, too; but then it derived its force not from the authority of the United States, but the consent of the people themselves. Being free to choose what government they pleased, they had as much right to submit to this as to any other. Their own consent was all that was wanting, and this was equally valid whether given tacitly or expressly. But, however given, it could impart no power, right or jurisdiction to the United States which had not *been delegated* by the articles of confederation. Consent cannot give jurisdiction to a court, and still less to a government prohibited from exercising any power, jurisdiction or right which had not been expressly delegated to it.

Although the State Government had only been in operation for four years, under the Constitution, the whole State was again thrown in commotion in consequence of efforts being made to elect members in favor of calling a Convention to amend the Constitution. Those in favor of the Convention not being able, at that time, to point out any particular defect in the form of government, were strongly suspected to have for their object the amendment of the Constitution so as to allow the introduction of slavery. This party was afraid to openly avow such a change to be their object, but failing to point out others sufficiently important to incur the expense and inconvenience from too frequent a change of the fundamental law of the land, the anti-slavery party was aroused; and never was a people more agitated than were the voters of the State, for the period commencing the latter end of 1821 and terminating after the election of 1824, which resulted in a triumphant majority against slavery. The anti-Convention party, through their newspapers, hand-bills, public addresses of candidates, politicians, and from the pulpit, proclaimed the object of the Convention, and opened their batteries against the evils of slavery. Those in favor of its introduction, although more secretly engaged, were more active in whispering into the ears of the settlers from the Southern States the advantage the State would derive from an immediate and rapid immigration from the Southern States. They referred to Missouri, into which, at that time, the emigration from the Southern States was very large; they appealed to their sympathies in favor of a population whose habits, manners and customs were more assimilated to their own; they endeavored to excite their prejudices against the 'Yankees,' by representing them to be a close, mean and niggardly set of people. Strange as it may seem, the most talented advocates of the proposed change were from the free States, whilst Gov. Edwards, Judge Pope and Daniel P. Cook, the avowed leaders of the anti-Convention party, were from slave States, and two of whom were slaveholders. There were, however, able co-operators with them from the free States, among whom were Judge Lockwood, Hon. David J. Baker, William H. Brown, Alfred Coules, and others. The prejudices among the Southern and Western people were, at that time, very great against the 'Yankees;' and to such an extent did this sentiment prevail, that it was generally believed that nearly all those seeking public favor, from that portion of the Union, denied that they were 'Yankees,' but claimed to be New-Yorkers! I have heard Mr. Cook say, that, on one occasion, he stayed all night with a farmer, in the southern portion of the State, and, during a conversation, he inquired of him the news; to which question the farmer replied that "there was none, except they were afraid that d—— little yankee, *Cook*, would be elected to Congress!" The conversation continued, on various subjects, during the evening; and on Mr. Cook's taking leave of him, in the morning, the farmer was so much pleased with him that he inquired of him *his name*. Mr. C. replied that he was "that d—— yankee, Cook," he alluded to the previous evening! From that time the farmer became his devoted friend.

From the fact that nearly all of the Northern and Eastern inhabitants were the friends of Gov. Edwards and Mr. Cook, they lost many supporters from the Western and Southern States.

In the year 1818, Gov. Coles came to Illinois, bringing a letter of introduction from President Monroe to Governor Edwards. The following is a copy of the letter:

WASHINGTON, *April* 13, 1818.

Dear Sir:

Mr. Edward Coles, intending to pass through Illinois, probably to remain some time there, I take much pleasure in introducing him to your acquaintance and kind attention. I have long known and highly respected him for his excellent qualities and good understanding. He was, several years, Private Secretary to the late President, and employed by him in a confidential message to Russia—in which trusts he discovered sound judgment, great industry and fidelity, and is generally beloved by those who know him best. Should he settle with you, you will find him a very useful acquisition—and I understand that is not an improbable event.

I hope that the arrangement made this winter will avail our country of your services, in the proposed treaty with the Indians, in a manner satisfactory to yourself; for success, on just principles, is the object of my most ardent wishes.

With great respect and esteem,

I am, dear sir, very sincerely yours,

JAMES MONROE.

In a very short time afterwards, Gov. Coles received the appointment of Register of the Land Office at Edwardsville. In this way he had a good opportunity of making the acquaintance of the people, and, being very polite and gentlemanly in his manners, he had a great many warm friends. On his arrival in the State, he also brought with him a very large family of negroes from Virginia, to whom he not only gave their freedom, but also aided in furnishing their houses. These circumstances, and his opposition to slavery, contributed in a great degree to his success in the election for Governor of the State, in 1822. He was afterwards sued, and judgment obtained against him, for the penalty imposed for a violation of the statute which prohibited the introduction of negroes into the State. The Legislature remitted the amount of the penalty for which a judgment had been obtained against him in favor of the county of Madison. The circuit court, over which Judge McRoberts (afterwards Senator in Congress) presided, denied the constitutional power of the Legislature to remit the fine, but the supreme court reversed this opinion.

At the session of 1822, a resolution passed recommending the electors, at the next election for members of the General Assembly, to vote "For" or "Against" a Convention for the purpose of amending the Constitution. I have already alluded to the object of calling the Convention, and to the arguments that were advanced in favor of making this a slave State. As the friends of slavery had succeeded in electing a very large majority of the members of the Legislature, they were confident, if they could succeed in securing a sufficient number of votes in favor of the Convention, they could also elect a majority of delegates in favor of amending the Constitution so as to allow the introduction of slavery. It, then, became a matter of great importance to point out the evils of the Constitution, and the necessary amendments to remedy them. Gov. Coles having called the attention of the Legislature, in his message, to the fact that slavery still existed in the State, notwithstanding the ordinance of 1787, the Convention party had so much of his message as related to that subject referred to a select committee. The committee, composed of those in favor of the Convention, made an elaborate report, sustaining the right of the settlers at the time of the cession of the territory, by Virginia, to the United States, to hold their slaves. They also contended that the descendants of such slaves could be held in perpetual bondage, and that there was no way by which slavery could be even gradually abolished, without an amendment to the Constitution. Their report, with resolutions sustaining this view of the subject, was adopted by a large majority of the House of Representatives. Thus we see that the right of the French to hold their slaves was conceded by the Legislature, not only by resolutions declaring this right, but by laws on various subjects referring to this class of our population as slaves. These resolutions and reports were intended to entrap the friends of freedom to vote for the Convention, by inducing them to believe that the Constitution could be amended so as to abolish instead of establishing slavery. The people were not so easily imposed upon, and the result was, as I have already stated, that the call for the Convention was defeated by a very large majority.

William H. Brown, Esq., of Chicago, at that time one of the editors of the "Illinois Intelligencer," in an editorial article of the 15th Feb., 1823, thus refers to the extraordinary proceedings of the Legislature that were adopted for the purpose of calling the Convention:

Since the commencement of the present General Assembly, the subject of calling a Convention to amend the Constitution has been a topic of conversation in and out of the State House; and although I knew that the sole aim and avowed object of this measure was to introduce into this State, by a legislative provision, that worst of all evils, the evil of slavery—for reasons best known to myself, during the pendency of this question, I have never penned one single sentence either for or against this contemplated change of policy. And even at this time, had not extraordinary means been resorted to, to effect the object, I am not prepared to say that, in my editorial capacity, I should have called in question the expediency or propriety of the measure.

It may be remembered by the reader that some days since, a resolution, recommending the people to vote for or against a Convention, was introduced into the House of Representatives, and found twenty-two votes in its favor and fourteen against it. At that time, there not being a constitutional majority, it was reconsidered and laid upon the table. From this period down to Tuesday last (by means which it does not become me to state) a change of two votes was effected, and on that day the House took up and proceeded to consider the resolution upon this subject from the Senate, which had passed that body by a bare constitutional majority. When the question was put in the House of Representatives, Mr. Hanson, the member from Pike county, who had on a former occasion voted for, now voted against it, and the question was lost. Mr. Darnwood of Gallatin, who had voted for the resolution, and was, of course, one of the constitutional minority, moved to reconsider the vote; which the Speaker correctly and promptly decided to be out of order. An appeal was taken from his decision, which was sustained by a decided vote.

It will be recollected that, during the first days of the session, John Shaw, a citizen of Pike county, contested the election of Mr. Hanson, and, after a full and fair investigation, the committee of elections recommended the right of Mr. Hanson, in which recommendation the House concurred. Mr. Hanson continued to occupy his seat, thus solemnly confirmed to him, until Wednesday last, when Mr. Ford, one of the committee on elections, moved to reconsider the vote taken on concurring in the report, and resolutions accompanying it, of the committee on elections, on this contested election. The question was put and decided in the affirmative, by a vote of 22 to 13. Upon Mr. Field's motion, John Shaw was permitted to a seat in the House, and the documents were again read. An additional document was introduced, purporting to be the affidavit of Levi Roberts, Esq., and sworn to the 28th of January last, (no notice of the taking of which was even pretended to be given,) which affidavit gave it as the opinion of the affiant that John Shaw received a larger number of votes than Mr. Hanson. Mr. Field then moved to strike out the name of "Nicholas Hanson," and insert in lieu thereof the name of "John Shaw." Mr. Hanson was turned out and John Shaw admitted to his seat. The question was soon taken upon concurring in the resolution, from the Senate, recommending a Convention, and carried by a constitutional majority—John Shaw supplying the place of Mr. Hanson.

At the next session, the General Assembly adopted the following resolutions, on the subject of slavery, to-wit:

WHEREAS the General Assembly of the State of Ohio did, on the 17th day of January, 1824, pass the following resolutions, by way of propositions to the States and Congress, viz:

"*Resolved*, That the consideration of a system providing for the gradual emancipation of the people of color, held in servitude in the United States, be recommended to the Legislatures of the several States of the American Union and to the Congress of the United States.

"*Resolved*, That, in the opinion of this General Assembly, a system of foreign colonization, with correspondent measures, might be adopted, that would, in due time, effect the entire emancipation of the slaves in our country, without any violation of the national compact or infringement of the rights of individuals, by the passage of a law by the General Government, (with the consent of the slaveholding States,) which would provide that all children of persons now held in slavery, born after the passage of such law, should be free at the age of twenty-one years, (being supported during their minority by the person claiming the service of the parent,) *provided*, they then consent to be transported to the place of colonization.

"*Resolved*, That it is expedient that such a system should be predicated on the principle that the evil of slavery is a national one, and that the people and the States of this Union ought mutually to participate in the duties and burthens of removing it." Therefore,

Resolved by the General Assembly of the State of Illinois, That it is expedient to concur in the plan proposed in the aforesaid resolutions.

By an act which passed in January, 1829, negroes and mulattoes, not being *citizens* of the United States, could gain a residence in the State by producing to the county commissioners' court a certificate of his or her freedom, and also by giving bond, with security, in the sum of $1,000, that would not become a charge upon the county, and would demean themselves in strict conformity with the laws of the State. If such persons were found in the State without a certificate of their freedom, they were liable to be taken up and sold for one year—on the expiration of which time, if no person claimed them, they were entitled to a certificate which would allow them to remain in the State, as free persons, until their owner claimed them.

FREE SCHOOLS FIRST ESTABLISHED IN UPPER ALTON.

The proprietors of Upper Alton having donated one hundred town lots, one-half for the support of the gospel and the other half for the support of public schools in said town, an act passed, in 1821, incorporating trustees, and authorizing them, in addition to the powers usually granted to towns, to lay a tax not exceeding seventy-five cents on each lot, (not including the one hundred lots donated by the proprietors,) to be applied to the support of teachers and the erection or repairing of buildings. This school was declared to be open and free to all, of a suitable age, within the limits of the town. Up to this period no school system had been adopted, and no provision had been made for the support of schools—with the exception of the small amount that might be realized from leasing the school lands—until the session of 1825, at which time an act passed for the establishment of free schools throughout the State.

As it will doubtless be interesting to the friends of education and free schools, I will give the outlines of that act. The preamble to the act, which was entitled "An act providing for the establishment of free schools," is as follows, viz: "To enjoy our rights and liberties, we must understand them: their security and protection ought to be the first object of a free people; and it is a well established fact, that no nation has ever continued long in the enjoyment of civil and political freedom, which was not both virtuous and enlightened. And believing that the advancement of literature always has been and ever will be the means of more fully developing the rights of man—that the mind of every citizen in a republic is the common property of society, and constitutes the basis of its strength and happiness—it is therefore considered the peculiar duty of a free government, like ours, to encourage and extend the improvement and cultivation of the intellectual energies of the whole. Therefore—

"SEC. 1. *Be it enacted, etc.*, That there shall be established a common school or schools in each of the counties of this State, which shall be open and free to every class of white citizens between the ages of five and twenty-one years: *Provided*, that persons over the age of twenty-one years may be admitted into such schools, on such terms as the trustees of the school districts may prescribe."

Section 2d provided that the county courts should form school districts, upon a petition for that purpose, by a majority of the qualified voters within the proposed district: *Provided*, that such districts shall contain not less than fifteen families.

Section 3d provided for the election, by the voters of the district, of three trustees, a clerk, treasurer, and assessor and collector, who were required to take an oath of office faithfully to discharge their respective duties.

The trustees were required to superintend the schools; to examine and employ the teachers; to lease the land; to call meetings of the voters whenever they deemed it expedient, or at any time when requested by five legal voters, by giving to each one at least five days' notice of the time and place of holding the same; to make an annual report, to the county court, of the number of children in their respective districts between the ages of five and twenty-one years, and the number of them actually attending school, with a certificate of the time a school has been kept in the district, and the probable expense of the same; to purchase or receive any property, real or personal, for the use of the district; to give orders on the treasurer for all sums expended in paying teachers, and all other expense incurred in establishing and supporting schools in the district; and at the regular meeting of the inhabitants, the trustees, as well as all other officers, were required to settle their accounts which accrued during the year for which they were elected. The duties of the respective officers were clearly defined, and the assessors were required to assess all such property, lying within and belonging to the inhabitants of the district, as he was directed to assess, by a vote of the majority of the voters of such district.

The legal voters of each district had power to appoint a time and place of holding annual meetings; to select school house sites; to levy a tax—either in cash or good merchantable produce, at cash price—upon the inhabitants of the district, not exceeding one-half per centum, nor amounting to more than ten dollars per annum on any one person; and to do all and everything necessary to the establishment and support of schools within the same.

The State appropriated, for the support of schools, two dollars out of every hundred received into the treasury, and five sixths of the interest arising from the school funds—which was divided annually between the different counties, in proportion to the number of white inhabitants in each county under twenty-one years of age. The treasurer of the county, to whom was paid the amount belonging to the county, was required to make a like distribution among such districts of the county as had kept a school in actual operation at least three months in the year, for which the appropriation was made.

The rents arising from the school lands were directed to be divided among such of the inhabitants of the township as had contributed, by tax, subscription or otherwise, to the support of a common school in or near the township, for at least three months within the last twelve months preceding the time of making such dividend; and such division was made in proportion to the sum contributed by each person to the support of such common school.

The commissioners of the school fund were directed to invest the same in the purchase of the indebtedness of the State, at its market value.

The county clerks were required to make an extract of the reports of the trustees, stating the number of children within each district, the number actually sent to school, the time a school had been kept in operation in each district, with an account of the expenditures of the same—and forward it to the Secretary of State on the 1st day of December, annually.

The inhabitants of the district were required to make regulations for building and repairing school houses, and for furnishing the same with furniture and fuel. They had power to class themselves, and agree upon the number of days each person or class should work in making improvements, and to make such other regulations as they might deem necessary for that purpose: *Provided*, that no person should be required to work, unless he had the care of a child who attended the school for the purpose of receiving instruction.

The collectors and treasurers were required to give a bond, with security, for the faithful application of the money received by them.

The free school system which had been adopted in 1825 was modified by an act which passed on the 17th February, 1827, in several important respects:

1. On the application of the inhabitants of any settlement which was partly situated in two counties, the commissioners' court of both counties could lay off a district to be formed out of territory taken from each of their counties.

2. The legal voters had power to cause either the whole or one-half of the sum required to keep a school, in such district, to be raised by taxation; and if only one-half shall be raised by taxation, the remainder might be required to be paid by those who sent pupils to the school: *Provided*, that no person could be taxed, for the support of any free school in the State, without his consent first had and obtained, in writing. No person was, however, permitted to send any scholar to such school as was supported either wholly or partly by taxation, unless such person had either consented to be taxed, or had obtained the permission of the trustees.

3. By an act, which passed on the same day, it was made the duty of the county court to appoint trustees for each township, whose duty was in most respects similar to that now conferred upon the trustees of schools.

At the session of 1829, an act passed—on the condition that Congress should assent to the sale of the sixteenth section—for the appointment, by the county court, of a school commissioner, who, on the petition of nine-tenths of the freeholders of any township, was authorized to sell the sixteenth section, in tracts of not greater than eighty acres, at public sale, and for any price not less than $1.25 per acre. After the lands had been offered at public sale, they could be entered at private sale by the payment of $1.25 per acre, in cash. It was the duty of the school commissioner to loan the money at as high an interest as he could get, by taking good security, for the use of the schools of the proper township—the interest of which was to be distributed, under such restrictions and regulations as the county court should deem right, by the trustees of schools, among the schools of the township. This was the origin of the present township fund. An act also passed, at this session, for the sale of the seminary lands.

The free school system was also virtually destroyed by the repeal of the appropriation, out of the State treasury, of two dollars out of every one hundred paid in, annually, by taxation, and by the law which prohibited the levy of a tax without the consent of the inhabitants.

Having given a general outline of the legislation of the Territorial and State Governments, the reader will be better prepared to understand and properly appreciate the following speech of Gov. Edwards, during his canvass for Governor, at the election held on the 1st Monday of August, 1826:

By the eighteenth section of the eighth article of our Constitution, it is declared that "a frequent recurrence to the fundamental principles of civil government is absolutely necessary to preserve the blessings of liberty." The experience of the whole world bears testimony to this great political truth. Unfortunately, such is the nature of man, that, in the fruition of the greatest blessings, he is most apt to become insensible to their intrinsic value, forgetful of the source from whence they emanate, and careless of the means of preserving them. As the individual who has always enjoyed uninterrupted health is, of all others, the most likely to forget its natural tendency to deterioration and decay, so communities, long blessed with the highest perfection of civil and religious liberty, are too prone to indulge in a false security against those dangers to which all human institutions are liable. The warning voice of experience admonishes us to guard against this disposition of our nature. However prosperous our condition, such are the wise dispensations of an overruling Providence, that our own exertions are necessary to preserve it; nor can the most vigilant precautions for that purpose be pretermitted with impunity. And hence arises the necessity of reviewing those great events which have contributed to the establishment of our liberty, and of frequently recurring to the fundamental principles of civil government, on which it is founded, to enable us to maintain it in its greatest purity, and to hand it down unimpaired as the most precious legacy to a grateful posterity.

No time seems to me more suitable for those purposes than an occasion which has a direct reference to the great and inestimable right of election—the vital principle of all free representative governments and the solid foundation of the mighty political fabric which we have erected. I therefore trust that a few general remarks, on those subjects, will not be unacceptable to you on the present occasion.

In the contemplation of our present prosperous and happy condition, compared with that of all other nations of the world, it seems to be impossible for any human heart not to dilate with gratitude to that Almighty Being, who has so signally smiled upon our efforts, and irradiated with the light of His countenance the path that has conducted us to our present glorious preëminence. Equally difficult is it for a rational and reflecting mind to resist the belief that we have been thus peculiarly favored, protected and supported for some great and wise purpose of His inscrutable providence. In the long period, of more than fifty-eight hundred years, which have elapsed since the creation of the world, neither tradition nor history furnishes any example of a nation that has been so blessed with every rational means of comfort and happiness, as we have been; and did our gratitude bear anything like a just proportion to these transcendent blessings, we should undoubtedly be the most moral and religious people on earth.

About two hundred and twenty years ago, these United States were one immense forest—the haunt of savage beasts and still more savage men. Deprived of their civil and religious liberties in their native land, our hardy ancestors sought, in these wilds, an asylum from persecution; and notwithstanding the awful dangers and appalling difficulties of settling in a savage and uncultivated country, at the distance of three thousand miles from the abodes of civilization, such was their invincible love of liberty, that, relying upon Divine Providence, they freely encountered overy peril, and, by surprising efforts of constancy and valor, overcame every obstacle. This noble and undaunted spirit, inculcated by precept and animated by example, was transmitted through all the succeeding generations to the period of our Revolution, when it produced that determined resistance of British aggression which secured to the American name imperishable renown, and made us a free and independent nation. It is consolatory to every patriotic bosom, in looking back through the vista of a few past ages only, to observe that, from a band of persecuted exiles, this mighty nation has arisen, of limits larger than those of any other, with a population now sufficient to defend us against the whole world, and still increasing with amazing rapidity; and whose progress in all the arts of civilized life, in science, in refinement, in physical and moral power, and in every species of national prosperity, transcends that of any that now is or that ever existed.

Having learned practical wisdom in the school of adversity, and moderating their views by the sober dictates of experience, our forefathers, equally avoiding the Charybdis of monarchy and the Sylla of anarchy, laid the foundations of civil liberty which have hitherto secured our happiness, and by which we have been enabled to exhibit to the world the sublime example of the entire practicability of a government founded upon the just and equal rights of man.

True, genuine, rational, well-regulated liberty may, therefore, be almost said to have had its birth in America. Matured and cherished by the affection and sustained by the blood of the first adventurers of this happy land—guarded by the patriotic vigilance and protected by the valor of their descendants—it has, by the care, integrity and wisdom of our Washingtons, Franklins, Jeffersons, Madisons, and their compatriots, been brought to that unparalleled perfection in which it is now our felicitous lot to enjoy it.

Our own direct interest, therefore, a proper respect for the memory of our virtuous and valiant ancestors, duty to our posterity, and our obligations to that Divine Providence by whose behests we seem to have been destined to become a shining light unto the world, all conspire to demand our most sedulous and devoted exertions to merit, to preserve and to perpetuate to all future generations the blessings of that precious boon which has thus descended to us; and, by the moral force of our example, to dispel the mists of error, to vindicate the rights of man, and to burst asunder all those chains of bondage that enslave the rest of the world.

Think you, my countrymen, because there is no enemy now thundering at our gates and demanding the surrender of the citadel of our liberties, that there is no danger?

If so, discard the dangerous, fatal delusion. Remember, that although all mankind were created with equal rights and with the love of liberty implanted in every human bosom, yet all, with the exception of ourselves, have, sooner or later, by the supineness and folly of themselves or their ancestors, fallen from this high estate and been compelled to bend their necks to the galling yoke of thraldom. Recollect, also, that although, for a nation to be free, it is only necessary that she herself wills it, yet ours is the only really free nation on the earth. Let us, therefore, look to the experience of others, as warning beacons, to guide from the dangerous vortices that have engulfed them in ruin. Just, as is the cause of free principles and equal rights, we should not forget that there is, at this day, an alliance (nicknamed holy) of some of the greatest potentates of the earth, to prevent its progress, and that, of all the nations of the old world, there is not one that is not arrayed against it.

Mankind has long been divided in opinion as to what form of government is best calculated to secure the welfare and promote the happiness of a nation ; and, strange as it may appear, there is too much reason to believe that, great as has been the triumph of our system over prejudice and opposition, it has not been sufficient to convince even all of our own fellow-citizens of its superiority. Men of sinister motives and inordinate ambition, disposed to aim at uncontrolled power, there ever have been and ever will be, whose talents will be united to compass the destruction of equal rights and to establish exclusive privileges and arbitrary power. Availing themselves of the unsuccessful experiments of all the ancient republics and of the disastrous issue of the late French revolution, the enemies of our system have labored and are incessantly laboring to demonstrate that it is Utopian, visionary and impracticable, and that we shall ultimately have to exchange our sentiments of liberty for the chains that hold other nations captive.

But while I admit that there is enough of similitude between the ancient republics and our own to induce us to take warning from their experience, and to awaken our vigilance to guard against their errors, I contend that we are not in the same imminent danger that they were—not only because we have all the advantage of their experience, but because our government is free from those inherent defects and imperfections which mainly contributed to the unfortunate catastrophies of theirs. These were not self-balanced, like ours, and of course were more liable to yield to violence and power—to the strategems of popular demagogues and to the momentary infatuation and sudden commotions of the people themselves; but, above all, they lacked that pure and genuine representative principle which constitutes the perfection of our system.

Ours is a compound republic, composed of two descriptions of government: the one federal, the other local and municipal—both being necessary to and instituted for the safety and happiness of the people, and equally dependent upon their will. The principal objects of the former are the common defense against internal convulsions and foreign aggression, the maintenance of a just and friendly intercourse between the different members of the Union, and the management of all our affairs, political and commercial, with foreign nations. The objects of the latter are all those domestic affairs that relate to the personal interests of the people and to the internal tranquillity, improvement and prosperity of the respective States.

This division of powers between the two governments renders them much less capable of being perverted to purposes of usurpation and oppression than if all those powers were concentrated in any one government, and, moving within their respective orbits, the barriers of our liberty are strengthened by their mutual tendency to prevent any dangerous aberrations by either. The powers surrendered to them, respectively, by the people, have been happily separated and distributed into different departments, which, mutually checking each other, insures cautious inquiry and deliberate investigation—while the people, who are the acknowledged source of all legitimate power, have a right to sit in judgment upon the conduct of all their public servants, and, by the power which they have retained by changing them at certain stated periods, can effect any other change they please—either in the Federal or State Government—in a tranquil, pacific and constitutional mode. This system, which is adapted to almost any extent of territory, already embraces such a widespread population, and such a multiplicity and variety of interests, as to render any dangerous internal combinations against our peace, safety and happiness extremely difficult. In all these respects, as well as in many others arising from the physical situation of our country, we possess decided advantages over all the ancient republics. Nor can our situation be justly assimilated to that of the late French republic. It is true that, when that nation commenced its republican career, the recollection of their past services to us in our struggle for freedom, sympathy for their situation, and a virtuous desire for the progress of our own principles, caused every American bosom to swell with anxiety for their success, and inspired us all with the animating hope of their emancipation of millions of our fellow creatures, and of seeing another bright and impressive example of the justice and practicability of free government. But if our disappointment has been mortifying, there is something consolatory and encouraging in the contrast between their conduct and ours, for while theirs affords an admonishing lesson of the danger of a nation's trusting to its own self-sufficiency to accomplish its happiness, it equally evinces the superior wisdom of ours, in looking to an overruling Providence, who holds the destinies of nations in the palm of His hand, to guide us in our duties and to crown our efforts with His blessing.

If any one doubt that wickedness and impiety have an inevitable tendency to the destruction of any nation, he need take very little trouble to find enough, both in profane and sacred history, to remove all his scepticism on this subject. He may find, in the histories of Babylon and Ninevah, and even in that of the highly favored Jews, themselves, such signal instances of Divine chastisements, as will leave him at no loss to account for the unfortunate issue of the French revolution. Suddenly emerging, as they did, from the lowest depths of despotism into uncontrolled liberty, and indulging all its licentiousness, their system itself had its origin in popular frenzy; and, relying upon their own self-sufficiency, instead of looking to Divine Providence for assistance, they endeavored to establish a new era, to be denominated "the age of reason"—and with an inconsiderate eagerness to explode all old systems and to free themselves from all those restraints which ever will be found necessary for the government of mankind, they impiously though vainly attempted to undermine the very foundations of religion itself. By which means, after shedding oceans of human blood, and passing through all the horrors of anarchy, they have been compelled to surrender that liberty which they had so grossly abused, and to sink again into the degrading condition of abject slavery.

On the other hand, throughout our whole revolutionary contest, our old Congress, our illustrious Washington, and all the distinguished actors upon the theater of our revolution, were in the constant habit, as may be seen by the records of that period, of imploring the aid of the Almighty, and of attributing their success to His divine beneficence. And our system of government, which was the result of steady habits, sedate reflection and progressive developments, is not only predicated on the reality of religion, but relies upon its sanctions for the faithful administration of our affairs. Comment surely cannot be necessary, either to demonstrate or to enforce the great moral lesson which this striking contrast teaches. But, my countrymen, although there is nothing in the cases referred to to produce despair in regard to the eventual success of the great cause in which we are engaged, there is yet enough to premonish us against supineness and inattention to its interests. Secure as it may be, at this time, in this favored land, against open assaults, it is not exempt, even here, from the danger of the insidious arts of the designing and ambitious, and we should at all times bear in mind that, as all our institutions depend for their support upon public virtue, whatever tends to lay the foundations of the latter, proportionably endangers the former. Our liberty should not be regarded as a mere exemption from bondage, but as a means of usefulness placed within our power, and imposing upon us the highest obligations to endeavor to improve our own condition and to advance the interests of mankind. Many talents have been committed to our charge; the opportunities of improving them are highly propitious. Let us, then, not act the part of the wicked and slothful servant, lest our unfaithfulness should provoke a similar condemnation. We have, indeed, a high destiny to fulfill. Liberty, though driven from all her abodes in the Old World, is, happily, extending her empire over this hemisphere. Twenty millions of the inhabitants of the southern part of this continent are beginning to enjoy her benign and happy influence. The most of them have adopted our system as their model. Our continued example is necessary to their permanent success; and if they and we act well our respective parts, we may reasonably indulge the pleasing, cheering hope that it is reserved to the New World, by the moral force of her example, to regenerate and reform the Old. Great, therefore, is our encouragement to persevere in that prudent and virtuous course by which we have attained our present happiness and glory. Having "tried it," and, by long experience, proved it to be "good," let us "hold fast to it."

Our local, not less than the general government, demands our care and attention; and with such abundant causes of felicitation in regard to the latter, I wish it were in my power to congratulate you upon an equally auspicious aspect of our domestic concerns—but this neither truth nor duty will permit. On the contrary, it is not to be disguised, we have, for some time past, and now are laboring under the paralyzing influence of a system of measures, equally oppressive to the people, ruinous to the resources of the State, and disgraceful to its character—results which must appear the more extraordinary and difficult to be justified, by contrasting our situation immediately after we became a State, with what it has subsequently been. At that time, owing to the paucity of our population and the limited objects of taxation, arising partly therefrom and partly from the exemption from taxation of the military bounty lands for three years after the date of the patents, and of the public lands for five years after the sale of them, there was a necessity for subjecting us to higher taxes than had ever been imposed upon any other part of the Western country, to enable the State to discharge certain Territorial arrearages, to defray the expenses of our Convention, and to meet the current demands of the Government. The taxes then imposed, however, were found sufficient for all these purposes; and nothing was more confidently anticipated than their speedy reduction.

At that time the expenses necessarily required, by the organization, are objects of the Government—with the exception of a trifling amount arising from the addition of a few members to the Legislature—were precisely the same that they were in the early part of last year, or at any intermediate period. Yet, notwithstanding the vast increase of our population, the great augmentation of our personal property, and the accession of the whole of the county and a considerable portion of other lands to the objects of taxation, our taxes have not yet been reduced; but our revenue, as if diminishing in an inverse ratio to the multiplication of our financial resources, was, at the close of the session of the Legislature in 1825, and before a single expense had been incurred in consequence of the new organization of the judiciary, found deficient in the means of meeting the demands on it to a very large amount, which had to be supplied by an emission of Auditor's warrants. Even now the current expenses of the Government do not exceed $25,000, which must be much less than the revenue arising from the military bounty land, alone, every acre of which has, for several years past, been subject to taxation. Of these lands there are 3,500,000, which, at one cent per acre, or one dollar per hundred acres, the lowest rate of taxation, amount to $35,000. Rated in the second class the amount would be $52,500, and in the first $70,000. What proportion has been entered in the first class, or whether any, I know not. It is certain, however, that a very large quantity has been listed in the second; so that it may be fairly inferred that the revenue which they ought to have yielded cannot be short of $40,000, which is $15,000 more than the whole amount of the current expenses of the Government.

It is evident, therefore, that with judicious management this source of revenue alone would havê been sufficient to have defrayed all our necessary expenses, and left in the treasury a large amount surplus, available for the purposes of internal improvement, or any other object of domestic prosperity. But when, with this source of revenue, we take into view all others that have accrued, in addition to the original objects of our taxation, which, of themselves, had been found sufficient to pay off all our Territorial arrearages and to defray the expenses of the Government, they not only increase the difficulty of accounting for so large a deficit in the treasury, but greatly highten the very reprehensible character of that wretched system of policy, which had its origin in the legislation of last year, of paying out our State paper at the enormous discount of three dollars for one.

By this wonderful expedient, our financial resources have been subjected to the same exhausting operation as if the Legislature had actually borrowed money, at two hundred per cent. interest, to pay the debts of the State and to defray every item of public expenditure—as will appear by the following consideration. According to the charter of the State Bank, the State has bound itself to redeem all the notes of the bank that may be presented to it, in gold and silver coins, in the year 1831, and in the meantime, to receive them in discharge of any debts to the State; and for the fulfilment of this contract the public faith, and all the lands, town lots, funds, revenue and other property of the State, have been solemnly and effectually pledged. This, then, is the contract between the State and the holders of the notes of the bank, and as the Constitution has expressly declared that "no law impairing the validity of contracts shall ever be made," it follows that all these notes must be redeemed with gold and silver within five years from this time, if not sooner done. When, therefore, they are thus received at par and paid out at three dollars for one, the public loss must necessarily be equivalent to the payment of 200 per cent. interest. To illustrate this subject to the entire conviction of any rational mind, a few examples of the practical operation of the system are all that can be necessary. The salary of a circuit judge is $600, for which he receives $1800 in State paper. In like manner a judge of the supreme court, whose salary is $800, receives $2400 in State paper, and the Governor, whose salary is $1000, receives $3000 in State paper—so that the people will have to pay $1800 for every circuit judge, $2400 for every supreme judge, and $3000 for the Governor. Upon the same principle, supposing the expenses of the

Government, including those for rebuilding the State House, for the twelve months ending with June last, to have amounted to $15,000 (and I am informed they were more), a debt of $150,000 for the payment of those expenses has been imposed upon the people which will eventually have to be wrung out of them by taxation, thereby producing a clear loss to them of $100,000 in one year, and this with no other consolation for it than that of a little indulgence as to the time of payment—at the expiration of which they may find it just as inconvenient to pay as it would now be.

Now, my countrymen, what is the effect of this system upon you individually? Stripped of its disguise, nothing is clearer than that it must render the taxes of each one of you three times as much as they would otherwise have been—for as a community is but an aggregate of individuals, so the debts of the former are due and payable in just and fair proportion by the latter; and as the State reserves a lien upon every man's property for its proportion of taxes, this unwisely accumulated debt attaches to the property of each of you, operating as a mortgage upon it, to secure the payment of your respective proportions thereof.

Are you, then, willing to have your property thus subjected, unnecessarily, to a triple tax? No State, whatever its energies and resources, could long withstand the destructive power of such a system. Nothing could more effectually check the population and prosperity of our own—for emigrants to a new country are generally of that description of people who are neither the most able nor the most willing to pay high taxes; and a public debt, increasing in this ratio, would soon swell to such magnitude as would not only be outrageously oppressive to our present inhabitants, but would effectually deter others from coming to reside among us.

Our situation at this time, though better than it was last year, is yet too bad to be patiently endured. Our Government is now receiving State paper at par, and paying it out at two dollars for one, which is equivalent to borrowing money at 100 per cent. interest; yet there are not wanting those, and of pretty high authority too, who profess to entertain and endeavor to inculcate the opinion that the State is not interested in the appreciation of its own paper—the absurdity of which is sufficiently manifest from this consideration, alone: that for every dollar paid out by the Government at fifty cents, we become liable to pay one hundred. And, who does not perceive that, as our government is now carried on with State paper, worth only fifty cents on the dollar, its appreciation to par value would render only half as much necessary, and of course would admit of the reduction of our taxes to one-half of the present amount, without producing the slightest diminution of our financial capacity.

A simple fact is sufficient to present a striking and impressive view of the wasteful, injudicious and humiliating character of those measures. It is this: that our revenue derivable from non-residents, alone, has, for years past, amounted to between $40,000 and $50,000—double, or very nearly double the whole amount of the current expenses of the Government; and yet, with this resource, and all the contributions that have been exacted from the inhabitants of the State, those deplorable defalcations as sacrifices, before mentioned, have taken place—and surely nothing can be more humiliating to our pride or disreputable to our character abroad, than that, with an income from non-residents, alone, sufficient to take up all our paper in about four years, it should have depreciated to one-half of its nominal value—since this can only be accounted for on the assumption of our want of good faith and moral honesty.

There has been, fellow-citizens, another feature in our anomalous revenue system, so abhorrent to my feelings that I find it difficult to speak of it, either with the moderation which becomes my years, or is due to the present occasion. This is odious, injurious and indefensible discrimination between the citizens of the State, and non-residents—whereby, while the last article of personal property, not exempt from execution for debt, which the poorest man among us owns, has constantly been liable to be taken and sold for his taxes every year, non-residents have not been compelled to pay theirs oftener than once in two years, and even then always leaving those due for one year uncollected. Now, although I should be one of the last men who would wish to disturb that fair equality, as to taxation, which they are entitled to, under our compact with the General Government, I must be permitted to observe that if any difference had been proper, reason and justice would have required that it should have been in favor of and not against the actual settlers of the State, on whom its defense, safety and prosperity depend.

Whether this measure was the result of design or proceeded from oversight, the want of foresight, or *no sight at all*, I will not pretend to decide. It is demonstrable, however, that its tendency has been to create, cherish and support speculation to the manifest detriment of your interests.

As the principal part of our revenue arises from the taxes of non-residents, human ingenuity could not have devised a more effectual scheme for producing an annual deficit in the treasury than by permitting these taxes always to remain one year in arrear; and this, by creating the necessity for new issues of Auditor's warrants, has constantly afforded opportunities of speculating on them, by which the public have lost precisely what the speculators have gained—whilst the two years indulgence has afforded to the purchasers of lands sold for taxes an opportunity of disposing of them at a profit, for that length of time, without being subject to the inconvenience of paying taxes upon their property, as you are bound to pay on yours. How, then, is this discrimination to be justified? Are speculators more meritorious and useful than the honest cultivators of the soil? If not, why should they have been so much more highly favored?

But these are not the only objections to this measure. It was calculated to withdraw State paper from circulation among us, to accumulate it in the hands of non-residents and speculators, and, ultimately, to insure to them the benefit of discharging their taxes in that medium, while the great body of our people would have been compelled, for the want of it, to pay theirs in cash. Depreciated, as our paper had been, by our legislation, to less than one-third of its nominal value, and thereby increasing the inducements to buy it up, so much of it had, in the early part of last year, passed into the hands of non-residents, that its scarcity was greatly felt throughout every part of the State. Judging of the future by the past, it is reasonable to infer, from the competition which has taken place at every public sale for taxes, and the evidently increasing disposition to engage in that speculation, that our paper would have been hoarded up for the purpose of being laid out in the purchase of lands, or in the payment of taxes on them, at the next sales. These were to have taken place in January, 1828, when there would have been three years taxes due, which would not have amounted to less than between $120,000 and $150,000. Taking into consideration, then, that the whole amount of our State paper is less than $200,000, and that, of this, $60,000 are required by law to be burnt before that time, you may well judge how much of it would have remained in circulation, available to our own people in the payment of their taxes.

Regarding the subject in this point of view, and happening to be at Vandalia, at the last session of the Legislature, I spared no pains to get this unwise and unjust distinction between our own citizens and non-residents abolished; and I am happy to have it in my power to say, that the sales for the taxes of the latter are hereafter to be annual, which (better late than never) will compel them to disburse, and enable the Government to get into circulation a large amount of paper, which, in the course of next year, cannot fail to afford great relief to the people, but which would otherwise have remained hoarded up for at least one year longer.

The taxes of those non-residents and speculators, for the last year, as well as our own, became due on the first day of last October; but while you have been compelled to pay yours, not a cent was exacted from them. Had they, like you, been required to pay them, there would have been no necessity for a new emission of Auditor's warrants; the State would have saved all the loss consequent upon the increase of its paper and paying it out at $2 for $1, and $40,000 more, at least, would have been paid into the treasury, which, by the operations and disbursements of the Government, would have been diffused throughout the State, thereby increasing our circulating medium and facilitating to you the means of paying your present year's taxes. But then this would have withered if not annihilated that speculation which has so long been luxuriating upon the spoilations that have been committed upon the resources of the State and the honest earnings of the sweat of your brows. Such impositions as these, upon a free, high-minded and independent people, I boldly assert have no parallel in the annals of free government, and they are only to be borne by that charity which hopeth all things, believeth all things, and endureth all things.

Nor are the innovations that have been introduced into our new-fangled revenue system, in regard to the listing of our lands and the payment of our taxes, among the least of our grievances. Visionary and impracticable, as their injurious effects upon the revenue and the confusion they have created have proved those new regulations to be, it is much to be feared that, by their preventing us from listing our own lands and at the same time subjecting them to be sold in the names of other persons, many an honest man may lose his land before he is apprised of his danger; but to say nothing of those other novelties and eccentricities which have given many of us much trouble, and puzzled the best informed among us to know how to act to save our property according to legal requirements, what reason, justice or propriety is there in requiring the lands of residents to be sold for taxes at Vandalia? If necessary to sell them at all, why not, as heretofore, permit them to be sold in the counties in which they lie? The taxes could be collected with equal certainty. An advertisement at the court house door would notify more of the inhabitants of a county than its publication for a whole year, much less three weeks only, in a paper printed at Vandalia; the lands would be less likely to be sold without the knowledge of the owners, and, being sold where they were known, less of them would probably be sacrificed. Is it not, then, outrageously and insufferably oppressive that a citizen residing at the mouth of the Ohio, or in the extreme northern parts of our settlement, should be subjected to the expense and trouble of going all the way to Vandalia, either to prevent the sale of his lands, to pay the taxes on them, or to redeem them? For my part, I can conceive of no one reason, in favor of this measure, except that it might multiply the chances of buying our lands for a trifle. And are we to be converted into "hewers of wood and drawers of water" to pamper a set of merciless speculators?

I had intended to have brought into review some of the topics of our domestic policy, but I fear I have already trespassed too long upon your patience. I will, therefore, in conclusion, only add, that with a sincere desire to preserve the blessings of liberty, and to assist in relieving our State from its present difficulties and embarrassments, I offer myself to your consideration as a candidate for the office of Governor, assuring you that if I shall be fortunate enough to be honored with the approbation of my fellow-citizens, now peculiarly desirable to me as well from personal as public considerations, my poor abilities shall be faithfully excited to protect your interests and to advance your happiness and prosperity—which is all I can promise.

It is, fellow-citizens, only in the sunshine of his prosperity that any man can boast of his trumpeters. In general all such auxiliaries are dead to him who has been overwhelmed by the rough storms of adversity; no time is more unpropitious for finding "a friend, indeed," than when "a friend's in need." With those, therefore, who consider me a prostrate man, I might be excused from saying a little in my own favor; but as I have never been put down by the people, and will not believe that I shall be until I am compelled to realize it, I shall not attempt to avail myself of that privilege. My public conduct is before you. It is not to be doubted that, in a long, uninterrupted course of public service of nearly twenty-eight years, in various highly important and responsible stations, I must have committed many errors which are liable to serious objections. Hoping, however, that your generosity will regard them with all those charitable interpretations and indulgencies which are due to human frailty, I shall rely exclusively upon your own recollection of such parts of my conduct as may have appeared to you meritorious and acceptable.

I must beg leave, however, to notice one objection urged against me, which relates entirely to the future, and, if true, involves no culpability on my part for its existence. This is that I am too old. Now, although I freely acknowledge that I am old enough to be much better and wiser than I am, and were it not for a very contented spirit with which I have been blessed, might even wish to be younger, yet if small things may be compared to great ones, I may be permitted to say that I am not as old, by between two and three years, as Gen. Washington was when he was appointed to the command of our revolutionary army; and, with all due deference for the more disinterested judgment of others, I cannot think that I am so entirely frail, leaky and unseaworthy as not to be trusted on one more voyage at least. I am indeed too old to be captivated or misled by the ruinous prospects and dangerous novelties which I have animadverted upon; and I am much mistaken if I shall not be found quite young enough to convince my fellow-citizens generally of the expediency, if not absolute necessity, of a thorough reform in all these particulars. There are many things, both in the moral and physical world, that grow better as time waneth. Even wisdom herself is often improved by the experience which age brings to her aid. Old whisky, old wine, old bacon, old servants, old acquaintances and old friends are quite agreeable to us all, and I should not be surprised if you should even like some of the good old ways by which we contrived to get along somehow or other while I had the honor of being your Governor. Everything, therefore, is not to be rejected merely because it is old; and among those good old things which you may not consider the less worthy of your regard on account of their age, I hope you will not forget to include the Old Ranger.

On another occasion, during the canvass for Governor in 1826, Governor Edwards, in a speech to his constituents, after making a few introductory remarks, proceeded as follows:

It is evident, however, that in connection with other measures adopted by our Legislature, it was calculated to render our miserable banking system almost exclusively subservient to the interest of non-residents and speculators, by its tendency to withdraw State paper from circulation among us, to accumulate it in their hands, and ultimately to insure to them the benefits of paying their taxes in that medium, while our own citizens would have been compelled, for the want of it, to pay theirs in cash.

As there could be no inducements to purchase our paper if it were at par, so it is only as it depreciates that it admits of any speculation whatever. The greater, therefore, its depreciation, the greater the speculation, and consequently the stronger must be the inducements of those who have money at command to purchase it, because, while they risk less, they have a fair prospect of gaining more than they could make under different circumstances. Upon whom then are these inducements calculated to operate the most powerfully? Most certainly upon those non-residents who hold such immense tracts of land within our State, and whose taxes alone would be sufficient to take up all of our paper within about four or five years at most. The great amount due by them is sufficient to awaken their vigilance to provide themselves at the earliest possible period with the means of discharging it; and thus while our own citizens, owing but comparatively small sums, and being generally scarce of money, think only of providing for the payment of their taxes about the time the sheriff is expected to demand them, these non-residents and speculators have had the opportunity of engrossing nearly all the State paper which in the meantime had been in market. Having once got it in their possession, either for the payment of their taxes or for the purchase of lands to be sold for taxes—the only uses that have heretofore rendered it valuable—they could have but little inducements to part with it, even for a much higher price than they gave for it, since they could have no certainty of obtaining adequate future supplies, and of course would be subjected to the danger of having themselves to replace it with specie. It has, therefore, constantly been their interest to hoard it up till they could apply it to the objects for which they obtained it, and you might just as well talk of catching birds by putting fresh salt upon their tails, as to expect to force men who have engrossed our paper for these purposes to part with it by reducing its value. This would, in fact, only throw so much more into their power. Were there any doubts as to these results, the woful experience we have already had is sufficient to remove them. The experiment of making our State paper more plenty and more accessible to those of our fellow-citizens who stand in need of it by depreciating it, has been fully tried, and the result of the experiment has been that it has almost entirely disappeared from among us. Depreciated, as it was by our legislation, to less than one-third of its nominal value in the early part of last year, non-residents having a large amount of taxes to pay, and well knowing that the State was and always will be bound to receive it at par with specie, employed so many agents and used such exertions to purchase it up, that its scarcity was soon perceived, and has been ever since severely felt throughout every part of the State. Judging of the future by the past, it is reasonable to conclude, from the great competition that has existed at every sale of lands for taxes at Vandalia, and from the evidently increasing disposition to engage in that speculation, as evinced at the last sales, that our paper would, as it has heretofore been, be hoarded up for the purpose of being laid out in the purchase of lands or in the payment of taxes on them at the next sales. These were to have taken place, according to the law under consideration, in January, 1828, when there would have been three years taxes due, which, according to the estimate in the report of the last Legislature, could not have amounted to less than $120,000. Taking into consideration, then, that the whole amount of our State paper is less than $200,000, and that of this amount more than $60,000 are required by law to be burnt before that time, you may well judge how much of it the policy of our legislation would have left in circulation available to our fellow-citizens in the payment of their taxes, or to the unfortunate bank debtors in the payment of their bank debts, whom the Legislature determined rigorously to coerce at the very time that its injudicious measures were so well calculated to lessen their means of payment, if not to render it utterly impracticable.

Experience has ever proved that a paper currency tends to prevent the circulation of the precious metals. A proof of this is found in the fact that not a cent of specie is now or has been for years past paid into our treasury. And thus, while we are deprived by this means of a sound circulating medium, the benefits of our miserable State currency are almost exclusively enjoyed by non-residents. The greatest evil we now labor under is the want of an adequate circulating medium of any kind. How unwise, then, must have been the policy of this extraordinary indulgence to non-residents which has so clearly tended to aggravate that evil? Seeing that our paper must have been hoarded up in their hands, the most natural and obvious policy would have been to have compelled them to disburse it in the payment of taxes as often as we could, consistently with our stipulations to place them upon a fair equality with ourselves. They might, indeed, have purchased it again, but not upon the same terms they did last year. They bought it then at an average of not more than 30 cents to the dollar: they would now have to give at least 50 cents; and as when once received into the treasury it could only get into market again through the medium of our citizens, its re-purchase would have been a clear gain to them of 20 per cent. upon the whole amount.

This extraordinary indulgence to non-residents has been practically extended to the purchasers of lands sold for taxes wherever they may have resided. The taxes of these non-residents and speculators, as well as our own, for the last year, became due on the first day of October last, but, while you have been compelled to pay yours, not a cent has been exacted from them, nor did the law to which I am objecting require them to pay a cent till January, 1828—an indulgence of two years and three months longer than has been allowed to you.

Unnatural as this partiality for non-residents and speculators seems to be, and unjustifiable upon principle as it surely would be, even if productive of no public loss, it is infinitely more reprehensible in consequence of its having been extended to them, as I shall presently show, at the sacrifice of your pecuniary interest.

It must indeed be humiliating to your pride to find that the sympathies of your own Legislature have been so much more strongly enlisted in favor of non-residents and speculators than yourselves. Such a predilection cannot fail to surprise all who are unable to penetrate the mysterious motives which have produced it. Congress, judging from the general disposition which the members of a Legislature would naturally be expected to cherish towards their immediate constituents, and aware of the ordinary springs and motives of human action, deemed it necessary to guard against what they supposed a much more probable bias—a partiality in favor of our own citizens—and hence insisted upon a stipulation, which we agreed to, for placing non-residents upon a bare equality, as to taxation, with ourselves. How much, then, must that enlightened body be surprised to find, not only that their precaution was wholly unnecessary, but that our Legislature, not content with placing non-residents upon a fair equality, and disdaining the maxim that "charity begins at home," have distinguished them by extraordinary indulgencies denied to our own citizens.

Such conduct certainly appears somewhat inexplicable. It is, however, susceptible of the clearest demonstration that a further tendency of this indulgence has been to create, to cherish and to support an abominable system of speculation to the manifest detriment of the public interest.

Let it be remembered that the principal part of our revenue is derived from the taxes of non-residents. This being the case, human ingenuity could not have devised a more effectual scheme for producing an annual deficit in the treasury than by permitting these taxes always to remain one year in arrear; and this, by creating the necessity for new issues of Auditor's warrants, has constantly afforded opportunities of speculating on them, by which the public have lost precisely what the speculators have gained, while the two years' indulgence, allowed to the purchasers of lands sold for taxes, has afforded them the opportunity of disposing of their lands so purchased at a profit, for that length of time, without being subjected to the inconvenience of paying taxes on their property as you are bound to pay on yours. How, then, is this discrimination to be justified? Are speculators more useful, more meritorious, more worthy of the forbearance, lenity and encouragement of the Government than the honest farmers and mechanics of the country, who make their livings by the sweat of their brows? If not, why should they have been so much more highly favored?

Had those non-residents and speculators been required to pay their taxes last October, as you were compelled to pay yours, there would then have been no necessity for new issues of Auditor's warrants, the State would have saved all the loss consequent upon the increase of its paper, and paying it out at two dollars for one, and forty thousand dollars more at least would have been received into the treasury, which, by the disbursement and operations of the Government, would have been diffused throughout the State, thereby increasing our circulating medium and facilitating to you the means of paying your present year's taxes; but then, this would have withered if not annihilated that speculation which has been too long luxuriating upon the spoilations that have been committed upon the resources of the State and the honest earnings of the sweat of your brows.

Were I to assert that you are taxed to support this indulgence to non-residents and speculators, would you not consider it too monstrous and incredible for belief? Or, believing it, would it not betray a mean, servile and abject spirit, which every independent freeman must abhor, to regard such oppression with anything short of the most indignant reprobation? It was not the trifling amount of the tax on tea, imposed by the British Parliament, but an opposition to the principle imposed by the elevated sentiments of freedom, that roused the spirit of resistance and animated the exertions of our noble sires in our glorious contest for independence. We should indeed disgrace our lineage, and deserve to be considered their degenerate sons, if we could feel reconciled to be placed, in our own State, and by our own Legislature, too, on inferior grounds to that of non-residents and speculators. But to be willing to be taxed to support a humiliating discrimination between them and us, which violates our just claims to a fair equality, would prove us worthy only to become their "hewers of wood and drawers of water."

Incredible, however, as it may appear, it is nevertheless true that you are, in fact, taxed to support this unjust inequality. The amount of the tax due last October, by non-residents, as assumed in the report of the Legislature, before alluded to, is $40,000. They had, then, this amount of our State paper in their hands, or like our own citizens they should have had it, which is the same thing to us. It bears an interest of two per cent., which, on $40,000, is $800 per year. The interest, therefore, for the two years' indulgence extended to non-residents, over and above what has been allowed to our own citizens, amounts to $1600, not a cent of which is chargeable to them, according to the practical operation of the system, provided their taxes be paid at any time within that period. Now, had those taxes been paid last October, as they ought to have been, the State would have saved that amount of interest, as our paper, when once received into the treasury, ceases thereafter to bear interest; but, instead of this, this sum of $1600 has been virtually offered as a premium to non-residents and speculators not to pay their taxes as you have been compelled to pay yours —for they will be allowed precisely that much more, as interest upon our paper, at the expiration of the two years' indulgence, than they would have received if they had paid it last October. Could it, then, be expected that they would be guilty of the egregious folly of overlooking and disregarding this singular advantage? And who, let me ask, has to pay for it? The interest thus allowed them, every man of common sense will see, must be made up by the State. I have already shown that the debts of the State are due and payable, in just and fair proportion, by the people of the State; and as the State has no means of raising revenue, paying debts or making up any losses whatever, but by taxation, which must necessarily fall equally upon all, it is evident that each one of you will be compelled to pay your respective proportion of the interest thus gratuitously allowed to non-residents and speculators. And if you are willing thus to be taxed to maintain a distinction which degrades you below their level, and from which no public benefit can possibly arise, it is hardly to be expected that you will, hereafter, feel or manifest any repugnance to the unnecessary multiplication of offices, or the addition of a few hundred dollars more or less to the salaries of our officers.

But this, my fellow-citizens, is but a bagatelle—a mere atom in the great mass of losses that have been sustained by this unfortunate measure, and for which you have been and still are, and for years to come must be taxed. I do not intend to be understood as assailing the motives of any particular individual for the projection of this measure, for I neither know nor have I sought to find out who was its original author; but believing it to be not less my duty than my right, as a free-born citizen, to point out its consequences, I will say that the powers of the human mind are utterly incapable of devising a more adroit and artful scheme for perpetrating and increasing the evils of our present paper system, and involving the State in hopeless bankruptcy and disgrace, than this indulgence to non-residents and speculators, with the auxiliary measures that have accompanied it. Nor can a stronger proof of the dextrous nature of this destructive policy be desired than is to be found in the fact that, although it has been in operation for years past, its ruinous consequences have hitherto escaped the general notice of the people.

Soon after the establishment of our State Bank, its deleterious influence on the prosperity of the State and its injurious effects upon our revenue became so manifest, that no one who had any reputation to hazard could have been found bold enough to have encountered the strong public sentiment against it, by even proposing to issue the additional $200,000 which the charter admitted; but our Legislature have stolen a march upon you, and have done infinitely worse in issuing Auditor's warrants, both because they never can answer the purposes of a circulating medium as well as the bank notes, and because the loss upon them to the State must necessarily be greater. According to the charter of the bank, it never was intended that the State should have sustained any loss. If the law had been executed in good faith, by taking security to double the value of the sums borrowed, it might have sustained none. In many cases it will sustain none. But in issuing Auditor's warrants, and paying them out at $3 for $1, a loss of two-thirds of their whole amount is realized on their issue, without any hope of receiving or any right to claim any indemnification whatever. Besides, all those warrants have tended to keep down the value of the notes of the bank, and of course to subject the State, which is bound to make them good, to all the eventual loss of their depreciation.

Every real friend of the State must deplore these accumulating evils; and while every patriotic bosom has been cherishing the fond hope of their gradual diminution and final termination, what has been the result? In five years about $100,000 of these bank notes have been withdrawn from circulation, but in a single year a larger amount of Auditor's warrants have been substituted in their place; for during the last year, only, warrants to the amount of $107,000 were issued. When, then, are our embarrassments to end, if as fast, only, as our bank notes are withdrawn from circulation, Auditor's warrants, at a much greater loss, are to be made to supply their place?

It has been supposed that this wretched policy was intended to favor bank debtors. If so, it would have been far better to have given up those debts altogether, for it can be demonstrated with mathematical certainty that an annual loss, equal to that which was produced last year by this policy, would, in less than five years, amount to one-third more than the whole sum due by bank debtors, and it would surely be wiser to give this up than to sacrifice one-third more on their account in so short a time, and this, too, without any additional assurance of making ultimate collections from them. It would, indeed, have been less grievous if this loss to the State had been the gain of the bank debtors, for then it would have been among our own citizens; but we have, unfortunately, no grounds to solace ourselves with this consolation, for the most of these warrants, like our State paper, were soon caught up by the agents of non-residents and speculators, who, like the eagle ready to pounce upon its prey, stood waiting and prepared for that purpose.

Let us, then, inquire whence arose the necessity or what furnished the pretext for issuing those warrants. Certainly, nothing else created the one or furnished the other than those deficits in the treasury which arose from the indulgence, granted to non-residents and speculators, in regard to the payment of their taxes. This pretext, thus obtained, may be made to operate with equal force forever, and keep us constantly issuing warrants and receiving nothing else from non-residents in the payment of their taxes—while they may hold our State paper, bearing an interest of two per cent., until the State is bound to redeem it with gold and silver.

In consequence of those non-residents and speculators not having been compelled to pay their taxes last October, it became necessary, as before observed, to issue warrants to the amount of those taxes. These warrants, bearing no interest, and the payment of them not being quite as well secured as that of our State paper, could of course be bought cheaper. What, then, was to prevent those non-residents and speculators from buying them up to pay those very taxes in January, 1828, which ought to have been paid last October? The warrants being thus paid into the treasury, the State would only have redeemed them, the treasury would still be as destitute of funds as ever, and the Government under the same necessity to issue new warrants as when these were issued. And again, new warrants might be paid and substituted in like manner, and thus, instead of gradually diminishing our responsibility for the notes of the bank, and saving at the rate of $800 a year in interest, the warrants so issued in advance might be made to pay the taxes of those non-residents and speculators, till the expiration of the charter of the bank, when our whole bank debt will fall due.

Let us now inquire how much has been realized to the State, by this system of policy, out of the taxes of non-residents, for the last three years. At the close of the

Legislature of 1825, neither their taxes for the year 1823 or 1824 had been required to be paid. Supposing them to have amounted, for these two years, to $80,000. This may be assumed as the amount of the warrants that were issued to supply the place of those taxes. These warrants being paid at $3 for $1, of course the State could only realize one-third of the amount of those taxes, which is but $2,666 66 out of the $80,000. The taxes due last October being $40,000, this may be assumed as the amount of the warrants to supply their place. These warrants being paid at $2 for $1, $20,000 only of these taxes can be saved to the State—thereby, without making any deduction for the loss of interest, as already explained, realizing only $46,666 66 out of $120,000, being at the average rate of a little upwards of $15,000 per year, which is not half the amount of last year's expenses. But nothing is more easy than, with a few strokes of the pen, to supply every deficiency, however produced, by Auditor's warrants at $3 for $1, which, however sportful to others, I am afraid you will find death to you, unless it can be speedily and effectually checked.

But let us further inquire how these warrants affect our interest in other respects. They were made receivable in payment of bank debts, at par, though issued at three times as much as they were paid out at. The amount of the bank debts collected annually is $30,000. Supposing this sum paid in warrants of the same nominal value, but issued at $3 for $1, the State would receive only $10,000 instead of $30,000, and from these $10,000 at least $5,000 must be deducted for the salaries of five cashiers, and other incidental expenses of the bank, so that the State would, in fact, receive only $5,000 out of the $30,000 for which it is accountable, and of course would still be liable on this account for the remaining $25,000, which, let it be remembered, could only be raised by taxation.

Supposing the whole debt settled in the same way, and what would be the loss which the State would sustain? The original amount was $300,000, which the State agreed to redeem, at the expiration of ten years, with gold and silver coins, and, to indemnify it for this responsibility, the borrowers were required to pay one-tenth of it, to-wit: $30,000, annually. But if, instead of receiving this sum, the State should only secure $5,000 per annum, these for ten years would amount to but $50,000, which would leave the State in debt, at the expiration of that period, for the remaining $250,000, which, if paid as our Legislature have paid our other debts of every description, in Auditor's warrants at $3 for $1, would involve us in a debt of precisely $750,000. If paid in Auditor's warrants, at the rate at which they are at present issued, to-wit: at $2 for $1, (and there would be the same apology and justification for paying this as any other debt in this way,) it would leave us involved in a debt of $500,000, which, let it not be forget, could only be raised by taxation.

Our losses necessarily arising from the policy that has been pursued by our Legislature are precisely in this proportion. And upon whom do they fall? You, who have had no agency in this indulgence to non-residents and speculators, nor anything to do with the bank—old residents, new settlers and future emigrants—will all have to be taxed to pay your respective proportions of these losses. Are you, then, willing to be taxed to support a partial and unjust system, or to pay other people's debts? If not, you must speak with the voice of authority, and at least forbid the issuing of any more warrants upon the ruinous terms upon which they are even now daily issued—for, independent of other losses, they must, on these terms, render your taxes twice as high as they would otherwise be. Such impositions as these upon a free, high-minded and independent people, I boldly assert have no parallels in the annals of free government, and they are only to be borne by that Christian charity which hopeth all things, believeth all things, and endureth all things; but with whatever fortitude they may be borne, truth and reason must forever consign them to the indignant reprobation of a people who have the judgment to discern, the sense to feel and the spirit to resist injustice and oppression.

Regarding this indulgence to non-residents and speculators with the objections which I have pointed out to you, and happening to be at Vandalia during the last session of the Legislature, I spared no pains and provoked no little hostility to myself in trying to get this unwise and unjust distinction, between them and our own citizens, abolished; and, although I could not accomplish all I wished in this respect, I am happy to say that the sales for their taxes are hereafter to be annual, which (better late than never) will compel them to disburse, and enable the Government to put into circulation a large amount of our paper—which cannot fail, in the course of next year, to afford great relief to the people, but which would otherwise have remained hoarded up for at least one year longer.

There is no danger, fellow-citizens, that I shall ever be deprived of the credit of having been the means of effecting this change, for this injurious measure had been in operation for years, and no member of the Legislature can acknowledge that he foresaw the consequences I have pointed out, without pronouncing his own condemnation for not having at least attempted its repeal at an earlier period. I ought to receive this credit at your hands, for my interposition on this subject has been denounced as an undue interference with the Legislature, and has elicited against me the angry, persecuting and relentless opposition of all those who, by such means, have promoted their own ambitious views or satiated their craving avarice. This is no wonder, since I have deprived them of the means of feasting sumptuously upon the spoils that have been committed upon your interest. But, whatever may be the consequences to myself, I glory in what I have done, and only long for an opportunity to complete the work of reformation, thus begun, by putting an entire stop to the issue of Auditor's warrants upon terms which now daily subject you to be taxed twice as high as you ought to be, or as there is any necessity for. I denounce the whole system of warrants, and never will give my consent, in any situation, either private or public, to the issue of one dollar's worth at any sacrifice whatever of your interest. I have ever been a fearless politician—probably too much so, on some occasions, for my interest—but I thank my God that I am not to be deterred by the log-rolling caucuses of big men assembled at Vandalia, who, arrogating to themselves the right of deciding for you, and undertaking to determine whom you shall be permitted to raise up and put down, issue their orders accordingly to their instruments throughout every part of the State. It is true that painful experience has taught me not to undervalue the power of such combinations, but I would infinitely rather be put down by them, in a manly struggle, than meanly succumb to them. And you may be assured the time has arrived when, if you do not set your faces against such bargaining systems, you will find your most essential rights bargained away from you.

My appeal from the self-constituted tribunals is directly to the people, in whose virtue, intelligence and ultimate justice I have the most implicit confidence, and on which I have ever found the safest dependence. It is, happily, your right to decide for yourselves, and whatever may be your decision, I shall be one of the last men in this world to complain of it. These powerful combinations hope to influence you to oppose me. They may succeed; but why should they? Few of those individuals, if any, have any just cause of hostility to me. Some of them may even owe much of their present power to injure me to my unrequited kindness to them. It would not be the first time that I have raised up a stick to break my own head with. It may be my misfortune to be considered as standing in the way of the gratification of their own views of personal ambition; but it would be asking too much of independent freemen, whom I have never injured or even intentionally offended, to become my enemies merely because this and that big man happen to be so from their own selfish motives. I have always taken the greatest pleasure in rendering any assistance in my power to my fellow-citizens. I am not conscious of ever having turned my back upon any man who has endeavored to seek justice, or the redress of any grievance, through my instrumentality. I may have offended some of you, but inexorable, indeed, must be the vengeance I have provoked, if the power of combinations have not already prostrated me sufficiently to satisfy it.

Have the people any interest to advance by assisting those who have brought them to the very brink of ruin, to keep down a man who boldly and fearlessly advocates their own cause, which each one of us knows to be just? What have I ever done to deserve your hostility? Let the time, place, and circumstances—the when, and where, and how—be distinctly stated, and I am ready to answer for myself. I disdain to notice the petty, contemptible, gossiping tales which falsehood and malignity are constanting inventing and circulating against me; but I challenge my enemies to show a single act of my whole public life that is as reprehensible as this indulgence to non-residents. I go further: I defy them to show that all my official misdeeds, throughout my long public service, put together, have been as injurious to the public interest as this single measure, with its auxiliary of Auditor's warrants at three dollars for one, or even at two for one. Could they do this, they would not spare me, for it has been my misfortune to owe as little as any man in the world to the courtesy and forbearance of my enemies. You do not hear them complaining against and denouncing the authors of those measures. Why, then, am I so much more obnoxious to their opposition than those whom they are obliged to admit have done worse than I have? I leave you to decide upon the motive.

Some of them pay me the compliment (probably an undeserved one) of admitting that no man in the State is more capable of devising the ways and means of freeing it from its present calamitous situation than myself; but then, with sinister premonition, they inquire, "Is he to be trusted?" I am willing for you to decide this question—am I to be trusted. I have been tried for many years—and when, or where, or how have I ever deceived the people? Was it during those Territorial times, that tried men's souls? was it when our frontiers were smoking with the blood and strewed with the mangled bodies of our men, women and children, indiscriminately slaughtered by ruthless savages? Did I then consult my own ease and comfort and interest, or shrink from the highest responsibility? Did I wait for authority to act? Did I not unhesitatingly act without it? and freely risk my commission, my reputation, my property and my life to defend my fellow-citizens and punish barbarian aggression? I have letters in possession from some of my present persecutors that contain satisfactory answers to all these questions. Did I, then, betray or deceive you on any of those great questions, so vitally affecting your interest, which were agitated in Congress during the period of my service in that body? Let my published speeches and the journals of the Senate answer.

No, my fellow-citizens, my enemies do not fear that I shall deceive you. They well know that if I were to try my best I could not possibly effect any measures more injurious to your interest than those which are now in daily operation before your own eyes, but they believe I possess the capacity to produce reform and they fear that I shall obtain the credit of effecting it—and this is a credit which, if my life and health is spared, they shall not deprive me of, for, so long as oppression continues to stalk through our land with such gigantic strides, you shall find one man, at least, in the State, whether you reject me or not, bold enough to cry aloud and spare not. You may abandon me, but I will not desert your cause; for an ambition to deserve to be considered as the people's friend is engrafted in my very nature, and no man can more strongly confide in their ultimate justice.

I am charged with attacking the members of the Legislature; but it is not my object to assail any individual whatever. I have explored no journals to see who voted this way or that way. It is measures, and not men, that I wish to be understood as opposing. I firmly believe the great majority of our Legislature to have been honest, virtuous and patriotic. Many of them, I know, have anxiously desired to get rid of all the evils of our paper system; but I have no doubt that, tired and discouraged by unavailing efforts for that purpose, and yielding to a listless despair, they have been deceived, and that few of them, if any, ever foresaw the consequences I have pointed out; nor is it to be wondered at that they should not. It falls to the lot of but few men to be good financiers; and did they possess the highest financial capacities, the opportunities of ascertaining the true state of our treasury, and the effects of particular measures upon it, during the session of the Legislature, when they have so much other business to attend to, are too limited, and hence it has been made by our constitution the duty of the executive, who has the requisite time for attention to these subjects, to communicate to the Legislature, from time to time, the true state of the government—besides all which, those measures have generally been adopted near the close of a session, in all the hurry and bustle usual about that period. If the evil consequences which I have portrayed escaped their notice, I cannot hesitate to believe, as true patriots and real friends to the State, they will rejoice, for the sake of the public good, that I have discovered and disclosed them. But, whether or not, if the measures are wrong, as I contend they are, I disclaim the authority of any gag-law, legal or moral, to restrain my animadversions upon them.

The combined powers of his political opponents, of the bank party, of the advocates of the circuit court system, aided by the co-operation of some of the most powerful men and purest patriots of the State, who then took an erroneous view of his course, but who were afterwards numbered among his warmest friends, were all brought to operate against his election. In attacking the policy of previous Legislatures, he also dissatisfied many of his warmest friends who had supported and voted for many of those measures. Against this powerful host he contended almost single-handed. But deploring the ruinous measures that had formerly prevailed, and the enormous taxes with which the people were at that time oppressed in consequence thereof, he determined, regardless of personal consequences, to produce reform; and neither consulting nor soliciting the aid of any individual, he took such bold grounds in all his addresses, that the politicians and many of his friends thought it too hazardous to be identified with him—yet he succeeded, though the candidate for Lieutenant-Governor and for Congress, on the same ticket, and many of his political friends, were defeated at the same election, and a majority opposed to them and himself were returned to the Legislature. This election, when it is considered that Mr. Cook, his son-in-law, was the candidate to represent the only Congressional district in the State; that both of them had represented the State, the one in the Senate and the other in the House of Representatives of the United States, for nearly the whole period since the admission of the State into the Union; that Judges Pope, Alexander, and Abner Field, relatives of Gov. Edwards, had also filled important offices—was, indeed, in the language of the Hon. William Wirt, "a noble victory." It proved to the nation at large that he was sustained by the people of his own State. Among his warmest supporters in this election may be numbered such men as Judges Lockwood, Wilson, Breese, Brown, Gov. Ford, George Forquer, William H. Brown and Hon. David J. Baker. For a history of the financial condition of the State, and other measures of policy which he advocated, the reader is referred to his messages and speeches; and, indeed, his correspondence and publications furnish such a complete history of his times, as to make it unnecessary to write much on the subject.

In his messages to the legislatures, he recommended the measures which he had advocated in his public addresses—most of which were adopted without much opposition.

In the year previous to his being elected Governor, Auditor's warrants, which the State was bound to redeem with gold and silver, to the amount of $107,000, were issued and paid out at three dollars for one, whereby the State sustained a loss in one single year of more than $70,000—a sum, at that time, sufficient to have carried on all the necessary operations of the government for three years. The result of the measures which he proposed, and which were adopted by the Legislature on his recommendation, were as follows: The taxes on lands of residents of the counties in which they were situated, which had previously been paid into the State treasury, were given up to those counties; the State was not losing one cent by its financial operations; and the taxes could be reduced to at least one-third of the amount previously levied. All of these measures were effected without the aid of any resources which were not in the power of the State previous to the commencement of his administration. Governor Ford, in his history of the State, says that he broke down all opposition to his administration, carried all his measures, and succeeded in having all his candidates elected.

Judging from the friendly and cordial feelings manifested towards him by the Legislature, at the close of his term of office; from letters he received from every portion of the State; from the kind and affectionate treatment he met with from his fellow-citizens, wherever he went among them, and from the undoubted fact that many who had opposed him were then his friends and supporters—he never stood better with the people of the State than he did at the close of his administration.

CHAPTER XI.

The Winnebago and Black Hawk Wars.

During Gov. Edwards' administration, as Executive of the State, the Indians upon the North-Western frontier began to be very troublesome. The different tribes not only commenced a warfare among themselves, in regard to their respective boundaries, but they extended their hostilities to the white settlements. A treaty of peace, in which the whites acted more as mediators than as a party, had been signed at Prairie du Chien, on the 19th day of August, 1825, by the terms of which the boundaries between the Winnebagoes and the Sioux, Chippeways, Sauks, Foxes, and and other tribes, were defined, but it failed to keep them quiet. Their depredations and murders continued frequent, and in the summer of 1827 their conduct, particularly of the Winnebagoes, became very alarming. There is no doubt, however, that the whites, who at this period were immigrating in large numbers to the North-West, and earnestly desired their removal further westward, purposely exasperated the Indians, at the same time that they greatly exaggerated the actual hostilities committed.

According to a letter written at this time, by Gen. Street, from Prairie du Chien, to Gov. Edwards, the Winnebagoes had been soured by the conduct of the adventurers flocking to and working the lead mines of Fever River and vicinity. Of those who went there by land, by far the greatest number passed through the country occupied by the Winnebagoes, and no doubt behaved very badly towards them. As to the right of that tribe to the lands in question, there seems to have been a misunderstanding. It appears, by a treaty made by Gen. Harrison, in 1804, that all the lands between the mouths of the Wisconsin and Illinois Rivers were purchased by the United States from the Sacs and Foxes. In 1816, Gen. Clark, Col. Chouteau and Gov. Edwards, as Commissioners of the United States, ceded, with certain reservations, all those lands which lie north of a due west line from the southern extremity of Lake Michigan to the Mississippi, to the Ottaways, Chippeways and Pottawottamies, (denominated the Indians of the Illinois River,) and who therefore appeared to be the *real* owners of the lands. But, according to the treaty of August 19th, 1825, the Commissioners seemed to have recognized the right of the Winnebagoes to this same land. Certainly, whether rightfully or not, the latter tribe were, and had been for years, in possession of the territory, and fully believed it belonged to them. But without regard to this claim, Mr. Thomas, the agent at the mines, freely granted permits to the miners collected there, and numerous diggings were industriously pushed far east of the line between the Winnebagoes and the Indians of the Illinois River. These trespassers procured and took away great quantities of mineral to the smelters. The Winnebagoes complained of this as an open violation of the treaty; no notice was, however, taken of their complaints. The permits continued to be given and the diggings progressed. At last the Indians attempted force, which was repelled; and very angry feelings, by consequence, were produced on both sides.

In this state of excitement some of the Indians left the neighborhood of the mines and made a journey above Prairie du Chien, for the purpose, as was supposed, of consulting some of their chiefs and influential men there, and also to invite the co-operation of the Sioux. They were there met by a Sioux Indian, called Waw-zee-kootee (he that shoots in the pine-tops), who told the Winnebagoes that the U. S. commander at Fort Snelling had delivered up several Sioux Indians to the Chippeways, by whom they had been cruelly murdered, and that at the same time two Winnebagoes, in confinement, charged with murder, had been butchered by the whites. It appears that just before this time a party of twenty-four Chippeways, while on their way to Fort Snelling, had been surprised by a band of Sioux and eight of them killed. The murderers had been captured by the U. S. commandant and turned over to the Chippeways, by whom they had been properly punished; but that there was no foundation whatever for the rest of the exaggerated story detailed to the Winnebago Indians. However, they were prevailed upon to seek revenge for the alleged murder of their two men—Waw-zee-kootee promising them that the Sioux would assist them, so soon as the first blow was struck. It is further evident that Red Bird, the chief of the Sioux, (who wished to retaliate on the whites for having, in the Fort Snelling murders, sided with the Chippeways,) was at the bottom of this contemplated alliance. The plan was to kill or drive off all the whites above Rock River.

With this understanding the Winnebagoes, on the 24th of July, killed two whites, in the vicinity of Prairie du Chien, and on the 30th of the same month they attacked two keel boats, which were conveying military stores to Fort Snelling—in which attack two of the crew were killed and four severely wounded. These murders greatly alarmed the frontier settlements at Galena and the mining country around that post.

As soon as intelligence of the hostile attitude which the northern Indians were manifesting, towards the whites, reached Gov. Edwards, and even before any blow was struck, as early as the 14th of July he issued an order to the commandants in Gen. Hanson's brigade, located on the east side of the Illinois River, (except the Twentieth Regiment,) commanding them to take immediate steps for detaching into service one-fourth of their respective regiments. Should any part of the frontier south of Rock River be found to be invested by the savages, the officer in command of the detachment was directed, with the least possible delay, to march to the support of any point attacked, without further orders.

On the same day he wrote to Col. Thomas M. Neale, of the Twentieth Regiment, mostly from the Sangamon country, in the course of which he said:

You will accept the services of any number of mounted volunteers, not exceeding 600, who will equip themselves, find their own subsistence, and continue in service thirty days unless sooner discharged. They will rendezvous, as soon as possible, at Fort Clark, where you will organize and take the command of them, and march, with all possible expedition, to the assistance of our fellow-citizens at Galena, where, if you find an officer of the United States army entitled to superior command to yourself, you will report to him and receive his orders. In your progress you will avoid rashly exposing your men to unequal contests, but it is expected that you will not overlook any proper opportunity of repelling any hostile incursions of the savages.

You will order the officer next you in command to take immediate steps for drafting from your regiment, according to law, and with the least possible delay, six companies of infantry, which are to be held in readiness to march, at a moment's warning, to any frontier that may be invaded; in which event, he is immediately to march them to the support of the point attacked, without further orders. None of the citizens, however, in the vicinity of the immediate frontier, are to be drafted.

On the 9th of August, Gov. Edwards wrote to Gen. Clark as follows:

There being the strongest reason for believing that the Pottawottamies of the Illinois River have been depredating upon the property of some of the citizens of this State, and the official communication of Dr. Wolcott, Indian agent at Chicago, leaving no doubt of their hostile dispositions, it is my duty to inform you that, if any future depredations should be committed by them, and immediate reparation refused, I will not hesitate to drive them from their present residence, which you know they have no right to occupy.

On the 20th of August, Gov. Edwards wrote to the Secretary of War as follows:

Gen. Cass, and other officers of the United States of great respectability, and with the best of opportunities of forming correct opinions on the subject, all concurring in the belief that the neighboring Indians intended making war upon us, and these Indians having committed several daring robberies and other depredations between Peoria and Galena, and commenced actual war in other parts, I have felt it my duty to call out about five hundred mounted volunteers to defend our frontiers.

I suppose not less than 1,500 men have been driven by these acts from the vicinity of Galena; and, but for the measures I adopted, several other parts of our frontier, from their defenceless situations, would have been depopulated. I, therefore, beg leave to ask how far it may be the pleasure of the President to recognize the defensive measures which I have been thus compelled to adopt, and what provisions will be made for paying the militia which have been called into service.

My power to act in such cases is limited to sudden emergencies. The defense of every State belongs to the General Government. I now beg leave to ask, in behalf of this State, of the President of the United States such measures of protection to our extensive frontier as its peculiar weakness demands. The measures adopted by Gen. Atkinson are, I presume, sufficient to insure safety to our western boundary; but they are not the least calculated, nor has he the kind of troops necessary to protect these settlements, which extend from the mouth of the Illinois River to Chicago.

I need scarcely remark to you what all experience has proved, that whenever the Indians have once made up their minds to commit hostilities, or have actually committed such as deserve chastisement, their pacific dispositions never can be safely relied upon until they have begged for peace—and begged it so earnestly as to leave no doubt of their sincerity. Nothing of this kind has yet occurred. The latter part of next month is, of all others, the most favorable time for concentrating their forces and striking the most formidable blow. I will add that I should be very happy to render, on the present occasion, any services that would be acceptable to the President.

The services of the men I have called out will expire in a few days, and until I hear from you I shall not adopt any other measures, but leave it to the General Government to provide for such protection and safety as the people have a right to expect from it.

In this crisis, Col. Abner Field, a gentleman of much intelligence and high respectability, was deputed by the population of Fever River Mines to apply to Gov. Edwards for further assistance to repel the hostilities of the Indians, with which they considered themselves daily threatened. He arrived at Belleville on the 2d of September, bringing very unfavorable news from the exposed frontier, which was fully confirmed by another express which arrived the next day from Peoria.

It appeared that the Winnebagoes had ultimately refused to come to any arrangements with Gov. Cass and Col. McKenney; that information had been received, which was believed, that a part at least of the Pottawottamies had determined to unite with the Winnebagoes in the war; and it was apprehended that the people of Fever River would be attacked before it would be possible to send them any aid; that Gen. Atkinson had sent an express to that place asking for all the mounted riflemen that could be spared from it, and had marched towards Green Bay with about 600 infantry and 130 mounted riflemen, to attack those Indians. Upon this information, Gov. Edwards wrote to the Secretary of War, on the 5th of September, as follows:

No doubt Gen. Atkinson will accomplish all that can be effected with the force under his command; but it is much to be regretted that he has not more mounted men; for if the hostile Indians are as numerous as Gov. Cass supposes, it is not possible that he can march such a distance through their own country, without having a hard fight at least. Should he be defeated or driven back, it may well be imagined that the consequences must be truly disastrous to our very extensive and exposed settlements all along the Illinois River and its waters. Whatever may be their fate, however, if you will only cast your eye upon the map and consider that all the hostile Indians, with the exception of one small band, reside between the line of march and those settlements, it must, I think, be obvious to you that there is either no danger at all, or that they are in very great danger. Regarding them in the latter point of view, I feel it my duty to reiterate my former application to the President for that protection which their situation demands—a protection, the necessity of which is just as apparent as that of any movement which has been made under the authority of the government, and which cannot be doubted without an utter disbelief of any hostile disposition on the part of those savages, nor without questioning the propriety of all those measures of the government which have been adopted upon that suggestion. For if the Indians are hostilely disposed, as they can attack no where else with the same prospect of success and so little risk to themselves, so none can be in more danger than these settlements. Besides their lives and property, the people, I humbly conceive, have a fair claim upon the Government for protection against those interruptions of their tranquillity by the savages, which are reasonably calculated to prevent them from resting under the shade of their own vines and fig trees without any one to make them afraid.

I learn from Col. Field that about 3,000 men have been driven from the mines, and but for the measures I adopted upon the first alarm, it is scarcely to be doubted that other parts of our frontier would have been entirely depopulated. I need not, I am sure, attempt to point out to a gentleman of your practical knowledge and experience the immense losses and sacrifices that must have resulted, both to individuals and the State, from this state of things.

My authority to act being limited to a sudden emergency, my measures were adopted with a view to such duration only as would be sufficient to enable the Government to get its own into operation; and I have now only between sixty and seventy men in service. Nor had I intended, under any circumstances, to have done more on my own responsibility, in consequence of there being no money in our State treasury; the impossibility of doing without it and the risk of pecuniary embarrassment, of which I had some experience during the late war, being greater than I have felt under any obligations to encounter. These views, however, have never been communicated to a single individual; and looking to consequences to the administration from adhering to them, which can scarcely escape your sagacity, I have concluded, should actual hostilities be committed on our frontier, immediately to repair to it, make it my headquarters, and endeavor, with my own funds and at my own risk, to provide subsistence for such volunteers as I may be able to call to my aid until I can receive your answer to my letter of the 20th ult. Whatever that may be, if it only shall afford reasonable ground to expect I shall be sustained, I will continue to do the best in my power until I receive your answer to this letter; otherwise, unless all danger shall entirely have disappeared, I shall be compelled to convene the Legislature and lay the case just as it is before them.

I beg leave to observe that the experience of three years' hard service on our frontiers, during the last war, has convinced me that no other force of any reasonable amount is available for such protection as they require than that of mounted riflemen. Your infantry on the Wisconsin is too remote to afford the least assistance. It would be scarcely less available to us if it were at Washington City.

On the strength of the information communicated by Col. Field, on the same day (5th of September), Gov. Edwards issued a further order to Brig. Gen. Hanson, commanding him immediately to take all legal measures necessary for enrolling in the militia all persons subject thereto, on Fever River or in the vicinity of the mines, and for organizing them according to law.

Before, however, this order was fully executed, intelligence was received that Gen. Atkinson, who had marched into the Winnebago country, in pursuit of the offending Indians, had returned to Prairie du Chien with Red Bird, a chief of much prominence, and six other Indians, among whom was Black Hawk, who became famous afterwards. They were all committed to jail, under the criminal charge of having committed the murderous attack upon the boats. They were kept in jail many months, awaiting their trial, and many threats were made by the Indians that if Red Bird should be executed, it would be the signal for a general uprising among the different tribes. In regard to Red Bird's capture and imprisonment, a letter from Gen. Street to Gov. Edwards, dated at Prairie du Chien, December 28th, gives the following account:

Red Bird is a favorite with his people and had obtained a high reputation among the whites previous to the late unprovoked murders. You, I doubt not, have had a particular account of his voluntary surrender of himself. This manly, chivalric act, his open, free and high bearing at the time, has something more than ordinary in it. Dressed in his Yanctonuni form of white, unsoiled skins, with a fine, white, dressed-skin robe cast loosely across his shoulder, and mounted on a fine mettlesome horse, with a white flag in his hand, and marching into the camp of Whistler, unconfined, with a pleasant, unclouded brow, to deliver himself up as a murderer, is a little out of the ordinary course of such things amongst us. You perhaps have seen him. He is a tall, well-made, straight Indian, about thirty or forty years old, and has a very pleasant countenance. There is nothing remarkable about the six other prisoners, if you except Red Bird's son, a lad of twelve or fifteen. He is a pleasant, smiling boy. Confinement goes hard with Red Bird, and he does not have good health, but if a white man calls to see him, all the nobility of a great savage appears to light up his fine and intelligent features, and a stranger would point to him as no every-day character.

I wish the trial and execution of the murderers was over. If a strong force is not present when Red Bird is to be hanged, if convicted, (of which I see no reason to doubt,) I shall not feel free of apprehensions of danger. There is an opinion prevalent at St. Louis, and amongst some here, that the Winnebagoes are greatly alarmed at the late events. They *were* much alarmed at the time Gen. Atkinson and the Illinois volunteers were in their country. The movement was sudden, beyond what the Indians had been accustomed to, and the expected reinforcements from Illinois, under your order for one-fourth the militia, was calculated to take them by surprise, and at the time it had its effect. Since then the Indians seem to be gradually awakening, as it were, from a deep sleep, until their fears are given to the winds and there is dead stillness—a portentious calm that all my secret endeavors cannot interpret. They cannot be induced to talk on the subject, and they come and go, ask no questions about the prisoners, and if told of their health, answer, to any mention of them, "Ugh." Say they are well, or sick, is immaterial—"Ugh!" is the answer, and it is evident they wish to avoid the mention of them. At the same time, the wives and and relatives of the prisoners are properly attended to. The wife of Red Bird, however, does not come near. I learn she is rich, as Red Bird was the best hunter in the nation, and great attention is paid to her by the nation.

But before his trial took place, the chief, Red Bird, whose lofty spirit could not brook confinement, died in prison. Of the other prisoners, a part were acquitted and a part convicted and hung. Their execution took place on the 26th of December, of the following year. Black Hawk, who was one of those acquitted, afterwards acknowledged his guilt and openly boasted of it.

With the death of Red Bird ended the Winnebago war. The tribe seemed to be thoroughly humbled by the result of the campaign; and although fears of further hostilities from them were for sometime after entertained, they continued peaceable. In regard to the lands, about which the difficulty with them originated, until the question of ownership could be adjusted amicably, they promised to keep away from the mines entirely. In regard to their disposition at this time, a letter from Gen. Street to Gov. Edwards says:

The chiefs who have visited me proffer their friendship, but anxiously inquire when they may expect their Great Father will settle the line, and mark it, between their country and the whites at the mines. They say they have left their country to keep their young men from having anything to do with the people at the mines, until they hear from their Great Father. "This," say they, "is our promise to Gen. Atkinson, and we will keep it." They add, "Gen. Atkinson promised us that next summer persons should come from our Great Father to consult with us about this matter, and we will wait and see them."

A talk was subsequently held with them, in which they abandoned all the country south of the Wisconsin River. After this there was a general peace with the Indians throughout the Western frontier.

Meanwhile, however, Gov. Edwards, who placed no confidence in Indian promises or Indian friendship, was not idle in his endeavors to rid the State of the different Indian tribes still within its borders. Having got rid of the Winnebagoes, he continued with much persistency to urge upon the War Department the pressing necessity for removing all the Indians beyond the State. He saw very clearly, from the events of the last few years, that the red and white men could not live together, in the same vicinity, without committing reprisals upon each other and provoking hostile feelings. His first communication to the Department, on the subject of the removal of the Indians, was written as early as the 4th of September, 1827, in the course of which he said that "the occupancy, by the different tribes, of the ceded lands, and their constantly traversing every part of it at their pleasure, without any right to do so, could no longer be submitted to." He particularly mentioned the Pottawottamies who resided near Peoria, on lands which had not only been ceded but actually granted by the Government to individuals. He regarded it as "a grievance inconsistent with the rights of the State," and the respect of the President for those rights ought not to permit him to hesitate to do his duty in the premises.

The Indians who resided at this time on the ceded lands, within the State, were the Kickapoos, Pottawottamies, Ottaways and Chippeways, of the Illinois River, and the Sacs and Foxes. These Indians, and occasionly large parties of Shawnees and Delawares, were in the habit of hunting extensively through the settled parts of the State, to the great annoyance of the citizens. They not only in a great measure exterminated all the wild game, or drove it from the State, but in their marauding expeditions they did not hesitate to kill the tame animals belonging to the settlers.

The Kickapoos were within the agency of Major R. Graham of Missouri. The Pottawottamies, Ottaways and Chippeways of the Illinois River were within the sub-agency of Mr. Peter Menard, Jr. The Sacs and Foxes were within the agency of Thomas Forsyth of St. Louis. The Shawnees and Delawares were within the sub-agency of Major Peter Menard of Kaskaskia; and the whole were within the superintendency of Gen. William Clark.

On the 13th of September, 1827, Gov. Edwards addressed a confidential letter to President Adams, on this subject, and proceeded to show that the Indians had no right, either by treaty or otherwise, to any of the lands in the State, and proceeded to assure the President that "their removal could not fail to give the greatest satisfaction to the people of the State, as being both popular and right."

On the 29th of October, following, Gov. Edwards received a letter from the Secretary of War, Gen. Barbour, informing him that "Gov. Cass had been instructed to take such measures as would fulfill the wishes of the State in reference to the removal of the Indians occupying the ceded lands." The order, he said, was that "the Indians should be removed with the least possible delay, consistent with humanity," and in case of insuperable difficulties he was to report forthwith to the Department.

Gov. Edwards replied, acknowledging the prompt attention on the part of the General Government to the interests and tranquillity of the State; but, at the same time, on account of the remoteness of Gov. Cass' residence and the Indians not being within his superintendency, he doubted if the proposed measure promised as speedy a redress of the grievance complained of as seemed to be anticipated or was desirable. He wrote that the people of Illinois would hope much more from the interposition of the Indian agents on the spot, or from General Clark (the Indian Superintendent for Illinois), than from that of any one at so great a distance from the State as Gov. Cass.

The measures adopted by the Government resulted almost as Gov. Edwards had predicted. The Indians still remained in the State, and kept up their marauding incursions through the settlements. On the 25th of May, of the following year, he wrote to Gen. Clark, Indian Superintendent, inquiring whether any and what arrangements had been made for removing the Indians in pursuance of the directions of the War Department—the letter of the Secretary having given the people of Illinois reason to believe that that measure would have been accomplished long before. The continued delay caused much indignation, and Gov. Edwards wrote, "the General Government has been applied to long enough for its own action to have freed us from so serious a grievance. If it declines acting with effect, it will soon learn that those Indians *will* be removed, and that very promptly."

Gen. Clark, (as would appear, also wearied with the want of energy displayed by Gov. Cass, or rather the General Government) had begun to use his personal exertions to prevail upon the Indians to remove, as the best means, in the excitement which prevailed, of preserving tranquillity between them and the citizens, and he did all he could to that end without using actual coercion. They continued to promise to go, but still remained. Gov. Edwards argued that as pursuasion would not accomplish it, *force* should be substituted. He wrote again to Gen. Clark, on the 29th, that "however justifiable might be a temporizing course on the part of the Government, were Illinois one of its territories, it has no right to authorize or permit, even temporarily, an invasion of the rights of a sovereign and independent State."

On the 17th of June he again addressed the Secretary of War, in which he stated that the former promises of that Department had justified a reasonable expectation, on the part of the people, that the energies of the Government would long before that time have been exerted to protect the State from further annoyance. He concluded by saying: "This grievance still continuing, and aggravated as it has become by recent occurrences, of which I am bound to presume you are informed, I feel it my duty to ask you what further measures, in regard to this matter, may be expected from the General Government."

It appears that, upon the urgent request of the Indians—who made all manner of fair promises—twelve months further time, within which to remove from the State, was accorded to them by the General Government. This extension was greatly deprecated by Gov. Edwards, who did not believe the Indians would, even at the end of that time, remove, without the employment of force; and he wrote to Gen. Clark that, at any rate, if any act of hostility should be committed on the frontiers, he [Edwards] would not hesitate to remove them on his own responsibility, as Governor of the State.

About this time the President issued his proclamation, according to law, and, in pursuance thereof, all the country above the mouth of Rock River (the ancient seat of the Sauk nation) was sold to American families, and in the year following it was taken possession of by them. To avoid difficulty with the tribes another treaty, confirming previous ones, was made with the Sacs and Foxes, on the 15th of July, 1830, by the provisions of which they were to remove peacefully from the Illinois country. A portion of the Sacs, with their principal chief, Keokuk, at their head, quietly retired across the Mississippi. With those who remained in the village at the mouth of Rock River, an arrangement was made by the Americans who had purchased the land, by which they were to live together as neighbors, the Indians still cultivating their old fields as formerly. Black Hawk, however, a restless and uneasy spirit, who had ceased to recognize Keokuk as chief, and who was known to be still under the pay of the British, emphatically refused either to remove from the lands or to respect the right of the Americans to them. He insisted that Keokuk had no authority for making such a treaty, and he proceeded to gather around him a large number of the warriors and young men of the tribe, who were anxious to distinguish themselves as "braves," and placing himself at their head, he determined to dispute with the whites the possession of the ancient seat of his nation. He had conceived the gigantic scheme, as appears by his own admissions, of uniting all the Indians, from the Rock River to the Gulf of Mexico, in a war against the United States, and he made use of every pretext for gaining accessions to his party.

In the spring of 1831, he recrossed the river, at the head of five hundred warriors of his own tribe, besides some allies from the Pottawottamies and Kickapoos, and, bringing with him his women and children, he declared his intention of re-establishing himself on the ancient hunting-grounds and in the principal village of his nation. He ordered the whites to leave, and, destroying their fields, tearing down their fences, and killing or driving off their cattle, he threatened the settlers with instant death if they remained.

The whites complained to the Governor, who thereupon declared the acts of the Indians to be a hostile invasion of the State, and he immediately called upon Gen. Gaines for troops to protect the Illinois frontier. At the same time, he ordered out seven hundred of the militia of the State, to be mounted, and report themselves immediately for service. They were placed under the command of Gen. Joseph Duncan, who marched them directly to Rock River, where they arrived on the 25th of June. Six companies of regular troops were also dispatched, by Gen. Gaines, from Jefferson Barracks, to the Sauk village, early in the same month.

Black Hawk and his party, alarmed at this formidable array of troops, fled across the river, and on the 26th the army took possession of the village without firing a gun. On the next day the Indians sent over a flag of truce. A parley ensued, and a treaty of peace was made on the spot—by the terms of which the Indians promised to remain forever on the west bank of the river, and the Americans guaranteed to them the payment of a large supply of corn in lieu of that which they were compelled to abandon in their fields.

But the trouble did not end here. Notwithstanding the treaty, early in the spring of 1832 Black Hawk recrossed the Mississippi, and commenced his march up Rock River Valley. Gen. Atkinson, who was stationed at Fort Armstrong, warned him against this aggression. His aim was to reach the countries of the Pottawottamies and Winnebagoes and make them his allies.

Upon being informed of the movements of Black Hawk, Gov. Reynolds issued an order for a thousand mounted volunteers, from the Central and Southern parts of the State, to rendezvous at Beardstown, on the Illinois River. In a short time (April 15th, 1832) a brigade, armed and equipped for service, under the command of Gen. Samuel Whiteside, accompanied, also, by Gov. Reynolds, commenced their march directly for Rock Island, where they joined Gen. Atkinson, with about four hundred regular troops under his command. From that point the mounted volunteers proceeded at once up Rock River, on the south side, by way of the Prophet's town, which, although deserted, they burned on their march. At the same time Gen. Atkinson ascended the river with the regulars, in boats, taking with him supplies for the entire army; but not reaching Dixon's Ferry as soon as the command under Gen. Whiteside, the latter were for several days entirely destitute of provisions, which rendered their position most embarrassing.

At Dixon's Gen. Whiteside was reinforced by a body of volunteers from the counties of Peoria, Tazewell, etc., under the command of Major Stillman. Immediately upon being mustered into service, at their own request, they were permitted to start on a tour of observation several miles up the river, but instead of returning to the encampment, as they were directed to do, they continued their "hunt for Indians" some twelve miles still further up. On the evening of the 14th of May, while making preparations to encamp, they discovered a body of a party of Indians, five in number. Black Hawk says they were the bearers of a white flag, but this is denied.

However this may be, Stillman's men immediately charged upon them in grand style; but just as they came up with them, a band of warriors, numbering several hundred, who were lying in ambush, with a terrible war-whoop suddenly sprang up, with Black Hawk at their head, and gave fight with so much energy and determination, that the whites faced directly about and fled in utter consternation and confusion, not stopping till they reached Gen. Whiteside's encampment, thirty miles distant—leaving their tents, camp equipage, baggage wagons, ammunition, and some of them even their saddles and bridles, to whomsoever chose to appropriate them. In this hasty and shameful retreat eleven whites were killed and several wounded. The Indians lost four or five killed.

Gen. Whiteside, convinced, from the exaggerated stories of the panic-stricken men, that an Indian force a thousand or two strong must be in the vicinity, immediately called a council of war, and determined to march forthwith to the fatal field of the previous evening's disaster. But although scouting parties were dispatched in all directions, no track or trace of the Indians could be found. The whole command then returned to Dixon, being almost famished from want of provisions. Here, after another day, Gen. Atkinson arrived with the boats, bringing reinforcements and supplies.

The affair at "Stillman's *run*," exaggerated as it was, alarmed the whole State, and Gov. Reynolds forthwith issued orders for three thousand volunteers, to rendezvous at Hennepin, "to subdue the Indians and drive them out of the State."

Peace was now hopeless, and both sides prepared for retaliation and reprisals. On the 21st of May, a party of Indians attacked the Indian Creek settlement, in LaSalle county, killed fifteen men, and took two young women prisoners. The latter were, however, afterwards, through the interposition of the Winnebagoes, given up. On the following day a party of spies were attacked and four of them slain. A number of other murders and outrages followed, in rapid succession; and several engagements between the Indians and armed bodies of whites took place at different points.

Gen. Whiteside marched immediately towards Ottawa, but the term of service of his brigade having expired, they were discharged, and Gen. Atkinson was compelled to await the arrival of the three thousand militia ordered by Gov. Reynolds.

On the 20th of June, the new army rendezvoused near Peru, and were organized into three brigades, of about a thousand men each, under the charge, respectively, of Gen. Henry, Gen. Alexander, and Gen. Posey. They marched forward directly to Rock River, where they were joined by the United States troops—the whole being under the command of Gen. Atkinson. Congress, also, in June, ordered out six hundred mounted men, to be raised for the defense of the frontier; while Gen. Scott, with nine companies of artillery, hastened from the seaboard, by way of the lakes, to Chicago.

A spy battalion of one hundred and fifty men, sent forward from Dixon's, under the command of Major Dement, in advancing towards Galena, was, on the 25th of June, attacked near Buffalo Grove by a party of two hundred warriors, under Black Hawk. The fight was hotly contested, and at one time the Americans were driven back, but, getting possession of the block-house, they finally made a stand against the Indians and after a fierce struggle, in which great bravery was displayed, they compelled them to retreat; but not being sufficiently strong they did not pursue them. In the fight several were killed on both sides.

The army continued its march up Rock River, near the sources of which it was represented that the main body of the Indians were collected. As provisions and army stores were scarce and difficult to convey in such a country, a detachment of a hundred and sixty men was sent, under the charge of Gen. Henry, to Fort Winnebago, at the portage between the Wisconsin and Fox Rivers, to procure supplies. This detachment, learning that Black Hawk's army was encamped up on the Whitewater, thirty miles distant, resolved to start in immediate pursuit, and overtook them on the evening of the 21st of July, near "Blue Mounds." Gen. Henry formed his troops into a hollow square, the opening being in the rear, and in this manner received the attack of the Indians. The latter first charged upon the right (Col. Fry's battalion), where, being repulsed, they attempted to break through the left (Col. Collins'), where they were again repulsed. The whole line was then ordered to charge the Indians, which order was promptly executed, both sides rushing to the rencounter with terrible yells and war whoops. The Indians were immediately driven from the field, leaving fifty-two of their number dead upon the spot, while only one American was killed and eight wounded. It being now quite dark, the Americans encamped upon the field without pursuing the enemy. The next day they marched to Blue Mounds, twenty-five miles distant, and two days after they were joined by Gen. Atkinson and the main body of the troops—Gen. Henry having, before the action, sent them word of his movements. On the 28th of July, the entire army crossed the Wisconsin River in pursuit of Black Hawk, who, with his forces, was hastily retiring towards the Mississippi. Upon the banks of that river, nearly opposite the Upper Iowa, the Indians were, on the 2d of August, again overtaken.

Here a decisive action, called the battle of "Bad Axe," took place, which resulted again in the defeat of the Indians. Gen. Atkinson, in his official account of the battle, says the loss of the Indians was about one hundred and fifty killed and thirty-nine women and children taken prisoners. The whites lost eighteen men. The remnant of the enemy, cut up and disheartened, crossed to the opposite side of the river and fled into the interior. This battle entirely broke the power of Black Hawk. He attempted to make his escape, but was seized by the Winnebagoes, (who, during the war, were allies of the Americans,) and, on the 27th, delivered up to the officers of the United States at Prairie du Chien. He and his family were afterwards sent as hostages to Fort Monroe, in the Chesapeake, where they were retained till June, 1833.

In September, the Indian troubles were closed by a treaty, which relinquished to the whites thirty millions of acres of land, constituting what is now the eastern portion of the State of Iowa. For this, stipulated annuities were to be paid, though it was well understood at the time that the Sacs and Foxes had no rightful claim to the land. Thus ended the Black Hawk war and the Indian troubles in the State of Illinois. The various tribes yet remaining found homes beyond the west bank of the Mississippi River.

The "Sangamon Journal," at Springfield, Illinois, published a letter of Gov. Edwards to our Senators in Congress, of June 5th, 1832, in reference to the distressed situation of the frontier settlements during this war with the Indians, accompanied with the following notice: "We give the communication of Gov. Edwards, above referred to. It shows that he is alive to the welfare of the State. Would to God that she could boast of more of such men, who are willing and able to sustain her rights. ...... The citizens of this State, and more especially of those of the northern counties, will feel themselves deeply indebted to Gov. Edwards for the able and independent manner in which he has stated to our Senators in Congress the distressed situation of our frontier settlements, and the causes of those distresses."

CHAPTER XII.

Gov. Edwards' Correspondence with the Secretary of the Treasury on the Subject of the Three Per Cent. Fund—His Private Character—His Pursuits—Management of his Personal Affairs—His Usefulness as a Citizen and Neighbor—Funeral Discourse of the Rev. J. M. Peck.

THREE PER CENT. FUND.

On the 9th of March, 1829, Gov. Edwards addressed a letter to the Commissioner of the General Land Office, advising him of his having drawn bills on account of the three per cent. fund due to the State, and requiring payment at the treasury. The letter was referred to Samuel D. Ingham, the Secretary of the Treasury, who replied to the Governor that the act of Congress directs " that an annual account of the application of the money shall be transmitted to the Secretary of the Treasury, and in default of such return being made, the Secretary of the Treasury is required to withhold the payment of any sums that may be due until a return shall be made as herein required. This provision of the act not having been complied with on the part of the State of Illinois, and the act seeming to leave no discretion, I have been constrained to decline the payment of one of the bills mentioned in your letter, which has this day been presented; but the holder has at the same time been informed that the bill is for part of a sum now due to the State of Illinois, and that immediately upon the receipt of the return required by law, payment would be made." On the receipt of this letter from Mr. Ingham, Gov. Edwards, on the 2d of July—and subsequently the Governor and Commissioners of the School Fund—wrote to the Secretary, inclosing an account of the disposition of the sums which had been paid to them for the encouragement of learning within the State of Illinois, under the act of the 12th of December, 1820. Mr. Asbury Dickens, the Acting Secretary, replied "that it would have afforded great satisfaction to the Department to have found in that account, and in the explanation presented, a justification for the payment of the drafts of the Commissioners, but the law must be the rule of action; and as the Department cannot consider the investment which the account shows to have been made of the moneys hitherto paid in purchasing the State debt, as an application of those moneys according to law, it deems itself prohibited by law from making any further payment until an account is presented showing the application of the sums already paid to the purposes for which the law declares they shall be applied......I have submitted the whole subject to the notice of the President, who has been pleased to approve of the course which has been adopted."

Gov. Edwards, considering the doctrines and assumptions in the letter of the Acting Secretary, although sanctioned by the President and Secretary of the Treasury, as subversive of the just rights and derogatory to the dignity and honor of the State, contended that Congress had no more right to confer such a power on the Secretary than the State would have a right to authorize the Auditor to require of the Government of the United States an annual account of the application of the money stipulated to be disbursed under the direction of Congress in making roads leading to the State. The following reply to the letter of the Secretary is an able exposition of the rights of the State, and satisfactorily demonstrated that no such power could be delegated to the Department as to authorize the withholding of this money:

BELLEVILLE, ILLINOIS, *June* 4, 1829.

SIR—I had the honor, a day or two ago, to receive your letter of the 13th ult., acknowledging and informing me that it would afford great satisfaction to the Department to have found in that account, and the explanation presented in my communications, a justification for the payment of the drafts of the Commissioners for the amount which has subsequently accrued; but that the law must be the rule of action, and as the Department cannot consider the investment which the account shows to have been made of the moneys hitherto paid, in the purchasing the State debt, as an application of those moneys according to law, it deems itself prohibited by law from making any further payment until an account is presented showing the application of the sums already paid to the purposes to which alone the law declares they shall be applied; that it is a cause of sincere regret to the Department; that with the strongest desire to regard as correct such a disposition of the funds in question as the authorities of the State of Illinois might have deemed proper, it has not found grounds to concur in the views which they have taken of the subject; and that, anxious on an occasion of so much delicacy and interest, that the State should not suffer by any error of judgment on your part, you had submitted the whole subject to the notice of the President, who has been pleased to approve of the course which has been adopted.

Not doubting in the least that it would have afforded you great satisfaction to have found in the account of the Commissioners a justification for a different decision, in a case of so much delicacy and interest to the State, and how great soever may have been your regret at finding yourself compelled, by your construction of the law referred to, to refuse the payment of the drafts in question, I can truly say it cannot have exceeded that which I sincerely feel at finding *myself* compelled, by a due regard to the high responsibilities which your decision devolves upon me, to endeavor to justify the part I have had in this business, and to protest in behalf of the State against the doctrines and assumptions of your letter, as equally subversive of its just rights and derogatory to its dignity and honor. In doing this, I must be understood as combatting your opinions only—for as the duty enjoined upon the Secretary of the Treasury in this case is purely ministerial, his responsibilities are so exclusive that even the President himself has no right to control, no power to justify him; and so long has this principle been established by the highest judicial decisions, so universally acquiesced in, and so uniformly acted upon by the Treasury Department itself, that I can but regard it as an extraordinary inadvertence that you, who have so long and often witnessed and participated in its practical operation, should have introduced the President's opinion with an official communication on a subject so clearly without the sphere of his authority.

The injuries which the State has already sustained by the decisions of the Department, and losses, greater than the whole amount drawn for, which must inevitably result to it, from an adherence to the determination expressed in your letter, will, I trust, fully justify the frankest examination, on my part, of the grounds you have assumed, and invite to a review by the Department of a decision too disastrous, in its present and ultimate consequences, to be insisted upon under every doubtful authority, or without the clearest, most perfect and irresistible conviction of its justice and propriety. In pursuance of a practical exposition which had been given to the compact between the United States and this State, and to the law you refer to, both by Mr. Crawford and by Mr. Rush, as Secretaries of the Treasury, and in conformity to the advice and every previous requisition of the Department, the drafts in question were drawn—none of the Commissioners anticipating that the Government or any department thereof would disown its own acts, and, by a sudden change of its conduct, without any previous notice thereof to the State, subject it to the severest losses consequent upon the protest of those drafts. These losses, however, it has sustained, by the decision of Mr. Ingham. Those which must result from yours, are far greater. He determined that the drafts could not be paid till "the return required by law" should be made; but by informing the holders of them that, immediately upon the receipt of such return, (knowing at the same time that annual ones were then impossible) payment would be made, he gave assurance that a strict compliance with the law would not be insisted upon. You say, "*the law must be the rule of action.*" He only decided that a return should be made. You claim the right to decide upon its consistency with the obligations of the State, and thereby to control its action and cause its submission to your own views of its duty. His decision amounted to no more than that payment should be postponed. Yours is equivalent to a determination that it shall never be made. For knowing, as you did, that the State had authorized and that the Commissioners had invested the moneys, hitherto paid, in purchases of the State debt—determining this to be illegal, insisting that "*the law must be the rule of action,*" and requiring returns which those purchases have rendered utterly impossible, can amount to nothing less than an absolute refusal to pay at all. Nothing was less anticipated than this result. Mr. Ingham's letter, with a perfect knowledge that no returns had been made for years past, and with the law of the State, authorizing those investments in the Department, containing an assurance that immediately upon the receipt of an account of the application of the moneys heretofore received, "payment would be made," and such amount having been transmitted, no danger was perceived in renewing the drafts; and they were renewed under a confident expectation that no further difficulty would occur. Your decision, however, has not only, a second time in the same year, subjected the State to an additional loss of ten per cent. upon the whole amount drawn for, but must, if persevered in, force it to incur the expenses of a call of the Legislature, far more considerable than the whole amount which you have thought fit to withhold. For as no doubt was entertained that the Legislature of the State might authorize this fund to be loaned upon interest, for the purpose of rendering it a productive source "for the encouragement of learning," or that it might authorize the Governor to borrow it from the Commissioners, for the use of the State, upon like terms, and for the same purpose, its appropriation in that way was so confidently relied on, as a provision for defraying the current expenses of the Government, that its operations must necessarily be suspended, without other resources—which the Legislature alone is competent to supply.

Is, then, the State to be subjected to such inconveniences, its interest to be thus sacrificed and its dignity prostrated at the feet of an acting Secretary of the Treasury —however distinguished for his intelligence, integrity and patriotism—merely because, "with the strongest desire to regard as correct such a disposition of the funds in question as the authorities of the State of Illinois might have deemed proper," he has not found grounds to concur in the views they have taken of the subject? Such results could hardly have been expected at any time; much less at a time and under circumstances so generally regarded as peculiarly auspicious to State rights. It must be admitted that there can be no more legitimate object of State authority and jurisdiction than the "encouragement of learning." What, then, could be more humiliating to the just pride of a free and independent State, than that its legislative action upon a subject, so unquestionably within the sphere of its sovereign powers, should be subjected to the supervision, control and negative of a subordinate officer of a different government? The degradation cannot but be most painfully felt in the present case. As none could have a deeper interest in or higher motives to the "encouragement of learning" than the State itself, the compact, with no more than reasonable confidence, has, without exacting security or providing any means of coercion whatever, submitted this business to the sound discretion and good faith of the Legislature of the State. The Legislature, with a disposition that has never been complained of but as too favorable to this object, has, in the exercise of its best judgment, endeavored to render this fund as available as possible to the purposes for which it was granted. The measures adopted with this view have been and still are approved by the people of the State, and their success is sufficiently evinced by the extraordinary augmentation of the fund itself. Yet, your decision, assuming that the Legislature was either too ignorant to perceive its duty or too faithless to perform it, requires that the State shall retrace its steps, and in default thereof denounces against it consequences only due to a faithless violation of the most solemn promises and engagements. And all this because it so happens that you cannot concur in the views that have been taken of this subject by those whose peculiar province it was to decide upon it.

If such a decision is to be persevered in, it will not, I trust, be without a favorable reception and a deliberate consideration of the objections which painful but imperious duty calls upon me to make against it. I will not urge the force of precedents. I will not rely upon the practical exposition of Mr. Crawford and Mr. Rush, and the acquiescence of the Government for eight successive years; but I may be permitted to say, that, if you are right, they must have been guilty of flagrant violations of their duty, and it is left to the Department to decide how far this serious inculpation of such distinguished and enlightened public officers should furnish an additional motive to that deliberate reconsideration which I have the honor most respectfully to solicit. I am perfectly willing to consider the case as *res integra*, and to test your decision upon principle.

And here let me be distinctly understood as not intending to include any objections to the decisions of Mr. Ingham. On that branch of the subject, I have nothing to add to the views contained in my letter to him of the 2d of April, last. But I contend that the Government of the United States is incompetent to confer upon the Secretary of the Treasury the right, which you have assumed, of deciding upon the validity of the account of the application of the fund in question, which the State is required to return; that no such power was intended to be or has been delegated to him, by the law referred to, and that, if it had been, your decision is erroneous.

The propositions offered by the United States were accepted and agreed to by the State on certain conditions. Now, sir, I need not, I am sure, quote authorities to show a gentleman of your intelligence that all treaties, conventions and agreements, however denominated, made between sovereigns, are public engagements, which, in regard to their validity, their execution, the dissolving of them, the rights they confer, the obligations they impose, are all subject to precisely the same rules. This compact, therefore, cannot be considered in an inferior light to that of a treaty, and a treaty, too, between equals: because, however different in splendor, pomp and power, equal in point of independence—which is all that is essential to sovereign equality. This equality, then, at once explodes your doctrine that the "law must be the rule of action," as applied to the rights and obligations of the State; for as law is nothing less than a rule of action prescribed by a superior to an inferior, whence can either party derive authority to give law to the other. The power of the United States to disengage themselves from their promises and nullify a compact, is not intended to be questioned; but the right, on their part, to interpolate into it conditions for which it has not provided, and to prescribe the duties of the State by law, cannot be conceded without dishonor. Sovereigns acknowledge no competent authority to decide between them, and have nothing to rely upon for the fulfillment of their mutual engagements but the faith of promises. Neither party has a right to construe the compact at its own pleasure, and any difference between them, growing out of it, necessarily becomes the subject of negotiation or must eventuate in its nullification. How, then, could Congress delegate to you the power to supervise, control and negative the legislative action of the State upon this subject? How authorize you to require the State to retrace its steps, and enforce its conformity to your own views of its duty, by a violation of the promises of the United States and the exaction of conditions which it had never bound itself to perform, and yet recognize the existence of the compact? The refusal of one party to fulfill its stipulation places them in a new attitude towards each other, from the very nature of things puts an end to the compact, and is only to be justified on the ground of a faithless violation of the promises of the other. The obligations of the compact are perfectly reciprocal; the rights of the parties under it equal. If, then, the United States can authorize their Secretary of the Treasury to require of the State an annual account of the application of the money, stipulated to be appropriated by the Legislature thereof, for the "encouragement of learning," and to withhold payment if he should think the money misapplied, permit me earnestly to ask of you (or of Mr. Ingham, if this letter shall be referred to him,) why may not the State authorize its Auditor of Accounts, or any other officer, to require of the United States an annual account of the application of the money stipulated to be disbursed, under the direction of Congress, in making roads leading to the State, and to suspend the execution of all the promises of the State if he should think this money misapplied?

To me, it appears that the rights of the State, and the propriety of such a requisition on its part, are far the most obvious and reasonable, because both these stipulations appear to have been offered as inducements to the State, were obviously intended for its benefit, and were granted only upon the condition of an ample equivalent, which it has faithfully rendered. Should this right be conceded to the State, there is every reason to believe the compact would be of short duration, since it is not probable that there is a single individual within its limits who really believes that the disbursements of this fund which have been made under the direction of Congress have been in conformity to the compact. At all events, they are not less questionable than those appropriations under the authority of the Legislature of the State, which you have denounced. It cannot be pretended that the State has not strictly complied with every condition on which the engagements of the United States were made to depend. Is it, then, reasonable to expect that the State should continue to perform those conditions, whilst the stipulated equivalents for them are thus arbitrarily withheld? I think not. Every article of a treaty or compact has the force of a condition, which, by a default of the party promising, is nullified—for neither party is bound by its promises but upon the honest and faithful fulfillment of the engagements of the other. The State may, therefore, rightfully and legally absolve itself from its obligations whenever the promises in its favor are violated, or the benefits intended to be secured to it are withheld; and as the bargain was a very disadvantageous one on its part, it is scarcely to be doubted that it will avail itself of this right, if this extraordinary refusal of payment shall be persisted in.

It cannot, therefore, be presumed that Congress could ever have intended to delegate to the Secretary of the Treasury power whose exercise involves such awful consequences; and the nature and importance of the case forbids any derivation of the power you have assumed from implication. Let us, then, see whether the power you claim has been conferred upon you. The law declares that the Secretary of the Treasury shall pay the money in question for the purposes mentioned in the compact; that an account of its application by the State shall be transmitted to him; and that in default of such returns being made to him, he shall withhold the payment of any sums that may then be due, or which may thereafter become due, until the return shall be made. All, then, that the Secretary is authorized to demand of the State is that it shall exhibit to him an account of its application of the money. This being done, whether he may think the application right or wrong, wise or unwise, he is bound to pay, since he has no right to withhold payment but in default of such return being made to him. The State is not required to account to him for its conduct, to satisfy him that the money has been properly applied; to submit to his control or dictation in a case confided to its own judgment by the compact itself, and undeniably included within its legitimate power. Nor has the law given him the power to decide upon the validity of the application of the money, to arraign the State for its ignorance, or to denounce it for its treachery, and subject it to punishment or force it to abandon measures which it knows to have been adopted in good faith and believes to be in conformity with the compact, and better calculated than any other to advance the very interest for which it was intended to provide. Had such an awful power been intended to be granted to the Secretary, its great importance and the obvious consequences to which it might lead, forbid the belief that it should have been left to any kind of implication, or that it would not have been distinctly expressed and guarded by every prudent precaution. It is far more reasonable to suppose that Congress intended to provide the means of ascertaining how the money should be disposed of, and to reserve to themselves, and not transfer from them to the head of a Department of the Government, the right of deciding upon such measures as should thereupon appear to be expedient and proper.

But if this extraordinary power has been granted to the Secretary, it is, with all due deference, confidently believed that you have decided erroneously.

Previously, however, to entering upon this branch of the subject, that I may not be personally involved in the censure implied by your decision, I may be permitted, in justice to myself, to remark that, as I never participated in the investment of the money in question in the purchase of the State debt, I am not entitled to any share of the merit or demerit of that measure. It is due, however, to candor to say that I have never seen, nor can I now see, any objection to the whole policy that has been pursued by the State in regard to this fund, than an over-anxiety to augment it for the purposes for which it was granted, and premature efforts to aid the interests of learning at the expense of other interests having equal claims.

In a new State, with a very sparse and greatly dispersed population, it may well be imagined that there may have been a time when a regular system for the encouragement of learning had not been adopted, and that with the utmost anxiety to effect so desirable an object, it may have been unavoidably retarded by circumstances which could not be controlled. This was, in fact, the situation of this State at the time the money in question was received. There were no existing institutions of learning to which it could properly be applied. Should it, then, on this account, have been withheld by the Secretary? If not, was it absolutely necessary that it should lie idle and unemployed, when it could be made to yield an increase that would greatly facilitate and accelerate the object for which it was intended? Or how should it have been used so as to have enabled the State to render an account of its application that would have satisfied your construction of the law? If I understand rightly the remarks in your letter, with the reference you make to mine of the 2d April, it is just as necessary to exhibit an account to satisfy you that the money had actually been literally applied to "the encouragement of learning," as that it had not been misapplied to any other object. And, indeed, if you have the right to decide upon the consistency of the return with the obligations of the State, there seems no reasonable distinction between those cases, since the cause of learning could not be less injured by withholding this fund from its aid than by otherwise applying it.

What then is the consequence of this construction? Being unable, and likely to continue so a long time, with its own funds exclusively to establish those institutions of learning which should be the objects of the stipulated appropriation, the State in the meantime, though held to a strict and continued performance of the equivalent conditions on its part, is to be altogether deprived of the use of this money. And this notwithstanding the law itself has declared that it shall be paid to it quarterly. Is it to be supposed that such a state of things could be acquiesced in by a free, highminded and independent people?

I had the honor to state to Mr. Ingham, in my letter of 2d April, to which you refer, as follows: "The several sums heretofore received, however, on this account, being as yet inadequate to the objects for which they were granted, have not been appropriated otherwise than in the purchase of the notes of the State Bank of Illinois and warrants upon its treasury at a great discount, which has considerably augmented this fund, all of which is deposited in the treasury of the State, to be appropriated in due time exclusively to the objects for which it was granted." Instead of a justification for making further payments, you find enough in this statement, and in the account of the Commissioners, to prohibit them. Why? Because you cannot regard as correct such a disposition as has been made of the fund in question, which as well includes the deposit of the whole amount of it, augmented as it has been, "in the treasury of the State, to be appropriated in due time exclusively to the objects for which it was granted," as the means by which its augmentation was effected. Speaking of the latter, as you do, in such close connection with the obligations of the State to appropriate the money to "the encouragement of learning," you seem to contend that it should, at all events and under all possible circumstances, be confined to a specific appropriation, that should directly and immediately and exclusively operate upon learning only; and hence it would appear that no deposit in the treasury of the State of any sum, under any circumstances, till the sums received should be adequate to the intended objects, would meet your approbation, since the deposit of the actual sum received could scarcely be more satisfactory than that of a much larger amount for the same purposes; and especially as the acknowledgment, by the State, of the receipt of the former from the Commissioners could afford no greater security than its acknowledgment of the receipt of the latter, with the most solemn pledges of its faith to appropriate it exclusively "to the encouragement of learning," and to no other object.

By the Legislature of the State, it has been supposed that this fund was intended to aid it in the establishment of institutions of learning, as well as to support them after their establishment; that it was under no imperative obligation, whether prepared or not, expedient or otherwise, to exhaust every cent received by immediate, direct and exclusive appropriations to "the encouragement of learning;" that it was under no absolute necessity to "rip open the goose to get the golden egg;" but that it might invest the money in any safe and productive funds, or loan it upon interest, and apply the proceeds to those objects. You would have the whole amount received annually exhausted, at all events. You would not permit it to be invested even in the stock of the Bank of the United States, since you object to its more profitable investment in the debt of the State, unless upon the degrading assumption that the former is worthy of all credit and the latter of none. It would seem that it could not be more safely loaned than to the State, whose honor and interest equally conspire to insure its fidelity to such an engagement; but you would not permit it to be loaned at all, since you refuse to allow the State to use it upon far more profitable terms, unless your objection arises from a particular want of confidence in the ability or good faith of the State. What, then, would you have the Commissioners of this fund to do? Would you wish them to release the State from its solemn and explicit obligation to pay the whole amount for which it has receipted in the lawful currency of the United States, and to diminish the fund so greatly increased, by accepting, in discharge of its obligation, the amount only which has been received from the United States? And can you believe that this would advance the interest which you are so careful to protect? How would you have that part of the fund which is required to be appropriated to a college or university disposed of? I confess, I cannot ever conjecture what, with your construction of the law, would satisfy you; and I would take it as a favor to be enlightened on the subject by the Department.

By the compact, it is declared that one-sixth part of the money contracted to be paid by the United States "shall be exclusively bestowed on a college or university." Now, suppose the amount received within the past year, after the passage of the law, to be one thousand dollars, one hundred and sixty-six dollars and sixty-six and two-thirds cents of this amount would be applicable to a college or university; but no such institutions were then in being, nor was the existence of either, at that early period, contemplated by either of the contracting parties. The money, therefore, could not be directly bestowed on a college or university. It would be insufficient for the erection of a suitable building for either; the annual application of such a sum to such a building could scarcely be expected to eventuate otherwise than in its entire loss; and you will not permit it to be idle or suffer it to be employed in any other manner than the strict letter of the compact; for the State is under precisely the same obligations to apply and account for the application of this part of the fund as the balance of it. What, then, should be done with it? The State will be greatly interested in being informed on the subject, should it find itself compelled to abandon its own, and adopt your views of its rights and obligations.

The Legislature of the State, composed, as it has been, of men who claim no exemption from the fallibility and imperfections common to all mankind, may, doubtless, have erred, but the most rigid scrutiny is defied to detect a single ground to justify the imputation, or even the faintest suspicion that it has in any manner whatever acted upon the subject without the most scrupulous regard to good faith. Influenced by its own construction of its rights and duties, and animated by an ardent, if not a rather too exclusive disposition to advance the interests of education, it seized with avidity the opportunity to make the investments to which you object, as the best possible expedient for rendering this fund the most available for those purposes. It authorized all the notes of the State Bank purchased by the Commissioners, to be canceled, and required the Auditor of Public Accounts to give them a certificate for their whole amount, payable in the legal currency of the United States—which certificate was delivered to and kept by the Commissioners "as an evidence of their claim upon the treasury of the State." It has sufficiently evinced its determination to appropriate this fund exclusively to the encouragement of learning, and to prevent its diminution in any other way, by having caused a sum of which it had been robbed, while it was in deposit for safe keeping in the Bank of the State, to be reimbursed to it; by providing by law that "no part of the said three per cent. fund shall ever be applied to any other purpose than the encouragement of learning in this State, and the expenses attending the receipt of any portion thereof shall be paid out of any moneys in the treasury not otherwise appropriated;" by establishing a system of free schools, and providing by law "that for the encouragement and support of schools respectively established in this State, according to this act, there shall be appropriated, for those purposes, two dollars out of every hundred hereafter to be received in the treasury of this State; also, five-sixths of the interest arising from the school fund (meaning the one in question), which shall be divided, annually, between the different counties of this State, in proportion to the number of white inhabitants in every county under the age," etc.

But I will press the subject no further. The whole case resolves itself into this simple question: Whether the State is to be compelled to abandon its own opinions, in which there is, probably, not a single dessentient within its limits, and to adopt yours? If this must be so, it cannot be less than a mortal blow to State rights; and whatever the consequences, I, for one, can never yield my assent to it.

I have only to add that, whatever may have been the freedom of the remarks which I have felt myself called upon to make, I beg leave candidly to assure you that they have proceeded, not from any unfriendly disposition, but from a sincere and anxious desire to avoid a collision but too well calculated to interrupt the peace and harmony of the Union itself.

I need not urge that the peculiar circumstances of the case render it extremely important to the State that I shall receive as early an answer to this communication as may suit the convenience of the Department.

I have the honor to be, very respectfully, sir,

Your most obedient servant,

N. EDWARDS.

To ASBURY DICKENS, Esq., *Acting Secretary of the Treasury.*

Having given a history of Gov. Edwards' character as a public man, and of his public services, I propose to say something of his private life—of his pursuits in the management of his personal affairs—and his usefulness as a neighbor and citizen.

At a very early age, as has been previously stated, he was sent by his father to Kentucky to take charge of his landed estate. Although only nineteen years of age, he took charge of the farm hands, opened and improved a farm upon which his father afterwards removed, with his numerous family, from the State of Maryland, built distilleries and tan-yards, and gave all the necessary instruction in relation to their construction. It was at this time that he indulged in habits of dissipation, from which, by a determined resolution, he was snatched like a fire-brand from the fire. He broke loose from his associates, removed to Logan county, Kentucky, where he devoted himself to the study and practice of his profession. Very soon after his appointment to the office of judge, he resided on a farm, and successfully carried it on until his appointment to the office of Governor of the Territory.

After the reformation of his habits, he was intrusted by his father with funds to locate lands in Kentucky, and his success was such that he laid the foundation for the fine estate which was afterwards realized by his brothers and sisters. Though his father was anxious to divide his property by giving him an equal share with his brothers and sisters, he insisted upon receiving nothing under the will. It appears, from a letter to Mr. Wirt, that he declined receiving anything from his father, as early as 1808. Mr. Wirt, in a letter of that year, thus alludes to it: "Your delicacy in relation to your father's will does you honor; but you are amply requited for it—for a testamentary compliment from such a man and such a father is the richest of legacies."

Although, in the year 1799, he was left without a dollar he could call his own, by his practice for the short space of only four years, and his prudent investment of the money realized from his profession, he amassed what was considered in that day a large fortune, consisting of lands, notes, farms and stock, previous to his leaving Kentucky for Illinois, in the year 1809. Many of his friends expressed surprise that he should leave Kentucky for the office of Governor of the Territory of Illinois. Speaking of his success in Kentucky, Mr. Wirt, in a letter written about that time, says, "I had supposed the Presidency of the Court of Appeals, connected with the society of your relatives and friends, and its dignity, upheld by your own splendid fortune, was an office much more desirable than that for which you have exchanged; and although it gave me great pleasure to state to Mr. Madison, at large, my impression of you, yet, I must confess, in secret, I half wished the application might fail, principally on your father's account, whose old age, I believed, reposed in a great degree on you. But of all these considerations, you, who was on the ground, are certainly best judge, and I will not doubt that you have decided correctly."

For a considerable portion of his time, after his removal to Illinois, he resided on his farm near Kaskaskia, to which he brought with him, from Kentucky, an improved stock of horses, cattle and sheep, from which the agricultural interests of the Territory were much benefited. He also had a choice collection of fruit trees, grape vines and shrubbery. He established saw and grist mills, and engaged extensively in the mercantile business—having no less than eight or ten stores in as many places in Missouri and Illinois; and, notwithstanding the arduous duties of his office, he almost always purchased his goods himself. He established stores in Kaskaskia, Belleville, Carlisle, Alton and Springfield, in this State; and in St. Louis, Franklin and Chariton, in Missouri.

He was equally useful to his fellow-citizens and neighbors as a physician; for, although he did not practice medicine as a profession, yet he was devoted to the study of it, and the writer knows of hundreds of instances of his visiting and prescribing for the sick without any charge; and it was not unusual for persons to come several hundred miles to consult him with regard to cases that were considered of a dangerous character by other physicians.

As in his public life righteousness and faithfulness were the rules of his conduct, so in his private affairs was he influenced by a love of justice, benevolence and truth. He was sued but once in his life, and in that he was successful. He was kind and compassionate to the unfortunate, never turned away the needy from his door, and was the friend of the widow, the fatherless and the poor. I know of widows and ministers of the gospel who were indebted to his liberality for their homes. A more affectionate and devoted husband, father, brother, or a kinder neighbor, never lived. His children so respected and loved him, that it was unusual for either of them ever to incur his displeasure by doing any act which they believed would not meet his approbation.

He resided at and in the vicinity of Kaskaskia from 1809 to 1818; in Edwardsville from the time of his removal from Kaskaskia until 1824; from which time, his place of residence was Belleville, St. Clair county, where he died on the 20th July, 1833.

In closing this memoir of Gov. Edwards, I may be permitted to say, what indeed can be said of few men who have been engaged so long in the public service, that his political opponents were never able to point to a single measure which he had supported which did not meet with almost the unanimous approbation of his fellow-citizens; nor to any measure, calculated to advance the interests of his constituents, which he did not propose or favor. At the time of his death, he had scarcely an enemy in the State. Gov. Bond, John McLean, (Senator in Congress from this State,) and nearly all his former political opponents, were his warmest personal friends. In the year 1828, he received a letter from the Hon. John McLean, of Illinois, in which he says, "But that you have always been true to your friends and faithful to your engagements, I am and have for a long time been fully satisfied; and it has always been to me a source of regret that we were, either with or without cause, in a state of collision. But that is over, and, on my part, I assure you that I only recollect it to regret that it ever existed."

The following sketch of Gov. Edwards' life, extracted from a discourse delivered by the Rev. Dr. J. M. Peck, on the 22d of December, 1833, is inserted here as embodying, not only some of the leading traits of his character, but facts of his history:

FUNERAL DISCOURSE.

"Her strong rods were broken and withered."—EZEKIAL—xix: 12.

Figures of speech were common in ancient times; the scriptures abound with them. Hence, to a right understanding of such expressions of scripture as my text, it is necessary to notice the application of the phraseology, and its connection with the subject over which the prophet was lamenting. He was here bewailing the ruin of the royal family of Judah, and the great calamities that had fallen upon the nation of Israel.

In the connection, the Jewish commonwealth is represented by the figure of a lioness—her whelps ensnared and taken.—(Verses 3-9.) Allusion appears to be had to Jehoahaz, whom the people had made king after Josiah was slain, and whom Pharaoh Necho carried, in chains, into Egypt. The people, seeing no hopes in his return, submitted to Jehoiakim, whom Pharaoh had made king. Like a young lion he used his power with great cruelty, till he fell under the provoked hostilities of the king of Babylon.

The next figure, to represent the condition of the Jewish nation and their rulers, is that of a vine, planted in a fruitful soil.—(Verses 10-14.) Their magistrates and chief men are compared to "strong rods."—(2-11.) The judgments of heaven had passed over the land. "The east wind had dried up her fruit." What the prophet alludes to here is not so readily determined. Was it the pestilence from the east that swept off the people and withered the strong rods? Or, was it the allusion to the invasion of Judea, by the king of Babylon?

"Strong rods" metaphorically denote leading men—rulers of the nation. This is manifest from the eleventh verse: "And she had strong rods for the sceptres of them that bore rule." Such a metaphor would describe those who had superior talents, and in other respects were well qualified to rule.

It is deserving of remark that such a rod should grow out of a weak vine; but God raised up from the Jews, even when the nation was in a low condition, many distinguished and mighty men. For there were periods, in the history of this nation, when the people had excellent and wise magistrates for their governors.

It is affirmed in the text that these strong rods were broken and withered. Death had removed them. Imbecility and corruption, or tyranny and cruelty, then characterized her rulers.

The loss of such public men, as were fitly described by the figure "strong rods," was deplored by the prophet as a public calamity. Hence, I regard the text as expressing this sentiment: that the death of an able statesman is a public calamity.

First—I shall contemplate the use and application of the metaphor.

A parent is a strong rod to his family. The companion of his bosom leans on him for support and happiness, and his children look up to him for counsel and example.

A minister of the gospel is a strong rod to the church over which he has been placed as overseer.

A man eminently qualified for public business and usefulness in a political community, is a strong rod to a nation or a state.

We will proceed to notice some of these properties in public men, which entitle them to the application of the figure "strong rods."

1. *Great natural talents.* These are to be found in strong reasoning powers and a vigorous understanding; a peculiar aptitude and genius for public business; a keen penetration into the tendencies of measures towards the welfare or injury of the community, and the speediest means to advance the one and counteract the other—with clear perceptions of right and justice, and the false colors in which unjust measures are often disguised. Though these abilities are susceptible of great improvement, by education, self-discipline and experience, yet their foundation seems to be laid in a naturally vigorous intellect.

2. *In an educated or well cultivated mind.* When great natural talents are well cultivated by close, systematic study, observation and experience, and by these means the mind has become enriched with a large fund of useful knowledge, the foundation is laid for a great man.

Public men should possess considerable knowledge of the history of men, nations and governments—knowledge of the whole circle of human affairs, (particularly of the condition, resources, policy and designs of neighboring nations)—that they may know how to direct the affairs of their own with advantage; and more particularly of the constitution, principles, history, laws, and peculiarities of their own Government.

The peculiar organization of our National Government, with the coördinate and subordinate relations of each State—the different circumstances in which each are placed in relation to others, and to the Confederate Republic—make it indispensable for a well qualified statesman to bring to this subject a mind habituated to severe and patient investigation, and well stored with previous reading.

Considerable knowledge of the nature, sources and obligations of law, and especially of the fundamental laws of our country, is a most important acquisition; so is the knowledge of human nature, in general—of our own hearts—of the human passions, and especially the power of influencing others to the adoption of important measures. A statesman must not only be capable of forming wise plans, but he must be able to carry them into effect by bringing the people to coöperate with him. He must also possess competent knowledge of the condition and resources of the country he serves, and skill to direct those resources to the best advantage.

It will now be perceived that, without an educated and well cultivated mind, a man can never become an eminent statesman, however great may be his native powers. Like that potent agent that propels our commerce and drives our machinery, a vigorous mind, without cultivation and discipline, may do great injury.

I am not here depreciating the properties of those minds who have not been classically or scientifically educated, or whose names have not been recorded on a college diploma. Shall I be told that eminent men, profound statesmen and able commanders have done honor to our own country and that of other nations, and yet have never entered the walls of a literary or scientific institution? Will the names of Washington, Franklin, Sherman, Rittenhouse, Patrick Henry, and a hundred more in the last or present generations, be arrayed before me to confute the position that an educated and well cultivated mind is necessary to eminence in public life? Let it be remarked that I have not made a collegiate education and the attendance of able instructors, in all cases, indispensable to these attainments. But it is denied that Washington, Franklin, and other sages and patriots of like character, were uneducated men, and that they attained to eminence and usefulness by mere natural genius, with uncultivated minds. They possessed, most unquestionably, great intellectual powers, but these were highly cultivated. They had not the advantages that many others possessed, in the means of acquiring their education. By pressure of circumstances they were forced, in a considerable degree, to educate themselves. Did such men ever arise by the mere flight of unaided genius? No; it was only by patient and long continued study—aided by much practical observation—that their mental powers became developed and exhibited such vigor.

We admonish young men to beware of the delusion that they can ever become "strong rods" in a political community, or eminent in any pursuit, without close study. Your partial friends may flatter your vanity by indiscreetly praising your genius and natural talents; but never expect to arise above the common level, without study and observation. "Give attendance to reading" is no less applicable to the young patriot than to the young preacher.

3. *Self-government is an important requisite in the character we are contemplating.* This implies the subjugation of our appetites and propensities—equanimity of temper—and such power over the passions as will enable the judgment and reason to retain the ascendency on every emergency. He who cannot rule himself, will rarely succeed in governing others and retaining their confidence.

4. *A noble, high-minded and generous disposition.* Nothing servile, base and cringing. Men of small talents, uncultivated minds and bad tempers are apt to be jealous, envious, malignant and revengeful, and are often guilty of low and mean conduct, especially towards their rivals.

In the collisions of party and the heat of political excitement, men of character and talents often say and do that which, in their sober and reflecting moments, they deeply regret; but the real statesman never will suffer such feelings to become habitual. A noble mind, conscious of its own tendency to undue excitement, makes allowances for the same infirmity in others. Such a character will possess self-respect; and the tendency of a due regard to one's own character will manifest itself in a proper respect to that of others. A man of real greatness of mind abhors those things that are mean and sordid. Artifice and clandestine management, to promote his own selfish designs, cannot be the governing principles of his soul. A just regard to future character is the duty of every one. This is far removed from the vices of pride, vainglory or ambition. It arises from self-respect. A man is as much bound to respect and preserve his own character, as he is to preserve the members of his body or his life; and he is equally bound to transmit the odor of a good name to posterity as to provide for the future happiness of his children. This duty devolves preëminently upon public men; and not only are their personal friends and families immediately concerned, but their services and their characters are alike the property of the nation.

5. *Firmness and decision of character are also important qualities.* In all governments there are broad, fundamental principles, which must be regarded and maintained, whatever may be the risk. On these principles the course of a statesman should never vacillate. The right of the people to instruct their representatives is unquestionable—for they in the aggregate, and not a privileged few, possess the governing power; but there may be occasional emergencies when a public man has to take the responsibility, and risk his popularity, for the benefit of his country. Such instances occurred in the gloomy period of the Revolutionary war. In some districts of the country a majority of the people fainted in the day of adversity, and would have submitted to British domination; but there were men of uncommon nerve who threw themselves into the breach and saved the country.

It is admitted that this call is not upon the topics of ordinary and common legislation, much less for the promotion of party designs. It is only when constitutional principles are at stake, the national compact to be preserved, or great and paramount interests are in jeopardy, that the firmness and integrity of the patriot should be brought in collision with the will of his constituents. Yet he should never be obstinate or self-willed, but proceed with due deliberation and make up his mind to fall a sacrifice to popular resentment, rather than betray his country or violate his conscience. There is a moral sublimity in the conduct of a public man who will risk this much for the public good.

He should also be firm and immovable in the administration of law and justice. Hence, unbending integrity and an inflexible regard to righteousness should mark his course under all circumstances. He should not be "a terror to good works, but to the evil." (Rom. xiii, 3)

6. *Patriotism is the last quality I will notice as belonging to a statesman.* A patriot is one who is actuated by love of his country, and who will sacrifice his own interests rather than the interests of the people. Private interests are merged in public good.

True patriotism does not annul or counteract the duty of universal benevolence, for it does not call us to regard our country's interest exclusively, at the expense of the general happiness of mankind. It does not abrogate the Divine injunction to love all mankind—to love our enemies. The laws of universal justice and equity require no one to promote the interests of the country, state, town or neighborhood where he resides, at the expense of justice, humanity and the happiness of mankind. A nation is exalted only by righteousness, and not by rapine, injustice and artifice. "Equal justice to all" has been recognized as the sentiment of this nation.

True patriotism in a citizen displays itself in zealously supporting the honor, interests and prosperity of our country and government on principles of equal justice. It never engages in plots or conspiracies to overturn or pervert constitutional principles—though individuals, equally patriotic, may honestly differ in opinion about the extent and application of those principles. It never seeks to bring the government or its constituted authorities into contempt; and though it may approve of one set of measures and disapprove of another—it may seek to elevate this man as more fitted to rule than that—yet it never takes pleasure in exposing the errors of rulers, or in defaming their characters. A dutiful son may see faults in his father, and affectionately remonstrate, but until all affection is extinguished, and self-respect is lost, he will not take pleasure in exposing him.

So with the real patriot. He delights not in exposing his country's faults.

But the man in office, above all others, is expected to be a true patriot. He must exhibit that unquenchable love of country that will prompt him to a cheerful sacrifice of his own interest when placed in competition with the public good. This will appear the more necessary when it is noticed that men of wealth as well as influence are frequently selected for the higher and more important offices. If such persons are not influenced by the spirit of the real patriot, the temptation to sacrifice the people's interest to their own will too easily prevail.

It is unnecessary here to particularize instances where the most elevated patriotism existed. Their names are found scattered over the records of antiquity. One of the most brilliant examples is that of Moses. For in renouncing the pleasures of Egypt, and his title, as the adopted son of the king's daughter, to the throne, and in preferring the interests of the Hebrew nation in their vassalage, his patriotism was not less conspicuous than his piety was elevated. The page of our revolutionary history furnishes evidence of entire devotion to the welfare of the nation. He, then, only deserves the name of a patriot who enters into public office with the fixed principle of promoting the good of his country and his fellow-men, and who continues to be governed by that principle. And, however important are natural talents, a well cultivated mind, self-control, magnanimity and high-souled feelings, and decision of character, if patriotism is wanting, he may be a great man, but we dare not pronounce him a great statesman.

Secondly—The death of such a man is a public calamity.

1. *Because such men are great benefits to society and government.* The prosperity of a nation depends much more on the character of its public men than is commonly imagined. They not only give direction to public sentiment, but, from the constitution of our natures, and the unavoidable habit of suffering ourselves to be influenced by those in whom we repose confidence, they often originate that sentiment. All the great, and many of the minor interests of society, are under their care and subject to their influence; and their opportunities to promote the public interest are great in every respect.

The direction they give to public affairs has a tendency to promote the wealth and prosperity of the nation, or to impoverish and cover it with the thick cloud of adversity.

The interest and happiness of the whole community, not excepting the humblest and most obscure, are materially affected by the character and conduct of those who are chosen to rule over the people. And as it is the intention and tendency of all good and upright governments to be a terror to all evil-doers and a protection to those who do well, public and private morals and virtue are promoted or retarded by the character of public men.

And while, in accordance with the principles of our national and state constitutions, we protest against all interference, on the part of the civil government, with the high and holy attributes of religion, as a subject entirely beyond its province, yet it is obvious to every reflecting mind that the character of public men cannot but affect materially the influence and prevalence of religious principles. Public virtue and sound morality are always affected by the course of human legislation. A most striking illustration of this truth is to be found in the history of France, when the national convention, controlled by a band of unprincipled atheists, denounced all religion, set up the Goddess of Reason, severed every bond of moral obligation, placed over the gates of the public cemetery the inscription, "Death is an eternal sleep," and thus broke over all the restraints that accountability to the Divine Being, and the influence of religious principles, have erected as a barrier to the depraved passions.

The butcheries and enormities which followed have furnished the world with a dreadful comment of a government without religious principles and moral ties.

Without belief in the general and leading principles of religion—such as the existence of a God, our accountability to him, and a future retribution—no laws, penalties or oaths will have efficient influence on mankind. Not to enlarge upon the importance of religion in exciting fear in the human heart of temporal judgments, passing by its high authority in communicating sanctity to oaths, and in restraining that class of offenses which human laws can neither detect or punish, we maintain it is of the utmost importance in softening the turbulent passions of men and collecting them together in friendly society.

Thus, the prosperity and safety of the people, under God, depend very much on such public men as we have described as "strong rods." Hence, when these are broken and withered, it is to be regarded as a mark of Divine displeasure, and submitted to as a public calamity.

2. *Wise, upright and talented men are, in a great degree, the defense of a nation.* Innumerable and great are the evils to which nations, states and communities are exposed in this sinful world. A people without government are like a city without walls or the means of defense, and yet encompassed on every side by enemies. They become unavoidably subject to confusion, misery and destruction.

Government is necessary to defend communities from intestine discord, injustice and violence. Its necessity springs from the ignorance, depravity and selfishness of human nature. It is equally indispensable to protection from the injustice or violence of other nations, and from those individuals who have thrown off the restraints of national government, and, as pirates or robbers, depredate upon the property of individuals and communities.

Qualified statesmen and rulers are equally indispensable to the administration of good government. They are the bulwarks of a people in time of war, and the chief instruments of their prosperity in time of peace. They see the evil approaching and throw themselves into the breach. They survey the resources of the country and aid the people in their development.

Strong rods are necessary to good government. Such was the virtuous Josiah to the nation of Israel, who probably was one of the "strong rods" alluded to by the prophet. When he fell in an unequal contest with the king of Egypt, "they brought him to Jerusalem, and he died and was buried in one of the sepulchres of his fathers, and all Judah and Jerusalem mourned for Josiah." With him fell the glory and strength of the nation.

APPLICATION.

It will be readily perceived by this audience that, in many particulars, our late distinguished fellow-citizen, Gov. Edwards, was a strong rod to this community and State. He was justly entitled to the appellation of Father of Illinois.

After giving a very brief sketch of his life, not materially different from that I have given in another part of this work, Dr. Peck proceeds as follows:

From the time of his first election to the Legislature of Kentucky, before he had quite attained his majority, up to this period, he had not been out of public office, and in every station he had acquitted himself with honor, and to the satisfaction of the people.

It was not to be expected that he would be permitted to remain long in retirement. The people of Illinois, who, in various ways, had expressed their acknowledgments of the value of his public services, still had claims upon him. He was elected Governor of the State in 1826, and whatever might have been the feelings of political opponents upon his entrance into this office, we believe few persons could be found who did not approve the general course of his administration. A candid and dispassionate review of his correspondence as Governor of the Territory, his speeches in Congress, and his messages to the Legislature, would convince even his opponents of the entire devotedness on his part to the interests of the State. History and posterity will pronounce him a true patriot, and point out many official acts in which private interest was sacrificed on the altar of the public welfare.

Upon the expiration of his constitutional term as Governor, it was his intention not to appear before the people again in any public capacity. Enjoying some share of his confidence and friendship, I feel authorized in this declaration. But he consented to suffer his name to be used as a candidate for Congress, at the election in 1832, by the repeated and urgent solicitations of many friends whose wishes he felt bound to respect. This was the first and only election he ever lost before the people, and at this time there were four other respectable candidates for the same office—two of whom were considered by the people as belonging to the same political party with himself, to whom many had committed themselves previous to the annunciation that Gov. Edwards was a candidate.

Much of the latter period of his life was devoted to the adjustment of his private affairs, and to acts of humanity and benevolence. And he possessed such method and system that, notwithstanding his estate was large and his business complicated, his affairs were left in such order as to admit of easy adjustment.

His neighbors and fellow-citizens can give ample testimony to his humane, liberal and benevolent character. Possessing considerable medical knowledge, with a sound discriminating judgment, he frequently administered and prescribed for the sick, visited the couch of the dying, and gave consolation to the afflicted. To the poor and distressed he was liberal in his personal services and benefactions. The poorest man in the State was as fully welcome to the hospitalities of his house and table as the most opulent and distinguished.

In his benefactions to purposes of benevolence and charity, Gov. Edwards was liberal without ostentation. It is known to the speaker that in many instances he gave liberal sums of which the public knew nothing.

He never made a public profession of religion, yet he was a believer in its doctrines, and there were times in the latter period of his life, known to the speaker, when he became unusually interested in its weighty truths, and was anxious about his personal salvation. On these occasions, his conversation was free and evinced deep feeling.

When that dreadful disease, the cholera, to which he fell a victim, first appeared amongst us, Gov. Edwards was indefatigable in obtaining the most valuable and accurate information of the nature of the disease, and the most successful mode of treatment, and in diffusing it among the people. When it approached the village where he resided, his anxiety for the preservation of others was great. Though of feeble health and of impaired constitution, and forewarned by his friends that an attack of the cholera in his system would prove fatal, yet, night and day, he was with the sick and dying, till he fell a victim to his humane and charitable exertions for the relief of others. The first attack on himself was in the form of dysentery, which greatly weakened his system, but produced no alarming symptoms. From this attack he recovered so far as to leave his room, prepare some papers on business, and converse with his family and friends, which he did for two days, with cheerfulness and with the prospect of a speedy recovery.

On Friday evening, July 19, he was attacked with the cholera in its regular form, under which he sunk rapidly till about seven o'clock on Saturday morning, July 20, when he expired. He left three sons and one daughter, to feel and mourn the irreparable loss of a kind father.

Were I to attempt a portraiture of his character, in its various colorings, I could say nothing new nor do it ample justice. Yet, it may be necessary to call into remembrance some of its prominent features, to excite your minds to profitable reflection:

First. Contemplate him again as a youth, a minor—ardent, impetuous, aspiring, and sent forth upon the world; journeying several hundreds of miles from his paternal guardian and home; entering upon a new and unformed state of society on the frontier of Kentucky, and exposed to all the temptations incident to youth in all places, with those peculiar to a new country. See him, falling before the tempter—the structure of a noble mind about to be thrown down in ruins—yielding to the seductive influences of youthful follies—lured on to the precipice by giddy and thoughtless companions—the hydra monster about to encircle him in his scaly and voluminous folds. Pause a moment! Here are brilliant prospects—promising talents—a fine imagination—a cultivated mind—a father's hope, a mother's joy—about to be crushed and withered in this deadly embrace, and, as worthless things, thrown down the precipice into the gulf of oblivion. And is escape from such toils common? Ah, no! Where one has escaped, thousands have perished. Gaze here, ye young men, accustomed to your nightly orgies! Look at that immolation about to be offered! And yet, from this horrid embrace, and these fascinating toils, he did escape—marvellously escape!

We pause again. A silent, secret resolution begins to heave his youthful breast; it wavers—it struggles—it falters, and struggles again. The hopes of father, mother, brother, sisters, and a long line of friends, are flickering—sending forth the last feeble rays. The voice of filial love is not quite silent. The voice of conscience is upraised. The cheering gleams of hope appear above the distant horizon. The struggle is renewed, and victory crowns the conqueror!

Let our young men here be admonished. Your success depends, not in imitating his youthful follies, but in escaping from the snare and devoting your minds to the acquisition of useful knowledge and forming habits of virtuous industry.

We know not which to admire the most—the merciful providence of God to this young man, or the uncommon decision and energy of character put forth. Now view him as a close, laborious and successful student, determined to qualify himself for the profession he had chosen. Breaking away from the fascinations of his youthful companions, he puts forth the vigor of manhood and enters upon a life of honor and usefulness.

Second. View him as a public man—ardently devoted to the interests of the people; receiving their confidence; chosen by them to important trusts, and, from the midst of a constellation of legal talent, placed on the bench of the circuit court at the age of twenty-seven—rising, both in the confidence and respect of the people and in the judicial station, till he reaches the elevated position of Chief Justice of the State of Kentucky before he is thirty-two years of age. Is here imbecility of mind, fickleness of purpose, neglect of study, time wasted in gossiping and listless folly? Is here anything like indecision? indolence? waywardness? Far otherwise. Here are talents of no common order—moral energies that press through every obstruction—steadiness of purpose that never fails of success—mental discipline that will cause the mind to grow brighter and brighter—time husbanded as an invaluable treasure. Here is decision of character sufficient for the noblest purposes, industry that never tires, and a soul subjected to the government of reason.

Contemplate him through his future public life. The same traits of character increase in vividness—the same intellect accumulates strength. All the virtues we have contemplated are called into active exercise in forming the character, modeling and administering the government of this Territory.

View him as a Senator. His weight of character and influence command the respect of the nation. His suggestions are listened to as the voice of wisdom and experience, while, through all his public services, the people cling to him, as a strong rod, for support.

Third. But it is not in the ardor and buoyancy of youth, nor in the halls of legislation, nor on the bench of justice, nor yet in the executive chair, that a man's whole character is exhibited to the best advantage. Go to the domestic circle, see him by the fire-side, around the family altar, and in the every-day dress of his character, if you wish to gain a full and distinct view of the picture of a man. Let us contemplate our friend in this interesting aspect. As the head of a family and a father, few persons have manifested stronger affections in the family circle—few fathers were more beloved by their children. Ask that desolate widow, whose affections have been scathed as with the lightning's blast, to count up the sum of her loss. Ask those disconsolate children how much they loved him. Let the circle of relatives, with the long line of personal friends, draw near, estimate his worth, and the loss they have sustained.

Fourth. Contemplate him as a neighbor and citizen. Though elevated to high offices and rank, he was truly your equal. Few men of his station in life ever possessed less of the pride of ostentation and greatness. While all trifling and mimicry were despicable in his eyes, it was his nature to be sociable, conversant and friendly with every class of citizens. As a neighbor, he was kind and obliging.

Were I to mark the prominent traits of his character, I would place in high relief great decision—determined, resistless perseverence—quickness in dispatch of business—sagacity to the public interest—a liberal and philanthropic disposition—and a sense of his accountability to God.

We have thus, fellow-citizens, attempted to give you a brief but imperfect sketch of the life and character of our distinguished friend; and while we are taught, from Divine revelation, to submit with humility to that calamity which a wise and mysterious Providence has brought upon this State, in the death of a fellow-citizen of such eminent abilities and usefulness, we shall close this discourse with a single reflection. "*For none of us liveth to himself*," is the declaration of an inspired apostle. We are not insulated beings. Our example, influence, wealth, talents and prayers are all to be employed for useful purposes, and should be directed in that way that will lessen the most misery and promote the most happiness in the world in which we dwell. Whatever be our rank—whether as legislators, jurists, magistrates, ministers of the gospel, or private citizens—we are capable of doing immense harm or immense good, and the influence of this good or evil is not expended upon the present generation, merely: ages to come will feel the effects. It will follow in the continuous line of succeeding generations; and future millions will arise to call us blessed, or invoke anathemas upon our memories. The laws that are now framed—the moral influence exerted—the national or state improvements attempted—the schools established—the churches gathered—the preachers ordained—the appointments to office—the public and private example of all—the humblest walk of the humblest citizen of this State—will prove the means of happiness to individuals and the community for years to come.

Filled and overwhelmed with a sense of this weighty responsibility, let each one act well his part in life, that blessings may water his memory when his ashes have commingled with their kindred dust.

CHAPTER XIII.

Memoir of the late Hon. Daniel P. Cook.

The following memoir of the late Hon. Daniel P. Cook, who had been a member of Congress from the State from 1819 to 1827, which, by the permission of William H. Brown, Esq , I give a place in this work, gives a brief sketch of the able and distinguished men who had been the prominent political opponents of both Mr. Cook and Gov. Edwards. Two of them, the Hon. Elias K. Kane, and John McLean, were the successors in the Senate of the United States of Gov. Edwards and Judge Thomas, and were both distinguished for their talents and usefulness to the State and the Nation. They both died while holding their seats in the Senate.

MEMOIR OF THE LATE HON. DANIEL P. COOK.

To the Members of the Chicago Historical Society:

At your request, I have prepared a brief memoir of the late Hon. Daniel P. Cook, our second representative in Congress from this State, and in honor of whom the county of Cook was appropriately named. I have undertaken the task the more readily because I deem it desirable and important to preserve our early statistics, and some facts of history in connection with this gentleman, and because I take pleasure in perpetuating the memory of one of my first and constant friends, and vindicating his character from some of the aspersions cast upon it in times of high political excitement. Though confessedly a labor of friendship, it is believed that no partial coloring has impaired the truthfulness of the picture ; and certainly no attempt is made to underrate the character or talents of Mr. Cook's competitors to enhance his merits or exalt his virtues.

An interval of thirty years is a potent anodyne. It gives time for many "second sober thoughts," and clears the vision of prejudice and passion. It obliterates the rough and angular points of character, and brings out the milder virtues of your adversary. Gradually and imperceptibly his failings and foibles are forgotten, and memory dwells only on what was lovely and of "good report."

Mr. Cook was born of very respectable parentage, in the county of Scott, in the State of Kentucky, about the year 1794. In his early youth, he enjoyed only such means of education as were afforded by the common schools of his native State. If he studied the classics at all, it must have been in the later years of his life, and after he had entered upon its arduous duties. It is, however, certain he pursued no collegiate course.

When quite young, he was placed by his parents in a mercantile establishment, but continued therein but a short time. This sphere was too limited for his high aspirations, and leaving trade and commerce to minds less ardent than his own, he commenced the study of the law with the late Hon. John Pope, of Kentucky, then in the zenith of his fame, and engaged in a large and lucrative practice.

Mr. Cook came to the Territory of Illinois in the latter part of the year 1815, and established himself in business at Kaskaskia, the seat of the Territorial Government, and the only considerable town in the country, embracing a population of from seven hundred to one thousand inhabitants, two-thirds of whom were native French. He entered successfully into the practice of the law, attending the courts in all the then organized counties* (except those upon the Wabash), and in the lower counties in the Territory of Missouri. The business of the courts at this period was comparatively small, owing to the few inhabitants in the Territory, and the limited business transacted by them. It is probable that few, if any, of the profession, at that day, supported themselves exclusively by their practice. Many were engaged in agricultural pursuits, and others occupied a portion of their time in land speculations.

In the early part of the year 1816, Mr. Cook became a joint owner in the office of the "Illinois Intelligencer," the only newspaper and printing office in the Territory, and assumed the duties of an editor. Unfortunately, the files of the paper of that period were not preserved, and no opportunity is now afforded to form an opinion of the manner in which those duties were discharged; but, from the known talents and industry of Mr. C., it may be safely assumed that, while under his management, the paper took a high rank amongst its contemporaries, and exerted a healthy influence in the community. With the printing of the laws and journals of the Territorial Legislatures, and blanks for the public offices, at prices which would now astonish a practical printer, it is certain the business was lucrative and yielded a competent support to its conductors.

It appears, by the record of appointments, that Gov. Edwards conferred upon Mr. C. the office of Auditor of Public Accounts, in the month of January of that year. If the office was accepted by him, he could have continued in it but for a short time.

Late in this year, or early in 1817, President Monroe selected Mr. C. as bearer of dispatches to the late John Quincy Adams, then Minister at the English Court, to recall that gentleman, preparatory to his assuming the office of Secretary of State, to which office he had been appointed upon the formation of Mr. Monroe's cabinet. Mr. C. performed that duty, and in due time returned and resumed his practice and other duties.

Shortly after his return, Mr. Cook was appointed a Circuit Judge. His district embraced the counties of Bond, Madison, St. Clair, Randolph and Monroe, containing a large territory of nearly one-third of the present limits of the State. He retained this office but a short time, and could have held but one or two terms of his courts. He acquired, however, an enviable reputation as a Judge, evincing talent, energy and promptness, and was as popular as a judicial officer as when pursuing his profession at the bar.

Upon the organization of the State Government, in December, 1818, Mr. C. was elected, by the Legislature, Attorney General for the new State, which office he held until October in the following year.

---

*These counties were Bond, Madison, St. Clair, Monroe, Randolph, Jackson, Franklin, Union, Johnson, Pope, Gallatin, White, Edwards, Crawford and Washington.

The State of Illinois was virtually admitted into the Union in October, 1818; but, by a provision in the Constitution, an election for State officers, and for a representative in Congress, was to be held on the third Thursday of September of that year, for the short session, expiring March 3, 1819. Mr. Cook became a candidate, and was opposed by the late Hon. John McLean, then a resident of Shawneetown. It is hardly necessary to say that, during the administration of Mr. Monroe, there was a remarkable political calm throughout the entire country. The great questions, which before had been eagerly and acrimoniously discussed by the people, and had divided the nation into the two great political parties of Democrats and Federalists, had either been decided, or, by general consent, postponed to an indefinite future. The course pursued by Mr. Monroe gave universal satisfaction, and the people enjoyed, for six or eight years, a political millennium. That quietude and peace, in common with others, was enjoyed by our early settlers. It is not, however, to be forgotten, that early in the territorial history, as well as in the first six years after Illinois became a State, the disturbing question of slavery formed an important element in the politics of that period. There was a strong party in favor of introducing slavery at the election of delegates to the Convention which formed the Constitution; but it is well known that the principles of liberty prevailed, and the whole question was set at rest by the decisive vote of 1824, when this subject was brought directly before the people.

Another element of division in our politics was personal preferences, or the existence of parties for the advancement of particular individuals or their friends. Thus there were the Edwards party and the Bond party, the respective adherents of either warmly contending and struggling for office and supremacy. The leaders of these parties were Gov. Edwards, Judge Nathaniel Pope and Mr. Cook, professed anti-slavery men (though the two first were slave-holders) on the one side, and Gov. Bond, Elias Kent Kane, his Secretary of State, and John McLean on the other. The former, of course, supported Mr. Cook, while the latter naturally fell into Mr. McLean's ranks. This gentleman was a Kentuckian by birth, and a leading member of the bar, in the south-eastern part of the State. Possessed of fine talents and an unblemished character, he was at that time, and continued to be until the day of his death, one of the most popular men in the State. He was subsequently speaker of our House of Representatives, and, in 1826, was elected a Senator in Congress. He died at an early age, possessing, in a rare degree, the confidence and esteem of all who enjoyed his personal acquaintance.

The election thus held in September, seems not to have excited general interest. The State ticket was a compromise one—composed of Col. Bond, for Governor, from the one side, and Col. Pierre Menard, an excellent and worthy French citizen, from the other. The contest was mainly for Congress, and Mr. McLean succeeded by only fourteen majority.

At the special election, in the summer of 1819, the same gentlemen were candidates for Congress, and great exertions were made by the candidates, themselves, and their respective friends. No election, before or since, caused more feeling and effort. The exciting Missouri question had, at the previous session, been brought into the halls of Congress, and, upon preliminary votes, Mr. McLean had favored the pro-slavery party, and indicated his desire that the State should be admitted without the proposed restriction. In addition to this, he had been so unfortunate, in some of his addresses before the people, as to offend some of the more recent immigrants from the Eastern States, and, as a general thing, lost their votes. Mr. Cook was elected by a fair majority. As in former contests, the old question of slavery was prominent. The anti-slavery party rallied around Mr. Cook's standard and insured his success.

In 1820 the contest was renewed. Mr. McLean, satisfied with the efforts of the previous year, and unwilling to risk another defeat, declined to be a candidate. The Hon. E. K Kane was brought out as Mr. Cook's competitor.

The question of the admission of the State of Missouri as a slave State was still more directly before the people. The old pro-slavery party, represented by Mr. Kane, were against imposing any restriction upon the proposed new State—while the other party were, to some extent, divided. Many, who theretofore had acted in our local struggles as anti-slavery men, were disposed to leave the question to the decision of those most immediately interested; others, and perhaps the larger portion, looked upon the admission of another slave State as a great evil, to be resisted at all hazards. Both candidates, however, were understood to be in favor of the admission of this State with a constitution admitting slavery—Mr. Kane from choice, and Mr. Cook from policy. The contest, therefore, in 1820, was mostly a personal one, depending mainly upon the popularity of the candidates. Mr. Kane was badly defeated, obtaining a majority in only one county in the State Mr. Cook's majority was two thousand four hundred and eighty-two, in a vote of less than eight thousand, or nearly two to one in his favor.

On his first entrance into Congress, Mr. C. was placed upon the committee on Public Lands—the most important to the people he represented. At this period, and before, the government lands were in market at two dollars per acre, one fourta in cash and the residue upon a credit of five years. The comparatively prosperous years, immediately before the formation of the State Government, had induced the wildest speculations in public lands. Every man who could command the sum of $80 (the cash payment upon 160 acres, then the smallest subdivision); became a *quasi* land holder, and a debtor to the government. The financial revulsion throughout the country, soon after the close of the war of 1812, reached the West in 1819. Men who had supposed themselves possessed of large wealth, suddenly discovered their error. They had, it is true, an equitable claim to many quarter sections of land, but the claim was valueless, and the land unsalable; and in addition to this embarrassment, they were largely indebted to the government for the sums remaining unpaid upon their purchases. It may be safely stated that, from this cause, at least one-half of those who had been considered the men of capital in the country, were reduced from supposed wealth to positive bankruptcy.

To relieve the country from this load of debt, Mr. Cook warmly advocated plans of relief, which resulted in a general law, abolishing the credit system and reducing the price of land to $1.25 per acre.* Former purchasers were permitted to consolidate their entries and relinquish the surplus quarter sections to the government By the operation of this law individuals secured, in fee simple, the number of acres of land they had actually paid for, at the rate of $2 per acre, and were released from their liabilities for further payments. Mr. Cook introduced and advocated, at the session of 1820–21, a resolution giving preëmption rights to settlers on the public land. It was the first effort made in this direction, and failed of success. It was, however, the germ of the policy thereafter adopted, and from which our citizens have derived great and incalculable advantages.

*At a subsequent election, Mr. Cook, a considerable land owner, under the $2 per acre law, was charged with opposition to the new law. The writer has abundant evidence in his possession to prove the falsity of this charge.

Mr. Cook voted in Congress against the admission of Missouri. As he had given the people to understand, during the canvass, that he would favor that measure, his vote excited surprise, and called forth from his opponents unmerited abuse and bitter denunciations. Bribery and corruption, the violation of pledges, deception and double-dealing, were rung upon all their various changes, and, for the time being, Mr C. apparently lost his hold upon the confidence and affections of the people.

His reasons for his change of mind were given in his speech in Congress when the bill was before that body; and, inasmuch as this is one of Mr. Cook's acts which has been loudly denounced, it is proper he should be heard in his defense and in his own words. The following extracts, it is thought, will place this subject in a proper light, and enable the reader to form an opinion as to the propriety of the course he saw fit to adopt:

* * * "When," said Mr. C., "he first arrived at Washington, he, for the first time, met the objection which was now urged against the Constitution of Missouri; and, perhaps, under the influence of a strong anxiety for her admission, had examined the question, as he thought, thoroughly, and for a considerable time saw no reason to change his determination. Under the conviction produced by that examination he had, as he hoped he always should do, fearlessly expressed his opinion in favor of her admission. He even now, notwithstanding his opinion was changed, freely declared that all his predilections were in favor of such a vote. Missouri, he said, was the near adjoining neighbor of Illinois; and, notwithstanding an unhappy difference of opinion upon political subjects, had created, between their respective citizens, a rancor and animosity which he well knew the vote he was about to give would not in the least allay—a vote at which he also knew many of his constituents would be greatly disturbed when they heard of it—yet he should be glad to see her admitted and placed upon an equal footing with the State he had the honor to represent.

* * * "In order to be a State in the Union, or to be entitled to become such, he considered it an indispensable pre-requisite, on her part, to form a constitution in conformity to the principles of the Federal Constitution, and in conformity to the conditions presented by the act in virtue of which her constitution, upon its face, professed to have been formed. That she had not formed such a constitution, he thought, was fairly deducible from the argument he was about to make.

"The constitution of the United States, said he, gives to 'Congress the power to dispose of and make all needful rules and regulations respecting the territory and other property of the United States.' This, said Mr. C., is a general power; and in its exercise, he apprehended that Congress had a right to dispose of that territory to whomsoever they pleased. He said it had been admitted, by gentlemen on both sides of the question, that free negroes and mulattoes were competent to hold real estate; and that they did hold it in almost, if not quite, every State in the Union. They are, therefore, competent, he observed, upon the admission of all parties, to purchase such estate from the United States. But the constitution of Missouri declares, 'that it shall be the duty of the Legislature, as soon as may be, to pass such laws as may be necessary to prevent free negroes and mulattoes from coming to and settling in that State, under any pretense whatsoever;' a provision, said he, which, notwithstanding their competency to purchase, and the indisputable power of Congress to sell to them, clearly asserts a controlling power over the rights of these individuals, and the paramount authority of Congress. * * * * Mr. C. said there was another view of that clause of the Missouri Constitution, under which it seemed still more obviously in violation of the Federal Constitution. Congress, he said, by virtue of the general power which it possessed to dispose of the territory of the United States, for the purpose of obtaining the military services of persons, as well of this as every other description, had offered them a land bounty—to many of whom, and embracing free negroes and mulattoes, patents had already been issued for lands in Missouri. He said persons of this description, to his own knowledge, had purchased land in Illinois, and he had no doubt such was the case in Missouri. Whether they had, or not, however, did not vary the case—the principle was the same. In the soldier, as well as the purchaser, therefore, he begged leave to say, the Government of the United States vested a fee simple estate in those lands. This title he considered to consist of the possession, the right of possession and the right of property; and he thought, when he asserted that the Government had guaranteed all these features of the right which it vested both in the soldier and purchaser, that no honorable member would hazard a denial of that assertion. Under this guaranty, he contended the United States incompetent, unless for public purposes—and then only by paying a fair equivalent therefor—to deprive them of this property. And yet Missouri, through a subordinate Legislature, if her constitution be allowed to operate, does virtually take it away without paying any equivalent whatever; for if a person be not allowed to enjoy the possession of his property, he is virtually deprived of it.

But the United States are bound, both to the soldier and purchaser, to protect him in the enjoyment of his property. It constitutes, by every principle of law and reason, a part of the original contract. The Government, for this obligation, has received a full consideration; and yet Missouri, in direct violation of that provision of the Federal Constitution which forbids any State to pass any '*ex post facto* law, or law impairing the obligation of contracts,' has virtually provided that those contracts, which have been completed by the issuing of patents, shall, by the *ex post facto* operation of her constitution, be annulled, and the force of the contract wholly impaired; and, by its prospective operation, as virtually impairs the obligation of those contracts which are as yet executory for the want of patents.

* * * "Mr. C. repeated that his feelings were in favor of the admission of Missouri—that both personal and political reasons combined to render it a desirable event—and were it consistent with his sense of the duty which he owed to the country and the Constitution, to give such a vote upon the resolution under consideration, he was sure no member on that floor would do it with more pleasure. But, while he considered the Constitution the rock upon which our temple of liberty must stand, and having sworn to support it, he felt himself called upon to forego all such considerations, and defend it against infringement. Should we suffer, said Mr. C., our individual feelings and wishes to enter into our deliberations and discussions, so far as to govern our public conduct, those feelings and wishes, like the imperceptible rising of the tide, will finally run over every principle of the Constitution, and we shall ultimately find ourselves floating at large upon the open sea of uncertainty, without a single landmark to guide us."

In the summer of 1821, Mr. Cook was united in marriage with Miss Julia Edwards (the eldest daughter of the late Gov. Edwards), a young lady of great personal charms and finished education—and in all respects fitted to be the companion of a statesman who bid so fair to attain high and commanding positions in the councils of the nation. Mrs. Cook survived her husband about three years, and died at Belleville, in the year 1830.

At the general election of 1822, Mr. McLean again run as a candidate for Congress against Mr. Cook. His hopes of success were, doubtless, predicated upon the "noise and confusion" consequent upon Mr. C.'s vote upon the Missouri question. So great was the clamor of interested partisans, that, at the commencement of the canvass, the chances of the respective candidates appeared to be nearly equal. In its progress, Mr. C. satisfied the people of at least the honesty of his intention in giving this vote, if not the propriety of the vote itself. His constituents triumphantly sustained him, giving him forty-seven hundred and sixty-four votes, and Mr McLean thirty-eight hundred and eleven—a majority of nine hundred and fifty-three.

The project of a canal, to unite the Illinois River with Lake Michigan, was started soon after the organization of the State Government. The Legislature of 1820–21 took initiatory steps in this matter, and it was brought before Congress by a report from the topographical corps, giving the results of a partial survey, and demonstrating its practicability. The canal project was a popular one in the eastern and western part of the State (there was no north at that period), and was opposed by representatives from the southern counties. Indeed, it found some opposition in the then great counties of Madison and St. Clair, growing out of sectional prejudices; for a Senator from one of those counties, in the Legislature of 1822–3, opposed it upon the ground that it would be an inlet for hordes of "blue-bellied Yankees," as he termed our eastern people.* The fears of that Senator have been realized, and the results are the extensive commerce of our lakes, our rich and populous north, and our young and enterprising cities, teeming with life, activity and business.

In 1822, this subject was brought directly before Congress. Mr. Cook labored to secure such aid from the General Government as would enable the State to prosecute this important work. He asked for bread and received a stone. The utmost extension of Congressional liberality was a grant of a strip of land, ninety feet wide, through the public domain, from the Illinois River to the Lake; and lest, by any means, the Congress of the United States, after such a *munificent* grant, should be further committed, a saving proviso was added, that the United States should in no wise become liable for any expense incurred by the State in "surveying or opening said canal."

In the intervening years, from 1822 to 1827, Mr. Cook urged this measure in Congress, as a national work, in which other States were as directly interested as his own, and affording to the Government, in time of war, great facilities in the movement of troops and transportation of stores. The result of his labors was the passage of the act of 1827 (the last session of his Congressional career), granting, in fee simple, to the State, and without any reservation, the alternate five sections upon each side of the canal, amounting to more than three hundred thousand acres of land, and embracing the site of the city of Chicago. This act was worthy of a Congress representing a great nation, and is wonderfully in contrast with that of

*To defeat or embarrass the canal bill, then before the Legislature, the Senator from St. Clair introduced a bill to drain certain lakes in the American Bottom, alleged to be injurious to the health of the people in their localities. In committee of the whole, the friends of the canal were adroit enough to include in the bill, by the aid of southern Senators, almost every inconsiderable pond in what would now be called Southern Illinois. Having thus loaded it to its utmost capacity, an amendment was proposed, by a canal man, to appropriate some thousand dollars to drain Lake Michigan, which also was incorporated in the bill. This was a little more than bargained for by the Senator, and he was compelled to aid in the destruction of his own bantling.

1822. But its greater and more enduring value was the precedent for future grants, embracing that for railroad purposes, the effect of which we now feel in the enhancement of the value of property, the increase of business, and the general prosperity of the State.

Upon the passage of the canal bill, that great and long desired improvement was considered as "a fixed fact," and the northern part of the State soon began to be settled by an enterprising class of people. It was not commenced until 1836, and, under many difficulties and adverse circumstances, was not completed until 1848.

The proposed national road, intended to have been built by Congress, from Washington through the several seats of governments of the Western States, excited great interest in the middle and eastern parts of the State. At this time, the road (a perfectly macadamized one) had been completed nearly to Wheeling, Va., upon its way to Columbus, O. It was a splendid undertaking on the part of the National Government, and, in the absence of railroads, would have been a very important and desirable improvement.

Mr. Cook urged appropriations to continue the surveys westward of Columbus, through Indiana and Illinois, to St. Louis. He succeeded to such an extent that the line of the road was located to Vandalia, in this State, the streams bridged, and the road partially graded. Before this great thoroughfare was fully completed, even as far west as the seat of government of Ohio, its use was suspended by the construction of railway lines, so much in advance of the best constructed carriage roads, that, by universal consent, the work was abandoned, and the portions finished and unfinished conveyed to the several States through which it run. Though never completed, enough work was done on that part of the road passing through this State, to render it useful to those residing in its vicinity, and to the public generally. Extensive and durable structures were thrown over all the streams it crossed, the low bottom lands raised to the proper grade, and the wet ground thrown up, so that a line of stages was put upon the road in 1837, and continued thereon to this day.

At the general election in 1824, Mr. C. was again a candidate for re-election to Congress. His uniform success and his great popularity rendered him a formidable competitor. None of his political adversaries were very desirous to enter the lists against him. He had twice beaten Mr. McLean, one of the strongest men in the opposition, and almost distanced the real leader of the Bond party, Mr. Kane. It was thought necessary, however, to preserve the integrity of the party, to bring out a candidate against him in the person of Gov. Bond—the ostensible head—who, two years before, had vacated the gubernatorial chair. This latter gentleman had spent the most of his life in the Territory and State, residing, until elected Governor, in the present county of Monroe. He was a man possessed of strong natural abilities but little improved by education. He stood deservedly high in the community, and, in his administration of the State Government, there was nothing particularly worthy of condemnation, unless that, in his appointments to office, his political friends, sometimes not the most capable, were the general recipients of gubernatorial favors.

Gov. Bond, though far behind Mr. McLean in talents and oratorical powers, had this advantage over him, in that, by a judicious bestowment of his patronage, he had created many political friends, who were bound to do battle in his behalf, and expend their energies, influence and time in securing his election. It was apparently the last card that could be played against Mr. C., and like desperate gamesters, a disposition was evinced to risk all upon the stake. A presidential election was also in progress, which might pass into the House of Representatives, and vest the vote of the State in its single representative. The Governor and his friends took great interest in the success of Mr. Crawford—then a candidate for the Presidency—who, though a member of Mr. Monroe's cabinet, had given evident tokens of opposition to the administration, and had created an active party of politicians, more intent, it was then believed, upon a division of the "loaves and fishes," than the promotion of the great interests of the country. Whoever Mr. C. might be for, in the contingency the vote came into the House, it was certain he would vote against Mr. Crawford. Thus impelled by personal and political motives, the Governor and his friends entered warmly into the canvass, and labored zealously, but without success. The vote for Mr. Cook was 7,460, while Gov. Bond received only 4,374.

It is well known that the presidential contest of 1824 resulted in the failure of the people to unite a majority of the votes on either of the four presidential candidates* before them. The question was therefore determined in the House of Representatives, and the vote of Illinois was given by Mr. Cook to Mr. Adams.

It is natural for those disappointed in their political aspirations, either by their own defeat or that of their favorite candidate, and the consequent loss of power and office in expectancy, to give vent to their wounded feelings and crushed hopes. Mr. C. had reason to expect that so important a vote as he gave upon this occasion would not escape notice or animadversion. Nor was he disappointed in this regard, for he was charged with betraying his constituents, of violating his pledges given at a previous election, and having basely sold his vote for office. It is, therefore, due to his memory, that this matter should be placed in a proper light, and facts substituted for reckless assertions—the more especially as, at a subsequent election, he was beaten for Congress, thus giving some color to the charges preferred against him.

The electoral college of this State, in December, 1824, gave two votes to Gen. Jackson and one to Mr. Adams;† and as Mr. C., when before the people in the summer of that year, had promised to be governed by the expressed will of his constitutents at the November election for electors, it was claimed that, as Gen. Jackson had obtained two electoral votes, he was therefore entitled to the vote of the State in Congress The fallacy of this assumption is a misunderstanding or a misrepresentation of Mr. C.'s pledge. He was too wise a man to make such a promise as would trammel his action in any given state of the electoral vote; for he well knew that, though a large majority of the people might favor the pretensions of one candidate, yet, by the division of the electoral districts, a comparatively small minority might secure the election of two electors, who would give their votes in opposition to the will of that majority.

What was the promise made by Mr. C. in relation to his vote in Congress? is the first question to be determined. It is contained in an address to his constituents, dated May 30th, 1824, and is in these words:

"On the subject of the approaching election of a Chief Magistrate of this country, inasmuch as it has become fashionable‡ for members of Congress to endeavor to dic-

*Messrs. Adams, Jackson, Clay and Crawford.

†The presidential vote in 1824, was given by districts—the State being divided into three.

‡Alluding to the nomination of Mr. Crawford by eighty odd members of Congress.

tate to their constituents for whom they shall vote, you probably may expect me to say something Influenced by the principles which govern me as your representative, I do not consider it my duty to attempt such dictation. You are as much interested as I can be in making a judicious choice. It is over your interests, as well as mine, that he is to preside. To each of you, therefore, as well as to me, it belongs to make a free and voluntary choice for yourselves. In voting, in my *individual* capacity as a citizen, for an elector in the district in which I reside, I shall surely vote for him who will, in the electoral college, support the individual that I believe to be the best calculated properly and faithfully to administer the executive government; but, should the electors chosen by the people fail to unite a majority of their suffrages on any individual, and thereby devolve the duty on the House of Representatives of choosing one for them, I shall feel it my duty to vote, *as a representative*, in accordance with the *clearly expressed sense of a majority* of those whose will I shall be called upon to express. This is all I have to say on that subject."

Mr. Cook, then, was to be governed by the "clearly expressed sense of a *majority* of those whose will" he was called upon to declare. Not, certainly, the *will of the electors*, who were but three of the many thousands of his constituents.

The next inquiry is, was the "sense of a majority" of his constituents *clearly expressed*, or was it expressed at all?

At the election in August, 1824, the aggregate vote for Congressmen was 11,834, and the aggregate vote upon the Convention question (for this was settled at this election) was 11,612.* The aggregate vote at the election in November, for all the candidates for electors, was 4,707—making a difference of 7,127 from the highest vote given in August, and showing that that number of voters had no will to express, or were so indifferent as to the success of the presidental candidates as to fail to express it at all. But if we take the number of votes given in November, 4,707, as an expression of the will of the people, "a clearly expressed sense of a majority" would have required 2,354 votes to have been given to one of the candidates, to have brought him within the rule laid down by Mr. C. for his future action. Did any one of the candidates receive that number of votes?

Of the clear and undisputed votes given upon that occasion, Mr. Adams, through his electors, received 1,541; Gen. Jackson 1,273; Mr. Clay 1,046; and Mr. Crawford 218. There were also given, at that election, for James Turney, Esq., who run in the first district professedly for Clay and Jackson, 629 votes. If Mr. Turney, and those who voted for him, were sincere in their preference for either Clay or Jackson, in such a calculation as the present one it would be but fair to divide these votes between those gentlemen, increasing Gen Jackson's vote (giving him the the odd one) to 1,588, and Mr. Clay's to 1,360; but giving Gen. Jackson *all* of Turney's vote, it would amount to but 1,901—leaving him in a minority of 453 votes.†

But it was contended, at the time, that Mr. Turney's candidacy, though ostensibly for Jackson and Clay, was really for Mr. Crawford. It was well understood that Mr. Adams' strength was mainly in the first district, embracing Fayette county on the south, and Sangamon on the north, and that no honest voting could prevent him from obtaining the electoral vote of that district. The friends of Mr. Clay and of Gen.

* The vote upon the Convention question was, For—4,972; Against—6,640.

† Gov. Reynolds, in his "Life and Times," p. 254, says Mr. Cook promised to "give the vote of the State for the presidential candidate who received from the people the most votes throughout the State." Comparing this *dictum* with Mr. Cook's address, shows that the Governor sometimes writes *ad libitum*.

Jackson had brought out candidates for electors in the first district for each of these gentlemen—Dr. John Todd of Springfield representing Mr. Clay, and Messrs. J. W. Scott and Jon. Berry, candidates for Gen. Jackson. Mr. Turney was nominated by a convention of politicians, convened at Edwardsville in October of that year, in which the principal Crawford men of the first district figured. The following is a part of one of the resolutions adopted at that meeting, disclosing, to some extent, the object desired to be obtained: "And this meeting, reposing their full confidence in the well-known republican principles and character of James Turney, Esq., the Attorney General of this State, do earnestly recommend him to the democratic-republican citizens of this district as a suitable person, to be supported at the ensuing election as an elector, whom the friends of Henry Clay and Andrew Jackson ought to support, with the fullest confidence that he will, in the electoral college, '*vote* [not for either Clay or Jackson, but] *for the one who, at the time of voting, will seem most likely to succeed against Mr. Adams.*' "

That part of the resolution italicised was evidently intended to pave the way for a vote for Mr. Crawford, if he was the one "most likely to succeed against Mr. Adams."

It was a notorious fact that, in the first district, Mr. Crawford had many strong and influential supporters, especially among the politicians* of that day; for, in addition to his supposed strong bias to recreate a new political party proper, it was deemed certain, from his appointments as Secretary of the Treasury, that the patronage of his administration would flow through the Gov. Bond party channel, and that those who gathered under the Bond banner would be the recipients of the many offices in the gift of the President. Notwithstanding, it was not considered politic by the leaders of that party to run a candidate in the first district for their chief, or make any open demonstration in his favor † The *true* friends of Mr. Clay and Gen. Jackson would have been slow to complicate the chances of *either*, by bringing out a candidate to run for *both*, while each had separate candidates in the field. The inference is considered a fair one that Mr. Turney was brought before the people, by the Crawford party, either to secure a vote for Mr. Crawford or lay the foundation for future attacks upon Mr. Cook, should he be called upon to vote, in Congress, for any of the presidential aspirants, and especially for Mr. Adams, whom he was known to favor.

It is conceded that, *after* the election, in January, 1825, Mr. Turney made a publication in one of the newspapers of the day, that, if elected, he should have given the electoral vote to Gen. Jackson. And, no doubt, he then would; for at the date of his publications, and, indeed, for some time before, the votes of the States had been ascertained, and though Mr. Crawford was, with Mr. Adams and Gen. Jackson, returned to the House of Representatives, they having the highest electoral vote, yet public sentiment had narrowed the contest to these latter gentlemen, and Mr. Crawford was virtually out of the question. Had Mr. Turney been as free to declare his preferences in October as he was in the following January, after the attempted election by the people was over, all doubts, in relation to the views of those who voted for him, would have been removed, and the question would have been one of figures only.‡

* Among these were the Hon. Jesse B. Thomas, then one of our Senators in Congress, Hon. T. W. Smith, late one of the Judges of the Supreme Court, Emanuel J. West, and others.

† Samuel Allen offered himself as a candidate for Mr. Crawford, and received *one* vote only.

‡ "Keep dark, Boone," was a common slang expression, and will be familiar to the older residents of the State. It originated from Mr. Turney's course in this election.

It may, therefore, be safely said that Mr. Cook, in giving his vote for Mr. Adams, violated no pledge previously given, nor did he act in opposition to the will of his constituents, as declared at the November election. The whole subject was referred to the people. They determined nothing. He was, therefore, left free to exercise his own judgement, and to vote for the man who, in his opinion, would best execute the functions of the Presidential office. If the doctrine of pluralities was to guide him, he was bound to vote as he did—Mr. Adams stood highest. His vote was clear and undisputed; that given to Gen. Jackson was complicated and doubtful. And was not the comparatively high vote given to Mr. Clay worthy of consideration in forming an opinion of the "sense of a majority" of the voters? If one vote might be transferred to another, was not the "elective affinity" of Clay and Adams stronger than that of Clay and Jackson?

It must also be remembered that, in 1825, Gen. Jackson was a new man for the Presidency. Though he had developed extraordinary military talents, his capacity for the civil administration of the Government was as yet untried and uncertain, and by many doubted. He certainly was not then the Gen. Jackson of 1832. Mr. Adams, on the other hand, had been educated as a statesman. The great powers of his mind were understood and acknowledged; and, from former precedent from the days of Jefferson, as Secretary of State, "he was the presumptive heir to the succession." Under all these circumstances, the error of Mr. Cook, if error at all, must be accounted as only venial—an error of the judgment, and not of the heart.*

*List of candidates for electors in 1824, as announced in the papers of that day:

FOR HENRY CLAY—Doct. John Todd, 1st Dist.; James Gray and Samuel H. Clubb, 2d Dist.; William H. Bradsby and H. B. Jones, 3d Dist.

FOR JOHN QUINCY ADAMS—William H. Harrison, 1st Dist.; Leonard White, 2d Dist.; Col. Pierre Menard, 3d Dist.

FOR GEN. JACKSON—Jon. Berry and J. W. Scott, 1st Dist.; Henry Eddy, J. M. Street, A. Ramsey and Daniel Boatright, 2d Dist.; A. P. Field and James S. Smith, 3d Dist.

FOR MR. CRAWFORD—A. G. S. Wight, 1st Dist.; Wm. M. Alexander, 3d Dist.

FOR JACKSON AND CLAY—James Turney.

The following shows the vote, at the November election, for electors for President in 1824:

FIRST DISTRICT.

Counties.	Harrison.	Scott.	Turney.	Berry.	Todd.	Allen.
Pike	193	6	1	....	....	....
Fulton	27	1	4	7	4	....
Sangamon	125	17	9	20	123	....
Morgan	86	12	21	3	11	....
Fayette	38	....	45	....	12	....
Greene	85	....	214	1	8	....
Madison	243	5	198	1	49	....
St. Clair	170	....	104	6	119	1
Bond	75	10	13	13	6	....
Montgomery	21	....	13	7	11	....
Total	1063	51	629	58	343	1

The last of the charges intimated, viz: that Mr. Cook sold his vote for office—is sufficiently answered by the fact, that Mr. C. neither sought nor received any post of honor or profit from the new administration. Had his valuable life been spared, it is hardly possible that a man of his industry and commanding talents could have remained long in private life. His views for the future were disclosed in the following extract of a letter to the writer of this article, dated April, 1827: "Of the proceedings of Congress, it is not necessary to say anything. You are already informed of all that has been done. Whatever of censure or credit I may be entitled, I leave to the calm decision of the people; and when they shall make that decision, with the knowledge of all the facts connected with each act, I shall not quarrel with them for it. But I am now on a tour to recover my health, if possible—and it may be that the voice of praise or censure will be alike unheard by me before any opinion shall be formed. The probability of such a result, however, does not repress the hope that I may yet pass, with the people of the State, through many changes of increasing prosperity; and, finally, before the curtain be drawn, see Illinois what even in one man's life she may be, and what my feeble exertions have always aimed to aid in making her.

SECOND DISTRICT.

Counties.	Eddy.	Grav.	White.	Clubb.	Boatright.	Street.
Wayne	62	18	6	....	....	....
Lawrence	31	65	16	....	....	....
Gallatin	199	41	47	1	1	28
Crawford	64	64	18	....	....	....
White	111	129	58	....	....	30
Hamilton	36	25	4	....	....	6
Clark	1	5	13	....	....	....
Edgar	37	26	34	....	....	....
Edwards	55	103	29	....	5	....
Total	596	476	225	1	6	64

THIRD DISTRICT.

Counties.	Field.	Menard.	Jones.	Alexander,	Bradsby.
Pope	41	11	32	....	....
Monroe	2	35	....	11	30
Randolph	47	149	2	177	12
Jackson	46	6	....	7	39
Union	153	15	....	3	10
Alexander	28	3	....	....	1
Johnson	40	2	....	....	4
Franklin	49	1	....	5	9
Jefferson	62	1	....	1	9
Washington	29	30	....	14	79
Total	497	253	34	218	193

RECAPITULATION.

	Adams.	Jackson.	Clay.	Crawford.	Clay and Jackson (Turney.)
1st Dist	1063	109	343	....	629
2d Dist	225	667	476	....	....
3d Dist	253	497	227	218	....
Total	1541	1273	1046	218	629

"Should I recover my health, so as to feel able to embark in the business of my profession, or any other business for which I am qualified, within a few months, I shall return to the State. But should it continue feeble, and yet improve, as I hope it will, in the mild and genial climate of Cuba, the place of my destination, I shall probably remain there a year or two, or till, at least, I have fairly tested its virtues."

Mr. Cook was a candidate for re-election to Congress in 1826. His old opponents would, doubtless, have suffered this election to go by default. No candidate was brought forward to oppose him. In the course of the summer, the people of the State were astonished at the temerity of a young gentleman, then but little known, in announcing himself as a competitor with Mr. Cook for this office.

Gen. Joseph Duncan was then a resident of Jackson county, and engaged in mercantile business. He had served in the regular army as a Lieutenant, in the war of 1812, and had acquired some distinction in the humble post he occupied. He had also been a member of the Senate of this State, from the county of his residence, and probably held that office at the time he announced himself for Congress. He was, however, but little known beyond the few counties adjacent to Jackson; and no one, at the time, supposed he was fitted, either by education or experience, to exercise the duties of the office to which he aspired. His chances of success were apparently hopeless; and it is supposed that a betting man, at that period, would not have risked one to one hundred dollars upon his election. He canvassed the State, however, with diligence and assiduity, and presented as bold a front as if assured of success. He was unaccustomed to public speaking, and in this respect compared very disadvantageously with Mr. Cook. Yet he had the faculty of presenting his ideas in a plain and simple way, easily understood by the masses, and, to a great extent, effective in such a population as then constituted the State.

The old opponents of Mr. Cook, of course, united upon him. As a candidate, he was a perfect God-send to them. If he failed in his election, it would be attributed not to the weakness of the party, but to the absence of all claims on the part of Gen. Duncan to such a position. To these were added the real friends of Gen. Jackson, who were dissatisfied with Mr. C. for his vote in Congress. Gen. Duncan received 6,321 votes, and Mr. Cook but 5,680.

No event excited greater surprise and amazement than the result of this election —it was totally unexpected to friends and foes. It may be safely said that if an election could have been held immediately after the result was known, the vote would have been materially changed. "We did not intend," was a very common remark, "to beat little Cook, but so to lessen his majority as to make him feel his dependence upon us." It is but just to Gen. Duncan to say, that his constituents were happily disappointed in his subsequent development of talents and tact, rendering him a worthy successor to our second representative.*

It may be confidently asserted, that Mr. Cook's defeat was not attributable to his vote upon the Presidential question. The small majority of 641 obtained by Gen. Duncan would indicate this fact. For if, as contended by many at that day, the choice of two electors for Gen. Jackson determined the political character of the State, a much larger majority would have attended Gen. Duncan's election. Taking, however, the votes cast for electors in 1824, as a test of the sentiments of the people,

*General Duncan remained in Congress until 1834, having been elected Governor in that year. Before this time, his original supporters had left him, and he was sustained mainly by Mr. Cook's old friends.

had the election of 1826 turned upon the Presidential question, it will be seen, that by adding the vote given to Mr. Clay, 1046 (nearly equal to that given to Gen. Jackson), to Mr. Adams' vote, 1541, Mr. Cook ought, upon this issue, to have received a majority as 2587 is to 4707, or over four-sevenths of the vote cast, giving to his opponent the excess of votes, 167, over the votes given for congressmen in 1824.

Matters of interest in Congress, connected with this State, have been briefly intimated in the foregoing pages. At the commencement of the session of 1825–6, Mr. C. was transferred from the Committee on the Public Lands, to that of the Committee of Ways and Means. The late Mr. McLane, of Delaware, was chairman of that committee, and the name of Mr. C was the second on the list of members. During the whole of the session of 1826–7, Mr. McLane was absent, and the duties of chairman devolved upon Mr. Cook. It was one of his cardinal principles to do well and thoroughly whatever he attempted; and naturally inclined to overtask his physical powers, and a desire to acquit himself with honor, led him to devote the hours of rest and recreation to examination and study. Occupied during the day in explanation of the varied and important measures presented to the House through this committee, every interval of time was spent in preparation for the public conflict. His feeble frame could not long endure the vast amount of labor he performed, and the last days of his Congressional life found him confined to a sick room. At the close of the session, he embarked, as before intimated, for Cuba, trusting to recover health and strength in the mild climate of that island. The journey was a vain one—and early in the month of June Mr. Cook returned, with his family, to his home at Edwardsville. During the summer, his health gradually declined; and he determined to return to the home of his nativity, and die upon the spot that gave him birth. He breathed his last on the 16th day of October, 1827, at the early age of thirty-four, and his remains repose in the soil of his native State.

From this brief statement of some of the incidents in the life of Mr. Cook, it will be seen that he was a self-made man. Without the aid of the schools, and by the mere force of the native powers of his mind, the few brief years of his public life developed intelligence and talent of no ordinary character. His powers seemed to expand with the occasion that called them forth. His mind was active and clear, and his command of language ready and copious, so as equally to interest the scholar, and enlighten the illiterate hearer. But few men, then constituting the Congress of the United States, notwithstanding his youth, stood higher in public estimation, or were listened to with more attention and interest. His voice, though soft and melodious, was of great compass and tone, equal to addresses in the open air or in the halls of legislation.

It has been said that Mr. Cook was a popular man. His popularity was not based upon the artifices of the demagogue, or upon assumed traits of character. His urbanity of manner and gentlemanly deportment were natural and constant. No one doubted his truthfulness or sincerity, and his benevolence and kindness of heart was universally conceded. Mr. Cook's conversational powers were remarkable, and he made himself an agreeable companion with all classes of society, preserving at the same time the dignity and attributes of a well bred gentleman. In all the exciting contests through which he passed, his manner toward his opponents was such as never to disturb social relations or friendly feelings. However strong the opposition for the time being, it ceased when the conflict ended; and if defeated, they preferred Mr. Cook's success to any other political opponent. Mr. Cook was generous to a fault. He was often imposed upon by the unworthy and deceived by the recital of imaginary sufferings. His kind heart forbid the withholding of pecuniary assistance whenever demanded; and he thought it safer to err, in his charities, on the wrong side, than fail to bestow them upon worthy objects.*

In his personal appearance, Mr. Cook was a small spare man, considerably under the ordinary hight. His usual weight did not, probably, exceed one hundred and twenty pounds. He was straight and erect in his person, and quick and active in his movements. His features were plain but marked—and so indicative of intelligence and kind feeling as to render them agreeable and pleasing. He left behind him but one child, a son, now a resident of the city of Springfield in this State, and late Mayor of that city.

In estimating the labors of Mr. Cook, it must be remembered that he was virtually the first Representative in Congress after the admission of the State: and that the settlement and arrangement of the various matters contained in the act of Congress changing our territorial to a State government, devolved mainly upon him. It is believed that all questions arising out of the change, through his tact, talent and perseverance, were decided more favorably to our interests than they probably would have been, if entrusted to other hands. Neither must it be forgotten, that in obtaining valuable concessions from the General Government, he had no precedent to urge, or landmark to guide him. It was subjecting the powers vested in Congress by the Constitution, to new tests, and applying them to new objects. It was an untried field of effort, in which every obstacle was to be overcome. The prejudice of opinion was to be combatted, and perhaps honest, but mistaken constitutional objections to be removed. To devote the public lands to any other purpose than that of replenishing the public treasury, was then deemed by many a political heresy. It is now a settled principle, mainly through Mr. Cook's efforts, that the public domain is to be used for public purposes, and devoted for the promotion of the general interests of the whole people—a principle which, as we have seen, in 1827, invigorated our waning energies, and in 1851 placed us in the front ranks of the States composing our Union, and promises us a future, unless marred by our own folly or effeminacy, prolific in all the sources of material wealth, and the highest moral and christian civilization.

Mr. Cook supported other measures, of great importance to his State, besides those alluded to in Mr. Brown's memoir.

On seeing, in the year 1820, an advertisement, in the public prints of Baltimore and Washington, over the signature of a Mr. Bond, announcing that he was not only authorized by the Treasurer of the State to receive the non-residents' land tax, due to the State, but to give receipts therefor, he addressed a letter to Mr. McLaughlin, the then Treasurer, admonishing him of the danger and impropriety of giving such authority. He said: "If Mr. Bond receives a considerable sum (the land tax from non-residents being then upwards of $20,000, annually,) and then refuses to pay it over,

*In one of his journeys to Washington, upon the Ohio River, as the steamer approached Wheeling, the point of debarkation, a well dressed person accosted Mr. C., a perfect stranger, and apologizing for his intrusion, said, "Sir, I am yet some distance from my home, and am out of money. I know no one on board the boat. I have closely scanned the countenances of my fellow passengers, and have discovered no gentleman more likely to assist me than yourself. Will you please, sir, make me a loan of $50?" "Certainly," Mr. C. immediately replied, and suiting the action to the word, opened his pocket book, and handed him the desired sum.

I cannot see by what means the State is to reach it, otherwise than by a suit against the Treasurer, which, in these times, might be a very precarious remedy. From the deep interest which I feel for the safety of the public money, and being in a situation to warn the Treasurer of the danger he is encountering, I conceive it both my right and duty to address a letter to him on the subject."

Congress had, in 1819, pledged the fund reserved to Indiana and Illinois, for the laying out and making roads to those States, for the repayment of the money advanced by the United States for constructing the Cumberland road to the Ohio River. On a resolution offered by Mr. Cook for the repeal of this provision, and asking its appropriation for the construction of roads to this State, he addressed the House as follows: "In offering this resolution to the consideration of the House, I beg leave to ask its attention to the act referred to. By that act, the fund reserved for the improvement of roads leading to the States of Indiana and Illinois has been pledged for the repayment of the money appropriated by Congress for the completion of the Cumberland road. This road was commenced, I believe, ten or twelve years ago. By the acts of 1816 and 1818, authorizing the admission of Indiana and Illinois, respectively, two per cent. of the net proceeds arising from the sale of the public lands in those States was reserved, by Congress, to the laying out and making roads leading to those States, respectively; and for the consideration of this appropriation, made by Congress, with others, which were understood, on all hands, to be for the benefit of those States, they respectively surrendered a part of their sovereignty: they agreed that the lands of the United States, then remaining to be sold, should be free from taxation for five years after the day of sale—and in Illinois, the bounty lands, given to the soldiers of the late army, were also to be exempted from taxation for three years from the date of their patents. This surrender of the sovereign right of Illinois to tax the lands thus exempted, was the consideration given for the fund now under consideration, as well as some other advantages which were granted to her, and for which she is grateful to the Government. This, with the other propositions made by Congress, are now matters of compact between Illinois and the United States, and to divert this fund from the channel in which I can but think it was intended to flow, Illinois will consider a violation of that compact. To appropriate that fund to the making a road terminating at Wheeling, a point several hundred miles from the borders of the State, never can be an appropriation in unison with the intention of Congress or of the State of Illinois. As well might you appropriate it to the making of a road leading from Missouri to Santa Fe, uniting those two sovereignties, as to the object for which it stands pledged—for that would be a road leading towards Illinois. From an examination of the subject,

I find that the revenue which Illinois would derive from a tax on the lands which may be sold within the State, and on the bounty land—which she cannot now derive in consequence of this compact—would, at a reasonable rate, amount to about $280,000, a large proportion of which would now be subject to be called into her coffers, and of which she really stands in great need. Can it be contended that this fund, which is reserved to Indiana and Illinois, respectively, to make roads leading to them—in the one case about ten and in the other twelve years after the Cumberland road was commenced—was at that time intended or understood, either by these States or by the United States, to be subject to defray the expenses of that road? It cannot be possible. It seems much more likely to have been reserved for the purposes contemplated by the resolution which I offered: to extend that road to the borders of those States; and unless it is so appropriated, or at least in making roads leading to and not towards them, I think they will have just cause of complaint against the Government. Since the admission of those States, I believe, a fund of about $50,000 has already accrued from the sale of lands, which should now be lying in the National treasury. This sum, although it would not complete the road, would defray the expense of marking and laying it out, and go far towards opening it so as to render it passable; and, as the fund continues to increase, it might be employed to complete it. Indeed, it seems to me to be so obvious that the intention of Congress was, that this money should be appropriated to the improvement of roads, to facilitate the entrance into those States, that reasoning cannot make it plainer; and any diversion of it to any other object, therefore, is a violation of the compact between those States and the United States. I trust the resolution will be considered and adopted." The resolution was then considered and unanimously adopted.

On the same day he offered the following resolution:

Resolved, That the Committee on Public Lands be instructed to inquire into the expediency of providing, by law, for the payment of so much of the money arising from the sale of the public lands in the State of Illinois, since the 1st day of January, 1819, as has been reserved by law for the encouragement of learning, to said State.

Mr. Cook observed that "the object of this resolution is, simply, to enable the State of Illinois to obtain the three per cent. fund arising from the sale of the public lands, which has been reserved by Congress, to be appropriated by the State to the encouragement of learning. This course has been considered necessary, since the Secretary of the Treasury might not, otherwise, feel authorized to pay it over."

This resolution was also adopted, and a law passed in accordance with its provisions.

After Mr. Cook's return to the United States, in 1817, with Mr. Adams, he remained for some time in Washington City, undetermined what business he would engage in. His health was not good. Mr. Adams had applied to the President to give him the appointment of Secretary of Alabama. Mr. Cook, in a letter to Gov. Edwards, dated October 2, 1817, says: "Had not my application for that office been too late, the President said, it would have received that attention which it merited, but that he had previously promised it to another. I could get into the State Department as a clerk; but experience tells me it will not do for me to engage in close, laborious writing, and it would not satisfy my ambition to be buried in an office, merely as a servant, where the world, perhaps, would never hear of me. Mr. Adams assures me he will, at any time, take pleasure in bringing me before the Government, when an opportunity offers. I am advised by my own judgment, as well as his, to return to the West, and remain there until an opportunity presents itself for my advancement."

Mr. Cook was, indeed, a very ambitious man. As early as 1824, he had a very high standing in Congress. In one of his letters to Gov. Edwards, during that session of Congress, he says: "There are none of the opposition but Forsyth, and McLane of Delaware, that I will meet, as deserving my special notice. This will be taking high ground, to be sure, but I will take it. Forsyth and I have had some sparring on the tariff. I think, although he has 'been in Spain,' I need not—I certainly do not—dread him."

Hon. John C. Calhoun, as early as 1821, spoke of him thus: "For Mr. Cook I have a most genuine respect, both for his character and talent. I have read his circular with pleasure; its independence and sound sense do him much honor. He has adopted the proper mode to build up a lasting popularity."

And again, in a letter dated August, 1822, he says: "I take much interest in Mr. Cook's election, and shall wait with great impatience to hear the result. He is honest, capable and bold—just such a man as the times require. His absence from Congress would be a serious loss."

Judge McLean spoke of him as follows: "He stands well with all parties, and is not excelled, in weight of character, talents and influence, by any member from the West. For his success in the late election (that of 1826) I felt a stronger interest than for the success of any other individual, not excepting my own brother. Mr. Cook's name is before the President for Minister to Columbia. It was placed there by me before the commencement of the session. If the President does not appoint him, he will forfeit all the claims of friendship and gratitude. So far as I have been informed no appointment could be made, in the same quarter, more acceptable to the friends of Gen. Jackson. I have heard many of them express great kindness for him, and some of them have expressed a strong wish for his success. The duties which devolved upon him, as Chairman of the Committee of

Ways and Means, were very arduous. The labor was more than his health could bear, independently of the long confinement every day to the unwholesome atmosphere of the hall. He, however, continued to exert himself until his physical powers gave way, and he was consequently confined for some weeks—the greater part of the time to his room. We were favored with his company, as one of the family, shortly after he became unwell, and I hope contributed, in some degree, to his comfort and restoration."

On hearing of his death, Judge McLean wrote to Gov. Edwards "that all my family were distressed at his loss, and deeply sympathise with his disconsolate partner. I fear your State cannot supply his place by a man equally useful and respected in public life. His race was short, but it has been honorable to himself and useful to his country. No man in Congress, from the West, had a higher standing or could exercise a more extensive influence."

The Hon. Tristram Burgess, in a speech delivered by him in Congress, on the 15th of January, 1831, speaks of Mr. Cook as follows: "Our relations with Cuba have long since been interesting and important. Gentlemen will call to mind that we have frequently heard, from Europe, that Cuba might be transferred from Spain to some other sovereignty. Such a report was rife in this country in the winter of 1826–7. It was believed, by the friends of the last administration, that a confidential agent was, by Mr. Adams, sent to Cuba, to ascertain, if possible, the truth of this report, and that Daniel P. Cook was that agent. * * Permit me to speak a word concerning Daniel P. Cook, because every man who hears me did not know him as many of us who sat in this House with him. He was a man whom the gentleman from New York would probably not call a genius; but his mind was of that cast and capacity, in the transaction of human affairs, to which every man would wish to commit the management of his own. His sense was that of the every-day intercourse of men, and would pass, like the most precious or useful metal, wherever such a commodity could be in request. A man, in whatever may be required of manhood; a child, in all that singleness of heart and purity of purpose which renders childhood so amiable—with those who knew him well, he had so fixed himself in their hearts, that, though they might wish to forget the pain of their loss, they can never cease to remember his useful public labors and many endearing social qualities.

"Mr. Cook, it was known, was in delicate health, and was about to visit Cuba for the benefit of the climate. In the examination of witnesses, the whole labor of the gentleman from New York was directed to prove that the state of his health would not permit his doing any public service. The gentleman was discontented by the result; for it came out in evidence that, feeble as was his health, he had performed all that was required of him. * * Mr. Cook was in delicate health, but that served to place him above suspicion of any sinister motive in visiting Cuba. His acquaintance with Gen. Vires (the Intendant-General of Cuba), while in this country, the known integrity and obvious simplicity of his character, the amenity of his manner, and even his delicate health, all combined, must have placed him at once in relations of entire confidence and frank intercourse with the Intendant, and enabled him to obtain speedily, from that Governor, all which it was proper for him to communicate or for our Executive to know. The man at whom the gentleman from New York magnanimously aimed his arrow, sleeps quietly in the green bosom of his own beloved Illinois."

Gov. Edwards, in a letter to Mr. Clay, says that Mr. Cook's defeat was not attributable to his vote for Mr. Adams, but that "he lost his election because both he and his friends felt too sure. None of them, with the exception of myself, could be induced to believe there was the least danger. His opponent did nothing else, for many months previously, but ride through the State and visit the people at their own houses. Mr. Cook was confined by sickness and could only visit a few counties. The greatest possible efforts were used to turn to both his and my disadvantage the circumstance of the father-in-law and the son-in-law being before the people at the same time for the two highest offices in their gift; but the circulation of thousands of hand-bills, ingeniously contrived, to produce the impression that both he and I voted against the reduction of the price of public land, at a period too late to be answered or contradicted, had far more influence than all other considerations united. A strong proof that his defeat was not produced by his vote on the Presidential election, is to be found in the fact that, in the strong Jackson counties (as they are called) which he visited, he obtained majorities. Gallatin, Pope, Greene and Morgan are the counties most highly distinguished by their partiality to Gen. Jackson, and there are no four counties in the State that would give him so large a majority—yet, Mr. Cook obtained decided majorities in all of them; while in some of the strongest Administration counties he got scarcely any support. Neither Mr. Cook's friends nor his foes believed that he would be defeated. The result has surprised everybody. The people are already disabused as to the land vote. A powerful reaction has already taken place, and very many that opposed him are anxious that he should become a candidate for the Senate. Should he do so, I think his election beyond doubt.

"As to myself, it is utterly false that I owed my election in the slightest degree to my forbearance, or any kind of temporizing in regard to the candidate for the Presidency. On the other hand, I openly declared that I would reserve to myself the right to vote for or oppose whom I pleased, and bid defiance to all kind of opposition."

CHAPTER XV.

Letters and Speeches of Ninian Edwards.

Letter to his constituents during his canvass for Congress against Matthew Lyon, in 1806.

I have been as busy as you ever saw any man about an election. My prospects in this quarter seem to brighten every day. I have just returned from Muhlenburg county, and I cannot tell what changes may take place hereafter, but at present I am well satisfied that Lyon cannot get thirty votes in that county. The circumstance of his neglecting his duty, the session before last, in going to Frankfort and spending a month there, merely for the purpose of getting the Legislature to remove the court house of his county from the centre of his own town in one corner, and thereby showing that he would let his private interest not only cause him to wish to do an injury to his own county, but to neglect his public duty by losing nearly two months during the session of Congress, is operating most powerfully against him; and at the last session he lost, about his gun-boats, near another month—having only arrived at the city about the last of December. Now, suppose every other Western member had done the same thing, our country might have suffered greatly, for he himself declares that there is a strong party against us; and as we had a difference with Spain, which affects the Western country more than any other part of the Union, surely every member ought to have been at his post, and the people through these counties are of opinion that there need not be any greater objection against him than neglect of public duty. There has also been much said about his being a contractor under the Post-master-General and the Secretary of the Navy, and still holding a seat in Congress. Even in the corrupt government of England this thing is not allowed, as you will see by the first volume of "Blackstone's Commentaries," page 178. Whether our Constitution will admit of it, has been tried by Congress. The subject was most lengthily discussed. A majority, however, were of opinion that they could not expel such members, but every man who spoke on the subject, both those in favor and those against the expulsion, unanimously agreed that such conduct was highly improper, unjustifiable and dangerous to liberty, and that it ought to be prohibited by some means, and the thing has ended in a proposition to amend the Constitution. At first the people seemed to think that those were objections merely raised by Lyon's enemies; but now they find all the best Republicans in Congress disapprove of such conduct in any member, and think it it necessary to amend the Constitution. They begin to think seriously about it. Do the people agree that such amendment should be made? If they think it ought, surely it would not be safe to send Col. Lyon back, because, if he thinks so, his conduct is in direct opposition to his opinion, and, for the sake of his interest, he has sinned against light and knowledge. It is wrong for contractors to be members of Congress, for many reasons. In the first place the great officers of State, those who are the President's council, have the making of those contracts; they have the power of favoring the members of Congress, and they have a chance of buying up the whole of them—for there are contracts enough for all of them. Suppose that these officers should greatly sacrifice the public interest and their duty, by granting such favors—where is the check upon them? By whom are they to be called to account? By Congress—by those very persons on whose account the malpractice took place—by those they have befriended by the very act of their friendship to them. If this were the case, there would be very little chance of impeaching a public officer. But further, if these officers are allowed to contract with members of Congress, the members of Congress may be disposed to favor them in various ways. It is well known that Col. Lyon voted to give the Postmaster-General $500 more than Congress would allow him, for he admits it in one of his circulars.

Further, if members of Congress are allowed to take contracts, they themselves have to vote for the compensation—for all money bills must originate in the House of Representatives—consequently they are voting for their own interest; and if a surveyor among us could not be allowed to hold a seat in the Legislature, because it would be blending the Executive and Legislative Departments, and would allow a vote for his own compensation for services, surely a member of Congress should not place himself in such a situation as to vote upon his own interests or disqualify himself from voting at all. But this is not all. Suppose a member of Congress should fail to comply with a contract, or apply for more money—alleging some unforseen occurrence. Congress must legislate upon the subject; they may grant more money, or free the person delinquent from suit for his failure. Will not everybody see that they would be voting directly upon their own interest? And where is the candid mind that will not admit it is wrong? But, you may depend on it, Lyon is more deeply engaged in contracts than is generally supposed—for it is pretty certain that he has some not in his own name, and to a great amount. This is improper in another point of view: it is taking an undue advantage of his constituents—for these contracts are generally made by them. He ought to give them notice that such contracts were to be made, that they might have an opportunity of getting them in the first instance—for if they are able to perform when contracting with him, they might as well do it with the Government at once, and let them derive the advantage of it, not himself, because he gets well paid for all his services, and it is his constituents who befriend him, and surely he ought to befriend them so far as to serve them in this way; but it is certainly taking an undue advantage, when he gets a contract for a certain sum, and lets it out to one of them for $500 or $1,000 less than he gets it at—for, if he gets more than it is worth, he actually wrongs the Government, and there is very little hope of his trying to right it, whilst he is himself the instrument of doing the wrong and derives the advantage of it; he would scarcely move to have a committee appointed to consider a proper remedy. If, on the other hand, he gets the contract at its actual value, he does a wrong and injury to the individual to whom he lets it, by letting it to him at so much less. This is a kind of speculation which, however pardonable in an individual, is clearly unjustifiable in a member of Congress. He is presumed to have enough to attend to the duties of his station; he cannot perform such contracts himself, and ought not to meddle with them on his own account.

But there is a charge of still greater magnitude than all those against him. The vast importance of the Floridas to us is universally admitted; without them we cannot enjoy the long navigation of the Mobile Bay and Tombigbee River. It is through that channel that we must expect all our imports to this country; and so soon as the country between the Tombigbee and Tennessee Rivers is settled, so that wagonage can be procured, there is no doubt but that all our goods will be imported that way. We are all equally sensible of the necessity of settling the country between Natchez and Orleans, for the purpose of defending our trade—for the whole proceeds of the sale of all the Western produce must return through that country; and, while it remains unsettled, we shall ever be subject to great inconveniencies and be infested by bands of robbers. A great part of this very country, and a part of that if not the whole that lies between the Bigbee and Tennessee, belongs to the Indians. By getting the Floridas, we remove entirely from our country any foreign nation which can have it in its power to set the Indians on us, or cause them to refuse to treat with us for such a part of their country as is absolutely necessary to us for the purpose of trade. When we shall be their only neighbors, it will be no difficult task to manage them. We shall, by the acquisition of this country, connect our disjointed territory, avoid the calamities of war, remove all danger of collision with Spain in future, and be able to command the whole West India trade—among which islands is the best market the United States enjoys for flour and all kinds of provisions. The secret proceedings of Congress are now published. It was this very business they engaged in with closed doors. They determined to try to purchase the Floridas of Spain, and thereby put an end to all disputes with that power; for which purpose they passed a law, appropriating two millions of dollars. To the astonishment of everybody, Col. Lyon is joined with every Federalist in Congress, without exception, opposed to the laws. Uniting with all those who were opposed to the purchase of Louisiana, at a former session, he is the only solitary Western member who opposed it. Findley and Smiley, two distinguished, well-tried Republicans from the western part of Pennsylvania, with others from the same quarter; Jackson, a leading member from the western part of Virginia; the representation from the State of Ohio; all from the State of Tennessee, and every one from this State except Col. Lyon, were in favor of the law, and surely no Western man of sound discernment, if he meant to do right, ought to have opposed this purchase. Each of the

United States will have to contribute its just proportion towards the payment.

The Western country will exclusively enjoy the benefit of the purchase. By a war (the other alternative) our citizens would have been drafted, put to much difficulty and great inconveniencies, and stationed in a most unhealthy climate, where disease alone might have vanquished them; and probably we might have been greatly delayed, at least, in obtaining possession of the country, if not defeated altogether, and had the mouth of the Mississippi blocked up by a ship or two of war. Particularly are we likely to be embroiled with England. But a war would have afforded many persons an opportunity of making contracts for gun-boats, victualing the army, etc. It would have been an advantage to persons engaged in such pursuits, but surely not to the people at large; they always have to bear the burthen, and get the least benefit from it. Is it possible the people will prefer Col. Lyon's opinions to all the other Western members? That they will suppose him entirely right, and the Republican members who voted against him wrong? Is it possible that, after they have lavished plaudits upon the present administration, who certainly were warmly in favor of this measure, that they will still think Col. Lyon's opinion superior to the whole of those I have mentioned? Is it possible that they will suppose that he has the prosperity of the Western country more at heart than the rest of the members from every part of it—particularly as they are not engaged in contracts under the government, are not supplying any garrison with provisions, or building any gun-boats and wishing to build more, etc. The people have now to judge for themselves. If they elect Col. Lyon, they say we are opposed to the purchase. Strange as this conduct may be thought, by those who have always considered the Colonel an intelligent, disinterested representative, yet it is no less true, that he did actually give this vote on the 14th day of last January, as may be seen by the journals.

But were these all the acts of inconsistency in the Colonel, he might still be thought, by his corresponding society, an unchangeable Republican, as they in their nocturnal essays describe him. In his circular of the 20th Dec., 1804, he says: "There is an old proverb which says, 'he that does evil hates the light.'" This, as it respects the Government, is perfectly correct. Everything that concerns the government of a nation, may be with safety as plain and simple as that of a family; and a nation should always be considered as a large family. Such is the true science of politics; and it is in governments, only, where the benefit of the few is aimed at, that the people are prohibited from knowing its minutest movements.

What will those say who have applauded the Colonel for this statement—who have professed to believe it correct—provided they should find that he has departed (most inconsistently, too,) from it—has actually violated the very principle that he contended for? Will they stick to him through thick and thin—right or wrong? Surely, if they will not, they must say, if he deserved credit for the above statement, he deserves condemnation if he has acted counter to it. And those who have been attached to him from principle, seeing his contradictions, will not feel bound to adhere to him any longer.

No! Honest, independent men will think and act for themselves, and will not steel their minds against conviction. Let such persons, then, know, that, notwithstanding the sentiment contained in his circular, Col. Lyon did, on the 31st March, 1806, vote against taking off the injunction of secrecy from the proceedings of Congress; did then vote against letting the people know what Congress had been doing, as appears by the journal itself.

Will the people not let his own words apply to him, "that he who does evil hates the light?" And that it is only those who aim at the benefit of these few very contractors, etc., that wish to prohibit the people from knowing the minutest movements of Government? For my own part, I am very strongly of the opinion contained in his circular: if the members of Congress conceal from the people what they have done, how are the people to know whether they have done right, or whether it would be proper to change them for others; and if they conceal one of their acts, what is to prevent them from concealing one-half of them, and finally all? It is a bad precedent, and I should like to see a representative, if he errs, err in favor of the people, not against them. For this vote of the Colonel there is no apology, and strong suspicions that he was afraid to let the people know what he had been doing —for on the 15th day of January he voted for taking off the injunction of secrecy; on the 16th, the law passed by a large majority. Finding, then, that he stood opposed to all the Western representatives, and united with those whom he has hitherto represented as the most hostile to our interests, he afterwards refused to take off the injunction of secrecy. Those on the Republican side who voted, with him, against letting the people know what had been done, except himself, urged, as their reason, that they were afraid that if they gave publicity to the proceedings, it might defeat the very object of the law. And this is the very reason, if he meant to be consistent and candid, that he should have voted for the measure—for as he voted against the law, if he did it upon proper principles he must have thought it wrong, and therefore should have tried to defeat it. From these considerations I infer that he was really afraid to let the people know how he had voted; that he really feared the light.

But since Col. Lyon has commenced to build gun-boats, his sentiments about a navy and commerce are entirely changed. In his magazine (commonly called his blue-book), where his sentiments are fully stated (pages 16, 17, 18, 19, 118), he represents commerce as merely the interest of merchants—of the few —and that we had better give up the carrying of goods than go to war for it, which must affect the people at large; that back-country people are not so much affected by a loss of commerce, and that it is *folly to build a navy*, and states the experience we had in this navy business at Lake Champlain and Penobscot, for which, he says, we are in debt many millions, although millions had been paid for the interest. And in the same book (pages 104–5) you will find that Mr. Jefferson, our beloved President, is of the same opinion; and, also, that we ought never to think of war unless invaded by land.

You will find in a newspaper (the "Expositor," No. 212, circulated by the Colonel himself) a speech of his, made in Congress, the 25th of March, in which he defends commerce as the interest of the farmers; and that, instead of giving up this same carrying trade, we had better fight for it; and that back-country people are deeply interested in commerce; and that we ought to have a navy, and to look forward to the day when we shall be the greatest naval power on earth.

Formerly, as observed above, he determined not to go to war with England or France, although they were then practicing worse treatment on us, or to a greater amount, than we have lately received; and yet, in another speech which he made in Congress, (appearing in the same paper, No. ——, circulated by himself through his district) he declares himself in favor of war, in the most pointed terms, in direct opposition to all his former declarations. And what is there to have changed his sentiments? The debt of the last war is not paid off, we have incurred a debt of thirteen millions for Louisiana, and are about to purchase the Floridas.

Let the people examine for themselves—they have the books and the papers; and let them candidly ask themselves if the Colonel has not completely turned about! Surely an inquiry of this kind is worth the trouble, and the people have the means of knowledge. Now, I ask, if the Colonel deserved credit for his former conduct, what must be said as to his present motives? If he was right before—and the people have all contended he was—must he not be wrong now? A war would now be an advantage to him individually. Let the midnight corresponding society look to these things, and say how unchangeable their friend is.

Letter to William Wirt, on the subject of the Expedition of Col. Burr.

COLLINA, LOGAN COUNTY, KY.,
January 5, 1807.

Dear Sir:

When I wrote you last I promised you another letter shortly, not doubting but that you would be anxious to hear further particulars relative to Col. Burr's enterprise, and expecting, before this time, to be able to communicate to you something interesting upon that subject; but in the latter I have been considerably disappointed, owing, as I suppose, to three successive failures in the Orleans mail, which the public voice attributes to Burr's machinations. He has excited so much suspicion and such feelings in this country, that everything improper in any of our civil or political relations, that cannot be otherwise readily accounted for, is attributed to him; and, however unjust such suspicions as exist against him may be, the promulgation of them is infinitely more injurious to the interest of our country than to him, individually—for, by magnifying his power, it fortifies him in the confidence of his adherents and well-wishers, strengthens their hopes, and gives more energy to his assertions; and I believe it is with this view, and for this purpose, that Gen. Wilkinson made such a pompous display of patriotism before the Chamber of Commerce in Orleans, about the 10th ult. He well knew that a great proportion of the population of Orleans Territory was disaffected to our Government, anxious for insurrection, impatiently waiting for a favorable conjunction, and devoted to Col. Burr; that, by giving to the conspiracy such uncommon extension and vast resources, and altogether such dangerous magnitude, he was most effectually cherishing the fondest hopes of the disaffected and preparing the minds of others for the moment of a successful attack upon them, and causing them to believe that, should he withdraw his support from them, their case would be hopeless—in order that when he determined upon this step, their efforts might become completely paralyzed. What greater encouragement could Burr's ignorant partisans require, than a knowledge that the brave and patriotic Gen. Wilkinson, being well-informed upon the subject, thought there was great danger of his succeeding—the forces of the United States, the non-erected fortifications, the little navy, the union of merchants, and the embargo, notwithstanding.

But there was something in the General's propositions extremely insidious, if he is not actually a patriot. He wishes to leave Orleans, march up the river, and meet Burr. He knew exactly the number of men Burr was to have had with him, which nothing but the vigilance of our Government deprived him of, and that could not have been foreseen by the General. He also expected forces up the river to attack Orleans, and still was for drawing out all the forces from Orleans to attack the malcontents descending the river. Suppose his scheme had been adopted. He had no ground to march his men on for 150 miles up the river, except the levee, about wide enough for twenty men to walk abreast. He could not have expected to have fought to advantage on such ground. He had no naval force adequate to the purpose of stopping or destroying Burr's fleet of boats. If he had, it was only necessary to have sent forward the gun-boats, without risking his land forces in such disadvantageous ground. If he had actually thought that fighting was necessary, he would have acted most injudiciously. A decisive battle in Burr's favor would have rendered him truly formidable, and if he thought there would be no fighting, it was a deceitful affectation of patriotism. Knowing, as he declared he did, that Burr had many friends in Orleans, he must have known that his design of marching up the river would have been communicated to Burr before his army and fleet could have reached their destination, and he could not have expected that Burr would have been so weak as to have rushed headlong upon his own ruin, or have been taken by any strategem that he could have devised in that situation. Such a project promised no solid advantage; the objections to it and the danger of it are self-evident. Wilkinson had to ascend the river; Burr was descending. The former could not travel in the night; the latter as expeditious as in the day time. In a dark night the latter, knowing the position of the former, could have descended silently and unobserved; or, if he chose to have landed in the night, what havoc might he not have made upon the General's encampment on the levee. A victory or a rout, which might have been effected had Burr been allowed to take down his recruits, would soon have made him master of Orleans. In fact, had Wilkinson's plan succeeded, there could not have been one so admirably devised to have insured success to Burr. The object was to take the Orleans volunteers and the well affected on the expedition—none others would have gone. The disaffected remained in the city, ready to receive him with open arms; and there was nothing to prevent the forces which were expected from New York, and some of the Southern States and the Floridas, from making a successful approach to the city from the Gulf of Mexico, even if the forces descending the river had been checked in their progress; and it ought to be remembered that the General declared he expected an attack in both directions. With Consul O'Brian, I think such a plan looked "squally."

No doubt any longer exists in this and the adjacent States that Burr and his partisans have meditated a deadly thrust at the prosperity of our happy country; and, however flattering his prospects appeared at first view, his scheme is now almost universally execrated, and both he and his satellites have sunk into merited contempt, though some of his supporters, his advocates and real friends have been among the most choice characters in our State. What his success has been in the lower territories, we have not heard a word, since his departure from the mouth of the Cumberland. Much speculation exists as to the part Gen. W. will now take. Some fear he will, at all hazards, join Burr, notwithstanding all his declarations to the contrary. Others, and probably the majority of those acquainted with his character, think his conduct will be entirely regulated by Burr's prospects of success; that if he should conceive that the enterprise can succeed, all his talents and energies will be devoted to it; if he sees that it will fail, he will be the most prompt to suppress it. But let him act as he may, he never can acquire the confidence of this Western country. He is, too, well known to have commenced an intrigue with the agents of Spain for a separation of this country from the Atlantic States, some years ago. No one that I have ever conversed with, on the subject, doubts his being a Spanish pensioner, and his conduct of the last two years has not lessened the suspicion of the present existence of his former intrigue. That he was known to have been upon the most intimate and friendly terms, and to have had many closetings with Col. Burr, when he made his first tour through this and the adjacent country; that he was one of Burr's partners in his Ohio Canal Company, an ostensible scheme to divert the attention of the public from the real object; that his greatest favorites, those whom he distinguished most by his patronage in the Territory over which he presided as Governor, have proved themselves Burr's warmest adherents—are circumstances very unfavorable to his excellency's character. The appointment and continuance of this man in so important an office—a man whose private character is as exceptionable as his public character is suspicious—a bankrupt, devoted to every species of pomp and pageantry, without an income adequate to his style of life—and as ambitious as Napoleon the first—is the only trait in the present Administration which does not meet with the approbation of the Western country. But this I think is the cause of universal regret. It is extremely unfortunate that this man should now be at the head of our army, even if he is as pure a patriot as I believe the President to be—for should any force be necessary from this country, for the purpose of either acting against the malcontents, insurgents or the Spanish troops below, the ardor of the true friends to their country would be considerably abated by the consideration that they would be subject to the command of a General in whom they have no confidence; and this circumstance would be a stimulus to those we should have to oppose—for they would derive encouragement from our suspicions and jealousies, even if they had no other assurances from the General or his friends. But these misfortunes they would actually hope for and expect from his defection as much as we would dread it. Were it not for this cause, should events render it necessary, the people of Kentucky would, by one universal impulse of patriotism, tender their support to the present Administration, and hosts of volunteers would be ready to suppress any insurrection or frustrate any traitorous scheme that may make its appearance in any part of the Western country; but I should really fear, if Wilkinson retains the command, that there would be but few volunteers who could be depended on. One description only could be procured with facility, and they would be those who are mere adventurers, whose circumstances cannot be worsted in any event, and whose principles would not restrain them from taking any side. And this is an opinion I entertain, not merely from what very probably would happen, but from what I know has actually happened. I know many who have already volunteered themselves, and I know them so well, that I should be extremely unwilling to be associated with them in defense of my country in opposition to Aaron Burr. They have been too sanguine for his success against Mexico, too ready to assist him in all his propositions, and too clamorous about arresting him after they knew that it was in vain to attempt it—after he was perfectly out of their reach. He, however, very narrowly escaped at the mouth of Cumberland; had he waited one day longer, I am well convinced we should have had no further trouble with him or about him. When the militia of Livingston county were ordered out, a certain Col. Benj. Hardin, of that county—a South Carolinian, who had been accustomed to killing tories in the American Revolution, and who, about five years ago, killed two men in this country for horse-stealing—ignorant enough to think it best, on such occasions, not to trouble the civil authority, hardy and bold enough to attempt anything that an uninformed mind or a misguided zeal should point out as beneficial to his country—had prepared himself and did actually go to the mouth of Cumberland for the express purpose of shooting Burr, having communicated his design to only a single individual; and I am confident he experienced a considerable chagrin and mortification at his disappointment, when he found the little apostate had left that place the day before his arrival.

The public mind is all impatient to hear from Orleans. Almost everybody expects to hear of some great action—some mighty revelation. This is not my case. My opinion is a singular one, such as it is. I hazard it with all the rest of my conjectures. I expect to hear nothing more important from Burr or Wilkinson than such a show of patriotism by the latter, with the consent of the former, as they conceive necessary to quiet suspicion and give more time for maturing and perfecting their plan. It is probable that Wilkinson will attempt to take Burr, or that Burr will surrender himself for trial at Orleans, where no testimony will be procured against him sufficient to convict him, unless the courts should put off his trial till Gen. Eaton could be procured—in which case every attempt will be made to excite the sympathy of the people in his favor, or by ingeniously portraying him as an innocent and persecuted man—thereby rendering them more favorable to his views, and furnishing an apology for any steps he may take. I cannot think he has explained himself to any man who can be procured (except Gen. Eaton) in such a manner as to render proof against him practicable; for I entertain an opinion similar to what he expressed at Nashville, viz: that Mr. Daviess, the attorney for the United States in this district, must think him a much greater fool than he really was, if he thought he had any unlawful enterprise in view, and had conducted it in such a manner as to give an opportunity of proving it upon him. Whether he may be acquitted, or any uncommon appearance of rigor be exercised against him in Orleans, the effects, I am confident, will be astonishing; for I think I am well acquainted with his standing in Orleans. All my information from that quarter—except such as is through the public agents—leaves no doubt upon my mind that his popularity is immensely great and dangerous to the Government; and I depend much more for correct information, as to the state of public sentiment in any particular place, upon men in the common walks of life, and who are disinterested, than I do upon those who move in superior circles, who are interested or who are placed in such a situation as to render concealment towards them indispensably necessary to the success of any intrigue. No man can conceive what an effect Burr's second acquittal in this State had upon the public mind in his favor for some time. To have any correct idea of it, a man must have witnessed it, and it will be proportionably greater at Orleans, as his popularity there is greater and his adherents more numerous than here.

Should either of the events I have suggested take place, and should Gen W. not apprehend any danger of removal, nothing decisive, I think, will be attempted for some time. Burr's men, owing to the vigilance of our Government, will not be able to join him shortly. They must have time and opportunity to collect. The prospect of a Spanish war will delay their operations. Should it take place, it will furnish all his adherents an opportunity of joining him unmolested and without much reproach. Should it not take place, they will await the event of another scheme—which is the proposed population by Congress of a tract of land on the west side of the Mississippi. Certain I am that unless Congress does encourage the settlement of that country, to a certain extent, with the natives of the United States, with men attached to the principles of our Government, those lower Territories will produce one continued scene of insurrection. I am sensible it is necessary at this time. But I know it is at this time dangerous, and any law for that purpose ought to be extremely well guarded; for, unless it is made so, the moment such a law passes is the moment at which Burr's adherents will set out for that country under the authority of that law, and will be collected at a proper point for action before the least hostility towards the United States will be indicated.

Upon this subject, I feel an uncommon solicitude, and extremely regret my want of personal acquaintance with any of the departments of the administration that would justify communication of such circumstances as have or may pass under my observation, with my sentiments upon them. I acknowledge that one of Burr's greatest and best informed friends calculated highly both upon such a law and the want of such a law, paradoxical as it may appear. If no permission to extend the settlements was allowed, he thought the old subjects of Spain would always be instruments to produce revolution. If such permission was given, it would afford the means of collecting individuals that would be favorable to the views of Col. Burr. Any law, therefore, for this purpose at this conjuncture, ought to be most cautiously enacted, for even if the present conspiracy should be crushed, the scheme will not be laid aside.

Truly your friend,
N. EDWARDS.

To WM. WIRT, ESQ.

ELVIRADE, *June* 18, 1811.

Sir:

I acknowledge the receipt of your letter by your son, Major Whiteside, and entirely approve the whole of your conduct.

Continue the party you have ordered out until further orders. I presume they will be sufficient for the purpose for which they were intended, being numerous enough to make discoveries and to resist mere stragglers.

Have the militia under your charge immediately classed out and prepared to march at a moment's warning.

Order every Captain—at least those on the frontiers—to be ready, should any depredation be committed within the bounds of his company, to repel the attack, or to follow and take those Indians who may commit those outrages. Should circumstances clearly justify a reasonable belief of an invasion by any tribe of Indians, you will designate such officers and such force as you may think adequate to repel it, and transmit an account thereof to me.

Should immediate pursuit be made after any Indians who may have stolen horses or committed murders, etc., and they be overtaken with the property in their possession, or be otherwise clearly ascertained to be the indentical persons who committed those offenses, your orders must be for the men to take them peaceably, if possible, that they may be brought to trial in a legal way, and be made examples of; but if they cannot otherwise be taken, not to let a single man escape alive.

As many men might be disposed to take advantage of the latitude here given, I shall request you to select as officers (where it is in your power) those in whose discretion you can best confide.

Enjoin it on the officers not to make an attack on any party of Indians, under any of the above orders, without being fully prepared and determined to make it successfully.

I wish you to employ some person as a spy, to go amongst the Indians most likely to have committed the late outrages—particularly those near Peoria, calling themselves Pottawottamies, under Main-pock. I wish to ascertain their numbers, their character, disposition, etc.—every information relative to their present settlement.

I wish particularly to ascertain who have committed those recent hostilities, which are the subject of your letter.

I am, sir, very respectfully,

Your most obedient servant,

NINIAN EDWARDS.

To Col. Wm. Whiteside.

Elvirade, Randolph County,
Illinois Territory, *June* 7, 1811.

Sir:

I have the honor to represent to you that, as Superintendent of Indian Affairs in this Territory, I have frequently been under the necessity of obtaining the aid of an interpreter, who deserves and expects some compensation for his services, but between whom and myself no positive stipulations have existed, nor do I know whether I should be authorized to draw for any sum, and, if any, how much for his use.

I have also the honor to represent to you that, on some occasions, I have been visited by Indians who reside in the upper parts of this Territory, on or near the Mississippi River. I have on those occasions detained them as short a time as possible, but have necessarily incurred some expense (which I have hitherto paid out of my own pocket) in furnishing them with provisions during their stay and making them some presents on their departure.

As, from the aspect of affairs with the Indians up the Mississippi, it is likely I shall have much more to do with them, I should be happy to receive some instructions from you on the subject of the Indian business under my superintendence.

I have good reason to believe that not less than forty horses have been recently stolen from this Territory by some of those Indians, the most lawless of whom is a small tribe calling themselves Pottawottamies, but principally composed of outcasts and vagabonds of the neighboring tribes, who seem to live by depredations, and whose audacity in them is unequalled.

Yesterday, I was informed, by unexceptionable authority, that one young man on the frontiers, in the county of St. Clair, had been killed and his sister carried off by some Indians, who also stole some horses.

I have been applied to send a belt of wampum and a talk to the chiefs of some of the tribes, for the purpose of obtaining restitution of some horses. I shall do the best I can in the business, but am not supplied with wampum or any other article usual and necessary in intercourse with Indians, nor can I procure any of them here.

The movements of a part of the Indians, in the uppermost part of this Territory, seem strongly indicative of a hostile disposition toward us, but the extent of it cannot yet be ascertained, though every means is pursuing for that purpose.

I have the honor to be,
Very respectfully, sir,
Your most obedient servant,
NINIAN EDWARDS.

To HON. WM. EUSTIS, *Secretary of War*, Washington City.

ELVIRADE, RANDOLPH COUNTY,
ILLINOIS TERRITORY, *June* 20, 1811.

Sir :

I have the honor to transmit to you a copy of an affidavit of Rebecca Cox —a respectable woman and a resident of St. Clair county—containing an account of the murder of her brother, the plundering of her father's property, and her being taken a prisoner and carried off by a party of Indians.

As soon as the outrages, which are the subject of the affidavit, were known, a party of our citizens were raised, who pursued the Indians and retook the young woman, but did not succeed in regaining any of the property that was taken with her.

In the engagement that took place one of our men was wounded, and an Indian was certainly killed or else badly wounded.

Of the truth of the foregoing facts there is no doubt, and I myself have entire confidence in the following statement: A young man, by the name of Lindley, was to have joined the party who pursued the Indians, but did not arrive at the place of rendezvous in time. On his return home, he states that he was pursued and overtaken by two Indians (supposed to be those spoken of by Miss Cox in her affidavit); that after running until he was nearly exhausted, he stopped in the midst of a fallen tree, from which he shot the foremost Indian and seized his gun, and with it shot the other Indian as he came up, and actually killed both.

From the character I have of this young man, and, among others, from the circumstance of his fetching in a gun which he did not carry with him, I strongly incline to the opinion (which seems very generally entertained) that he has told the truth.

Since my letter to you of the 7th inst., I have received more circumstantial accounts of the horses that were said to have been stolen by a party of Pottawottamie Indians settled near Peoria, under a chief named Main-pock or Man-shot.

Those complaints of the people are corroborated by statements made to Gen. Clark by some Pottawottamies now in St. Louis, by similar statements of other Indians to the United States Indian interpreter at Chicago, and by the testimony of an Indian trader, who saw some of those Indians in possession of about eighteen horses which they have stolen at one time. The information which the interpreter at Chicago has received, induces him to suppose that the principal actors in these depredations are two brothers of the wife of Main-pock, the chief. These are the same Indians who committed the depredations about which I had the honor to write you last summer. They are certainly gaining confidence from impunity, and their conduct is getting entirely insufferable.

As nothing can be a stronger indication of determined hostility than the taking of prisoners, and it is reasonable to suppose that the Indians will be disposed to resort to retaliation in consequence of the death of those who were killed, and the people on the frontier are getting very much alarmed, I deemed it proper to order out a few men, who would be sufficient merely to make discoveries or resist stragglers—and issued orders, of which the inclosed is a copy, to the Colonels of St. Clair county. In the meantime, I have dispatched a spy, and am taking every means in my power to ascertain what Indians they were who committed the outrage upon Cox's family and property.

We have every reason to believe that the celebrated Indian Prophet is but too successful in exciting hostility toward the United States, in various tribes of Indians.

I have the honor to be,
Very respectfully, sir,
Your most obedient servant,
NINIAN EDWARDS.

To Hon. Wm. Eustis, *Secretary War*, Washington City.

Elvirade, Randolph County,
Illinois Territory, *June* 22, 1811.

Sir :

I have this moment received a communication from Col. Wm. Whiteside, of the county of St. Clair, of which the annexed is a copy, and by which it will appear that one more of our citizens was actually killed and the other, though living, mortally wounded by some Indians.

Great alarm exists among the people, and many are quitting their farms and seeking safety in the most populous settlements.

I shall immediately order out a full Captain's company, to protect the frontiers of St. Clair county and quiet the alarms of the people.

I have the honor to be,
With the highest respect, etc., etc.,
NINIAN EDWARDS.

To Hon. Wm. Eustis, *Secretary of War*, Washington City.

Elvirade, Randolph County,
June 22, 1811.

Sir :

I have this moment had the honor to receive your letter of yesterday. I must repeat my wish, that the militia under your command be immediately organized, so as to be ready to march at a moment's warning.

If Major William B. Whiteside is willing to take command as a Captain, stipulating only for Captain's pay, and Samuel Judy should be willing to take command under him as a Lieutenant, with the same stipulation, they may select any other officer to act as their ensign, and raise as many volunteers, not exceeding a full Captain's company, as they can. In that case you are hereby required to order them to the frontiers, with instructions to resist all invasions, repel all attacks and aggressions from the Indians, and afford protection to the settlers on the frontiers in the most effectual manner in their power—to remain in service for thirty days, unless sooner therefrom discharged.

Should it not be possible to raise volunteers enough, you must direct a draft according to law.

Should this arrangement not be agreeable to Major Whiteside, then order Capt. Judy to take the command of a company, to be raised in like manner, and for like service.

Should the arrangement not be satisfactory to Capt. Judy, Major Whiteside is, nevertheless, (if willing) to take the command of the company, and in that case you will select two subalterns to act under him.

I have the honor, etc., etc.,

NINIAN EDWARDS.

TO COL. WM. WHITESIDE.

ELVIRADE, RANDOLPH COUNTY,
ILLINOIS TERRITORY, *October* 16, 1811.

Sir :

I have the honor to inclose you the proceedings of the citizens of St. Clair county, and their address to you—all of which I am convinced is the result of apprehensions of danger entertained, not merely by timid minds, but by men well acquainted with the geographical situations, habits and dispositions of the Indians alluded to—experienced in Indian warfare, and as much distinguished by their valor as any other citizens in the Western country.

The principal facts stated in the address, I have already had the honor to communicate to the War Department.

The Indians residing about Lake Michigan, and on the Illinois River and its waters, are those who have committed the depredations which have so much alarmed and agitated this Territory, the north-western parts of which are very much exposed to their attacks. Whether those Indians visit our frontiers by land or water, they pass through Peoria or its immediate vicinity both in coming and returning. A garrison, therefore, at that place, would, in my opinion, hold in check all those from whom we have most danger to apprehend, and in several respects be attended with very beneficial consequences.

Believing the proposed measures to be expedient and necessary to the safety of the Territory, I have thought it my duty thus far to support the prayer of the inclosed petition; but I had no knowledge that any such was contemplated, till I received the inclosed papers.

I have the honor to be,
With the highest respect, sir,
Your most obedient servant,
NINIAN EDWARDS.

To the President of the United States.

Proceedings of Citizens of St. Clair County, Illinois, and their Address to the President of the United States.

At a large meeting of the inhabitants of St. Clair county, Illinois Territory, where Col. Whiteside was conducted to the chair, and Samuel Davidson, Esq., appointed Secretary—

Resolved, unanimously, That the following memorial be presented to Ninian Edwards, Governor of the Territory aforesaid, as the joint sense of the meeting, to be signed by the chairman: which humbly showeth that we are highly gratified in the prompt, speedy and prudential manner in which your excellency has issued your orders for the defense of the exposed frontiers of said county, to oppose the repetition of Indian hostilities; and that we have the utmost and incontrovertible confidence in your abilities and patriotism for our safety in the present alarming times, as the constitutional channel between the General Government and us.

Wherefore we do confidingly request your excellency to forward the annexed memorial to the President of the United States, with such statements as may appear reasonable and just to gain the object prayed for—as we are confident your excellency must feel and see, with us, that one or more garrisons, established and defended by veterans of the United States, would be of the utmost safety to the extensive and exposed frontiers of both the Louisiana and Illinois Territories—in a more particular manner, as the great and numerous tribes of Indians, who had the hardihood and insolence to wage war against the United States (and in some instances with effect) a few years since, infest this region.

That, by the treaty of Greenville, and other subsequent treaties, they have relinquished their title to their former hunting grounds, (which is now transformed into substantial plantations,) and are changing their habitations fast, from the lakes and waters of the Ohio, down the Illinois River to the Mississippi, where undoubtedly it would be necessary to establish a fort, in order to set reasonable bounds to their savage fury and unprovoked disturbance. We beg leave to refer your excellency to a view of the great and manifest benefits lately obtained by the garrisons established far up on the two great rivers, several hundred miles above their junction, where, before the establishing these strengths, there did not a season pass by but some innocent person fell a victim to their savage barbarity on both sides of the river; and we confidently believe it would have the same salutary effect in establishing one fort or block-house on the first eminence above either the mouths of the Missouri or the Illinois Rivers, and another in the seditious village of Peoria—the great nursery of hostile Indians and traitorous British Indian traders.

We hope it will not be thought superfluous to mention that the above request is not to gratify our pride or avarice, in obtaining military pomp to decorate our streets, or the expenditures of the public money to buy our produce; but it is to keep the improving citizen in peace in a remote region of the United States, who is now working to convert the fertile and extensive plains of the Mississippi into the fairest portion of the Union. From different circumstances the inhabitants of this county are not in possession of a sufficiency of arms to repel any attacks that may be offered; owing to the present alarm it is not in our power to buy any, and a considerable portion of the militia are not circumstanced to buy. If your excellency will be pleased to make use of your good offices to obtain from the General Government the use of what rifles and muskets as may be thought, in your wisdom, needful, it certainly would be of great service to this frontier country.

WILLIAM WHITESIDE, *Chairman.*
SAMUEL D. DAVIDSON, *Secretary.*

To His Excellency Ninian Edwards.

At a numerous meeting of the militia officers, and other inhabitants of St. Clair county, Illinois Territory, at the court house, the —— day of ———, 1811, to take into consideration the alarming situation of the frontiers of said county, from the numerous and horrid depredations lately committed by the Indians, Col. Whiteside was conducted to the chair, and Samuel Davidson was appointed secretary.

Resolved, That there be a memorial immediately signed by the chairman of this meeting, and countersigned by the secretary, stating to the President of the United States the necessity of his ordering what regular troops he, in his wisdom, may think requisite, to be stationed for the defense of said county.

Resolved, That said memorial be sent to the Governor of said Territory, requesting him to forward the same to the President of the United States, and make such statement (to accompany said memorial) as the urgency of the subject may require.

To James Madison, *President of the United States*—Greeting:

The memorial of the inhabitants of the aforesaid county most humbly showeth—That the inhabitants residing on the frontiers aforesaid have sustained frequent and repeated damages from the different and numerous tribes of Indians on and in the neighborhood of the Illinois River, these five or six years past, by stealing their horses and other property, as well as the cruel murder of some few of the citizens. In lieu of retaliation, that said citizens have curbed their passions and restrained their resentment, lest they should be so unfortunate as to draw a stigma on the Government by punishing the innocent for the transgressions of the guilty, and in one instance restrained the vindictive spirit by taking two Indians prisoners, in possession of stolen property, after a chase of one hundred miles, and gave them up to the law. We have become the victims of savage cruelty in a more hasty and general manner than what has lately been experienced by the citizens of the United States. The last spring there have been numbers of horses stolen. On the 2d of June, the house of Mr. Cox was robbed and plundered of valuable effects, five horses stolen, a young man massacred, and his sister taken prisoner (sad and conclusive effects and presages of war), and likewise one other man severely wounded when following said Indians.

On the 20th of the same month, one other man was killed and scalped and another mortally wounded, which can be more fully stated by the Executive of said Territory

—all those who suffered being no intruders, but living on their own farms, on the north-western frontier of said county.

From our knowledge of the danger we are in and our long sufferance, we think we ask nothing but what is reasonable, and what will be advantageous to the United States, when we implore you to station what number of soldiers you may think sufficient to establish a garrison at the village of Peoria (commonly called Opea), on the Illinois River, and one other on the eastern bank of the Mississippi, at or near the place once viewed and adopted by Captains Stodard and Bisswell, six or eight miles below the mouth of said Illinois River—both sites being covered by treaty. We beg to refer you to the Governor of said Territory, concerning the urgency and necessity of the above calamities, not doubting but that you will grant our request if you think it will be for the good of the Union.

WILLIAM WHITESIDE,
SAMUEL D. DAVIDSON.

ELVIRADE, RANDOLPH COUNTY,
ILLINOIS TERRITORY, *October* 22, 1811.

Sir:

I have had the honor to receive the proceedings of a meeting of the citizens of St. Clair county, at which you were chairman, and have transmitted the papers to the President of the United States, supported by my opinion in favor of the measure which you solicit.

I beg leave to express to you, and through you to those who united with you, the peculiar gratification which I feel at finding the measures I had pursued, for the safety and protection of the Territory, so highly approved by gentlemen of experience, valor and patriotism.

This answer has been delayed only by my indisposition.

I am, very respectfully, sir,
Your most obedient servant,
NINIAN EDWARDS.

To COL. WM. WHITESIDE.

ELVIRADE, RANDOLPH COUNTY,
ILLINOIS TERRITORY, *October* 29, 1811.

Sir:

I have the honor to inclose you a receipt from the Kaskaskia tribe of Indians, including all the payments that have been made them for their annuities since I have had the honor to administer the government.

I have, also, the honor to inclose you a receipt from the priest who was, according to treaty, employed to preach to the Kaskaskia Indians, including all the payments that have been made to him by me. The first year's annuity to him, I paid in one hundred dollars which were sent me by Governor Harrison, and the second payment was made out of the proceeds of a draft of one hundred dollars, which I had the honor to draw on you for. I am not enabled to ascertain whether or not he is entitled to another year's annuity, because I cannot ascertain how many he has received.

Not having sent forward the receipts last year, because I thought it possible I might receive some instructions on the subject, I have thought it advisable to send them now in their present form.

I have the honor to be,

Very respectfully, sir,

Your most obedient servant,

NINIAN EDWARDS.

To Hon. Wm. Eustis, Esq., *War Department*, Washington City.

Elvirade, Illinois Territory,
December 14, 1811.

To the principal Chiefs of the Pottawottamies residing on the Illinois River and its waters:

My Children, there seems to be some misunderstanding between you and your white brethren. I wish to prevent any bad consequences, and, if possible, to cause you and your white brethren to unite your hands in friendship. This is the wish of your Great Father, the President of the United States. You have seen that he does not fear war, because his strength is great; but he loves peace, and will always do justice to those who treat him well.

I have many things to say to you, which it would be inconvenient to write. I therefore wish Gomo, and one or two more chiefs, to come and hear my words.

Capt. Hebert will conduct you, and he will prevent any one from hurting you.

It is your own safety that makes me wish to see you. I will send you back again safely.

NINIAN EDWARDS.

Elvirade, *December* 14, 1811.

To the principal Chiefs of the Kickapoos:

My Children, I wrote you last summer that your Great Father, the President of the United States, wished to be at peace with you. You must know that he is too strong to fear war; but I tell you again he still wishes for peace, because it is a good thing, in itself, and is best for your happiness and that of your people.

That great deceiver, the Shawnee Prophet, has misled some of your people, and caused them to make war on their white brethren. Your people were told that the Shawnee Prophet was a bad man—that he was hired by the British to tell lies—but they had no ears to hear those things. Their eyes must now be opened. They know the Prophet deceived them, and, if they will now abandon that bad man, all will still be well. They may have peace or war—which they please.

Many of you, I have reason to believe, did not join the Prophet, but hated him the more for deceiving your friends and brothers.

I wish a few of you to come and hear my words, because then I can say more than it is convenient to write. This may explain all things and place us again on the footing of confidence as well as friendship.

Major Whiteside will conduct you, and I will send you back safely.

NINIAN EDWARDS.

ELVIRADE, RANDOLPH COUNTY,
ILLINOIS TERRITORY, *Jan.* 18, 1812.

Sir:

I have the honor to state to you that the militia, who were called out by me to defend this country during the last summer, are constantly importuning me on the subject of their pay.

The unexampled unhealthiness of the season, and the attention necessary at that time to their crops, made the sacrifice on their part very considerable; and it is now no longer doubted by the most incredulous that their services were important to their country, by preventing the savage attacks with which it was menaced. Under these circumstances, I fear, if those people cannot obtain some remuneration, it will have a most unhappy effect upon a population too weak, at best, at a time when there is the strongest probability that similar services will again be wanting.

I therefore should be happy to be informed whether they will be paid, and, if so, what steps are necessary to be pursued for that purpose.

I have the honor to be, etc., etc.,

NINIAN EDWARDS.

To HON. WM. EUSTIS, *War Department*, Washington City.

ELVIRADE, RANDOLPH COUNTY,
ILLINOIS TERRITORY, *Jan.* 10, 1812.

Sir:

I have the honor to state to you, that Col. John Grant, formerly of the State of Kentucky, desires, through me, to apply to the President for a lease of a tract of land at the lower ripple on the Saline Creek, where he now resides, with a view to prepare houses for the reception of salt, which is constantly sent to that place for deposit till the rise of the water is sufficient to carry it out of the creek.

He states that he has made a contract to receive and take charge of very considerable quantities of salt at that place, that the contract is to continue two years, and that the houses are necessary to secure it from the weather and from thieves, and that he wishes to erect them at his own expense, provided he can be permitted to do so.

For my own part I see no injury that would arise from such a lease, and think it very probable that, if it were sufficiently guarded, it might be attended with great public conveniences. But I suppose that a permission to remain as *tenant at will* would be sufficient for him, and would most effectually guard against any injury to the public interest, etc.

NINIAN EDWARDS.

To ALBERT GALLATIN, *Secretary, etc.*

ELVIRADE, RANDOLPH COUNTY,
ILLINOIS TERRITORY, *Jan.* 25, 1812.

Sir:

I have the honor to inform you that, from a knowledge both of the exposed situation of our North-western frontier and of the disposition of Indians to retaliate upon the white people for the loss of their friends and relations, I, shortly after Gov. Harrison's battle, thought it necessary to send out a few spies, who have since been kept out in consequence of the hostile threats which the Indians are known to have made, and the proximity of the hunting ground they were about to occupy to our frontiers.

Such have been the apprehensions and irritation of the people of St. Clair county (those most exposed), that it has been found very difficult to restrain them from commencing hostilities, as you may perceive from the inclosed letter from Col. Whiteside, who, though not blessed with a good education, possesses a strong discriminating mind, is highly distinguished as an Indian fighter, and has all the influence that such characters never fail to command on a frontier, in times of danger. Upon the receipt of the letter, I immediately dispatched the Brigade-Major (express) with orders to put a stop to the contemplated expedition. He, however, did not arrive in time, and eighty-six well mounted riflemen actually started in search of the Pottawottamies, who, either suspecting an attack or having some previous intimation of it, had removed and could not be found. Otherwise there certainly would have been a hard fight.

In this state of things I thought it advisable to send for some of the Kickapoos and some of the Pottawottamies of the Illinois River, as well to ascertain their disposition towards us as to make arrangements that would conduce to their safety, provided they should be disposed to be friendly. Neither of my messengers have yet arrived, although more than two weeks have elapsed beyond the time appointed by each of them for his return. This delay occasions great uneasiness among their friends and much speculation among the people at large.

I have also the honor to inform you that I have received information (which I am very certain may be relied on) that the Puants, or Winnebago Indians, on the 1st inst. attacked the trading establishments on the Mississippi, below Prairie du Chien, plundered them of their property, killed several men, and declared that they would kill every American that they could find—alleging that they had lost a number of their men at the late battle at the Prophet's town.

Perilous is the situation of a great portion of this Territory, at least; but the danger is greater from the negative state in which we find ourselves, being neither at peace nor at war.

Notwithstanding the repeated depredations of the bands of Indians on the Illinois River, the murders they have committed, and their refusal to deliver up the offenders or make any satisfaction, though solemnly demanded of them —and notwithstanding the daily expectations universally pervading the country of a renewal of these hostilities—we cannot legally take any measures of offense against them, but must wait for another attack, not knowing when or where it may be made. For my own part I have not a doubt that our north-western frontier at least will be greatly annoyed as soon as the weather becomes a little more moderate. Many of these Indians certainly contemplate joining the British. They are in the habit of visiting Fort Maulden, annually, and as soon as they are prepared for their departure thither, they will (as I believe they have already declared) make inroads upon our settlements, as well to take scalps as to steal horses.

If, under these circumstances, we could be authorized to break up their settlements on the Illinois River by volunteer expeditions of mounted riflemen, taking them by surprise, as was the case in Kentucky during the former Indian war, it would, in my opinion, be attended with the most salutary consequences. Without this, or a garrison at Peoria, or some other measure of offense, a great number of our inhabitants will without doubt be forced to abandon their settlements. Peoria is the great highway through which all the Illinois Indians and all those about Lake Michigan make their incursions into this country, and the latter Indians derive great encouragement from the asylum which the villages on the Illinois affords them.

I beg you, sir, to believe I have felt myself constrained to make these observations from the perfect conviction I feel of the dangers to which the people of this Territory are exposed, and my knowledge of their defenseless situation.

I have the honor, also, to state to you that I have received a letter from the Military Agent at Newport, Ky., advising me that he had forwarded me 116 muskets, bayonets and cartridge boxes, and 46 pairs of pistols. He stated to me that Gov. Harrison had drawn for the rifles, which you had authorized me to receive.

I should be happy to have your order for some rifles and some more arms for cavalry, particularly swords, of which there were none forwarded to me.

I have the honor to be,

Very respectfully, sir,

Your most obedient servant,

NINIAN EDWARDS.

To Hon. Wm. Eustis, *Secretary of War.*

ELVIRADE, RANDOLPH COUNTY,
ILLINOIS TERRITORY, *January* 26, 1812.

Sir:

Although I am sensible of the claims which the most important business must have upon your attention at this time, I beg leave, most respectfully, to solicit of you any information which you can, with propriety and convenience to yourself, communicate to me relative to the probable period when the land office in this district, for the sale of public lands, will be opened; and I flatter myself that a plain statement of facts will convince you that neither an indecorous or impertinent curiosity forms any part of my motives in requesting this information.

At no time have the people been better satisfied with their Territorial officers than at the present period; yet a combination of interests and of views, differing materially in their ultimate object, have united the majority of the freeholders of all parties in wishing for the second grade of Territorial Government, that they may thereby obtain a delegate to Congress, through and by whom they may make known and support their various wishes, complaints and demands. The memorials upon this subject are not yet delivered to me, but I am in the daily expectation of receiving them.

The freeholders of this Territory are a very inconsiderable portion of its population. Of the respectable farmers of the country who have made arrangements and appear to be disposed to be permanent residents, they do not, I am sure, constitute the one-tenth—yet they can decide upon the change of government, with all the accumulation of taxes it will bring with it. Afterwards, they have the exclusive right of voting for the representatives in the Legislature, who will be elected for two years, with the right to nominate the Council to be appointed for five years. By which means, a small minority will have the power to fix upon a very large and respectable majority of their fellow-citizens a course of measures which may not be changed, however disagreeable to the majority, for five years. Although this danger may be considered problematical, yet such are the jealous and independent dispositions of freemen, that they will never be satisfied to depend for the security and protection of their rights upon the mere courtesy of others.

The situation of the settlers on the Ohio, and between it and Kaskaskia, is peculiarly unfortunate at this juncture. They are in general respectable, independent in their circumstances, and anxious to have an opportunity to purchase the lands on which they reside, and to be admitted to an equal participation in all the rights of citizens. They constitute nearly one-third of the whole population of the Territory, and ought shortly to have a new county, yet, among them, there are not more—as far as I can ascertain—than three or four freeholders; so that, while the other counties will have representatives by reason of freeholders living interspersed through them, this portion of the Territory will have none.

I, therefore, have thought that if the public sales should be likely to commence shortly, it would be proper in me, as a necessary means of conciliating the affections of those people to the Government, when I come to act on the contemplated change, to defer the elections till after the public sales are over, and thereby afford them the opportunity to become freeholders, in which light they would be considered by purchasing at the sales.

I beg leave, also, to suggest that, if it be possible to make some provision by law, favorable to settlers, previous to the commencement of the sales, such a measure would tend greatly to tranquilize the Territory, already extremely agitated upon this subject, and to which the principles and doctrines contained in the printed papers herewith sent, inculcated and enforced by means of associations already formed, have greatly contributed.

The appointment of a Register and Receiver to this district created a general impression that lands would shortly thereafter be exposed to sale, and many persons settled with the belief that they would have the opportunity to purchase land before their improvements of it would so far enhance its value as to render it an object with others to bid against them; and since then, either from necessity or with a hope that something would finally be done for their security, they have increased these improvements till they have become objects of real importance.

As the United States would not wish to receive more than the value of the land in its unimproved State, or that its increased value from the improvements of others should fall into the hands of speculators, the public interest, I think, cannot suffer by giving to the settlers the pre-emption right to purchase at the price fixed by Congress. Admitting that they, by having the first choice, had occupied the best lands, still the price is high enough; for land of the first quality in the Mississippi Bottom, with indisputable titles, has been and now can be bought at that price, with liberal credit. Judges Stuart and Thomas, Secretary Pope and myself, have purchased first rate tracts and elegant situations, in the American Bottom, adjoining each other, without giving more.

But the supposition, as it relates to the settlers, is not true. Proximity to springs and what is called good range for stock—objects not generally found in the richest lands—have had a much more decided influence upon them than the fertility of the soil or the intrinsic value of the land.

If, however, it should not be deemed proper to extend to the settlers this or some other indulgence, it might be advisable—their numbers being so considerable—for the agents of the sale to make such arrangements as would enable those people, with the least inconvenience to themselves, to attend to bid for the lands they occupy. As the sales must continue six weeks, the district offered for sale might be divided into six parts. Each division could be well described, and the week in which it would be offered for sale might be specified—of all which, notice might be given, and every man be thereby freed from the necessity of attending longer than one week.

Since writing the above, I have ascertained for the first time, from Gen. Rector, the tract of country which was last summer recommended by the commissioners for satisfying unlocated claims, and believe it will include nearly every settlement in the county of St. Clair, and also the principal part of those in this county, with the exception of those toward the Ohio.

I am far from wishing to suggest anything to the injury of the holders of unlocated claims; for, although those rights have sometimes been purchased at low rates, yet it is very certain some of them are in the hands of the original *bona fide* holders. Many others have been traded for adequate and valuable considerations; and all, I presume, have passed a rigid scrutiny by the commissioners—notwithstanding which, I cannot refrain from communicating the facts and expressing the apprehensions I feel for the tranquillity of the Territory, hoping that the wisdom of Government may thereupon be able to devise and adopt such measures as ought to satisfy the reasonable demands of all persons, and, at the same time, preserve peace and harmony in the Territory.

In an abstract point of view, it may be considered that the settlers were trespassers, and that no claim upon the Government could grow out of their own wrong. But may not an evil, when suffered to increase too long, render the application of mere unbending, abstract principles inconsonant with the dictates of true practical policy?

At a time when delusive theories and captivating plans are dispersed among the people with success, when, also, the interest of so many is involved, while their services are absolutely necessary to repel the attacks of savages, and in the crisis in which we find ourselves in regard to foreign nations, I cannot but think it true policy to conciliate attachment to our Government, if it can be effected without too great a sacrifice of the public interests.

If, sir, in this communication, I shall be considered as having improperly made any suggestions or transgressed any rules of propriety, I sincerely hope it will be attributed to the true cause—to an anxiety, honest and sincere, for the welfare of my country.

I have the honor to be,
Very respectfully, sir,
Your most obedient servant,
NINIAN EDWARDS.

ELVIRADE, RANDOLPH COUNTY,
ILLINOIS TERRITORY, *February* 10, 1812.

Sir:

The arms, which you advised me that you had forwarded, are not yet arrived, but I expect them very shortly.

As soon as it is in your power, I shall be very glad if you would send on some more arms for cavalry—particularly swords, without which I cannot equip a single man.

If you feel authorized to do so, and if it is in your power, I should also be very glad to receive rifles enough for one complete rifle company, at least.

I wish, also, to be furnished, as soon as possible, with powder. I am at a loss about the quantity that may be wanting, but that some will be required I have every reason to think more than probable. Lead is cheaper here than with you, and I shall have no difficulty in procuring a sufficient quantity for bullets, but I wish to be furnished with shot for muskets.

Very respectfully, sir,
Your obedient servant,
NINIAN EDWARDS.

MAJOR THOS. MARTIN, *Military Agent*, Newport, Ky.

ELVIRADE, RANDOLPH COUNTY,
ILLINOIS TERRITORY, *February* 10, 1812.

Sir:

Understanding that Congress is about to authorize the President of the United States to raise several companies of rangers for the protection of the frontiers, I beg leave to recommend Major William Boling Whiteside, of this Territory, as pre-eminently qualified to command one of those companies.

He has been raised on our northwestern frontiers, with which he is well acquainted; and on several occasions of the greatest danger and difficulty, he has manifested so much prudence, self-command and intrepid bravery, that he has both acquired the confidence of his fellow-citizens and become a terror to the savages.

In times of danger, he is one of the most active and useful men in the Territory—his reputation and influence enabling him to associate his fellow-citizens with him in the most hazardous enterprises, in which he is always foremost to volunteer his own services—and I do him but justice to acknowledge that I myself have received essential aid from him in the protection of this country.

In recommending him, I am alone influenced by a knowledge of the satisfaction which his appointment would give to the exposed parts of the Territory, and a firm belief that no other man's services will be more useful

I have never spoken to him or one of his friends on the subject, but I have no doubt he would accept the appointment with pleasure. And I sincerely hope that if this application should not be successful, he may succeed in obtaining some other military appointment of the grade of Captain.

If it should be deemed advisable to station a company at Peoria, during the existence of the present dangers, for the protection of our northwestern frontier, he, I think, would be well qualified for the command—could soon raise the proper kind of men for that service, is well acquainted with the country, and extremely dreaded by the Indians in that quarter.

I have the honor to be,
Very respectfully, sir,
Your most obedient servant,
NINIAN EDWARDS.

To HON. WILLIAM EUSTIS, *Secretary of War*, Washington City.

ELVIRADE, RANDOLPH COUNTY,
ILLINOIS TERRITORY, *February* 10, 1812.

Sir:

Understanding that it is probable several companies of rangers will shortly be raised for the protection of the frontiers of the United States, I have recommended Major Boling Whiteside, of this Territory, for the command of one of them. I shall be happy to have your aid in procuring the appointment for him.

In times of danger, he is one of the most useful men in the Western country, is distinguished for his bravery, possesses as great qualifications for Indian warfare as any man I ever knew, and has been accustomed to it from his infancy.

I never spoke to him on the subject. I really recommend him for the good of the country, and from no other motive. I refer you to John Rice Jones for further particulars concerning him.

The chiefs whom I sent for to meet me in council have evaded my request, which augurs badly. The principal chief on the Illinois River sent me word that he wished for peace, but that the Winnebagoes would attack our frontiers. This may be true, but I am sure he also intends it as a cover to the depredations which his own party will commit.

The people are in great alarm, and if troops are not immediately sent to our exposed frontier, I repeat again to you, this country will in two months lose nearly one-half of its inhabitants. Every day, I hear of their removing in all quarters.

Your friend,
NINIAN EDWARDS.

TO HON. JOHN POPE.

ELVIRADE, RANDOLPH COUNTY,
ILLINOIS TERRITORY, *February* 10, 1812.

Sir:

I have the honor to inform you that the messengers whom I sent for the chiefs of the Kickapoos and Pottawottamies of the Illinois River have returned without being able to prevail on them to visit me according to my request.

Gomo, the principal chief of those bands on the Illinois, sent me word that he could do nothing until he could have a conference with all the Indians who are connected, by alliances and friendship, with those of his own particular party.

In the meantime, he advises me to be on my guard against the Winnebagoes, who, he says, will certainly attack our frontiers to revenge themselves for the loss and injury of many of their men, who were killed or wounded in the late battle at the Prophet's town.

His thus evading my request augurs unfavorably. If he is not sincere in wishing a previous consultation with the chiefs, etc., his conduct is an evidence of settled and decided hostility. If he actually thought such a consultation necessary, it clearly indicated his opinion that hostility was contem plated by others, if not by himself. And it evidences that their dispositions towards us are of so doubtful a character, at least, that we have no security against their attacks.

He had no inducement to conceal the hostile intentions of the Winnebagoes, since they had not only openly and boldly avowed them, but had, in part, carried their threats into execution, by attacking the trading establishments below Prairie du Chein; and I strongly suspect his admonition, to be prepared for them, was designed by him as a cover to the depredations which he expected his own party would commit.

His sincerity cannot in the least be depended upon; for, notwithstanding all his declarations to the contrary, the Indians who committed the murders in this Territory last year are certainly of his party—were present at the time I demanded them—have continued to reside with him since, and were seen and conversed with by my late messengers.

The alarms and apprehensions of the people are becoming so universal, that really I should not be surprised if we should, in three months, lose more than one-half of our present population. In places, in my opinion, entirely out of danger, many are removing. In other parts, large settlements are about to be totally deserted. Even in my own neighborhood, several families have removed, and others are preparing to do so in a week or two. A few days past, a gentleman of respectability arrived here from Kentucky, and he informed me that he saw on the road, in one day, upwards of twenty wagons conveying families out of this Territory. Every effort to check the prevalence of such terror seems to be ineffectual, and although much of it is unreasonably indulged, yet it is very certain the Territory will very shortly be in considerable danger. Its physical force is very inconsiderable, and is growing weaker, while it presents numerous points of attack.

The Winnebagoes, Kickapoos and Pottawottamies comprise the principal strength of the Prophet's army, and are certainly greatly irritated by their losses. The two former, and a large portion of the latter, reside in this Territory, and can, with great facility, make hostile incursions into our settlements, and they will most certainly do so unless our differences with England are speedily adjusted; for, till that event, whatever professions they may make, I am convinced we need not flatter ourselves with safety, unless, by waging war against them and perpetually harrassing them, we convince them that it is their interest to sue for peace. Independent of their present causes of irritation, it is very certain that the British emissaries, who are certainly among them, have infinitely more influence with them than we have.

Under these circumstances, I cannot forbear to solicit a portion of the regular force for the protection of this Territory.

My own opinion, which I submit with great deference, is that two complete companies at least are necessary, and if they were composed of what is commonly called backwoods' riflemen, they would furnish the cheapest and most effectual defense by having stations somewhere on the frontier, from which parties should be constantly detached, in different directions, as spies, always leaving enough to defend the station.

If, with this, we should be authorized to carry on some offensive operations, and the communication between the Indians and Fort Madison could be intercepted, and all our own traders be withdrawn from among them, their wants and necessities would soon constrain them to ask for peace.

I have the honor to be,
Very respectfully, sir,
Your obedient servant,
NINIAN EDWARDS.

To HON. WM. EUSTIS, *Secretary of War*, Washington City.

ELVIRADE, RANDOLPH COUNTY,
ILLINOIS TERRITORY, *February* 13, 1812.

Sir :

Gov. Howard and myself have recently received information from various quarters, which convinces both of us that formidable combinations of the savages will very shortly attack the frontier of this and Louisiana Territory.

Under these circumstances, I shall wish—if it shall eventually appear to be necessary—to raise some volunteers in the southern parts of Kentucky, provided the measure meets your approbation, which I most respectfully solicit.

I have the honor to be,
Very respectfully, sir,
Your most obedient servant,
NINIAN EDWARDS.

His Excellency Gov. SCOTT, Frankfort, Ky.

ELVIRADE, RANDOLPH COUNTY,
ILLINOIS TERRITORY, *February* 15, 1812.

Sir :

I think it my duty to transmit you the inclosed proceedings, as they tend strongly to corroborate the statements I have heretofore had the honor to make relative to the apprehensions of the people of this Territory.

Their extreme uneasiness seems to have led them into an opinion that I had not made the proper representations on the subject, as it appears by their 4th resolution; and, therefore, I inclose copies of my letter of the 16th of October last and its inclosures.

For my own part, I have never flattered myself with the belief that Gov. Harrison's victory would produce permanent peace with the Indians. It may produce a momentary impression upon the neighboring tribes, but I have no doubt but this will eventually yield to British policy and British influence.

The British emissaries, who are constantly among the Indians, will endeavor to cause our frontier to be attacked by distant tribes, over which we have no influence, hoping that our people may become so irritated that they will not —if they could do so—discriminate between those who are friendly and those who are hostile, and that, therefore, all may be compelled to fight in their own defense.

I have the honor, etc.,
N. EDWARDS.

To the SECRETARY OF WAR, Washington City.

Circular.

ELVIRADE, RANDOLPH COUNTY,
February 15, 1812.

Sir :

You are hereby requested to take a census of all the free male inhabitants in your county, above the age of twenty-one, and return the same to me as soon as possible after the last day of March next.

I request that you will use the utmost diligence to take in all persons of the above description.

If, however, any whom you take in should hereafter, and before you make your return, remove, and this should come to your knowledge, you will take especial care to make the correction, as it is my object to know, precisely as possible, the number of actual inhabitants above the age of twenty-one at the date of your return.

I have the honor to be,
Very respectfully, sir,
Your obedient servant,
NINIAN EDWARDS.

To JOHN HAYS, ESQ., *Sheriff of St. Clair County.*

Extract of a letter to Gov. Howard and Gov. Clark.

ELVIRADE, 16*th February*, 1812.

* * * By the exercise of the plainest common sense I had foreseen, contrary to the general expectation, that Gov. Harrison's victory would not be attended with all the good consequences that were fondly anticipated. I regret very much that the President seems to have fallen into the same error.

It is in vain to attribute all the hostility of the Prophet's associates to fanaticism. Facts do not justify the conclusion. Religion was totally out of the question with many of them, and I doubt very much whether all the Prophet's praying and priest-craft had half as much influence in exciting the enthusiasm of the Indians as the enterprising spirit, the undaunted valor and the bold designs of Tecumseh, who, in conjuncture with British emissaries, has long been endeavoring to inspire them with the opinion that we had wronged and oppressed them and would continue to do so, unless they boldly resisted our encroachments.

Admitting this supposition to be true, how is their unfriendly disposition towards us to be affected by the exposure of all the Prophet's juggling arts. They may hate him for deceiving them, but it will not make them love us, who have not yielded them the lands they claimed or conceded to them any other demand.

The Prophet's pretended conversation with the Great Spirit did not generate those hostilities; only gave a new spring to it, not more efficacious than British presents, arms, ammunition and promises may be hereafter.

A defeat may have dampened their ardor for a while, but the momentary terror over, revenge, the predominant passion, will occupy its place, and they who have so valiantly relied upon their own strength alone, will hardly dispair when flattered with all the British nation can furnish, nor will they who have reposed so much faith in the necromancy of an impostor, have less reliance on British power and resources.

I am convinced, in consequence of the momentary impression that may have been produced in the neighboring tribes, the British policy will now be, to set upon us those who are more distant and over whom we have no influence, hoping that by these means our people may become so irritated that they will not (if they could do so) discriminate between the innocent and the guilty, and that eventually all may be found to fight in their own defense.

Such have been the views which I have fully communicated to the Secretary of War. I have portrayed, in the strongest colors, the dangers of the negative state we are in (being neither at war or peace); I have pressed the necessity of an expedition against the bands of Illinois, who still retain among them the murderers, and refuse to deliver them up, or make any satisfaction for their depredations; I have advised that there should be a strong garrison at Peoria; I have stated the universal terror that pervades and is desolating the Territory; I have solicited the aid of two regular companies of back-woods riflemen, with a view to put them in two stations on the frontiers, from which parties as spies, in all directions, shall be constantly detached, always taking care to leave enough to defend the stations; in fact, I have said so much on the subject of danger and the necessity of preparations, that I derive great consolation from being fortified by your opinions, for I was growing afraid that my representations might be attributed to timidity, seeing that the papers, in all directions, held a contrary language.

For several weeks I have been endeavoring to organize a force for active service, and I am assured that there are three companies of volunteers on the Ohio awaiting my orders. I have also written to Gen. Scott for his approbation to raise a few men, if necessary, in the southern parts of Kentucky. Major Whiteside has directions to raise a company for immediate service. I have kept out a few spies, since Harrison's battle, and you may rely on it that I am willing to enter on any danger, risk or responsibility for the safety of our exposed frontiers.

I am, etc.,

NINIAN EDWARDS.

P. S.—I shall be at St. Louis in a day or two—this week at all events.

ELVIRADE, RANDOLPH COUNTY,
February 18, 1812.

Sir :

I have the honor to inform you that Indian hostility remains no longer a matter of conjecture.

You will have seen, from one of my last communications, that the Winnebagoes were collecting their forces to attack Chicago, Fort Madison, the settlements on Salt River, and those below that place.

On the 10th inst. they attacked and killed a family, consisting of ten persons, residing about thirty miles below the mouth of Salt River. An express, coming from Fort Madison, was also fired at, and several traces of Indians have been discovered in that quarter. Of all this there is no doubt. I have seen and conversed with people who have been at the very place where the murders were committed, since that unfortunate event.

I have also heard of another encounter that those Indians have had with seven white men, but cannot learn the particulars. We have not heard from the settlements on Salt River, but I have great fears on account of those people.

All these hostilities will now be charged to the Winnebagoes exclusively, like the depredations of last year were wholly charged to the Prophet's own proper party; but I am convinced that the bands of Pottawottamies on the Illinois, and some of the Chippeways, Ottaways and Kickapoos, will be equally guilty, and I should not be surprised at a general and open combination among them.

Under these circumstances Gov. Howard and myself have thought it would be improper in us to remain inactive, waiting for orders, and permit those fellows to murder our fellow-citizens with impunity. We have therefore determined to order out a force, consisting of rangers, sufficient to protect the frontiers; and I trust, sir, if our conduct in this particular shall not be disapproved, that provision may be made to meet the expense that may be necessarily incurred, as we have been obliged to pledge our words for the payment of it.

I have the honor to be, etc.,

NINIAN EDWARDS.

To WILLIAM EUSTIS, ESQ.

P. S.—If you should wish to acquire any information relative to this country, with a view to any military establishments, there is now a gentleman in your city who is probably better acquainted with its history and geography than any other person you can meet with. This is John Rice Jones, who, I presume, has very probably been introduced to you.—N. EDWARDS.

ELVIRADE, *February* 21, 1812.

Sir :

Every information I have received indicates the hostile disposition of the neighboring Indians. In consequence of which you are hereby required to cause to be enrolled and classed every militia man in your Regiment, and to make such preparations in giving notices according to law, as will enable you to detach at least one-half of your Regiment into actual service at a moment's warning.

The necessity that compels me to go immediately into the upper country, to put it into a proper attitude of defense, will greatly increase your responsibility, because, should circumstances require it, it will be your duty to call out the militia and defend this country, during my absence, as you will perceive by a reference to the law.

The danger at present is considerable, but I expect it will be of short duration, as every effort in my power has been used to procure assistance. I doubt not those efforts will be crowned with success.

At present it is not proper that either you or I should merely content ourselves with issuing orders. We must turn out actively and help to execute them.

Yours, etc.,

NINIAN EDWARDS.

To COL. THOS. LEVINS, *Commanding 1st Regiment Militia, R. C.*

ELVIRADE, RANDOLPH COUNTY,
March 14, 1812.

Dear Sir :

I hope the sincere desire which I feel to serve the people of this Territory, and their having no delegate in Congress, will be accepted as an apology for the trouble which this letter will give you.

At no time, since the organization of this government, have the people, as far as I can learn, been better satisfied with their Territorial officers than at the present juncture. But a variety of different wishes and motives have combined to induce them to wish to enter the second grade of Territorial government, merely for the purpose of obtaining a delegate to Congress, which I always supposed might with as much propriety have been allowed them, without their being obliged to incur, for that purpose alone, the expenses of the second grade—more especially since, if the same rights should be extended to them that are enjoyed by the Indiana Territory, the delegate will be wholly independent of the Legislature.

The population of this Territory, as appears by the late census, amounts to 12,282, in the whole of which there does not exceed between two and three hundred freeholders, (two hundred and twenty, I am convinced, is the extent.) This is owing to the sale of public lands being postponed much beyond any period that was anticipated, from the appointment of a Register and Receiver to this District. This very small portion of freeholders have the exclusive right of determining upon the contemplated change of government, after which they alone will have the right to vote for the members of the Legislature, who will be elected for two years, with the right to nominate the Council, who will be appointed for five years, by which a small minority will have the power to fix upon a very large and respectable majority of their fellow citizens a course of measures which may not be changed, however disagreeable to the majority, for five years. Even if the danger to be apprehended should be problematical, still such is the jealousy and independence of freemen, that they never will be satisfied to depend for the security of their rights upon the courtesy of others.

A number of petitions have been presented to me, by the freeholders, in favor of organizing a General Assembly, and not one against the measure has been received—so that there is no doubt that the change will very soon take place; and I have this day issued a proclamation for taking, in a formal manner, the sense of the freeholders on this subject.

Under these circumstances I am sure I do not miscalculate, when I suppose your attachment to republican principles will lead you to wish to extend their salutary influence to the people of this Territory, by enlarging the right of suffrage. It is the more just and necessary because it is not the fault of the people that they are not freeholders, for many of them are able and anxiously waiting to buy land, as soon as the public sales shall be opened. These sales will certainly commence shortly, and the number of freeholders will thereby be greatly augmented. Yet, unless immediate provision be made for them, they may, for the reasons before given, be excluded from the benefits of representation for five years.

These considerations also demonstrate the propriety of giving the people of this Territory the right to elect their delegate to Congress, as was done for Indiana whilst this Territory was an integral part of that. A delegate was designed to represent thewhole people of the Territory, and not any particular description of citizens only. Except as to the right of voting in Congress, he stands precisely in the same relation to the people of a territory that any representative in Congress does to the people of his district. Why, then, should the election of the one be made by the Legislature, and the other by the people themselves? It is more necessary that the people here should have this right secured to them, than any where else; for, owing to the peculiar situation of this Territory, in consequence of the sale of public lands being so long delayed, one hundred and thirty freeholders, having an interest distinct from that of the great body of the people, by uniting would constitute the majority of the freeholders, and could elect the delegate in opposition to the interest and wishes of all the rest of a population consisting of 12,382 persons. It surely is enough that such an inconsiderable minority should possess the power of legislating for the whole Territory; but to secure, also, the additional advantage of a delegate to Congress, is a reason strongly urged to pass into the second grade of government before the public sales shall open, and thereby increase the number of persons who could participate in the equal rights of free government.

Independent of the reasons growing out of the peculiarity of our situation, in favor of the measure, it is strongly recommended by considerations of justice and policy, upon general principles. Our House of Representatives will consist of seven members, the Legislative Council of five—making, in the aggregate, twelve. While these men have the sole right to elect the delegate, scenes of intrigue will constantly present themselves, which, while they may gratify the ambition of individuals, will greatly disturb the repose and tranquillity of our Territorial government, and hazard much of the best interests of the best citizens thereof.

The situation of the settlers between Kaskaskia and the Ohio most cogently demands consideration. The appointment of a Register and Receiver to this District, several years ago, induced the people to believe (as the obvious and common duty of such officers is to sell lands and receive money) that the sale would very shortly thereafter commence—by which means they were induced to settle on the lands they proposed to buy. They now constitute at least one-third of the whole population of the Territory, and a great portion of them will become freeholders as soon as the sales shall be open. Yet, unless Congress interposes to extend to them the rights of suffrage, etc., they must be deprived of the benefits of representation. The ordinance, and laws amendatory thereof, require that so soon as the Governor shall receive satisfactory evidence that the organization of the General Assembly in the Territory is the wish of the majority of the freeholders, he shall order an election for representatives, whose numbers shall not be less than seven or more than nine, and these he shall apportion to the several counties in the Territory according to the number of free males above the age of twenty-one years. At present there are but two counties in the Territory, so that I must give at least four representatives to one and three to the other. This power is given to the Governor for the purpose of getting the second grade of government into operation, after which he has no power to apportion the representation by taking a member from one or both the counties to which he had previously given them. This must depend on the Legislature, which will consist of the representatives of two counties only, and it is not a safe calculation that they will have magnanimity enough to relinquish all that justice would require. The people of whom I have spoken as residing between Kaskaskia and the Ohio, in Randolph county, will be counted for it in the apportionment of representatives, and yet will have no vote. If I separate those people from Randolph by laying off a new county, (which I have only been prevented from doing in consequence of their being, in legal estimation, intruders on the public land,) and should apportion to them their share of representatives, still I do not know that there is one man among them who is qualified to be a representative by having a freehold of two hundred acres of land, and not more than three or four qualified to vote by having a freehold in fifty acres—which are the qualifications fixed by the ordinance.

Convinced, as I am, that nothing more than a fair representation of the situation of the people of this Territory, at the present time, to Congress, can be necessary to procure the justice which their situation imperiously calls for, I beg leave in this behalf most earnestly to entreat your aid in procuring the passage of a law to extend the right of suffrage *in all cases*, and for the election of a delegate to Congress by the people at large, instead of by the Legislature. An early passage of the law, alone, can secure the advantages which it may propose, or otherwise the second grade will be forced on, so as to defeat its beneficial purposes. The business of Territories, however urgent, it is understood is too often postponed, when they are unfortunately not represented, because no one particularly feels sufficient interest to take upon himself, exclusively, the trouble of preparing and attending to it.

If, under such circumstances, the people should be fortunate enough to obtain your aid, I am sure they will feel and be proud to acknowledge everlasting obligations to you. I would thank you to inform me what may be the prospect of having the right of suffrage extended, because, should I be assured that that event would certainly take place, I would postpone the elections a little beyond the period I should otherwise appoint for them. I therefore shall be greatly obliged if you can find it convenient to write me on the receipt hereof.

Your friend,

NINIAN EDWARDS.

To HON. R. M. JOHNSON, *in Congress.*

ELVIRADE, RANDOLPH COUNTY,
March 15, 1812.

Dear Sir:

I received your letter yesterday, by Mr. Moore, and although it furnishes no ground to question the correctness of your motives, yet I learn with extreme regret that you should have felt it necessary to have called any court-martial for the trial of any officers, for speaking disrespectfully "of the Executive of the Territory and their superior officers," without intending any reflection of the least unfriendly nature. I am fearful that a little too much hastiness of temper, or too much zeal if possible, or the want of due reflection as to the nature of the late orders, have had rather too great influence on your mind.

At a time when the pressure of circumstances require much individual sacrifice, it is natural that feelings and not reason should predominate among those from whom those sacrifices are necessarily required; and, being one of the defects of our natures, great allowance should be made for it. For my own part, I feel such sensibility to the privations, inconveniences and sacrifices that a call on the militia always produces on my fellow-citizens, however necessary it may be, that I can bear their complaints without the least resentment.

As to the late orders—so far as they were for the purpose of raising volunteers, their very essence and nature implied a liberty as free as air itself, and no opposition from any quarter whatever could, therefore, in this view of the subject, be at all illegal, nor consequently any offense. Being a matter of mere choice, one man had as great a right to advise against it as another in favor of it; and when men exercise *a right*, however injudicious it may be, they are liable to no official censure.

As to myself, I certainly desire very much that no charge may be exhibited against any man for any abuse of me.

If I am misrepresented, time and the uniform tenor of my conduct will prove a corrective. Many a worthy man, seeing my actions through a false medium, may innocently mistake my views and motives. Many may have had erroneous information, and all are liable to the domination of prejudice in a greater or less degree. Force always aggravates these errors and false views, but never corrects them; and from any opinion the people may be led to entertain, concerning me, I can apprehend no danger—for whenever it may become actually necessary, I shall completely have it in my power to silence clamor and convince them that their substantial interests have, at all times, occupied my thoughts and engaged my most industrious exertions.

These things are always best attempted when clamor has exhausted its utmost fury. The times are now pretty hard at best, and, from the most friendly motives, I advise great moderation and forbearance, having no doubt that my candor and frankness will not be misconstrued by you.

Your most obedient,

NINIAN EDWARDS.

To Col. Wm. Whiteside.

P. S.—I am informed that the militia were greatly dissatisfied at not seeing me on the 3d of March. I had certainly not promised to attend, but there is nothing that would have gratified me more, had I not been obliged to return home to send off for arms, which I actually did. It must be understood that when my duty calls, I must obey; and no reasonable man can be dissatisfied, on reflection. I wish this thing understood.—N. Edwards.

Elvirade, Randolph County,
March 15, 1812.

Sir:

I am gratified by the faithful and attentive manner in which you have executed my orders in your town up the Illinois River. If Major Whiteside has any thoughts of going to Peoria, or invading the Indian territory at present, I certainly wish him stopped. This would have a very bad effect, when I have sent a messenger to the Indians who reside there, and might jeopardize his life.

I wish Major Whiteside strictly to execute the orders I gave him, but not to exceed them.

NINIAN EDWARDS.

To Col. Wm. Whiteside.

St. Louis, *February* 27, 1812.

Sir:

I have had information that a Mr. Lucas is now trading with the Indians on the Mississippi, at a point nearly opposite the mouth of Jefferson, and that certain other gentlemen are trading on the Illinois River—with all or some of whom, I am informed, you are interested. Not being at home, I cannot now ascertain whether those gentlemen have a license from me, and, if you have any interest in their adventure, I should be glad to hear from you on the subject.

Whether those gentlemen are licensed, or not, our relations with those Indians are of such a character that a continuation of further intercourse with them, for the present, is wholly inexpedient and must be discontinued. A letter addressed to me at Cahokia will reach me, as I shall continue there some days.

Your obedient servant,

NINIAN EDWARDS.

To GOV. HOWARD, *St. Louis, Mo.*

ELVIRADE, *March* 23, 1812.

Sir:

I have the honor to inform you that I have this moment received communications from Chicago, Peoria and Fort Madison, which leave no rational doubt of the decidedly hostile views of the major part of the Indians between the Lakes and the Illinois and Mississippi Rivers.

Strong circumstances are stated which seem to justify a belief that the Sioux have joined or are about joining the hostile confederacy, and, if so, it will be the most formidable one with which the Western country has had to contend.

One of the soldiers at Fort Madison was murdered on the 3d inst., in the most barbarous manner, within a mile and a half of the fort. An attempt was also made to shoot one of the guard. No one dare venture out of the fort; and every one within believes it in danger of being taken.

Yours, etc.,

NINIAN EDWARDS.

To HON. WM. EUSTIS, *Secretary of War.*

P. S.—I have a company of rangers still out to defend the frontiers, co-operating with those that Gov. Howard has ordered into service. I have taken this measure upon my own responsibility, from the urgency of the case, and I stand personally pledged to pay the men. My situation is very unpleasant, and unless I shall be shortly authorized, they will abandon the service, in spite of every effort I can make.—NINIAN EDWARDS.

ELVIRADE, RANDOLPH COUNTY,
March 2, 1812.

Sir:

Herewith I send you the commission which I have just received from Hon. William Eustis, Secretary of War, appointing you a Captain of Rangers.

Accompanying the said commission was a letter from the Secretary, from which I give you extracts.

If you accept the commission, you may take the oath of fidelity to the United States, and the oath of office, before some judge or justice of the peace.

You must return a muster-roll and pay-roll of all the men that have been in service, under any order, from the 3d of March to 14th of April, at which time you were directed to organize your company under the law of Congress.

From the 14th inst. you will consider your company as enlisted, according to the forms herewith sent. These, certified by you and countersigned by myself, will constitute the proper voucher for payment.

You may discharge those men who were enlisted, by any order, for three months, as fast you can supply their places by the enlistment of others for twelve months, according to the foregoing instructions—always observing to muster your men when you discharge any, upon receiving new recruits, and be very particular to note the term of enlistment of each man.

You are so to arrange matters as to subject the three months' men to as little inconvenience in discharging them as possible. You may discharge any of them who wish it, provided your company will not, in your opinion, be too much weakened by it.

Considering the service you are, by existing orders, required to perform, your company must not exceed sixty-eight men, including the non-commissioned officers. As often as you have an opportunity, let me hear from you. I presume opportunities will frequently occur from Fort Madison. Request Mr. Payton to keep notes of everything remarkable in the geography and situation of that part of the country in which you are now stationed. He is very competent, and the information will be useful to me.

NINIAN EDWARDS.

To Capt. Wm. B. Whiteside.

Elvirade, Randolph County,
May 6, 1812.

Sir:

About four weeks ago I had the honor to receive your letters of the 28th of February and 11th of March last, just as I was starting to the county of St. Clair, to hold a council with the Ottaways, Chippeways, Kickapoos and Pottawottamies. After the council was over I found it absolutely necessary to visit our extreme frontiers, from which I returned only two days past, considerably indisposed and enfeebled by fatigue and a severe attack of intermittent fever. On my return home I had the honor to receive another letter from you, of the 16th of March, and shall proceed to reply to the whole of them as well as my health and strength admit.

For the leading features of the council I beg leave to refer you to the inclosed newspapers, which also contain other important information that can be relied on. In my speech to the Indians I intended, also, to operate on the traders (many of whom attended) by convincing them that their trade depended on the preservation of peace. I was, so far, successful, and I have no doubt all of them will use their utmost exertions to promote our views in regard to the Indians. I endeavored to satisfy them that we had no intention or wish to take their lands from them. Upon this subject they had great uneasiness, and I fear that our policy of buying their land too frequently has given rise to it. My own opinion is, that no contract of the kind ought to be attempted with the chiefs, unless the whole tribe had previously manifested a willingness to it.

On the receipt of your letter, of the 11th of March, I at once determined to take Captain Whiteside's rangers and a company of militia with me to the River Sainquemon, and to have built a fort where the trail from Cahokia to Peoria crosses the river. This I designed, for the present, as a station for the rangers. It is about one and a half day's march from Peoria. I could have thrown any quantity of provisions into it, and the whole body of troops intended to build the fort at Peoria, without giving them the least ground to suspect my intentions. I also intended to direct Mr. Forsyth (the sub-agent), or some other reliable person at Peoria, to procure a quantity of logs, for the apparent purpose of building for himself two large cabins, and to have them all collected at a proper point, when, everything being in readiness, I contemplated a forced march to Peoria, to seize the logs, split them, and instantly have erected a fortification that we could have defended. From this plan I was diverted by the necessity I found myself under of giving an entirely different direction to the rangers to repel the attacks of the Winnebagoes and others.

I am now using all the address in my power to get the Indians to consent to the erection of the contemplated fort without being seen or suspected in it. If they do not consent, I can assure you that one thousand picked men will not be sufficient to effect it. It might have been easily done in the spring, before the Indians returned from their hunt, but they are all now concentrating their forces about Peoria, and, with five days' previous notice, can rally a force of 1000 warriors, independent of any assistance from the Prophet, whose village is only four days' march from theirs; and it ought to be observed that, though the Prophet cannot prevail upon all those Indians to unite with him on the Wabash, because they have not taken a decided part against us, yet there would be no difficulty in their procuring his aid, and he would gladly change the seat of war, in consequence of the prospects which their invitation would hold out to him.

Whatever may be the difficulties of building the fort, the advantages will be in proportion to them—which will be obvious to you from the rough geographical notes I intend to send herewith, if I shall be able to set up long enough. I have heretofore taken great pains to acquire necessary information for any object the Administration may contemplate in this quarter, and shall continue to do so; that which I intend to transmit I am sure is substantially correct. Information from the Indians with whom I held the council, from the Sacs and Foxes, from Prairie du Chien, from Peoria, Chicago and a number of traders in different directions, confirms the hostile machinations of the Prophet and the determined hostilities of the Winnebagoes, who, it was agreed, were approaching our frontiers in different directions with hostile intentions, which the Indians above mentioned say nothing but death can prevent them from executing.

Under these circumstances, Gov. Howard and myself held a conference and concerted measures of coöperation: his rangers to guard the usual ingress to Louisiana, about 120 miles above St. Louis, on the Mississippi, and Capt. Whiteside to occupy the ground from the same point on the Mississippi to the mouth of Sangamon, on the Illinois River—the point on the Mississippi and that on the Illinois, required to be occupied, not exceeding a day and a half's march. To complete the measure of defense, I was obliged to order out a volunteer company of mounted riflemen, to range from the mouth of Sangamon, up it and in an eastern direction to the heads of the Kaskaskia, a distance of between 70 and 100 miles, covering our north-western frontier. With one-half of the company of mounted riflemen, the Captain regularly commences his route from the mouth of Sangamon, while the Lieutenant, at the same time, with the residue of the company, commences his from the heads of the Kaskaskia, and they alternately pass to each others. The ground thus occupied by Whiteside and the mounted riflemen, by an arrangement with the Indians, was agreed on as the boundary for them, and us also, till some change of circumstances should take place.

I could have no difficulty, if I could have a personal interview with you, in convincing you of the propriety and absolute necessity of those arrangements; and even in the imperfect mode of satisfying you that is alone allowed me, I still hope I shall not have much difficulty. But it will not long be possible for me, without I shall be enabled to give the people some assurance that they will be paid by the Government, to turn out, upon any sudden emergency, a force sufficient to meet it. Already have I had great difficulties, independent of performing almost the drudgery of a corporal, to effect as much as I have done, and in organizing Whiteside's company upon my own responsibility, I had to pledge my private fortune for the payment of them. It is now well understood that had not Gov. Howard and myself taken those measures on our own responsibility, our frontiers would have been deluged with the blood of our fellow-citizens. About that time a party of Indians, (under White-hair, a Pottawottamie chief,) consisting of about sixty, were within thirty miles of the frontier, and had actually agreed to commence hostilities and retreat to the head of the Illinois River. One hundred and fifty warriors were below Peoria, on the river, many of whom would have followed White-hair's example. The Kickapoos certainly did murder O'Neal's family on the Mississippi, thus affording melancholy evidences to fortify the opinion, that I have constantly maintained since Gov. Harrison's battle, *that the danger was not over*, and that all the benefits of that battle would be lost unless it should be succeeded by measures to coerce satisfaction for all past aggressions. Should we have war with England, peace with the Indians need not be expected till, by excluding them from all British trade, withdrawing all our own traders and pushing a vigorous campaign against them, they shall be brought to their senses—which these measures would soon effect. None of the rangers destined for the defense of the frontier have yet arrived. The present is the time when, of all others, we have cause to apprehend most danger, and I hope, under such circumstances, I shall stand justified in calling out the company of mounted riflemen and continuing them in service till the arrival of some company of rangers. I feel anxious on this subject. Had I a right to exercise any discretion, I should have no dread of the responsibility; but I have no such right.

Whiteside, under my order, mustered into service seventy-two men on the 3d of March, enlisted for three months. These continued until the 14th ult., when I received your letter and directed the organization of the company conformably thereto.

It is impossible for the rangers to supply themselves with rations and be as serviceable as they otherwise might be. I have already had to become responsible for a deposit for them at their station on the Mississippi, which they agree shall be deducted out of their pay—a measure they at all times prefer. I most sincerely hope those men called out by my order may be paid: without which, either they or myself must be greatly injured; and I believe Gov. Howard and his rangers are in precisely the same situation.

Capt. Whiteside accepts his commission, and I think will do honor to it.

I recommended William Savage as First and Isaac Hill as Second Lieutenants. They were chosen by the company, and I have since become acquainted with them and approve the choice. Mr. Greene, whom I mentioned in my last letter, was chosen Ensign. He is a very brave man, but I cannot recommend him as an officer. For Ensign I recommend Craven Peyton, who was one of the first men who joined the company, has already distinguished himself, and, in my opinion, will make a first rate officer. Should a commission come for Greene, I shall not deliver it till I receive an answer to this letter, hoping that Peyton's will not be delayed for the return of Greene's.

I have a relation living with me, whom I have been educating—the son of a man who spent his best days and his whole fortune in the American Revolution. This youth is between seventeen and eighteen years of age. His name is Benjamin Sanford Edwards. I am very desirous of getting him into the military school, and will thank you to inform me whether my wishes in this particular can be gratified.

I have the honor, etc., etc.,

NINIAN EDWARDS.

To HON. WM. EUSTIS, *Secretary of War.*

P. S.—Two rangers of Louisiana a few days ago attacked and killed two Indians, on the east of the Mississippi, without receiving any injury. The Indians are said to be Winnebagoes.—N. E.

ELVIRADE, RANDOLPH COUNTY,
ILLINOIS TERRITORY, *May* —, 1812.

Sir :

The Pottawottamies of the Illinois River are divided into three bands, viz: That of Gomo, the principal Chief, consisting of about one hundred and fifty men, who now reside on the Peoria Lake, seven leagues above Peoria. Pepper's band, at Sand River, about two leagues below the Quin-que-que, consisting of about two hundred men, of different nations—Pottawottamies, Chippeways and Ottaways. Little Chief was, last year, head of this band. He is now dead, and Pepper has succeeded him. Letourney and Mettetat, brothers, both Ottaways, are war chiefs of this band, under Pepper. Their village is fifty leagues above Peoria and twenty below Lake Michigan.

Main-pock's band, consisting of fifty men, residing seven leagues up the Quin-que-que. This chief is reputed brave and desperate, although his number of men is less than either Pepper's or Gomo's. He is said to have more influence, in collecting followers for an enterprise of any kind, than both the others. His influence is very considerable with some of the bands on the south and east of Lake Michigan.

At Little Makina, a river on the south side of Illinois, five leagues below Peoria, is a band, consisting of Kickapoos, Chippeways, Ottaways and Pottawottamies. They are called *warriors*, and their head man is Lebourse or Sulky. Their number is sixty men, all desperate fellows and great plunderers.

On Fox River, which empties into the Illinois River at the Charbonierè, or Coal-pit, about thirty-five leagues above Peoria, there is another band, consisting of Pottawottamies, Chippeways and Ottaways. Wa-bee-sous is their leader. Their number is not less than thirty. The river on which they reside takes its source from Mil-waa-kee. The principal part of the other Pottawottamies reside on the River St. Joseph, that empties into Lake Michigan, and they have on that river three or four villages.

The Kickapoos in the Illinois Territory are divided into three bands. Pam-a-wa-tam is the principal chief. His band consists of one hundred and fifty men. They have left their old village, and are now building a village on Peoria Lake, three leagues from Peoria.

Little Deer has also left the great village, and is now building one opposite Gomo's village. His band consists of one hundred and twenty.

The other Kickapoos are those above described, who live at Little Makina below Peoria. From these three bands of Kickapoos there are now with the Prophet about one hundred men.

At Mil-waa kee, thirty leagues from Chicago, just on the west of Lake Michigan, there are several villages of Pottawottamies and Fulsowines.

At Sauk River, on the same side of the lake, is a village of Ottaways and Chippeways. At Sha-boi-ee-gan is another village of Ottaways and Chippe ways. From this river to Green Bay it is twelve leagues. At Two Rivers there is another village of Ottaways. Between Two Rivers and Little Detroit there are two villages of Ottaways. At the Little Detroit there is another village of Ottaways. This is fifty leagues from Michillimacinac. At Manisteé, thirty leagues from Michillimacinac, is another village.

The Winnebago village of Rock River is between thirty and forty leagues above the mouth of the river; it is about two days' march from Peoria. The country is prairie, or very fine, open woodland.

From the village of Rock River to the old Winnebago village on Lake App-quay, or the Fox River of Green Bay, it is one day's journey; and to Milwaa-kee, can be traveled in one day and a half.

From Peoria to the villages of the Sacs and Foxes, it can be traveled in three days at most. The Sacs have eight hundred and the Foxes six hundred warriors.

From Peoria to the Prophet's town, it is about four days' journey, over fine, high, dry country.

At the carrying place at Chicago, three leagues from the fort, is a village of Pottawottamies and Ottaways, of three hundred men.

Five leagues from Chicago, on the south side of Lake Michigan, is a river called the Little Calamick, on which there is a village, consisting of about one hundred men, of Pottawottamies, Chippeways and Ottaways. Old Cam-pig-nam was their chief last year. One of his hands has been greatly injured by a burn, and his nose has been broken or cut to pieces. It was reported that he was killed this spring in going from Detroit to Niagara. Nan-non-quy was the second chief, and, probably, will be the first.

Thirty leagues from Chicago is the river St. Joseph. Ten leagues up that river is a village of about ten Pottawottamies; no particular chief to lead them.

At the Terrecoupé is a village of about one hundred Pottawottamies. This village is ten leagues, by land, to the lake. It is also about thirty leagues to Chicago, over fine, open country and good traveling.

On the St. Joseph, about forty leagues from its mouth, is another small village of Pottawottamies, at the mouth of a small river called the Riviere Pivellee (or Speckled River.) The chief is called Nan-neck-quai-bee.

On Stag-heart River, ten leagues from its mouth, is another small village of Pottawottamies. Their chief is Nan-quai-sai. Stag-heart River empties into the St. Joseph. The most of those Indians described as being on the south of Lake Michigan and on the St. Joseph or its waters, are now with the Prophet, on the Wabash.

At the mouth of the River Kick-kaa-la-maa-zo, which empties into the lake fifteen leagues beyond St. Joseph, is a village of seven or eight men. About twenty-five leagues up the river is a village of Pottawottamies and Ottaways, of sixty or seventy men.

On Grand River, which empties into the lake ten leagues beyond the Kick-kaa-la-maa-zo, there are four villages of Ottaways, altogether containing about two hundred men. The first village is about three leagues from the mouth, the second about fifteen, the third about twenty-five, and the fourth about forty leagues. This last is on a small river called Riviere des Plains. Grande Riviere goes near Detroit.

On Mush-kee-gom River, which is four leagues beyond Grande Riviere, there are two villages of Ottaways. The first, about fifteen leagues from the mouth, numbers about ten men. Peck-keoo-nai (or The Snake) is their chief. The others are about fifteen leagues up, and number about twenty-five men. Wampum is their chief.

On the bluffs, one league beyond White River, which itself is four leagues beyond the Mush-kee-gom, is a village of Ottaways, called the Bluff Village; number of men about seventy or eighty. On Pierre Marquette River, which is twelve leagues beyond White River, is another small village of Ottaways; number of men about ten.

The total number of the Indians of the Illinois, including those of the portage of Chicago, is, therefore, 790 men, viz:

At the Portage	30	men.
Pepper's band	200	"
Main-pock's band	50	"
Wa-bee-sau's band	30	"
Gomo's band	150	"
P.'s band	150	"
Little Deer's band	120	"
At Makina, under Sulky	60	"
In all	790	men.

Those Indians, in the late council I held with them, told me they were about to settle themselves together in a large town at or near Peoria.

The facility with which those about the lake and St. Joseph's can join them is obvious, as they can transport themselves in canoes all the way, are constantly in the habit of passing in that manner, and most decidedly prefer it to any other mode of travel.

The proximity of the Indians between Lake Michigan and the Mississippi to Peoria, would enable all those bands to unite their forces in a very few days. If the Prophet should be driven from his present ground, or the Illinois Indians become decidedly hostile, he will rally all his forces on the Illinois River, from which he can do more injury to our people, with less danger to himself and his followers, than from his present station.

These notes already show that this is the most vulnerable frontier that belongs to the United States. But I will add further ones in regard to the Illinois River and its waters.

Names of the rivers emptying into the Illinois: River Fouchai is the first on the south side, and two leagues above the mouth of the latter; River Makapinn two leagues above Fouchai, south side; River Lenois four leagues from Mee ka-pinn, south side; River A'la Pomme two leagues from Lenois, south side; River Cha-bot two leagues above A'la Pomme, north side, (from here to the mouth of Salt River, on the Mississippi, the Indians can go and come in a day on foot); Mouse River four leagues above Cha-bot, south side, (one day's march, on foot, to the Mississippi—fine, open country); Blue River two and a half leagues above Mouse River, north side; Arrowstone River two leagues above Blue River, south side; Mauvaisterre River one and a half leagues above Negro River, north side, (from here near ten days' march to the Mississippi—fine, open country); Le Ballanson four leagues above Mauvaisterre, south side; Mine River, two leagues above Le Ballanson, north side, one and a half days' march to the Mississippi.

N. EDWARDS.

To the SECRETARY OF WAR.

ELVIRADE, RANDOLPH COUNTY,
ILLINOIS TERRITORY, *May* 12, 1812.

Sir:

I have the honor to acknowledge the receipt of your letter of the 7th ult., but as yet I have heard nothing from any of the companies of rangers that you informed me were to repair to this quarter for the protection and defense of the frontier.

This is particularly unfortunate at the present conjuncture, because a great part of the very object contemplated in providing this force will be lost by the delay. Every person acquainted with the Indian customs and habits knows very well that the present is the time to apprehend the most danger from their predatory parties. Their hunt is over, they are done making sugar, their women are all collected at their villages and preparing to make their corn. The men have now nothing to do but make war, and a thick foliage favors their mode of warfare—objects at all times appreciated by them.

Hitherto, with nothing to mislead or guide me beyond very humble pretensions to common sense, I have invariably held the opinion that there was no prospect of peace with the Indians, and that nothing could produce it but rigorous coercive measures on the part of Government. Others of superior information and experience have thought otherwise, and I find a difference of opinion must still prevail—not as to the existence of danger, but as to the nature of it. My own opinion is that the war will be carried on by the Indians, for some time to come, in small parties, who will infest the frontiers, attack all exposed parts, and surprise and murder men, women and children. A general attack upon some of our towns and villages may possibly happen, but I do not consider it a probable event at the present time. The Indians would not undertake such a measure without collecting a great force; and, although they can live on very little, yet I cannot foresee how they could calculate on providing enough for their support when collected together. They cannot depend on hunting; this is the time to supply themselves by plundering. The Prophet's store of corn was destroyed last fall. His ammunition and many guns were taken, and so serious were the consequences of the battle, that his party had enough to do to keep themselves from starving, and, therefore, had very little opportunity, by their hunt, to supply provisions sufficient for a campaign against one of our towns.

If, however, such a measure as this should be adopted, and the Illinois Indians should become decidedly hostile, the greatest danger is to this or Louisiana Territory. Many of these Indians were not in the battle of Tippecanoe. All of them cultivated their corn and none of them lost any, nor had they to encounter any extraordinary difficulties in their hunt. They are, therefore, better prepared. Their force is superior to the Prophet's, and, if the facility of traveling by water is any temptation to them, the Illinois is more easily navigated than any other water-course that could be used, and has no garrison on it to command or guard it. If they travel by land to St. Louis, of Louisiana Territory, and Cahokia of this, both are nearer to the

Illinois villages and to the Prophet's town than Vincennes is, as I am well informed; and it is well known that neither of those Territories can, with the same facility, obtain assistance from the neighboring States; and, moreover, a considerable portion of our population cannot so far lose sight of old customs and their former government, as to be sincerely friendly to ours.

The danger of these Territories will be greatly increased should the Prophet be driven from his present ground, and the Illinois Indians be hostile; for they will most certainly unite on the Illinois, from which they can do us immense injury. This consideration has led me to exert myself as much as possible to maintain peace with those on the Illinois, and nothing would contribute so much to aid those efforts as the display of military force. With that, I do believe they would be decisively successful. Otherwise, those Indians will openly declare war against us.

I may be wrong in all my conjectures, and the respect I feel for the opinions of others of more experience induces me to entertain my own with great diffidence; but till convinced of my error, I feel it my duty (although I may be mistaken) to suggest, most respectfully, to you, those opinions and impressions that I have deliberately formed, not upon a few isolated facts, but upon a combination of all circumstances that have come within my knowledge.

I do not think we have the less danger to apprehend in consequence of believing that a general attack will not be made on our towns, for already I think it highly probable that as many have been killed in this year as we lost in Gov. Harrison's battle. I do not recollect the exact number of either, and I cannot ascertain our late losses; but since I wrote you last, I have ascertained an additional account of murders committed in this Territory, containing men, women and children.

I am informed by a Colonel of militia that considerable mischief was lately done within between forty and sixty miles of the United States saline. By a letter of the 3d inst., he states that two militia Captains in that quarter had raised a party and had pursued the murderers, but had not returned on the date of his letter. In this way, we shall lose more than we should lose by a battle. Such repetitions of outrages will, I fear, embolden the hostile and fix the wavering against us. We have no security against those attacks but by carrying the war into the Indian country, and this we shall, in a few weeks, be unable to do; for then, the hot season comes on, and during its continuance it is utterly impossible to carry on any expedition on horseback through the prairies. Unless the Indians should be arrested in this kind of warfare, they will continue it till the corn begins to ripen, and then, I have no doubt, they will embody and attempt to strike some decisive blow.

I am extremely much in hopes that the protection, which has hitherto been contemplated for this quarter, will not be withdrawn. The people have been led to calculate on it, which has prevented many from leaving the country; and were it withdrawn, I should be charged with exciting false hopes, and rendering them victims to those expectations.

Our north-western frontier, I presume, is well understood. We are now very much imposed on by our eastern frontier. The settlements in this country generally extend up the Mississippi, with the exception of those on the Ohio; those settlements extend no where very far from the Mississippi. Their width is very inconsiderable, being bounded on the one side by the river, and on the other by the great prairies, that cannot be inhabited for want of wood and water. Every part, therefore, appears to be equally exposed; and so great and so just are the general apprehensions of danger, that it is impossible to draw out and embody the militia for any general measure of defense —each particular part being so much exposed, that it has no men to spare from its own defense.

The notes I promised to send you, by the last mail, I was then unable, from sickness, to prepare. I now send them—and, if it is desired, I will continue to send all such information as I may be able to collect hereafter. The ignorance which I labored under, on those subjects, when I first came here, has rendered me indefatigable in exploring all the sources of information that were accessible to me; but it is hardly probable that it can be equally important to you, and I have some fears that, from an anxiety, honest and sincere, to discharge my whole duty, I have sometimes been rather troublesome. If so, in my motives I hope you will see some apology.

I have the honor to be,
Very respectfully, sir,
Your most obedient servant,
NINIAN EDWARDS.

To HON. WILLIAM EUSTIS, *Secretary of War*, Washington City.

ELVIRADE, *May* 16, 1812.

Sir:

I have completely ascertained that the murder of the family, mentioned in my letter of February 18th, was perpetrated by a party of Kickapoos, residing near Peoria; the Indians acknowledge the fact. The great chief of the tribe has frankly communicated it to one of my agents, with a request that I should be informed of it. Gov. Howard has demanded these murderers of me, and I now await directions how to proceed. A demand at present, under existing circumstances, would, I think, be attended with no good effect and much expense. It might aggravate hostility and hasten the war, when we are totally unprepared to meet it—no troops of any description having yet arrived. Nothing but a display of military force can induce the Indians to surrender such number of murderers.

Yours, etc.,
NINIAN EDWARDS.

To HON. WM. EUSTIS, *Secretary of War*.

P. S.—Finding it necessary, I appointed Jacques Mette a resident interpreter, on the 17th of last month, at a salary of one dollar per day and one and a half rations.—N. E.

ELVIRADE, *May* 20, 1812.

Sir:

Some time last month I had the honor to receive your letter of the 10th of October last, requesting me to forward to the War Department a statement of the articles which the Indians under my superintendence wished to receive as their annuity for the present year.

Although I supposed the letter had reached me too late to answer the intended purpose, I immediately dispatched a letter to the Kaskaskia tribe, but could receive no answer in consequence of the absence of the chief, who had gone to the Delaware villages in Louisiana. They will, however, be content with the same articles they received last year. Hitherto no annuities have been sent to me for any other tribe, and really great confusion exists in our Indian department in this country. All except a small band of the Kickapoos reside in this Territory, and also a very large portion of the Pottawottamies, as you will perceive by the notes I have forwarded by the last mail. I am, *ex-officio*, Superintendent of Indian Affairs in this Territory, and I am destitute of that control and influence which the payment of annuities always produces, and the Indians themselves are distracted by the confusion of having a Father here and another at Vincennes. I beg leave to suggest that it would, in my opinion, be best to combine the whole business in the hands of Gov. Harrison or myself exclusively.

The annuities can be very conveniently sent to the Indians from this quarter, and I dare say they would prefer receiving them here.

Gen. Clark can give you every necessary information on the subject, etc.

NINIAN EDWARDS.

To HON. WILLIAM EUSTIS, *Secretary of War.*

P. S.—I have, as yet, heard nothing from the companies of rangers that you informed me were ordered on. The appearances of hostilities continue to increase. Some of our people have killed, as I am informed, about five Indians. The particulars I have not yet learned. I have removed all the Indians from this quarter who had not a right to reside here; and, to protect the Kaskaskia tribe, I have been obliged to call them in, and am now furnishing them rations at the public expense. This measure is absolutely necessary for our safety, as well as theirs.—N. EDWARDS.

ELVIRADE, *May* 20, 1812.

Sir:

I had the honor, a short time ago, to receive your letters of the 26th and 27th of March. Not a moment was lost in complying with the requisitions contained in the first, and the contents of the latter have been communicated to Col. Grant, etc.

N. EDWARDS.

To HON. ALBERT GALLATIN, *Secretary of Treasury.*

ELVIRADE, *May* 22, 1812.

Sir :

An express from the United States Saline has just reached me, with the inclosed communications, which tend to show the embarrassing situation in which I am placed—having no authority from the President to call out the militia, and believing the whole country to be in imminent danger. Acting, however, for the best, I shall sanction the order of Col. Trammul, and continue the men in service until I can hear from you on the subject, etc.

NINIAN EDWARDS.

To HON. WM. EUSTIS, *Secretary of War*, Washington City.

ELVIRADE, *May* 24, 1812.

Sir :

You will pay great attention to the movements of the Illinois Indians and all those in the neighborhood.

You will take every means in your power to ascertain when Main-pock will return and what his disposition may be towards the United States, and, if hostile, what forces he will be likely to raise. You will, on your return, employ Mr. LeClair to make a tour through the country between Lake Michigan and the Mississippi, visiting all the villages that you may deem necessary, particularly those of Milwaukee and the Winnebagoes. You will apprise him that it will be expected that he ascertain the dispositions and intentions of the Indians, as far as possible, and that, on his return, the best geographical description he can give of the country will be expected.

You are also to collect information, as far as practicable, of the designs of the Prophet's party—their operations and their force. You will transmit to me, as often as possible, such information as you may be able to collect. If anything important should transpire, you will hire an *express*, taking care that the news shall reach me in the least possible time.

You will have to incur some expenses for friendly Indians who may visit you. In all these things you will make the best contracts that you can, and be as economical in your expenditures as possible, consistently with the public interest and advantage. Those expenses I shall pay. Transmit to me, as often as possible, a list of your contracts and expenses.

Yours, etc.,

NINIAN EDWARDS.

To THOS. FORSYTH, ESQ.

ELVIRADE, RANDOLPH COUNTY,
May 26, 1812.

Sir :

I have the honor to inform you that, since my last letter to you, I have received communications from Terre Blanch, on the Peoria River, about thirty miles from the Prophet's town, dated the 3d and 27th of April, from which it appears that a large majority of the Indians of that quarter were at that time decidedly in favor of war with us, and that, within the space of a month, they had carried to that place about fifty stolen horses.

I have also received communications from Chicago, containing the account of the murder of two men at that place, and other hostile indications on the part of the Indians. By these communications I have also been informed that, on the first of this month, a man by the name of Francis Keneaum, a subject of Great Britain, and an inhabitant of the town of Maulden, in Upper Canada, with two Chippeway Indians, arrived at Chicago, where he was arrested as a spy or British emissary; and I now have in my possession a copy of on affidavit, made by him, in which he swears that, about the 14th of April, a Mr. Innis, a merchant, and brother-in-law to Capt. Matthew Elliott, Indian agent in Canada, applied to him to go to Green Bay on secret business, which he then refused; that afterwards he was employed by the same person, and was then on his way to Green Bay to meet Mr. Robert Dixon, merchant, of Mackina; that the two Indians were provided as guards for him; that he received a quantity of wrought silver, of British manufacture, consisting of brooches and ear-bobs (or ear-rings), was promised £25 in cash for his trouble, and that he believed the nature of his journey was relative to Indian affairs and sanctioned by Capt. Elliott. The Indians also acknowledged that they had been employed to accompany him.

I have also received a great deal of information from Peoria, consisting of movements at the Prophet's town, the passage of a number of Indians on their way to join him, etc., etc.—all tending to prove the intentions of hostility and the increasing strength of the Prophet's party. Every account I have received, lately, makes his number greater than it was last year.

The chiefs of the Indians on the Illinois are wavering—they do not take a decided part. I hope for the best; but I know there is no trusting to professions or appearances among them. In consequence, however, of some expressions contained in a letter I received from them since I wrote, I have determined to start my interpreter to them to-morrow with a demand for the murderers of O'Neal's family.

Mr. Forsyth, of Peoria, left my house yesterday. He thinks the murderers will be delivered up. He is a very intelligent, gentlemanly man, has a perfect knowledge of the Indians, and would make a first rate agent; but he positively refuses to take $700 per annum and one ration per day for his services as sub-agent, which, I understand, was what Gen. Clark was authorized to offer him. Finding him decided on this point, and determined to go to Detroit on his private business, I offered to pay him an increase of $200 per annum and two rations per day, out of my private funds (provided the Government would not increase his salary), if he would stay—believing, as I do, that Peoria is now a most important point to collect information of every kind calculated for our success, and to facilitate our intercourse with and command a control over the Indians. I am not bound for the above mentioned increase of salary any longer than I can hear from you on the subject; but I should be very happy if you would take the trouble of making some inquiries of Gen. Clark, whom you will shortly see. He is personally acquainted with Mr. Forsyth, and knows the importance of the point at which the services are required.

I believe Peoria to be the most eligible point, at or near the frontiers of the United States, that could be occupied. It is more central to a great number of Indians, and it is not so remote from our settlements but that they would derive nearly as much security from troops there, as if they were nearer —thus combining the usual advantages of troops at such places with the positive protection of our frontiers, which is never the case where garrisons are fixed too far in the interior of the Indian country.

I have the honor to be,
Very respectfully, sir,
Your most obedient servant,
NINIAN EDWARDS.

To Hon. Wm. Eustis, *Secretary of War*, Washington City.

Elvirade, Randolph County,
Illinois Territory, *June* 2, 1812.

Sir:

I have the honor to transmit, herewith, a "talk," which I sent a few days since to the Kickapoos. So much depends on the proper management of those Indians and their confederates on the Illinois, that I believe it is to be both an embarrassing and critical business, and, therefore, I feel desirous to exhibit to you not only what I have done, but the manner of doing it.

I should not have made the demand, but that it appeared so evidently invited by the chiefs, that silence might have been mistaken by them for an abandonment of any requisition for satisfaction. The whole of their professions may be, however, designed to lull us into a false security, whilst they are concentrating their forces and preparing for hostilities.

If they do not surrender the murderers, I am convinced they will immediately commence war. If they should comply with my demand, it will make an everlasting breach between them and the Prophet's party, and confirm them in a pacific disposition towards us.

If the Illinois Indians become hostile, they will over-run this Territory. They are able to do so, for our population is very much dispersed, and cannot be drawn out to any one point of danger; and in an enumeration which I caused to be made, some time since, there were only about 2,000 male inhabitants above the age of twenty-one in the whole Territory, and since that time the population is considerably diminished. Great alarm exists in the Ohio settlements, in consequence of an extraordinary assemblage of southern Indians, on the opposite side of that river. I have heard many particulars about these Indians, and have received some expresses from that quarter; but the accounts I have heard are not sufficiently authenticated to be depended on.

I have sent out spies to make discoveries, and shall probably be able, by the next mail, to transmit correct information on this subject.

Our danger does not seem in the least diminished, and, as yet, no company of any kind has arrived.

I have the honor to be,
Very respectfully, sir,
Your most obedient servant,
NINIAN EDWARDS.

To Hon. Wm. Eustis, *War Department*, Washington City.

Elvirade, Randolph County, *June* 16, 1812.

Sir :

Two days ago I received the answer of the Kickapoos to my demand for the murderers of O'Neal's family, consisting of ten persons. It abounds with complaints and recriminations, and contains a decided refusal to deliver up the murderers, contrary to expectation which they themselves had authorized by their previous communication to me, and by their conversations with Mr. Forsyth and Mr. Mette, my interpreter.

The Indians with whom I held my late council have failed to comply with the promises they made me. Large numbers are now collected together at the head of Peoria Lake. They have killed a number of cattle belonging to the inhabitants of the village, and have exhibited strong indications of a hostile disposition towards us. This change in their conduct is attributable to their communications with the Prophet's party, and to the influence of a party of Miamis that have lately joined them.

From the above and other circumstances, I am convinced they will commence hostilities as soon as they hear of a declaration of war against England, or as soon as they may be told that such an event will certainly happen; and with only about 1,700 militia men in the whole Territory, dispersed from one end of it to the other, I can see but little prospect of opposing them with success. But nothing in my power to do shall be left undone.

For further particulars, I beg leave to refer you to Mr. Forsyth's letter which I have the honor to inclose.

I have the honor to be yours, etc.,
NINIAN EDWARDS.

To Hon. William Eustis.

P. S.—Gov. Howard and myself have sent out a force to oppose three parties of Indians that have lately been discovered on the Mississippi River. One party below where O'Neal's family was killed, one on the east and the other on the west bank of the river, above Fort Madison, on which they are supposed to have some design.—N. Edwards.

ELVIRADE, ILLINOIS TERRITORY,
June 17, 1812.

Sir:

Some time past, I had the honor to receive a letter from the Honorable Secretary of War, stating that a force would be organized for the defense of our frontiers, which he supposed would remove the apprehensions of the people of this quarter, etc.

I lately received another letter from the same gentleman, informing me that you were to take the command of five companies of the rangers, authorized by law to be raised for the defense of the frontiers, viz: those of Ohio, Kentucky, Indiana and this Territory. And having understood that you left Frankfort, a short time since, for Vincennes, I address you at that place, supposing it probable my letter may reach you there.

I have, within a few days, received very interesting information relative to the Indians, which induces me to believe that not only our frontier, but the whole Territory is in great danger—on which account as well as another, your presence here, if convenient, would be very desirable. In five days, my functions as Governor expire. The Secretary is not here, and if he were, could not act till it is known whether I shall be re-appointed or not. Intending to do the best I can, I do not wish that my want of power to act should be known at a time when it may be highly important to act at all hazards.

I shall be very happy to hear from you, and would be much pleased to see you at my house.

Your most obedient,
NINIAN EDWARDS.

To COL. RUSSELL.

ELVIRADE, *June* 23, 1812.

Sir:

On Saturday last, I received official notice from Col. Russell that he had arrived at Vincennes for the purpose of taking measures for defending the frontier—in consequence of which, I have issued orders for discharging the force I have had in service, and which I had previously ordered out from the necessity of the case, till the measures contemplated by the Government could be got into operation.

The Colonel having stated that he was directed to confer with me, I have given him the best and most candid view which I was able to take of our situation, and have promised all the aid and co-operation in my power. My powers as Governor of the Territory have, however, expired.

The Prophet and his emissaries have been latterly very active in endeavoring to stir up all the Indians between Lake Michigan and the Mississippi. Several general councils have been held. The Chippeways and Sioux have been applied to.

Dixon, the British trader, has returned, with a considerable number of Indians, to Green Bay.

I have reason to believe that the point of communication between the British and the Indians, from whom we have everything to apprehend, will be on the St. Mary's, between Lakes Huron and Superior. This, together with the movements of the army in Michigan, will add to the inducements (now, I think, strong enough) to the Prophet to unite his party with the Illinois Indians; and if so, the whole weight of the hostile confederacy will be thrown on this Territory.

How such a number can remained embodied with the Prophet, I know not. The difficulty of procuring provisions must be very great, much more so than on the Illinois, for at the latter place the lake abounds with fish, on which the Indians can and do live; and if they should find it necessary to take the cattle that belong to the people of Peoria, there are enough to last them a long time.

Hitherto I have apprehended most danger from mere predatory parties; and, knowing the effects which the movements of troops have upon the Indians, I have kept my small force constantly in motion, ranging generally from the Mississippi to the Kaskaskia, and sometimes between the latter and the Wabash. These measures have been, so far, very successful, and, I think, in consequence, their small parties will be deterred from coming in; and as it can hardly be expected such extraordinarily large numbers of Indians can remain much longer assembled together without attempting something, a general attack is rendered much more probable than I have heretofore believed it.

By a communication I received since I forwarded Forsyth's letter, it appears that the number of Indians now embodied near Peoria is not less than seven hundred, and with the boats now in the river and the canoes in their possession, they could transport themselves to Kaskaskia in four or five days.

Respectfully, your obedient servant,

NINIAN EDWARDS.

To Hon. Wm. Eustis, *Secretary of War*, Washington City.

Elvirade, *June* 30, 1812.

Sir:

I had the honor to inform you, in my letter of May 6th, that I had found it necessary to call out a company of mounted riflemen to co-operate with the rangers in guarding our frontier. I presume the number of men, women and children who have fallen, bleeding victims, to the ruthless ferocity of the savages, and the concurring testimony of various spies, agents and sub-agents in support of the further hostile intentions of the Indians and their preparations to invade us, must be considered as having rendered the measure I have adopted not only justifiable, but an act of positive duty, independent of any sanction it might seem to derive from the law of Congress, which admits the danger upon less authority, by providing for our protection. A personal influence which I was fortunate enough to have with the volunteers I called into service, together with the most solemn pledges to exert myself to procure them compensation, alone enabled me to effect my plan. I soon found that it would be impossible to keep out any one company for any length of time, and I organized two volunteer companies, one under the command of Capt Moore and the other under Capt. Short—two as meritorious militia officers as I ever knew. These have regularly relieved each other every fifteen days, except during Capt. Short's last term, which was longer than usual. I was obliged to call out Capt. Moore's company to oppose a party of Indians who had collected near a different part of our frontier.

These men, I will venture to say, have performed as arduous services as ever were performed in the same length of time. They have ranged to a great distance—principally between the Illinois and the Kaskaskia rivers, and sometimes between the Kaskaskia and the Wabash—always keeping their line of march never less than one and sometimes three days' journey outside of all the settlements. They have sometimes been divided—one part marching in one direction and the other in an opposite way—with a view to distract the attention and produce the greatest possible effect on the Indians. And while the danger was only to be apprehended from small bands, intending to approach us from different directions, this plan was the only one, of a defensive character, that could insure any security. Its propriety is sufficiently tested by its success; for since it has been in operation, not a life has been lost on an extensive and the most exposed frontier that belongs to the United States.

By the arrangement of each of these companies relieving each other, it will be the same in effect as if only one company had been in the service; but as they had necessarily to keep in a state of preparation, and always lost time in collecting at the place of rendezvous, they may possibly be considered by you as having a claim to more compensation than for the actual time they were ranging. Many of them had to incur debts in equipping themselves, and their pay ought to pass through the hands of their Captains, one of whom has incurred expenses to the amount of about three hundred dollars for his men, depending on their receiving pay to reimburse him.

I have the honor to send, herewith, muster and pay-rolls for those companies—although in the pay-rolls the amount due is not stated, because I knew not what would be allowed.

After the depredations were committed on the Wabash, a company was ordered into service from the neighborhood of the United States saline, under circumstances which I have had the honor to communicate to you. From that company I have not yet received the muster and pay-rolls.

My measures having been wholly precautionary, and adopted till those contemplated by the Government could be got into operation, were abandoned and the whole force discharged as soon as I received a notification from Col. Russell that he had arrived at Vincennes for the purpose of defending the frontiers.

Very respectfully, yours, etc.,

N. EDWARDS.

To Hon. Wm. Eustis.

ELVIRADE, *June* 29, 1812.

Sir :

Since my letter of the 23d inst., I have received information, which I am sure can be relied on, that the plan which the British now mean to adopt for introducing their goods into the Indian country is to send them from their deposit in the Straits of St. Mary's, between Lakes Huron and Superior, by Indians in canoes, to Green Bay, where an agent will remain to receive them. The Indians who went on with Dixon are to be employed in this service, and it is supposed the non-importation will not be enforced against them, if they should even happen to pass undiscovered. If, however, this plan fails, the same Indians are to be employed in carrying the goods by land to some point on Lake Michigan.

A few days past, I received a communication from Gov. Harrison, stating that he had received information that twenty Pottawottamies had left their village to commit depredations "on the Kaskaskia road." I know not what road is meant; but from the manner in which Gov. H. received the information, I think it very probable that I shall hear of mischief being done somewhere in a few days.

Yours, etc.

N. EDWARDS.

TO HON. WM. EUSTIS.

CAHOKIA, *June* 29, 1812.

Governor :

Since I had the honor of writing you last, I have seen it stated, in the "Argus of Western America," of the 10th inst., that sometime previous Col. Wm. Russell had received orders to go to the Indiana Territory for the purpose of taking command of the six companies of rangers and the regulars of the U. S. Army. It is also stated that he is requested to correspond with Gov. Harrison, etc., on the subject relative to the situation of our affairs with the Indians. As all the information that can be procured, on that subject, will be desirable, I humby submit to you my observations—especially as it affects the community at large.

It appears to me that the great and principal object has been overlooked, to which you may probably procure some remedy. I think if all those Indians that I mentioned in my last to you, living about Lake Michigan, cannot be supplied by the British traders according to the President's proclamation, all their traders will therefore retire to their own country, and then all those tribes, amounting to some thousands, will consider themselves as abandoned and as it were, dead, and through despair immediately they will assemble all the nations around them, determined to conquer or die, and destroy us, our wives and children, before necessary assistance can be obtained. Thank God I may be mistaken, and if I am, it will be when the United States will send factors or traders among those Indians to supply them with merchandise and powder, etc., to support them and their families, for which they will exchange their peltries—then and not till then will they be peaceful.

But under our present regulation, we have not only taken from them our traders, but in their place we have supplied them with no others.

This far I have ventured to give you my opinion, and

Remain, with due respect,

Your most humble and obedient servant,

JARROTT.

ELVIRADE, RANDOLPH COUNTY,
ILLINOIS TERRITORY, *July* 7, 1812.

Sir:

I had the honor to receive yours of the 4th ult., by the last mail.

Nothing new has occurred since my last letter, except that one of the Captains was ranging fell in with a trail of Indians, near the settlements, which is supposed to have been made by the Pottawottamies. The trail was pursued without success, the Indians having separated, and very heavy rains having fallen about that time.

I have the honor to inclose you a letter from Major Jarrott, of Cahokia, to myself. He is one of the most intelligent, wealthy and respectable French citizens; was at Prairie du Chien when Mr. Dixon left there on his return. The letter to which the inclosed refers I cannot now lay my hands on. It, however, states that there were collected at Prairie du Chien, of different tribes of Indians, 3,377, and these I suppose are the Indians he speaks of as being collected on Lake Michigan.

I have forwarded returns from the militia, etc., agreeably to your instructions. Some of them were transmitted, under cover, to yourself, having been sent off before I received directions to send them to the paymaster of the army in the city of Washington.

The militia who have been in service have performed the duties of mounted rangers, and furnished themselves at their own expense with every thing.

Very respectfully, etc.,

NINIAN EDWARDS.

To HON. WM. EUSTIS, *War Department.*

ELVIRADE, RANDOLPH COUNTY,
ILLINOIS TERRITORY, *July* 20, 1812.

Sir:

I had the honor to receive by the last mail your letters of the 11th and 19th, to the contents of which I lost not a moment in giving the necessary attention. On the same day I dispatched a messenger to Peoria with a "talk," to the Indians assembled near that place, and urged them, by every inducement which I thought likely to succeed, to visit the Commissioners from the President at Piqua-town, in the State of Ohio. I also enjoined on my messenger to exert his influence with them to the same effect. I sincerely hope they will comply with the request; but I cannot flatter myself with a belief that they will certainly do so.

As some objection might be made, on their part, to the want of timely notice, I requested that they should set out as soon as possible, and go on, even if they should not be able to arrive by the 1st of August, but in this I have not, in the least, committed the President.

The Indians have, for some time past, been in real want of powder. They, however, are induced to believe that they will receive all their supplies at the British Fort of St. Josephs, between the Lakes Huron and Superior; and the British traders calculate upon carrying goods from Montreal to that place. It is owing to these circumstances, most probably, that such uncommonly large numbers are collected and collecting on the western borders of Lake Michigan.

I continue to believe that we may expect an attack in this quarter as soon as corn gets into roasting ears, which will be very shortly. The Indians remain embodied near Peoria, and have lately killed about twenty head of cattle, belonging to the inhabitants of that village.

Should Congress have passed a law for raising additional companies of rangers, and it be considered advisable to raise them in this quarter, I could have at least two companies raised and organized in a week's notice.

The situation of the principal settlements in this Territory and Louisiana, in relation to the Indians, is such as to require a concert and union of operations; for the danger of the one is completely identified with the other, which all former experience has proved, and which is sufficiently obvious from the Mississippi being the great highway of the Indians and the residence of those from whom we have most danger to apprehend—being either on it or some other river which empties into it above St. Louis—and wherever they can transport themselves by water, they will not travel by land.

I beg leave to recommend Capt. James Moore, of this Territory, as a gentleman well qualified to command a company of rangers.

I have the honor to be,
Very respectfully, sir,
Your most obedient servant,
NINIAN EDWARDS.

To Hon. Wm. Eustis, *Secretary of War*, Washington City.

Elvirade, Randolph County, Illinois Territory, *August* 4, 1812.

Sir :

On the receipt of the information which I had the honor to transmit to you with my last letter, I immediately proceeded to organize some companies of militia to oppose the threatened invasion, and went to the upper county of the Territory for the purpose of putting that force in operation, in which I succeeded with great ease, although I had no legal authority to act at all.

Whiteside's company of rangers has gone up to the Illinois River, in a well fortified boat, with a view to prevent the Indians from descending the river. This measure was rendered necessary by the impossibility of watching the river any other way, as, for miles above its mouth, swamp lakes and ponds prevent any access to it by land, and the well known habits of the Indians and the history of the country render it almost positively certain that, if they invade us, they will come by water.

Since my last letter I have received information from every quarter with which we have any communication, on either side of the Mississippi—all of which is confirmatory of that which was forwarded to you.

In April last I informed you that Dixon, the celebrated British trader, who spent the last winter on the river St. Peters, calculated with certainty that in the event of a British war, he could make peace between the Chippeways and the Sioux, and bring both these powerful nations into the hostile confederacy against us, and that of course all others in this part of America would be coerced to join it, if they were not inclined to do it as a matter of choice. It now very satisfactorily appears that those nations have made peace, and the Sioux are making a very conspicuous figure in the hostile confederacy.

The two Chippeway Indians who were apprehended at Chicago, as I informed you in my letter of May 26th, had taken the precaution to put their letters in their moccasins and bury them in the ground. After they were discharged they proceeded to Green Bay, where they delivered the letters to Dixon. A Mr. Frazier, of Prairie du Chien, who accompanied Dixon from that place, states that the latter was informed, in the letters alluded to, that he might expect to hear of the British flag flying on the American garrison of Michilimacinac.

Dixon wrote to his clerk, a Mr. Anderson, in Prairie du Chien, that the Indians had collected on Lake Michigan to receive guns, ammunition and merchandize, from the British.

Letters from Fort Madison, dated 21st ultimo, state that the Indians frequently threaten hostilities as soon as their corn is ripe, and that the Sacs set out for their villages on the 19th to make sweet corn—so, as they say, the critical time is drawing near.

I send herewith a speech that was made, in a late council which was held at the Sacs' village, by a Kickapoo, who spoke for the Winnebagoes, Kickapoos, Pottawottamies, Shawnees and Miamies, who were present.

The messenger whom I sent to Peoria to invite the Indians on the Illinois River to Piqua-town, returned last night with the answer of Gomo, the principal chief. He tries to evade the request, and states that if they go, they are afraid that if their Great Father should give them presents, he will say he has bought their lands.

He acknowledged to my messenger that the Indians had all tendered their services to the British. It is now well understood at Peoria that the Indians are for war, and are only waiting for directions from the British.

They contemplate an attack upon four different points at the same time: one party (and a very strong one, too,) is to attack the settlements on the Mississippi; another party (those east of Lake Michigan) to join against Gen. Hull's army; another to attack Chicago; and another to attack the Indiana Territory. Those near Peoria are now constantly killing and eating the cattle of that village.

The Sacs, Osages and Winnebagoes have all made peace, which itself is a very striking circumstance in considering our situation.

The Indians on the Illinois are well supplied with English powder, and have been selling some of it to the white people. A few days ago, they sent some of their party with five horses to the Sac village, for lead. Pamwotam, the great chief of the Kickapoos, was hourly expected to return from Canada.

In consequence of having received information from Fort Madison, Peoria and the Ohio, of some of the southern Indians intending shortly to join the hostile confederacy, and the report also being confirmed by information from a Shawnee at St. Louis, I dispatched a confidential Indian to the Shawnee village, near Cape Girardeau, in Missouri Territory, to collect all the information in his power. He returned last night, and informed me that there are now about 1,000 Indians on White River, and another river that empties into the Arkansas, consisting of Cherokees, Chickasaws, Chocktaws, Catawbas, and Creeks; that they are shortly to have a great meeting on White River, within about three days' journey from St. Genevieve; that the southern Indians who joined the Cherokees, in the course of the present year, crossed the Mississippi near Chickasaw Bluffs; that about two months ago the Creeks were carrying belts of wampum among the Shawnees, Delawares, Osages, Cherokees, etc., and that all of those Indians had been very friendly and had lately been intermarrying. He also states that the Shawnees have left their villages, and are going up the Missouri to hunt with the Osages; that the Cherokees expect to go shortly to the same place, with the same intentions, but he could not learn that they had any hostile views. These facts, when combined with others, admonish us to be prepared for the worst.

At the same time that I received the information that the Prophet and his companies were active in stirring up the hostility of the Indians between Lake Michigan and the Mississippi, which was communicated in my letter of June 23d, I was informed that a party of Creeks had left the Prophet's town and gone down the Wabash; and, from the coincidences of time and circumstances, I suspect they are the same persons who were engaged in carrying the belts of wampum among the Indians on the west of the Mississippi. The conduct pursued on each side of the river seems to be exactly similar; and another fact furnishes strong evidence that the belts of wampum were carried by hostile Indians—for the confidential Indian I employed also stated to me that it was some of those Creeks who were carrying those belts that committed the murders near Chickasaw Bluffs.

The Sacs are known to be decidedly hostile; and the Osages, with whom they were so lately at war, are, at this time, freely mixing with them, as I am positively informed by my messenger just from Peoria. This union certainly does not augur anything favorable to us; and to the same course that has produced it may be attributed the close connection or intimacy that has lately been cultivated between those Indians west of the Mississippi, which now appears to be leading them all to the same hunting ground. The suspicion I entertain derives some support, also, from the circumstance of the discontent manifested last year by the Osages, concerning their treaty with us.

About two weeks ago I was informed, by two Indians, who I think can be depended on, that the Cherokees of White River had proposed to the Shawnees and Delawares to remove and settle among them, and unite in the war against us; that the Shawnees and Delawares had refused, and the reply of the Cherokees was, that, if they would not join them, they should share the same fate of the white people. Connecting this circumstance with the silence of the Shawnees on the subject—their leaving their villages at this season of the year—their going among the Osages, where the Cherokees also propose shortly to go—and the conduct that has been practiced among the Indians generally, of late—suspicion is unavoidable with me.

In short, I believe there is a universal combination among the Indians. It has, in a great measure, been produced by the jealousy excited among the British fur companies by companies that have been organized among ourselves for similar purposes, and by the state of war.

Dixon, and the most intelligent of the British traders, have openly declared that, as they have been exclusively in the habit of supplying the great bodies of Chippeways and Sioux, all they had to do, to make them take part in the war, would be to threaten them that they would withdraw all their traders. Independent of the Indians west of the Mississippi and three hundred lodges of Sioux on the Wisconsin, we may certainly count on 4,400 who can reach the settlements on the Mississippi in six or eight days, and come all the way by water. Our danger is, therefore, very evident, and it is equal on both sides of the river.

The principal settlements of this Territory being on the Mississippi, are at least one hundred and fifty miles from those of Indiana, and immense prairies intervene between them. There can, therefore, be no concert of operations for the protection of their frontiers and ours. I have been obliged to write in great haste.

I have the honor to be, etc.,

NINIAN EDWARDS.

TO HON. WM. EUSTIS, *Secretary of War*.

P. S.—No troops of any kind have yet arrived in this Territory, and I think you may count on hearing of a bloody stroke upon us very soon. I have been extremely reluctant to send my family away, but, unless I hear shortly of more assistance than a few rangers, I shall bury my papers in the ground, send my family off, and stand my ground as long as possible.—N. EDWARDS.

ELVIRADE, RANDOLPH COUNTY,
ILLINOIS TERRITORY, *August* 8, 1812.

Sir:

In my letters of May 6th and 12th, and June 23d, I suggested the probability of the Prophet's uniting his force with the Illinois Indians, in the event of their becoming hostile.

In my letter of June 16th I informed you of a party of Miamies having gone to Illinois—since which, I have been informed, at different times, that more Miamies, the Kickapoos, Ottaways, and Pottawottamies have also left the

Prophet, and collected at the same place. Still later I was informed that the Prophet's party had dispersed; and all the above information is fully confirmed by a communication which I have seen from Mr. Wells, at Fort Wayne, dated July 29th.

He states that, on the 17th June, Tecumseh passed that place, on his way to Malden, to receive from the British twelve horse-loads of ammunition. He arrived at Malden a few days before Gen. Hull reached Detroit, and immediately declared he would join the British against the United States.

On the 12th of July, the Prophet arrived at Fort Wayne, with about one hundred of his followers. Seven days afterwards an express from Tecumseh arrived at the Prophet's camp, with directions to him to rally his adherents, send their women and children towards the Mississippi, and strike a heavy blow upon Indiana Territory, stating, also, that he (Tecumseh), if he lived, would join the Prophet in the country of the Winnebagoes, which is on Rock River between Lake Michigan and the Mississippi, and in this Territory. The succeeding day the Prophet dispatched two Kickapoos to execute the orders of Tecumseh, and they stole two of Mr. Wells' horses. Mr. Wells states that he has received the above information from a quarter that cannot be doubted. He thinks that if the Prophet should fail in rallying his followers, he, with some of them, will meet the Commissioners at Piqua-town. Whether he does so or not, and whatever his professions may be, I can place no reliance on him. He will probably attempt to temporize at that place, whilst his partisans on the Illinois and Mississippi are waging the most bloody war. My reasons for thinking so are, that such has been his insidious course hitherto. He will send off his women and children to the most hostile Indians, who refused to meet the Commissioners. Tecumseh is the real efficient man of the Prophet's party. He is going, also, to those Indians, having declared his hostility. The Prophet will not be our friend while Tecumseh is our enemy; and we have traced the Prophet in his hostile machinations in every quarter, in the course of this year, and it is hardly presumable that he will peaceably abandon the measures that he has been so diligent and laborious in maturing.

But this information, together with that which has been hitherto transmitted, proves that the great danger from the Indians is in this quarter. Particular circumstances have rendered the Wabash more conspicuous as a point of danger, but there never was a worse selected spot for the Indians, and they well know that they cannot, in a time of war, maintain it. It is too near Kentucky and it is too far from the residence of the most hostile Indians. Nothing hitherto has induced the Indians to rally there but because it was the only place where the hostile standard had been erected. The Prophet's main strength was composed of Winnebagoes, Kickapoos and Pottawottamies. They joined him whilst the tribes to which they belonged professed to be at peace; but, once let those tribes raise the standard, and there ceases to be any inducement for any part of them going elsewhere for the mere purpose of war.

This opinion is well fortified by the present movements of the Indians and the evidences they give of an intention to abandon the Wabash.

So intimately connected is the danger of this and Mississippi Territory, that Gov. Howard has requested my permission to remove a part of his troops into this Territory, which I have consented to, knowing it to be absolutely necessary to the safety of that Territory.

Col. Russell has arrived with his company of rangers, from Kentucky—about one-third of them sick. Some new recruits—less than a company—are expected daily to arrive. This is all the force we can calculate on in this quarter, as those at Vincennes are wanted at that place.

I have the honor, etc., etc.,

NINIAN EDWARDS.

To Hon. William Eustis, *Secretary of War.*

Elvirade, *August* 15, 1812.

Sir:

By Col. Rector, who is just from St. Louis, I am informed a report had reached that place that Gen. Hull had taken Fort Malden, and that information has also been received that it had rendered the Indians very pacific, particularly the Sacs. For my own part I hope for the best, while I think it indispensably necessary to be prepared for the worst. I cannot flatter myself that the capture of Malden, which is seven hundred miles at least from the Mississippi, will afford us any security, whilst Fort St. Joseph remains in possession of the British, who can keep up their communication with it by the Ottawa River, without the least danger from our troops. At the latter fort large deposits of Indian goods have been made, and you may be assured that the Indians have all received their present year's supplies. I confess, however, that I am greatly embarrassed by the prevalence of a general opinion, on this subject, adverse to mine; and I am extremely unwilling to incur unnecessary expenses to the General Government. But, relying upon my own judgment, which I cannot honestly abandon, and believing that the critical moment is rapidly approaching, I avail myself of your letter, received by the last mail, so far as to ask Gov. Scott for a regiment of infantry for our protection, although I have had no opportunity of conferring with Gov. Harrison on the subject.

Ever since June 24th, I have been acting as Governor, without any commission; and as I had the honor to communicate my situation to you, I am lost in conjecture as to the cause, etc., etc.

N. EDWARDS.

To Hon. Wm. Eustis, *Secretary of War*, Washington City.

Elvirade, *August* 25, 1812.

Sir:

Last evening I received a letter from Gov. Harrison, covering a copy of his of the 10th inst. to yourself, and I am sorry that I cannot concur with him in recommending what he calls the Fort Wayne Expedition. I cannot believe that Gen. Hull's situation, when he receives the reinforcements marching to his aid, can be as bad as is supposed, and I do believe that the very best means of preventing the collection of Indians from which the danger is apprehended, would be to march directly into their own country, to which they would immediately return to protect their property and their women and children. But suppose the expedition to march to Fort Wayne. It would, of course, deter the Indians from that quarter and turn their attacks upon this, where they might easily take several villages equally as important as Detroit; but for reasons which I have given in my letter to Gov. Scott, of which I inclose a copy, I have no apprehensions that our Indians will travel so far to unite with the British. As to the establishment of the chain of forts, it would be probably a good plan, provided we were not able to fight the Indians; but it would be vastly expensive to the United States.

I would recommend a different one. I would march an army to Peoria and there establish a fort; thence to the Wisconsin and establish another, and thus coöperate with the Michigan army, whose operations will tend to check the British from going amongst the Indians, while ours would effectually prevent the Indians from going to them.

By the plan of the chain of forts we would gain no ground, and it would be more expensive than a vigorous campaign, which, in my opinion, would in a short time dissolve the whole hostile confederacy and produce permanent peace with the Indians.

Something, however, I think, must be done, or the country will suffer greatly. Even if we were authorized to attack the Indians, it would be some security. And I cannot see what ought to prevent us from attacking them, for I will pledge myself to prove that all those now collected on the Illinois River have declared their hostility. They have the advantage of a declaration of war, whilst we are obliged to wait for the first stroke, however deadly, before we can attack them.

I am so unwell that I can add nothing further.

I have the honor to be, sir, etc., etc.,

NINIAN EDWARDS.

To Hon. Wm. Eustis, *Secretary of War*, Washington City.

P. S.—If it were proper in me to do so, I could, I think, assign many reasons to prove this: The defense of this Territory, Indiana and Missouri should be combined, and intrusted to some one person, provided a campaign should be directed.—N. E.

Elvirade, Randolph County,
Illinois Territory, *August* 26, 1812.

Dear Sir:

My own inclinations, as well as the directions I have received from the Honorable Secretary of War, combine sufficient inducements with me to comply with your particular request, of opening myself freely to you on the subject of your letter.

As to what personally concerns myself, I must say, I do not understand the Secretary's letters to you, Gov. Scott and myself, exactly as you appear to do· I conceive the power given to me to call for assistance from Kentucky for the purpose of mere defense, precisely equal to yours, which seems to be contrary to your opinion, so far as I can infer it from the manner in which you express yourself relative to Col. Barbour's regiment. So long as those troops remain in this Territory, and are engaged in its particular defense, I claim the right of the exclusive control of them. Whenever the defensive system shall be exchanged for offensive operations—for a campaign or expedition—then it will be my duty to comply with the Secretary's request.

Giving this construction to the Secretary's letter—and I highly approve of your being selected for the purpose contemplated—I well know that I have no claims which could be put in competition with yours. But if I am wrong in my construction of the letter, much as I appreciate your merits, and willing as I have always been to do the most ample justice to them, I am free to declare that I will not consent to anything further than I have suggested.

Believing that my frankness will not be considered inconsistent with the friendship I profess, I will as candidly state my wishes, provided a campaign should be determined on—hoping that you will, if it should be inyour power, aid me in the gratification of them.

I am extremely anxious to accompany you as second in command, whereby, with your assistance, I flatter myself I should soon supply by my industry the want of experience.

You will perceive, by copies of my letters to Gov. Scott, that my opinion must be, that what you term the Fort Wayne Expedition would leave this country too much exposed, or, in other words, that an expedition is more necessary in another quarter.

I cannot believe that Gov. Hull's situation, when he receives the reinforcements going to his aid, can be as bad as you suppose; and I do believe the very best means of preventing the collection of Indians from which the danger is apprehended would be to march directly into their own country, to which they would immediately return to protect their property and their women and children.

Suppose the expedition to march to Fort Wayne. It would, of course, deter the Indians from that quarter and turn their attacks upon this, for if they are hostile, they will attack somewhere; and if they are formidable enough to endanger Gen. Hull, they could easily take several villages on the Mississippi equally as important as Detroit. But, for the reasons mentioned in my letter to Gov. Scott, I have no apprehension that our Indians will travel so far to unite with the British at Malden.

As to the chain of forts, it would probably be a good plan, if we were not able to fight the Indians; but it would be a very expensive one to the United States.

Nothing will, I think, sufficiently guard against their hostile incursions, but one of two plans—an actual attack upon them, or such an exhibition and display of military force as will constantly keep up the apprehension of an attack on their villages, and thereby induce them to concentrate their forces for defense.

The plan which I should prefer would be to march an army to Peoria, establish a strong garrison there, and thence to Wisconsin and establish another, and thus coöperate with the Michigan army, whose operations will tend to check the British from going among the Indians, while ours would effectually prevent the Indians from going to them.

By the plan of the chain of forts we could gain no ground, and it would be more expensive than a vigorous campaign, which, in my opinion, would still dissolve the whole hostile confederacy, and produce permanent peace with the Indians.

Those of Illinois River have openly declared their hostility; and I do think that a just regard for the dangerous situation of our Territories commands prompt and decisive measures with regard to them.

I have the honor to be, sir,
Yours respectfully,
NINIAN EDWARDS.

To Gov. Harrison.

Elvirade, *August* 26, 1812.

Brig. Gen. Rector is hereby required to take the most prompt and effectual means for calling into actual service, according to law, four classes of the militia from each Company in the First, Second and Fourth Regiments of the Militia of this Territory.

All those now enrolled as volunteers are to be excepted from the draft.

The detachments from the First Regiment will rendezvous at Kaskaskia; that from the Second at the station in St. Clair, now occupied by Col. Russell, and that of the Fourth at the United States Saline, at which respective places those detachments will be mustered according to law, and await further orders.

The Commander-in-Chief requests to be notified of the earliest period at which those respective detachments can be prepared to march.

NINIAN EDWARDS,
Commander-in-Chief.

Camp Russell,
Frontiers Illinois Territory, *Sept.* 6, 1812.

Sir:

I am now at this place at the head of a considerable detachment of militia that I have ordered out for the defense of the Territory. In consequence of an order from Gov. Harrison, Col. Russell, with Capt. Moderal's company of rangers, start this day for Vincennes, and thus leave us without the aid of a single man who has not been raised in the Territory, whilst there seems to be a large force concentrated at Vincennes. I cannot perceive the propriety of such a procedure. Vincennes has never appeared to be in a particle of danger from any quarter except the Prophet's town. That danger is too inconsiderable to justify the claim of that place to such a proportion of the rangers. The Prophet's town is not a place that the Indians will pretend to maintain in time of war. Many years ago the Kentuckians destroyed the town at Tippecanoe twice in one year, and the force now collected there is, I am convinced, very inconsiderable. Hitherto it was a rallying point to all of every nation who wished to go to war, because no hostile standard had been erected elsewhere. But let the war become genuine, all will find a rallying point among their own tribes, and will have no inducement to go to the Prophet's town for the purpose of war.

It is well known here that Vincennes is not in as much danger as this country; and if it be asked from what Indians the danger to that place is apprehended, I will venture to assert that, if they are once specified, it can be shown that they are inconsiderable, or that a vast majority of them are so situated as to be able to attack the settlements on the Mississippi with infinitely more ease, and with better prospects of success, than those on the Wabash; and, if so, it is inconceivable why they should prefer Vincennes.

Gov. Harrison and myself do not understand your letter of the 9th. He takes it for granted that the Government had determined upon offensive measures against the Indians, whereas it appears to me that that question was left to rest upon future events. I have thought the President might prefer our acting on the defensive till it shall be seen what effect will be produced on the Indians by the operations of Gen. Hull's army.

Gov. H. seems to consider you as intending to supersede my military command altogether in this Territory, by saying that his may be extended to it with my consent. I consider you as having contemplated no such thing, but in the event of a campaign, and then only in so far as might be necessary to the most effectual operations of the campaign alone. With this I am content. But if his construction be correct, I am free to declare that I never will lose sight of self-respect so far as to subscribe to my own disgrace by consenting to anything so humiliating; and I trust that such injustice to my feelings has never been contemplated by the President, having always been, from principle, not only an approver, but a zealous supporter of his administration. My communications to you prove the diligence with which I have discharged my duty in my present situation; and I have it in my power to prove, by facts which have subsequently developed themselves, that the opinions which I have given you relative to the Indians have been consistent and uniformly correct.

And it cannot be denied that my measures so far, for the defense of the Territory, have been planned with much good judgment, and executed with as much success as those of any other Governor. If all this be true, the distinction supposed to be made between Gov. Harrison and myself seems to me to be too degrading to have been really intended.

I beg leave to tender my testimony in favor of Col. Russell's conduct in this quarter. It has gained him the esteem of all who have had an opportunity of knowing him; and I should be very happy if he could be ordered back here. Indeed, I should have been well pleased if he, having the defense of the frontier under his particular charge, had been permitted to have carried on all the hostile measures against the belligerent Indians. As a really practical military man, there are few, if any, who are his superiors. He was one of the heroes of King Mountain, and has had as much or more experience in Indian fighting than any man in the Western country; and he has profited by his experience.

Very respectfully,
Your obedient servant,
NINIAN EDWARDS.

To THE SECRETARY OF WAR, Washington City.

HEADQUARTERS, CAMP RUSSELL,
ST. CLAIR COUNTY, *September* 8, 1812.

Sir:

Gov. Harrison writes to me that you had put Col. Russell under his command; that he has ordered him to repair to Vincennes, and that he must go there.

The Colonel has gone and has now three companies of the rangers with him at that place, leaving but one company here, viz: the one that was raised here; and these, as well as all the regular troops in this Territory, he considers he has a right to call off at any time he pleases. Under such circumstances I feel most awkwardly situated, and I cannot persuade myself that it was intended to vest Gov. Harrison with such exclusive control in this quarter, whilst he is discharging the most important duties in another, far distant. And I would wish to be informed whether I have a right to take any control over the rangers and regular troops within my own Territory.

By a letter received yesterday, from Mr. Forsyth, of Peoria, it appears that the Indians are coming in considerable force to attack us.

Very respectfully,
Your obedient servant,
NINIAN EDWARDS.

To THE SECRETARY OF WAR.

ST. CLAIR COUNTY, *Sept.* 12, 1812.

Sir:

I am extremely apprehensive that you will fail in supplies for the troops under my command. In peaceable times it will do to trust a little to chance, but in war times, absolute certainty is requisite.

I wish you always to keep a supply which will be sufficient for any service that may be required. I shall want, in a very few days, to be furnished, at a moment's warning, rations sufficient for a detachment of five hundred men, who may be ordered on a tour of duty for fifteen or twenty days.

I sincerely hope that the public service will not suffer for the want of provisions. Suppose the whole body were now to move, have you a store sufficient for their supply? I shall expect you to be able, at any moment, to supply the whole of the troops under my command, during their present tour, with thirty days' provisions.

In haste,

Your obedient servant,

NINIAN EDWARDS.

To Major Wm. Morrison.

Headquarters, Camp Russell,
Madison County, Illinois Territory, *Oct.* 4, 1811.

Sir:

We are considerably harrassed by the Indians in this quarter. Two nights ago a party attacked a fort on Shoal Creek, into which I had but the day before thrown a reinforcement. They attempted to tear down the pickets, wounded two of our men, stole eight horses, and then retired. Several other parties have made their appearance within a few miles of this place, and are now hotly pursued by detachments of mounted riflemen.

Large numbers are embodied within a day's ride of this place. The Illinois is now and always has been as dangerous a point as the Wabash, and yet, while there are more men in that quarter than can be advantageously employed, not a single man from Kentucky has arrived to our assistance. I have had to depend wholly on the local militia and the volunteer companies, which I have had influence enough to raise. The latter are mounted and kept constantly ranging; but their spirit is a good deal broken, having had to lead the life of rangers by being almost constantly in the woods, and neither they nor Capt. Whiteside's company of rangers having as yet received a cent of pay.

I have the honor to be,

Very respectfully,

Your obedient servant,

NINIAN EDWARDS.

To Hon. Wm. Eustis, *Secretary of War*, Washington City.

Kaskaskia, Illinois Territory,
December, 25 1812.

Sir:

I had the honor to receive your letter of the 24th October last, on the 20th inst. In saying that it was my fault that there was not a sufficient force in this quarter, Gen. Harrison has said what cannot be supported. According to the authority given me by you, I called upon the Governor of Kentucky for a regiment of infantry, but before it could reach this place it was called off to Vincennes. Col. Russell came on with one company, in the month of

August, but before the expiration of this month they were also called away to Vincennes—leaving me no alternative but to rely on the citizens of this Territory for its defense. With such limited means I defended it against a formidable invasion, and finally carried on an expedition against the Indians with as much success as has been accomplished under similar circumstances in the Western country; and even after being reduced to the necessity of encountering the most uncommon difficulties and of acting upon my own responsibility for the salvation of the country, I discover that some pitiful attempts are making to deprive me of the credit I am entitled to, by giving it to Col. Russell, who happened to join me (about three days before I commenced my march) with fifty rangers. The injustice of this is known and attested by the whole of my little army, and there is not a man of common sense in this country who does not believe my measures have saved it, nor a a man of common honesty who will not acknowledge it.

The letters alluded to by Gen. Harrison never reached me till the 9th of October, when I was busily engaged in preparing for my expedition, and when the season was too far advanced to derive any advantage from troops, for whom I should have had to send all the way to Knoxville.

Several British traders, with large quantities of goods, are now on the Mississippi and St. Peters Rivers. The consequences of this fact you will readily perceive. Col. Menard, the President of the Legislative Council, has received information from one of his correspondents that Dickson is now at St. Josephs preparing to head a large body of Indians and British subjects in an attack upon this country, as soon as the weather will permit.

I have received a letter from his excellency, Gov. Blount, stating that two regiments are ready to march here upon my requisition, but that they are not yet furnished with arms. If called for, he requires that I shall provide for their march, after they pass the limits of Tennessee. I have requested that one regiment should be sent on immediately, and have agreed to supply it with provisions on its march from any point on the Ohio. In requiring these troops, I have acted more from necessity than the dictates of my own judgment. Troops are, certainly, necessary; but these are not the kind I prefer. Mounted men I could have raised if authorized so to do. In a Territory of this description, half the number would have been more useful, and taking into consideration the length of time consumed and the great expenses incurred in those long marches, they would cost the United States less. Infantry may do to build and guard forts—horsemen alone can pursue invaders. If, however, these troops arrive, I will, so long as I have anything to do with the frontier, endeavor to turn their services to the best advantage, and at present I propose, with their aid, to build a fort on the Illinois River, about one hundred miles above its mouth. The advantage of this position cannot be properly appreciated without a correct knowledge of the geography of the country. The course of the Illinois is most erroneously represented on every map that I have seen; and you may rely upon it, that Peoria lies about due north of Kaskaskia.

The Legislature of this Territory has petitioned the President for a battalion of mounted men, and has proposed a plan for raising them. I would not, in any event, wish to make any objections to the gentlemen they recommend; but if I were to have anything to do with the military operations of this frontier in the approaching season, I should dislike to be embarrassed by any such plan. I would prefer raising the men in my own way, because I know I could succeed. I would ask for a regiment and would be glad to command it in person.

Mr. B., one of the unfortunate men who was wounded on the late expedition, is since dead. Mr. Teter, another of the wounded, is and always will be disabled in the arm, and it is hoped provision will be made for the latter and for the family of the former.

Some wagons and teams were employed and some kettles and axes were purchased for the use of the late detachment of the militia of this Territory. I should be glad to be informed how they are all to be paid for. The horses that were lost in the service of the United States are returned on the muster rolls, which have been transmitted to the paymaster of the army of the United States in Washington City.

Very respectfully,

Your obedient servant,

NINIAN EDWARDS.

ELVIRADE, RANDOLPH COUNTY,
ILLINOIS TERRITORY, *January* 2, 1813.

Sir:

On the 26th ult. I had the honor to receive your letter of Oct. 7, with its inclosure. The delay in its reaching Kaskaskia was so extraordinary, that I required the postmaster at that place to indorse the time of its arrival, which was accordingly done.

Upon a review of my letter with your answer, it appears that you must have considered Gov. Harrison's arrangements as amply sufficient for the protection of this Territory, and consequently could not have received in a favorable manner the representations which I thought the obligations of duty and patriotism imperiously called upon me to make to you. It is very probable that I may have manifested too much sensibility and have been rather importunate upon the subject. If my conduct has appeared to you in that light, you may be assured my motives were both honorable and patriotic, which, added to the history of facts now before you, will, I persuade myself, arrest any unfavorable impressions which you might have previously conceived. Very far indeed is it from my wish to criminate any one, but of nothing do I feel more confident than that I can completely justify my own conduct, and nothing do I desire more ardently than a fair and honorable opportunity of doing so.

Of the contemplated operations of the army at Vincennes, I never received any information till the 9th of October, when I was preparing for my expedition to Peoria Lake. At that time I received a letter from one of Gen. Hopkins' aids, and another from Gen. Harrison. By the first I was informed that the army would march (I could hardly tell where) on the 30th of September or 1st of October, and that if I wanted aid it should be sent to me. By the last I was authorized to call on the Governor of Tennessee for forces, with a view to a particular object, which Gen. Harrison, as early as September 6th (the date of his letter), thought it would be too late to attempt (this was building a chain of forts, recommended in his letter to you of August last). He, however, referred it to Gov. Howard and myself, who, I believe, thought alike upon the subject.

These propositions came, indeed, a little too late. One-half of the local militia had been engaged in repelling a most serious invasion. That force would not have been sufficient, if I had not contrived to make an impression upon the minds of the Indians that we had several other companies in service. Not a man from the Kentucky militia had arrived, and Gov. Shelby writes me that he is sure the force ordered by him for my assistance was prevented from coming by dishonorable steps. The danger of invasion was over, the season began to promise security, and it really would have appeared a Quixotic attempt in me to have sent for the aid promised by Gen. Hopkins' aid-de-camp, when, judging by his letter, the troops from which it was to be furnished should have marched nine days before I received the notice.

Sir, I have had serious difficulties to encounter. With as ardent a desire as any man ever felt to serve his country, I have the consolation of knowing that my exertions have been useful as well as honorable to it; but I know I must calculate on being misrepresented—and although I am not indifferent to the opinions which my Government and country may entertain of me, yet I feel all the support of conscious rectitude and am prepared for the worst.

Respectfully, your obedient servant,

N. EDWARDS.

To The Secretary of War, Washington City.

Kaskaskia, Randolph County, Illinois Territory, *March* 27, 1813.

Sir :

That state of things which was to be expected, from the communications I have had the honor to make to the department over which you preside, seems about to be dreadfully realized. The savages have already committed murders within the bounds of every regiment in this Territory. This week a party of twenty or thirty killed five persons in this county, and camped on the ground the whole of the succeeding night. One of the volunteer companies is in pursuit of them. Another party of Indians has been discovered between this place and the United States saline. It is so dangerous traveling to Kentucky, that the mail has been delayed several days and will start to-morrow morning with a guard. In this state of things, I feel considerable regret that I have not only never received a word of approbation or disapprobation of my conduct, since I adopted measures of defense last year upon my own responsibility, but that I am now totally without any instructions or authority to act. I have, however, eight volunteer companies, from the militia, in service, and have them as well employed as possible.

Hitherto the defense of this and Indiana Territory has been combined; but there has been and still is a most unjust division of the force provided for that object. I never have asked more than an equal division, although I am very able to prove that this Territory is much the most exposed—and I will prove it if any high official agent of the Government, in any of these Territories, will hazard his reputation by asserting the contrary. It is a fact —which of itself is enough—that whenever a force shall be marched from Vincennes or St. Louis against the most threatening and hostile confederacy, it must march through this Territory, which is equally exposed with the neighboring ones to an invasion by water, and more so to one by land. Should an army march to the mouth of the Wisconsin, it must go by Peoria and the mouth of the Rock River.

The Indians of the Illinois and its waters amount to about fifteen hundred warriors. Rock River, the residence of the Sauks and Winnebagoes, is two days' journey from Peoria. The Sauks are eight hundred and the Foxes six hundred strong. The Winnebagoes about four hundred and fifty. Besides, there are a great number of bands of Pottawottamies, Ottaways, Chippeways and Menominies residing between Lake Michigan and the Mississippi, all of whom can attack this Territory more conveniently than either of the adjoining ones, and all I ask is an equal share of the force so long as it shall be confined to defensive operations.

If the British erect a fort at the mouth of the Wisconsin, and should be able to retain it two years, this and Missouri Territory will be totally deserted —in other words, conquered.

I have the honor to be,

Your obedient servant,

N. EDWARDS.

To The Secretary of War, Washington City.

Elvirade, Randolph County, Illinois Territory, *May* 4, 1813.

Sir:

A short time ago I received a letter from Col. Bond, informing me that you had authorized him to request me to raise and organize three additional companies of rangers. I immediately wrote you that I supposed what had been done would be sufficient, and that those three companies who, through me, tendered the President their services as rangers, would be accepted. They have been notified by me that they were accepted, but, lest some accident may have prevented my letters from reaching you, I will here give the names of these officers—all of whom have been chosen by their companies and are approved of by me.

James B. Moore, Captain; David Robinson, First Lieutenant; Arthur Morgan, Second Lieutenant; John Huitt, Ensign.

Samuel Whiteside, Captain; Joseph Borough, First Lieutenant; Samuel Gilbaur, Second Lieutenant; Arthur Armstrong, Ensign.

Jacob Short, Captain; Nathaniel Jorvey, First Lieutenant; Andrew Bankston, Second Lieutenant; John Journey, Ensign.

These officers, and those of the companies raised here last year, are all exceedingly anxious to be commanded by Benjamin Stephenson as their Major. With the exception of an Ensign and a Lieutenant, who were absent at the time, they have unanimously petitioned me on this subject. The privates composing the battalion are equally desirous of it, and I can most conscientiously say that, in my opinion, the Territory does not admit of a better choice.

The Legislature of this Territory, at its last session, by the solicitations of certain individuals, was induced to ask for this force and to recommend John Murdock to be authorized to raise and command it. But I beg leave to observe that the force which I have raised has been upon a different plan altogether. Murdock has not raised a man, and has endeavored to throw every impediment in my way. He is not qualified, either by his knowledge or experience, for the command; and those who have recommended him will not pretend to say that his habits do not furnish a most important objection.

I have the honor to be,

Your obedient servant,

N. EDWARDS.

To THE SECRETARY OF WAR, Washington City.

MOUNT VERNON, *July* 14, 1827.

The commanders of the different regiments and odd battalions of Gen. Hanson's brigade, on the eastern side of the Illinois River (except the 20th Regiment), will take immediate steps for detaching into service, according to law, one-fourth of their respective commands. And should any part of the frontier, south of Rock River, be invaded by the savages, the Colonel entitled by law to command the detachment will march it, with the least possible delay, to the support of the point attacked, without waiting for further orders.

NINIAN EDWARDS,

Commander-in-Chief, etc.

MOUNT VERNON, *July* 14, 1827.

Sir:

I have this moment received, by express, intelligence of the Indian depredations, to which your letter of the 11th inst. refers, and I lose not a moment in transmitting, by express, such orders as appear to be most indispensable.

Promptness and energy are all that are necessary to meet every danger which can possibly threaten the frontiers. Your letter gives me reason to expect that neither will be wanting in your regiment. You will accept the services of any number of mounted volunteers, not exceeding six hundred, who will equip themselves, find their own subsistence and continue in service thirty days, unless sooner discharged. They will rendezvous, as fast as possible, at Fort Clark, where you will organize and take the command of them, and march with all possible expedition to the assistance of our fellow-citizens at Galena, where, if you find an officer of the United States army entitled to a superior command to yourself, you will report to him and receive his orders.

In your progress, you will avoid rashly exposing your men to unequal contests, but it is expected that you will not overlook any proper opportunity of repelling any hostile incursions of the savages.

You will order the officer next you in command to take immediate steps for drafting from your regiment, according to law, and with the least possible delay, six companies of infantry, which are to be held in readiness to march at a moment's warning to any point of the frontier that may be invaded, in which event he is immediately to march them to the support of the point attacked, without waiting for further orders. None of the citizens, however, in the vicinity of the immediate frontier are to be drafted.

Your obedient servant,

N. EDWARDS,

Commander-in-Chief.

To COL. THOS. M. NEAL, *Commanding 20th Regiment Illinois Militia.*

BELLEVILLE, *August* 9, 1827.

Dear Sir :

There being the strongest reasons for believing that the Pottawottamies of the Illinois River have been depredating upon the property of some of the citizens of this State, and the official communications of Dr. Wolcott, the Indian Agent at Chicago, as well as a variety of circumstances, leaving no doubt of their hostile dispositions, I think it my duty to inform you that if any future depredations shall be committed by them, and immediate reparation refused, I will not hesitate to drive them from their present residence, which you well know they have no right to occupy.

I have also to request that measures may be adopted for removing all the Indians who, without any right, now occupy any part of the ceded lands of this State, and to prevent further intrusions of all others on them. I have no confidence in any of them, and will not, by a hazardous forbearance, jeopardize the property or lives of my fellow-citizens. I trust, however, that you will find it proper and convenient to adopt such measures as may render my interposition wholly unnecessary.

I have the honor to be,

Your most obedient servant,

N. EDWARDS.

To GEN. CLARK.

BELLEVILLE, ILLINOIS, *August* 20, 1827.

Sir:

Gov. Cass, and other officers of the United States of great respectability, and with the best opportunities of forming correct opinions on the subject, all concurring in the belief that the neighboring Indians intend to make war upon us, and those Indians having committed several daring robberies and other depredations between Peoria and Galena, and commenced actual war in other parts, I have felt it my duty to call out about five hundred mounted volunteers to defend our frontiers. I suppose not less than 1,500 men have been driven by those acts of hostility from the vicinity of Galena, and but for the measures I have adopted, several other parts of our frontier, from their defenseless situations, would have been depopulated. I, therefore, beg leave to ask how far it may be the pleasure of the President to recognize the defensive measures which I have been compelled to adopt, and what provisions will be made for paying the militia that have been called into service. My power to act in such cases is limited to sudden emergencies—the defense of every State belonging to the General Government. I now beg leave to ask, in behalf of this State, of the President of the United States, such measures of protection to our extensive frontier as its peculiar weakness demands. The measures adopted by Gen. Atkinson, are, I presume, sufficient to insure safety to our western borders, but they are not the least calculated, nor has he the kind of troops necessary to protect those settlements which extend from the mouth of the Illinois River to Chicago.

I need scarcely remark to you what all experience has proved, that whenever the Indians have once made up their minds to commit hostilities, or have actually committed such as deserve chastisement, their pacific disposition never can be safely relied on till they have begged for peace, and begged it so earnestly as to leave no doubt of their sincerity. Nothing of this kind has yet occurred. The latter part of the next month is of all others the most favorable time for concentrating their forces and striking the most formidable blow.

I will only add that I should be very happy to render, on the present occasion, any services that may be acceptable to the President.

Hoping for as early an answer as possible,

I have the honor to be, sir,

Very respectfully,

Your most obedient servant,

NINIAN EDWARDS.

TO THE SECRETARY OF WAR.

N. B.—Presuming that you must have been informed, by official communications of officers of the United States, of the danger that has, at least, threatened us, and that no one could be more sensible of the necessity of a force different from that under the command of Gen. Atkinson, to afford the necessary protection of such a frontier as that of this State, I have constantly expected to hear from you on the subject. The services of the men whom I have called out will expire in a few days, and, until I hear from you, I shall not adopt any other measures, but leave it to the General Government to provide for such protection and safety as the people have a right to expect from it.—N. E.

BELLEVILLE, *September* 3, 1827.

Dear Sir:

Your account of the situation of our fellow-citizens on Fever River would induce me to risk much for their protection, but as this cannot be adequately provided for according to strict law, the influence of an organized opposition to all the measures I have already adopted for that purpose leaves me little ground to hope that I shall be able to furnish the necessary assistance in time, and therefore my advice is that they should rely upon their forts, during the present moon. In the meantime I will see what I can do.

Very respectfully,

Your most obedient servant,

NINIAN EDWARDS.

To COL. ABNER FIELD.

BELLEVILLE, ILLINOIS, *Sept.* 4, 1827.

Sir:

Col. Field, a gentleman of much intelligence and high respectability, having been deputed by the population of the Fever River Mines to apply to me for assistance to repel the hostility of the savages, with which they consider themselves daily threatened, arrived at this place night before last, bringing very unfavorable news in regard to that and other parts of our frontier, which is fully confirmed by another express that reached here last night from Peoria.

It appears that the Winnebagoes had ultimately refused to come to any arrangements with Gov. Cass and Col. McKenney; that the Governor had received information, which he believed, that a part, at least, of the Pottawottamies had determined to unite with the Winnebagoes in the war; that he apprehended the people of Fever River would be attacked before it would be possible to send them any aid; that Gen. Atkinson had sent an express to that place, asking for all the mounted riflemen that could be spared from it, and had marched towards Green Bay with about six hundred infantry and one hundred and thirty mounted riflemen to attack those Indians. No doubt the General will accomplish all that can be effected with the force under his command, but it is much to be regretted that he had not more mounted men, for, if the hostile Indians are as numerous as Gov. Cass supposes, it is not probable that the General can march such a distance through their own country without having a hard fight at least. Should he be defeated or driven back, it may well be imagined that the consequences must be truly disastrous to our very extensive and exposed settlements all along the Illinois River and its waters. Whatever may be his fate, however, if you will only cast your eye upon the map, and consider that all the hostile Indians, with the exception of one small band, reside between his line of march and those settlements, it must, I think, be obvious to you, that there is either no danger at all, or that they are in very great danger. Regarding them in the latter point of view, I feel it my duty to reiterate my application to the President for that protection which their situation demands—a protection, the necessity of which is as apparent as that of any movement that has been made under the authority of the Governor, and which cannot be doubted without an utter disbelief of any hostile disposition on the part of those savages, nor without questioning the propriety of all those measures of the Governor which have been adopted upon that supposition. For, if the Indians are hostilely disposed, as they can attack no where else with the same prospects of success and with so little risk to themselves, so none can be in more danger than those settlements. Besides their lives and property, the people, I humbly conceive, have a fair claim on the Government for protection against those interruptions of their tranquillity by the savages which are reasonably calculated to prevent them from resting under the shade of their own vines and fig-trees, without any one to make them afraid.

I learn, from Col. Field, that about 3,000 men have been driven from the mines, and, but for the measures I adopted, upon the first alarm, it is scarcely to be doubted that many other parts of our frontier would have been entirely depopulated. I need not, I am sure, attempt to point out, to a gentleman of your practical knowledge and experience, the immense losses and sacrifices that must have resulted, both to individuals and to the State, from this state of things.

My authority being limited to a sudden emergency, my measures were adopted with a view to such duration only as would be sufficient to enable the Government to get its own into operation; and I have now only between sixty and seventy men in service. Nor had I intended, under any circumstances, to have done more on my own responsibility, in consequence of their being no money in our State Treasury—the impossibility of doing with ut it and the risk of pecuniary embarrassment, of which I had some experience during the late war, being greater than I have felt under any obligations to encounter. These views, however, have never been communicated to a single individual; and looking to consequences to the administration from adhering to them which can scarcely escape your sagacity, I have concluded, should actual hostilities be commenced on our frontier, immediately to repair to it, make it my headquarters, and endeavor, with my own funds and at my own risk, to provide subsistence for such volunteers as I may be able to call to my aid, until I receive your answer to my letter of the 20th ult. Whatever that may be, if it shall only afford reasonable ground to expect that I shall be sustained, I will continue to do the best in my power until I receive your answer to this letter; otherwise, unless all dangers shall have entirely disappeared, I shall be compelled to convene the Legislature and lay the case, just as it may be, before them.

I beg leave to observe, that the experience of three years' hard service on our frontiers, during the last war, has convinced me that no other force of any reasonable amount is available, for such protection as they require, than that of mounted riflemen. Your infantry on the Wisconsin is too remote to afford the least protection. It would be scarcely less available to us, if it were at Washington City.

I must beg leave to call the President's attention to another grievance, somewhat connected with this subject, that has been borne by the people for a few years past with great impatience, and cannot be submitted to much longer: that is the occupancy by different tribes of Indians of various portions of the ceded lands of this State, and their constantly traversing every part of it at their pleasure, for the purpose of hunting, without any right so to do. A large number of Pottawottamies, particularly, have been for several years past residing within about twenty miles of Peoria, on lands not only ceded, but which have actually been granted by the Government to individuals—an illegal occupancy which has been in some measure countenanced by the Government, by making it the seat of an Indian agency—the place of paying those Indians their annuities, etc. I now, sir, have to ask of the President that a grievance so inconsistent with the rights of the State may no longer be permitted, and that these Indians, in particular, be removed with as little delay as possible. I shall be happy to assist in the accomplishment of this object by the most pacific means, if they will answer. I will not say what would probably be the result if the President were to decline a compliance with this specific request, because I do not believe his respect for the rights of the State will permit him to hesitate about it.

Respectfully,

Your obedient servant,

NINIAN EDWARDS.

TO THE SECRETARY OF WAR.

BELLEVILLE, ILLINOIS, *Sept.* 5, 1827.

Brig. Gen. Hanson will immediately take all legal and necessary measures for enrolling in the militia all persons subject thereto, who are now residing at the Lead Mines on Fever River or in that vicinity, and for their organization according to law.

NINIAN EDWARDS, *Governor,*
Commander-in-Chief.

Confidential.

BELLEVILLE, ILLINOIS, *Sept.* 13, 1827.

Dear Sir:

I perceive that the "Louisville Public Advertiser," in announcing the arrival of Gen. Gaines at that place, states that the administration has determined that the Winnebagoes shall surrender all those of their tribe who were concerned in the murders at Prairie du Chien, the attack upon the boats, etc., and that to prevent a recurrence of similar enormities, they shall abandon all the country on this side of the Wisconsin River. If this is the case, it cannot fail to give the greatest satisfaction to the largest portion of this State. In fact nothing could be more popular—nothing is more just. Even the "Advertiser" highly applauds this course and assigns the best of reasons in its favor.

As to the lands themselves, I believe there has been some great oversight or misunderstanding at Washington concerning them. I have only time for a hint or two on the subject.

In 1803 or 1804, Gen. Harrison purchased of the Sacs and Foxes all the lands between the mouths of the Wisconsin and Illinois Rivers. In 1816, Gov. Clark, Col. Choteau and myself, as commissioners of the United States, ceded all those lands which lie north of a due west line from the southern extremity of Lake Michigan to the Mississippi, to the Ottaways, Chippeways and Pottawottamies (all making one nation and generally denominated the Indians of Illinois River) with certain reservations. These Indians derive their claim from the United States, and are the real owners of the land about which the Winnebagoes have made so much disturbance. The latter have no claim to any part of these lands, unless some right has been recognized to them inadvertently by the United States since 1816, of which I know nothing, but which, if it exists, was a clear and palpable violation of the treaty with the Ottaways, Chippeways and Pottawottamies aforesaid, unless their consent was previously obtained, which I do not suppose was the case. It would in fact amount to nothing less than this—that the United States, after having made a solemn cession of certain lands to those Indians, involving a pledge of good faith to protect them in the enjoyment thereof, have violated their treaty.

Respectfully,

Your most obedient servant,

NINIAN EDWARDS.

To President Adams.

Belleville, Illinois, *September*, 1827.

Sir:

The rumor of eighteen men having been killed at Fever River, by the Indians, as mentioned in my last letter to you, was brought to this neighborhood by a decent looking man, who professed to have left that place the second day afterwards. I hasten, however, to inform you that the whole story has proved to be a sheer fabrication. No news from Gen. Atkinson has reached here since he commenced his march.

I cannot but observe that it appears somewhat singular that, while the Indian agents and other officers of the Government have been writing to the citizens of different parts of this State, warning them of their danger, recommending this and that precaution and mode of defense, and the General in command has even called for mounted riflemen from one of our organized counties, I have not received a single line from any one of them (except Gen.

Clark, of St. Louis,) nor from yourself, nor any other officer of the Government. Should the same course be pursued by Gen. Gaines, who arrived at St. Louis some days ago, I shall owe it both to the State and to myself to ask of you an explanation of a course of conduct as little to be expected from the General Government as disrespectful to the State.

I have the honor to be,
Very respectfully, sir,
Your most obedient servant,
NINIAN EDWARDS.

To The Secretary of War.

Belleville, Illinois, *October* 29, 1827.

Sir:

I have just had the honor to receive your letter of the 9th inst., in which you inform me that you had instructed Gov. Cass to take such measures as will fulfill my wishes in regard to the removal of the Indians occupying the ceded lands of this State, with the least possible delay consistent with humanity, or, if insuperable difficulties present themselves, to report to you forthwith thereon.

The prompt attention, on your part, to the interest, rights and tranquillity of this State, in the cases referred to, is duly appreciated. But I must beg leave to remark that the remoteness of Gov. Cass' residence, and the Indians alluded to not being within his superintendency, do not promise as speedy a redress of the grievance complained of as seems to have been anticipated, or as is desirable.

The Indians residing on the ceded lands within this State are the Kickapoos, Pottawottamies, Ottaways, and Chippeways of the Illinois River, and the Sacs and Foxes. These Indians, and occasionally large parties of the Shawnese and Delawares, are in the habit of hunting extensively through the settled parts of the State, to the great annoyance of the citizens thereof. It would seem strange that; while the old States have found it expedient, for the sake of preserving their game, to restrain their own citizens from hunting at pleasure, we should be expected to permit large bands of marauding savages, without any right whatever, to be constantly traversing this State, for the total destruction of ours. But the evil more immediately felt, and which has been too long practiced with impunity, is that they scarcely ever take this liberty without killing tame animals—an evil which cannot and will not be endured, though we shall patiently await the result of those measures of the General Government which you authorize us to hope for.

The Kickapoos are understood to be within the agency of Major Richard Graham of Missouri; the Pottawottamies, Ottaways and Chippeways of the Illinois River, within the sub-agency of Mr. Peter Menard, Jr.; the Sacs and Foxes, within the agency of Mr. Thomas Forsyth of St. Louis; the Shawnese and Delawares, within the sub-agency of Major Peter Menard of Kaskaskia; and the whole, within the superintendency of Gen. William

Clark. We should hope much more from the interposition of these gentlemen, or from the latter alone, than from that of any one at so great a distance from us as Gov. Cass.

I have the honor to be,
Very respectfully, sir,
Your most obedient servant,
NINIAN EDWARDS.

To HON. JAMES BARBOUR, *Secretary of War.*

BELLEVILLE, ILLINOIS, *October* 29, 1827.

Sir:

I have received your letter of the 15th inst., and lest certain inferences, which seem obviously deducible from it, may be erroneous, I have to request that you will, as soon as practicable, furnish me a statement:

1st. Of the date and amount of each loan made to the Directors of the Brownsville Branch Bank, and the names of the members of the Board which granted the same.

2d. A copy of the orders under which they respectively drew the money.

3d. The date and amount of each note and mortgage; the description of the property mortgaged to secure each of said loans; the amount at which it was valued, and by whom valued.

4th. The date and amount of each payment made by the said Directors, respectively; and if any of them were otherwise than direct payments into the Bank of its own notes, by the said Directors, or any one of them, how such payments are made.

5th. The amount now due by each of said Directors, the steps that have been taken to coerce payment from them, the dates when commenced, how long continued, how terminated, and all and every circumstance which has retarded and is likely to retard the collection of said notes, respectively.

If you know, or in the course of your business have found reason to believe, that any of said Directors did, either directly or indirectly, render himself or themselves responsible for, or come under any obligations to pay the debt or debts of any other person to the Bank, which debts remain unpaid, I trust that a due regard for the interest of the institution which is committed to your charge will induce you to communicate to me all the information you possess on the subject, since you must be sensible that the knowledge of such a circumstance would be more likely to insure payment to the community—whose agent you are—than any other measure of coercion that could be adopted. Nor can you doubt that, while it wrongs no one, it is just and right that the Governor of the State should be made acquainted with every circumstance that affects its interest even in the slightest degree. And from whom should such information so naturally be expected as from him to whose agency the particular interest affected has been specially intrusted?

You will please direct your answer to this place, and I hope it will not be long before I shall have the pleasure of receiving it.

Very respectfully,
Your obedient servant,
NINIAN EDWARDS.

To the CASHIER OF THE BROWNSVILLE BRANCH BANK.

EXECUTIVE DEPARTMENT, ILLINOIS,
January 28, 1828.

Sir :

It is understood that a letter from you, to my predecessor or myself, prescribing the manner in which the President required the unlocated part of the lands granted by the United States to this State, for the use of a seminary of learning, to be selected, was received at the State Department of the Government, and has been subsequently mislaid or lost. I regret exceedingly that it cannot be found, and have no other alternative than to request the favor of fresh instructions—hoping that since Missouri has been permitted to locate her lands, granted for a similar purpose, in unconnected sections, the President will extend the same indulgence to this State, which is now the more necessary to its interests from the long postponement of the location of these lands, and the consequently diminished range of selection.

I have the honor to be, etc.,
N. EDWARDS.

To THE SECRETARY OF THE TREASURY.

BELLEVILLE, ILLINOIS, *August* 20, 1829.

Sir :

The mail has just now brought me Mr. P. Bradley's letter, of the 1st inst., in answer to mine, to you, of the 16th inst. In addressing myself to you, in reply to his letter, I beg leave to premise that, as I entertain no other feelings towards you than those of respect and friendship, I trust that the remarks which I feel myself called upon to make will not be considered inconsistent with either the one or the other.

Great as your capacities may be, and no one appreciates them more highly than I do, you must necessarily have been dependent, in some degree, upon others for information as to localities and topography essential to the correct operations of your Department. It is not to be imputed to you as a fault that you may have been misinformed by designing individuals, or that, for the want of information, which it was the special duty of others to lay before you, this State is made to exhibit a degrading contrast which none of its citizens, who are worthy of its confidence or friendship, can regard with indifference. Collisions on such subjects are as unpleasant to me as to any other man, but I have never seen the day that I would not risk any personal consequences rather than submit to have the affairs of my own State controlled by members of Congress from other States, or to see it degraded and overlooked as though it were an inferior. Though older in every respect, and superior in the number of free population, and the extent of agricultural improvements and productions, to Missouri, the interest, convenience and accommodation of the latter have, of late years, been so much more favorably regarded by the Government, that certain magnates of St. Louis, who are in the habit of speaking of us, reproachfully, as "the free State," seem to consider us unworthy, on that account, of the equal regard of the Government; and hope, by their influence with the present administration, to impress upon us the stamp of degradation. It is to be hoped, however, that our own members of Congress will not permit their machinations to succeed without a vigorous struggle, at least.

It would be very unnecessary to exhibit in this letter the palpable partiality alluded to in all its different phases; but besides the conspicuous instances of it in relation to Indian affairs, I will venture to say it will be difficult to find any one equal to the task of demonstrating that better and more eligible locations for the troops now stationed at Jefferson Barracks and for the arsenal erecting near St. Louis, than the sites of either, might not have been had in the vicinities of Kaskaskia or Alton, and had we not been "the free State" they would doubtless have been preferred. Without, however, referring to any other subjects than the mail arrangements themselves, enough may be found to furnish just ground of complaint. The manner in which the accommodation of our seat of government has been postponed to that of St. Louis, and the shabby two-horse vehicles in which the mail is carried to and from it, contrasted with the superior style in which the mail is transported from St. Louis to Franklin (an inconsiderable, dilapidated town on the Missouri River), is calculated to inflict a deep wound upon the just pride of the whole State. If it be necessary that the mail be thus transported twice a week to this last mentioned town, on account of the population west of St. Louis, it is inconceivable why it should not be transported in like manner through Vandalia to our northern settlements, which are far more populous and equally respectable. Considering the proximity of numerous tribes of restless savages to the upper Mississippi, the superior facilities which British traders and agents there possess of operating upon them, the vast extent of the mineral country, the rapidity with which the Northwestern Territory is settling, the important Indian agencies located within it, and its bordering upon the territory of the only nation in the world from whom we have anything to apprehend, it cannot be contended with the semblance of plausibility that the Government is not more interested in a direct communication on the latter than the former route. It is evident, then, that the Government has no interest of its own to advance by this discrimination. As little is it to be justified by any reference to St. Louis as a place of trade or commerce, for no man of information, that has any regard for his reputation, will deny that the people of our northern settlements have much more direct commercial intercourse with St. Louis than those of the Missouri River. As, then, the former are more numerous, equally respectable, and can be accommodated as consistently with the interest of the Government, it would seem due to them that the mail should be carried direct from St. Louis, through the counties of Madison, Greene, Morgan and Sangamon, and even to Jo Daviess county, as often and in the same manner that it is carried to Franklin. There are no counties through which it passes to the latter place that are to be compared, in point of population and agricultural productions, to these; nor is there any reason to believe that, if, instead of the go-carts that figure in this State, equal accommodations were afforded, there would not be more traveling in the stage on the route here suggested than upon that one.

These, however, are not the only instances in which this mortifying discrimination and humiliating contrast are exhibited. Shawneetown, as to mail arrangements, is probably far the most important point in this State. Besides the multitudes of people who have occasion to go from a distance in all directions to the extensive salt works in its immediate vicinity, being the great landing place of traders, emigrants and travelers who come by water, it is to this State and Missouri precisely what you have known Maysville to be to Kentucky and Tennessee. A moment's reflection would therefore seem to be sufficient to satisfy any one that stage accommodation must necessarily be more in demand there than from St. Louis to the westward; and that a line of stages from thence through the interior of the State to the northern parts thereof, into which the streams of emigration are pouring their copious currents in a manner that never has been more successful in any country, is as necessary, and would afford greater accommodation than the line from St. Louis to Franklin. Yet there is nothing but a two-horse vehicle to fetch the mail from Shawneetown once a week; and this poor accommodation is not permitted to extend even to Vandalia, but is required to stop at Carlyle, the first point of intersection with the line to St. Louis, so that travelers and others visiting our seat of Government or our most populous settlements are to be forced from fifty to one hundred miles out of the way, to be deprived of such stage accommodation as is extended to other places with inferior claims to it.

But limiting our views of the discrimination made between the two States to a smaller circle, it will appear sufficiently striking by comparing the accommodation which your advertisement proposes for the village of St. Charles, in Missouri, with that which it contemplates for this place. Much superior in the number of its population and the amount of its agricultural productions, and importing more extensively from Atlantic cities, this county has not only far more trading and commercial intercourse with St. Louis than that of St. Charles, but more, in fact, than any other county in the two States; and this no respectable man in St. Louis will deny. And yet, while a four-horse mail stage is to run three times a week between St. Louis and that village, the mail is to be carried but once a week between this place and St. Louis, and this on an entirely unnecessary and circuitous route by Cahokia; and we are to have no stage at all, or be subjected to the delay and additional expense of traveling between six and seven miles out of the way. But what is, if possible, still more extraordinary, this four-horse stage, "of sufficient size to accommodate seven passengers," is, for the convenience of different neighborhoods in St. Louis county, to make its three trips a week on three different routes—one by Florisant, one by Jamestown, and one on the direct road, departing from its regular direction, for the first of these places, five miles, and for the second ten or eleven miles—all of which has been procured through the influence of some of the most conspicuous of those individuals out of the State alluded to by Mr. Bradley, who have been but too successful in convincing you that a much less deviation from the "direct road" should not be admitted in this "free State" in favor of the county seat of its oldest and one of its most populous and important counties.

But even if it be right to distinguish the people of St. Louis and St. Charles counties, in Missouri, by this marked preference, it is not easy to perceive on what just grounds the plain, reputable "free State" farmers, merchants and mechanics of this county, who, from their exportations, importations, commercial and other pursuits, are more interested in receiving the mail from St. Louis than any other quarter, should not be entitled to equal accommodation with a few gentlemen-officers at Jefferson Barracks, for whose benefit the mail is to be carried three times a week between that place and St. Louis. Similar comparisons might be made with Edwardsville and other places; but this is particularly referred to, because in withdrawing from us, at the instance of individuals residing out of the State, and probably a few of our own misguided citizens (who, on reflection, will be sorry for, if not ashamed of it), an accommodation deliberately granted by your predecessor, and which has not cost an additional cent, as documents in your Department will show, the expenses of the Government must necessarily be increased by the arrangements which you have deemed necessary in consequence of the change.

In accounting for this measure Mr. Bradley says: "An objection has been made by many individuals, in and out of your State, to the Department sending the important western mail out of its way or regular direction, to the inconvenience of the traveler and delay of the mail; and in consequence of those objections the route has been advertised, as it was heretofore, to the exclusion of Belleville."

As it is to be presumed that you would not have determined to reverse the deliberate decision of your predecessor and deprive us of a convenience and accommodation conceded by him on due consideration, merely because certain individuals have thought proper to object to it, or without being satisfied of the validity of their objections, it must have been proved to your satisfaction, or gratuitously assumed, that the departure of the mail from its regular direction, the inconvenience of the traveler, and the delay of the mail itself, have all been so great as to render the change necessary. Deeply affected as we are by this decision, it is hoped that a few brief remarks upon the several objections on which it is predicated will not be deemed too obtrusive. First, then, as to the sending the mail out of its way or regular direction. Whatever may be the principle adopted in regard to this matter, if equal in its operation none has a right to complain; but if it is to be made to tend to the convenience and accommodation of the citizens of one State, and to be rigidly and inflexibly inforced to the exclusion of the equal claims of the citizens of another, it degrades the latter, and stamps upon them an odious distinction which they would well deserve if they could meanly acquiesce in it. As a freeman, entitled to equal rights, I would, if I stood alone and unassisted, resist it by all proper means to the last extremity; and I should consider myself a traitor to the good people of this State if I could stand by with folded arms and patiently see it fixed upon them. What idea was meant to be conveyed in speaking of the "regular direction" of the mail, I do not clearly comprehend. But be it what it may, it cannot affect the comparisons I had made and intend to make between this and other places, since it must equally apply to them all. If it was intended to refer to the ordinary route on which the mail has been heretofore carried, then the answer is, that since the first establishment of the line it has never been transported more than two years on any other route than through this place, and that it has *regularly* been brought this way ever since the stage commenced running three times a week. If the phrase "regular direction" was meant to refer to a straight line, then, sir, the maps in your Department will show that there is no town through which the mail passes as near to a straight line between Louisville and St. Louis as this; and really it does not appear very reasonable that a departure from the "regular direction," so considered, for the accommodation of other places, should interpose such insuperable objections to a half an hour's delay in returning to the regular direction for the accommodation of the large and respectable population that inhabits this county.

But let us see how far the mail now comes out of the way. There is no dispute about its coming through Lebanon, nor would I, if in my power, prevent its passage through that flourishing village, nor any other place through which it is now transported. The road from Lebanon to St. Louis—and the only road—passes a Mr. Westfield's, where it forks, the one going directly to St. Louis, and the other coming this way. Measuring straight lines from Westfield's to the ferry opposite St. Louis, and from the same point to this place, and thence to the ferry, and comparing the distances, the difference is only three and three-tenths miles, as appears by the inclosed statement of John Messenger, Esq., our county surveyor, one of the most respectable men and the best practical mathematician in the State. If, however, there should be any doubt of the correctness of his calculations, my letter of the 16th ult. will enable you to have its accuracy completely tested by the maps in the General Land Office. This is presumed to be as fair a way of ascertaining the difference in the distance as our opponents could desire, because this route is at least as susceptible of being shortened as the other; and contemporaneous efforts are now making to shorten both. The improvement upon this route is certain to be made; that upon the other is, by an act of our Legislature, made to depend upon Congress "granting to this State scrip or other means expressly to improve said road," of the probability of which grant you can judge as correctly as any one else. On the direct road there is no postoffice; and running as it does through a very thinly settled part of our county, the

—46

mail in that way (if my recollection is correct, and I think I cannot be mistaken,) would pass by only four little houses or colonies between Westfield's and the little village through which both roads pass; and it is not probable that the occupants of these houses ever subscribed for a newspaper in their lives. The present route passes through the heart of the thickest settlement in the State, and accommodates this village, which imports more goods direct from Atlantic cities than all the towns through which the mail passes from Vincennes to St. Louis, and supplies one of the most important postoffices on the whole of the line through the State.

But supposing the difference of the distance to be *four* miles. The change upon your plan, even if, contrary to every reasonable expectation, you should continue to refuse more than one mail a week to St. Louis, would considerably increase the expenses of the Government, for by continuing the present arrangements there would be no necessity of carrying the mail by Cahokia to St. Louis, or twice a week between this place and Lebanon, as contemplated by your advertisement. By the change you can only save the expense of transportation on twenty-four miles, at most, a week, while you incur it on eighty-eight miles for the same length of time, the distance of the first of these new routes being twenty and that of the latter being twelve miles. But it is not believed that there would be any necessity for giving one cent more for the transportation of the mail on the present route than on the direct road, the difference in the number of stage-passengers on the former being more than equivalent to the distance. If I am not greatly misinformed, your Department will show that the proposals of the present contractor were to carry it on either of these routes for the same price. It happens that I well know that your predecessor could have made other contracts for carrying it on this route without any additional expense; and with the same disposition it is in your power to do the same thing. Why, then, should we, under such circumstances, be deprived of an accommodation extended to others with even inferior claims to it? Why apply to the people of this State one rule, and to those of Missouri another? Fort Osage is the termination of the western mail.

The maps, including the whole of the line you have advertised, are before you. You can easily see extraordinary instances of its sinuosities, from St. Louis to its termination; but it would be difficult to show a single one of them more justifiable than the small deviation from "the regular direction" which has brought the mail through this place. It would be a waste of time to specify the multitude of cases in which deviations from "the regular direction" have been and now are sanctioned by law, or authorized by your Department. They are numerous not only in Missouri, but in your own State. The slightest reference to a few of them will be fully sufficient to portray, in striking colors, the partial and injurious nature of the exception which is made in our case. If this be right, why should the mail, in its transit to Fayette, the county seat of the most important county on the Missouri, be made to go so far "out of its way or regular direction," and travel a much worse road, merely for the sake of passing the decaying little village of Franklin? Why require it to go so circuitously from Franklin to Chariton? And upon what principle are the people of the nominal village of Florisant, or of the almost houseless Jamestown, in Missouri, more entitled to have the mail in a "four-horse stage," "suitable for seven passengers," sent "out of its way or regular direction," than the people of this village, the seat of justice of one of the most fertile and flourishing counties in the Western world? Human imagination, I should think, can conceive none, unless it may be supposed that because the people of Missouri have negroes to work for them, they are to be considered as gentlefolks, entitled to higher consideration and superior privileges to us plain "free State" folks, who have to work for ourselves. That such is the opinion of a distinguished "individual out of the State," who has taken a very active part in this business, is scarcely to be doubted—nor is it intended to question his right to entertain and act upon it; but if any of our own citizens have countenanced and coöperated in his efforts to fix such a stigma upon the State, their labors will doubtless, in due time, be properly appreciated by an indignant people, conscious of their rights and too proud and high-minded to acknowledge inferiority to the citizens of any State in the Union. I hope I shall be pardoned for respectfully referring to a single one of the instances of departure of the mail from its "regular direction" in your own State. It will not be denied that, even in its transit from Frankfort to Paris, it is sent more "out of its way or regular direction," for the convenience and accommodation of your own county, than in our case. It is true that your county has at present more population than ours—an advantage, however, which it cannot long retain; but, bordering, as this does, on the Mississippi River, navigable at all seasons of the year—possessing superior commercial facilities—being of greater extent, and, incredible as you think it, of superior fertility—its want of mail and stage accommodations is scarcely less at present, and ere long must be greater, than that of yours. And if the convenience of "the traveler," or such alleged "delay of the mail," is to control its direction, its deviation from its "regular direction," through your county, would appear far the most objectionable, in consequence of the greater number of persons to be affected by it—which must be in proportion to the difference in the population west of Lexington and that which is west of this place, or to the inducements to traveling or demands for the mail westwardly of these points, respectively; but, without extending the comparison to all the places to which it is applicable, I beg leave to ask, why, if the people of St. Louis have a right to demand a change in the one case, those of Frankfort and Louisville have not at least an equal right in the other?

As to "the inconvenience of the traveler," it is an entirely new idea that the convenience of travelers is to control the direction, arrivals or departures of the mail; but were it otherwise, where is the proof that a single traveler has had to pay an additional cent, or been delayed a moment beyond the periods fixed by your Department for arrivals and departures to and from Vincennes and St. Louis, respectively, or that any change has ever been made in either, in consequence of the mails being sent through this place? It is confidently believed that no such proof has been or can be made; and it does not appear to be just that we should be subjected to such serious deprivations upon a mere naked, unsupported allegation, which the very returns, officially received, both by law and the practice of your Department, sufficiently falsify. But suppose some travelers have been kept on this road a half an hour longer than they would have been on the other: many others, equally entitled to the favors of the Government, have been accommodated by this arrangement; for it is susceptible of the clearest proof, and I pledge myself to produce it, if required, not only that the number of passengers between this town and St. Louis has been double if not quadruple what it has been on any other part of the line, but that this place has produced more traveling in the stages than all the towns and every other place through which the route passes, from one extremity of it to the other. But, whatever may be the force of this objection, it is equally applicable to any of the places to which this has been compared, and is much more so to some of them. It cannot, therefore, be considered harmless as to them, and so disastrous to us, without fixing upon us "free State" people an ignominious mark, which, I trust, the "distinguished individual out of the State," before alluded to, with all the strange and unaccountable assistance which he has hitherto got or may hereafter receive, in this State, will not be able ultimately to effect.

As to "the delay of the mail," this is a grave objection, and should not be assumed upon slight grounds, since it cannot have existed, to such an extent as to render the intended change necessary, without seriously implicating the official integrity of your distinguished predecessor, whose administration of the Department has commanded such universal approbation and applause, and whose popularity in this and the adjoining States is second only to that of the illustrious patriot who fills the Presidential chair. If such an evil has existed, it was his unquestionable duty to have corrected it. If it has been gratuitously assumed, it is not less unjust to him than injurious to us. How, then, stands the fact? It is known to you that the times of arrival and departure of the mail had been arranged and prescribed for the whole route without any reference to this place, and that none of them had been changed or any additional delay authorized in consequence of sending the mail this way. The contractor was just as liable to forfeitures for delays, as if the mail had been sent on the direct road; and it has been the constant duty of every postmaster throughout the whole route to report all failures. Did a single one of them make any report, during Mr. McLean's administration, to justify this assumption? Have any of them done so since you succeeded him—or a single forfeiture been enforced for a delinquency of this kind? It is unhesitatingly assumed, that all these questions must be answered negatively. Unless, then, all those postmasters have violated their oaths, this alleged objection is utterly unfounded. Nor, sir, will there be the least difficulty in fulfilling all the arrangements proposed in your own advertisement, should the mail continue to be transported as it has been under the present contract? But, were it otherwise, what would be the hardship of requiring it to start a half an hour sooner from some one of its night stands, or a few minutes earlier from more than one? Or, what important interest is to be jeopardized should it even arrive at St. Louis a half an hour later?

In addition to this view of the subject, though I feel the greatest deference for your superior legal attainments, I cannot avoid thinking your decision illegal. I take it that no executive can lawfully do that which the Legislature clearly intended *should not be done*—or disregard, control or set aside that which it obviously intended *should be done;* and nothing is clearer, to me, than that Congress, by establishing a route from Shawneetown to this place, intended that it *should not* be extended any further, and that it *should* here be connected with the line from Vincennes to St. Louis; and, therefore, I doubt your authority to destroy the whole of this intended arrangement by extending the line from Shawneetown to St. Louis, adding a new route to Lebanon, and withdrawing "the important western mail" from that on which it was then transferred.

Connected with the efforts to induce you to change the present route, there seems to have been a corresponding plan, of which you were doubtless unapprized, to destroy all the important objections of another one—which plan is calculated to subserve no interest, unless it may be that of a company who may intend to bid for the transportation of the mail on the whole line from Vincennes to St. Louis, and whose interest, should they succeed in obtaining the contemplated contracts, would be greatly advanced by the destruction of a rival establishment. The mail is now, and has been for some time past, brought from Louisville to Shawneetown in stages. It was intended by your predecessor to extend that stage line to this place, and, by connecting it from Equality to Centreville, in Kentucky, with the line from the mouth of Cumberland to Nashville, to establish a direct stage route from the latter to St. Louis, on the best and usually traveled road between those places. Your own personal knowledge of the country will enable you to judge of the vast population in the southern parts of Kentucky, Tennessee, Alabama, etc., which this route would accommodate; and, considering the prodigious emigration which Missouri and this State are both receiving from those States, the markets they afford for our surplus horses, mules, beef cattle and hogs, and the considerable and increasing commerce between them and this country, there seems to be no reason to doubt that a stage line from Nashville to St. Louis would be fully as important and not less desirable than the one from Louisville to St. Louis; and that such a line has been contemplated by yourself is inferrable from the stage route you have advertised from Frankfort, in this State, to Salem, in Kentucky.

Let us, then, see how this route is provided for. Beginning at St. Louis, it comes six or seven miles out of the way, by Cahokia, to this place, and thence, departing from the State road to Georgetown, the seat of justice of Washington county, at the passage of the law establishing the route, and through which it was intended to pass, it goes to Covington; thence, without any reference to the State road, on which the law intended it to be carried, to Frankfort; and thence to Salem, in Kentucky. Now, sir, had human ingenuity been taxed to the utmost to preserve the appearance of intending to run stages on this route as established by law, and yet to disappoint that expectation, nothing more effectual could have been devised than this arrangement; for the route, as advertised, is impracticable for stages, and if it were not, its course is so zigzag that no one would travel it. That you have been most awfully deceived, misinformed and imposed upon, as to the localities and topography in reference to this route, there can be no doubt; and it is to be deplored that there should be found "individuals in this State" so regardless of its interest, and the convenience and accommodation of their fellow-citizens, as to be willing to sacrifice or postpone them all for the sake of a personal interest in reference to the line from Vincennes to St. Louis, which never can be a commercial route nor half as important to this State as would be one from the town of America, on the Ohio River, to our northern settlements, corresponding with the great and only channel of exportation for this whole country.

But to return to the change under consideration. Mr. Bradley says: "Yet propositions may be so favorably made as to induce the Postmaster-General to forego partial engagements made to individuals on the subject."

As the experience of nearly two years affords abundant proof that sending the mail by this place need not delay its arrivals or departures a moment beyond the times prescribed by yourself, and it is demonstrable that the contemplated change cannot fail to increase the expenses of the Government, it is rather difficult to imagine the nature and objects of such propositions as Mr. Bradley supposes might be "so favorably made" as to induce you to change your present determination. But, be this as it may, since our just equality of rights has been drawn into question, and a celebrated member of Congress from another State, backed by certain individuals in this, is understood to stand pledged to deprive us of it, I, for one, am inclined to rely exclusively upon the intrinsic merits of our case, trusting that, upon a review of it, you yourself will do us ample justice, or, if not, that more good will result from letting the people see and feel how our affairs are permitted to be managed by members of Congress from other States, than could be obtained by occupying less elevated ground.

Although no consideration could induce me to withhold this remonstrance, I should be very happy not to be misunderstood. It is not my object to impute blame to your Department; for had the rights of this State been pressed with the same energy that those of other States have been, we all have had reason enough to feel assured that they would have been equally respected by your predecessor, and I have not the least doubt of a disposition equally just and favorable on your part.

Identified, as we are, with all great interests, with Missouri, and particularly so in reference to the prosperity of St. Louis, we entertain no other feelings towards our brethren of that State or city than those of friendship, nor do we doubt the candid reciprocation of the great body of them; and as to myself, far rather would I contribute, with the best of my poor abilities, as I have often endeavored to do, to advance their interests, than deprive them, if in my power, of any accommodation that has ever been extended to them or any part of them; but we claim an equality of rights with them. This nothing shall induce me to relinquish; for great is the debt of gratitude which I owe to the good people of this State, and they have never been seen to shrink when their rights and interests have been called into question, and, with the permission of Divine Providence, they never shall.

I have the honor to be,

Your most obedient servant,

N. EDWARDS.

To THE POSTMASTER-GENERAL, Washington City.

BELLEVILLE, ILLINOIS, *June* 11, 1832.

Mr. Breath:

At a period of such intense interest to all who have hearts to feel for the calamities which now afflict, and must, without prompt relief, finally overwhelm a large portion of our population, the inclosed letters, though not intended for publication, have been freely submitted to the inspection of all who have desired to see them, and particularly to many who have been disposed actually to coöperate in the objects they have in view. This has produced solicitations and importunities for their publication which I am bound to respect, and do not feel at liberty to refuse, and hence they are transmitted to you for that purpose. It is to be hoped that they may contribute to afford to our fellow-citizens of other States such information of our actual situation as may be sufficient to induce them to follow the example so laudably set by the city of St. Louis. Whatever the carnage and desolation which savage ferocity may inflict upon our northern counties, they cannot equal the calamities which are threatened by famine. This is our greatest danger. The General Government will doubtless provide for it as soon as expedient; but, in the meantime, great suffering, if not the most dreadful catastrophies, can only be prevented by active individual benevolence and charity. Unless they can see some other means of saving our suffering fellow-citizens from actual starvation, humanity requires that every editor in the State should spare no pains to make their situation known in its true colors.

NINIAN EDWARDS.

LOWER ALTON, ILLINOIS, *April* 19, 1832.

Gentlemen:

Ere this reaches you, you will doubtless have heard of the hostile deportment of the Sauks, Winnebagoes, etc. Even if no blow should be struck, the consequences cannot fail to be extremely disastrous to our northern settlements. The alarm is universal, the northern frontier weak and exposed and the inhabitants thereof are fleeing into the interior for protection. This, at this time of putting in their crops, will be ruinous and afflictive to many. If it should not reduce them to absolute starvation, they will be left without any resource but the bounty of others, who, in this new country, have enough to do to support themselves and their own families. I deplore this state of things, as well on those accounts as its inevitable tendency to check immigration. Such conduct ought to be submitted to no longer, and I trust that the wonted energy of the President will promptly apply the proper corrective. Those Indians were let off too easily last year, and they will for a long time to come continue to annoy us, if we do not utterly abandon the unwise policy of regarding one part of the tribe as friends while another part is warring upon us. I opposed this policy during the whole of the late war, and all subsequent experience has strengthened the opinion I then entertained. I doubt whether there is one informed candid man, who witnessed the events of the late war on the frontiers of this State and Missouri, that does not believe we suffered more from the peace party than from the war party. Nothing will do but to consider the whole tribe as answerable for the conduct of its members—unless, indeed, there was a permanent separation between, as well in peace as in war.

The Government ought to afford such adequate protection as would relieve the State from the necessity of calling out the militia so frequently, and particularly at such a season of the year as the present. The losses they must sustain by being taken from their farms at the time for planting corn are too serious and oppressive to be slightly regarded. Yet there is no other alternative at present—and this should powerfully recommend the employment of a mounted force, as proposed by the present Secretary of War. Should this plan be adopted, I cannot forbear, on the present occasion, to present to your consideration the preëminent qualifications of Gen. Samuel Whiteside for a service of this kind. His assistance is ever ready to be afforded, and can never be dispensed with on occurrences like the present. He will doubtless have a high command on the present expedition. It will be some reparation for the injuries they must sustain by the present call, if our militia be promptly paid; and as Congress is now in session, it is to be hoped that you may be able to obtain provision for that purpose.

I have only time to add that, although I am a decided tariff man, I highly approve your course on that subject, and will sustain it with the best of my poor abilities.

In great haste,

I am, respectfully,

Your most obedient servant,

NINIAN EDWARDS.

To Hon. Elias K. Kane and Hon. I. M. Robinson, *Senators in Congress*, Washington City, D. C.

A letter of Gov. Edwards in relation to the Black Hawk War, in 1832.

Belleville, Illinois, *June* 5, 1832.

Dear Sirs:

Nothing can be more deplorable than the dreadful situation to which the failure of crops last year and the present Indian war have reduced our fellow-citizens in the northern part of the State. Equally threatened with starvation and the ruthless tomahawk, they have, of themselves, no means of escaping the latter without encountering all the horrors of the former. Fanciful as these alternatives may seem to some, none can doubt their appalling reality who are acquainted with the circumstances and situation of those people, and know the undeniable fact that, owing to the severity of the two last winters and the failure of the last year's crop, there was not within the State, even before the present disturbances commenced, a sufficiency of provisions for our own consumption. No part of the State has escaped great difficulties and privations in consequence of this extraordinary scarcity, but so much greater and more universal has it been in the northern counties, that it was scarcely to be hoped, under the most favorable circumstances, that many of their inhabitants would not suffer such melancholy consequences of an actual deficiency of subsistence as humanity must shudder to think of. Dependent upon their own labor for the means of obtaining articles of the first necessity, the failure of their crops had left them penniless. But no amount of money could command, in those counties, the requisite supplies. Not a solitary inhabitant having more than enough for himself and his own family, none had any to spare to his neighbor. In this situation, these unfortunate people have, at the very time for commencing their crops, been driven from their homes by savage atrocities that have never been surpassed, leaving all their cattle, hogs and other property behind them, which have fallen into the hands of the savages, and compelled to seek refuge in forts where they cannot earn a cent, and must remain till the time for making their crops will have entirely elapsed. This is literally the situation of the people of Jo-Daviess county. Not a man remains on his farm, nor, from present appearances, can return to it for many weeks to come. Multitudes are in a like situation in other counties. How, then, are they, with the losses of property which they have already sustained, to be saved from actual starvation? Certainly by no other means than the interposition of Government, or the benevolence and charity of our neighboring States.

Shall, then, such a number of meritorious men, women and children be permitted, in this great Republic, this Christian land, to starve to death? Can the Government hesitate a moment to afford them all the relief which their distress and suffering so loudly demand? I should think not, for it is difficult to conceive of a more legitimate object for its action, or one that could impose upon it a more indispensable duty, than that of providing against a famine too extensive to be controlled by individual exertions, and which threatens calamities too awful to be safely trusted to the gratuitous relief of others. It has ever been the practice of all nations to afford relief in such cases. The citizens of Alexandria, who had suffered by fire—the subjects of a foreign power, reduced to want by an earthquake—and the starving Indians of the South—have all received the bounty of our own; and shall it be denied to our own suffering citizens, whose calamities have, in a great degree, been produced by measures which the Government itself has found it necessary to adopt?

Not only has this portion of our population suffered by those measures, but they have so injuriously affected every part of the State as to give us just and fair claim to remuneration from the General Government; all of which have been produced by the failure of Congress to provide for the raising of a corps of mounted rangers, as recommended by the Secretary of War. No other description of force is adequate to protection against Indian hostilities; and if anything could justify the placing of such a corps at the disposal of the President, as a measure of reasonable precaution, nothing could have more powerfully recommended it than the unsettled state of affairs on our northern frontier, the universal discontent of the Indians, and the disposition which they have constantly manifested to break out, upon the slightest encouragement, into their usual horrid excesses ever since the first settlement of Galena.

Forbidden by the Constitution to provide for their own safety, every State is entitled to the protection of the United States, and has an indisputable right to claim ample indemnity for injuries and losses sustained for the want of it. Were it otherwise, the Union would be scarcely worth preserving. But instead of that protection which we had a right to claim, and of the want of which the events of the last year had given sufficient warning, their measures have involved us in dangers and require us to fight, not our own, but their battles—for the immediate cause of the present war was the insult, indignity and outrage offered to the United States by the attack upon the Menomonies and murdering twenty-eight of them at Prairie du Chien, by Black Hawk and his party. To submit to an offense so heinous, would have been disgraceful to the United States, and hence it was very properly determined to demand those murderers for punishment. But atrocious as was this conduct, having been committed upon the lands of the United States and within their jurisdiction, it constituted an offense to them exclusively, and not to this or any other individual State. They, therefore, being at peace with all the rest of the world and having an overflowing treasury, should, without relying upon drafted militia from any State, have proposed not only to avenge their own injuries, but to protect the citizens of this State from all dangers justly to be apprehended from a conflict with the Indians about their own affair.

That a severe conflict should have been expected does not seem to admit of a doubt; for, while the pressing of the demand for the murderers, with threats of coercion, could not fail to increase the hostile disposition of the Indians, there was as little reason to believe that they would comply with it, as that the President would abandon it and permit those to escape with entire impunity. Who were demanded? Black Hawk, the most influential man of the tribe, and those distinguished chiefs and warriors who have been united with him ever since the commencement of the late war. For what purpose were they demanded? Not as hostages of peace, but to be tried for murders. As well might it have been expected that the whole tribe would consent to its utter annihilation as that these men would be surrendered for such a purpose. And it is not to be supposed that the President would be satisfied to permit these principal offenders to escape the punishment due to their crimes by the delivery of a few of their humble and comparatively innocent instruments.

But be all this as it may, the United States had no more right to devolve the burthens and hardships of this contest upon this State than upon Maine or Louisiana, and might just as well have required our militia to fight their battles for an attack offered to them in Arkansas or Florida, as in Michigan. Should it become necessary to fight for our north-eastern boundary, Maine, though directly interested in the cause of the war, if ever so competent to the task, would hardly be left to do all the fighting merely on account of her proximity to the scene of action. I therefore trust that, if the war is to be protracted, as it seems likely to be, our militia will no longer be exclusively required for that purpose.

Great are the losses which they must necessarily sustain by the requisitions that have already been made upon them. Called out and kept in service during the whole time for making their crops, they will be thrown out of business for the balance of the year, and deprived of all opportunity of providing food for their families and provender for their horses, cattle and hogs, many of which must inevitably perish in the course of the coming winter.

But the losses occasioned by these heavy requisitions are not confined to those who are detached into the service of the United States. Citizens who remain at home are taxed more than twice as much for, every drafted man, as the United States pay him, and are obliged to make prompt payment—for no man can, according to our laws be drafted, whatever the term of service, without having a right to recover $50 of the class to which he belongs; so that while the United States are only bound to pay for the services of drafted men at the rate of $6.66 per month, some four or five private individuals are responsible to him for $50, which, according to the term of service of the late detachment, requires the latter to pay for each man $36.68 more than the former—a burthen not only unjust, but intolerable and oppressive.

Disastrous, however, as have been all these events, the savage barbarities that have been perpetrated in the face of the large force that has been in the field, clearly evince that our situation would have been infinitely worse had not the Governor so promptly called out the militia. But for this all the settlements beyond the Illinois River must have been precipitately abandoned, in which case universal terror and consternation would have pervaded and to a great extent depopulated all the counties bordering on that river on this side, and thus, by accumulating vast supplies of all kinds, have enabled them to protract the war at their own pleasure. As it is, there is reason to believe the cattle and hogs that have fallen into their hands will enable them to continue it beyond the present year. That it will not end shortly, at any rate, is much to be feared, since, though Gen. Atkinson may march through every part of the country they occupy, such is its nature and extent that he cannot force them into a general engagement; and fighting them with such detachments of raw militia and inexperienced officers as they would not seek to elude, cannot but be extremely hazardous.

In these overwhelming difficulties, great consolation is found in the long experience and unrivaled judgment and energy of the President in such affairs; and trusting that he will be made fully acquainted with our actual situation, we confidently look to him for all the relief which it is in his province to afford—hoping, at the same time, that Congress will immediately provide for the raising of a competent number of mounted rangers and for relieving the wants, repairing the wrongs and adequately compensating the services and losses of our distressed and harassed population.

It is much to be feared that the appropriation proposed by the House of Representatives for defraying the expenses of that bloody war, will be insufficient. Any mistake of this kind would be extremely unfortunate, for nothing could be more unjust and oppressive than to withhold from our militia prompt payment for services rendered at such monstrous sacrifices. Those who were detached into the service of the United States last year, have not, as yet, received a cent of pay. Poor men, dependent upon the sweat of their brows for the support of themselves and their families, cannot withstand such delays, and, as might have been expected, the most of these have since been compelled to part with their claims for about one-half their amounts—for which losses, thus inflicted upon them by the Government at a time of profound peace and with a full treasury, justice cannot deny them equivalent compensation.

I have the honor to be, sir,
Respectfully,
Your obedient servant,
NINIAN EDWARDS.

TO HON. ELIAS K. KANE and HON. I. M. ROBINSON, *Senators in Congress*, Washington, D. C.

Speech when a Candidate for Congress against Matthew Lyon, in 1806, in Kentucky.—His opinions on "treating" at Elections, and on Secret Societies.

If there is any gentleman here who has indulged himself in secret whispers, in saying he has secrets to tell that will astonish my friends, let him speak them out. If they lessen my pretensions, the public should know them; if they do not, they must be told to gratify malignity.

Open attacks can be openly met, but the obscure insinuation, like the worm that penetrates the ship, proceeds without the possibility of resistance. The poisoned arrow is shot in the dark, so that no abilities can repel the blow—no innocence shield from its approach. If he will not do this, I hope you will say, let the weak and ill-natured enjoy the poor pleasure of whispering calumny and detraction, and let the man of sense display his wisdom in disregarding it. The dog bays at the moon, but it still shines in all its beautiful benignity and moves in its undisturbed regularity. There are some who see my acts with a jaundiced eye, and represent them to others in the same color in which they behold them. Their tale of slander passes over my mind as the shadow over the earth.

It may be asked, why I offer my services? The reason is, I have been solicited and not a man has requested me to decline. It is said that I can do the most good, but that I will not. Compare my conduct with that of my opponent's. Have I not, by my acts, promoted the population of the country? Did I not, while a lawyer, try to put an end to controversies? Have I not a general interest in common with the rest of you? Have I not been faithful as a lawyer and did I not faithfully represent your interests in the Legislature? I wish not this mushroom, this ephemeral popularity, which ends the day of its birth! You are are instructed by a corresponding society how to act. They declare that they have had a general meeting and that they came to unanimous resolutions, and yet they do not give the sanction of one name to their proceedings—were they ashamed? If they meant to make no improper impressions—if they meant the public good and not the gratification of private malignity, or the attainment of certain selfish, interested views—why conceal their names? 'Tis only the insidious, the treacherous and designing that shroud themselves with darkness or mystery. They mean to dictate to you, to control you, and yet they are ashamed to let you know who they are, lest you should blush to find yourselves following such blind or self-interested guides into the ditch, or as the instruments by which they obviously intend you shall advance their interests, being separate and distinct from that of yours and the public at large. Let them unmask themselves, and how many do you think you would find among them whose profession is agriculture? Not one; you will find them men of soft hands, active fingers, with fine clothes and always living in the shade. Are you willing to believe that they tell you the truth in what they say? Do you know them? Do you know whether they are entitled to credibility? Surely, if you do not, the act of concealing their names is a very unfavorable evidence of it. If a man intends to tell a truth which the public ought to know, and therefore which is his duty to tell, surely he should not be ashamed or refuse to give up his name and be considered as the author; and if he has not independence or integrity enough to give up his name, is it safe in you to confide in him? No; I am sure you will spurn from you, with contempt, the man who obtrudes his counsel on you and tells you he is led to it from patriotism, and yet would not let you see his face or tell his name. The great prototype of this society assumed the mysterious shape of a serpent, to deceive Eve, and those men are attempting to beguile you in the same way. They are known; and depend upon it, if you shall ever find them out, you will then be satisfied that they had your and the public good about as much at heart as the serpent had the happiness of Eve. They express their joy at the independence of the people; I rejoice at it, also. It is the only foundation of my hopes that they will not suffer themselves to be lead and deceived by men who have so little of that virtue, that they are unwilling to let their names accompany their acts. Would they only avow their names, you would have as little difficulty in discovering the motives of their conduct as if they were before the celebrated Temple of Truth. You would then discover the predominancy of a peculiar and separate interest, totally distinct from the public good, and circumscribed by particular views of private emolument.

They wish for the purity of election, yet they have attempted to misguide the public mind—for they speak of information they never possessed, of communications they never received, of a meeting that never took place: and this can be proved to the satisfaction of any candid mind; and if the contrary is contended, they are now challenged to come from their hiding places and contend the point before those upon whom they intended to dictate to, and for whose welfare they felt such disinterested sensibility. If they cannot do this, let them come forth and show the propriety of attempting to deceive the people for their good. What! shall they attempt to deceive the people, in order to make them do right? Such is sometimes the method of treating children—such conduct might suit the degraded slaves of the East—such may be justifiable conduct in monarchical governments; but in this enlightened age—in a Government predicated upon the information, integrity, independence and virtue of the people—every independent freeman must recoil at such an idea. His mind must be filled with an honest indignation at an attempt to feed him with pap—this slave-like, this childish victuals. An independent man has no palate for it. What! not trust you with naked, open truth, lest it might not answer the purpose? Not rely upon the strength of your own minds? They pay a poor compliment to your understanding, when they suppose you are to be influenced by them merely from the words "*general meeting*," "*unanimous resolves*," etc.—as if *they* possessed all the force and efficacy of a magical rod. But if it is admitted that they have a right to deceive you for your good, they will next claim and exercise the right of deceiving you for other purposes. This is the best apology that can be made for this attempt to deceive you with the magnitude of their meeting and the unanimity of their resolves; but are you willing to admit its truth? To concede this point, finding that they have deceived you on one or two points, what security is there that they have not done so throughout, and have intended to deceive you for their own and not your good? Let them remember the fable of the little boy who cried "wolves!" and you can make the application. I cannot, for my part, confide in any man who I know has attempted to deceive me; nor can I ever believe that any man's object is a laudable one, when he attempts to attain it at the expense of truth and sincerity, and on the ruins of the best principles of sound morality. They might as well contend for the right of taking off my head to prevent me from going to Congress, or deprive you of a vote because you were not disposed to vote as they wished, as to contend that they have a right to deceive and mislead you in order that you might vote as they wished. They deprecate the idea of converting the election into a mere trick, as they call it; and yet, you never discovered a greater disposition to make use of tricks than they have attempted—and all they lacked is the power of executing it with success; and the only obstacle to it is the good sense of the people. Men who discover, with ease, unworthy motives in others, are very apt to be led into the belief from the operations of their own minds. Thus we find these men endeavoring to practice the most shallow trick, which they are charging upon others—like the thief, when pursued, cries "stop thief!" to direct the attention of the people from himself. This trick, they say, will be produced, if the people give up their right to a "*circling junta.*" I confess that, although the epithet *circling*, as applied to *junta*, is borrowed, I cannot discover its beauty or force in this case; but I am not disposed to dispute about terms. The members of this society are not, I presume, perfectly free from superstitious notions, or they could not have calculated so much from the talismanic operation of "general meeting" and "unanimous resolves;" and as a circle was familiar to the magic art, and indeed, according to vulgar ideas, necessary to its operation, they may have very naturally associated the idea with juntas of which there are none, and I sincerely hope there never will be any but their own. That their society has every requisite appertaining to junta, is evident. It is a clandestine association, composed of not more than five members, and has for its object certain ends, to which any means will be subservient. It is not necessary for me to point out the danger to be apprehended from such an association; they have done it themselves. They confess it will convert elections into a "mere trick," by which ambitious men may pass silently into power. The people, being thus warned, I hope will at least be on their guard, and prevent this junta from effecting their object, unless they will come forward unmasked, like the rest of their fellow-citizens. They say they are afraid their brethren may relax in their efforts to serve their friend, and they stimulate them by an assurance that they are determined to support him with all their influence; and still they say he does not need it, because he has gained ground. Do you believe this? If they thought so, why their extraordinary efforts—why their uncommon exertions? But then, they say, the people are determined to vote as becomes freemen, and will not be influenced by any man or set of men. If they think so, where is the necessity for the efforts of their brethren? Surely it would be absurd for them to try to influence the people, if they were determined to disregard it. How do they intend to support his election, if the people are determined not to listen to their arguments? If, as they say, the people are determined to do right, why not let them alone? The truth is, they think all do right who do as they wish them; they will not allow any other man to support his friend, but they must be allowed to support theirs; they are opposed to all juntas but their own; they claim the exclusive right of forming a junta, and I seriously hope none others will follow so pernicious an example. I hope they will be left in the undisturbed enjoyment of plots, tricks, etc.; but I also hope that the good sense of the people will not be misled by them. I hope they will first show their claim to the privilege of directing the people how to vote—and, if it is not unfounded, that they may be left to the enjoyment of their own creed, and the people to their independence.

But it is not only the interest and the duty of each individual to act correctly himself, but also to use his influence in society to prevent any violation of the letter and spirit of our Constitution. That the success of our Government and the preservation of liberty depend upon the purity of election, is self-evident. Our greatest patriots, and best and wisest men, have proven incontrovertibly that such was their belief; and the influence of their opinion should be very great—for we find that there is scarcely a Constitution in the

United States under which treating at an election, or anything like it, is not made a disqualification to the person guilty thereof from holding a seat in any body to which he might be elected. Is there any one that does not consider this a wise regulation? If it is a wise regulation, it is surely your interest that it should exist in practice, and not merely have a place on paper. It will bind the virtuous and conscientious man; for I can scarcely conceive how any man, who has sworn to support the Constitution of his country, can reconcile it to himself to violate it in its most essential provisions. It is evident that it will bind the virtuous men; for them no such provision is necessary. It was intended to restrain the vicious and ambitious, who would be disposed to make use of any means to attain their end; and unless it is made to operate as a check on them, the provision will be perfectly nugatory, and this will be the same thing as if it did not exist at all; nay, infinitely worse, because it gives to those who have no conscience an advantage over those who have, inasmuch as the restraint of the virtuous adds additional strength to those of the other class. If, then, you do not discountenance those who are disposed to practice this corruption—if you do not withhold from such men your confidence, and teach them that it is their interest to act otherwise, in order to gain your approbation—instead of inspiring the minds of your fellow-citizens with a laudable and patriotic ambition to serve their country and excel in virtue, you cherish their vices by rewarding them; you establish a school of vice and depravity in our country, tending to contaminate not only the present, but succeeding generations; you foster in your own bosoms the deadly adder, which, sooner or later, will sting you to death. The deadly poison will insinuate itself into the heart of society, and from thence diffuse itself throughout all parts of it. Let it be once conceded that you are willing to see the practice of "treating" for an election once introduced among us, and what will be the consequence? The precedent, once established, will become less and less objectionable by becoming more familiar to you—it will finally become fashionable, and ultimately necessary to success. I ask you, then, where is your boasted equality? Where is the fair and open field in which talents and merit may successfully exert themselves and receive their just reward? It will vanish forever, or only remain as a dream upon the mind. All distinctions will then be confined to the rich—for they alone will be able to meet the expenses of an election. A man in moderate circumstances, be his talent ever so great, will not be able to contend with his more wealthy competitor; and we shall find ourselves completely under the dominion of an aristocracy, while we are only amused with the name of a free government! He who has paid the least attention to the current of events, or histories of other countries, may be satisfied that unless this most formidable enemy to freedom, *corruption*, is successfully repelled, by the virtue and wisdom of the people, in his first attempt to invade us, he will rise in his strength, like a mighty torrent, and tear down everything before him.

Even in England treating for an election to the House of Commons, that branch of the legislature of that country which consists of the immediate representatives of the people, is severely prohibited, and made, also, a disqualification of the person guilty thereof; and had the regulation been strictly adhered to, that country would have been free compared to what it now is—such oppression as their people now feel could not have reared its gigantic head among them. The treating in England commenced, in the first instance, as it seems to be commencing in the United States: as a harmless thing. It was thought that the independent minds of the Britons were not to be influenced by it. It was practiced by the most indirect means—it was masked under various pretences—till at length it has become the only engine of procuring an election; and it is no extraordinary thing, now, to hear of an election costing a candidate £500.

Such has been the progress of it in England. Most dearly have the people there paid for their toleration of it, till it became so formidable that they cannot now resist it. Such will, I fear, be its progress in this country, unless the people at large are disposed to benefit by the example and fatal experience of others. For the sake of guarding against the evils that have befallen them—for the sake of public virtue on its own account—they should therefore discourage the practice in any shape in which it can make its appearance. No man in England ever said to another, "I give you this treat to vote for me," but, on the contrary, were he charged with it, he would deny it; he would speak of his right to spend his money as he pleased, and resort to many other evasions. So it is in this country. But inquire into the case as rational men. If you find a man profusely spending his money in treating, while an election is pending, what construction can you put on his conduct than that he is, indirectly, attempting to buy your votes? You should ask yourself, "would this man practice so much liberality, unless he had some object in view? Is it his constant habit on all occasions?" If so, you must think him immensely rich or very prodigal and imprudent, and very little calculated to manage his own business; and surely a man incapable of managing his own affairs is not very well qualified to manage the affairs of a nation. Therefore, if you find him prodigal, there is no hopeful presage of his rendering the nation any great services; for we can scarcely expect that a man who is very prodigal of his own money, will be very careful of yours—at least there is danger. If, on the other hand, you find his profusion only to exist during the pendency of an election, you can draw no other conclusion than that it is for the purpose of advancing his election. Let it, then, be conceded that it must be to promote his election—for surely he would not do so unless he had some object in it, and this can be the only one—with whom does he expect to advance his election, by this means? Surely, with those who drink his whisky! He could not think it would benefit him, unless it was to do it in this way. How, then, is it to benefit his election, unless he supposes that more people will vote for him, in consequence of his whisky, than otherwise would do so? Does he not, then, attempt to buy their votes? Certainly; for he buys the whisky, and this he gives for the purpose of getting votes, and all he receives in consequence of it are as much bought as if, instead of the whisky, he had paid the value of it in money. Whether he succeeds, or not, it must be evident to all thinking men that this is his object; for his giving the whisky does not render him any better qualified to serve you, and he evidently shows that he considers that your minds are to be influenced by it. Would he give it unless he thought so? and is there anything that ought to fill the minds of enlightened and independent freemen with more indignation, than an attempt of this kind? Is there anything more degrading to them than such a supposition? Can a man insult them more than to show that he conceives them so mean and mercenary? And can you suppose that a man is not influenced by other motives than the public good, when he endeavors to succeed in his election by purchasing it—in other words, by bribery and corruption?

This is the only view I am capable of taking of the subject, and I hope my observations will be received as a sufficient apology for my not falling into this too common practice. I cannot but feel too great respect for my fellow-citizens to show that I conceived them capable of being, either directly or indirectly, corrupted; and if I did conceive them so, I cannot reconcile it to my conscience either to practice it upon any one, or to violate that Constitution which I have sworn to support. I love rational liberty; I esteem the practice of which I am speaking as the most formidable engine of attacking it; and if we ever do lose our liberties, I will venture to predict that it will only be effected by destroying the purity of elections.

No man is fonder of the approbation of his fellow-citizens than I am. My disposition and habits have always led me to cultivate their friendship; I esteem it a most distinguished honor, and a most valuable and desirable acquisition; I am anxious to attain the honor of serving my country; I have endeavored to qualify myself for it. But I am not disposed to attain this honor by any other than the most honorable means! I can never sacrifice my integrity, my ideas of propriety, or my independence, to procure it. I do most sincerely wish your approbation, but I only wish it upon proper principles; and I am sure it is not your interest to give it upon any other. I therefore submit myself to your consideration, as a candidate for the honor I solicit, upon the very small stock of merit you may conceive I possess. I pretend to no superiority over any other gentleman; I am sensible of my own deficiency; I am influenced by no personal opposition to any man; nor shall I attack the pretensions of any other person or say anything against him, unless it shall be rendered necessary to my own defense. I will hold myself ready to repel, and not commence, any attack—for this is the office of the people, and not the candidate; it is your province, and not his, to decide to whom the preference ought to be given. But, being a freeman, I have a right to offer myself to the district, and this I hope is not just cause of offense to any one. It should not be to the people, for I enlarge their choice—and if they do not choose to accept my services, I will cheerfully submit; and I do sincerely hope that those who cannot reconcile it to themselves to vote for me, will not consider me as their enemy on that account. I assure you I shall consider no man my enemy merely because he does not prefer me, on this occasion; but I may even indulge the hope that, though he cannot now prefer me, yet, probably, at some future period, when we may be better acquainted, or with some other competitor, I may have his approbation.

It is generally known throughout this country that I have exerted myself on all occasions, hitherto, to promote the real interest of this district. This I did while I was a representative from Nelson county, before I ever came among you; and I was then influenced by the purest republican views. My wish was that every man might have an opportunity of procuring a freehold of his own—that there might be as few tenants as possible—as I have always considered tenants too subject to the influence of their landlords, and landlords in general so much disposed to abuse that influence, as to render it dangerous and highly inimical to republicanism.

With these views I have zealously persevered in exerting the small portion of the influence I possessed to ameliorate the situation of all the citizens of this district, and to promote its general prosperity in every point of view whatever; and I indulge the pleasing hope, the animating expectation and the firmest persuasion that, from the particular manner in which our district has been settled—from the facility with which the people could get and have procured lands of their own—we shall be amongst the last people in America to surrender our liberty and independence. And in whatever way I may be treated by the people—even if I should not get a single vote at the approaching election—it shall not diminish in the least degree my zeal for the welfare of the district, or my exertions to promote the public good. I hope I shall be permitted to say that, if such was my conduct before I came among you, or possessed the least interest in the country, it is unreasonable to suppose that I should depart from it, after I had identified my interest with yours, by having permanently settled among you and concentrated in the district every particle of property I possess in the world. No, sirs; my interest being similar to that of the great mass of my fellow-citizens—having no interest separate and distinct from theirs—deriving my principal support, at this very time, from the cultivation of the earth—there is no measure that could be adopted, that would be oppressive upon them, but would be equally so upon me. You have, therefore, the best security for my fidelity—inasmuch as, by promoting your interest in the best manner possible, I at the same time should, in equal proportion, advance my own. As to my qualifications to serve you, I say nothing—you must judge for yourselves; but, as far as they extend, they shall be exerted with the utmost zeal to promote yours and the public good. More I cannot promise.

Speech delivered in the Senate of the United States, on the bill to abolish Credit in the sale of the Public Lands.

Mr. PRESIDENT:

It has not been nor is it now my object to defeat the bill, as it has been suggested. Indeed, I am so far reconciled to its principles, that, if liberal and equitable provisions were contained in it in favor of persons actually settled upon public land, it should have my support; but these I have not deemed it practicable to obtain, and therefore I have limited my views to the proposition which I have submitted, not hitherto doubting that, from its reasonableness, it would succeed; and in that event I have felt disposed, during the whole of the present session, to acquiesce in the proposed arrangement.

The objects of my proposition are to dispose of public lands which will not sell for cash; to accommodate actual settlers who have not cash to give; and to promote the settlement of the public lands. I cannot but feel astonished that objects so just and reasonable should excite any serious opposition, more especially with gentlemen from that section of the country in which those lands are situated. I am not one of those who are disposed to contend that the law of nature is paramount to and should control the positive institutions of society; but I do contend that those institutions should, as far as practicable, be predicated upon and consistent with this law; and that as all men have a natural right, according to the beneficent intention of the Creator of the world to a portion of the land which He has made for their benefit, no government, having large tracts of waste and unappropriated land, can, without acting flagrantly unjust, and contrary to the Divine intention and will, withhold from those of its citizens who are unable to advance cash, such a portion of land as they may need, upon the terms proposed by my amendment. The case might be put in a much stronger point of view, but this is sufficient for my present purpose, and I hope it will not be denied by those whose veneration and respect for natural law and the Divine will have been so recently exhibited before this house.

In opposition to the amendment which I have submitted, it has been stated, by the Honorable Chairman of the Committee on Public Lands, that the object of it is to defeat the bill, and that, if agreed to, it would produce a mongrel system I can assure the gentleman that I had no hopes of defeating the bill, that I had no intention of attempting it, and that I had reconciled my mind to submission upon the subject, with a sincere desire that the change might not excite those discontents and evil consequences which I feared it might produce. But, sir, there is not that incongruity between my amendment and the bill, which the gentleman seems to suppose. His plan is to sell, for prompt payment, all the lands that will command cash; mine is a limited appropriation of a small part of those lands which will not sell under his system, and to extend credit to those poor people who may be actual settlers thereon, and who are otherwise unable to acquire a home. And really, considering the quantity of land in the gentleman's own State, which he himself knows will not sell for cash, and supposing it probable that there might be a portion of the population of that as well as other States who might be accommodated by the measure I propose, I was somewhat surprised to find that the gentleman was not equally anxious with myself to extend the settlement of his own State, and provide as far as practicable, consistently with natural justice, for all classes of the citizens thereof.

As to its being a mongrel system, because a part of the public lands will be sold for cash and a small portion upon a credit—if experience can be relied upon, there is nothing very substantial in this objection. I need not, I am sure, remind the honorable gentleman that for many years such a mongrel system has prevailed, and under the present law more land has, from time to time, been sold for prompt payment, than will probably be sold on credit if my amendment should prevail; and that hitherto experience has not demonstrated any very great inconvenience or objection from selling lands at the same office for cash as well as upon credit.

When I had the honor, a few days since, of submitting to the Senate the amendment now under consideration, I expressly declared my intention to abstain from all discussion of the merits of the proposed change in the manner of disposing of the public lands—not because I did not think that weighty and important considerations forbid the contemplated change, particularly in the present crisis of our affairs, but from the resistless conviction, which was forced upon me by circumstances not necessary to be repeated, that all efforts to arrest the measure in this house, at the present moment, would be utterly fruitless. Strong, however, as was that conviction, I did not expect to witness that impatience and anxiety to precipitate the measure, which I thought was evinced not less by the manner of pressing it than the nature of the opposition to the amendment offered by the gentleman from Alabama, as well as the one offered by myself. His amendment, having the most natural affinity to several provisions contained in the bill itself, embraces the very debt from which so much is apprehended—proposed a natural and rational remedy for the very evil which is said to demand the contemplated change—and related directly to the sale of the public lands, the object of the bill itself; yet gentlemen seriously contend that it would be better and more appropriate to engraft it in a bill hereafter to be acted upon, whose sole object is to extend certain additional credits upon installments now due, and with which object no other has hitherto been permitted to be united on any of the similar occasions that have presented themselves in the course of several years' legislation upon the subject.

Little did I expect such an innovation upon all former precedents to be recommended by gentlemen whose transcendent abilities have so lately been exerted to advocate what has been called single legislation, and to demonstrate the impropriety of uniting two distinct objects in the same bill. But, were their recommendation to be followed, I do not think it more probable that their objections to the union of Maine and Missouri would have vanished, if the restriction they so much desired had been imposed upon the latter, than that they would then be as zealous to defeat the object of the amendment as they now are; for while, without attempting to impugn the merits of our amendments, or to show that they have not a natural connection with the subject of the bill, they earnestly advise us to change our position, they do not, even in that event, promise us their support—and for my own part I cannot consent, in these inauspicious times, to camp upon the ground selected by my enemy. Let it be remembered that I have as much reason to believe that their object is to defeat my amendment, as they have to assert that my object in offering the amendment is merely to defeat their bill.

I am sorry that the honorable gentleman from Alabama thought proper to withdraw his amendment, and am happy to learn that it is his intention again to offer it. I am decidedly of the opinion that the cases which it presents loudly call for the interposition of the National Legislature. All of us must be convinced of the folly and delusion with which those persons for whose benefit it was intended were misled. Nothing, since the days of the celebrated South Sea and Mississippi schemes, has been more fallacious and visionary than the calculations with which those deluded persons have been betrayed; and the Government I hope will be too magnanimous to wish to profit by the folly of its own citizens, or to take advantage, like a ruthless sharper, of those indiscretions which it has, in a great degree, been instrumental in encouraging—especially when it can abstain from doing so without being placed in a worse condition than it would have been in if those sales had never taken place. I cannot, however, think that the gentleman's amendment has any suitable connection with the bill in which it has been proposed to incorporate it; and I apprehend the gentleman would find himself greatly mistaken, if, either in a separate or any other bill, he should suppose it would be more likely to succeed than in the one now under consideration, which relates to and provides a mode of disposing of the very lands for which his amendment was intended to provide.

The alleged ground for all this eagerness to change the present system of disposing of the public lands is, that our fellow-citizens, during a period of extraordinary and general delusion, purchased more lands than it is supposed they can conveniently pay for—and, therefore, to save others who are wholly guiltless of such indiscretion, you determine to abolish the system, lest they should hereafter be tempted to injure themselves in like manner.

Following up those principles with the same parental care, and I ask whether they would not equally admonish you to abolish foreign commerce abandon manufactures, and prostrate all your banking systems which have demoralized and disgraced your country? Have the temptations presented by these objects, during the period alluded to, been less alluring and seductive, or less disastrous to individuals or the Government, than those of your land system? So far from it, your commerce and your banks may be justly considered as the primary cause of the evils that are supposed to have resulted from that system, as well as of many others of infinitely more importance; but it seems that the lessons of experience are thought to be sufficient to produce every requisite correction on this side of the mountains, whilst it is presumed that all its admonitions will be totally lost upon the people of the West, unless it be kindly aided by the interposition of your coercive guardianship over them—which is indeed a species of kindness that gentlemen in a certain quarter of our country would have been very willing to have dispensed with, in certain restrictive and embargo times, when it was thought that people should be permitted to judge of and pursue their own interest according to their own notions.

That excessive purchases, as they were called, of foreign goods, as well as land, have been made, and that the former have been attended with consequences much the most injurious, will, I presume, hardly be denied; yet, I believe there is very little prospect of withholding that positive encouragement which is given to the purchases by the credit on merchants' bonds, from which the Government is liable to lose, and no doubt has lost greatly—whereas it is impossible to lose by the credit given under your land system, because the land is always liable for the debt that may be due upon it. And really, sir, I think that large debts due by merchants to the Government are as likely to produce an influence upon its councils, as debt due by the plain and honest agriculturists of the West.

The gentleman from New York foresees great political dangers from the debt now due and to become due for public lands, and has frequently endeavored to illustrate his apprehensions by a reference to the case of the settlers on the south side of Green River, in the State of Kentucky. No man is more minutely acquainted with that case than I am; and did I not know how hopeless a task it is to try to convince gentlemen against their wills, I think I could most satisfactorily demonstrate that his apprehensions are without foundation, and that, in the very case alluded to, the lands could neither have been kept out of the market, nor disposed of in any other way, so as to have produced more general satisfaction or less injurious political consequences. Sir, it is the public land, not the debt, which is the most liable to create those political dangers that are so much to be deprecated; as an illustration of which, I can refer the gentleman to a case much less equivocal than the one on which he relies—I mean the celebrated contests relative to the agrarian law, from their first commencement throughout all the convulsive struggles to which they gave rise. In spite of the theories to the contrary, the best practical expedient to guard against those dangers is to facilitate the acquisition of land to all those who are disposed to purchase. But, supposing the debt now due to be as ruinous to individuals and as dangerous to the Government as the gentleman presumes—what could be a more appropriate remedy, or more just and politic on the part of the Government, than to cancel the contracts as proposed by the gentleman from Alabama, when it can do so and still be placed in a better situation than it would have been if those debts had never been contracted? Surely, sir, we ought not to be alarmed at dangers that are capable of being so easily avoided by so small a sacrifice.

Resolutions, prepared by Gov. Edwards, against relinquishing to Great Britain any part of the provinces of Canada that we may acquire by conquest.

Although, at the time, a citizen of Illinois, Gov. Edwards prepared the following resolutions, to be submitted at a public meeting of the citizens of Logan county, in the State of Kentucky, convened upon previous notice, for the purpose of taking into consideration our difficulties with Great Britain during the late war:

WHEREAS, in the prosecution of the present just and necessary war, which has been forced upon these United States by the persevering injustice of Great Britain, it has pleased the Almighty Disposer of Events to crown our arms with success in the province of Upper Canada—and confidently relying upon the justice of our cause and the blessing of the same Almighty Being, we anticipate like success in Lower Canada; and whereas, we have seen, in the newspapers published in different parts of the Union, strong remonstrances against relinquishing to Great Britain any part of their provinces which we either have conquered or may conquer, during the war; thereby implying a doubt of the steadfast determination of our Government to retain the same; we deem it not less our privilege than our duty to express our opinion upon the subject. And, therefore,

Resolved (as our opinion), That the entire conquest of the Canadas is required by the injustice of Great Britain towards us. That their acquisition is expedient for us, by opening to us new sources of wealth and prosperity in the vast fur trade of North-western America; in facilitating intercourse between the waters of the Rivers St Lawrence, Mississippi, Missouri and Ohio; in expelling from our border an unprincipled neighbor, whose hostility has even increased with our increase of prosperity, and who, regardless of his own honor, and callous to the dictates of humanity, has heretofore employed and would on any future occasion employ and encourage his merciless savage allies to commit their ruthless barbarities upon wounded prisoners, unoffending citizens, and helpless women and children. And, therefore, it is our opinion, that the relinquishment of the Canadas (or any other of their provinces which we may conquer) to Great Britain, after the treasures that have been spent and the precious blood which has been and must be profusely shed, in obtaining them, would forego all those advantages, produce recurrence of those calamities which we have witnessed and deplored, be injurious to the character of the United States and particularly oppressive upon the Western country, whose citizens would ere long be called on to make the same conquests, then rendered more difficult by those precautions which the enemy's late experience would teach him to adopt.

Resolved, That a copy of these resolutions, signed by the chairman and countersigned by the secretary of this meeting, be transmitted to our brave and patriotic Governor, to the representatives of this county in the Legislature, and to our representatives in Congress—all of whom are respectfully requested to take such measures as to them may appear most proper, to give to the foregoing sentiments permanency and efficiency.

The substance of the remarks of Mr. Edwards, of Illinois, in the Senate of the United States, on the following resolution, viz:

"*Resolved*, That appropriations of territory, for the purpose of Education, should be made to those States, in whose favor no such appropriations have been made, corresponding in just proportion with those heretofore made to other States in the Union."

Mr. President: Notwithstanding that any opposition to the resolution upon your table, on the part of the representatives of the new States, has been denounced as "disreputable to their characters for honesty and justice," not only by many of our most distinguished and patriotic public journals, but also by one of the most respectable States of the Union, yet, sir, a sense of duty will not permit me to decline an investigation of the subject, hopeless as it may be, to oppose my feeble efforts to the transcendent abilities with which the proposition under consideration has been supported, and, unpleasant as it is, to subject myself to imputations which the zeal of many of its ablest advocates affords me but little prospect of escaping. I shall, however, carefully endeavor to follow the example of the honorable gentleman who has just resumed his seat (Mr. Lloyd), in treating the subject with such deference to the feelings of others, as to furnish no ground of exception to any gentleman with whom it may be my misfortune to differ in opinion. And permit me to say, sir, that, equally with the gentleman from Maryland, appreciating the advantages of education—regarding it as a most efficient means of increasing the virtue, knowledge and happiness of mankind and of imparting additional moral power, stability and embellishment to our republican institutions—it would afford me the sincerest gratification to unite with him in any just and proper measure for the advancement of that important object. But, sir, it appears to me to be doubtful, at least, whether Congress can rightfully adopt, for that purpose, the measure now under consideration.

The appropriation which we are asked to make is avowed to be for a mere State purpose, and in that point of view I shall proceed to consider it under every modification of which it is susceptible. The question, then, is, *can the resources of this nation be thus applied?* This should be tested by principle, rather than by the "precedents upon precedents" referred to and relied upon by the gentleman from Maryland, for this Government is much too young to acknowledge the force of any precedents, not founded upon, and much less of those which are in opposition to, principle; and gentlemen who are disposed to avail themselves of an argument deduced from mere precedents, in the present case, ought to recollect how little inclined they would be to respect such authority, in a variety of other cases that might be referred to.

In discussing this subject, I may, I presume, safely premise that the duties, powers and objects of the Federal and State Governments are separate and distinct, and that the success of our whole govermental experiment, and the prosperity and happiness of this nation, depend upon the fidelity and wisdom with which those governments respectively discharge their appropriate functions. Each government has, for those important purposes, and as necessary thereto, its own particular resources, which cannot be yielded up or misapplied without impairing its capacity to fulfill the objects of its institution, for nothing could be more nugatory than a grant of powers without the means of executing them. The resources of this Government are found from experience to be, at this time, inadequate to its wants; any measure, therefore, whose tendency would be, further to embarrass and cripple its operations, must be deemed highly inexpedient at least.

Mr. President, the gentleman from Maryland appears to have reviewed, with critical accuracy, all the events connected with the acquisition of the national domain, and he has with great perspicuity traced out the origin and demonstrated the validity of our title to it. But, sir, whether it has been acquired by conquest, cessions from particular States, or purchases from foreign powers, one thing is undeniable—it has doubtless been acquired by and exclusively belongs to the Confederation or Union. It must, therefore, be considered as National and not State property, and by fair inference is applicable only to National and not State objects. It is true, as contended by the honorable gentleman, that it is a common fund, in which all the States are interested. So, sir, is the revenue, and every other species of property belonging to the United States, in relation to all of which the interest of the States is precisely the same. Being a common fund, applicable to the use and support of the General Government, the States can enjoy the benefits of it only in its just and legitimate application to national purposes. I hold, therefore, that no State can rightfully claim, and of course to none can be granted, the separate and distinct use and enjoyment of the property or funds of the nation, in consequence of a right to a common participation therein.

Independent, however, of these general considerations, the adoption of the proposed measure is, I think, forbidden by a just regard to the positive stipulations of the United States with the States which ceded the public domain on the east side of the Mississippi River. Let us, for a moment, attend to the circumstances under which those cessions were made, which have been so eloquently narrated and commented upon by the gentleman from Maryland.

During our revolutionary struggle, which eventuated so happily in the establishment of our liberty and independence, the pecuniary resources of the nation had been exhausted; and, at the close of the contest, it found itself loaded with a heavy debt, incurred in the prosecution of the war, which it had not the means of discharging, but which every dictate of justice, honor and gratitude required should be provided for, at the earliest practicable period, by every means which the nation could command.

Several of the States claimed large tracts of waste and unappropriated territory, in the Western country, as being within their chartered limits. These claims had long been the subject of much animated and sometimes irritating discussion, as is sufficiently obvious from the authorities read by the gentleman from Maryland. The States which had no part in those lands had earnestly insisted that, if the dominion over them should be established by the common force and treasure of the United States, they ought to be appropriated as a common fund for defraying the expenses of the war. Congress, appealing to the generosity, magnanimity and patriotism of the States having those claims, had recommended and solicited liberal cessions of a portion of them, for the same purpose—promising, as inducements thereto, by the very resolution which the honorable gentleman has read to you, that all the lands which might be so ceded or relinquished, should be disposed of for the common benefit of the United States; that they should be settled and formed into distinct republican States, which should be admitted into the Federal Union; and, that the regulations for granting and for settling those lands should be prescribed by Congress.

The States thus appealed to yielding, at length, to a laudable spirit of harmony and conciliation, made the cessions which had been requested of them—not, however, without stipulating, very explicitly, that those lands should be considered as a common fund for the use and benefit of the Union, as it then was or thereafter might be; and that they should be faithfully and *bona fide* disposed of for that common purpose, "and for no other use or purpose whatsoever."

The United States, therefore, having solicited and accepted the cessions upon such terms—under such circumstances—having bound themselves, by solemn compact, to dispose of those lands for the use and benefit of the Union, "and for no other use or purpose whatsoever," Congress cannot now, I think, consistently with good faith and honor, disregard those solemn engagements by withdrawing the whole or any part of the fund so surrendered from the use of the Union, and appropriating it to that of any one or more States.

Sir, the stipulations of the United States embrace the whole of those lands. If, then, you can withdraw any part of them from the use for which they were specially solicited, ceded and accepted, where, I beg leave to ask the gentleman from Maryland, is the limit to your power over them? Why may you not as well make partition of the whole of them among the several States of the Union? And how, then, would you fulfill the stipulations of the United States? First, that the regulations for granting and for settling those lands should be prescribed by Congress. Secondly, that they should be settled. Thirdly, that being settled, they should be formed into distinct republican States, and admitted into the Federal Union. It cannot be contended that we are competent to delegate powers for such purposes to the States; for, if that be the case, there are no powers with which we are invested that might not, with equal propriety, be transferred.

Mr. President, it is no answer to these objections to contend, as the gentleman from Maryland seems to do, that the claims of the ceding States were not just and valid, for, however defective they may have been originally, the United States, by accepting the cessions upon special conditions, must be considered as having admitted the right and bound themselves to comply with the conditions—otherwise there could be no faith and confidence reposed in any adjustment, arrangement or contract with the Government. [Here Mr. Lloyd rose and explained the remarks he had made; and, having resumed his seat, Mr. Edwards again proceeded.]

Mr. President, in consequence of the explanations of the honorable gentleman, I shall forbear the remarks I had intended to make upon this part of the subject. But, sir, let it even be admitted that the claims of those States were wholly defective—that they had never made any cessions whatever—that the United States had never entered into any stipulations in relation to the subject—and that the public domain had actually been conquered by the united valor of all the States—still it would have been an acquisition, made, not in their State but in their Federal character, in which latter character, only, could they participate in the use and benefits of it. For, being a Federal acquisition, it could not, without a total prostration of our whole system of Government, be annihilated as such, by being partitioned out, in due proportion, among the several States of the Union. Where, sir, is delegated the power that is competent to make such a division, either of the whole or a part? The State Governments most assuredly have no control over the subject; and surely those, to whom the powers of the Federal Government are entrusted, never could, rightfully, annihilate its own resources for any such purpose.

If, however, sir, the gentleman from Maryland is correct in the opinions which he has supported with equal zeal and ability, then, indeed, sir, may the States rightfully claim and Congress rightfully grant partition of all the territory purchased of France and Spain with the common funds of the nation, to be appropriated to objects to which powers of Federal legislation are not pretended to extend. Then, indeed, sir, may the revenue, and every other species of property belonging to the United States, receive a similar destination: for they all constitute "the common funds of the nation," in which the States are interested; and the powers and objects of appropriation, as granted to Congress by the Constitution of the United States, are equally precise, defined and limited, in relation to all the funds of the nation, without discrimination.

In the specification of those powers, there is none, either expressed or implied, to warrant the appropriation now asked for. It cannot be inferred, from the general power to make all needful rules and regulations for disposing of the territory and other property of the United States; for candor must admit that the plain and natural inference from this want of power is, that the property of the Union should be disposed of for the use and benefit of the Union—and that, too, in strict conformity with the legitimate powers of Federal legislation—and, solely, in aid of the great objects thereof. If, then, the States, respectively, have no right to the separate and distinct use and enjoyment of the common property and funds of the nation, whence do we derive the power to confer such a right upon them? And if the control over those funds be intrusted to the Federal Legislature for National and not for State purposes, I beg leave, also, seriously to ask gentlemen whether we can appropriate them to the latter without a most palpable violation of the trust confided to us?

In addition to all these objections, there is one more which cannot be disregarded, so long as we retain the slightest respect for the just and lawful acts of our predecessors, or consider the high character for justice, honor and good faith, which this Government has hitherto so justly acquired and maintained, both at home and abroad, as worth preserving.

The first Congress, composed principally of the venerable sages and patriots of the revolution, duly considering the purposes for which the public lands had been ceded, and disposed fairly to fulfill the stipulations of the United States in relation to them, by the act of 1790, solemnly pledged, not only those, but all other lands which the United States might thereafter acquire, for the payment of the public debts, expressly declaring that they should be applied solely to that use, until those debts should be fully satisfied.

By the act of 1795, this pledge is again repeated in language still more energetic, for the faith of the United States is therein also expressly pledged that those lands shall remain inviolably apppropriated to the payment of those debts, until the same shall be completely effected.

At various other periods, between 1790 and 1817, inclusive, has this subject been brought under the review of different Congresses, and as often has the same pledge been renewed. And thus has been created a solemn compact between the United States and the public creditors. Seeing it, then, supported by so many repeated enactments, and sanctioned as it has been, to this day, by the public sentiment of the nation, shall we now violate it? Have our predecessors acted unjustly or unwisely in making it? If not, we ourselves, though bound by no previous obligations, ought, for the sake of justice, to be willing to do the same thing, if it were now to be acted upon for the first time; for the Government ought to be just before it pretends to be generous, especially at the expense of others.

[Mr. E. here read several sections of the laws containing the pledges referred to, and contended that the faith of the United States being pledged that the whole of the public lands should remain inviolably appropriated to the payment of public debts, they should be appropriated solely to that use, until those debts should be fully satisfied; and a vast amount of them still remaining unpaid, no part of the national domain could be rightfully appropriated to the purposes contemplated by the resolution under consideration.]

And if, indeed, sir, we have on any former occasion, through inadvertence or from other causes, misapplied any part of this fund, so far from furnishing an argument in favor of persevering in a course so unjustifiable, I appeal to the candor of the gentleman from Maryland, as he does to mine, to say whether it does not, incontestably, give to the public creditors an additional claim upon us to forbear all further willful misapplications?

But, sir, let us inquire into the extent of the application we are called upon to make. Instead of the "small slice," as described by the gentleman from Maryland, it is to the enormous amount of about ten millions of acres of the national domain; which, at the average price at which those lands have hitherto been sold, would produce a sum nearly equal, if not entirely so, to the whole amount of the net proceeds of the sale of public lands received into the treasury of the United States, during the last nineteen or twenty years. It would be needless to review the extraordinary circumstances which, in this period, so powerfully contributed to augment the receipts of the treasury, from this source of our revenue. Similar causes are not likely to recur for many years to come, and calculating upon the sales that have been made since those causes have ceased to operate, a much longer period, probably not less than double that length of time, would be requisite to effect sales to the same amount.

What, then, Mr. President, is to be the consequence of granting this quantity of land to the States, in whose favor it is applied for? It surely cannot be, seriously, intended to vest the old States with power to plant colonies of tenants in the new ones. This would be impracticable, and to those States utterly useless. Waiving other important considerations, which I forbear even to allude to, the vast extent of the national domain, and the cheapness of unimproved lands, thank God for it, afford but little prospect of renting such lands to advantage, or even of having them settled and improved for the use of them.

The object, then, must be either to authorize the States to dispose of the land, or that this Government shall become their auctioneer for that purpose. The former would be transferring to those States a power exclusively delegated to Congress; a right to do that, which, according to the stipulations before referred to, can only be performed by Congress. For I take it for granted that, if you cannot vest in the States the right to dispose of their respective interests in the whole of the public lands, you can transfer to them no power to dispose of any part of them. But, sir, supposing there is nothing solid in this objection, what is to be the effect upon your treasury, of authorizing the States to sell the land proposed to be granted to them? They must enter into competition with you. In proportion to the extent of their sales, whatever they may be, yours must be diminished, because not only the price, but the sale of land must depend upon the relation which supply bears to demand; for if the price be so low and the supply so great that it ceases to be an object of speculation, there can be no motive to purchase it but for cultivation. As the Government, however, would still have an infinitely greater variety of lands to select from, the States could not sell at all, to any extent, without underselling the Government. This, therefore, they must do—otherwise their lands would be of no use to them. Recollect, sir, the millions of acres which you have granted in military bounties. These have already come into competition with you at the reduced price of from twenty to forty dollars a quarter section, and have most materially curtailed your sales. Add to them the ten millions of acres now proposed to be granted, you must abolish your present system of sales, and abandon your minimum price altogether or close up your land offices for twenty, thirty or forty years to come.

Take, then, sir, if you please, the other alternative, that the Government shall dispose of the land for the benefit of those States. To this, some gentlemen seem to think there can be no objection, because the Constitution has delegated to Congress the power of disposing of the property of the United States, though that power is, by express stipulation and plain and obvious inference, coupled with the positive duty of disposing of such property for the benefit of the Union. By this plan, however, the injurious effects of competition might be avoided and the present minimum price preserved. But, as has already been shown, it would require some twenty years at least to dispose of the land, though not an acre should, in the meantime, be sold for the benefit of the Union. This would, indeed, be transforming Federal into State agents; abstracting them from duties for whose performance they were solely created, and devoting them to a pretty long servitude to mere State purposes. Now, sir, admitting we have a right to give away land to the States, whence do we derive the power to constitute ourselves, and our successors too, their agents and trustees? Or to convert this Government into such State machinery?

But, sir, putting the best possible aspect upon this plan, it can amount to nothing less than a virtual grant of money, to be paid out of the public treasury, with a pledge of our already pledged, repledged, triple, quadruple, quintruple pledged public lands for its payment. Is, then, that a proper time for making such an appropriation, when the receipts of the treasury are not more than adequate to the current expenses of the Government? when the Government has to support itself by loans of five millions at a time? and when every man in the nation, of ordinary sagacity, must be convinced that we must soon resort to a permanent system of internal taxation. Sir, it cannot be disguised from the people of this nation that, in proportion as we misapply or impair any of the ordinary sources of revenue, additional burthens must be imposed upon them; and can it be supposed that they will be reconciled to an appropriation to such an amount—attended with such consequences—without even the pretense of power on the part of Congress to enforce its application to the objects for which it is to be granted?

But, sir, what is to be the extent to which the new doctrines upon which the present proposition is supported are to lead us? One false step begets another. If, because one thirty-sixth part of the national domain in the new States has been appropriated to the support of education therein, the States in which there is no public land are entitled to an appropriation of equal amount, as contended by the gentleman from Maryland, why may they not, with equal propriety and justice, claim a much larger proportion of the net proceeds of the sale of public land for a different purpose, and one, too, which has not escaped the attention of the honorable gentleman, but has been several times referred to by him in the course of his remarks. By stipulations with the new States, one-twentieth of those proceeds is appropriated to the making of roads in and leading to them. Are not roads, as well as education, equally necessary to every State in the Union? And if you grant the proposed appropriation for the support of education upon the principles contended for by the gentleman from Maryland—not asked as a favor, but, according to his own language, "demanded as a right"—upon what ground can you refuse the suggested appropriation for public roads? If the latter be granted, then will not only this source of national revenue be completely annihilated, but other sources must be rendered tributary to the States; for if a sum equal to one-twentieth of the proceeds of the sale of public land is to be granted to each State, then as certainly as twenty-twentieths are the whole, those proceeds can only satisfy twenty States, and the balance must be paid out of some other branch of the revenue.

In short, sir, it appears to me that we have no more right to grant to the States the funds than the powers of this Government, for take from it its pecuniary resources and destroy its character for good faith, and it would be idle mockery to pretend to talk about its powers.

Mr. President, in the remarks which I have had the honor to submit to your consideration, I have attempted to show that, upon principle, the proposition under consideration ought not to be acceded to. But, says the gentleman from Maryland, similar donations have been made to the new States.

Admit it, sir—what then? If the cases be analogous, and my argument be well founded, that also is wrong. And can we derive from one error a just and lawful right to commit another of still greater magnitude? If our predecessors have violated the fundamental principles of the Government, disregarded its most sacred obligations, prostrated its faith, and assumed powers never delegated to them, does this confer upon us the right of further usurpations? If that be the case, then truly have we discovered a most convenient means of acquiring power—after which, man at all times lusteth a little too strongly. Such a principle, however, never can be recognized by this enlightened Senate. The precedent referred to therefore, if in point, I contend is destitute of all authority, because, as such, it would be most palpably erroneous. But it will not, I think, upon a fair and candid examination, be found to warrant the argument that is attempted to be drawn from it.

I shall endeavor to show that the parallel between those cases does not run quite as far as seems to have been imagined by the gentleman from Maryland, but that there are striking diversities in them, affording ground for such an honest difference of opinion, at least, as requires the exercise of a very moderate portion of common charity to believe that gentlemen may support the one and oppose the other, without intentional injustice or inconsistency. The one, sir, is a case decided upwards of thirty-six years ago, by the gentleman's own showing; confirmed by repeated subsequent decisions, and universally acquiesced in. The other is a case purely *res integra*, never before acted upon, or even agitated. In supporting the former, we are, therefore, fortified with the concurring sentiment of the nation, and the positive approbation of all our predecessors since the year 1785. In forbearing to adopt the latter, we are equally supported by their example—and opinion, too, sir, as far as it can be inferred from their conduct; and it would not, I think, be a very modest pretension, on our own part, to claim for ourselves more wisdom to discern or virtue to execute our duties, than was possessed by so many of the wisest heads and best hearts that ever adorned any nation. Appreciating the advantages of education, as they must have done, and not less devoted to the interests of their respective States than ourselves, had they considered those cases as presenting equal claims upon them, they never would have provided for the one so promptly, and have postponed and totally neglected the other so long. The gentleman from Maryland, therefore, in his eloquent appeals to the magnanimity of the members from the new States, ought not to forget that, whatever disapprobation is fairly due to their opposition to the particular measure which he presses with so much ardor and ability, equally applies to those distinguished sages and patriots who have retired from the stage of public action with so much honor and glory, or whose souls have fled to another and better world to receive the rewards of the virtues they practiced in this.

Sir, the great and leading distinction between those cases is, that the one had for its object the common benefit and advantage of all the States, in their federal character; the other is intended for the particular use and benefit of certain States in their State character. The former was conformable to the powers and objects of federal legislation, and consistent with the stipulations of the United States with the States which ceded their lands, and can only be justified upon such grounds; the latter is warranted by no delegation of authority whatever, either expressed or implied, and would be in direct contravention of those stipulations, and, therefore, cannot be supported at all. The one involved no breach of engagements with the public creditors, since the pledge of the proceeds of the sale of public lands imposed no obligation to change a mode of disposing of them, which had then been five years in operation; the other would be a most flagrant violation of the faith of the United States, solemnly pledged to those creditors.

The gentleman from Maryland contends that there has been no contemporaneous construction to warrant a distinction between those cases. But, sir, never, perhaps, was there a case in which the evidences of such a construction were stronger, or its authority entitled to more respect, than is evinced by all the circumstances attending the cessions of our public lands—the mode of disposing of them which was shortly afterwards adopted—and the constant adherence to the same system from that time to the present period.

In the adoption of this system, under which the reservations for the support of education were made, the most enlightened patriots of the nation, who had taken an active part in relation to those lands, the States which insisted that the cessions ought to be made, the States that made them, and Congress which accepted them, all concurred. This general concurrence, therefore, was the best possible practical exposition of the intentions of all parties in relation to the manner in which this fund might be fairly and justly disposed of for the common use and benefit of the Union.

Sir, it cannot be supposed that the States which had so strenuously insisted that those lands should be appropriated as a common fund for defraying the expenses of the war—the States which stipulated, with such jealous caution, that they should be faithfully disposed of for the common use and benefit of the Union, and for no other use or purpose whatsoever—and Congress, which accepted them upon that express condition, should so soon afterwards have intended to make a partial disposition of any portion of them.

Virginia, sir, had made much the most important and valuable cession—not, however, without some apparent hesitation at least. If then the system for disposing of those lands had been understood to contain any unjust and partial appropriation of them, in favor of any State or States, to the exclusion of Virginia, it is particularly extraordinary, not only that her wise and sagacious representation, by which she has always been eminently distinguished, should have acquiesced in it, but that, two years afterwards, two of her most distinguished representatives—and Mr. Madison himself one of those two—should have united in a report to Congress strongly recommending the same system, with the additional reservation of the twenty-ninth section of each township to be given in perpetuity for religious purposes. It is evident, therefore, that the system was adopted for the common benefit and advantage of all the States, and that it furnishes neither precedent nor apology for an

—50

appropriation of the national funds to the particular use and benefit of any State.

Sir, it must be manifest, from this view of the subject, that the distinction I have endeavored tô draw between those cases is supported by the practical exposition which has been given to all the cessions of public land and the stipulations connected therewith by those of all others best qualified to interpret them—by the parties themselves; while, on the other hand, the forbearance of all of them to insist upon, or any of them to adopt, such a measure as the one now proposed, with the most powerful inducements thereto, had it been proper, affords the strongest ground to believe that they considered any such disposition of the national funds as wholly inadmissible.

Independent, however, of the very high authority of a decision thus given by those who were so eminently qualified to judge correctly upon the subject, it is easy to demonstrate, not only that the reservations for the support of education were justifiable upon strict national principles, but that even much greater encouragement to the settlement of the national domain, had circumstances required it, might have been afforded by the Government with perfect fairness and impartial justice.

In vain, sir, would Maryland and the rest of the States, which originally set up no claim to those lands, have insisted that they should be appropriated as a common fund for defraying the expenses of the war, or the States that ceded them have stipulated that they should be disposed of for the common use and benefit of the Union, and fruitless would have been the pledge of them to the public creditors, if they had been permitted to remain in the condition in which they were received—waste and unappropriated, the haunts of ferocious beasts and the habitations of blood-thirsty savages.

In this situation, neither the Union itself nor any State whatever could derive any possible benefit from them; hence, it became not less the interest than the duty of the Government to encourage emigration to them. And if, for this purpose, it had been necessary to have actually given away a moiety of them to settlers thereon, according to the policy pursued by some of the older States in similar cases, such a measure would have been equally demanded by the engagements of the Government and the real interest of every State.

But, sir, without insisting upon what might have been done, it is sufficient for my purpose to show that the reservations which have heretofore been made for the support of education, were proper, expedient and just, in relation to all the States. This I shall endeavor to do.

The conditions which the United States bound themselves to perform, in relation to the ceded territory, seem to have had two principal objects in view.

First, that those lands should be rendered available, as a common fund, for paying the debts, defraying the expenses, and advancing the interest of the United States. And, secondly, that they should, at the same time, be so disposed of for those purposes as to promote the formation of new States within their limits, to be admitted into the Federal Union. Both these objects equally depending upon the same stipulations, neither could properly be provided for to the exclusion of the other; for, as the new States could not, consistently with the conditions agreed upon, be formed and admitted into the Union without previously disposing of a suitable proportion of the territory, so, neither could the territory be disposed to a foreign power or in any other manner so as to prevent the formation of new States. Nor could any other measure have been correctly adopted in relation to one of these objects without a correspondent regard to the other. The first contemplated a transfer of the land; the second was intended to provide the means of enjoying it with the utmost safety, comfort and happiness. Thus understood, they were calculated mutually to aid each other. The promise to establish distinct republican States, and to admit them into the Union upon an equal footing with the original States in all respects whatever, as soon as might be practicable, could not fail to promote the sale and settlement of the land; whilst every other inducement that could be afforded to the latter would equally contribute to hasten the accomplishment of the former.

It would, therefore, have been a violation of good faith, if, in disposing of the lands, due regard had not been paid to the formation of the new States; and a most culpable neglect of duty, if all necessary and practicable means of rendering them useful members of the Union had not been adopted. This, evidently, was the opinion of the old Congress, and hence we find one ordinance for disposing of the Territory, and another for the government of its inhabitants. The former, among other things, provides for the support of education—doubtless with a view to promote both of the objects referred to. The latter contains an explicit avowal of the moral benefits expected from those reservations; for, in one of the six articles, which are declared to be articles of compact between the original States and the people of the ceded Territory, unalterable, unless by common consent, it is expressly said, "that religion, morality and knowledge, being necessary to good government and the happiness of mankind, schools, and the means of education, shall forever be encouraged."

As, then, it was not less the duty of Congress to provide for the establishment of the new States than to dispose of the lands, it may be considered a fortunate circumstance that those two objects were so well calculated to harmonize with each other; since, had it been otherwise, the obligations to provide for both would not have been the less imperative. Nor would any of the original States have had just cause of complaint if the formation of the new ones had even required sacrifices on the part of the Union; for that, being one of the conditions of those grants or cessions, must be considered as a part of the consideration thereof, and none could, fairly or honestly, claim the benefit of the one without contributing in just proportion to the other.

In order, therefore, to do justice to the wisdom, foresight and profound policy which dictated the reservation of a part of the national domain for the support of education, it is necessary that that measure should be considered in relation to both of the objects referred to.

I will not, Mr. President, consume your time by attempting to demonstrate the general political considerations which must have recommended its adoption. The influence of education upon the happiness, moral power, good government and prosperity of any community, is too obvious to require illustration. Nor, indeed, sir, could any one, much less myself, add anything upon the subject more eloquent and convincing than what we have already heard from the honorable gentleman from Maryland.

Considering the measure merely in relation to the sale of the lands, it derives equal justification from the intentions with which it must have been adopted and the success that has attended it; for it can neither be doubted that it was intended to render those lands more valuable and available to the Union, nor that it has been eminently successful in producing those effects.

But, sir, in whatever point of view it can be fairly considered, it seems to me to be difficult, at least, to discern any principle, upon which it can be justified, that can support, or which, indeed, does not exclude the claim now contended for on the part of the original States.

That the encouragement of education, as a means of diffusing useful knowledge, of suppressing vice and immorality, and of promoting religion, would, as contended by the gentleman from Maryland, be eminently calculated to insure the safety, happiness and prosperity of our common country, is most readily admitted; but it does not therefore follow that we have a right to adopt the proposed measure for such purposes; for, if that be the case, the powers of Congress must be admitted to extend to all those objects, and would equally authorize any other means calculated to promote the same ends.

It is quite a familiar axiom, in politics as well as in law, that a grant of power includes an implied authority to adopt the necessary means of executing it. But it would really be somewhat novel, I think, to contend that Congress has a right to adopt the means of promoting, advancing, or providing for objects over which *all power* has been withheld from the Federal Government, and retained exclusively to the States. And I trust, sir, that the Republicans of the school of 1798, now dominant, are not themselves about to revive the exploded doctrine of a general, undefined power in Congress to provide for the general welfare. No, sir, recent demonstrations of increasing vigilance over State rights, and strong indications of a jealousy of Federal encroachments [alluding to an argument made by a gentleman of the Senate, a day or two before] forbid any such supposition. I therefore discard from my view of the subject all arguments deduced from any such supposed grant of power.

The power to provide for such objects in the new States results from the engagements of the United States, under the old confederation, and from that clause of our present Constitution which declares that all engagements entered into by them, before its adoption, shall be valid against them. These engagements were, first, with the States which ceded their lands, as has been already explained; and, secondly, with the inhabitants of the ceded Territory, to whom a promise, declared to be irrevocable, unless by common consent, had been made in the ordinance for their government, "that schools, and the means of education, should forever be encouraged."

Congress having a right to legislate for those inhabitants, and being *bound* to provide for their admission into the Union, unquestionably must have had the power to adopt the necessary means of training them up in correct principles; and, in the language of the ordinance, religion, morality and knowledge being necessary to good government and the happiness of mankind, it was fit and proper that education should have been encouraged for such purposes in the cases referred to.

But, sir, the original States, having the exclusive right to legislate for themselves upon such subjects, and Congress having no superintendence over morals, religion, education, or other objects of municipal regulation within the several States, has no authority to interfere with them in any manner whatever. Such objects are, as to Congress, *coram non judice*, and therefore we can neither legislate upon them to their benefit or to their injury. Let us not forget, sir, that the power to do the one admits the possibility, at least, of doing the other, since all power is liable to abuse. And if ever the day shall arrive when the authority of this Government shall be admitted to extend to such subjects, then adieu to all State sovereignty. It will be completely swallowed up in the great vortex of a grand consolidated National Government. In this point of view, therefore, it is evident there is no analogy between those cases, and that the claim of the original States can derive no possible support from any of the considerations that have been referred to.

Let us now, Mr. President, inquire whether the claim of the original States can be better supported upon any other principles that could have led to the adoption of the present system of disposing of the public lands.

By this system, all those lands are divided into townships of six miles square. These, again, are subdivided into thirty-six sections of one mile square, one of which is reserved to be granted to the inhabitants of the township, for the use and support of a common school therein. But, sir, as all settlements upon the public lands are prohibited, under severe penalties, the township must be *sold* before it can be *inhabited*. The citizens of the new States, therefore, can only enjoy the full benefit of a reserved section upon the condition of purchasing the remaining thirty-five sections of the township. Would it, then, comport with "impartial justice" to grant such a benefit to the citizens of other States, without requiring any condition whatever? Would it be right, sir, to punish the citizens of the new States for daring to intrude upon a reserved section, without having previously purchased thirty-five sections, and at the same time to bestow a section gratuitously upon others, merely because you had allowed the former the privilege of acquiring one upon the terms I have mentioned? Surely not, sir.

I contend that those reservations have, undoubtedly, increased the intrinsic value of the residue of the land—and that, on the other hand, its value and productiveness, as a national fund, would as certainly be greatly deteriorated by the proposed donations to the old States.

I acknowledge, sir, that the proportion in which the reserved sections have enhanced the value of the residue cannot be ascertained with anything like mathematical certainty, but, judging from all the lights which many years' experience have shed upon the subject, there seems to be no doubt that townships with those reservations have commanded and will continue to command a higher price than they would sell for without them. And considering how highly the gentleman from Maryland estimates the value and advantages of education, it is surprising that he should have any doubt of the correctness of this conclusion. If, then, such be the fact that those reservations lose all the character of donations because they are more than paid for in the sale of the residue of the land, of course they furnish no precedent for the *pure* donations now proposed to be granted.

Again, sir, no citizen of the new States can enjoy or derive the slightest benefit from the reserved sections without paying for it, since no privilege, interest, right or title in them, can be acquired, without purchasing land at a higher price than it would sell for without them. This difference, therefore, whatever it may be, is the price actually paid for the interest acquired in them, which must be in exact proportion to the quantity of land purchased. Even upon the improbable supposition, that the consideration thus given were an inadequate one, still, I presume, it can hardly be contended, by the honorable gentleman from Maryland, that this circumstance can justify grants in favor of the citizens of other States, without any consideration at all.

But, sir, settlement, as well as purchase, is an indispensible prerequisite to the right of enjoying the use and benefit of the reservations. Its importance to the Union may well be imagined by contrasting the present value of the national domain with what would probably have been its value had it remained to this time waste and uninhabited. And this is certainly but a fair and just view of the subject; for if the new States are to be charged with the reserved sections, they surely ought to have credit for the value which their settlements and improvements have imparted to the residue.

Sir, with the settlement of the country its improvements must progress. These, by multiplying the comforts, conveniencies and advantages of a residence in it, will continue to render the vacant residue more desirable, more valuable and available, till the whole of it shall be disposed of. The policy, therefore, which has hitherto required the condition of settlement, must continue to prevail so long as the United States retain any of those lands, and are desirous of disposing of them to the best advantage. But this requisite, also, is to be dispensed with in favor of the citizens of the original States, without requiring anything whatever of them to counterbalance it. Would this be "fair and impartial justice?"

According to any correct view of the subject, it is manifest that the citizens of the original States participate largely in the benefits of the present reservations in support of education. But those of the new States can have no such corresponding interest in the proposed donations; these are intended for the exclusive benefit of the former. Nor is anything proposed, in favor of the latter, as a counterpoise or equivalent for this want of reciprocity and glaring inequality—and surely, they who have reposed in perfect safety under their own vines and fig-trees, at their native homes, are not entitled to be placed in a more eligible situation, in relation to the national domain, than those who braved the dangers, encountered the difficulties and submitted to all the privations incident to the settlement of it.

It is admitted, sir, that one of the principal objects of the reservations was to encourage emigration, and the policy of the measure, in that respect, is not questioned; yet, it is contended that the right of the original States to an equal portion of the public lands, for the support of education within their respective limits, grew out of the adoption of that measure, is coevil with it, and is not at all impaired by the delay in asserting it. But, really, sir, it appears to me that those cases not only do not rest upon the same foundation, but that the latter is entirely inconsistent with and calculated to defeat the very policy of the former. To adopt a measure to promote emigration, and at the same time to grant equal advantages to all those who might not choose to emigrate, would be very much like a sport which many of us have witnessed in our younger days: building up with one hand for the mere pleasure of knocking down with the other. No one could be attracted to a remote wilderness by advantages which he could equally enjoy without going there. In this respect, therefore, the policy of those measures is so directly hostile to each other, that the one must necessarily exclude the other.

But, sir, with whatever objects or motives the presentsystem for disposing of the public lands may have been adopted, let it be remembered that, though now complained of as if it had been the decision of some partial, unjust corrupt, foreign tribunal, it was a measure of the original, now complaining States, themselves—and unless communities, when the sole arbiters in their own cases, are infinitely more liable than individuals to lose sight of their interests altogether, and be unjust to themselves, it must have been adopted for their own benefit, and fully have they realized all the advantages anticipated from it. It could not have been intended to operate upon persons who had gone to the public domain, if there were any such; but only upon those who could be induced to go there. All the advantages and inducements which it tendered were then, constantly have been, and still are offered alike to the free acceptance of every citizen of the Union, and consequently it was in its origin, has continued to be, and still is, equally fair and just in relation to all of them. Nothing, therefore, can be more unreasonable than to consider those reservations as partial donations to States that had no existence, or to a Territory unpeopled but by savages, to be subdued and expelled.

Permit me here, sir, to avail myself of the example of the honorable gentleman from Virginia, in referring to that portion of the national domain that lies upon the Pacific Ocean. In its present situation, as a source of revenue, it is not now nor can it ever be of any manner of use to us. As was correctly stated by the gentleman to whom I refer, a project for establishing a colony upon it has already engaged the deliberations of one branch of the National Legislature. Suppose, then, that Congress, with a view to revenue, to commercial advantages, to the security of our traders, and to prevent the encroachments of rival powers, should determine to colonize this section of our territory, and for that purpose should, with universal consent and approbation, tender to every citizen of the United States any inducements whatever to emigrate thither: for whose, but the benefit of the Union, would this measure be adopted? How, and in favor of whom, could it be considered unjust and partial, even before the terms of it had been accepted by a solitary individual? If fair and just in its origin, how could it become otherwise, merely by effecting the very objects it was intended to accomplish? Could mere inducements to emigration, in this case, be considered as originating a claim to equal advantages in favor of all those who might not choose to emigrate? How wonderfully efficient, sir, would be a measure for such a purpose, which should promise every citizen the same benefits for staying at home, with which it intended to tempt his removal to a distant, unsettled country, through a trackless wilderness of vast extent. As well, sir, might every citizen of the United States now demand of you a quarter section of land, because you gave that quantity to the soldiers of your late army. Nor could anything be more outrageously unjust than to promise your fellow-citizens a gratuity for settling upon the public land, and then to make them pay for it by deducting its full value from their proportion of a common stock, as is proposed to be done by the proposition upon your table.

Sir, the claim of the original States has been particularly insisted upon, because, in the encouragement which they themselves afforded to emigration, for the sake of their own interests, too, they have, forsooth, lost a part of their population and wealth. An argument so sectional and anti-national in its character surely comes with a bad grace from those who, with a perseverance threatening the most disastrous consequences to our common country, at a most awful crisis, insisted that those lands should be ceded, settled and formed into separate States, for the purpose of paying the debts, promoting the interest and advancing the security of the Union. How, sir, could any one of these objects be accomplished without disposing of the land? Who would have bought it without a view to its settlement by himself or others? And by whom, but citizens of the United States, was it intended to be settled? It is not to be supposed that any of the States could, for a moment, have yielded to a policy so contracted and selfish, as to have wished to have exempted themselves from the disadvantages common to all of them in consequence of those cessions; or to have enjoyed the full benefits of them at the exclusive cost of others. No State, in fact, would have submitted, or would now submit, to the exclusion of her citizens from the right of emigrating to the public lands. The original States, therefore, cannot justly claim an equivalent for a privilege which they themselves secured to their own citizens, and which they would not now be so unjust as to relinquish, were it in their power to do so.

The motive, sir, to encourage emigration being the advantages expected to be derived from it, these must have been the only equivalent contemplated for any encouragement given to it. The benefits, therefore, offered to emigrants, depending upon a condition from which the States expected correspondent advantages, at least, when that condition was fulfilled, the consideration of those benefits was fully discharged, and no other equivalent can in reason or justice be demanded.

Nor have the original States any reason to complain that their citizens have exercised and enjoyed the benefits of the privilege thus secured to them, for such were not only the necessary and intended consequences of their own measure, but they were the very essence of the contracts upon which the public lands were ceded. Sir, you took them upon those terms, "for better, for worse," and have infinitely less reason to complain, than the man who sought to be absolved from his matrimonial obligations because he had found his wife all of the worse and none of the better. You have realized important advantages in the increased value and utility of the land, the improved condition of your population, the development of the resources of your country, the extension of your commerce and navigation, the augmentation of your revenue, the support of public credit, and the security of your borders. These advantages, however, are much less the result of your own liberality than of the bold, enterprising, adventurous and aspiring character of your population, and the superior liberality of some of the States whose lands adjoined yours. No Government, I will venture to say, has ever yet established a distant colony, similarly situated, upon terms more advantageous to itself. None has ever given less to emigrants or exacted more from them.

England, France and Spain have all held a part of our present domain, and, by their superior regard to the law of nature and the Divine will in the distribution of those western lands, whilst they held them, have exhibited a contrast between monarchies and the freest government in the world which, I am sorry to say, is by no means favorable to the latter.

Mr. President, had Pennsylvania, Virginia, North Carolina and Kentucky demanded two dollars per acre, in good money, as the minimum price of their lands, and subjected all intruders to legal prosecution and removal by military force, much of your great north-western territory now so thickly populated—so highly cultivated and improved—so richly embellished with cities, towns and villages—every where exhibiting monuments of the advance of science, the progress of the arts, and the multiplication of the comforts and elegancies of civilized life—would still have been a waste, uncultivated wilderness. The territory of those States being unoccupied, yours could never have been inhabited. They, therefore, by the population which they attracted to theirs, and by their wars to maintain it, expelled the savages from a large portion of yours, and thereby contributed more to its settlement than all that you have ever done towards it.

Yet, sir, some of the States seem to think they have had a hard bargain in taking the land at all, because they have lost a part of their population by it. But, sir, had it been retained by England, France or Spain, it is by no means certain that those States would have lost less. Had it remained the property of Virginia, owing to her superior liberality in such cases, as is evinced by her uniform conduct, there is every reason to suppose they would have lost more and gained nothing.

I know, sir, it has been very gravely asserted by one most respectable State that, if the original States had been governed by a selfish policy, they would have thrown every impediment in the way of emigration to the national domain. This, however, does not appear to me to be very consistent with the motives which induced them so zealously to insist upon its being surrendered as a national fund; and, besides the breach of faith involved in such a policy, it would have been just about as rational as the Japanese mode of duelling, in which one man rips open his own bowels for the pleasure of imposing an obligation on another to follow his example. None could have lost more or gained less by such a measure than those very States; and little can be known of the immense tracts of land in the Western country which yet remain to be settled, if it can be supposed that any measure of that kind could have had any other material effect upon emigration than to have changed its direction and swelled the population of some of the other Western States. It is evident, therefore, that the inducements afforded to emigration by the original States have neither been so purely gratuitous, nor its effects, which they so deeply deplore, so exclusively the results of their liberal forbearance to impede it, as seems to have been imagined.

In the enumeration of the grievances and injuries for which they demand indemnification, we find them complaining that the sale of their western lands "has prevented an increase in the price of lands in the Atlantic States," though they have not a single acre of land of their own to dispose of in those States. Regretting exceedingly, sir, that my remaining strength does not admit of my entering into a full investigation of this singular ground of complaint, I will barely remark that the high price of land so much desired can only result from a density of population, from which much dependence and wretchedness would be inseparable; that there is nothing in the history of our own or any other country to authorize the opinion that it would be more auspicious to the interest and happiness of the great mass of our population or to the preservation of the free principles of our Government; that its tendency would be to advance the interest of the few that have land to sell at the expense of the many who have it to buy; and that, instead of impeding, it would be calculated to increase emigration—since, in proportion to the difficulty of obtaining lands in the old States, there would be additional motives to seek it elsewhere.

[Mr. Edwards here remarked that, being greatly fatigued, and fearing he had exhausted the patience of the Senate, he should be compelled to omit or postpone to a future stage of the discussion, other views of the subject which he was anxious to present to the consideration of the Senate.]

I have, sir, contrasted the relative situations of the citizens of the new and the old States in relation to the proposed appropriation. I had intended to have presented similar contrasts between the claims of the new and the old States themselves, and between the grants made to the former and those proposed to be made to the latter. I had also intended to have shown that, even admitting the principle contended for by the honorable gentleman from Maryland, the contemplated apportionment and distribution of the land would be manifestly unequal and unjust; that the demand on the part of the original States of an equivalent for the "particular" advantages which the new States derive from the present system of disposing of the public lands for the benefit of the Union, is inconsistent with every idea of national government, and that the latter States might, with equal propriety, demand an equivalent for the "particular" advantages which the former derive from the vast expenditure of public money within their limits, or from any other measure of national policy.

I find, however, I must content myself with remarking that you have granted to the new States nothing more than a mere naked trust to execute your own previous obligations or to promote your future interest. So far as the public lands had been sold, the right to the reserved sections had vested in the inhabitants of the respective townships, and did not depend at all for its validity upon the grants to the States—for you neither could have withheld nor impaired it, nor can those States now do so. So far as the lands have not been sold, no right to the reserved sections has vested or can vest, either in those States or the inhabitants thereof, but upon conditions hereafter to be performed highly conducive to your own interest.

Suppose, sir, the new States had refused to become your trustees, you would not on that account have changed your present system of disposing of the public lands; and you could not have sold a single reserved section in any township in which a solitary sale of eighty acres only had been made. What then have you given to the new States? Nothing that you could or would have retained.

But in whatever light those grants are to be viewed, they are founded upon compacts which neither party is now at liberty to revoke, annul or disregard. On the part of the new States, they have, I think, manifested great liberality in giving a full equivalent for advantages that either would not or could not have been withheld from them if they had refused to give anything. The State which I have the honor, in part, to represent, has probably had a pretty hard bargain in agreeing to forbear to tax the lands of individuals, and in the consequent burdens imposed upon her own citizens, for all the consideration she received. She agreed to exempt from all taxation three millions five hundred thousand acres of military bounty lands for three years after the emanation of the grants, and at least thirty millions of acres of the public land for five years after the sale of it—which, according to the State taxation, at first rate, would be equal to $3,210,000; second rate, $2,250,000; third rate, $1,650,000; and at the average rate, $2,370,000.

If then, sir, any of the old States insist upon having as much land as they contend has been granted to Illinois, let them first purchase the same quantity of land which she either has purchased or is bound to purchase to perfect her title to the supposed grants—and let them also agree to pay the taxes upon the same quantity of land which she has exempted from taxation, and for the same length of time—or talk no more about "fair and impartial justice."

CHAPTER XVI.

Letters from William Wirt, Attorney-General of the United States; John McLean, Postmaster-General and Judge of the Supreme Court of the United States; John C. Calhoun, Secretary of War, United States Senator and Vice-President of the United States; Samuel D. Ingham, Secretary of the United States' Treasury; Gabriel Moore of Alabama, Member of Congress, Governor, and United States' Senator; William Kelley of Louisiana, Representative and Senator in Congress; David S. Morrill, United States' Senator from Maine; Isham Talbott, United States' Senator from Kentucky; James Monroe, President of the United States; John Quincy Adams, President of the United States; Thos. B. Read, Senator in Congress from Mississippi; Felix Grundy, Senator in Congress from Tennessee; Richard M. Johnson, Senator in Congress, and Vice-President of the United States; Almy McLean, Member of Congress from Kentucky; John J. Crittenden, United States Senator, and Attorney-General of United States; Thomas H. Benton, Senator in Congress; Charles Fisher, Member of Congress from North Carolina; John Crowell, Member of Congress from Alabama; Samuel L. Southard, Senator in Congress, and Secretary of the Navy; Rufus King, Senator in Congress, and Minister to England; George M. Bibb, Senator in Congress, Chief Justice of the Court of Appeals in Kentucky, and Secretary of the Treasury; Albert Gallatin, Secretary of the Treasury; William Eustis, Governor of Massachusetts, and Secretary of War; Edward Tiffin, Commissioner General Land Office; A. J. Dallas, Secretary of the Treasury; W. H. Crawford, Secretary of Treasury and War Department; and others.*

WILLIAMSBURGH, *January* 10, 1802.

My Dear Sir:

I inclose several letters, which I hope will arrive in time to promote their purpose. Wishing you success in the appointment, and that you may find it advantageous in every point of view, I beg leave to return to my own business.

I am ultimately resolved on my Kentucky project, and have nothing further to do than to make preparations for the trip and to decide on the time of starting. On these subjects I must trouble you with a few questions:

*Some of the letters from Wm. Wirt, in this Chapter, are addressed to Benjamin Edwards, the father of Ninian Edwards.

What kind of furniture will it be necessary for me to carry to Frankfort? In other words, are manufactures in such a state there that every article immediately necessary to house-keeping may be procured on my arrival—I mean tables, chairs, beds, table-furniture, etc.

When do the superior courts sit?—for I wish to be there at the spring terms, if possible.

Would it be practicable to procure the Constitution, and acts of Assembly passed there since the erection of the State?—that is, so as to have them here in a month or two.

If you decline the Indiana election, or if the appointment should have been otherwise disposed of, suppose, on your return to Kentucky, you visit this country. It is worth seeing in a historical point of view. Within eight miles of this place was the first Christian settlement made in the United States—I mean Jamestown. Besides, Norfolk is worth the journey, as being one of the most flourishing towns on the Atlantic frontier; and, among other inducements, we wish very much to see you. The interview would, at least to me, be very highly useful. I wish to ask a thousand questions about your State, which would do only for conversation; one, though, I will ask even on paper, viz: In what are lawyers' fees paid, in Kentucky, *i. e.*, in cash or specifics? This I ask to assist me in adjusting some previous movements in this State. I have not yet heard from your father, or any of my other friends in Kentucky, to whom I wrote early in November; but you have had such opportunities of possessing all the facts necessary to decide on the prudence of my removal, that I shall rely exclusively on you—so that if you have decided too soon, in the advice which you have given me, it will be but charitable to retract before I shall have taken any irretrievable step.

I am, my dear sir,
Your friend,
WILLIAM WIRT.

P. S.—My acquaintance with the members of Congress and the Secretary of State would enable me to inclose you more letters, but I apprehend they would scarcely pay the postage, and for this reason I have declined sending them.—W. W.

To NINIAN EDWARDS, ESQ., Montgomery Court-house, Maryland.

WILLIAMSBURGH, *December* 16, 1802.

My Dear Sir:

Your very interesting and obliging favor, of the 7th of October, was received about the last of that month. I sat down and answered it immediately; but as you had informed me, in yours, that your visit to Philadelphia would keep you from Maryland until the first of January, my scroll was thrown by in my drawer, with the view of being sent to meet you in Montgomery, on your return. It has been lying so long by me that it has grown stale, even to its author, and I find that it contains a circumstantial narrative of my life since I came to Virginia which could afford very little entertainment to you.

I have determined, therefore, as the 1st of January is drawing near, to give you a letter at least fresh, and more concise than that which I prepared in October.

The account which you gave me of your father's health, spirits, settlement and prospects, administer the most sensible pleasure to me. When I saw him last, in Maryland, I had the most gloomy forebodings as to his health; and he seemed, himself, to apprehend that his restoration was hopeless. Instead of those sincere bursts of laughter, which used to bespeak his mind void of care, he was, I thought, pensive and desponding. I rejoice at his recovery, and would most heartily join in his laugh even at my *rencontre* with Chase.

Your mother's recollection and account of my visit to Mount Pleasant is exquisitely grateful to me. To be remembered and esteemed by the early friends of my youth—by those who led me upon the theater of the world—affects me in a manner which does no discredit to my sensibility, however it may dishonor the sternness of manhood. But I must acknowledge that I am not made of those rugged and inflexible materials which constituted the character of Cato and his brother stoics. The passing glory of the world, and even the dismemberment of a once happy and beloved neighborhood, touches me acutely; the remembrance of Seneca—of my friends once collected, healthy and gay, but now dead or dispersed over the earth—strikes with force on the chords of my heart. Enough!

The general prosperity of your sisters and brothers affords me very great pleasure. What obligations have your parents conferred on Kentucky, by transferring to it so hopeful a little colony! It is but just that the State should requite the favor to their children.

The variety of scenes through which you have passed will do you no disservice. Dissipation can never again lure you to ruin; she possesses no charm which you have not proved to be hollow and sepulchral. You are fortified, therefore, against any further temptation from that quarter. Your professional success, I doubt not, is merely commensurable to your desert—for, notwithstanding all your disqualifying observations on yourself, I do not believe that the people of Kentucky are to be imposed on by any Jenkinsonian pretensions to wisdom; they are too conversant with those beautiful landscapes called "connected plots," to be plotted out of $30,000 by an imposter. I am sorry, however, that your pursuits have been interrupted by ill health; but the man who mines for gold must expect these little rubs. By this time I trust that your recovery is complete; yet, considering the seat of your disorder, I should have more sanguine hopes from a trip to a Southern climate.

I heartily wish you success in your election for Congress. You complain of the want of political information, to meet your competitor in public. If the acquirement of that information is not immediately practicable, you must try Chesterfield's trick on the question for reforming the calendar: he acknowledges that he gleaned from a noble friend a few scanty ideas on this astronomical subject; but he clothed these few ideas to such advantage, that he bore away the palm from the very friend who had furnished him with his lights. It is incredible, to the man who has not tried, how much may be done in a popular harangue by the mere force of harmonious periods, new and striking metaphors and spirited apostrophes, with very little solid matter. It is, to be sure, a shameful artifice for the man who has any alternative; and it ought, besides, to be considered, if these mere embellishments are capable, by their own intrinsic force, to produce such effects, what would they work if one could breathe into them the soul of wisdom and information—*sapiente verbum sat.* On this head of information I will merely hint, that, for the purpose of the "spouting" campaign which you meditate, on your return to Kentucky, it will be perhaps more material to show the people that you understand the proper interests of the State, than to convince them of your historical exactitude in past events—inasmuch as the man who knows what *ought* to be done, is better qualified to legislate than he who merely knows what *has* been done; but to know both is certainly best. Besides that, the knowledge of what *has* been done, constitutes the sound experimental test of what is proper to be done in future.

I never received your pamphlet by Dr. Rumsay, and I am mortified at his having deprived me of that gratification. I wish I may have an opportunity of claiming it from him.

Of my little exhibition on the Fourth of July I have not a single copy, nor do I know where one is to be procured. I believe that, like other ephemera, it perished at the close of its day.

From the superscription of your letter, I infer that you are apprised of the office which I hold in this State. It is, to be sure, one of the most honorable that Virginia can confer, but it is almost literally a post of mere honor—the salary attached to it is not sufficient to support my family; and, to my shame, I have not been industrious and economical enough to have laid up any subsidiary resource from the practice of law. The consequence is that I shall be compelled to resign and go back to the bar. This I meditate to do very shortly; and where do you conjecture I mean to resume the office of lawyer? In Kentucky, sir—unless I am differently advised by your father and some other friends there, to whom I have written for counsel. But, for *your* opinion I should be particularly thankful, because, having been, yourself, of the profession, you best know the profits on which I could calculate, and you best know what station would be more advantageous for me, if you should incline to the opinion that the project of removing to Kentucky is a discreet one at all. When I accepted the office of Chancellor for this State, I was a single man; and I could have well lived and supported myself and my niece on $1500 per annum. I accepted the office, too, under the impression that I should never again be married—for I had addressed the only girl on earth who could govern my heart; and although her attachment, even then, was not less ardent and sincere than mine, yet, for certain reasons *of state*, I was discarded. But, about three months ago, I pressed her to my heart as my wife. My situation thus unexpectedly changed, I can resign my office without the fair imputation of too much versatility; and I must resign it, or ignominiously perish with the girl of my heart! I shall return to the bar with more determined zeal and with much better qualification than I have ever before possessed. I shall be impelled by two of the most powerful springs which can actuate the soul of man: the pride of vindicating the opinion which the Legislature of Virginia has passed on me—and the pride of dignifying one of the most angelic girls that ever filled the enraptured arms of man! I feel the consciousness that I am capable of far greater exertion, and of more patient and inflexible perseverence, than I ever was; and if the world has not flattered most imprudently, I have reason to hope that my exertions will not be lost.

Thus determined, I would know of you (and I expect you will answer not to please, but *candidly to advise*) what prospects I might expect in Kentucky? For fifteen years, if my life and health are spared, I will labor most indefatigably. In that time, might I expect an independence in Kentucky? Are the land disputes over? or how are they? Are the lawyers very formidably eminent? for I mean not to shrink into the country practice; on the contrary, I am resolved, if not otherwise advised, to *take a dash* at the highest courts. If you think my removal to that State expedient, would you advise me to reside at Lexington, or Frankfort? Lexington is said to be the most populous and flourishing, but Frankfort is the seat of Government. How slight these circumstances, to affect my determination! In which place would my progress to wealth be most early and rapid? Pray deliberate maturely on these points, and give me your ingenuous and friendly advice. In Virginia, I could live well by the profession: but Ed. Randolph merely *lived;* I wish to go to some country where I can provide for sickness, old age and death—so that, when I am gathered to the tomb, I may leave my family in circumstances at all events independent, and, if possible, affluent. I am attracted to Kentucky, not more by the wish to get an honest subsistence for my family, than by the desire to belong to that State. I love Kentucky; I am charmed by her republican spirit; I am delighted by the energy with which she sustains her rank in the Union. Virginia has the same advantages; but Virginia is an old and well-established dominion, full of veterans, who are fortified against the possibility of want of honorable service. I am not wanted here. I wish to go where I shall be able to render service to the State —in a small circle, to fan the flame of liberty—in the narrow sphere of my associates, to assist in repelling sentiments hostile to the freedom and happiness of the country; and if I fasten only one leaf on the cap of liberty, I shall think my existence not in vain.

If I determine ultimately to remove to Kentucky, I shall endeavor very strenuously to effect my removal in the spring. There can be but one obstacle, which, however, by the aid of my wife's father (Col. Gamble of Richmond), I hope I shall be able to surmount.

I wish it were possible for you to extend your journey to Williamsburgh—we should be able to communicate on the preceding subjects much more minutely and satisfactorily than by letter; and if you are not absolutely compelled to return directly home, I shall cherish at least a faint hope that you will do me this pleasure.

The subject of my resolution is a secret in this State, and I wish it to remain so here; yet, if Kentucky is certainly my destination, I do not know that it will be necessary to keep my intention a secret there.

One question, before I conclude: Are houses to be had in Frankfort and Lexington, for rent? Because I do not know that I shall be immediately able to purchase, and I might perhaps find it necessary to prevent embarrassments, on my arrival, by engaging a house beforehand.

Wishing you health and prosperity,

I am, dear sir, very sincerely,

Your friend,

WILLIAM WIRT.

To NINIAN EDWARDS, ESQ., Montgomery Court-house, Maryland.

WILLIAMSBURGH, *March* 2, 1803.

Dear Sir:

I was on a visit in Richmond, my dear friend, when yours of the 5th January, from Montgomery Court-house, in Maryland, reached this place, so that I did not receive it until last Friday—at which time, also, I had the delightfully good fortune to receive a letter from your father, in Kentucky. You tell me, in the conclusion to yours, that you proposed very shortly after its date to go home, but that you would wait eight or ten days longer than you had intended, to receive my answer. At all events you direct me to write to you as if in Maryland, and that, if you should be gone before the arrival of my letter, you would leave directions with the postmaster to send it on to you. This I had determined to do when I wrote to your father, as he will inform you; but, on farther reflection, the delay in receiving your letter was so much greater than you could have calculated, that I suppose there is very little probability of your being, at this time, in Maryland. To save, therefore, the time which would be lost in this letter taking a circuit through Maryland, I write directly to Bardstown, to the care of your father.

In the first place, I hope you will do me the justice to believe that the kindness with which you have answered my inquiries, and tendered your aid in facilitating my establishment in Kentucky, has made the proper impression on my mind and on my heart. The time may come—though, for your sake, I hope it never will—when the impression may be manifested by other evidence than words. At present, however, I do not know that I shall have any need to avail myself of your generous offer of service in Frankfort; if I should need it, on my arrival there, I shall use the freedom of a friend in claiming your engagement.

The prospect which you point out to me in Kentucky is so fair, and so firmly established by the actual experience of others, that I see no reason and feel no disposition to repress the delightful expansion of hope with which I look to that country. I feel the sweet presage that the inauspicious gloom of want and dependence, which has lowered over my past life, is about to break away forever; and I look, with emotions little short of transport, to the sun-gilt calm of ease and plenty. The month of November gave me birth—my morn of life was winter indeed; the lucid spring of it is, I hope, fast advancing, and I trust in God that I shall not survive the autumn of my age. I would fain gather the fruits of my labor, but I wish not to see the withering and fall of my leaves—much less to endure again the piercing frosts which had nearly blasted me in the bud. The reflection which crowns my sweet anticipations in Kentucky is, that I shall conduct to prosperity, and, I hope, to happiness as pure and perfect as mortals can know it, a wife who has realized and even surpassed the fondest expectation of a lover. Connected with this is another reflection, which, as Coriolanus says of his wounds, "shall be yours in private," and which feeds the flame of rapture in my breast. In short, on whichever side I view the subject, I am delighted—inexpressibly delighted—with it, and regard Kentucky in the same light as a careworn Mahometan does his paradise. At the same time I am not so ignorant of the flattery of hope, and the fallacy of the brightest earthly appearances, as to be unprepared to meet, with that fortitude and dignity which become a man, a diminution and even reverse of my expectations in Kentucky. If adversity meets me, she will be no stranger—habit has instructed me how to receive and entertain her; but if prosperity, she will be a welcome guest, and I shall practice all the arts of hospitality to detain her.

I concur with you perfectly in the opinion that Frankfort is the most eligible stand. In addition to the reasons which you adduce, my residence there will give me a command of the records of the Court of Appeals, and enable me to inform myself of the principles which govern the decision of your land cases—for I suppose, from the manner in which your country has been settled, that there must be principles of adjudication on this head peculiar to Kentucky; and, indeed, considering the number and variety of causes which your Court of Appeals has adjusted, I shall be somewhat disappointed if I do not find in their records one principle or other to fit any future question relative to the title of lands. In England, where there is such a multitude and such a countless diversity of tenures, it is not surprising that a case shall now and then occur on which a precedent can be brought to bear; but I should suppose that in Kentucky, where the kinds of title, and the modes of acquiring them, were so free and uniform, the judicial difficulty would be, not in inventing new principles, but in applying those which have been already settled. But I shall know more of this, I hope, in the course of the summer. I should endeavor to meet you, as you kindly hoped, on the first Monday in May, in Frankfort, but for the consideration that the April term of the Chancery Court, here, will find the business at a stage which would render my immediate resignation an inconvenience and an injury to the district—and Virginia has deserved no injuries at my hands. On this account, I will be obliged to defer my resignation until the last of April; and then I propose to set out as soon as possible.

Accept my congratulations on your appointment to the judicial bench of Kentucky. I have no doubt you will give lustre to the office—in point of health I presume the change will be greatly to your advantage. I imagine there is no labor connected with it, except in term time—so that you will have leisure to pursue your studies as far as you please, and to mingle in that pursuit as much exercise as your health will require. That you may succeed in the pursuit of both science and health, is my most ardent wish. It will be no small addition to the happiness which may await me in Kentucky, that it will bring me within striking distance of your father's family, and that my profession and your office will bring you so often in contact with

Your much obliged and sincere friend,

WILLIAM WIRT.

NINIAN EDWARDS, Bardstown, Kentucky.

RICHMOND, *Sept.* 17, 1805.

My Dear Friend:

Your favor of the 29th July reached me on the morning of the last day of August. On the evening of that day I had to set off for the District Court of Moorfield, on the south branch of the Potomac, from which place I have just returned—so that I lose no time in acknowledging the receipt of your letter, and thanking you for the genuine pleasure which it afforded me. Your father's transmitting my letter, for the inspection of his children, in the quarter in which you live, and his urging them to regard and treat me as a brother, administer the most exquisite gratification to me, and convince me that he is still the same obliging friend I have ever found him. I can truly say, in the presence of that God who knows the secrets of all hearts, that the approbation of such a man as your father is far more soothing and delightful to me, than all the plaudits and acclamations would be which Shakspeare represents as having made the welkin ring in Cæsar's rejection of the crown, tendered him by Mark Anthony: for I know your father is too penetrating and judicious to be imposed on by mere surfaces, and too virtuous to approve of anything but virtue. I am made happy, therefore, in thinking well of myself, when I remember that such a man is my friend and would even be willing to let me consider him as a father. Let me entreat you, as a brother, to help me maintain my place in his good opinion, and if, by chance, hereafter—by the agency of calumny, or any other fiend—there should be danger of losing his esteem, that you will be my advocate with him until I have a chance of advocating myself; and let me hope that you will ever be to me the friend you so obligingly declare yourself in this letter—relying that, on my part, there shall be no want of the feelings of friendship, although, for your sake, I hope that the continuance of your prosperity may render any practical exertion of it, towards you, forever unnecessary.

One evidence of your friendship I shall continue to insist on: I mean your correspondence—nor do I admit the soundness of your apology for having, hitherto, been remiss in this particular. My want of knowledge of Kentucky, and the fewness of my acquaintances there, should, on the contrary, have been inducements with you to write—for my ignorance in these respects would have given you a new and fresh field for description, and you might have introduced me, on paper, to your country and its prominent characters. Besides, while Mr. Morse and Mr. Scott, together with the Kentucky papers are open, I cannot be supposed altogether ignorant of your State, so far as relates to the boundaries, climate, soil, productions, trade, constitution, jurisprudence, etc., and of those who, I suppose, ought to be your prominent characters. I knew Duval, Haden, Edwards, Gerard, Fortunatus Cosby, William Wallace, and a few others. It may be that some of these men are in obscurity: for it is not always that men fulfill the promise of their youth. Indolence, and worse vices, have blasted many of the fairest geniuses that ever graced the earth. It is really mournful to look back on their school days, count up the brilliant companions of their youth, and observe how many of them have been lost to themselves and to the world—the victims of idleness or intemperance, or both. How few of them have come out with honor; and even of those whose habits have been temperate and studious, how rarely the autumnal fruit has corresponded with the luxuriant flowering of the spring—resulting more frequently, I believe, from an error in the mode of culture, than from any defect in the original stamina or any declension in the faculties themselves. I will be obliged to you, however, to give me, in your next, some account of the gentlemen whose names I have mentioned, and to inquire for another friend of mine—James Bell—who used to practice law in Orange and the adjacent counties, in this State, and who now, I believe, lives somewhere in your Green River country. One of the best of men, and with very respectable talents, he was the victim of unvanquishable diffidence. If you can hear of him, pray let me know how he prospers in Kentucky.

I am extremely sorry that there is anything so disagreeable in your judicial office as to make you think of resigning it—more especially as you seem to entertain some idea of following up your resignation by a removal to Louisiana. I like this last idea less than the other, because I should be afraid of the effect of the climate on your health and that of your family. I doubt, too, the advantageous effect of the removal on your fortune. Your salary as a judge in Louisiana would not, I apprehend, be higher than it is in Kentucky—and as to the progressive value of land there, I apprehend it must be very slow, because the value of land can only rise with the pressure of population, and the consequent pressure in the demand for land; but Louisiana is, itself, such a *world*, that it must be a very long time before there can be any pressure of population felt. I suppose (for on this subject I am, of necessity, all hypothesis,) that the acquisition of Louisiana must lessen the value of lands in Kentucky, because it opens a sluice to drain off your population, and relieves the little pressure which you might have already begun to feel. It presents, too, a new object and a new theatre for your land speculators and our emigrants, and will withdraw from your market much of the influence which they have produced.

Admitting that the cheapness of living in Kentucky would enable you to maintain your family and educate your children there on your salary and the income of your estate, I incline to think that you had better remain as you are. You are in a country filled with civilized and polite people—a country in which you are known, respected and established. Your place gives you time for the culture of science, the superintendence of your children's education and the blandishments of conjugal and paternal bliss. Your wife and children will soon have found their select circle of associates, among a people who, I presume, so far from *Indianizing*, may tend to form the manners of your young ones to advantage. As for yourself, you may attain all the eminence of the judicial character in a country capable of estimating your worth. Why, then, should you sacrifice all these certain blessings, which are now in a great measure in actual possession, and run the hazard of their renewal in Louisiana?—on a mere speculation of fortune, as I understand it, to get more lands, when you have already more than you can turn to advantage. As to your two elbow associates, is it clear that you will have more elbow room in Louisiana, or better company on the bench? *Quære de hoc.* For my own part I am a good deal of Hamlet's way of thinking, and had much rather "bear the ills that I have, than fly to others *that I know not of.*" All this may only serve to convince you that I am tendering advice which I do not understand; but, you know "*ubi intentio bona, actio non mala,*" and at all events these hints may lead *you* to consider this subject of your *transmigration* a little more closely and earnestly.

For my own part, I begin to think that my lot is cast for life in Virginia; but not with an eye to the Presidency of the United States, your solemn mention of which has afforded me a hearty laugh and reminded me of some talk your father used to hold with me, when I was about sixteen years old, on the same subject, with the view, as I *then* knew, merely to stimulate me to study and emulation. Far different reasons induce me to believe that my lot is finally cast here. My wife's parents and relatives are extremely anxious that I should come to Richmond to live, and, by way of inducement, my father-in-law talks of building a house and improving a very beautiful lot for me here. If he does so, as I believe he will, I shall not be long in Norfolk, probably not longer than a year or two. By this means I shall get rid of all the objections to Virginia arising from the climate of Norfolk; I shall have every advantage of education for my children; and, if my professional prosperity continues, shall be able to retire from the bar in fifteen or twenty years with a sufficient fortune for my wife and daughters. My sons must do as I have done—shift for themselves; daughters cannot. As to Kentucky, my wife's objection to the removal will be insuperable, as long as her parents live; and by the time they are no more, if they reach the usual period, I hope to be so well fixed here as to render a removal altogether unnecessary. I presume that, when I am established in Richmond, I may anticipate an average practice of $5,000 per annum. My experience has already convinced me that I can live economically; and I imagine the calculation of expense sufficiently liberal when I estimate it annually at $3,000. I shall be thus able to lay up, from my practice, $2,000 per annum; and as money, you know, begets money, and in this commercial country many modes of employing money securely and advantageously present themselves, I expect that, by these means, and another that I shall presently mention, I may, if I am spared fifteen years, possess a capital of as many thousand pounds. I mention fifteen years as the limit of my forensic toils; but if my son is spared to me, and I also am spared, I shall continue at the bar until he shall be ready to take my place—which will be six years longer than I have mentioned. In the course of fifteen or twenty years I hope the people of this country will see the folly of the pitiful salaries which they have attached to the bench, and tender something worthy of a man's acceptance. In that event, when my son comes to the bar, I may possibly be again invited to the bench.

And here you have the whole scheme of my life, in expectancy. You see that it is obviously projected on the supposition that the political affairs of this country go on quietly in the beaten track. The example of France, however, teaches us how precarious this must be. It surely would not be matter of more surprise if the twentieth year from this should find an Emperor enthroned in America, than that ten or twelve years should have conducted France through a complete revolution from despotism, through anarchy, democracy and aristocracy, back to despotism again! Heaven avert such a calamity from us; but really it is not easy to determine what may be the fate of this country, when all those eminent characters shall die off whose respective grades were fixed by our revolution, and who seem to have a kind of acknowledged title, in succession, to the first honors of the country. Is there not some reason to dread that State jealousies, faction, corruption, ambition, may then disturb the halcyon sea on which we are riding, and change our peaceful elections into a military operation; then disunion, anarchy, civil war, and the fate of divided Greece; subjugation to some Macedonian Philip, Coriscan usurper, or some other foreign martial tyrant, or perhaps some Cæsar or Cromwell at home? I know the American character is a sedate and reflecting one, and, in this, very unlike the character of France; but it is to be remembered that the English have always been pronounced phlegmatic and saturnine—yet, that even they were capable of all the excitement which I dread in America: witness the bloody wars of York and Lancaster, and the tragedy of 1645. Nay—if we are truly informed, Pennsylvania, at this moment, on the subject of the election of Governor, betrays an excitability and an actual excitement which, if it were the temper of the country in a Presidential election, would soon bring about the national catastrophe of which I am speaking. These apprehensions may be visionary; they seem to me, however, to be too well justified by the history of mankind, and to be too strongly countenanced by the spirit which has sometimes manifested itself already, even in the American Congress. What a pity it is that our young men who are rising into notice, and who soon will be the political leaders of our country, have so false an idea of personal greatness of character. I speak of those in Virginia, whom alone I know. According to them, heat, rashness, intemperance and intolerance constitute the patriot and statesman. This has not been the character of our greatest men. Our Washington, Franklin, Jefferson, Madison, etc., were and are cool, calm, temperate, thoughtful, deliberative, tolerant and benevolent. I am afraid of those young men. Our Legislature is, this year, full of them. I tremble for my country when I see so many State bomb-shells, fraught with combustion and death, with their fuses already lighted; but Heaven, I hope and trust, will protect us.

As for me, I have not the most remote idea of going into public life. My sole object is to place my dear wife and children above the reluctant charity and still more insulting pity of a cold, proud and selfish world. This object I will pursue with unremitting ardor. I consider it my first duty (next to that which I owe to my Creator), and no vain idea of public honors shall take me off from the discharge of it. In this I make no sacrifice of feeling, for I have no *penchant* for political life; my feelings dispose me to tranquillity, the bosom of my family, and my books. I cannot say that I am indifferent to professional fame; but I can truly say that I love it less, for itself, than as the means of attaining my *summum bonum*: competence for my family. This is so truly the case, that, if I knew any other honest means by which I could acquire competence and independence more rapidly, I could relinquish the bar, not only without a sigh, but with pleasure. The truth is that, as yet, it is very little indeed that I know of professional fame or its accompanying sweets, except by the report of others; when I know more I may perhaps have a better relish for it.

According to your desire, I send you the "British Spy." I would send a copy of it to your father, but I apprehend, from his having mentioned it in his letter to me, that he already has a copy. It is strange how easily the multitude are taken by a little glitter. I can declare with the utmost sincerity that I had no conception that the soap-bubbles would have survived the newspaper in which they first appeared. I did not project them with a view to duration, or to anything else than a momentary amusement to myself and to the equally idle readers of newspapers. The printer, however, knew a little more of mankind, it seems; for you perceive that this is the third edition, which he is selling off very rapidly, and I presume he has cleared several thousand dollars by the adventure. This affair has induced me to consider whether, in those intervals of professional labor which would otherwise be spent in idleness, I cannot execute some little work in this way, by which I may earn both money and fame. I am accordingly preparing materials for the lives of our Virginian revolutionary characters of eminence; and if I can succeed in collecting them, I propose to myself to become their biographer. I shall probably send out the life of Patrick Henry, next fall, as Noah did the dove out of the ark, to see what foothold the country affords. If he succeeds, the other lives will follow in succession, or all together, something on the plan of "Plutarch's Lives." If I can do justice to this work, it will pay a just tribute of honor to the dead, will perpetuate their memory, stimulate the rising generation and present them with the best models by which to form their own characters, besides affording to myself a decent harvest of reputation and—*cash!* It is said, here, that John D. Burk, who is writing a third-rate history of Virginia, has sold the right for $10,000. I will not vouch for this, although I had it from a bishop; but if it be true, as is rendered highly probable by the immense profits which the author and the other parties concerned have derived from the "Life of Washington," it presents a very flattering evidence of the profits of book-making in this State; and if my own experiment shall be successful, the term of my labors at the bar may be perhaps considerably shortened. In the meantime, I am not so deeply infected with the *cacœthes scribendi* as to permit it to interfere with my profession. I shall ply this without intermission, considering it as my chief dependence. The other shall come in collaterally, merely to fill a chasm in the toils of the law.

I am much gratified to hear of Presley's progress in his education, and feel myself most delicately and poignantly flattered by the wish you express to place him under my direction, in the fall of 1806. Most welcome shall he be to every advantage that I can impart to him. I only wish that I could be living in this town next fall—for then I should hope that the examples which he would see at the superior courts of this State might fix themselves, as models, in his mind: whereas I fear that the little sort of questions which form the principal part of our Norfolk business, and the pettifogging discussions which he will hear at the bar there, will be scarcely considered, either by him or you, as compensating him for the time. I will promise, however, to show him, as distinctly as I can, the way in which he should walk in order to be eminent. I cannot, indeed, say to him, like Henry the Fourth of France to his soldiers, "when you find yourself in disorder, and at a loss what course to take, look upon my white plume—you will always find it on the road to honor and glory." I cannot even say to him, in the charging order of our Col. Washington, "follow me, my boy," which I am told was the practice of our Col. (now Gen.) Henry Lee. I can point out the plan, and tell him, "go on my boys." I will write to him as soon as my fall circuit will be over and I get back to Norfolk—which, however, never happens until about the 20th November.

It will delight me to see you, as you promise, and I hope you will not easily permit yourself to be diverted from taking Norfolk in your route. By the time this reaches you, your expected son will be born. Let me congratulate you, by anticipation, on this joyous event, and beg that you will give my love to him, your lady (who is my old-young acquaintance) and to your daughter; and let me be remembered, in terms of filial respect and affection, to our father, mother, sisters and brothers. Heaven bless and prosper you.

Believe me, ever,

Your friend,

WILLIAM WIRT.

To Hon. Ninian Edwards.

Norfolk, *Jan.* 10, 1806.

My Friend and Father:

It was not longer than five or six days ago that I sat myself down to complain of your long silence; but, in writing a folio page, I made myself so melancholy with the idea that we were never more to meet, that I found I was incapable of writing anything but what was calculated to infect you with my own hypo., and I determined to wait for a flood-tide of spirits. Your letter of the 6th ultimo, which was brought to me this morning, while I was at breakfast with my wife and little daughter, has affected me in such a manner as to disqualify me for thinking of anything but you and yours, or doing anything but writing to you. Without waiting, therefore, any longer for flood- or ebb-tides, I sit myself down to pour out to you the feelings of my heart and the vagaries of my brain, without reserve.

I see, by your letter, that you have not forgotten how fond I used to be of your praise—you are right in supposing that I love it still; but, indeed, your partiality has betrayed you into very great extravagancies about me. I look upon the picture which your friendship has drawn of me, in this letter, as the traveler in Germany does on his own gigantic image, reflected by the rising sun from the mist of the mountains: in size and grandeur the phantom surpasses him so far, that he wonders how his own little self could have produced such a phenomena, and whether it be not self-existent, without any prototype in the human creation. No, my dear Mr. Edwards; my vanity has had too many castigations to permit me, at this time of day, to suppose myself anything uncommon. I have, too often, occasion to feel my own defects, and I meet with too many superiors, to believe that I am born for peculiar honors or distinctions. In this borough resides a man, a practitioner of law—one of the best curers of vanity that I have ever met with. I am opposed to him at the bar; and very rarely am I so, without the most sensible humiliation. He is, indeed, an uncommon man—a young one too—that is, about my own age; and the only comfort I have, when I compare myself with him, is the reflection of the superior advantages which he has had. His name is Littleton Waller Tazewell. His father was a judge of the General Court of this Commonwealth, then a judge of the Supreme Court of Appeals, and died as a member of the Senate of the United States for Virginia. These honors show the estimation in which the virtues and talents of the father were held, and justly held, by the country. The son is confessedly very far the father's superior in point of native talents, and he has had an education unequaled by any in the State. He was not more than seven years of age when he was placed in the family of Bishop Madison, the President of William and Mary College, and the particular friend of his father. Under the instruction of this gentleman, and the various professors in that seminary, he became master of the dead languages and of several living ones, and, by the time he was seventeen years of age, was a veteran in all the sciences and a first-rate historian. So that while I, with a little knowledge of Latin and less of Greek, was mounted upon a bench in the Seneca meeting house, teaching a parcel of little girls and boys to *sol-fa* it, this gentleman was conversing with the planetary system, ranging through all nature, and learning wisdom from the experience of nations that are no more. Thus accomplished, he was, at the age of seventeen, placed by his father in the office of Mr. Wickham, a relation by affinity—the rival of Marshall and of Washington, and their superior before a jury. In the office of this gentleman he had the advantage of a most extensive and judiciously selected library; he heard the daily and hourly counsel given by this eminent advocate in every variety of cases; he learned all the technical and practical parts of the profession, acquired the best system of arranging his papers and going through the routine of professional duties, and, being in the metropolis, he had before him not only the most finished models of forensic argument and eloquence in the superior courts of the State, but he had an opportunity of lighting his genius at the altar of a Henry and a Lee in the Virginia Legislature.

Much about this time Ninian, poor Andrew Lane, and myself, were living with William P. Hunt, himself a novice in the profession—his library consisting of three or perhaps six books, no clients to consult him, and no examples of oratory before us much superior to Baker Johnson's pike-staff—nor of these half a dozen law books or Baker Johnson's staff did we think a thousandth part as often as of the bright eyes and angel smiles of the Misses Turner & Co.!

I am ashamed to pursue the parallel any farther—but this gentleman came to the bar, where he found himself the master of every question that was started; whither he brought with him the law learning and address of his master, and all the stores and treasures which he had amassed at college; whither he brought with him what is, if possible, more important than them all: the firmly-rooted habits of industrious application and of close and forcible thinking. Here he soon felt what it was to be touched with the animating beam of public applause and admiration, and he had the still more exquisite pleasure of gladdening the heart of a father and filling it with proud and rapturous anticipations. Of all these pleasures my evil stars and my own imprudence deprived me. Against all my disadvantages of education and of habit I have yet to struggle. I have, indeed, with the aid of Divine Providence, cast off the debauchee; but when I compare the neat and systematic operations of this gentleman—his papers, his pleas, his arguments—with the chaos which I contrive to create around me, and my loose, irregular and desultory mode of acting and of speaking, I am so far from finding occasion of vanity, that I am humbled unto the dust.

Dugald Stewart (a professor in the University of Edinburgh) observes that every man, when he grows up and enters upon life, finds and feels some error which was committed in his education; and he adds that we ought never to think it too late to begin to educate ourselves anew. Heaven knows how sensibly I feel the truth of the first part of this observation; and, were I in circumstances to educate myself anew, I would enter the office of some automaton of a clerk or merchant—the creature of habit, a mere machine—where I would remain until I had gotten the habit of keeping my papers in the most exact arrangement. I would then study the mathematics until my brain became mathematically methodical—until I could find a pleasure in hanging over intricate problems and winding through the most perplexed and extensive mazes of logical deduction. These are the two wants which hang like a dead weight about my neck, and which must always prevent me from rising much higher in my profession than I now am. Beware of them, my dear friend, in the education of your younger sons; rely upon it, that these two habits are of more importance to a lawyer than all the genius of a Cicero or Demosthenes. For my own part, I am persuaded that there is scarcely any solid basis of intellectual greatness and utility, other than the mathematics. If Providence spares my son, I am determined, if it be in my power to have it so, that he shall be sufficiently qualified to be a professor of mathematics in a university. It is for the want of this acquirement, and of those habits of business and of close, systematic and persevering thought and application which it never fails to generate, that my progress at the bar has resembled and will continue to resemble more the lambent motions of the flame of a candle, than the steady emersion of a planet, gradually increasing in light as it rises, until its glories blaze in the zenith. This, my dear friend, is not affected depression of myself. It would be a very silly piece of affectation, and very unworthy of that perfect candor and openness which I wish to subsist between us. I have thought it my duty to be thus full about myself, in order to undeceive you as to the estimate in which you seem to suppose I am held in this country, and more especially as I may have myself contributed, though innocently, to produce the deception—for I find, by your letter, that I stated myself to have received an accession of character from the letters of the "British Spy." This was true: those letters made me known to many to whom I was before a stranger, and known to my advantage, too, as the *bagatelle* had the good luck to hit the capricious taste of the public. But on the roll of fame I am far, very far, behind the Tullys and Hortensius of Virginia, and indeed, comparatively, am little more than a cypher. Yet, let not my sincerity rob me of your esteem: it was your own benevolence, and, I doubt not, your sympathy for my desolate and unfriended situation, which first attached you to me. I am no longer, indeed, desolate or unfriended, but I should almost believe myself so, if I thought I were to be discarded from your esteem and affection. Continue, then, I beseech you, to think of me as a son. Your solicitude for my prosperity and fame will be a strong incentive to exertion; and if nothing less than fame can insure me your heart, I will struggle to overleap the barrier of mediocrity, which, hitherto, has been my limit. I fancy that, by this time, you will not think that I paid you any great compliment in attributing to you the formation of my mind and character. The fact is that, on the dissolution of Parson Hunt's school, your invitation drew me from the whirlpool of vice in Bladensburgh, in which, but for you, I should have been irretrievably lost; nor is this all: if, on my taking up my abode at Mt. Pleasant, your character had been a negative one—a neutral between vice and virtue and destitute of dignity—my levity and immoral propensities would still have ruined me. It was the decision, the energy, the dignity of your mind and character, that restrained my follies and levities. The praise which you bestowed on my genius, and the opinions which you expressed of what I was capable of attaining, awakened in me a greater respect for myself and kindled my emulation. The warmth, let me add (without the imputation of flattery, for I speak from my heart) the eloquence—the natural, ardent and impressive eloquence—with which you delivered your sentiments on virtue, public and private—on morals, on the glory of patriotism as exemplified in Brutus and Cato—and this very frequently too—gave a shape and fashion to my own sentiments on those subjects, which finally mixed with my constitution and became a part of my character. It was thus that you erected a court of *oyer and terminer* in my own breast, and commissioned a self-accuser. It was before this tribunal and this accuser that, during the days of dissipation into which I was betrayed, on first coming to this State, my conduct was, every morning, arraigned and punished—until the salutary punishment and my anxiety for the happiness of another wrought a reformation in me, and brought me back to the ground on which you placed me.

How can you speak so disrespectfully of your own powers? I doubt if there ever was a mind more highly endowed by nature, or a man who would have shone more splendidly than you would have done, if you had devoted yourself to public life; but you preferred the peace and quiet of private life. I approve your choice, and, as far as it is in my power, shall follow your example. Like Shakspeare's Falstaff, "I like not such grinning honor as Sir Walter hath," neither have I any very strong appetite for those highly-seasoned dishes of calumny with which I see the President and his secretaries regularly regaled, by half the presses in America. I would not give the dance which I have just witnessed between my wife and children (for it is now night, and I am a fiddler) for a thousand such high and honorable banquets! Give me independence, the peaceful bosom of my family, a friend, and books—I ask no more! The rest I leave to those who love public honors more than tranquillity.

You have said something about your own health: I hope, therefore, that you continue well, and more especially that you have no return of that malady which made it necessary for you to submit to the surgeon's knife, in Fredericktown. You talk, indeed, of religion "supporting you in solitude, and enabling you to bear your afflictions without a murmur;" but, with such a flock of children around you, and within three miles of Bardstown, I should hope you were not much oppressed by solitude; and as for afflictions, I trust you introduced them only to complete the quotation, and not because you have in reality any afflictions to contend with, other indeed than those "little, whiffling cares and vexations," as Sterne calls them, which are the inevitable lot of the most fortunate life.

What pleasure it would give me to place my dear wife and our little ones around your hospitable board—to see and converse with you and Mrs. Edwards, and your children—I leave to your imagination; I cannot figure to myself a higher or more exquisite enjoyment in this world. But, alas! that enjoyment cannot be mine; for, besides her parents, my wife has a sister (the wife of the present Governor of the State) and two brothers stationed for life in Virginia, and I believe she could not leave them without a sacrifice which I have no right or wish to ask. Much, indeed, do I long to be stationed in Kentucky, because it is there that, I think, I should the soonest be enabled to relinquish the laborious, harassing and degrading profession in which I am embarked. I perhaps receive more money here than I should in Kentucky; but I have no genius for speculation or turning that money in any way to advantage; and I am persuaded, in order to become wealthy in this State, a lawyer must have some source of profit other than the mere revenue arising from his profession. In Kentucky, lands present a subject of easy speculation and certain profit, in which it would be difficult if not impossible to err. I must own to you that I am impatient to be released from the wrangles of the bar. It is, indeed, possible that if I were perfectly at liberty to indulge in those studies and pursuits for which I feel a very ardent passion, I might be of some service to my fellow-creatures—so at least I think; and I often sigh for that liberty which would enable me to make the experiment, but which I fear cannot be mine—at least until all the vigor of mind as well as body, and "all the life of life," is flown. But it is in vain to repine at our destiny, and can produce no other possible effect than to aggravate the troubles with which we are already surrounded. There is no conduct on such occasions, worthy either of the philosopher or Christian, but to kiss the rod with a smile of resignation, and console ourselves by doing all the good we can within the sphere of our action.

I think your remarks on the profession of the law, in the general, correct. The necessity of defending wrong with a face and manner of earnestness and sincerity, and of laboring with zeal to deceive judges and jurors, has certainly a tendency to sully the sanctity of the moral sense—more especially when it is seen that eulogies and honors are lavished on the bright and victorious eloquence which can the most successfully produce those deceptions. Deception indeed, is, half our time, the very traffic in which we deal—fashion and opinion have made it not only a justifiable, but even an honorable traffic; nor is it much to be wondered at, if some members of the profession in this country and very many in England, urged by want, transfer the habits of the bar into private life. There are, however, few if any instances in this country of men, virtuously educated, who have been rendered base and corrupt by the practice of the law.

There is no revolution in my family since I wrote you last. My daughter and son continue to grow more and more interesting every day. I shall teach them to love and respect you and Mrs. Edwards, and to consider you and your children as their paternal relations; and from you I shall claim the fulfillment of your promise, that you will teach yours to regard me as a brother; they shall indeed find me one, if an occasion shall present itself.

Ninian, in his letter, talked of bringing on Presley and leaving him with me this winter, and perhaps longer. If it be your impression and Ninian's that his residence with me will be serviceable to him, you know me, I am sure, well enough to be convinced that it would afford me one of the most delightful gratifications in the world. The only objections to it are such as arise from a consideration of Presley's benefit, and which I think I mentioned to Ninian: my library is, as yet, on a small scale—the practice of these courts is too loose to afford him any information as to the technical parts of the profession—and the yellow fever assails the town every fall. If these difficulties can be obviated to your satisfaction, my house, my books, my best instructions, and the bosom of an affectionate brother, are at his service. When I wrote to Ninian, I had, I think, a pretty near prospect of going to Richmond to settle. That, however, is removed further off; and even if I should go while Presley is living with me, he can accompany me without any inconvenience or difficulty. When I state that my library is small, you must not understand it to be quite as small as William P. Hunt's. I suppose I have five or six hundred dollars' worth of well chosen books, and I am constantly augmenting the number. I hope Presley has not been confining his attention to law, solely, but that, independent of his education at college, he has attended to general science, to history (both ancient and modern), and to poetry—the latter by way of raising his imagination and acquainting him with the melody of the English language; an important acquirement for a public speaker.

My Betsey returns her dutiful acknowledgments to yourself and Mrs. E. for your affectionate mention of her, and begs you both, and her adopted sisters and brothers, to accept of her love. My little Laura, whom I have just asked if I should give her love to you, too, answers that I "must *do* (for *go*) and tell you!" Little does she know what happiness it would give me to be able to do so. My love and duty to you, Mrs. E., and all the children, with their husbands and wives. (Elisha, I suppose, is married by this time.) Pray let me hear from you again, soon—every month at least—and prompt Ninian. I don't know how to quit you, and yet I have not said half I wished; but I must. Adieu, my friend and father.

WILLIAM WIRT.

To BENJAMIN EDWARDS, ESQ., near Bardstown, Kentucky.

RICHMOND, *February* 2, 1807.

My Dear Sir:

I am indebted to you for your favor of the 5th ult., which I received to-day. A combination of causes have made me a defaulter towards you lately; be assured, however, that a diminution of my respect and affection for you is not amongst those causes. You do not, indeed, notice my defalcation in this letter, and I infer pardon. I shall be happy to hear from Mr. Trigg, and to serve him by any means in my power; the particulars of his case you tell me I shall have from himself.

I have seen the papers from your State, and marked with regret the number of respectable names involved in the Spanish intrigue. We hope that the work of expurgation, which is begun among you, will go on until the body politic is thoroughly cleansed. To say the least of Innis, his virtue was in a capitulating mood; he ought to follow the steps of Sebastian. Poor Nicholas! death has dropped the curtain over him; let us not raise it. I am glad to find that those who are on the spot, and have therefore the best opportunity of judging, concur in extolling the vigilance and patriotism of Mr. Daviess. He has been very strongly suspected, in this State, of being touched with the Spanish disease; and even his late efforts against Burr, for which he received such distinguished honor in Frankfort, appeared to us so poorly concerted and weakly sustained that they were regarded as feints to give a moment's relief to the reputation of the culprit and favor his escape. I am pleased to find you think otherwise, and hope you may see no cause to change your present opinion of him. Poor Burr! what an inglorious fall for genius and science! The example of Sylla, Cataline, Cæsar, Augustus, Bonaparte, etc., appear to have had the same effect, on his brain, which those of Orlando Furioso and other knights-errant had on that of Don Quixote: more especially if we believe him to have projected the extended and magnificent project to which Gen. Eaton has just sworn—(not knowing whether you take the Richmond papers, I inclose the "Enquirer," of this day, containing Eaton's and others' depositions, together with the President's last communication touching this conspiracy, and suppose it may probably reach you as soon as through another channel). Hitherto, Wilkinson has behaved well in this affair; but, admitting that nothing had been understood between him and Burr, before the arrival of Swartwout and Bollman at Orleans, this is a curious departure from the generally supposed style of Burr's negotiations—sending agents there to confer with Wilkinson, and sending them under the impression that W. had been previously gained; writing to him, too, in a manner which shows that he himself was under the same impression! If there had been no previous understanding between Wilkinson and Burr, all that can be said for it is, that the latter has assailed his virtue with as little ceremony as if he had been a common prostitute, and was always ready when the money was offered. There is, indeed, reason to suspect Wilkinson; but if he is disposed, "by hearty repentance and true faith, to turn unto his" duty, should he not be received? Would it not afford just cause for clamor against the tyranny of the Government? And even if Wilkinson be pure, at present, would it not naturally force him, with all his influence, into the arms of Burr, and palliate his treason? It is a critical situation in which the Government is placed. Perhaps the course adopted by the President, towards him, is not only the most just but the safest: the show of a magnanimous confidence has been known to confirm even a wavering faith. If Wilkinson is innocent, removal would be cruelty not to be surpassed, for it would blast his character forever, or else the blow would recoil on the Administration. "*Sed non nobis est, tantas componere lites.*" The danger we believe is now over; for if Wilkinson has been merely playing the patriot all this time, and "mouthing at Cæsar" in order that he may be retained at his post until he can surrender Orleans and the army to Burr, it is believed that they will find the fallacy of calculating on the conduct of an army of freemen and Americans, from the example of the corrupt and mercenary legions of Rome.

I saw, some time ago, in the "Western World," a paragraph stating the resignation of Sebastian, and expressing a hope that Judge Wallace would follow his example. Who is this Judge Wallace? Not, I am sure, my old friend and schoolmate; and yet, knowing no other Wallace in Kentucky likely to be a judge, I felt considerable uneasiness on his account. You would have increased it if you had stopped at informing me that my friend Wallace had succeeded you on the bench of the General Court, but you have relieved me entirely by speaking so warmly of his virtues. I am happy to hear of his promotion, so far as honors are concerned; but how can he support his family on the salary of a judge of your General Court? and would he not have found it his interest to have continued at the bar? Your lawyers get rich; Wallace, certainly, could not have failed in a country in which Daviess succeeds! or else Daviess must be a very different man from what he was when he was in Richmond, about seven years ago. I think Wallace has talents which would have enrolled his name amongst advocates of the first order, if he had energy enough to throw off that flattering and hurried manner, which he learned in his childhood, and cultivate a talent for speaking. He had but to practice that slow and deliberate enunciation which Lord Bacon so strongly inculcates, and which Plato is said to have exemplified so beautifully and sweetly. But how easy is it to give these lessons; how difficult to practice them! I have been trying all my life to learn to speak in the time of Lady Coventry's minuet, but I began with a Virginia jig, and shall go on shuffling all the days of my life. I have a little son, just two years old, who is beginning to talk handsomely. I labor before him to speak in proper time, knowing the decisive importance of parental example; but the moment my attention is withdrawn from my own enunciation, my tongue breaks loose like one of those windmills with which they frighten crows from a corn field, and so my poor boy, I fear, must be a jig-dancer too.

And Presley is at the bar, while I was expecting him in Richmond! What pleasure it would give me to hear his maiden efforts; and how shall I rejoice to hear the echo of his fame reverberating to our Atlantic coast! He will have a good deal to do to fulfill the expectations which were formed of him in his childhood. Your father, I remember, got Brooks' novel called "The Fool of Quality," about the time Presley was five or six years old, and we were all struck with the resemblance which he bore to the character of "Henry Clinton." I suspect I can repeat, to this day, the first set-speech he ever made—and that was borrowed from an almanac:

"Man's but a vapor and full of woes—
Just cuts a caper, and down he goes."

Pray, give him my love and best wishes. It will make me happy to see your cousin, Mr. Pope, in Richmond. There is not the least probability of my going to Washington next winter. I am no politician. I have not that fondness for politics which I perhaps would have, if nature had given me talents to make a figure in them, and a temper to endure the buffetings and humiliations which I see all politicians are doomed to suffer. As it is, my ambition is bounded by the single desire of finding ease and peace for my old age and independence for my family; and this I have a prospect of compassing if I live out the usual lot of man. I very sincerely wish you success in your desire to get on the Federal bench. I have no influence on the appointments of the Cabinet. I know Mr. Jefferson and Mr. Madison, indeed, both very well, and, if it be necessary, might perhaps be justified in stating to them my impression of you, but have no reason to flatter myself that such statement would produce any effect in changing the destination of honors and offices; but if you think otherwise, or it would afford you any manner of gratification, I will write with pleasure to either or both of them. Pray what is the salary of a judge of the Court of Appeals of Kentucky? The manner of your appointment was certainly very honorable; you must have out-Jenkinized Goldsmith's hero! One and the same speech would not always serve your turn, and nothing can be more different than your catastrophies; but perhaps you are not at the end of your journey.

You give but a poor account of the net proceeds of my little school. Carlton is, however, full as smart as I expected; and Sol. has maintained his character throughout the drama—which, you know, is a matter of great merit among the critics. It was kind in his wife, since she was predetermined to beat him, to furnish him with a fortification of horn-works against her own assaults. Mr. Addison's idea is verified in the example of the two boys—they make the same figure, now, in relation to society, which they formerly made in relation to their school-mates. Sol. was always, you know, a smiling, Jerry-sneak sort of a fellow, and Carlton a giggling one, who asked no more than a slight provocation to laugh to be perfectly happy. It is possible that Watkins' vanity may be corrected by age, and Catlett's temper by prosperity; I wish they may. I am of the opinion that Catlett is the cleverest fellow of the two; he has more volubility, but it is all commonplace, and an affected imitation of the gay, fashionable rake and debauchee, who has been the object of comic satire ever since the reign of Charles the Second; his glitter is mere isinglass. I am glad to hear that Dr. Jones is doing even so well as you represent; pray remember me to him affectionately. Give my love to my old schoolmate and favorite, Doct. Wallace; he was always amiable, in spite of Latin and Maguire, both of whom he hated as much as he is capable of hating anything. This Maguire was our usher; and, by-the-by, Wallace can tell you a good story of him, which now I have neither time nor paper to give you.

I am afraid Elisha is going to be an old batchelor; it is high time he was contributing to de-forest and people Kentucky. Betsey married, and Peggy has had offers! When I read this I felt disposed to look into a glass and see if I was not as hoary, wrinkled and emaciated as Father Priam, or even Methusalem; and yet I am but thirty-four, if there be any truth in family chronicles! You have not told me the name of Betsey's husband, which you ought to have done. I have no objection to Peggy's being a little romantic, for I think it spreads the charm of delicacy with a fine effect over a female character; but it will not do to carry it so far as Mrs. Radcliffe, the celebrated moralist, who, I am told, is at last crazed by the offspring of her own fancy. I am surprised at your saying my old friend Kelly moved to that country, a few days past—for if, by that country, you mean Kentucky, I thought he had been there ten years ago, at least; but perhaps you mean that he had moved to Logan county. Pray recall me to his recollection, and assure him I take the most friendly interest in his welfare.

I presume you will expect to hear something about me and my prospects, in so long a letter. Providence has still favored me since my removal to this place. I have more of reputation and business than I deserve; still maintain my family, and have a little surplus cash to invest in an advantageous speculation, now and then. The Legislature, lately in session here, solicited me by some of their members to take a place in the Council of State, which I declined, as interfering too much with my pursuits. I have been much pressed, too, to represent this city in the Legislature, but I have declined it, and mean not to be diverted from my object of an affluent old age, exempt from political storms, and indulged in the innocent pleasures of retirement and books. This may be thought an ingloriously indolent scheme; but I think it quite as desirable, though perhaps not so glorious, as the exit of Cato, Cicero or Demosthenes. My soul is entirely too unambitious to be pleased with the prospect of falling on my own sword, being the victim of tyrants' myrmidons, or stealing into the grave by sucking poison from a pen; nay, I am torpid enough to love solitude and peace more than the glory of running the gauntlet of all the scandalous presses in America. I have three children—the youngest, a girl, near five months old; this is an effectual way of serving my country! and I have a prospect of serving her very effectually in that way, which is quite enough to satisfy my ambition! Besides this, there is no necessity for my embarking in the vessel of State: there are candidates enough, anxious for the service, even to stand before the mast; and I do not see why I, who know nothing of political navigation—scarcely the names of the ropes and sails—should be pushing and elbowing to become a mariner. These are the motives which have determined me to private life.

I beg you, if you should have an opportunity, that you will offer my love, respects and duty at Shiloh. Mr. Edwards has seen so many of his children married and colonized, that, I imagine, he is beginning to look forward to the time when he and Mrs. E. may sit in opposite corners and play "Darby" and "Joan!" What a patriarch he will be in a few years, with his children and his children's children swarming in hosts around him, until it will require as good a chronicler as Moses to enumerate, through all of their ramifications, the descendants of the new tribe of Benjamin! I hope he still enjoys his health, and has had no symptoms of the return of his Maryland complaint.

Pray what has become of those geniuses, Haden Edwards and Gerard, or Garrett as he was called, who frightened me so much when they were at your father's, on their way to Carlisle College? I remember I was almost afraid to open my lips before them; and as for Garrett, I expected to have heard before this that he had set the Ohio, Mississippi, Missouri and Gulf of Mexico on fire! I hope he has not returned into water himself, like one of Ovid's metamorphoses.

Give the love of a brother and friend to Mr. and Mrs. Whitaker, your sister Polly, and all your brothers and sisters. Remember that you promise, in this last letter, to write to me again shortly. Adieu!

WILLIAM WIRT.

To HON. NINIAN EDWARDS, Logan county, Kentucky.

RICHMOND, *February* 22, 1807.

Dear Sir:

The mail of this morning has brought me your favor, without date, but bearing in the postmark that of the 29th ultimo. So far from an apology being necessary for your letters, I am extremely obliged to you for them, both on account of the facts and the speculations which they contain. As the best return which I am now able to make, I inclose you a handbill, struck from one of our papers of yesterday morning, and which may probably bring you the news of Burr's surrender, Monroe's treaty with Great Britain, and the construction of Bonaparte's proclamation-blockade of that kingdom and her dependencies. If I were able to write, I would not trouble you with the inclosure; but this is the first time I have written a line for a week past, owing to a distracting pain over my right eye, and I now find writing so painful that I have barely power to reassure you that I am,

Your friend,

WILLIAM WIRT.

To Hon. Ninian Edwards, Collina, Logan county, Kentucky.

Richmond, *August* 2, 1807.

My Dear Sir:

I dare say, my good friend, you begin to think me a Godwinian, in point of gratitude—seeing how diligently you detailed the operations of Aaron Burr, while he was in your quarter, whereas he has been near four months in our metropolis and you have not heard a word from me. I can only assure you that my silence has resulted from the importunity of my engagements, and from that cause solely.

While he was wandering over the United States, brought before grand juries in Kentucky and the Mississippi, and finally under proclamation for flying from his recognizance, I could not help often imagining, "suppose that chance had brought him on his trial in Richmond, and chance still greater had embarked me in his cause—what course would I pursue?" Little did I suppose that *that* imagination was so soon to be realized. I had gone from Richmond about the last of March to wind up old causes in Norfolk, and to defend a criminal by whom I was called to Northumberland District Court. Burr arrived in my absence. At Williamsburg, I received an express to engage me on behalf of the United States, and I did engage. At Northumberland Court-house I was met by an express from Burr, which was of course too late. From this solicitude to engage me, you will readily see that I am playing the "Jenkinsonian" successfully in Virginia, as you represented yourself to have done in Kentucky. On the 22d of May the Federal Court met. Burr challenged some of the grand jury for favor, on the authority of Hawkins' Pleas of the Crown and Bacon's Abridgement. The propriety of the challenge was admitted, I think most wrongfully—the authorities setting out a class of causes of challenge totally distinct from favor, and the year books, on which Hawkins founds himself, flatly disproving the principle in the latitude of construction allowed to it here. Others of the grand jury were set aside as having been improperly summoned. After the marshal had summoned the twenty-four required by law, some of the twenty-four having declared their inability to attend, it was decided by the court that the marshal had exhausted his power by summoning the twenty-four; that having no power to touch another man, the rest were not, in law, summoned, and consequently were not grand jurors. By these acts the grand jury was reduced to its lowest number, sixteen, and consequently the chance of the concurrence of twelve in finding a bill, was reduced to its minimum. Of these sixteen, too, several were Federalists and several *minority* men, and among the latter John Randolph, who had spoken of the affair, in Congress, as a petty intrigue. Burr and his counsel were filled with triumph at the prospect that there would be no bill found; they displayed this triumph very injudiciously, and went so far as to declare out of doors that there was no chance of finding a bill—representing the whole as a military project, to take place only in the event of a war declared between the United States and Spain. Meantime, while the grand jury were engaged in examining the evidence, Burr amused us with a series of interludes in court—motion upon motion —argument upon argument, for upwards of thirty days—the principal policy of which was to turn the current of popular indignation from Burr against the Administration, by representing Burr as a victim of envy, malignity and persecution. These arts had no effect beneficial to Burr, except upon a few Federalists, who were predisposed to believe anything and everything dishonorable to the Administration; but upon the community at large, from whom Burr's jury must come, the effect was most inauspicious.

In the midst of all this hurly-burly came Wilkinson and his suit, like Pope's fame, "unlooked for," at least by Burr's partisans. I was anxious to to mark the interview between Burr and Wilkinson. There was no nature in it; they had anticipated the meeting, and resolved upon the countenances they would wear. Wilkinson had been some time within the bar before Burr would look towards him, affecting not to know he was there, until Hay introduced him by saying to the court, "it is my wish that Gen. Wilkinson, who is now before the court, should be qualified and sent up to the grand jury." At the words "who is now before the court," Burr started in his chair, turned quickly around, and fixed a look of scorn and contempt on Wilkinson. Wilkinson, bowing to the court on his introduction, did not receive Burr's first glance, but his bow finished, he turned his face down on Burr and looked with all the sullenness and proteuity of a big black bull. Burr withdrew his eyes composedly, and there was the end if it. When the grand jury came down with the bills against Burr and Blennerhassett, I never saw such a group of shocked faces. The Chief Justice, who is a very dark man, shrunk back with horror upon his seat and turned black; he kept his eyes fixed upon Burr with an expression of sympathy so agonizing and horror so deep and overwhelming, that he seemed, for two or three seconds, to have forgotten where and who he was. I observed him, and saw him start from his reverie, under the consciousness that he was giving way too much to his feelings, and looked around upon the multitude to see if he had been noticed. He is, I believe, one of the greatest and best of men; some of our political friends, warped by their prejudices, think him too much warped by his—if he is so, he does not know it, for never did I know a man who was more solicitous to cast every bias from his mind and decide every proposition on its abstract merits. I think he has sometimes decided wrong, but it is much more probable that I myself am wrong. The great Luther Martin was here all the while. He may have been eminent, but I think he has nothing but the fame of his greatness to recommend him; he is all sing-song—a most loose, careless, slubbering speaker; his style is very coarse and very often incorrect; his conceptions half-formed, and without grace, spirit or force. Jonathan Dayton, being amongst those against whom the grand jury found bills, is also some where about town, *incog.*, and my brother, Robert Gamble, who has just arrived from Orleans *via* Rhode Island, informs me that Ingersoll and Lewis are coming on for the purpose of defending him (Dayton), so that we shall have the grand climacteric characters of the American bar to cope with. "O! the blood more stirs to rouse a lion than to start a hare."

Love to Mrs. Edwards and to your father and family. To-morrow the trial in chief comes on; the witnesses are parading; Martin has arrived. You shall hear from me again.

In haste,

Your friend,

WILLIAM WIRT.

To Hon. Ninian Edwards, Logan county, Kentucky.

Richmond, *December* 26, 1807.

My Dear Friend:

The last mail brought me your favor of the 14th November, accompanied by Joseph H. Daviess' pamphlet. I had received, also, in due course of mail, your former letter, describing the indisposition of your father, and immediately on the receipt of it sat down to write to him, under all the oppression of spirits which your letter was calculated to produce; nor was it until I had discharged my heart on three pages, that it occurred to me I was not in a proper frame of mind to write to a sick man. I am glad I did not send the letter, for I find, on looking at it now, that it would very probably have given your father the *hypo*, even if it had found him in health. Since that time I have been almost afraid to inquire about Kentucky, lest I should hear that the benefactor and father of my youth was no more. But about four weeks ago I dined in company with a Major Duvall, of this place, then just from Kentucky, who began, of his own accord, to tell me of his having been several days at our father's, and that he had left him in full and perfect health and spirits. Your last letter has banished this pleasing illusion and added the afflicting account of your own ill health. Thus is something ever occurring to remind us of the frail tenure by which we hold our earthly enjoyments. I have had some sever lessons on this text during the fall: In October we lost a little girl thirteen months old, one of the sweetest and most fascinating children I ever saw; and in the following month a beautiful infant of four weeks old. We have only our two first left. They are, thank Heaven, very healthy, very sprightly and very entertaining. My wife and myself enjoy our health, and endeavor to learn resignation to the will of Heaven. I very much hope that the winter will bring you and your father up again and brace and restore you to health. A short time ago I had some hope of seeing you both in Kentucky. Mr. Rodney, the Attorney General of the United States, proposed to me to attend the court at Chilicothe and aid in the prosecution of Aaron

Burr there; but the lowest sum which would have indemnified me for the trip was higher than the treasury could afford, at a time when we were threatened with war. If I had gone I was half resolved, while on the wing, to take a flight to your State, and shake you all by the hand once more. As I cannot go myself, I send you, inclosed, my representation; it is the work of a French artist here, by the name of Memin, and is thought an excellent likeness. I shall inclose one, also, to your father. How gratifying would it be to me, if, in exchange, I could receive likenesses of you both, since I now believe that I shall never see you more! The distance which separates us, and the duties which confine us to our respective homes, have placed a gulf between us which we never can pass; and to this the prospect of war adds another barrier. The return of our Minister from London, and the embargo laid by Congress, which was announced to us on yesterday morning, have cast a deep gloom over the country. War is considered as inevitable; and who can tell whether we will survive it. Bonaparte has given us as much cause of offense as Great Britain, saving the impressment of our seamen: our commerce is equally a subject of plunder and our flag of insult with both nations; but whether we go to war with one or both, the war will be no trifling one. It seems to be the wretched destiny of every State, that intermeddles with either of them, to fall sooner or later under the tyranny of the Corsican; whether friend or foe, this is equally the case. We just hear, through a respectable channel, that Bonaparte is in Madrid, at the head of 100,000 Frenchmen, and among other exploits, that he has imprisoned two hundred Spanish nobles. This is his friendship: what his hostility is, all Europe can tell. Is not this man bent on realizing the chimera, as it was thought of Louis XIV—universal dominion? He will pay dearly for us, if he gets us at all; we will give him the flag of St. Domingo on a grander scale: our mountains and our forests shall stand us in newstead.

I am much obliged to you for Daviess' pamphlet; it is a curious production. I should not suppose that, in the cast of his talents, judgment was his predominant faculty, or it would scarcely have permitted him to mix such a quantity of trash, and sometimes low trash, with the sounder parts of his publication. But he wrote under the influence of spleen and resentment, and his judgment, perhaps, had not its usual ascendency. However this may be, he seems to have consulted his own personal dignity as little as he did that of the Administration, and his pamphlet, I suspect, will do him more harm than it will them. It is strange that man cannot have a little more wit in his anger: but that he will permit his revenge to range so licentiously abroad, as to defeat its own purposes. Herein he resembles more the wounded serpent, which, in the anguish of pain and fury of resentment, turns its envenomed fangs upon itself. Genius will, sometimes, run mad.

I am extremely gratified, but not surprised, at the interest which your father takes in my welfare. Since he can find a pleasure in the skeletons of my speeches, as given him by the newspapers, I will, in two or three weeks, inclose him a pamphlet containing a pretty faithful statement of my two principal arguments in the course of the proceedings against Burr and his associates. He will be enabled, by this pamphlet, to form a correct idea of my public speaking. I will, at the same time, inclose a copy to you, and you will see on how small a foundation it is sometimes the pleasure of fame to stand. I have heard no man whom I think eminent as a public speaker: they are either too declamatory and frothy, or too argumentative and dry; if those who argue attempt also to adorn, the ornaments are too obviously studied and too detached from the body of the argument. It is rare, I suspect, in any country, to find a man so variously accomplished as to speak to the judgment, the fancy and the heart with full effect. Such an one, I am told, was Mirabeau, the great leader of the French revolution. Lord Chatham spoke to the judgment and the heart—seldom if ever to the fancy. So, also, Fox, Burke and Sheridan paid their chief homage to the fancy and the heart; they rarely, if ever, made a powerful appeal to the judgment. The late William Pitt assailed the judgment principally, if not solely. Our Patrick Henry had very little to do except with the heart; and our John Marshall confined himself exclusively to the judgment. So rare is it to find a man who can reason irresistibly, and, also, when the occasion shall require it, can paint to the fancy and to the heart like a master! The faculties are totally distinct, and it seems to require almost the study of a lifetime to bring any of them to perfection. It is not wonderful, therefore, that their union is so seldom seen. There is certainly no man now before the public, in this State, who can make this high pretension. We have very able lawyers, good reasoners, astute and ingenious advocates, and fluent and elegant speakers; but we have no man who can fire the fancy by an evolution of new and sublime images, or who can melt the heart by the simple of nature. As to me, you will see how very small are my pretensions to the possession of any one of these faculties. The newspapers have spoken of me as eloquent, and on a recent occasion the members of the Assembly, now in session here, placed me, in their debates, above the heads of Demosthenes and Cicero! It would divert you after this, if your friendship would not be too much mortified to permit of your being diverted, to hear me speak. With a tongue two inches thick, and an articulation so rapid and indistinct, as a friend candidly told me the other day, that, in the middle of my sentences, I am perfectly unintelligible, it is only by putting together the beginning and end of the period, that the middle is to be guessed at! I have some briskness and vivacity of fancy, but it has not the originality, the fertility, the boldness and the awful grandeur which the orator requires; and as to moving the heart, I have no more of it than a child. This is not affectation: it is the ingenuous openness and frankness of friendship. I think myself unfortunate that the exertions of mere duty, during the trial of Burr, have imposed on me a superstructure of character which I know I cannot bear. This is too apt to be the case. The world is agreeably surprised by a man from whom they expected little or nothing: they puff him to the stars. Expectations are thus excited which it is impossible to fulfill; he disappoints them, and very probably falls below the point at which he ought to stand, and at which he would have stood if he had never been extolled beyond his deserts, but had been permitted to rise quietly and gradually, under the mere impulse of his talents. I have seen these things happen,

If I write anything for the public on any occasion, I will certainly comply with our father's obliging request. At present I have nothing in view, except the biography of Patrick Henry, which, by one cause or another, and indolence among the rest, I have had on the anvil for two years. I expect to finish it this winter, unless war should come in earnest to divert me from my purpose. If I can satisfy myself and the public with "Patrick Henry," I propose to pursue the "lives" of our other distinguished men, on Plutarch's plan.

Inculcate your young brothers, who are intended for public speakers, with the mathematics and Lock's Essay on the Human Understanding (they give the key to the human judgment), and epic and dramatic poetry, together with a close observation of the manners of men and the various motives and springs of human action. Inculcate in them the necessity of knowing the history of every country as intimately as if they belonged to each country; and inculcate in them the incalculating importance of the early habit of examining nothing superficially, but of engraving deeply on the memory a clear, distinct and full knowledge of every subject to which they turn their attention. I sigh deeply while I write these precepts: they remind me of advantages which I might have had, but which are gone forever. But these are auricular confessions, and in catholic confidence.

My Betsey and her children join me in love to you and Mrs. Edwards. Your good lady, I imagine, scarcely remembers me—she was very young when I saw her last; pray recall me to her, and assure her that she is very dear to me, both for her own and her mother's sake.

Your friend and brother,

WILLIAM WIRT.

To Hon. Ninian Edwards, Frankfort, Kentucky.

Richmond, *September* 12, 1808.

My Dear Friend:

The last mail brought me your favor of the 26th July. * * * I am glad to understand you purpose coming on this year. I hope you will take Richmond in your way, and let me see you once more in my life. If you come in December, you will find the Assembly in session, and may pass a week or ten days here very comfortably.

Daviess, being so eminent a man, I wish he was a less bitter opponent of the Administration—yet his extravagance, perhaps, renders his opposition the more harmless. He seems to me, from his book, to have a bold and strong mind, but as undisciplined and illy regulated as a raw body of militia. I am glad to hear of the footing Mr. Madison has in your State. What I think of him you will learn from an accompanying pamphlet, comprising a very hasty and crude reply to John Randolph's protest. It was scribbled off with great precipitation, in a few moments stolen from professional pursuits; hence you will find it unpolished and rough—passable merely as a newspaper essay. I think so little of it that I would not send it to you, if you had not desired me to send all I wrote.

I believe all the States, but the New England ones, will stand the embargo. New Hampshire and Rhode Island have already flown that way in their late elections; Massachusetts is said not to be fairly represented in the State. The people here sustain the privations with all the patriotism of '76. I hope Kentucky will be true to the Administration—Wilkinson, notwithstanding. How would it do for the President to displace him, since his acquittal? His situation (the President's) is a trying one. I think that the general want of confidence in Wilkinson is such as to make it very improper for him to be retained at the head of the army. It is much to be regretted that he cannot be got rid of, without the appearance of his being sacrificed to the public clamor. Horace's "*prava ardor jubentium*," if the warmth which is felt against him on this occasion deserves the epithet of *prava*. Heaven bless you!

WILLIAM WIRT.

To Hon. Ninian Edwards, Franklin county, Kentucky.

Richmond, *November* 26, 1808.

Dear Friend:

The last mail brought me yours of the 20th ult. I hasten to acknowledge, because I wish you to be sensible how much I value your correspondence. The indulgence with which you have read the pamphlet signed "One of the People," is very obliging, but nevertheless cannot remove my own consciousness that those essays are not in the tone of calm dignity which would better have become the vindicator of Mr. Madison. He is, himself, so totally free from asperity, so dispassionate, so purely intellectual and argumentative, that the example is a reproof to any advocate who uses heat and declamation in his defense. If the character of the piece could find any justification in the character and conduct of those to whom it is addressed, it is most amply justified; but I believe it would better have served the purpose, and would certainly have given a more advantageous impression of the person and dignity of the writer, if it had been more in the spirit of Mr. Madison's own pamphlet on "neutral rights." While we are on the subject of political essays, I cannot help expressing my surprise at the apprehension which you seem to have of the effect of Daviess' "Citizen." I should think that either "Regulus," who is understood to be Mr. Clay, or the eccentric "Doctor" who edits one of your papers, would have point and force enough to blow forty such *citizens* out of the water. Let my old acquaintance, Bibb, at him; if he is only half the man he promised to be when fifteen, he would scatter him like chaff before the winds of heaven. I am sure there must be at least a thousand men in Kentucky capable of refuting so gross a sophist and so blind a politician as Daviess either is by nature or has been rendered by the poison of political prejudice. The insolent confidence which he seems to feel, and the lordly tone in which he affects to dictate to the people of your country, amaze me. Such a bullying blade would be sufficiently answered by being rendered ridiculous. If I were living in your State, and thereby had a right to interfere in your politics, instead of inflating the gentleman with more importance, by

—55

a solemn answer, I would laugh at him and his arguments till the canopy cracked; I would not get mad with him, as I did with "Protestus," but would tickle him into convulsions with a peacock's feather. The people ought to see him in his true light of a Briton in politics and a despot in temper, and it is no matter how ludicrous the representation of him is made—*ridiculum acri, fortius et melius secat res.* Your proposition for me to answer him resulted from the heart with which you wrote. A moment's consideration would have satisfied you that such an intrusion would neither be modest nor decorous in me; it would have implied an opinion that there was destitution of talents in Kentucky and a superabundance in myself, which would have rendered me as fair a target for ridicule as Joseph Hamilton Daviess, himself. I am, moreover, so pressed with business, that I shall have to lay aside a political sketch of the Republican minority, which I had meditated; but we have now three superior courts in session, and they will run into the session of the Legislature which begins ten days hence—so you see the impossibility of my complying with your request, even if it were proper or necessary, and I think it can be no more necessary than proper. Yet, you give me a grievous account of the ascendancy of Federal talents in your State. If this opinion be not the effect of your own patriotic fears, it is grievous indeed, for it will have a most unpropitious effect on the opinions of young men of genius: they will begin to consider federalism, as they used to do deism, the proof and badge of talents, and will coincide with your Federal leaders with the same readiness that they would with Voltaire and Bolingbroke—to be thought like them in that respect.

I do not much like the idea of our judges embarking very actively in political feuds, yet I should hope that, without subjecting yourself to reproach, you might cull the prime and flower of the Republicans, give concert to their movements, and inspirit them to resist intrepidly and firmly the machinations of the Federalists in every part of the State. They require but to be met foot to foot and bearded with facts, to make them "shrink from the storm and steal to rest." They crow and plume themselves on the tame and passive silence of the Republicans. Joseph Hamilton Daviess no doubt already imagines that he "bestrides the State like a Colossus, and that you petty men are forced to peep about between his legs to find yourselves dishonorable graves;" and the danger is that the people, seeing him everywhere uncontradicted, will at length believe that it is because he cannot be contradicted with truth. He, in concert with the other Federalists throughout the United States, has laid hold of the embargo, and they fancy it the lever of Archimedes, with which they will overturn the Republican world; yet, the measure is so obviously dictated by the true interest and soundest policy of the Union, that even some of the most prominent men of their party are its advocates. Such is John Adams, his son John Quincy Adams, William Smith of South Carolina (whose political consideration of the subject is aided by a personal knowledge of foreign courts), Oliver Wolcott, and others. Federalists who oppose the measure declaim against it as weak and inefficient; yet it is a truth, asserted and reiterated by American merchants in London (and

Federalists too), that nothing prevented the measure from having its immediate effect but the clamor and uproar raised against it here, and the very menacing attitude taken by our Eastern brethren, on the occasion. This is the effect of several letters which have been received in this city and Georgetown, from several of our Federal merchants in London, and among the rest my brother John Gamble, of this place, and Wm. Murdock of the other. Thus, according to the evidence of their own party, it is the Federalists who have frustrated the measure, and made the continuance of it until this time necessary; and of those very effects, produced by themselves, are they now making handles against us. This may be policy, but it is not honor or even honesty. The truth is that the Federal opponents of the embargo are, in their political principles and feelings, as truly British as if we had already gone back to the darkest ages of our colonial servitude. Of the same color is Jo. Daviess' proposition, to suffer foreign nations to come here and buy our produce, although we will not buy theirs. They themselves say that the British fleet is our shield against France, and so omnipotent is her power on the ocean that they will not suffer the French to come here and hurt us. Suppose, then, our ports are open for foreign ships to come and buy; the ships of Great Britain and her colonies might be seen here, but where would be that vast competition for our products which has hitherto resulted from France and the countries connected with her? Our object, then, is to punish Great Britain for the wrongs she has done us; and how do Federalists propose that we shall effect it? By giving up to her the whole of the American carrying trade! Our object is to starve and impoverish her until she does us justice; and how do the Federalists propose that we shall effect this? By giving up to her, at her own price, the whole of our surplus produce, thereby feeding her at a much cheaper rate than before she wronged us—and furnishing her, moreover, with a productive subject of speculation on those nations whom she keeps from our ports. This view of the subject, so simple and so plain, must surely occur to every reader of Daviess' proposition, and defeat its effect; for can it be conceived that there is anywhere one American so tame and so mean as to reward Great Britain for the slaughter of our brethren on board of the "Chesapeake," for the captivity of the thousands whom she holds in her ships, for the unprincipled tyranny by which she has driven our seamen from the ocean, and the thousand wrongs and insults which she is daily offering us, by making her a present of the complete monopoly of our whole carrying trade and surplus produce! This was one of the very grounds on which our patriotic forefathers took up arms against her; and yet the virtuous Federalists propose that we shall return to our bondage—and that in requital of British murder and rapine. You will see by the President's message the overture which has been made to that court to take off the embargo, if she will rescind her orders of council; and by Canning's reply (compared with the hiss of the President of the United States at the dinner lately given to the Spanish delegates) you will see the respect which they entertain for us. Congress is debating with closed doors—it is supposed a proposition for war; but, whether the word is war or embargo, I cannot help believing, with the President of the United States, that there is in the country a fund of virtue sufficient to match the crisis. If there is war with England, what confidence can we have in these British-Americans of whom I have been speaking? I think such men as your Daviess would repine at the success of the American arms, if directed by a Republican administration against Great Britain. Whatever would contribute to give luster and *eclat* to Jefferson or Madison, would be poison or death to him; and I believe he would rejoice in his country's ruin, if republicanism were to fall with it. I do not doubt but that the whole gang would sooner see this country under the administration of George III, than either of the pure and virtuous patriots whom I have just named! I write to you without reserve, and I write my cool and deliberate opinion of those incendiaries. I do not mean to embrace in the censure every man who has the name of Federalist, because I know many in this State who are as pure and patriotic as any Republican; but I mean those fire-brands of faction who have chosen this perilous and fearful crisis to foment disunion and discontent, and to erect themselves upon the ruins of republicanism and the Union. For the principles, either moral or political, of such men, I have no respect.

I will make another effort to get you a copy of my arguments on Burr's trial. The whole report of the case is coming out, taken in short-hand by Robertson, who took down the debates of the Convention. I have not much opinion of his stenographic excellence, from the samples I have seen.

I beg you to present my compliments to Mr. Bibb, with the inclosed profile, and assure him I am much gratified by his friendly remembrance of me. I had indeed a great partiality for him, and looked upon him as a prodigy of genius and literature, considering his age. I am happy to hear, both for his sake and yours, that he is on the bench of the appeals. He must be a pleasing as well as an able associate.

I have, for sometime past, received both the "Palladium" and the "Western World," in consequence of your direction, as I presume. How am I to remit the subscription money? Do you take the "Enquirer," of this place, or shall I send it to you?

You talk of my seeing you this winter; and being here, myself, confined for the winter as a member of the Assembly, I take it for granted that I am to see you here—at which I shall very greatly rejoice. If you can come before February, you will see Richmond in its highest state of animation, and you will see how wofully the legislative council has fallen since the days of Pendleton, Wythe, Henry, Jefferson, Richard Henry Lee, etc. This last you will perceive I do not say by way of attraction, but to prevent disappointment by preparing you for the more humble figure which our House really makes at this time.

I observe, in Toulmin's collection of your "Acts of Assembly," page 239, an act allowing aliens to hold lands in fee simple, in your Commonwealth. I should suppose, from the language of the act, that its benefits are only intended for the benefit of aliens who should have been resident in the State two years previous to the falling of the title, and that no alien could, by going now to reside in Kentucky, acquire by two years' residence a title which has already fallen. A gentleman in this place died lately, entitled to lands in your State; his relations here are aliens. They are willing to go and live in Kentucky, if, by so doing, they could acquire a title to these lands. I have given them my impression of this law as above stated, and now write to you, not to know your exposition of the statute, because that would be indelicate, considering that the question may be brought before you, but I write to know whether the law has actually received a judicial exposition either against or in favor of my clients—or if there be any later explanatory or amendatory act providing for the case? Either of these questions I think you might answer with perfect propriety. If you think otherwise I hope you will not answer them. Be pleased to let me hear from you as soon as possible on this point.

I am extremely pleased with your remarks on the embargo, and peculiarly as it relates to Kentucky. Why do you not expand those ideas and propagate them in the form of essays? The people, I am persuaded, need but to be enlightened on the subject, and they will submit without a murmur. Daviess must be exposed, and the people must be prevented from being misled by false views of the subject. The nature of the British acts in council, and French decrees, ought to be simplified and made plain. The unjust aggressions of those nations ought to be depicted in detail, in order to show the policy of the embargo and the insidious and infamous arts by which the Federalists themselves have rendered the measure abortive. These subjects well explained, and colored only to the life, would make them execrate the Federalists, admire and applaud the Administration, and support with the gallant and patriotic spirit of their fathers every measure which the Government might take. It is not virtue, but correct information, that the people want; and those who are capable of giving it to them ought to feel it a sacred duty to do so.

I have just seen the "Western World," which was brought in this morning. I postponed my letter in the hope that something might arrive from Kentucky indicative of their resentment at the proud and insulting repulsion of the President's offer to the British council, touching the orders of council. I see that Mr. Street, or the writers, concur in Canning's sentiment of contempt for our Government; and my opinion is that they are just as well entitled to a coat of tar and feathers as any British tory at the beginning of the last war. It will not be long before such men will get it.

Pray give my love to your wife and children, and all friends.

Yours affectionately,

WILLIAM WIRT.

To HON. NINIAN EDWARDS, near Frankfort, Kentucky.

RICHMOND, *Feb.* 17, 1809.

Dear Sir:

I thank you for the trouble which you were so good as to take relative to my question on your "alien" statute. That question arose upon the death of a gentleman of this place, a naturalized Scotchman, who died intestate seized of a vast estate, consisting, in part, of Kentucky lands. His next of kin were nephews and nieces, part of whom were native Virginians and other part aliens. The aliens were willing to go to Kentucky if, by doing so, they could come in, *pari passu*, for those lands; but as they were not capable of receiving the title when it fell, and the other nephews and nieces were, I presume the latter will take the whole estate. Is there any doubt of this? You will see, by the statement, that the services you so kindly offer will be unavailing. The offer, however, is not the less sensibly felt.

I hope you will not be hindered from performing an act of piety in accompanying your father to the Virginia Springs, next summer, for his health. For my own part, I have already met you in imagination several times, and held long ideal conversations with you. Let me beseech you not to disappoint me. You could not have chosen a subject half so grateful to me as the description which you give of your father's attachment. His partiality for me is indeed excessive, and if I were politic, I should refuse to meet him at the Springs, where a personal interview would dissipate all the extravagance of his opinion and reduce me to my proper size. Nevertheless, I do long to meet him. You must tell me, for you have still time enough for the communication, at which of the Springs I may expect to find you, about the 25th of July; for, as I shall have only three, or at the farthest, four weeks to be with you, I should not like to lose any part of the precious time in hunting you from one watering place to another. Pray let me hear from you explicitly on this subject.

The session of our Assembly has just closed. It is my first experiment and I confess that it has not left me very highly enamored of legislative life. I was, indeed, clerk of the House of Delegates for two or three years, about eight or nine years ago, and may be supposed not to have come into the House totally ignorant of the nature of such a body; yet, when clerk, I was so insulated and had so little time to observe the springs of action in the House, or to mix my feelings with the ordinary business, that I really found myself in an element totally new when I entered it this winter as a delegate. So much inattention, so much servile dread of ayes and noes, so much of blind and sudden impulse, of prejudice deaf as an adder and almost as rancorous, too—such a sordid, avaricious, mean-spirited regard to the public purse, to the sacrifice of everything like just and wise policy—that, for my own part, I am heartily sick of the life of a legislator. We have had a great number of offices to fill in the executive, in the judiciary, in the militia, besides a treasurer and register to appoint. This has opened another scene of disgust—low and petty intrigues among the members, for office. The scene has been wound up by expelling from the office of superintendent of our manufactory of arms one of the finest artists that this or any other country has ever possessed, on charges without foundation, and in a manner as cruel and despotic as was ever practiced by the Jacobin convention of France, save only that they have not called in the guillotine. In short, my dear friend, that happiness which is to be derived from a communion with wise and virtuous men, is not to be derived, I fear, from communion with large popular assemblies. Faction, heat, intrigue, rashness and folly are not the agents to which a good man would appeal for happiness. I have spoken several times in the House this winter; they have heard me with deep silence and great respect. Sometimes they have decided with me; at other times, when the decision was upon the surface, palpable to the merest observer, I have seen them yielding, in a manner the most shameful and degrading, to their fears for their popularity or some less tolerable motive This is a sad picture, but a true one. My happiness, I believe, will be only found in the bosom of my family, and in the zealous cultivation of professional eminence. These will leave me at liberty to select my company and my occupations; they will leave my breast calm and composed, my mind unagitated by the tumult of popular passion and frenzy; they will put it in my power, too, to effect an object which ought to be the first with every man —that is, to make my wife and children independent of a scurvy world. This I hope to achieve in a few years.

I hope your apprehensions about the storm you suppose is brewing in Kentucky will be found to arise only from your patriotic concern for your country. Burr is said to be, certainly, in England, and it is thought is negotiating for his Mexican empire. His business is mere matter of conjecture.

Congress is giving ground unwisely to the insolence of Massachusetts; the repeal of the embargo, without a more rigorous substitute, will call the original wisdom of the measure into question. I fear the Union is not to be of long continuance; but the issues of political as well as physical life are in the hands of a Being who will direct everything for the best.

Remember me affectionately to Mrs. Edwards, your father, mother and family. I have had a little daughter born about three weeks ago. My family is not well, and unless their constitutions recruit greatly, there will be another object at the Springs next summer, besides the pleasure of meeting my friends.

Yours affectionately,

WILLIAM WIRT.

To HON. NINIAN EDWARDS, Franklin county, Kentucky.

RICHMOND, *March* 12, 1808.

Dear Friend:

I received by the last mail your favor of the 29th January, from Frankfort.

Your delicacy in relation to your father's will does you honor—but you are amply requited for it; for a testamentary compliment from such a man and such a father is the richest of legacies. You distress me extremely by your account of his ill health. I had flattered myself that Kentucky had restored and confirmed his health, which was seriously attacked in Maryland, and that he would live to a good old age—that he would see his posterity increasing and flourishing around him to the third and fourth generation—and that I might myself live to see him full of years and happiness. I will not yet dismiss this hope.

I wrote to him lately and inclosed to him a copy of my speeches in Burr's trial, of which a printer here had taken it into his head to form a pamphlet. I now send you one. I think they are taken down with sufficient accuracy to afford a just idea of my speaking. They would have had more dignity if I could have listened to the virulence of Burr and his counsel with indifference. But this was an effort beyond humanity—at least beyond my humanity. I suspect my face has altered so much since you saw me that you will scarcely see the likeness of the plate in the frontispiece. It is done by a very eminent artist here, and is thought an excellent likeness. Upon recollection, I think I inclosed you an impression from my plate, in a letter; if so, as you will have one to spare, you can give it to one of your brothers or sisters.

As to Wilkinson, my opinion of him is just yours. I have forborne to make this opinion public during his trial, and wish you not to proclaim it. It may be supposed that my opportunity of examining his guilt or innocence lately has been greater than that of the community at large, and a weight might be attached to my opinion, from that circumstance, which might excite prejudice against him. Let him have fair play. A member of the Executive Council of this State, who left the city of Washington last Thursday, has been sitting with me to-day, and states that Wilkinson is rising rapidly in the public estimation and that Clark is sinking—*sed quere de hoc.* I think it most probable that they will both sink together.

The gentleman stated to me that he had sat with the President a few evenings ago, and that he stated the negotiation with the British Minister to be at an end for the present—that it would be at least four months before it would be known it would be successfully resumed—during which time we should have a continuance of peace and the embargo; that Congress was about passing an act authorizing the President to remove the embargo, on the happening of certain events in their recess; that the bill to augment the military establishment would certainly pass into a law. The President seemed to think it probable that the rival powers—France and England—would be reciprocally cautious in striking a blow against us which would force us into hostilities and throw our weight into the scale of her adversary. That policy must keep them both at peace with us; and if one relaxed in her maritime regulations the other would probably relax too—from the same policy—and thus there was still a hope of honorable peace. The same gentleman also stated it as his impression, at headquarters, that if we arranged our differences with one only of those powers, our merchantmen would be permitted to arm and repel the hostilities of the other.

We have had some disagreeable collisions on the subject of the next Presidential election—the State has been in some degree split between Madison and Monroe; but a serious push being made in some of the Northern States in behalf of Mr. Clinton, Col. Monroe will probably be dropped, and the contest will lie between Madison and Clinton—between meridian light and intelligence, and orefuscular dimness and dotage.

Give my sincerest love to your parents, brothers, sisters, and to your own good lady and family.

Your friend,

WILLIAM WIRT.

To HON. NINIAN EDWARDS, near Frankfort, Kentucky.

WARM SPRINGS, *August* 24, 1809.

My Dear Friend:

I have been the tour of the Springs with my family, and am thus far on my return to Richmond. I lost all hope of meeting you on this route, but still entertained some faint expectation of seeing our father. That also is baffled, and I have no resort but to write to you in revenge. This inclination, which I before had, is quickened by a letter just received from my much valued friend, Mr. Stuart, in which he makes honorable mention of you, and says he flatters himself that he has made some progress in your esteem. You know me too well to believe that I would recommend any man to your friendship whom I did not thoroughly know, and know to be worthy of it. I have been acquainted with Mr. Stuart for thirteen or fourteen years—during ten of them I have lived with him on the footing not merely of a friend but of a brother. It is upon this intimate knowledge that I had "grappled him to my heart with hooks of steel." He is among the most valuable men that I have ever known in this world. A warmer, honester and more exquisitely impassioned heart never throbbed in the breast of a man; and with this sensibility, so acute and sometimes almost infantile, he unites the most undaunted firmness of spirit, and a judgment which, in point of vigor and solidity, has rarely been surpassed. He will seldom err—I may venture to say never, unless when betrayed by the honest warmth and impetuosity of his feelings. He is separated from all his friends—so are you from yours; you are thrown together in a new world—you are each in want of a friend; let me assure you that you will find no man on whose honor, prudence and ardent susceptibility of friendship you can more safely rely than on Alexander Stuart's. I am thus full and anxiously minute about him because I fervently wish the happiness of you both, and am convinced that you require only to be intimately known to each other to conceive the mutual attachment which I wish. His manner, perhaps, may not please you at first, but you will soon be reconciled to it; and you have been long enough in the world to look through the manner to the man.

I have not, I believe, yet had the pleasure of tendering my congratulations on your appointment: this I now do, rather on your estimate of the office than my own. I had supposed the Presidency of the Court of Appeals—connected with the society of your relatives and friends, and its dignity upheld by your own splendid fortune—was an office much more desirable than that for which you have exchanged it; and although it gave me great pleasure to state to Mr. Madison at large my impressions of you, yet, I must confess, in secret I half wished the application might fail, principally on your father's account, whose old age I believed reposed in a great degree on you. But of all these considerations, you, "who saw the whole ground," are certainly the best judge, and I will not doubt that you have decided correctly.

My friend Stuart thinks that money might be advantageously invested in lands in your country, and has obligingly offered me his services in this way. What think you on this head? You would oblige me by a full and detailed opinion. For be it known to you that the rich harvest of collections which has enriched Wickham and one or two others of our lawyers has passed away, and the mere profits of the bar present but a long and tedious road to independence. I am at a time of life when it is requisite to hasten my progress by some auxiliary means, or old age will find me, if not poor and destitute, at least in narrow circumstances. Yet my share of the practice is a very flattering one, and continues to increase annually. I should be gratified by a pretty full account of your Territory—its population, manners, amusements, intellectual improvements, agricultural productions, trade, etc.

Make my respects to Mrs. E., and believe me, as ever,

Your friend,

WILLIAM WIRT.

To NINIAN EDWARDS, *Governor of Illinois Territory*, Kaskaskia.

RICHMOND, *August* 28, 1810.

My Dear Sir:

I received, some days back, yours of the 30th June. * * * The circumstances which you mention as showing the prudence for investiture of money in lands in your valley at two dollars per acre, would be decisive but for two circumstances: 1. The ill health of the country, which will always hang like a mill-stone upon the neck of your lands; 2. That you yourself wind up your encomium on the land with a "but," which I do not well understand. After speaking of the public rise of the land in ten years, you say, "I hesitate not to say that a large fortune might be made of it—*but* some other objects would also present themselves"—I suppose as superior to the purchase of those lands. You do not say what they are, and from your snapping off the paragraph so short at the words which I have quoted, I am to suppose you did not mean to say what they were, and therefore I do not inquire.

My friend S. might very safely promise to communicate that same proof of your confidence if ever we should all meet—he knew that that was very improbable. I have a strong impression of the subject matter of the secret—and if my conjecture be right he will never tell me of it; for the act was a direct infraction of an engagement of honor which we both made when we were widowers together. He is one of the best of men—his only fault being that he is too much of one—in a political light. I do not know that it will be held a fault *in a new Territory*; but I will say no more lest I should have missed your aim and be unveiling a trait which you have not suspected.

I have a letter from him lately in Lexington, Kentucky, and am delighted to hear of the good understanding that exists between you. I think you will be more and more pleased with him the longer you know him. He is one of the good fellows who will wear well.

I have a letter from your father dated 3d July, by which I am very glad to find that his health is much improved. I have one also from your sister Margaret, of date the 25th July—and an elegant one, too—by which I discover that I have made a *faux pas* in imparting to her, on your information, a passion for novels; so I have saddled you with it, and holding the evidence of the fact it will be in vain for you to deny it.

I have heard, although not from you, that there was a Wirt in your family—by which I find that you are not of Mr. Shandy's opinion as to the influence of names on the fortunes of a house. You did well, however, to stick it in the middle, between two very auspicious ones, where I hope it will remain harmless, at least, to its owner. I will not be so formal with a friend as to thank him for this compliment—it is not necessary that I should, for you know I feel it.

Mr. Stuart talks of paying us a visit in about eighteen months from this time. Would it not be possible for you to join him? I think that we could make two or three months very agreeable to you. Should it be in the winter time I would go on with you to Washington, if you were so disposed to diversify the trip; if in the summer and after July, I would go with you to the seaboard, hire a vessel and run out a few leagues on the Atlantic. What say you?

Remember me affectionately to Mrs. E., and if you are a kissing man, kiss your children for me—if not, ask Mrs. E. to do it.

Your friend,

WILLIAM WIRT.

To Ninian Edwards, *Governor of Illinois Territory*, Kaskaskia.

Richmond, *May* 12, 1816.

My Dear and Ever-honored Friend:

Judge Fleming, the President of our Court of Appeals, has been so obliging as to apprise me of his intention of paying a visit to your part of Kentucky, and to request that I will make him the bearer of a letter to you. I cannot deny this pleasure either to him or to myself—for he is quite enraptured with your former reception of him, and has never failed, whensoever or wheresoever I have fallen into his company, to make you the subject of his conversation and warmest eulogies. He is, himself, one of the most excellent of the human family—as pure of soul as a ray of light—and though age has considerably impaired the springs of his faculties, yet his understanding is still respectable, and his virtues and past services make him universally venerated. He is extremely fond of conversation—and it is much to be lamented, for his own sake as well as that of his associates, that his deafness renders this pleasure so difficult of attainment. But he is an old patriot—worn out in the service of his country—and I am therefore sure that you will overlook every inconvenience which may attend his entertainment.

And why, my dear friend, have I not heard from you for so many, many months—I might almost say years? Has anything occurred to diminish your esteem for me? I hope not; nay, I am sure that you would not permit anything to work this effect on you, without communicating it and hearing my defense. * * * * * * * * *

I am sure it will give you pleasure to know that my professional prosperity is still in its flood. I have received an appointment—that of United States Attorney for the District of Virginia—which is said to be worth from $1,500 to $2,000 per annum, but which I have a well founded hope of being able to render worth three times the latter sum, and to add to it a civil practice of equal value. I consider my property in this place as worth from $80,000 to $90,000; and I am engaged in a series of prosecutions for the recovery of a vast landed estate for the heirs of the late Col. Byrd, of Western Virginia, in which, if I succeed (a point thought very clear by Mr. Wickham and myself), I shall derive an addition to my present property of from $40,000 to $50,000; so that, with the blessing of Providence, I hope, when I shall be called away, to leave my wife and children independent—no trifling acquisition to a man who started from nothing, and commenced his gains with a family on his back, and who has a prospect of at least sixteen children to provide for—one-half of that number being now in full life and health. The last Legislature of Virginia offered to make me a Senator of the United States, and had my family been sufficiently provided for, I would certainly have accepted it; but a sense of domestic duty compelled me to decline it, and the same cause will keep me chained to my profession for seven or eight years more—so that whatever figure I might have made as a politician, I consider the door as now closed and the color of my destiny as finally fixed for life. Nor am I at all dissatisfied with it; on the contrary I think I have abundant cause to bless the Author of all Good that he has raised me from insignificance and obscurity, even to the station which I now hold in society. The imprudence and errors of my youth, the worse than waste of those golden hours which I ought to have devoted to intellectual improvement, and the manner in which I have slighted the vantage grounds to which Providence has so often raised me, as it were, by force, at least without any effort on my part, ought to have consigned me, if I had received my deserts merely, to poverty and obscurity. Have I not far greater reason, then, to bless the beneficent Disposer of Events for what I am, than to repine over the unavailing speculation of what I might have been? I think—I often think—over those friendly predictions which you used to make for me at Mt. Pleasant. You said, when I was not more than sixteen years of age, that I might be the President of the United States, if I chose! I believe I have never told you the impression which such remarks used to make on me at the time. I will tell you now, and with a freshness and certainty of recollection which seems to have been improved even by time. I never thought it flattery, for I knew, young as I was, that your spirit was too lofty to flatter the proudest of mortals, much less such a thing as I was. I never thought it wrong, either, for I knew you too generous and sympathetic to wound me, in the humble situation in which I was placed. My conclusion, therefore, was that you had a friendly wish to excite my emulation, and make the most of me, by leading me to aspire after what you knew, at the time, was far beyond my reach. Sometimes I thought (for I am going to be very candid with you) that you were disposed to amuse yourself, in a vacant hour, by seeing how far the credulous vanity of a boy could be influenced; but, although I dare say that I gave, at that day, many proofs of vanity, capriciousness and folly, I tell you now sincerely that I never, even then, thought myself possessed of any uncommon powers of intellect, much less such as your glowing eloquence sometimes ascribed to me; and every subsequent year of my life has confirmed the rectitude of my own judgment at that early day. I have since become very intimately acquainted with Mr. Jefferson and Mr. Madison—men who travel, in one sentence, over an extent of region which it would take me days to explore. I have coped with men much inferior to them, at the bar, whose promptitude and resources have made me feel my own littleness—my want of information—my want of readiness—my want of that quick and resistless vigor of conception, cool self-possession and commanding survey of the whole ground which are the true characteristics of a mind formed for the great business of life. You must, therefore, excuse me, my ever dear and revered friend, if I have baffled prophecies which you may have most seriously meant; and let me not lose your affection by having forfeited a part of your admiration. By way of palliation for my deficiencies, I beg leave to inclose you a pamphlet which has just made its appearance, and which may tend to show you that I have not entirely neglected the little talent which the bountiful Father of us all vouchsafed to give me. It is right, however, to tell you, by way of correcting any inordinate conclusions in my favor, that the book is reported to be written by a young gentleman who read law with me, Francis W. Gilman, a brother of my first wife.

Here is a letter of egotism from beginning to end—from which I hope you will infer no more than that I still think myself and my concerns matters of some consequence to the friend of my youth—the only father, in feeling, that my youth ever knew. I shall think of you, till the last gasp of life, with gratitude, affection and veneration. I recall, with feelings which your manly firmness and dignity of character might deem childish or effeminate, our many, many conversations, serious and sportive, at Mt. Pleasant; and at this moment every object there—every apartment of the house, the yard, the road, gate, store and neighboring fields, and the sugar-loaf mountain—bring you and all your dear family, with tears of recollection, to my fancy. Has Mrs. Edwards, have your sons, your daughters entirely forgotten me? I shall never forget them—never, never till memory, itself, is no more! May Heaven bless you all, and make you as happy as my heart wishes you to be.

I am told that your health is much better than it used to be. How fortunate is this, and that you still enjoy that best of intellectual banquets—for which Heaven so eminently fitted you—social conversation. All this is happy; but that conversation I must never more enjoy—unless Providence, by one of those strange turns which has marked my life, should carry me to Kentucky. How should I enjoy such a visit? I have seen several of your countrymen this winter, at Washington, of whom I have become very fond, and of whom I should have had much to say to you if I had thought of it sooner; but I have already tired your patience, I fear, and I have now to pack up for a journey in the stage, to-night, to a distant court. I must tell you, though, that my dear wife, who considers you and Mrs. Edwards as her second parents, assures you of her love and duty, and begs to be affectionately remembered to our brothers and sisters. I pray you to present me most tenderly to them all, one by one, and to believe me, as ever,

Your grateful and affectionate friend,

WILLIAM WIRT.

To BENJAMIN EDWARDS, Esq., Shiloh, near Bardstown, Kentucky.

P. S.—My wife has just begged me to present, in her name and with her love, two little books—"The British Spy" and "The Old Bachelor"—to her sister Margaret. The latter has all the numbers which proceeded from my pen marked with a W. The rest I am not at liberty to disclose.—W. W.

WASHINGTON, *January* 17, 1821.

My Dear Friend:

I received, last night, your letter of yesterday, and after reading your feeling and solemn injunction that I would say no more on a certain subject, I regretted extremely that I had said so much in two letters received by you on yesterday, and which, but for an accident, you would have received two days sooner.

With regard to your determination to retire from public life, I should consider myself a traitor in friendship if I did not say, in spite of your injunction to the contrary, that I consider you as standing in your own light, in coming to that resolution, and as committing political suicide. No man, who has been for so short a time in Congress, has more hopeful or brilliant prospects than you have. This is only a shadow that flits across your path; why should you mistake it for eternal night? If you are right in your view of things, the rectitude of that view will ere long appear, and your political sun will break out with redoubled lustre. Were I constituted for public life as I believe you to be (with the exception, I fear, of a little too much sensibility), neither the machinations of enemies nor the mistakes of friends should lead me to devote myself to voluntary obscurity. In reading Homes' "Sketches of Man," many years ago, I was struck with a trait in the character of the people of Japan, which, *outre* and ludicrous as it is, finds many a parallel in more enlightened nations. The Japanese, when he is insulted, takes revenge upon himself: he rips up his own bowels; and, according to the laws of honor, in

Japan, is considered to be as nobly avenged as a knight of the fourteenth century would be in meeting his enemy in a duel. I dare say I have mentioned this to you before; the truth is that something is continually occurring to recall it to my mind, and even my children have it by heart. Need I make this application to your case? You cannot but be struck with it. The truth is that your feelings are too quick and acute. A politician should have the hide of a rhinoceros, instead of the uncovered and agonizing nerves of Marsyas, after he was fleeced. This is, I confess, preaching unsupported by practice. In imputing this soreness of nerve to you, I am describing myself. Enough! Think better of this matter—think twice—and do not permit irritation, impatience and disgust to sit, much less to preside, at the council board at which the question is to be decided. A man in a passion never says or does anything right. Consult your wise and excellent father and let him decide—by whom I would rather be directed, after he knows the whole ground, than by a whole battalion of Congressmen. Don't take the advice of younger men than yourself in this matter: they are too hot for counselors in such a case; nor that of inferior men, who will always think themselves wise in echoing your own opinions. And now I shall nevermore touch this forbidden subject, 'till you yourself dissolve the injunction.

Your speech is excellent, manly, strong and sound. Farewell. May God bless and direct you.

Your sincere friend,

WILLIAM WIRT.

To HON. NINIAN EDWARDS.

WASHINGTON, *January* 31, 1822.

Dear Sir:

The rumor, which you mentioned last evening, that I had charged the Government $400 for an official opinion in regard to the claim of the Messrs. Johnson on the United States, is of too serious a nature to be left on the very short verbal explanation which I then gave you. It is due to my feelings and character to acquit myself of so injurious an imputation—for I take the liberty to say that there is no honor nor profit in the gift, either of the Government or the people, which could induce me to do the act which this rumor imputes to me.

It is proper, for a correct understanding of this case, to show you, in the first place, what acts *do* belong to the official duties of the Attorney-General, that, with this standard in your hands, you may compare the service in question.

The judiciary act of 1789 defines the duties of the Attorney-General in the following terms: "Whose duty it shall be to prosecute and conduct all suits *in the Supreme Court*, in which the United States shall be concerned; and to give his *advice and opinion upon questions of law*, when required by the President of the United States or requested by the heads of any of the Departments, touching any matters that may concern their Departments." A subsequent law makes the Attorney-General a commissioner of the sinking-fund. He is, also, regularly summoned, together with the heads of Departments, to attend the President in council, whenever a meeting of the members of the administration is required. These are the duties of the office—and they are all the duties.

In the case in question, I was called on by *Gen. Jessup*, the Quartermaster-General, with a request *that I would prepare a written argument to be laid before the arbitrators to whom the claim of the Messrs. Johnson had been submitted.* I stated to Gen. Jessup, in the most explicit terms, that if my opinion on the legality of the claim was wanted, the Secretary of War had a right to call for it, and was bound, *ex-officio*, to furnish it; but if he wished me to *argue the cause*, either *viva voce* or by writing, before the tribunal to which it had been referred, it was no part of my official duty. He answered that he was aware of the distinction; that he called upon me, *not officially, but professionally*; that the contract with the Messrs. Johnson having occurred in his Department, the superintendence of the controversy had been placed under his immediate care; that the opposite party had procured written arguments, on their side, from two eminent counsel (Messrs. Pinckney and Clay), to be used before the arbitrators; that he was desirous that these arguments should be answered by some professional gentleman, and that a full *argumentative* view of the whole subject, both *of the facts and law* of the case, should be furnished for use before the arbitrators; that the service must be rendered by some professional gentleman, who would of course be entitled to compensation for it; and that, being a service entirely distinct from my official duties, it was perfectly understood that I was to be compensated for the service as any other professional gentleman must be who should be called to perform it. With the clear and distinct understanding on both sides, all the documents, depositions, etc., together with the arguments of the opposite counsel, were placed by him in my hands; the case was studied by me, in all its aspects, as elaborately as if the argument were to take place before the Supreme Court, and the argument drawn out, *in extenso*, with a full discussion both *of the facts and the law*, with a labor far more oppressive, as all professional men of my experience know, than if the argument had been delivered *ore tenas* in court.

The rate of compensation for this service had not been previously fixed. When it had been rendered, and the *quantum* of the service thereby ascertained, it was left to Gen. Jessup to fix the compensation. I stated to him that there was no scale of compensation fixed, either by law or practice, for such a case (a written argument for arbitrators); that, so far as I was informed, the average fee for argument in the supreme Court, in cases involving such heavy sums (hundreds of thousands of dollars) might be considered to be five hundred dollars, and that, to my knowledge, it was frequently more than this; and that I had much rather have argued the same cause before the supreme or any other court than to have undergone the labor which I have had with it; that, however, I demanded neither that nor any other sum, but should be content with whatever was thought a reasonable compensation for the labor.

Gen. Jessup took full time to consider of it, and tendered me four hundred dollars, which I accepted—and I will add that it is not one-half the sum which I have repeatedly received, both before I held this office and since, for a much less troublesome professional service.

In determining on the form of the argument, I suggested to Gen. Jessup that, as the opinion which I was required to advocate was my sincere opinion, and not one which our profession are sometimes required to advocate from motives merely professional, the argument might have more weight with the arbitrators and be thought entitled to more respect, if this truth were known to them; and with this view I proposed to give it an official stamp by addressing it to the Secretary of War. He said that he left the form entirely to my own judgment—he being solicitous only to have the argument in that form in which it would best advance the purposes of justice. With this understanding, equally clear and explicit with every other part of the transaction, the argument was prepared as it stands, and submitted to the arbitrators. And if the form, adopted on this explanation and with this view, can change the inherent character of the service, and take away the right of compensation, thus expressly stipulated, then I was wrong in receiving the compensation thus stipulated: otherwise the act was just and proper, and I am not afraid of the decision of any correct and unprejudiced mind. It is most certain that I never did and never could have considered it an official opinion for the guidance of the Secretary of War. Had I done so, it would have been copied into my official opinion book, where it is not to be found. The Secretary of War had asked me for no advice or opinion for his guidance—he had no act to perform in which he required advice—the subject had passed out of his hands into those of the arbitrators, and all that remained for him to do was to await their award. The Secretary had asked me for no opinion, for he wanted none. He could not have asked for an opinion on the facts, much less for an argumentative discussion of the facts; for the law has given him no power to make any such call. He has a right to my opinion on questions of law on a given state of facts—here his right and my duty end; and it seems to me that the mind must be willfully blind which can confound such an argument, drawn from me on an understanding and a contract so full, clear and explicit, and that, too, for the exclusive use of the tribunal to which the case had been referred, with an opinion on a question of law called for by the Secretary for his guidance.

Give me leave, in conclusion, to state that the heads of my official duties are easily enumerated, but the execution in detail renders this, I believe, (and I know that I am not singular in the opinion) the most laborious office in the Government. There is no other officer, from the heads of departments down to the lowest clerk, who has it not in his power to devote his evenings to relaxation, to social or domestic intercourse, and to the care of his health. I alone am obliged, by the nature of my duties and my anxiety to discharge them in a manner satisfactory at least to my own conscience, to come into my office before breakfast, and to remain in it from nine till ten o'clock at night; and yet, if I am not misinformed, there are those who consider the office as a sinecure, and who are disposed to throw an additional mass of duties on the load already almost insupportable, with one hand, and at the same time to withdraw the salary gradually with the other. Would it not be wiser and more just to abolish the office at once? If it be unnecessary, why not abolish it? But before it be abolished, would it not be still wiser to ascertain its utility by inquiries of those who are best able to judge—the President and heads of departments?—and if it be found not only useful, but highly so, and one of the most effective offices under the Government, on account of the wide scope of its duties and the controlling authority of the opinions of the law officer, would it not be wise, as it regards the public interest, to render the office comfortable enough for the acceptance, and occupancy of a man qualified to discharge its duties? These are questions which relate to the public, and not to me. I have, thank Heaven, a profession and a standing in it, by which I can live without the office; and there are, I know, many others who could discharge its duties more wisely, but not more faithfully. But this I will venture to predict: that the man of professional standing who holds it at its present salary, under its present load of duties, and with the annoyance and humiliation of continual and unfounded censures, must be actuated by very different motives than a sordid regard for his own interests or happiness.

I am, dear sir,
With ancient regard and esteem,
Your friend and servant,
WILLIAM WIRT.

TO HON. NINIAN EDWARDS.

P. S.—Will you have the kindness to show this explanation to Mr. Galliard, from whom you had the report, and to any other gentleman who may have been in the way of hearing it. General Jessup is, at present, not in Washington, but is, I understand, expected. When he returns, I will make it my business to furnish you with his statement of the facts.—W. W.

WASHINGTON, *Oct.* 2, 1824.

Dear Sir:

The President, in answer to my letter, says that the two statements, to-wit: First, that you had denied to him the authorship of the "A. B." letters, and thereby obtained your nomination to Mexico, and, second, that you had applied, through Mr. Adams, to be permitted to wait on him, and had been refused, are unfounded—the first most certainly, the last according to his best recollection. He thinks, also, that Dr. Everett could not have spoken by his authority in making the communication which you say he did to Mr. Cook.

The President, however, is extremely unwilling to take any step which could be construed into a personal interference in your controversy with the Secretary of the Treasury—more especially at this point of time, when the affair seems to have died away, and when any movement on his part, although intended as a mere act of justice to you, would be certainly interpreted into a disposition on his part to revive the dispute to the prejudice of Mr. C. He thinks that very purpose you have in view will be answered by your own denial of these statements in the papers published here; which, under the silence observed on his part, will be considered as true. And, moreover, if any one should personally apply to him for information on the subject, he will say of the statements what I have said above.

In great haste,

Yours, truly,

WILLIAM WIRT.

HON. NINIAN EDWARDS, Brown's Hotel.

ANNAPOLIS, *November* 19, 1826.

Dear Sir:

I received, some time since, under a black envelope, the inclosed letter, which I take it for granted came from you. I wrote immediately to your honored father—whom I reverence with all the devotion of a son—taking his address from Cyrus' letter, which I suppose was correct.

It is needless to suggest to a mind so strong as yours, that this is one of those dispensations to which all must submit, and against which it is unavailing to murmur. Your dear mother has died with a well-founded confidence which leaves us nothing to mourn on her account. That she is at this moment in the enjoyment of perfect bliss, I have no more doubt than I have of my own existence. But the state of desolation in which she has left her bereaved husband wrings my heart to think of. What is life, and what this poor world, that we should care so much for them? You and I were boys the other day—up at Seneca—and now we are old and gray; we shall soon be gone, and our children after us will moralize in the same way, and follow us to the grave. And what of it all? It is the will of that great Being of whose creation we form but a small part, who best knows His own wise designs, and who deals with us at His pleasure, and always for the best, as I believe. What remains for us, then, but to submit with resignation to that order of events which no wish of ours can arrest or alter? Would to God that we could only do our duty on earth as faithfully as your dear and honored parents have done theirs, and that we could die with the same well-founded confidence of a happy futurity! I should ask no better fate. These reflections, I am sure, are needless to you, through whose mind they have long since passed, and I suggest them only to assure you of my sympathy and condolence.

Your friends (and I among the foremost) have rejoiced at the recent proof of respect which you have received from your State. It must have been balm to your feelings as it is to ours. But I regret exceedingly Mr. Cook's discomfiture, both on his own account and on account of the reason which is assigned for it in this quarter—which is, that it proceeded from his avowed support to the measures of the present administration. Of the question between Mr. Adams and Gen. Jackson, at the next election, it might not become me to speak. But surely so long as the measures of the existing administration are sound and judicious, no discredit ought to be attached to any politician for supporting them—unless our country is nothing and individuals are everything. But I profess to know nothing of political matters, so far as management and machinery to carry a given election, as you very well know; and what is more, I am contented to remain in ignorance of all such matters—being quite content myself if I shall be able, as duty may require, to give a sound opinion as to the effect of a public measure on the interests of the country.

I beg my affectionate remembrance to Mrs. Edwards and Mrs. Cook, and remain, with sincere regard,

Your old friend,

WILLIAM WIRT.

To Hon. Ninian Edwards.

Letter from Wm. Wirt on the death of Gov. Edwards' father.

Baltimore, *December* 20, 1826.

* * * * * * * * * *

And most dearly did I love him! I have lost one of my best and dearest friends, and the world has in consequence lost to me much of its interest. He loved me when a poor, obscure and destitute orphan. He took me by the hand when there was no one else to do it, and in all my wanderings, his affection never lost sight of me—nor amid all my silence did I ever lose sight of him. On the contrary, I never met a bright turn of fortune that one of its sweetest concomitant reflections was not the pleasure I knew it would give him.

A day or two before I left Washington, I received, myself, a letter from Presley, announcing this desolation; and, under the pressure of the moment, I wrote an obituary notice of him, which I sent to Mr. Green, the editor of the "Telegraph," requesting him, if he approved of it, to insert it in his paper and send me a copy of it, and to send the original, with my request indorsed, to Messrs. Gales and Seaton, requesting their insertion of it in the "Intelligencer." Having heard nothing from Mr. Green since, I fear it did not meet his approbation; and I have been so much occupied here, that I have not had time to inquire of him—which, however, I will do in a few days. He told me, indeed, when I verbally proposed to do this, that he was engaged himself in preparing something on the subject; and probably mine was too long for convenient insertion—or less to his taste than his own. It was, indeed, a very hasty effusion, and full of the feelings of the moment, which were, perhaps, too particular and individual for a newspaper obituary.

I am interrupted by a gentleman on business. God bless you. Make my love acceptable to your wife and children, and believe me,

Your friend,

WILLIAM WIRT.

Gov. Ninian Edwards, Belleville, Illinois.

ANNAPOLIS, *October* 11, 1827.

My Dear Sir :

Just before I left home, I received your letter of the 13th ulto., and had barely time before I started to leave a letter, in favor of Hardage, for Mr. Secretary Barbour, who was then daily expected from Virginia. It will always give me pleasure, while I continue to live and breathe upon this ball of earth, to render any act of kindness I can to those who were so kind to me in my destitute and unprotected youth. I remember those days rather with increasing than diminished gratitude, by the lapse of time and the advance of old age. As I contrast that kindness to a poor, obscure, orphan boy with the heartless maxims of the present age, what a change in the morals and charities of the world since those days! I know not how it may be in the country, but in towns, where I have lived, it is not the same world—or at least there are no longer such men as your father in it, and very few such women as your mother known to me. I remember them as belonging to a golden age—so far at least as human charities and sympathies are concerned—and I shall be pleased with every opportunity that may present itself, during the short sequel of my life, to show to their posterity that kindness which they showed to me.

I really cannot tell you what is the tone of Mr. Secretary Barbour's feelings towards you. He did belong, you know, to the Crawford party, and those of that party, I suppose, have not forgotten or forgiven the Parthian arrow, as they called it, shot at their chief. But there has been such a strange jumble and mixture of parties, that I, who never understood political management, and hope I never shall understand it, really cannot tell you, with confidence, the feelings of any one man towards any other. The time seems to be at hand, if it has not already arrived, when, in the reckless scramble for public honors, all private honor will be forgotten, and mutual distrust, jealousy and hatred, or interested, hollow and transient factions, will be the only relations that will subsist among men. The public good, the love of country, which were the ruling principles of the men of the Revolution, are old-fashioned things, which men mouth in public now to serve their own views, as they do religion, and laugh at in private as fit only for fools, women and children. I am really very sick of the whole affair, and long for some retreat where I may get clear of the din and strife of party. This, I dare say, sounds very weak to you who have a *gusto* for these things, but there is no disputing, you know, about tastes. For my own part, while I hope I shall be ever ready and willing to serve my country, never will I be the servant of any party till a party shall arise who have no other object at heart but their country, and its happiness, honor and glory. Such a party as that, I should be proud to join, but such a party is, I fear, not to be expected in these days.

How is your health, and that of your family? I shall be very glad to hear from you, if you can find time to write to such an unworldly man as myself—I use the expression in no vain sense, but in that in which you know me, as a man who has neither turn nor taste for the working of what is called political machinery, which seems to me to make up the whole interest of this American world.

Pray remember me affectionately to Mrs. Edwards and Mrs. Cook, and believe me, with the kindest feelings of the olden time,

Your friend,

WILLIAM WIRT.

To Hon. Ninian Edwards.

Washington, *March* 22, 1828.

My Dear Sir:

The pressure of the Supreme Court has prevented me from attending to your letter inclosing the case between A and B. You have now Mr. Webster's opinion and mine, which you will find concurrent with your own. It is certainly a very plain case, and I am much surprised there should have been a doubt on it.

I am much rejoiced, in common with your other friends, at the honorable demonstration you have received of the confidence of your State, so bravely and so nobly won; but when you talk of quitting politics you do not know yourself as well as I do. You will find that you will realize the fable of the cat transformed into a lady, whenever a political mouse runs across the floor. The man who has been a fox hunter from the time he was first able to resist the cry of the pack, will continue to love the sport so long as he can throw a leg over the saddle. Habits so inveterate become a part of our nature, and we can no more give them up than we can give up breathing. I, who was never a political sportsman, but have found my happiness in my fireside and literature, am so far from being excited, by the uproar of the chase, to join in it, that I shrink from it intuitively, as I would from the pelting of any other pitiless storm, and press my wife and children closer to my heart. If the political contest were one only for the good of the country, and the candidates were only of that noble kind of "who should do most good," I should like it; but when it degenerates into a coarse, ignoble, vulgar contest for personal power, and is carried on by lying, abuse, intrigue and all manner of vile practices, I shrink from it as I would from the taste of human flesh. I have no cannibal propensities, and ask only for peace and competency— a clear fireside, a book, and my affectionate family. I know that all this is very poor-spirited and tame to the Bedouin Arabs, whose delight is in political rapine and mischief. So be it—every man to his taste. I prefer my life and death to theirs'—for I shall live peaceably and die quietly, none offending and offended by none.

Among the many evils growing out of this species of political warfare, there is one which has touched me in a tender point. Your sister, Mrs. Green, is living here. We exchanged a visit or two with her on her arrival, and we should have been most happy to have kept up the intercourse. She reminded me most strongly of Mt. Pleasant, and of your dear and honored father and mother; but the tone of Mr. Green's paper, and my political connection with the Administration, rendered it impossible for me to keep up the intercourse, without exciting suspicions that would have been too painful to have been borne by me, and I have been obliged to discontinue it. You understand these matters, and I need say no more on so delicate a subject.

You do only justice to Mr. Clay; he has been scandalously treated, I think. I dare say you are aware that my predilections in his favor were not stronger than your own. The political course which he held towards that excellent man, Mr. Monroe, used to shock and offend me almost past endurance. He is a very different man in the Cabinet from what I expected to find him; all that wildness of judgment which seemed to me to govern him, when a demagogue in the House, has left him, and he is one of the most safe and prudent counsellors I have known, and very cautious, kind and cordial in his intercourse with his associates and with the world. I was so much gratified by the paragraph in which you mention him, that I could not forbear showing it him. It had all the effect I intended and expected. "The manner in which the Governor mentions his sense of injustice done me, does honor to his own heart, and I cannot but hope that he may feel himself prompted to lend his powerful aid and support, at this crisis, to the cause which the most enlightened men throughout the community consider as the cause of our country." He speaks, of course, of the Presidential contest. I merely state his suggestion, and leave it to your own disposal. My only motive for doing so is the pleasure I derived from the light in which he views you.

We have had a tough campaign of eight or nine weeks in the Supreme Court; thank heaven I have survived it, and find my health quite good, for my time of life. I have a little of the dyspepsia now and then, but it is not very troublesome. I live abstemiously, take exercise, and work hard at my profession.

My eldest daughter is married to Judge Randall of Florida, a fine, honorable, noble-spirited, high-minded young man, in whom I have the most unbounded confidence. For $5000 I have been able to give him 1000 acres of prime lands, to build a good frame dwelling house, and give him ten working hands—five of them men, the rest young women—and a good tailoress. He had two young men of his own. His lands are first rate sugar and sea-island cotton lands, and I have no fear of his doing well. I mention these details because I know you will take an interest in them.

Mrs. Wirt and family are well and desire to be affectionately remembered to you and yours. If Mrs. Edwards has not forgotten me, greet her fraternally in my name.

Your old friend,

WILLIAM WIRT.

To Hon. Ninian Edwards.

Norfolk, *March* 17, 1805.

Dear Friend:

I cannot describe to you, my dear Mr. Edwards, the sensations with which I have just read your most welcome and obliging letter of the 17th ult., from Shiloh. I need not be ashamed to tell you that my tears bore witness to the sincerity and force of my feelings. You have taught me to love you like a parent. Well, indeed, may I do so; since to you, to the influence of your conversation, your precepts, and your example in the most critical and decisive period of my life, I owe whatever of useful or good there may be in the bias of my mind and character. Continue then, I implore you, to think of me as a son, and teach your children to regard me as a brother: they shall find me one, indeed, if the wonder-working dispensations of Providence should ever place them in want of a brother's arm, or mind, or bosom.

You could not more strongly have expected my wife and me to partake of your Christmas turkey in 1803, than we ourselves expected it when I wrote you last. I was sensible that I owed you and my friend Ninian an apology, or rather an explanation, of the abrupt change of my plan in relation to Kentucky, and this explanation would have been certainly made at the proper time, but for a point of delicacy arising from the nature of the explanation itself. But now that the project is over, and with you, I fear, forever, I may explain to you without reserve.

The first obstacle which I had to encounter arose from the difficulty of compassing so much cash as would enable me to make my *debut* sufficiently respectable. To have disclosed this obstacle either to you or Ninian, after the strong desire which I had manifested to migrate to your State, might have been liable to an interpretation, which, either from true or false pride, I chose to avoid. As I could not state to you this primary obstacle, I thought it would be disingenuous to amuse you with an account of merely subordinate ones; but now you shall know the whole truth. My wife, who was thoroughly convinced of the propriety of our removal to Kentucky, had consented to it, from the dictates of reason and judgment, whilst her heart and affections secretly revolted against the measure. Most dutifully and delicately, however, she concealed her repugnance from me, and I should never have known it, but for an accident. Waking one night, at midnight, while this journey was contemplated, I found her in tears; and, after much importunity, drew from her an acknowledgment that her distress proceeded from the idea of such a distant, and most probably final, separation from her parents and family.

I will not affect to deny that I believe this discovery and the manner of it, would have been decisive with me against the removal, even if the first objection had not existed. Fortune and fame are, indeed, considerations of great weight with me; but they are light, compared with the happiness of the best of wives. About the time of this discovery, and while the current of my own inclinations had been thus checked and brought to an eddy, a young gentleman (a son of the late Judge Tazewell) who was at the head of the practice in this part of the State, very generously and disinterestedly waited on me at Williamsburg, opposed my removal by every argument that friendship or ingenuity could suggest, offered to recede, in my favor, from several of his most productive courts, painted the progressive prosperity of Norfolk in colors so strong and alluring, and exhibited such irresistible evidence of the present profits of the practice in this borough and district, that my mind was left in equipoise between Kentucky and Norfolk.

At this critical juncture came a letter from you, in which you very amicably exhorted me against the indulgence of a too sanguine imagination in regard to Kentucky. You stated that the specie had almost disappeared from the State, owing to the occlusion of Orleans by the Spanish Intendant against your deposits—an inconvenience whose duration it was impossible to calculate, and represented that the gentlemen of my profession, like the other inhabitants of the State, carried on their business by barter, receiving their fees in negroes, horses, etc. Under the joint action of all these obstacles, difficulties, considerations and motives of policy and expediency, I was led to the adoption of the resolution which brought me here. And so here I am, abreast with the van of the profession in this quarter, with the brightest hopes and prospects; duping the people by a most Jenkinsonian exterior, using "words of learned length and thundering sound," puffed by the newspapers as an orator, to which I have no pretensions, and honored and applauded far beyond my deserts. It is only for the humiliation with which I see and hear what is written and said in my praise, that I give myself any credit. I have formed in my own imagination a model of professional greatness, which I am far, very far, below, but to which I will never cease to aspire. It is to this model that I compare myself, whenever the world applauds, and the comparison humbles me to the dust. If ever I should rise to this imaginary prototype, I shall rest in peace. Herculean enterprise!—But I must not despair, since it is only by aiming at perfection that a man can attain his highest practicable point.

If a fortune is to be made by the profession in this country, I believe I shall do it. It must require, however, fifteen or twenty years to effect this. Norfolk, as you guess, is very expensive. I keep, for instance, a pair of horses here, which cost me eight pounds per month. Wood is from four to eight dollars per cord; Indian meal, through the winter, nine shillings per bushel—this summer it is supposed it will be fifteen; flour eleven and twelve dollars per barrel, a leg of mutton three dollars, butter three shillings per pound, eggs two shillings and three pence per dozen, and so on. Having set out, however, with a view of making a provision for my family, in the event of my being called away from them, I live as economically as I can, so as to avoid giving my wife any reason for regret at the recollection of her father's house and table. After this year, I hope it will be in my power to net annually two thousand dollars, by the practice, but I do not expect ever to do more than this. I shall be content to leave the bar whenever my capital will net me an annual revenue of four thousand dollars, and not till then.

I am indeed sometimes very apprehensive that the yellow fever, which you mention, may cut this operation short, by removing me from this scene of things; or protract it, by driving me from my business into annual exile, as was the case last summer and fall. If I find this latter event likely to take place, I shall certainly use all my influence with my wife to reconcile her to Kentucky; for even now, I will not conceal it from you, propitious as is the face of my affairs, your letter makes me sigh at the thought of your State. It is not, however, the idea of being "a comet in a naked horizon," which I long to realize. I have seen too many luminaries, infinitely my superiors in magnitude and splendor, to believe myself a comet; nor can I believe *that* horizon naked which is adorned and lighted up with a Breckenridge, a Brown, a Maury and N. Edwards. Besides, if I were ambitious, and it were true that this part of the hemisphere were gilded with the brightest stars, I should, for that reason, choose this part. A glow-worm would be distinguished amid total darkness; but it requires a sun indeed to eclipse the starry firmament. No, sir. It is the Green River land which makes me sigh; the idea of being released from the toils of my profession by independence, in six or eight years, and of pursuing it afterwards at my ease, and only on great occasions, and for great fees; of having it in my power to indulge myself in the cultivation of general science; of luxuriating in literary amusements, and seeking literary eminence. These are the objects which I have been accustomed to look to, as the most desirable companions in the meridian of life; and six or eight years more would just bring me to that age at which Parson Hunt and his son William used to predict, in moments of displeasure and reproof, that I should begin to be a man—viz., at forty. It is because your letter holds out probabilities like these, that I sigh. For I know that, by the practice of this country, independence by my profession is a great way off.

How much it would delight me to live once more within eye and earshot of you! To be able to talk over with you the affairs of Mount Pleasant, and of my youth; to hear your raillery and your laugh. These are things that I could think of until I should be quite unmanned—but enough. My wife has given me two children in little more than two years. We were married on the 7th September, 1802, and on the 3d September, 1803, she gave me a daughter, now a lovely child, going on nineteen months old, with the romantic name of Laura Henrietta, the first the favorite of Petrarch, the last the christian name of my mother. On the 31st day of last January she gave me a son, who is certainly a *very* handsome child, and, if there be any truth in physiognomy, a fellow whose native sheet of intellectual paper is of as fine a texture and as lustrous a white as the fond heart even of a parent could desire. My fancy is already beginning to build for him some of those airy tenements, in the erection of which my youth has been wasted. My wife wants to call this boy Robert Gamble; and as this is a matter altogether within the lady's department, I shall give way. She was just twenty-one the 30th day of last January, and I was thirty-two the 8th day of last November; so I hope we may reach my wished for number of twelve, and be almost as patriarchal, by and by, as yourself.

How much you gratify me by the circumstantial description of your children—their prosperity now, and their hopeful prospects! May all your wishes in regard to them be fulfilled! I hope and pray so, from my inmost soul! I have a kind of dim presage that I shall yet be in Kentucky time enough for your Benjamin Franklin, if not for Cyrus. Heaven send I may ever have it in my power to be of any use to either of your children! Pray remember me to them all, with the regard of a brother, and present me to Mrs. Edwards with the respect and dutiful affection of a son. Shall I ever see you again in the midst of them, on your farm, disengaged from all care, and happy as you deserve to be? You cannot think with what tenderness my memory dwells on Mount Pleasant and the neighborhood. I remember, indeed, very many follies to blush at and be ashamed of, yet still it is one of those "sunny spots" in the course of my life, in which recollection dearly loves to bask. Let me be free with you, for you used to make me so. To this day, the image of B. S—— is as fresh in my mind as if she had just left Mount Pleasant, on Sunday evening, on the bay mare, and my eyes had followed her through the gate, and as far around as she was visible, on her way home. And the investigation which you once made of the difference between K——'s passion for her and mine, is just as vivid as if it had passed on yesterday. By-the-by, you have not said a word of my friend K——, and as I take a very strong interest in his welfare, let me hear of him when you write next.

I thank you very much for your mention of several of my old acquaintances. Among them all, Jack Wallace (if he is the son of James) is my favorite. Nature, indeed, had not taken much pains in the caste of his genius, but she gave him one of the sweetest tempers, and one of the finest and noblest hearts that ever warmed a human breast.

Major W——, I presume, is my schoolmate, William, who used to live at Montgomery Court-house. When we were at school together, about the year 1785, he was thought one of the world's wonders, or rather a new wonder, in point of genius. Where is the hopeful promise of his youth? Smothered under the leaden atmosphere of indolence? Or has it faded, like the first flowers of spring, to bud and bloom no more? * * * * *

Of Q. M—— I only remember that he was a large-faced, well-grown boy, who learnt the Latin grammar until he came to *penna-a-pen*, where he stuck fast, and his father took him away in despair. But it is possible that I may be mistaken, and am confounding him with some other boy. One other thing I am sure of, that he had a very pretty sister, whose name was L——, with whom I was very much in love one whole night, at an exhibition ball, in the neighborhood of Parson Hunt's. E. M——, I do not remember at all. I could not have been acquainted with him, nor, I think, with M. L——. I well remember the family of the latter, who lived on a hill, near a mill-pond of Samuel W. Magruder's. There were five or six of us, of the family of Magruder, who, after bathing of a Sunday in the pond, used to go up and see a sister of Matthew's, whose name was Betsey (a name always fatal to me!) I was then about twelve years old, and I remember that for one whole summer that girl disturbed my peace considerably. The sex, I believe, never had an earlier or more fervent votary; but it was all light work till I came to B. S——. To this moment I think kindly of her, even in the grave. * *

I have already used a good deal of egotism in this letter: but it is unavoidable in letters between friends; and it certainly is not *desirable* to avoid it between friends so far sundered as we are, who are obliged to resort to letters as a substitute for conversation. For my own part, I sat down with the determination to write just as I would talk with you, in order that I might approach as near as possible to the enjoyment of your company; and, as I should certainly have talked a great deal of levity and nonsense, so have I written, and so I shall still write, although I know that I am taxing you with a heavy postage.

But to myself again. I find that you have read "The British Spy," and, from your allusion to it, I presume you have understood me to be the author. It is true. I wrote those letters to while away six anxious weeks which preceded the birth of my daughter. In one respect they were imprudent. They inflicted wounds which I did not intend. * * * * * *

In the esteem of a penetrating and learned man, "The British Spy" would injure me, because it would lead him to believe my mind light and superficial; but its effect on the body of the people here (on whom I depend for my fortune) has, I believe, been very advantageous. It was bought up with great avidity; a second edition called for and bought up; and the editor, when I saw him last, talked of striking a third edition. It has been the means of making me extensively known, and known to my advantage, except, perhaps, with such men as Jefferson and Jay, whose just minds readily ascertain the difference between bullion and chaff. * * * * *

The title of this fiction was adopted for concealment, that thereby I might have an opportunity of hearing myself criticised without restraint. But I was surprised to find myself known after the third letter appeared. Having once adopted the character of an Englishman, it was necessary to support that character throughout, by expressing only British sentiments; yet, there were some men weak enough, in this State, to suspect, from this single cause, that I had apostatized from the Republican faith. The suspicion, however, is now pretty well over. * * * * * * * * *

I am your friend, and
Your son by election,
WILLIAM WIRT.

To Benjamin Edwards, Esq.

Richmond, *July* 2, 1808.

My Dear and Ever-honored Friend and Father:

I have read, half a dozen times, with swimming eyes, your precious letter of the 8th of April last. Our courts have been sitting, without intermission, ever since the 1st of February till the 28th of last month, or I should sooner have acknowledged your goodness in writing to me under so much pain. Your friendship and affection for me are among the purest and sweetest sources of happiness that I have upon this earth. Judge, then, with what feelings I hear of your ill health. Yet I trust that the same gracious Providence "who makes the good his care," and who raised you once before from the bed of torture, will spare you still to your family and friends. I have been afraid that you do not take exercise enough, yet Mr. Street, the editor of "The Western World," handed me, the day before yesterday, a letter from my brother Ninian, dated April 11th, three days after yours, in which he says that you had been, lately, at his house. That, I apprehend, is nearly as long a journey as would bring you to the mineral waters in Virginia. Would not this excursion, aided by the waters and the animation of the company, promise to give a tone to your system, and remove the torpor and debility of which you complain?

I wish you could believe it prudent and advisable for you to take such a step, because I should then have it in my power to see you once more. I would certainly meet you at the Springs, and receive your blessing; and my wife and children, from the sentiments they have for you, would accompany me, with all the piety of pilgrims. My imagination has dwelt upon this meeting, until I begin to feel a strong presentiment that it will certainly take place. My brother Ninian and his family would, I dare say, attend you. What a happy group should we form! How would we talk over the days that are past, till torpor and debility, and sickness and sorrow would fly and leave us to our enjoyments. What do you say to this project? I have a san guine hope that you will find it as judicious in reference to your health, as I am sure it would be exquisitely grateful to your feelings. And if we meet once, and your health should become settled again, might we not devise a scheme of meeting at the same place every two or three years? By these means our children would become acquainted, and the friendship which has subsisted between us would be continued in them.

I leave it to your heart and your fancy to develope this idea, through all its consequences. To me, *the anticipation*, merely, is delightful; and, in spite of Mr. Harvie's doctrine to the contrary, I believe *the reality* would be still more so. Will you not think of this? Take medical counsel upon it, and let me know the result.

Yes!—there is nothing more true than what you say. "When we must die, there is nothing like a well-grounded hope of future happiness, except a perfect faith, which removes all doubt." I thank God that I have lived long enough, and seen sorrow enough, to be convinced that religion is the proper element of the soul, where alone it is at home and at rest. That to any other state, it is an alien, vagrant, restless, perturbed and miserable—dazzled for an hour by a dream of temporal glory, but awakening to disappointment and permanent anguish. It is the bed of death which chases away all these illusive vapors of the brain which have cheated us through life, and which shows us to ourselves, naked as we are. Then, if not sooner, every man finds the truth of your sentiment, the importance of a well-grounded Christian hope of future happiness. We need not, indeed, so awful a monitor as a death-bed, to convince us of the instability of *earthly* hopes of any kind. We have but to look upon nations abroad, and men at home, to see that everything under the sun is uncertain and fluctuating; that prosperity is a cheat, and virtue often but a name. Look upon the map of Europe. See what it was fifty or sixty years ago—what it has since been, and what it is likely to become. Formerly partitioned into separate, independent and energetic monarchies, with vigorous chiefs at their head, maintaining with infinite policy the balance of power among them, and believing that balance eternal: France, in the agonies of the birth of liberty, her *campus martius* resounding with *fetes*, in celebration of that event: the contagion spreading into other nations: monarchs trembling for their crowns, and combining to resist the diffusion of the example: the champions of liberty, and Bonaparte among the rest, victorious everywhere, and everywhere carrying with them the wishes and prayers of America. Yet now see, all at once, the revolution *gone*, like a flash of lightning; France suddenly buried beneath the darkness of despotism, and the voracious tyrant swallowing up kingdom after kingdom. The combining monarchs thought that they were in danger of nothing but the propagation of the doctrines of liberty; but ruin has come upon them from another quarter. The doctrines of liberty are at an end, and so are the monarchies of Europe—all fused and melted down into one great and consolidated despotism. How often have I drunk that Cæsar's health, with a kind of religious devotion! How did all America stand on tiptoe, during his brilliant campaigns in Italy at the head of the army of the republic! With what rapture did we follow his career; and how did our bosoms bound at the prospect of an emancipated world! Yet see in what it has all ended! The total extinction of European liberty, and the too probable prospect of an *enslaved* world! Alas! what are human calculations of happiness; and who can ever more rely upon them!

If we look to the state of things in our own country, still we shall be forced to cry, "all is vanity and vexation of spirit." Look at the public prints with which our country is deluged, and see the merciless massacre of public and private character, of social and domestic peace and happiness. Look at the debates in Congress. Where is the coolness, the decorum, the cordial comparison of ideas for the public good, which you would look for in an assembly of patriots and freemen, such as were seen in the old Congress of 1776? Nothing of it is now to be seen. All is rancor, abuse, hostility and hatred, confusion and ruin. * * * * * * * * *

According to my present impressions of happiness, I would not exchange the good opinion of one virtuous and judicious man, for the acclamation of the millions that inhabit our country; not that these would not be grateful—but as for taking them as a basis of happiness, I would as soon think of building a house on the billows of the sea. * * * * *

Yours most sincerely,

WILLIAM WIRT.

To Benjamin Edwards, Esq.

Richmond, *February* 26, 1809.

Dear Sir:

* * * And now let me tell how grateful I feel for this "the longest letter that you have written since the commencement of your disease." It is so perfectly in the style of your conversation, that I heard the sound of your voice in every line, and saw every turn in the well remembered expression of your face. * * * * * * * *

There are parts of your letter which make me smile. You wish me to aspire to the Presidency of the United States! This is so much like your Mount Pleasant talk! *Then*, it was extravagant enough, although at that time I was but sixteen or seventeen years of age, and had a whole life before me to work wonders in; but *now*, you seem to forget that I am in my six-and-thirtieth year, by which time the color of a man's destiny is pretty well fixed, and that, besides being so old, I have yet a fortune to make for my family before I could turn my thoughts to politics. No, no, my dear friend, I make no such extravagant calculations of future greatness. If I can make my family independent, and leave to my children the inheritance of a respectable name, my expectations and, believe me, my wishes will be fulfilled. For the office of Secretary of State, under Mr. Madison, I am just about as fit as I am to be the Pope of Rome. Nor ought I, nor would I, accept it in my present circumstances. It would be to sacrifice my wife and children on the altar of political ambition. I have no such ambition; and my not having it is one among a thousand proofs that I am unfit for that kind of life; for nature, I believe, never yet gave the capacity without the inclination. I am writing unaffectedly and from my heart. I know enough of the world to know that political power is not happiness, and that my happiness is nowhere but in private life and in the bosom of my beloved family. I think I may be able to attain distinction enough in my profession to have it in my power, in ten years, to retire from the bar into the country, and give myself up to the luxury of literature and my fireside. You will say that this is selfish—that a man's first duty is to his country—and you will tell me of Curtius, and Cato, and Brutus. I admit the grandeur of their virtues, but I am neither a Curtius, a Cato, nor a Brutus. There are thousands of my countrymen better qualified than myself for those high offices, and as willing as capable. Should I attempt to give myself the precedence to such men, it would not be love of country, but self, that would impel me. The wish to see my country prosper is not compatible with a wish to see the reins of government in hands that are unfit to hold them; and to wish them in my own, would be to wish them in such hands. Hence my duty to my country is so far from opposing, that it accords with the real wish of my heart for independence and domestic peace. These are the principles by which I am regulating my life, and I should be almost as sorry to have them disturbed as a Christian would the foundations of his faith.

Monroe is certainly a virtuous and excellent man. I opposed his election, but my opinion of him is unaltered. (By-the-by, my dear wife, who is a good Federalist by inheritance, drew her pencil through that part of your letter in which you speak of the Federalists and Tories who supported his election. She wanted to show your letter to her mother; but as both her father and mother are Federalists of the first water, and supported Monroe, she was afraid that this passage would defeat the effect which she wished the letter to produce—that is, to inspire them with the same love and respect for you which she feels herself.) I think it a misfortune to Monroe that he had the support of which you speak; but as it was unsolicited and undesired by him, I do not think he ought to be blamed for it. I wish the Federalists were all like you—Madisonian Federalists; and I wish the Republicans were all like him—that is, tolerant, candid, charitable and dispassionate. I should then have some hopes of the duration of the Republic; but as it is, may Heaven protect us! If you knew Mr. Jefferson personally and intimately, you would know him to be among the most simple and artless characters upon earth. His fault is, that he is too unguarded. If he had more of Gen. Washington's reserve, he would be less in the power of his enemies than he is. I do not know that this would make him a more amiable man, but it would make him a happier one. * * * * * * *

I am delighted with the account you give of Cyrus' parts. Has he read Locke's "Essay on the Human Understanding?" If not, I wish he would try it. I consider it a pretty good test of a young man's vigor. When I was about fourteen years old, a friend made me very flattering promises if I would read Locke through twice, and produce a certificate from a gentleman, whom he named, that I was master of his meaning. He intimated that I should be considered as a sort of phenomenon if I achieved this task. It was on Sunday, I recollect, when I received this letter; and I went instantly to Parson Hunt's library, took out the book, and, spreading a blanket on the floor, up stairs, laid down flat on my breast—the posture in which I had been accustomed to get my Homer's lesson, and which I therefore supposed was peculiarly favorable to the exertion of the mind. I was soon heels over head among "innate ideas"—subjects which I had never before heard of, and on which I had not a single idea of any kind, either innate or acquired. I stuck to him, however, manfully, and plunged on, pretty intelligently, till I got to his chapter on "Identity and Diversity," and there I stuck fast in the most hopeless despair; nor did I ever get out of that mire until I again met with the book in Albemarle, when I was about twenty-three years of age. Even then, as I approached the chapter on "Identity and Diversity," I felt as shy as the Scotch parson's horse did when repassing, in summer, part of a road in which he had stuck fast the preceding winter. Cyrus is two years beyond the time at which I made the experiment, and I do not doubt that he will bound over it like the reindeer over the snows of Lapland. Locke is certainly a frigid writer to a young man of high fancy; but whoever wishes to train himself to address the human judgment successfully, ought to make Locke his bosom friend and constant companion. He introduces his reader to a most intimate acquaintance with the structure and constitution of the mind; unfolds every property which belongs to it; shows how alone the judgment can be approached and acted on; through what avenues and with what degrees of proof a man may calculate with certainty on its different degrees of assent. Besides this, Locke's book is auxiliary to the same process for which I have been so earnestly recommending the mathematics—that is, giving to the mind a fixed and rooted habit of clear, close, cogent and irresistible reasoning. The man who can read Locke for an hour or two, and then lay him down and argue feebly upon any subject, may hang up his fiddle for life: to such a one nature must have denied the original stamina of a great mind. * *

That Heaven may restore and confirm your health, and continue to smile with beneficence upon yourself and your family (who, I believe, are as dear to my heart as the closest consanguinity could make them), is the devout and fervent prayer of Your friend,

WILLIAM WIRT.

To Benjamin Edwards, Esq.

Richmond, *June* 23, 1809.

My Ever-honored Friend:

Yours of the 15th ult. reached this place a week ago. I was then in Norfolk, in the Admiralty Court, and learned, with sorrow, by a letter from my wife, your inability to meet us at the Springs. In consequence of this our own resolution of going thither is very much shaken; and I doubt much whether we shall go higher up the country than to my wife's sister's, Mrs. Cabell, who lives in Buckingham, a county bounded to the west by the Blue Ridge. There we shall get the mountain air, avoid a hot journey and a good deal of expense—which we would have encountered cheerfully in the hope of meeting you and some portion of your family. This inducement removed, the objections to the jaunt remain without a counterpoise; and we must submit with as good a grace as possible to the disappointment, still cherishing the hope that, by some means or other, at some place or other, we shall yet meet before we bid adieu to the world. In the meantime, lest it should be otherwise, from your parental anxiety for me I am sure you would be glad to know what is to become of me, and how I am to pass through life. I have looked into this subject of my future life with a vision as steady and distinct as I can command, and I now give you the result. In the course of ten years, without some great and signal misfortune, I have reason to hope that I shall be worth near upon or quite $100,000 in cash, besides having an elegant and well-furnished establishment in this town. I propose to vest $25,000 in the purchase, improvement and stocking of a farm somewhere on James River, in as healthy a country as I can find, having also the advantage of fertility. There I will have my books, and with my family spend three seasons of the year—spring, summer and fall. Those months I shall devote to the improvement of my children, the amusement of my wife, and perhaps the endeavor to raise by my pen a monument to my name. The winter we will spend in Richmond—if Richmond shall present superior attractions to the country. The remainder of my cash I will invest in some stable and productive fund, to raise portions for my children.

In these few words you have the scheme of my future life. You see there is no noisy ambition in it; there is none, I believe, in my nature. It is true I love distinction, but I can only enjoy it in tranquillity and innocence. My soul sickens at the idea of political intrigue and faction: I would not choose to be the innocent victim of it, much less the criminal agent. Observe, I do not propose to be useless to society. My ambition will lie in opening, raising, refining and improving the understandings of my countrymen by means of light and cheap publications. I do not think that I am Atlas enough to sustain a ponderous work: while a speculation of fifty or a hundred pages on any subject—theological, philosophical, political, moral or literary—would afford me very great delight, and be executed at least with spirit. Thus I hope to be employed, if alive, ten years hence, and so to the day of my death, or as long as I can write anything worth the reading. Voltaire (voluminous as his works now are, as bound up together,) used to publish, in this way, detached pamphlets; and so did many others of the most distinguished writers in Europe—all the essayists and dramatists, of course, and many of the philosophers. This mode of publication is calculated to give wider currency to a work. There is nothing terrible in the price or the massive bulk of the volume. The price is so cheap and the reading so light, as to command a reader in every one who can read at all—and thereby to embrace the whole country. May not a man, employed in this way, be as useful to his country as by haranguing eloquently in the Senate? The harangue and the harangue-maker produce a transient benefit, and then perish together. The writer, if he have merit, speaks to all countries and to all ages; and the benefits which he produces flow on forever. To enjoy them both would be, indeed, desirable to a man who could feel sufficient delight in the applause of his eloquence to counterbalance the pain which the cabals, intrigues, calumnies and lies of the envious and malignant would be sure to inflict upon him. This, I think, I could never do; and I shall, therefore, attempt that kind of fame which alone I can find reconcilable with my happiness.

By perusing these two pages you may look forward through futurity to the end of my life, and, from the point on which you now stand, take in my whole prospect. One thing, at least, your adopted son promises you: that he will transmit to his posterity a name of unblemished honor; and he flatters himself that, in future time, they will look back to him as the founder of a race that will have done no discredit to their country. This is vanity, but, I hope, not vexation to your spirit; for with whom can I be free, if not with you? I flatter myself that you have that kind of love for me which would make you desirous of seeing how I shall conduct myself through life; but since, in the ordinary course of things, this cannot be, the next degree of enjoyment is to see it by anticipation, and for this purpose it is that I have been trying to lead you to the summit of Pisgah, and show you my promised land.

But enough of it. Your letter gives a view of the advanced life of parents, not the most cheering that could be imagined. But then, those children whom you went to Kentucky to live with, although widely dispersed, are all in the road of honor, prosperity and happiness. They could not have remained with you always: you should not have desired it. They were to be established in the world; and you have the delightful knowledge that they are well-established. What a feast is this reflection to a heart like yours! Contrast it with the idea of their always having remained about your house, your daughters old maids, and your sons lazy old bachelors. You would have had their company, indeed—but what sort of company would it have been? And if you once admitted the idea that they were to be married and settled, I am sure you were not chimerical enough to expect that they would all settle around Shiloh, like so many small bubbles surrounding a large one. I doubt very much the happiness of a neighborhood so constructed, even if it were reasonable to expect such a construction. I incline to think that distance gives you a juster value for each other, and that when you do meet, your happiness makes up in intenseness what it wants in frequency; so that, upon the whole, the sum of your happiness is pretty much the same.

But, my ever-honored friend, any man with your practical judgment must have foreseen this result—that your children would marry, and that their own parental duties would force them to follow their fortune wherever she pointed the way. And how happy is your fate compared with that of hundreds, thousands and millions of other parents. No child has ever wounded the honor of your house. You have no reprobate son to mourn: no daughter's ruin to bring down your gray hairs with sorrow to the grave. How many are there who have! When I think of these agonizing, soul-rending calamities, I almost shudder at the idea of being a father. "Yet in Providence I trust."

I had heard of Ninian's wish for the governorship of the Illinois, from himself, and had written to Mr. Madison (whom I know very well) my impressions of his (Ninian's) character. I know not whether the change of office is for better or worse; and am sorry to learn that you think it against reason and judgment. The office, I presume, will impose more labor upon him, and be more likely to embroil him in quarrels and trouble. But will not these be balanced by the power which he will have of providing for his children, and ushering them advantageously into life?

I am happy to hear that Cyrus has laid siege to the mathematics. He will, no doubt, soon be tired of it, and when he is so, he ought to turn to Rollin's account of his namesake's siege of Babylon, to see what patience, enterprise and heroism can achieve; and, though he may not see at present the benefit which is to result from his labors, he will feel it by-and by, when the arguments of his adversaries fall before him like the walls of Jericho at the sound of the horns.

By-the-by, my wife is afraid that you took too gravely her little gayety in penciling some of the lines of your letter touching the Federalists. I told her that, *to my sorrow*, you were a Federalist too; and that your observation could scarcely have been intended to cover the whole of a party to which you yourself belonged. The act was, as it related to herself, a mere sally of sportiveness; and in this light she begs you to consider it. I have some hopes that, in time, I shall have better luck with her than Paul had with Felix: that I shall altogether persuade her to be a good Republican. This will be the effect, however, of living long together, and wearing down, by slow degrees, the little Federal asperities which her parents gave her; that is to say, if my own political asperities, as being made of softer stuff, do not give way first. You know that in rencontres of this sort, men have not much to expect beyond the pleasure of being vanquished. * * *

Here is another long and vapid letter. No wonder this time, for I have written under the pressure of about ninety-six degrees of heat. My wife and children unite with me in love to you, Mrs. E., and our brothers and sisters. Heaven bless you, restore you to health, and preserve you to your family.

Yours,

WILLIAM WIRT.

To BENJAMIN EDWARDS, ESQ.

RICHMOND, *December* 22, 1809.

My Dear Friend:

* * * * I think you are rather hard upon my brother Ninian, when you speak of the Quixotic schemes which he has carried to his Territory. It strikes me that a fellow who has made his way through the presidency of a Court of Appeals, to the government of a Territory, deserves to have his solidity a little better thought of. I suspect that the Knight of La Mancha would never have achieved such adventures as those. I own that I cannot see what he will gain by the exchange, except (what I should suppose he has no need of) land: but he has displayed so much soundness of judgment that I do not doubt motives exist sufficient to justify his conduct. I am sorry that Cyrus is deprived of McAllister. I hear this man everywhere spoken of as a prodigy of learning and mental force; not very well qualified perhaps for the instruction of children, but highly so for the instruction of young men —and Cyrus is now a young man. McAllister, I am told, is distinguished for the clearness and cogency of his style of reasoning. What a treasure would such a man be to a young man of genius and enterprise who was destined for the bar! This power of analysis, the power of simplifying a complex subject, and showing all its parts clearly and distinctly, is the *forte* of Chief Justice Marshall, and is the great *desideratum* of every man who aims at eminence in the law. Genius, fancy and taste may fashion the drapery and put it on; but reason alone is the grand sculptor, that can form the statue itself. Hence it is that I have been so anxious for Cyrus to cultivate the mathematics—not for the sake of being a mathematician, but to give to his mind the habit of close and conclusive reasoning. I hope he will still be placed in some situation where he may pursue this science. I would have him mathematician enough to be able to comprehend and repeat, with ease, by calculations of his own, Sir Isaac Newton's mathematical demonstrations of the principles of natural philosophy. Locke says, if you would have your son a reasoner, let him read Chillingworth: I say, if you would have him a reasoner let him read Locke. I think you will find that the mathematics and Locke will put a head in his tub; for, what you censure is not, I apprehend, any defect in the faculty of memory, but rather the inattention and volatility so natural to his time of life, for which there is no better cure than what I am recommending. * * * * * * * * * *

As to my country's calling for my aid, you make me smile! yet, if such an improbable thing should ever come to pass, you will find that your lectures on patriotism have not been lost upon me. Alas! poor country! what is to become of it? In the wisdom and virtue of the Administration I have the most unbounded confidence. My apprehensions, therefore, have no reference to them, nor to any event very near at hand. And yet, can any man who looks upon the state of public virtue in this country, and then casts his eyes upon what is doing in Europe, believe that this confederated republic is to last for ever? Can he doubt that its probable dissolution is less than a century off? Think of Burr's conspiracy, within thirty-five years of the birth of the republic; think of the characters implicated with him; think of the state of political parties and of the presses in this country; think of the execrable falsehoods, virulent abuse, villainous means by which they strive to carry their points. Will not the people get tired and heart-sick of this perpetual commotion and agitation, and long for a change, even for king Log, so that they may get rid of their demagogues, the storks, that destroy their peace and quiet? These are my fears. Heaven grant that they may prove groundless! It may be for the want of that political intrepidity which is essential to a statesman, that these fears have found their way into my mind —yet I confess they do sometimes fill it with awe and dismay. I am sure that the body of the people is virtuous; and were they as enlightened as virtuous, I should think the republic insured against ruin from within. But they are not enlightened, and therefore are liable to imposition from the more knowing, crafty and vicious emissaries of faction; and the very honesty of the people, by rendering them unsuspicious and credulous, promotes the cheat. They are told, for instance, that this Administration is in French pay, or under French influence; and that this country, although nominally free, is, in effect, a dependent and a province of France. That the taxes which they pay to support this Government, instead of being applied to these purposes, are remitted to their master in France, to enable him to complete the conquest of Europe, and hasten the time of his taking open possession here. The people who live amid the solitude and innocence of the country, who read or hear of this tale, well vamped up, and see general items pointed out, in the annual accounts of expenditure, which are declared to cover these traitorous remittances—what are they to think—especially when the tale is connected with a long train of circumstances, partly true and partly false, growing out of the actual embarrassments of the country? Would it be surprising, if, thus worked upon for four years, with the vile and infamous slander sanctioned by assertions on the floor of Congress, they should precipitate Mr. Madison from the Presidential seat, and place one of his calumniators in the chair of State? And then, when "vice prevails and wicked men bear sway," "what ills may follow." Heaven only can foretell. * * * * * *

Yours, forever and aye,

WILLIAM WIRT.

To BENJAMIN EDWARDS, ESQ.

RICHMOND, *May* 8, 1810.

My Dear and Revered Friend:

* * * * * I have, indeed, great cause of gratitude to Heaven. I will not say that Providence has *led* me, but that, in spite of the reluctant and rebellious propensities of my nature, it has *dragged* me from obscurity and vice, to respectability and earthly happiness.

In reviewing the short course of my life, I can see where I made plunges from which it seems clearly to me that nothing less than a Divine hand could ever have raised me; but I have been raised, and I trust that my feet are now upon a rock. Yet can I never cease to deplore the years of my youth, that I have murdered in idleness and folly. I can only fancy, with a sigh of unwilling regret, the figure which I might have made had I devoted to study those hours which I gave up to giddy dissipation, and which now cannot be recalled. I have read enough to show me, dimly and at a distance, the great outline of that scheme of literary conquest which it was once in my power to fill up in detail. I have got to the foot of the mountain, and see the road which passes over its summit, and leads to the promised land; but it is too late in life for me. I must be content to lay my bones on the hither side, and point out the path to my son. Do not charge these sentiments either to a weak and spiritless despondency or to sluggish indolence. I know that a good deal may yet be done, and I mean, as far as I can, that it shall be done; yet, comparatively, it will be but a drop in the bucket. Seven-and-thirty is rather too late for a man to begin his education; more especially when he is hampered by the duties of a profession, and in this age of the world, when every science covers so much ground by itself. What a spur should this reflection be to young men! Yet there is scarcely one in ten thousand of them who will understand or believe it, until, as in my case, it comes home to the heart, when it is too late. I now think that I know all the flaws and weak places of my mind. I know which of the muscles want tone and vigor, and which are braced beyond the point of health. I also think I know what course of *early* training would have brought them all to perform their proper functions in harmonious concert. But now the character of my mind is fixed; and as to any beneficial change, one might as well call upon a tailor, who has sat upon his shop-board until the calves of his legs are shriveled, to carry the burthens of a porter; or upon a man whose hand is violently shaken with the palsy, to split hairs with a razor. Such as it is it will probably remain, with a little accession, perhaps, of knowledge. You will do me injustice if you infer, from what I have said, that I am sighing with regret at those distant hights of political honors which lie beyond my reach. I do not know whether to consider it as a vice or virtue of my nature—but so far am I from sighing for political honors, that I pant only for seclusion and tranquillity, in which I may enjoy the sweets of domestic and social love; raise my faculties, by assiduous cultivation, to their highest attainable point, and prepare for that state of future existence to which I know I am hastening. Nor should I propose to myself, in such solitude, to forget what I owe to my country: on the contrary, I think I could be much more solidly useful, in that situation, than in one more public and active. So strongly are my hopes and wishes fixed on this life of sequestration and peace, that if you ever hear of my having entered on a political course, you may rely upon it that it is a painful and heart-rending sacrifice to a sense of public duty. I hope and trust that such an emergency is scarcely possible. I am sure that it is very improbable; because I believe there will always be those who are much better qualified for public offices, and certainly far more anxious for them than I am. At the same time, I think our country is, at present, very badly supplied with materials for future legislation and government. I cast my eyes over the continent, in vain, in quest of successors to our present patriots. There seems to me a most miserable and alarming dearth of talents and acquirements among the young men of the United States. I have sometimes sat down and endeavored to fill the various offices in the Government with characters drawn from those who are made known to us, either personally or by fame. But so far am I from finding among them a man fit for a President, that I cannot even find persons fit for the heads of Departments. What has become of the talents of the country? Are they utterly extinct? or do they merely slumber; and does it require another great convulsion, like our revolutionary war, to rouse their dormant energies? I myself think that it proceeds, in a very great degree, if not altogether, from defective education. Our teachers themselves either want learning, or they want the address necessary to excite into vigorous action the powers of the mind. Young men are everywhere turned loose in the various professions, with minds half awake, and their surface merely a little disturbed with science. This is not the way great men have been made, either in Europe or America. As long as this system is pursued we shall never have anything but political quacks. * * * *

You will no doubt have seen, in the public papers, the loss we have suffered in the premature death of my wife's father, Col. Robert Gamble. In the full enjoyment of health and strength, of uncommon mental and corporeal vigor, in the active and prosperous pursuit of his business, his children all established, surrounded by his grandchildren and an extensive circle of sincere and fervent friends, and with the fairest prospects of earthly happiness opening around him on every hand, he was suddenly killed, on the morning of the 12th instant, by a fall from his horse. He was a faithful soldier of the revolution, a sincere and zealous Christian, one of the best of fathers, and honestest of men. * * * * * * * * * *

Yours,
WILLIAM WIRT.

To BENJAMIN EDWARDS, ESQ.

NORFOLK, *May* 6, 1806.

My Dear Sir:

* * * You see I have not gotten rid of my levities, and most certainly I never shall while I live; they make an essential part of my constitution. I catch myself sometimes singing and dancing about the house like a madman, to the very great amusement of my wife and children, and probably of the passengers who are incidentally going along the street. This is very little like the wise conduct which Shakspeare makes Henry IV recommend to his son; but the harebrained find some consolation in the figure which Henry V made in spite of his father's maxims of gravity. Yet I hope you will not believe that I either sing or dance in the street or in the court-house. I know the indispensable importance of a little state, to draw the magic circle of respect around one's self, and repel intrusion and vulgarity.
* * * * * * * * * *

To be sure, in a letter, it is not so material if a man cuts an eccentric caper here and there; but I feel the same propensity when I am arguing a cause before a court and jury—although I see the track plainly before me, yet, like an ill-disciplined race-horse, I am perpetually bolting or flying the way—and this, too, perhaps in the very crisis of the argument. After having laid my premises to advantage—often having gone through an elaborate deduction of principles—in the very instant when I am about to reap the fruit of my toil, by drawing my conclusion, and when everybody is on tiptoe expectation of it, some meteor springs up before me, and, in spite of me, I am off, like Commodore Trunnion's hunter, when the pack of hounds crossed him so unpropitiously, just as he was arriving at church to seize the hand of his anxious and expecting bride. I was in conversation the other day with a very intimate friend of mine on this subject, and was lamenting to him this laxity of intellect, which I was sure arose from the want of a well-directed education. He admitted that I had ascribed it to its proper cause, but doubted whether it ought to be lamented as a defect, suggesting that the man in whose imagination these meteors were always shooting bid much fairer, both for fame and fortune, than the rigid logician, however close and cogent. In reply, it was but necessary for me to appeal to examples before our eyes to disprove his suggestion. One was Alexander Campbell, whose voice had all the softness and melody of the harp; whose mind was at once an orchard and a flower garden, loaded with the best fruits and smiling in all the many-colored bloom of spring; whose delivery, action, style and manner were perfectly Ciceronian, and who, with all these advantages, died by his own hand. * * * On the other hand: here is John Marshall, whose mind seems to be little else than a mountain of barren and stupendous rocks—an inexhaustible quarry, from which he draws his materials and builds his fabrics, rude and Gothic, but of such strength that neither time nor force can beat them down—a fellow who would not turn off a single step from the right line of his argument though a Paradise should rise to tempt him; who, it appears to me, if a flower were to spring in his mind, would strike it up with his spade as indignantly as a farmer would a noxious plant from his meadow; yet who, all dry and rigid as he is, has acquired all the wealth, fame and honor that a man need desire. There is no theorizing against facts: Marshall's certainly is the true road to solid and lasting reputation in courts of law. The habits of his mind are directly those which an accurate and familiar acquaintance with the mathematics generates. * * * * * * *

I feel so sensibly my own deficiencies in this mathematical study, that, if Heaven spares my son and enables me to educate him, I will qualify him to be a professor in it, before he shall know what poetry and rhetoric are. If he turns out to have fancy and imagination, he will then be in less danger of being run away with and unhorsed by them. If he is for the bar, I shall never cease to inculcate Marshall's method—being perfectly persuaded that for courts (and especially superior and appellate courts, where there are no juries), it is the only true method. It is true that, if I had my choice, I would much rather have my son, as to mind, a Mirabeau than a Marshall—if such a prodigy, as I have heard Mirabeau described by Mr. Jefferson, did ever really exist; for he spoke of him as uniting two distinct and perfect characters in himself, whenever he pleased: the mere logician, with a mind apparently as sterile and desolate as the sands of Arabia, but reasoning at such times with an Herculean force, which nothing could resist; at other times bursting out with a flood of eloquence more sublime than Milton ever imputed to the cherubim and seraphim, and bearing all before him. I can easily conceive that a man might have either of these characters in perfection, or some portion of each; but that the same mind should unite them both, and *each in perfection*, appears to me, considering the strong contrast in their essence and operation, to be indeed a prodigy. Yet I suppose it is true, "for Brutus is an honorable man." * * * * * * * *

No, my dear friend, I shall certainly never become famous by burning a temple or despising the religion of Christ. On these subjects, in the heat, vanity and ostentation of youth, I once thought and spoke, to my shame, too loosely. A series of rescues from the brink of ruin, to which, whenever left to myself, I madly rushed, convinced me that there was an invisible, benevolent power, who was taking an interest in my preservation. I hope that ingratitude is not one of my vices. The conviction which I have just mentioned no sooner struck my heart, than it was filled with a sentiment which, I hope, will save me from the fate of a Voltaire or a Domitian.

The friendly hope which you express, that you will live to hear me toasted at every political dinner, for superior virtues and wisdom, is indeed very obliging, but very unfounded. You know how poor I have always been. The rocks and shoals of poverty and bankruptcy lie very near to the whirlpool of dishonor and infamy. Among these rocks and shoals I have been tossing and beating ever since I entered upon the world. The whirlpool I have escaped, and, thank Heaven, feel myself now out of danger; but that horrible danger I shall never forget, nor shall I cease struggling till I place my children out of its reach. This cannot be done if I give myself up to politics. This latter might be the road to distinction, but not to independence, either for myself or my children. When I have placed my wife and children beyond the reach of this world's cold and reluctant charity, unfeeling insolence, or more insulting pity, then my country shall have all the little service which I am capable of rendering. But while I have opportunities of hearing, seeing and reading, and making comparisons between other men and myself, I cannot believe that the little all of my services will ever make a political toast. Nor, indeed, do I envy that distinction to any man; for I remember how Miltiades, Aristides, Cicero, Demosthenes and many others were once idolized by their countrymen; and I remember the disastrous proof which their examples afforded of the fickleness of popular favor, and the danger of aspiring to political distinctions even by the exercise of virtues. Yet I would not shrink from their fate, if my countrymen required the sacrifice at my hands. All I mean to say is, that I shall never enter on the political highway in quest of happiness. Thank Heaven, I have it at home! A wife, in whose praise, if I were to indulge it, my pen would grow as wanton as Juba's tongue in praise of his Marcia; two cherub children; a revenue which puts us quite at ease in the article of living; and the respect and esteem of my acquaintances and, I may say, of Virginia. A man who has blessings like these in his possession will not be very wise to jeopard them all by launching on the stormy Baltic of politics.

Ever your friend and servant,
WILLIAM WIRT.

To BENJAMIN EDWARDS, ESQ.

ANNAPOLIS, *October* 22, 1826.

My Ever-dear Friend and Benefactor:

Ninian has been so kindly thoughtful as to send me Cyrus' letter of the 22d July last, from Elkton (Illinois), announcing the sad bereavement you have encountered. The letter found me, about ten days ago, at Washington, whither I had returned from a long excursion to the South-western Springs of Virginia, for the benefit of my own health and that of one of my daughters; and it came to me at a time when I was most intensely engaged in preparing to meet a public engagement arising from the deaths of Mr. Jefferson and Mr. Adams. The shock which it gave me disarmed me for the day, and I would have poured out my heart to you at once, if my grief could have had any other effect than to increase your own. I reached this place about an hour ago, and although I have a cause now under argument in the Court of Appeals at this place, which demands my immediate attention, I cannot sit down to business until I have lightened my breast by giving you this evidence of my sympathy. Poor dear Mrs. Edwards! it is now thirty-eight years since I first saw her at Mount Pleasant. I was, then, in my sixteenth year, a volatile and thoughtless young boy, looking on the world and life before me, with all those brightning hopes and expectations of youth that painted it as a fairy scene whose pleasures would never end. I am now old and gray, the illusion is long since over, and I have been taught, by mournful experience, to know the world as it is, a poor and miserable stage-play, in which there is nothing of any value but those pure attachments which bind us to one another and those which bind us to our God and Saviour. If this life were all, the former, sweet and endearing as they are, would be but poor things: they are "flowers of the forest" withered and gone very often before we have had time to know their value. I lost a dear boy, in his nineteenth year. Two years, this fall, he died far away from me, in France, where he had gone for his health. He was the pride and hope of my heart and family, and an object of admiration and love to all who knew him. My dear friend, I cannot think of him, and never shall I be able to think of him, without tears. He was the third of my children I had lost; the two former in the tender and attaching age of infancy. But Robert was growing to be a man, and had displayed such a noble soul and mind, that I have said to myself a hundred times, if my dear old friend Mr. Edwards could but know this boy, what an augury would he not make for *him*, who made so bright a one on the inferior evidence presented by his father in the days of *his* youth! Dear Mrs. Edwards too—how kind *she* always was to me—how respectful and tender to a poor orphan boy, of obscure parentage, who had no other claims to her respect and tenderness than those which her own native kindness suggested! How well do I remember her looks, her voice, her movements, her manners—the natural dignity, and excellent understanding, and unaffected warmth and tenderness of feeling, that reigned in her character and conduct—the pleasure and just pride with which she listened to your conversation, my dear friend, and enjoyed the admiration of the circle around you, of which I was one, and not less proud of you, myself, than if you had been my own father! The family sitting-room at Mount Pleasant, the large and cheerful fireside, the lighted candles, the eloquent, varied and charming conversation, the fine healthy circle of children, the laugh, the jest, Kelly, myself, how forcibly the whole scene stands revealed to me at this moment! And yet it is near forty years ago. Where are they all? Through what scenes have I, myself, since passed? And all our neighbors, the Lanes, the Gassaways, the Catletts, only think of the desolation that has mowed them all down! Wm. Smith and his family, old Mr. Turner and his, and old Mr. Orme and his, and the Perrys, all gone! Have you not been rather favored, my dear friend, to have been so long blessed with the society of your most excellent and beloved companion? Come whenever it might, the blow must, indeed, have been most deeply felt. But, considering the fate of your old neighbors, and the certainty of that fate to all, has not Heaven been kind and merciful in suspending it so long? You enjoyed her society for near fifty-four years. The poor orphan boy you protected experienced the same bereavement before he was thirty years of age. And although your having lived so long together must have drawn the cords the closer and made it more agonizing to sever them, yet the separation must at last have come. Has it not been merciful in Heaven to have made it for so short a time as in the ordinary course of nature it must now be? for, according to the lot of humanity, it cannot be long before you will be united to part no more. Both believers in Christ, and as faithful followers of his as you could be, to what a speedy re-union may you not look in that world of bliss where you will know sorrow no more. Strange, when we reflect upon it, that we should mourn such a separation at all! But our natural earthly affections cannot be extinguished either by reason or even faith; and that Being who knows our infirmities will not fail to look upon them with mercy and pardon. Mrs. Edwards' confidence in her interest in the Saviour, can leave no doubt of the happy change she has experienced, and it does not become us to mourn as those who have no hope. * * * * *

I dare say, you have long since marked me down as having lost the heart of friendship I have always professed for you. Indeed, my occupations, I know, have subjected me fairly to this suspicion. But you, who know me as well as I know myself, will believe me when I assure you that I never think of you without the deepest feelings of reverence and gratitude; and though I have not been able to write as often as formerly, I have never ceased to regard you with the love and veneration of an affectionate child. I can now only pray to Heaven to strengthen and support you, and to spare you for the sake of your dear family yet a few years longer; feeling, on my own part, the most perfect assurance that death, come when it will, will open to you the gates of life and restore you to your partner in the bosom of your Saviour. May I not have a place in your prayers? And will you not do me the justice to regard me as among the most affectionate of your children?

WILLIAM WIRT.

To BENJAMIN EDWARDS, ESQ.

POSTOFFICE DEPARTMENT,
January 7, 1825.

Sir:

Some complaints have reached me from Illinois that Mr. Mills does not run his stages on the main route to St. Louis, and also on the one by Vandalia, when the road will admit. On every stage route in the Union, the contractor is authorized, by special instructions, when the road is so bad as to render the running of stages impracticable, to convey the mail on horse, in a boat, or in any other manner which will protect it from the weather. The great object is to deliver the mail as regularly as possible at the points designated, and where this cannot be done in stages, it is required to be done in some other manner.

Mr. Mills has no exemption above any other contractor in the Union, but is required to fulfill his contract the same as every other contractor, and if he fail, he shall be punished to the extent of the powers vested in me.

In no part of the Western country, I believe, has a stage been run regularly through the winter and spring, because it has been found impracticable to do so. But this license must not be abused. When the roads will admit of stages being run on all stage routes, they must be run, and a failure to do so will subject the contractor to a penalty and the censure of the Department. Knowing that you reside on the main route to St. Louis, from Louisville, and may have some knowledge of the manner in which the mail is carried on the route through Vandalia, I will thank you, at any time, to advise me when Mr. Mills or any other contractor shall fail in the performance of his duty, as above defined.

I have been induced to trouble you with this communication from the knowledge I have of your wish, in every particular, to promote the public interest.

JOHN McLEAN,
Postmaster-General.

GOV. EDWARDS, Belleville, Illinois.

GEORGETOWN, *April* 25, 1825.

My Dear Sir:

Having a few minutes leisure, I do not know how I can employ it more pleasantly to myself than by communicating to you the aspect of our political affairs, for I am persuaded it will not be wholly uninteresting to you. I may have noticed some facts which have escaped your observation.

Upon a full and impartial view, I think that the Administration has no ground to complain of the disposition which has been generally manifested towards it. There are but few persons, in my section of the country, who do not feel disposed to judge of it by its measures. This is all that any Administration ought to ask or expect to receive. Indeed, I think, to a very great extent, a friendly feeling has been shown—at least so far as to judge most favorably of the acts of the Administration; and it appears that a great majority of the public journals would rather praise than censure. It is not, however, to be concealed that there is a considerable party hostile to Mr Clay, and, on this account, will not be disposed to support with zeal the Administration. Of this you were fully aware before you left here. Circumstances which have since transpired render certain that which was, a few weeks ago, founded partly on conjecture. The "Richmond Enquirer," as you may have observed, is in opposition; and I think it will be found to speak the sentiments of a majority of the citizens of Virginia. In this, however, I may be mistaken. I judge principally from the great influence which that paper has had on the politics of Virginia, and of the avowed sentiments of several of the most distinguished men of the State. The late appointment of Mr. King will go very far to fix the position of Virginia on this subject. Perhaps no citizen could have been more objectionable to this State, for this mission, than Mr. King. The course he took on the Missouri question and the late proposition which he made in the Senate respecting Havery, have created a feeling that will not very soon be forgotten. But above all, the fact of Mr. King's having been at the head of the Federal party, and high in office and influence under the older Adams, form objections to the appointment which Virginia can never surmount. You know on many topics our friends of Virginia are somewhat extravagant in their notions, and they have never been charged with moderation in politics. North Carolina, South Carolina, Georgia, and all the ground in the north-west covered by Gen. Jackson, will of course incline to oppose the Administration, so far as it may be considered necessary to defeat the future prospects of Mr. Clay. Towards the President, it does not appear to me that much hostility is cherished, but he may be considered as having so intimately connected his fortunes with Mr. Clay, that the opposition may be directed against them both. From the representation in Maryland, I think the Administration may expect support, and also from several of the members from most of the States I have referred to.

Pennsylvania remains as she was—firmly opposed. New York may be considered doubtful—probably a majority will be against the Administration. The appointment of Mr. King was not fortunate for the Administration in this State, though I have no doubt Mr. Clay, and perhaps Mr. Adams, believed it would give them much strength. Mr. King, you are aware, is very unpopular with the dominant party in New York, and for some years has had no influence in that State with any party. The Clintonian party and the Republicans, who have been opposed to Clinton, will cordially unite in opposition to this appointment. Mr. King is upwards of seventy years of age, and has failed, it is thought, very much, both physically and mentally. He is thought by some, rather to belong to the past than the present age, and that his views are greatly behind the advances of our country. I heard Webster observe, better than a year ago, that King had no idea that the country west of the Alleghany formed any part of the United States—that his views of policy and feelings were confined to the "old thirteen." There was much truth in the remark. Mr. King has always evinced a want of liberality to the West, and has appeared anxious to check its rapid growth. Mr. Monroe once remarked to me that this disposition was evinced by Mr. King on almost every land bill that was discussed by the Senate. This appointment will be well received in England; but Mr. King will find that country, as well as this, vastly changed from what it was when he resided there, as a Minister from this Government.

On the other side of the question, it may be said that Mr. King, from his public services and high character, will be thought in many parts of the Union a most fit representative of this country to the most important foreign court. In New England, this appointment seems to be pretty well received. But I am not mistaken in saying, that in New York it weakens instead of gives strength to the Administration. Mr. Clay out of the question, Mr. Adams would have experienced little or no opposition in New York.

You have probably noticed the great effort that has been made by Mr. Webster and others, at Boston, to get up a new amalgamation party. This scheme has succeeded partially in Massachusetts in their late elections, but it has failed in New Hampshire, and will not probably generally succeed in New England. The object of this policy is very manifest. It is to destroy the Democratic or Republican party, by uniting it with the Federalists, who in a very short time would assume the entire direction of affairs, and show the same intolerance that cost them the power many years since. Their principles are not changed, nor has any alteration taken place in their disposition.

I have always believed that between Republicans and Federalists there was a radical difference of principle; and that great injustice is done the former by awarding to each applause and censure alike. No one who observed the movements of the Federal party during the late war, will differ with me in opinion on this subject. I confess, when I call into recollection the scenes which I then witnessed, that I can never repose entire confidence in many of the Federalists who were then the leaders of their party, but now the strong advocates of amalgamation. Throughout the whole war, the most systematic opposition was given to every measure calculated to give energy to our military operations. I shall never forget the expression of one of their most distinguished leaders, nor the occasion which called it forth. The public credit was next to the lowest state of depression, and unless a resuscitation speedily took place, our armies must have left the field and our Government been driven to an inglorious peace. At this time, I heard Timothy Pickering say that he was more than anxious that public credit should not be revived. In this he was supported by all his party, Mr. Webster included. The cause had then become the cause of the country, whatever might have been thought of it at the previous stages; and any man who would array himself against his country, under such circumstances, must hold the triumph of a party more desirable than the triumph of his country.

If the Federal party are willing to come over to the Republican party and occupy the same ground, I would most cheerfully receive them; but it seems they always stipulate that the advantage of the union should result exclusively to themselves. Where they have the majority, little is said of union, but when they are vastly in the minority, they are willing to unite, on condition that the offices shall be divided. I should rather see a union without such a stipulation and on Republican ground. In due time the meritorious would be confided in by the people. On amalgamation or any other principle, I view it as very objectionable, and hope that it may never take place.

Mr. Clay is still here and most industriously engaged in making out instructions for our Ministers. His health has become much worse than it was, and, unless he shall regain his health, I doubt very much whether the labors of his office will not be more than he can bear. I have no doubt that he will faithfully support Mr. Adams to the utmost of his power. In New England, the papers generally speak favorably of him.

You have read Mr. Clay's address, and no doubt the various publications which have followed it. The address is very well written, and from the remarks in the journals, it seems to be well received by a great majority. Upon the whole, it may remove some of the prejudices existing against Mr. Clay. He has been very fortunate in not having it reviewed by any one having a decent pretension to talents—unless it be a short address from Mr. Ingham, which I have this day read. This, however, only refers to such parts as go to implicate him with Mr. Kremer. Mr. Clay avowed his determination, to Dr. Drake and others, before he left Kentucky last fall, to vote for Mr. Adams, and that under no circumstances would he vote for Gen. Jackson. How then could he, in January, deliberate on the subject, and make up his opinion, as represented, from facts which were not known to exist, when his determination was expressed in Kentucky, etc., etc.

I have already said more than I intended, and will conclude this topic by saying that I have never doubted that injustice was done to Mr. Clay in many of the charges made against him.

Calhoun has gone to the South. I have not heard from him since his departure.

Mrs. McLean desires her respects to Mrs. Cook. Present my respects to Mrs. C.

Sincerely your friend,

JOHN McLEAN.

To Gov. Edwards.

WASHINGTON, *March* 24, 1826.

Dear Sir:

For your friendly letter, which has been long since received and should have been long since answered, I thank you. My apology for this seeming inattention is found in the labors of my office, which require my utmost exertions both night and day. In the approbation which is kindly given by the public, I find an ample compensation for my toils, and encouragement to persevere.

I have pleasure in informing you that I have made an arrangement for the mail, two trips weekly, in the stage between Louisville and St. Louis. Five days is the time fixed for each trip. The principal stage will run on the direct road from Vincennes to St. Louis, but the stage will be continued by the way of Vandalia and Edwardsville, as at present.

This increased accommodation, with what may be given by adding to the speed of the conveyance of the mail by way of Shawneetown, so as to make it correspond in time with the conveyance by the way of Vincennes, and give a third trip weekly between Louisville and St. Louis. I hope to satisfy public expectation on this subject.

I regret to see so much party feeling at this early stage of the present Administration. Both sides may have committed blunders, and time will determine what will be the effect of the course taken during the present session of Congress. Every judicious man, I should think, will admit that a change of the Chief Magistrate every four years, upon party ground, resulting from personal preferences, or important differences in policy, must essentially retard the rising prosperity of the country. Strange combinations may grow out of the present contest. I should rejoice most to see each party emulous in advancing the general interest.

From the certainty of your success in the approaching election I derive sincere pleasure. It will be a triumph to yourself and your friends. I believe almost all of that virulence of feeling which was so generally evinced by the caucus party against you, has disappeared, and to a considerable extent has been succeeded by feelings of a very different nature. Mr. Crawford will never be again presented on the political arena. His friends will generally support Gen. Jackson.

I presume Mr. Cook gives you all that is of any interest, which you do not receive in the public papers. He stands well with all parties, and is not excelled in weight of character, talents and influence, by any member from the West.

With sincere regard,

Your friend,

JOHN McLEAN.

TO HON. NINIAN EDWARDS.

WASHINGTON, *Nov.* 1, 1826.

Dear Sir:

An unusual press of official duties has prevented my answering your letter of the 17th of September until now. The contents of this letter produced no small degree of surprise and regret, and had it not been for the strong assurances of the most friendly motives, at the conclusion, it would have been impossible for me to view it in any other light than an attack upon my official integrity. The intimation that Mr. Cook might think it due to himself and his friends to make a thorough investigation of the subject referred to, which could be done in no other way than by a call in Congress, and of such a nature as to impeach my integrity, filled me with astonishment. I cannot suppose that Mr. Cook has thought of such a course; for admitting that the appointment of ——— was incorrect, could he believe that, in making it, I had acted corruptly, or was influenced by hostility to him? If I believed it possible for him to form such an estimate of me, I should not care how soon the investigation was commenced. But it is impossible—he neither doubts my integrity nor friendship. For his success I felt a stronger interest, in the late election, than for the success of any other individual, not excepting my own brother. In fact, my feelings towards him ever since our acquaintance have been of the warmest kind, and every word that I have ever spoken respecting him has evinced it.

Your letter was the first intimation I had of ——— being hostile either to him or yourself. I believed him to be friendly. If you will read with attention the publication of ———, which you inclosed, you will find, or I am greatly mistaken, that he does not refer to my act of re-appointing him as a mode of reversing the decisions of courts and juries, but to *public opinion.*

You have been too long conversant with the proceedings of courts not to know that they may sometimes err in their decision, and that juries are often led into error by the malice or mistake of witnesses. The innocent have often been convicted of the highest offenses; and it is presumed that this may happen so long as imperfection belongs to human nature. If one individual may be innocently convicted of an offense, may he not look to *public opinion* for justice? Is it criminal or even objectionable in him to refer to this tribunal, as the last resort. The appeal of ——— does not, it appears to me, place me in collision with the court and jury who tried his case. He refers to *public opinion* as sustaining him, and exhibits the evidence of being elected to the important office of Sheriff, by the unanimous suffrage of his county. This office is one of high trust, and in the discharge of its important duties great integrity is required. In ordinary cases, I submit to you, whether an appeal like this would not be considered conclusive of a man's standing and character. You will observe that I speak of any case presenting the same facts, without referring to the circumstances detailed in your letter.

I have never seen, as you suppose, the indictment against ———, but understand that it charged him with detaining a letter, for which the statute subjects him to a penalty. You will observe, however, that a removal from office forms no part of this penalty. This is a matter to be determined by the discretion of the Postmaster-General. How, then, could I have been brought into collision with the court and jury had I not removed ——? Might not a case exist where, on an indictment for the mere detention of a letter, a postmaster might be convicted, and after the trial it would be in his power to convince, by indubitable testimony, every impartial man of his innocence? And in such a case, would the court and jury, who tried and convicted him, be censurable; or would I cast an implied censure on them by appointing such an individual to an inconsiderable postoffice?

I have known members of the bench indicted for larceny, and in one instance for forgery. The evidence of innocence was complete, and yet no one ever thought of censuring the grand jury for finding the bills of indictment. I take it for granted, therefore, that you can entertain no feeling on this subject from the circumstance of your having been a member of the grand jury who found the indictment against ——.

It does not follow that a postmaster must be removed. But this is a charge which may be made against any postmaster in the Union, and has been made against hundreds of them; and if full credit had been given to the statements of malicious persons, without explanation from any quarter, many of the most estimable citizens in the community would have been removed from office in disgrace.

I know of very few large offices in the Union against which such charges have not been made within three years past; and these charges have often been supported by one or more affidavits. On investigating them I have sometimes found that letters were actually in the office which were not found on the first examination by the postmaster, and after an inquiry, where he undertook to answer in the negative, from memory, without making an examination. In some of these cases I have found grounds for censure, and in such instances I have never withheld what appeared to be merited.

On a late occasion the Postmaster at New York informed me, in the most positive manner, that a certain letter was not in his office. This assurance was given in a second answer to me, and the fact stated of several examinations of the office having been made for the letter to no effect. After a lapse of some weeks the identical letter was found in the office, it having been placed among the letters to be advertised. This letter contained money to a considerable amount. Now you can at once see that a malicious witness might make a strong case against the postmaster out of the above facts; and as the letter contained *money*, the motive, in the estimation of such a witness, would be clear. I have, for years, daily investigated charges against postmasters; and I am ignorant of having been once charged with exercising too much lenity. But I have found that no officers of the Government were so liable to be assailed as postmasters, and that the greatest caution was necessary to prevent their becoming the victims of malicious individuals.

An instance lately occurred in Connecticut, where an assistant postmaster was indicted in the Circuit Court of the United States, for breaking open a letter. This, you will observe, is a much more serious offense than the one charged against ——. The traverse jury found this person guilty, at the court where Judge Thompson presided, and the judgment was arrested for a defect in the indictment.

In this case the defendant was a person of respectability, and he sustained little or no injury from the prosecution. The suffrages of his fellow-citizens were conferred upon him at one or two popular elections, and the highest confidence was felt by the community in his integrity. I was requested to appoint him Postmaster by the united recommendation of the Connecticut delegation, and by many of the most respectable citizens of the town in which he lived. I should unquestionably have appointed him if I could have done so without doing injustice to the incumbent by removing him; and whenever a vacancy in the town may occur, I shall give him the appointment. When the indictment was found, I dismissed him from the office, as was done in the case of ——, after his conviction. In the case alluded to, a letter, which proved to be, I think, a lottery circular, directed to the postoffice, was opened by the accused; and the malicious prosecutor contrived to state a great many circumstances of concealment, etc., which aggravated the offense. These, after the trial, were well understood, and by the public properly appreciated.

This case is referred to for the purpose of showing that the finding of a grand jury and a conviction by a petit jury do not always seal the doom of the accused; that public opinion, to which Mr. —— refers, in some possible cases, may so sustain an individual as to place him on higher ground than he before occupied, notwithstanding his accusers, by malice and falsehood, have, through the legal forms of the law, gained a triumph over him.

I argue from cases that may occur, without meaning to give any opinion as to the proceeding against ——. This case I wish to present to your mind as it was presented to mine when I made the appointment.

It is true, I knew —— had been convicted of detaining a letter; but I had before me a letter from the Attorney-General of your State, and one from your Lieutenant-Governor, which speak on the subject in no equivocal language. Of these gentlemen I knew nothing personally, but from the offices they held I was bound to respect their representations—at least so far as regarded Mr. ——'s standing and character. I had also a letter on the same subject from a postmaster of respectable standing. In addition to these, the fact of —— being Sheriff of the county, and possessing in a high degree the confidence of its citizens, was not to be lightly regarded. The petition of about ninety persons, expressing, in his integrity, the highest confidence, and strongly urging his re-appointment, was before me. From all these evidences I could not doubt that he possessed the confidence of his fellow-citizens in a high degree, and that his re-appointment would receive the united approbation of all who were directly interested in the office. Indeed, it appeared to me that a proper regard to public sentiment required his re-appointment. At the time, there was nothing in the office against him, except the late prosecution and some remarks made by the late Postmaster referring to the difficulty he experienced in obtaining from the assistant of —— the property belonging to the office. This, however, had been satisfactorily explained.

I knew nothing of the extensive combination of which you speak; nothing of the military disgrace which you refer to. All these things have been since disclosed to me. You have now the principal facts before you on which I acted. Judge the case on the facts presented. If you would have acted differently from what I did, I doubt whether you could find stronger reasons for doing so than those that may be assigned in justification of the re-appointment.

——— seems never to have been Postmaster, as you have heard, in Massachusetts. I have applied to the War Department for the facts respecting the manner of his leaving the army. Had he, however, been cashiered, it was unknown to me, as it was, also, of his having once been Postmaster, if such had been the fact.

I do not believe that you and I will differ widely in this matter—it would be strange indeed, after looking back to past scenes, if we should.

In all my official conduct, I disdain any other motive than that of a conscientious discharge of my duty—with an eye single to the public welfare. I mistake myself if this is not the case.

Had your letter been received before I re-appointed ———, I should, as I have always done, have appointed the person you named. Had Mr. Cook named a person, he should have been appointed. This has been done, I believe, without a single exception. I felt sincere regret that I had made the appointment before the reception of your letter; but it was then too late, and I did not think it necessary to express my regret in my answer to you. I name this fact, from the disappointment which this answer seems to have given you.

For your success in the late election, although your competitor was an old, and, I believe, a sincere friend of mine, I felt a deep interest. It has been often referred to by me as a triumphant refutation of the scandal which had been so extensively circulated against you.

As Mr. Cook will soon be here, I shall take no step in the case of ———, until his arrival. If he be disposed, I will have a full and free consultation with him on the subject.

With great regard, yours,

JOHN McLEAN.

To His Excellency NINIAN EDWARDS.

P. S.—Since writing the above I have received a communication from the War Department, from which it appears that ——— was not tried by a court martial and dismissed from the service, as has been alleged against him.—J. McL.

WASHINGTON, *November* 17, 1826.

Dear Sir:

I have just received your letter respecting the irregularity of the mail. At this I am astonished and have directed a rigid investigation, and shall not spare delinquents.

The paragraph inclosed is ungenerous to Mr. Cook; as to myself, there is no man in the West whose wishes I have more pleasure in gratifying. I have given him everything he has asked, so far as I now remember, and shall continue to do so, if consistent with the public interest. When he arrives, I will consult him as to giving you a more satisfactory recommendation.

Your friend,
JOHN McLEAN.

GOV. EDWARDS, Belleville, Illinois.

WASHINGTON, *January* 11, 1827.

My Dear Sir:

You have mistaken my disposition. A friend cannot talk too plainly, and I esteem him the more for his frankness. It is true your first letter, respecting the appointment, led me to conclude that you was displeased at not having the person named by you appointed, when I thought I had informed you that, had your letter been received in time, it would have been done, etc.; but, all this aside, I have no doubt of your friendly feeling,

Mr. Cook's name is before the President for Minister to Columbia; it was placed there by me before the commencement of the session. If the President does not appoint him, he will forfeit all the claims of friendship and gratitude. I fear Clay is opposed to the appointment, and, if so, it will not be made. This is only conjecture on my part. I think that Clay could not object to the appointment on the ground of Mr. Cook's vote. So far as I have been informed, no appointment could be made, in the same quarter, more acceptable to the friends of Gen. Jackson. I have heard many of them express great kindness for Mr. Cook, and some of them have expressed a strong wish for his success. His health would be benefited by a journey to the South. This is a consideration which ought to have weight with the President, when everything else is favorable.

Your friend,
JOHN McLEAN.

GOV. N. EDWARDS, Vandalia, Illinois.

WASHINGTON, *March* 19, 1827.

Dear Sir:

A few days since, Mr. Cook left us for Baltimore, with the intention of sailing thence to Havana. He goes there as a secret agent of the Government, and is charged with very important duties. The compensation is $4,500 a year, exclusive of his traveling expenses.

The duties which devolved upon Mr. Cook, as Chairman of the Committee of Ways and Means, after McLane was excused from serving on the committee, were very arduous. The labors were more than his health could bear, independently of the long confinement, every day, to the unwholesome atmosphere of the hall. He, however, continued to exert himself until his physical powers gave way, and he was consequently confined for some weeks, the greater part of the time to his room. We were favored with his company, as one of the family, shortly after he became unwell, and I hope contributed, in some degree, to his comfort and restoration. The business in which he is now engaged is of great importance to the country, and I strongly advised him to go immediately to Cuba, as did also his physician, on account of his health. We entertain a sanguine expectation that this voyage, and a short residence at Havana, will give him better health than he has enjoyed for years. At the same time he will perform public duties important to the country. He will only remain on the island a few weeks, and will then return to Illinois and take Mrs. Cook with him to spend the next winter at Havana. I am sure you will approve of this arrangement; and although the disappointment to Mrs. Cook may be great, at his not returning immediately, yet, on reflection, I trust she will be reconciled and see that it is best. I do not think there is anything in Mr. Cook's health that should excite, in her, alarm; and I shall be greatly disappointed if she does not meet with him in August next, or perhaps in July, in better health than she has seen him for years. He left us in fine spirits, and, in a letter he wrote to me from Baltimore, states that he stood the ride well, and being disappointed in finding a vessel at that place, he was going to Philadelphia. Judge Barton goes with him to Havana, and will return with him to the United States. He has an excellent servant, and, I think, will be as pleasantly situated as could be expected, in the absence of his family. All things considered, I am much pleased at this agency being given to him. He retires from the political contest that now rages, and, standing well with both parties, will be able, in a short time, again to enter into political life with great advantage to his country and to himself.

It is, of course, unnecessary to suggest that this mission should remain a secret, as its great object may be defeated, if it were made public.

Your friend,

JOHN McLEAN.

Gov. Edwards, Vandalia, Illinois.

Washington, *May* 10, 1827.

Dear Sir:

Should a vacancy of Postmaster take place at Carlyle, I have directed the person named by you to be appointed. Mr. Clempson has been informed that the contract for the route he refers to cannot be made, until after public notice shall be given; that this with other routes would shortly be advertised, and that he might bid for a stage with a prospect of success.

I shall certainly take great pleasure in gratifying your wishes in regard to the public accommodation, on this route, that may be necessary, and shall be particularly gratified if the bid of Mr. Clempson shall enable me to give him the contract. As I feel myself bound to make the contract with the lowest responsible bidder, it would be well for Mr. ——— to offer to transport the mail in a two-horse stage on the route, as low as it can be done; and, at the same time, he might bid for a horse transportation on the same route—so that, if he should fail in one, he might have a chance of success on the other bid.

I have not heard from Mr. Cook since he left New York.

Your friend,

JOHN McLEAN.

GOV. EDWARDS, Carlyle, Illinois.

WASHINGTON, *November* 1, 1827.

My Dear Sir:

I have just heard the melancholy intelligence of the death of Mr. Cook. This event is not the less lamented because it was expected. I had cherished a hope, from some recent account, that the waters in Kentucky might restore him to a moderate degree of health, which would enable him to take another southern voyage, which might be the means of restoring him; but we must bow with submission to this afflictive dispensation of Providence. All my family are distressed at his loss, and deeply sympathize with his disconsolate partner. Her sorrows will be mitigated by the soothing advice and protection of her parents. I fear your State cannot supply his place, by a man equally useful and respected, in public life. His race was short, but it has been honorable to himself and useful to his country. No man in Congress, from the West, had a higher standing or could exercise a more extensive influence.

I hope that my late mail arrangements in Illinois have been such as to meet your wishes.

Your sincere friend,

JOHN McLEAN.

GOV. EDWARDS, Belleville, Illinois.

WASHINGTON, *January* 7, 1831.

My Dear Sir:

Your favor of the 14th ult. was received yesterday, and I take great pleasure in informing you that your friend, McKee, has been reappointed to the office he now holds.

The political horizon at this place is overcast. To the man who loves his country, there is no pleasing prospect for the future. I cannot state what I see, much less what I fear. I will, however, continue to hope, even against hope. A more important crisis than the present has not occurred in the annals of our Government. Parties are arrayed against each other, in conflict, on questions of national policy; and unless there be magnanimity and forbearance on both sides, there is ground to fear that the contest may end in the dissolution of the Union. If this shall take place, there is no hope for free government.

The truth is, selfish considerations have too much influence in our public measures. The affairs of the Government should be managed for the benefit of the stockholders, and not the directors. If the patronage of the Government shall be considered as the private property of him who may happen to possess the power, and it be used to advance his views, or any other selfish end, to the neglect of the public service, it will not be long before the moral force of our institutions will be destroyed, and after that they will not be worth preserving.

Mankind can only be governed by moral or physical force. The latter is incompatible with free government. I wish to see the public mind tranquilized by acts of moderation and patriotism on all sides. Our Government was formed on the principles of compromise, and it can only be successfully administered by a constant reference to the foundation on which it rests. If such a policy be opposed to the course of the heated partisan, it will advance the vital interests of the country. The Government was established for the people, and the officers of the Government should never forget that they are the equals of the people. But I need not theorize upon these subjects. They have, no doubt, occupied much of your reflection.

With great respect,

Truly yours,

JOHN McLEAN.

Gov. Edwards, Belleville, Illinois.

War Department, *July* 3, 1821.

Dear Sir:

I have received your favor of the 22d May, and as the reason assigned sufficiently explains the non-attendance of Mr. Whiteside at West Point, he will be allowed till the first of September to report himself there—beyond which period, under the regulations, he cannot be admitted, at least this year.

Should you desire it, your son may be admitted next spring; but if you will permit me to offer you an opinion, I would advise you against his admittance under sixteen years of age, and before he is thoroughly grounded in his English and classical education. With such a preparation, I consider the education at the Military Academy the best which our country affords.

I offer you the most sincere congratulations on the happy connection which your daughter has formed. For Mr. Cook I have a most genuine respect, both for his character and talent; and you have, I think, every reason to hope that the connection will prove propitious. I have read his circular with pleasure. Its independence and sound sense do him much honor. He has adopted the proper mode to build up a lasting popularity.

You do not write to me with more familiarity than what is perfectly acceptable. Thinking, as I do, of the justness of your views and your experience of men and things, your opinion will always be acceptable. I know of but few who judge of life as it really is, so much as yourself; who see it divested of those thousand circumstances which the art and intent of many endeavor to throw about it.

I cannot but think that the movement to hold up the Vice-President, from the quarter to which you refer, is a feint. It may be adopted, but it will be in the last resort, and in despair of anything else. The real object, I should suppose, is founded on a belief that he cannot succeed, and the hope, when it becomes apparent, that he and his friends will support them who apparently were so well disposed to support him. As to myself my course is clear. I think I may say, without the imputation of vanity, that I am much more attached to principle than promotion. The result of this temper is, not to be unduly solicitous about my own advancement, and to form no connection but to advance what I deem the solid and lasting interest of our country. As to the next Presidential election, I have formed no connection with any one, and my ultimate course will be governed by the principle which I have stated.

With sincere respect and esteem,

I am, etc.,

J. C. CALHOUN.

HON. NINIAN EDWARDS, Edwardsville, Illinois.

WASHINGTON, *June* 12, 1822.

My Dear Sir :

I have received your favor of the 22d May, with its inclosure for Mr. Ingham, to which I gave the directions you required.

The information which you communicate as to public sentiment, is very agreeable, and accords with that which I have received from others from the West. Mr. C———d, it seems to me, has now but a single circumstance to hang his hope on: the giving over the Bucktails of New York to his interest. To effect this, his friends in that State are making great efforts to prove that he is more purely of the Jefferson school of politics than any other candidate. If Van Buren can see his way clearly, either as to him or Clay, he will doubtless come out on that side, which may do much mischief in that State. I think Noah gives some indications on that side, but I am told his standing with the party in the city is such as to make it critical for him to make a bold stand. The information from the State is, that her course is not yet taken, but that at present my hold on the public sentiment is much the strongest, particularly out of the city. I understand that Yates, who will be Governor, has expressed himself favorably. It is quite probable that the State will not take any decided stand for any one, but that she will ultimately unite with Pennsylvania in her course. Great changes are taking place in Massachusetts, which will terminate in the entire prostration of the Federal interest in that State, in all probability. A middle interest has grown up. The fruits already are a Republican speaker and a partial Republican representation from Boston, itself. This change must have, in New England, a very considerable bearing on the Presidential election. It will give to that section more weight, which I should suppose would be, in the first instance, in favoring Mr. Adams; and if he cannot be elected, in my favor. Mr. Crawford, or Clay, I suppose, have very little hold on the public sentiment in that portion of the Union.

From South Carolina the information is favorable. Mr. L.'s friends have not yet yielded all hopes, but they are willing to pledge themselves in favor of a candidate from the State. Hayne, the Attorney-General, and one of the first men in the State, will oppose Smith, and, it is said, will doubtless be elected. This is a great point. The election for Senators, which will take place before the 6th of March next, is of the utmost importance. Most of the vacancies will occur in the South and West. Poindexter, I understand, will oppose Williams of Mississippi. What is Thomas' prospect? Will you leave him out? Though he is a man of moderate talents, yet much depends on his being left out.

The radical paper in this place continues its attacks on me with great violence. It is doubtless under the influence of Mr. Crawford, who, I perceive, gives it the treasury advertisements, though its circulation is so limited. It is perhaps as well that they should spend their ammunition at long shot. The necessity of a paper here, however, becomes more apparent, even from their feeble attacks. The establishment of an able and active paper in the city is almost everything, in fact, in the coming contest. Col McKinney, who is a very honest and honorable man, has proposed to establish such an one. He informs me that he has associated with him a first rate writer, and that he will be devoted to the cause of the Administration. I send you several copies of his prospectus, which you will perceive is written with spirit. I believe nothing but a respectable list of subscribers is wanting to put a powerful engine in action. In this you can do much in the West, particularly in your State, Kentucky and Missouri. The arrangement ought to be so made, that whatever subscribers are obtained may be returned in due time.

Our friend, Mr. McDuffie, will meet, in all probability, Col. Cumming, on the 7th inst., between Augusta and Savannah, on the Carolina side of the river. God grant that he may be safe! I have, however, a strange foreboding, which I put to the account of great solicitude for him. We will hear the result in three days at the farthest.

I am glad to hear that Col. McKee remains sound. Spain declines running the line for the present, of which he has been apprized, with the strongest assurance that the President will be glad of any opportunity of promoting his wishes.

I will be anxious to hear from you after your arrival at home. Much will depend on the West.

The Ministers to our Southern neghbors will not, in all probability, be selected till the meeting of Congress. I am decidedly of the opinion that one ought to be from the West, and that you ought to be the man. I will act accordingly.

My best respects to Mr. Cook; and believe me to be,

Yours, truly,

J. C. CALHOUN.

HON. NINIAN EDWARDS, Edwardsville, Illinois.

WAR DEPARTMENT, *August* 20, 1822.

My Dear Sir:

Since I wrote to you last, your several communications of the 13th June, and 5th, 14th and 27th of July, have been received. I take much interest in Mr. Cook's election, and shall wait with great impatience to learn the result. He is honest, capable and bold—just such a man as the times require; his absence from Congress would be a serious loss.

Since the return of the President to the city, I have urged on his attention the subject of making appointments to the offices to which you referred, and brought before him the names which you mentioned. He took the names down, and informed me that so soon as he had finished the investigation of the proceedings of the court-martial in the case of Lieut. Abbott, which he was then investigating, he would attend to the subject, and requested me so to inform you. I do trust that he begins to feel the necessity of taking a decided stand. I agree with you that it is much easier to put down the opposition, where its existence is once acknowledged, than to prove, to the satisfaction of the people, its existence. Until the President shall uniformly make the distinction between friends and foes, in his appointments, this cannot be done. If he will not see the opposition as it is, or if he did not, the country will be incredulous as to its existence. These ideas I have urged on him. That he fully comprehends the opposition I cannot doubt, and do hope he will act in such a manner as to leave no doubt, on the minds of the people, that he knows what is the continual state of things. For myself, I care less for my own prospects than I do for the welfare of the Administration. Identified, as I am, with it, approving its policy, I shall use every effort to maintain it in the good opinion of the people. The new paper here, if supported by a decided course on the part of the President, will aid much in bringing out the opposition. You will see that its tone is decisive, and that it knows what it is about.

Since the adjournment, no great change has occurred on this side of the mountains. Pennsylvania is firm. The symptoms in Maryland, Delaware New Jersey, Connecticut, and the New England States, generally appear favorable. In Virginia and North Carolina, they are also fully as much so as at the adjournment. The same cannot be said of New York; Van Beuren, for the present, has taken his stand in favor of Mr. C——d, as being the most suitable to his purpose of opposing the Administration. The "Advocate," which is under his influence, has made a demonstration the same way. He has not openly taken his grounds, but leaves no doubt as to his course. It is, however, the opinion of Noah (I have it from a letter of his to a particular friend of his) that neither Mr. C——d or myself will be elected, but that some third person, whom he does not name, will be. With this impression his zeal will not be great, and he will take care, at least for the present, not to commit himself too fully to prevent him from going back.

It seems, by the papers, that Tennessee has put Gen. Jackson in nomination. What will be the effect of this step, particularly in the West? It is certainly adverse to Mr. Clay; but how will it affect others? We now exhibit the extraordinary fact of five persons from the slaveholding States being before the people for the highest office in their gift, and but one from the non-slaveholding States. This gives Mr. Adams great advantages, if he knew how to improve them.

It is strange, after the appointment of Thomas, that Mr. C——d should have appointed Lourie's brother to inspect the land offices. He wants discretion in an extraordinary degreee, and ought to be made to feel the effects of it in this case. I am told he has conferred an appointment on another brother of Lourie. If any evidence could be had of Thomas having electionered for him, while engaged in making his inspection last year, it would have a strong effect on the public mind. His intrigue and management would make his election dangerous to the country. The appointments to South America will not be made, unless something should occur, till after the next meeting of Congress. On many accounts it would be imprudent to make them now.

I am much gratified with your statement as to the public feelings in the West in relation to the subject of lead mines. You have seen the course adopted by the Department, and I hope it is such as to meet your approbation. That Benton has been counteracted I attribute wholly to you, who, alone, fully understood the subject in the Senate, and had the energy to meet it boldly. Benton had been long in maturing his plan of attack, and no doubt anticipated much success from it against the Administration.

Your friend, Fisher, of North Carolina, I see is elected a member of the State Legislature. I mention the fact so that you might avail yourself of it, in your correspondence with him. North Carolina will doubtless become the scene of much political intrigue, on the part of Mr. C——d and his friends. It is, as yet, unoccupied ground.

Yours, truly,

J. C. CALHOUN.

To Hon. Ninian Edwards, Edwardsville, Illinois.

War Department, *Oct.* 5, 1822.

Dear Sir:

I have, since my last to you, received your several favors from the 3d August to the 14th September, and I am very happy to learn, from the last, that your health, which had been bad, has improved. I hope by your next to hear of its entire restoration.

The President left this city for Albemarle, a few days since, and will probably be absent till the 20th of this month. I forwarded your letter to him on the day which I received it. He has not yet made the appointments, which I suppose he has communicated to you, as he informed me that he would write to you on the subject. Had returns of the survey been made, the appointments would doubtless have been made also; none, however, have been received, and I believe no reason has been assigned for the delay. Without the official returns, the President felt a delicacy in acting.

That he has taken his stand to support his administration I cannot doubt. It is high time that he should. If longer delayed, the worst of consequences must result. With firmness, his administration must terminate in a manner honorable to himself and fortunate for the country; without it, the very reverse must follow.

The "Republican" has already affected a prodigious change. The *administration* is no longer assailed by the papers which support Mr. C——d. This they dare not do, while he remains *a member* of the administration. His present attempt is to attribute the *disposition* to *those who espouse* the opposition, and not to him and his friends, who have been the *authors* of it. A few articles in the Western papers, anticipating this course and showing its futility, would be of *much service.*

Things have reached, or will at least, at the next session, reach, a crisis. This, then, is an important moment. No one can have a greater influence or render to the country more important service than yourself. The struggle is between cunning and wisdom—political virtue and vice. The opposition to the Administration is unprincipled, and its overthrow by such an opposition would give a fatal example. Much will depend on the course pursued by the States, and they again will be much under the influence of the messages of the respective Governors. You know Adair, McNair and several others, and have it, I suppose, in your power to give a right direction to their messages. If no more can be done, it would be a great point for them to come out in favor of the Administration, but still more *to notice* the opposition to it. In fact, I think it would be decisive. If you correspond with Jackson, much of the same kind might be done through him. In the South it can be easily attended to.

Cook's election has afforded much gratification. He not only has talents, but is bold and resolute. The reëlection of Thomas would have a very bad effect. You must run but one, and if necessary you ought to come to an understanding. As connected with this subject, I hope the return of the survey may be received in time to make the appointments before it is too late to have the proper effect. The President directed their return forthwith. I do not in the least doubt that he will select the very respectable gentlemen whom you recommended.

You must take care of your health. It is valuable not only to yourself and family, but to the country. To give a right direction at this moment to our politics, is of the highest importance to the lasting interest of the republic Almost as much depends on it as on the late war.

Yours truly,

J. C. CALHOUN.

To Hon. Ninian Edwards, Edwardsville, Illinois.

WASHINGTON, *May* 21, 1823.

My Dear Sir:

I have been prevented from acknowledging your letter of the 16th April as early as I expected, by various causes—among which is an indisposition, from which I am just recovering. You write in a spirit of frankness which is very gratifying. I have no doubt that Mr. Adams has advanced much in popularity, within the last few months, and that he is particularly strong; still he has great difficulties to encounter, which time only can determine whether he can surmount. As to myself, I do not suppose that, at this moment, I am as strong as Mr. Adams; still, should the latter not take New York or Virginia, it would be more difficult to elect him than myself. The position which I occupy in Pennsylvania is in many respects more favorable than that which he does in New England, which, with the fact that there are fewer objections against me than him, may not improbably give me a final advantage.

As to Mr. C——d, he visibly declines. North Carolina, it is generally thought, is against him; he is doubtful in Virginia; and it is thought that he has but a slight chance of taking New York. His party is in a clear minority of the Republicans in the city, and, as the opposite side is now organized, it is expected that it will extend its influence rapidly over the State, things being ripe for change. Mr. Clay gains nothing on this side, and is now but little spoken of. He is not strong in a single Atlantic State.

* * * * * * I have often conversed with the President in relation to you, and he has ever spoken as your friend. I have every reason to believe that he intends to give due proof of it before the expiration of his term. I suggested your name for Mexico, not knowing whether you would approve of it or not. Believing that you possess qualities which are well calculated to advance the interest and honor of the country in a foreign mission, I would be highly gratified if the most important of all the appointments of that kind, connected with this continent, should be conferred on you. I must, at the same time, express my belief that few men are more important, at this moment, as connected with our domestic politics; few are so well acquainted with the actual state of things, with the character, the means and views of that faction which has reared its head among us—or with the means of resisting it with effect. I do trust that, if not otherwise engaged in the public service, you will by all means be in your place at the next session. We must remember that the faction has directed its efforts to carry that body, mainly, and that in it is the principal seat of its power. The standing or prospect of every public man must in a great degree depend on the issue of the struggle; and none more than yourself.

With sincere regard,

J. C. CALHOUN.

To HON. NINIAN EDWARDS, Edwardsville, Illinois.

WASHINGTON, *July* 20, 1823.

My Dear Sir:

I fear that your indisposition has continued, or that your letters miscarry. I have heard from you but once since you left the city, and that while you were on your way home. Placing, as I do, the highest confidence in your judgment and friendship, your letters are read with peculiar gratification, and I never fail to acknowledge them as early as circumstances will permit.

Events are progressing steadily in the course which all anticipated when you left the city. The Radical cause, with its head, is daily declining. I consider it as certain that Mr. C——d is now in a minority in every State—Georgia and perhaps Virginia, excepted. He does not stand, in New York, higher than third best. The "Advocate" has been discarded by the Republican party, and a new and able paper, the "Patriot," adopted in its place. It is decidedly hostile to C——d. In North Carolina the change has gone on steadily in my favor, and I am now decidedly ahead in that State. I hold it certain that our side must prevail; but whether it will be under myself, may be more doubtful. That, I think, will depend on New York; should she declare for either Adams or myself, the election will be decided by the people without going to the House of Representatives.

You see there is a new Postmaster-General. I hope the appointment will give satisfaction. I did not fail to bring up your name for consideration; and though, as between you and Judge McLean, I could take no active part —believing you both to be highly qualified—I would certainly have been not less gratified with your appointment than his. I believe that the scale was principally turned by the apprehension that the precarious state of your health might prevent you from bestowing that incessant labor and attention which the extensive duties and the greatly disordered state of the Department render indispensable. It was in arrear $40,000 the last quarter, with a prospect of a heavy deficit in the third and fourth quarters.

You may be assured there is no one whose advancement would give me more sincere pleasure than yourself. I believe there is no one whose zeal and abilities give a stronger claim on the Administration.

With sincere regard,

J. C. CALHOUN.

To HON. NINIAN EDWARDS, Edwardsville, Illinois.

WASHINGTON, *September* 23, 1823.

My Dear Sir:

I have been much pleased with Gen. Green. He is intelligent and decisive, and must, in time, become important in the West. I have conversed with him freely, and he can give you full information of the state of things in this quarter. Great changes have taken place. I now consider my prospect at least equal in New York; in fact, I feel confident it is much the best. In Pennsylvania, I hold my own; Jackson and myself divide the State. In New Jersey, I am at least as strong as Adams; there is no other interest there.

In New England, a strange state of things exists; though Adams is the strongest, there is a strong feeling that his position is not a firm one. North Carolina has began the contest at last. Of twelve papers in that State, six are for me; two for C———d; one for Adams, but preferring me to C———d; another for him, but not decided between C———d and myself; another against C———d, but not decided between A——— and myself; and another not yet out. My friends all say that I will certainly take the State.

I hope that you will not think of retiring. Your efforts in the present crisis are of the greatest importance. Few men can have greater influence over the destiny of the country than yourself, at this time. Your capacity, intelligence and firmness are all important.

With sincere respect,

I am, etc., etc.,

J. C. CALHOUN.

To Hon. Ninian Edwards, Edwardsville, Illinois.

Washington, *February* 15, 1831.

Dear Sir:

I inclose a copy of the correspondence between Gen. Jackson and myself, which has been the subject of so much speculation of late. The publication became indispensable in self-defense.

You will see that the whole affair was got up for my political destruction, and that an individual who has heretofore been so much misunderstood by the people (I mean Mr. Crawford), makes a capital but certainly not a very enviable figure in the plot. The publication places his character in its true light, and he is abandoned here even by his former friends and supporters.

It is really surprising that Gen. Jackson should have surrendered himself so entirely to those who were formerly his most bitter enemies. By what art it has been effected, the correspondence will in part explain; but to unfold it fully would require a volume. It remains to be seen whether the force of public indignation will not open his eyes to his thraldom.

As to myself, I may say, with truth, that I never stood stronger. The correspondence is considered by all sides a complete vindication.

I have received the letters, which you addressed to me, and am under obligations to you for your friendly feelings towards me. I did not answer them, because things were so situated that I could say nothing satisfactory. There is one point in your correspondence which I must, in duty to a friend, notice. I do not think you do justice to Mr. Ingham. I believe I may say that, had he had his own way, things would not have gone, on all points, in the same direction in his Department.

With great respect,

I am, etc., etc.,

J. C. CALHOUN.

To Hon. N. Edwards, Belleville, Illinois.

[NOTE.—The letters and papers in my possession give the following facts in regard to the occupation of Pensacola and St. Marks, from which it will be seen that Gen. Jackson had no just ground for being dissatisfied with Mr. Calhoun:

When Mr. Monroe called a Cabinet council to determine on the answer to be given to the Spanish Minister, in reply to his complaint of the occupation of Pensacola and St. Marks, Mr. Calhoun, being Secretary of War, was of the opinion that his orders did not authorize the occupation of those posts; that instructions to seize them would be an act of war, which the Secretary of War had no right to make; and in this opinion the Cabinet, with the exception of Mr. Adams, were unanimous. The next proposition was, how far was Gen. Jackson justifiable in taking those posts? Upon this point Mr. Calhoun was of opinion that the propriety of the conduct of the Commander-in-Chief, depending upon contingencies happening upon the spot, that Gen. Jackson, in the field, might do what he, as Secretary of War, had no right to order him to do, and that, as an act of justice to Gen. Jackson, a court of inquiry would afford him (Gen. Jackson) the means of placing the facts of the case in an official shape before the Cabinet, and thus enable the Administration to give a proper answer to the Spanish Minister. Upon this point Mr. Monroe suggested that there were considerations, growing out of the existing relations between the United States and Spain, which might make it proper to sustain Gen. Jackson without a court of inquiry; and after mature deliberation, which lasted three days, the entire Cabinet, consisting of Mr. Crawford, Mr. Wirt, Mr. Adams and Mr. Calhoun (Mr. Crowninshield being absent), concurred. During the discussion of the Seminole question in Congress, in 1819, Gen. Jackson having expressed his determination to go to the House of Representatives, "threatening to cut off the ears of some of the members," in a general consultation among his friends, Gov. Edwards having expressed his opinion that there was no one whose friends could, in a proper manner, use greater freedom than could Gen. Jackson's with him, was unanimously selected to communicate to him the views and wishes of his friends on the subject of his determination. The result showed that Gov. Edwards properly appreciated Gen. Jackson's character.—N. W. EDWARDS.]

NEW HOPE, *August* 20, 1823.

Dear Sir:

It is long since I intended to have written to you, but have wanted some special impulse, and things have been approaching so gradually to the point you so much desire, that there was no more motive for writing on any one day than on the preceding, and hence the delay. I have seen intelligent men from various parts of this State, from New Jersey and from New York, and have had an extensive correspondence in some of the other States. Nothing can be more clearly ascertained than that Mr. Crawford is completely prostrate. He has been on an inclined plane for some time, but has been descending with an accelerated velocity every moment, since he received the propelling stroke from "A. B." Van Buren, who had taken his cue from the Treasury, instead of watching public opinion, came out the moment he got home in the spring; but his own paper at Albany, and Noah's, are the only ones he has yet got out in New York. Root and Yates incline with him, but they are extremely cautious how they commit themselves. Latterly, however, all the papers that have been tinged with radicalism seems to have lost sight of Mr. Crawford, and affect to regard the salvation of the Republican party as their only wish—and, with this view, throw themselves on a caucus. They have been lead to believe that Mr. C——d would have a majority there; and here rests their hope. The only misfortune resulting from this is, that they prevent that free discussion which would otherwise take place. My opinion is that we ought to meet them in caucus, and show to the nation that he can-

—63

not succeed there. None would be nominated, I grant; but better so than leave them in possession of the caucus and perhaps one-half of the Republican party to rally upon, which, with the aid of Mr. Clay, in the West, would soon form a new coalition that would be troublesome hereafter. I hear that about ten of the New York delegation will be opposed to Crawford, in caucus; others uncertain. In New Jersey he will get but one, and in Pennsylvania none; Maryland three or four; in Ohio I can hear of none; in all New England not one, if we have a *viva voce* vote, which ought to be a *sine qua non.* What can we have to fear, then, of putting them down in caucus? They have been driven from all their Democratic pretensions, and now rely upon this usage alone to sustain them. Shall we beat them, as heretofore, by pre-occupying their ground, or leave it to them to rally upon? You will have seen the result of the Pittsburg meeting, where Mr. C——d was induced to believe he had a hold: not even a friend to receive him. This has given them a sore stroke, and not less so to Mr. Clay, who had hopes there. I should not be much surprised if Jackson were to supersede C—y in the West, to a great extent. Here he is not much talked about, as their own enemies pretend to push Mr. Gregg along on his back. We have no doubt of carrying our Governor. Every thing, in that respect, looks well, and will give a strong ground to rally upon.

Yours, respectfully,

S. D. INGHAM.

To Hon. Ninian Edwards, Edwardsville, Illinois.

P. S.—Mrs. Ingham joins in her respects to you. She will *scarcely be in Washington this winter.* Let me hear from you. Ought not the caucus meeting (which I have no doubt will break up without a nomination) be held early in the session, to give the papers more time afterwards?—S. D. I.

New Hope, *June* 5, 1824.

Dear Sir:

I have just now heard of your expected arrival at Washington. I do not suppose that any hint from me would add to your stock of intellectual powder in the present crisis. You will of course send a replication, and as the committee have adopted all of Mr. Crawford's excuses but one, viz: that deficiency upon his definition of *cash*—you will have an opportunity of rebutting the committee's reasoning under the cover of a replication to Mr. Crawford. Do not forget that you are writing for the popular eye and ear, which requires things to be made plain. By picking the committee thus covertly, they will be thrown upon their own defense. W—— is understood, but I much mistake if he believes in the estimate of Mr. Crawford's management by a percentage. They have made a sad blunder; the loss, instead of being estimated on eight years' receipts, as I suppose it is, viz: three years after these losses have accrued, and two years before they commenced—ought to have been estimated on three or at most four years' receipts, and then for public lands with a small amount of internal tax. But, again, these losses are upon moneys actually paid, and have accrued by reason of the credit extended to banks. If we make an estimate upon the debt accrued in the same time, or for any portion of it before 1821, we shall find that the whole was sponged to avoid loss to the Government and ruin to the debtors. Let your reply be mild, and forbear to draw any conclusions as to motives; and wage a defensive war by *an offensive operation.*

A committee who could excuse the receipt of the uncurrent notes from the Missouri Bank, as has been done, you may rest assured will acquit Mr. C——d of any motive that is improper.

Your reply will be read by everybody. You cannot, therefore, take too much pains. If Cook is at W———, tell him to write me. Also a line from you will be useful.

Yours, truly,

S. D. INGHAM.

To HON. N. EDWARDS, Washington.

P. S.—I have written Taylor to give him my opinion of the report. The *quo animo* is too apparent. The more I examine it, the less I think of the author. Things plain are obscured with much address to screen even the blunder of the Secretary. Among the members it was considered as a declaration of *peccavit* and a studied effort to excuse him.

Do not fail to inquire, in your reply, how the Tennessee notes were cashed? viz: in payment of pensions!!—S. D. I.

NEW HOPE, *June* 8, 1824.

Dear Cook:

I have this moment received your favor of the 3d, and hasten to comply with your request—but with all the disadvantage of not having Mr. Crawford's answer, as to the Mitchell case, before me. I failed to bring the printed report of the committee, and our papers have not republished the documents which accompanied the report. In such case, and for other good reasons, I shall not attempt to suggest a formal answer to the Secretary on the M———l case, but, as you have suggested it, I will endeavor to suggest the points which appear to me most material to be presented.

I think Gov. E. has acted wisely in declaring his determination not to be drawn into an accusation of Mr. Crawford. In this he ought to persevere, and place himself strongly on the voluntary and gratuitous character of Mr. C——d's attacks upon him—uncalled for by circumstances and more especially uncalled by the resolution. The greatest difficulty in maintaining this position will be found in the Mitchell case. As he has charged Mr. C——d with a desire to "screen his friend," if I recollect the memorial (I have it not before me) upon this point, he may rest upon the *probable cause* for the imputation, which will be found in an editorial answer to this charge which was published in the "City Gazette," in (I think) June last, where the reason given for withholding the document was that Mitchell was Mr. C——d's friend, and as there was a disposition to persecute him by others, he (Mr. C——d) would not aid them by sending the document. I believe the "City

Gazette" article was republished *in extenso* in the "Washington Republican" last summer, with comments. The character of the "City Gazette," its relation to Mr. C——d, and every thing, gives the defense a stamp of authority which would justify any one in supposing that it had his sanction. To suppose that he would permit such a defense to pass unnoticed, from a press so devoted to his interests, would be to impute to him a pretense of double-dealing more discreditable to him than the motive alleged in the "Gazette," viz: that of *screening his friend*—having laid the foundation for a probable ground for the imputation in that publication under his eye, etc. You have his admission that Mitchell was his *intimate friend*, with whom he was in the habit of private correspondence—which being notorious, left no other explanation so natural of Mr. C——d's motive for withholding the document; because, without the benefit of the Secretary's declaration that the omission was truly accidental, it could scarcely have been believed, after so serious a charge had been made against so intimate a friend, and a call from the House of Representatives for all the information relating to it had been made, that the Secretary could have forgotten that he had received the document withheld; and unless he had forgotten it, there was no way of accounting for his omission to inform the House, in his report, that there were other important and material documents which were mislaid. After placing these facts in strong colors, to justify the *probable ground* for the belief that the suppression of these documents could have been for no other purpose than to screen his friend, I would concede to his declaration all the verity which the high responsibility of the Secretary, etc., etc., ought to demand. This position would probably acquire additional strength by adverting to another defense of the Secretary, which appeared in the "National Intelligencer" last winter, which wholly omits to mention the *accidental* cause of the suppression. The two grounds of defense are, that Mitchell's letters were private and that McIntosh's was *substantially* communicated. I have not the papers before me, and can, therefore, only advert generally, but I think it would be well to make extracts from both articles and incorporate them into the answer. You will perceive that I suppose you to understand the facts in the case. I therefore confine my remarks to such matters as are suggested by reflection on the facts. Mr. C——d's labors to show that he could not have had any view to screening his friend, because the letter withheld was calculated to exculpate him—the use made of this letter by the Attorney-General—will destroy such a probability. It (the letter of 25th Dec.) constitutes the main ground on which *he* convicts Mitchell. But it will be impossible to put the public fully in possession of this subject, without a development of the Cabinet measures in relation to it.

I have understood, from various quarters, from desultory conversations on this subject, that Mr. Crawford submitted certain documents relating to Mitchell to the Attorney-General, before the call of Congress; that the Attorney-General advised a prosecution of Mitchell, which was never done. Next came the call of Congress. Soon after it was answered, Gov. Clark made formal charges against Mitchell. These were referred to the Attorney-General, who recommended that the whole papers be sent to Congress in answer to the call. This matter was considered in Cabinet council, and it was determined inexpedient to send the papers; but the whole subject was referred to the Attorney-General, who reported at large against M——l, whereupon he was removed by the President. This proceeding was therefore independent of the call of Congress, and the document sent by Gov. Clark not embraced within it.

The documents withheld are two letters of Mitchell's, dated 25th Dec., 1817, and 3d Feb., 1818 (both of which are noticed in the Attorney-General's report as letters *not before him*—that of the 25th Dec. "misplaced"); another letter from McIntosh, the Collector, with an inclosure from McIntosh, the Surveyor. These directly charged Mitchell, while the *letters sent* did not.

Mr. C——d says they were private letters from Mitchell. This is not the fact. Their contents import them to be public; and as the correspondence related to Treasury duties, and part of it was from a Treasury officer—the Collector at Darien—it was proper for the public files of the Department. All these matters may be introduced into the answer or replication, by way of showing that the defense made in the "National Intelligencer," during the last winter, which I have adverted to, did not explain the true reason for withholding the documents, which had been before given in the "City Gazette," or at least the most probable and consistent reason—the accidental misplacing of the documents not having been noticed in either of those defenses, nor anywhere else in public, though public attention was often called to the fact, or the suppression could not have been thought of by Gov. E., nor the extreme *forgetfulness* of the Secretary, when he answered the call, to which alone can now be attributed his failure to inform Congress of the existence of the misplaced documents. Gov. E., I think, may now rest himself very strongly upon the charge of *forgetfulness*. The case is nearly as strong a one as that which occurred some years ago, of a woman who was moving to the Western country with her family, and having stopped at a tavern, started again, leaving a sucking child asleep, wholly *forgotten*, till the wagons had passed a mile on the road and the landlord had overtaken her!

It appears to me there will be no difficulty in disposing of this matter, by establishing the *probable cause* as to the desire to screen his friend, and thus to place him in a most awkward and weak position, resting wholly for an excuse upon the most extraordinary and incredible forgetfulness; which excuse will have been rendered all but contemptible by the argument maintaining the *probable cause*.

I have written in such haste and so desultory, relying upon your seeing through the same medium that I do, that I fear I may not be understood. To prevent this, I should remark that the character of the reply should be made *defensive*, on this point, as well as the others, which is done by substituting C——d's own defense in the "City Gazette," for the charge of improper motive, contained in the memorial; by resisting the ground of defense taken in the "National Intelligencer," as highly improbable, because it admits the existence of documents of which the Secretary gave no notice in his answer to the call of the House; which failure was wholly inexplicable, without the knowledge of the accidental loss of the documents, and the supposition that their existence was wholly forgotten by the Secretary at the time he made his report to the House. It appears to me, that as a main object is to make the original position strong, the reply should rest upon facts within the knowledge of Gov. E. when he wrote the address; and subsequent matter, developed in Mr. C.'s answer, or the documents, or the reasoning of the committee used for illustration, or combatted (without being referred to) by arguments founded on facts previously known.

I do not perceive the least objection to using the newspaper articles I have mentioned in the way proposed. It was held, in Pennsylvania, in a case of impeachment, that an anonymous newspaper article was good ground to institute an official inquiry into the conduct of a public officer.

I must close, as the mail will not serve me again for two days, and if this can be of any use you must have it soon.

The documents in M——l's case, are the report of the Attorney-General, the resolutions and answer. Then see Gov. Clark's correspondence with McIntosh, Mitchell's defense in pamphlet, two articles in the "W—— Republican," early in February last.

Give my best respects to the Governor, to which add those of Mrs. Ingham, and

Believe me,

Sincerely yours,

S. D. INGHAM.

To Daniel P. Cook.

New Hope, *July* 8, 1824.

My Dear Sir:

I duly received your letter. Its advent had been somewhat anticipated, but was not on that account neglected.

When we consider that the committee had published their opinion of Mr. Crawford's conduct, I cannot but think the last report a triumph for you, not only over Mr. C——d, but the committee. The latter are in a most awkward predicament; they have admitted too many facts to justify their conclusion as to the *general correctness* of his fiscal management, which, by the size, is too qualified a commendation to do him any good. The loans to the District banks seem to be understood everywhere—they are too plain to be mystified by any cunning, after the acknowledged *illegality* and dangerous tendency of the measure.

I would have written to you sooner, but did not know that you remained at Washington. I left my documents with Mr. Cook, who had forgotten to forward them. I have not the Secretary's report and documents, nor your memorial, nor the report of the committee; if they are left with you, be so good as to have them forwarded.

I was pleased with the scrutiny of Reddick, by Cook; but he ought to have asked him whether several of the banks whose bills were transferred under the negotiation of March 2d, 1820, did not stop payment after the 9th of August, 1819, and before the 2d of March, 1820. His answer clearly shows that the deposits were not *specific*, according to any definition of that word given by any witness; they were, of course, *general*, *i. e. cash*. Such was the intention of the contract, *no doubt;* but if it were not, what sort of contract was it? Was it prudent and safe for the United States? Was it lawful to allow a bank, or any body, to use public money for one or two years, or a single day, and return it in depreciated notes?

The committee say there is no evidence that Mr. Crawford knew of the payment of the Tennessee notes to pensioners—the committee are very prompt in deciding points upon *absent* testimony. There is, however, a letter, among the correspondence last published, from Mr. Crawford to the cashier of one of the Tennessee banks, written after that bank had *stopped*, in which he proposes to him to disburse the notes about to be transferred from Missouri (March 2, 1820) as heretofore; referring to a previous letter by date, which directs the *disbursement to pensioners*. Mr. Cook was aware of this letter. I called his attention to it.

I feel anxious to see your reply. I cannot understand your motive for resigning. I fear it will give your enemies some advantage, unless the investigation is progressing before another tribunal which will do you more ample justice; but in that case, would you not have stood as well without resigning? But as I do not understand, I cannot judge.

Let me hear from you. There is no danger but the public will do you justice.

Respectfully, yours,

S. D. INGHAM.

To HON. NINIAN EDWARDS, Washington.

NEW HOPE, *July* 20, 1824.

My Dear Sir:

I duly received your favor of the 16th, and the same mail brought the report of the committee, and documents, which is the first view I have had of your whole defense. Upon all the charges and specifications, you have made out your case completely. * * * * * * * *

I would not dwell on Noble's testimony. Those who believe him will consider it no unusual *finesse* among politicians, and it will have much less effect than you suppose. You have already given it the proper answer—"Let the charge be made and you will meet it;" but do not avoid meeting them on the matters which concern Mr. Crawford most vitally. I think Mr. Webster must have winced under your exposition of his report on the uncurrent notes. I am not sure you have done right by resigning. * * * *

So far as the testimony has been published, where I have been, the current is most decidedly against the Secretary, and especially on account of his loan to the District banks. Had it been published a little sooner, and more generally, our Fourth of July toasts would have been full of it. I shall do what I can to have your defense published, and will give a summary of the case for our country papers, as soon as I can get my documents. Cook has not sent them, and I have written to Mr. Clark for a set entire of this good and able report.

If you do not go West, you ought to go North—as far as Saratoga. It would have a good effect.

Very respectfully, yours,

S. D. INGHAM.

To Hon. Ninian Edwards, Shepardstown, Virginia.

Donaldsonville, Louisiana, *Aug.* 10, 1823.

My Dear Sir :

In consequence of my absence from this place, during the greater part of the summer, your letter of the 10th of May did not reach me until yesterday.

* * * * * * * * * *

The Presidential election does not excite much interest in this State, as yet, but the public sentiment seems to be in favor of Clay and Adams, and I think that one of them will receive the vote of the State; and it is most probable that Adams will be supported by the State of Mississippi. *Entre nous.* Our friend Calhoun cannot succeed at the next election. Since Adams' contest with Russell I have considered Calhoun's chance as hopeless. He has as many personal friends and is as much admired as either of the candidates, but being a young man, he was not generally thought of for the Presidency.

With sincere regard and esteem, I am, sir,

Your friend and obedient servant,

H. JOHNSON.

To Hon. Ninian Edwards, United States Senate, Washington.

Near Huntsville, Madison County, Alabama, *August* 8, 1824.

Dear Sir :

I received your favor, dated 18th ulto., by last mail, since which time I have not had a personal interview with Judge Kelly, and probably may not shortly, as he is frequently absent on professional business. I would suggest the propriety of your addressing him on the subject to which you refer. Nothing of a similar nature ever astonished me more than the general character of the testimony given before the committee by Gen. Noble, and particularly that part of it which has relation to the authorship of the "A. B." publications, not only because I know that among the members of Congress it was generally if not universally understood and believed that you were the author, but because I had some conversation with Gen. Noble, pending your nomination, in relation to this subject, in which a reference having been made to the authorship as forming some objection to the confirmation of your nomination by some of the friends of Mr. Crawford, I am clearly and decidedly of opinion that, on this occasion, I was authorized, from the general tenor of Mr. Noble's remarks, to infer that whether you were the author or not would have or had produced no influence on his mind; that he thought you were capable, and, although he was friendly to Mr. Crawford, he would still support your nomination—intimating, at the same time, that the President might have made a more judicious selection, as he had also done in reference to his nomination of Mr. Southard for the Navy Department. As respects the conversation of which he speaks as having occurred between you and himself at his room, I can only say that, as to the time he came to board with Mrs. Queen, I think it was about the 20th of February, and a few days after your nomination to the Senate, and while you were very much indisposed and confined to your bed. As to your indisposition when he came, for some time before and afterwards, I know I cannot be mistaken, because I was in the habit of calling to see you every night and morning. It is also perfectly in my recollection that the day on the evening of which I informed you Gen. Noble had moved to take up your nomination, I had been informed you had experienced a severe shake of the ague, and at the time I gave you this information you were confined to your bed, and appeared much exhausted, and continued confined and much weakened and debilitated, I think, for six or eight days, and perhaps more.

If the publicity of any circumstance within my recollection, relative to this transaction, may be thought necessary, to do justice to an individual whom an unprincipled set of politicians have oppressed and persecuted, and whose crime has been his conviction, conscientiously formed, that Wm. H. Crawford, *a political apostate*, was unworthy the confidence of the people of the United States, I can have no objection.

The information I gave as coming from Gen. Noble, relative to his having moved the consideration of your nomination, as it may involve a breach of confidence *implied only* from the nature of the transaction, I would, unless very essential, except.

And as I was also in the habit of conversing with Judge Kelly on the same subject, it may have been from him I received it.

With sincere regard and esteem,

Very respectfully,

Your obedient servant,

GABRIEL MOORE.

To Hon. Ninian Edwards.

Near Huntsville, Madison County, Alabama, *October* 10, 1825.

Dear Friend:

I have received your favor dated 18th June. Judge Kelly was, at the time of its reception, absent—having taken a trip on professional business to Mobile. On his return, I addressed him on the subject of your communication, and took the liberty to inclose your letter, and his reply I herewith inclose you. His recollection on the subject referred to seems not as distinct as I had presumed it would have been.

I am much gratified to hear of the favorable prospect of your restoration to health; and let me assure you it will at all times give me great pleasure to hear of your prosperity and welfare. My hearty prayers have been with you in all difficulty and persecution, and I still hope to see you prosper, and to know the decline and decay of the standing of your enemies, which has been so unworthily obtained.

I can give you nothing of a political character, from this quarter, which would be interesting. The Alabamians and, I believe, the Tennesseans also, at this time, have it strongly in contemplation to make a hard struggle to supplant Mr. Adams with "Old Hickory" at the expiration of the first term. His Administration, in this section of the country, has become extremely unpopular recently. The appointment of Mr. King and the unmerited treatment of Porter have been the principal grounds upon which the enemies of Mr. Adams have acquired much strength and exercised much influence. A few more similar events will settle the point with Mr. Adams in the South.

My recent election, although more warmly contested than heretofore, was more honorable. My opponent, Judge Clay, was not only highly respectable, but it was given up, upon all hands, he was the strongest man the opposition could select. My majority was respectable in every county in the district. In Madison, where we both reside, my majority was 975; in Jackson, where 1,517 were taken, I received 1,325; the aggregate majority, 3,611. My enemies, as usual, left nothing which was unmanly undone; resorted to certificates of some poor, servile, unprincipled Crawfordites, as to my general standing, etc. At the city it was also stated that Floyd treated me with indignity and this passed unresented, etc., etc. But the result has mortified some silk and purple gentry beyond conception.

You will please tender my respects to Mr. Cook, and believe me to be,

With sincere respect,

Your friend and obedient servant,

GABRIEL MOORE.

GOV. N. EDWARDS, Belleville, Illinois.

WASHINGTON CITY, *April* 14, 1828.

My Dear Sir:

Your favor, dated 12th ulto., has been duly received. I have inquired of my colleagues and some other gentlemen from the South for Dr. Bowers, but have heard nothing of him with certainty. Mr. Owen thinks a gentleman of this name and character was in the southern part of Alabama about eighteen months since, but is of the opinion that he has removed, and he is not informed to what quarter.

The papers will give you all the interesting political intelligence of the day. The tariff bill, as is now generally believed, will finally succeed. Some increase of duty has been added to wool and woolens, and five cents upon cotton bagging added; which vary the bill from the original shape in which it was first presented, and this is the only material alteration.

As you very correctly imagine, much is said and done here, both in and out of the two branches of the National Legislature, with a view to produce effect upon the pending Presidential election. The friends of Gen. Jackson consider now that the result is almost inevitably decreed in their favor. I am greatly inclined to this opinion myself from all we learn from other quarters. I may be, however, as I have no doubt others are, too sanguine. We frequently have different opinions as to the result in your State, Missouri and Indiana. As you have opportunity for forming a pretty correct opinion of the probable result in these States, I would be glad if you would give me your views on the subject. If you think proper to require it, I will consider them as confidential.

I have transmitted you such public documents as I presumed you would view as the most interesting, which were within my reach. If there are any others which you wish, and you will signify the same, it will afford me great pleasure to furnish them.

Be pleased to accept the best wishes, for your prosperity and happiness, of

Your sincere friend and obedient servant,

GABRIEL MOORE.

To Gov. Ninian Edwards, Belleville, Illinois.

Washington City, *December* 27, 1828.

Dear Governor:

Your esteemed favor of 29th November has been duly received, since which time I have had the pleasure of receiving the newspaper containing your valuable message, for which you will please accept my acknowledgments.

"That the United States, by admission of the new States into the Federal compact upon an equal footing with the old States, have released all claim to the public domain within their limits," is a doctrine not only agreeable and acceptable to me, but founded in the soundest republican principles, and supported by a fair interpretation of the constitution, as you have well and satisfactorily established. Since this subject was first agitated, I have given it my feeble support. The Legislature of Alabama have the subject now under consideration, by a resolution instructing the proper committee to inquire into the propriety of memorializing Congress on the subject. But my fears are that the General Government, having the power in a matter so intimately connected with their interest, "will *forget right*," although the reason and argument should be legitimate and conclusive.

You ask for information "as to the formation of the new cabinet." I can give you nothing on this topic except general rumor. Van Buren and Tazewell are spoken of as aspirants for the State Department; Woodbury for the Navy, but some say (and the knowing ones too) that he must not be taken from the Senate, lest an Adams' man (or an anti-Adams' man now) should succeed him, and thereby add to the opposition which is said is now about to be organized in the Senate in order to paralyze the *Executive arm*. Whether this reasoning will predominate, and thus prevent the promotion of Mr. W., which the General's friends admit he is entitled to, I cannot say. Cheves, Gallatin, McLean, Postmaster-General, are spoken of for the Treasury. Livingston, Benton, H. L. White, Drayton, Hayne, Eaton, Ingham, Pope or Barry of Kentucky, and a host of others, for the War Department, Attorney-General, etc. Crittenden of Kentucky is now nominated to the Senate to fill the vacancy on the Supreme Court bench occasioned by the death of Judge Trimble. From what I have accidentally learned, this nomination will not be finally disposed of before the fourth of March, and then you can judge of the sequel as well or better than I can predict.

My friends have recently given my name to the public as a candidate for Governor. I anticipate warm opposition. My enemies will attempt to assail me on the ground of my heretical notions relative to internal improvements. My political experience is somewhat limited, and I may be at some loss probably for the strongest documents and arguments to sustain me. Any references or intimations which your long experience may suggest would be thankfully received.

I shall, with great pleasure, give you an account of the times here as anything may occur calculated to interest you.

I am, sir,
With respect and esteem,
Your obedient servant,
GABRIEL MOORE.

GOV. N. EDWARDS, Vandalia, Illinois.

CITY OF WASHINGTON, *Dec.* 31, 1831.

Dear Friend:

I acknowledge with cheerfulness the receipt of your letter, under date 10th inst., together with the communication addressed to your General Assembly —for which you will be pleased to accept my thanks.

I am unable to refer you to the sources from which you can obtain the information inquired for relative to the cessions of public lands, by the States, to the United States, etc. I would, with great pleasure, render you any aid in the prosecution of your object (which I view as highly meritorious and important to the new States) in my power.

While I occupied the office of Chief Magistrate in the State, I made an ineffectual effort to induce some of the leading members of the General Assembly to take up the subject which you have broached in claiming right, in behalf of the States, to the public domain, etc. Their resistance has been predicated entirely upon the solemn act of the Convention in the adoption of the ordinance disclaiming ownership over the soil, etc. I discovered that in our State the project would not be sanctioned, and I therefore declined bringing it to their view. All, however, admitted that, except for this ordinance, your views (for I distributed your message among them) were irresistible.

You will see, from the papers, that at this time various projects are under discussion in the House of Representatives for distributing the public domain among the several States, for as many distinct objects as there are gentlemen who feel an interest in the matter. Some say appropriate for internal improvements, others for purposes of education, and a third class for a portion of them to each of these objects, etc., etc. The diversity of opinion which seems to exist induces me to believe that nothing varying the established order of practice on this subject will be effected, until the public debt be extinct. At that time I am of opinion, from all I learn here, that there will be a disposition to establish some great and important change on this subject.

Although thus far all things have progressed smoothly—Mr. Clay having exhibited a most courteous and conciliatory deportment to all his great political opponents, (I mean Calhoun, Hayne, etc.)—has induced a belief with many that we should not experience that excitement which has been generally anticipated. Yet, if I am not much mistaken "in the signs of the times," the political horizon *now* begins to indicate most strongly that an angry cloud is beginning to make its appearance, the pernicious effects of which I cannot pretend to anticipate.

Some have thought Mr. C. would relax somewhat in his former *heresies* in relation to his abominable "*American system*;" but in a short discussion which occurred, the other day, on the proposition to reduce the duty on alum salt, he has removed all grounds for any hope of this character, and the parties *pro* and *con* are now making preparation for a general and spirited discussion on the proposition for a modification of the tariff. You, sir, are more competent to form a correct opinion as to the result, than I am (a junior member) to pretend to prophecy.

It is stated here, generally, that as to the nominations of the new Cabinet, on the question for confirmation there will not be any doubt, but as regards Mr. Van Buren, great doubts have been expressed. The wise ones here pretend to be able to count noses, and say, if all are present, he will either be rejected by *one* majority or by the casting vote of the Vice-President. In this calculation I am informed I am placed for the nomination. My mind, however, is not decidedly made up. I have a great repugnance personally to indorse Van B's nomination, but some other considerations, connected with the wishes of those who have placed me here, or what is said to be their wishes, will produce difficulty. King will go for him, or do any other act for the "*powers that be.*" The consequences of the State being divided, etc., is deemed by me a subject worthy of mature deliberation. If, however, it should so turn out *that a committee should be instructed*, among other subjects for their consideration, to *inquire into the causes which produced* the late dissolution of the Cabinet, and they should furnish some light calculated to lead to a correct conclusion as to the proper estimate to be placed upon this individual's worth or his demerits, which would enable me to give satisfaction at home, then all the doubts would be removed. No such proposition, as yet, has been made, *but it is by no means improbable that it may be made.*

Provided you should wish any particular document within my reach, or any other matter to be transacted within my power to do, you will be pleased to designate it, and it will afford me pleasure to oblige you.

I have, in consequence of your letter to Mr. Shackford, supported him warmly, and I did not fail to give him some others' support, and informed him I was influenced from your letter.

Respectfully and sincerely,
Your friend and obedient servant,
GABRIEL MOORE.

To Gov. Edwards.

Concord, N. H., *April* 26, 1832.

Dear Sir :

Your communication of the 20th ult. has been received. It not being directed to this place, where I reside, it has probably taken circuitous direction and may have been delayed in its arrival. The circumstance to which you allude, respecting the particular bill reported by Mr. Morrow, is most perfectly within my recollection—at least so far as this: I distinctly remember we were sitting in Old Congress Hall; that Mr. Morrow was Chairman of the Committee on Public Lands; that he reported a bill relating to that subject, the express provisions of which I do not now distinctly recollect, but this I fully remember: that, when the bill was read, you offered six or eight amendments, all of which, I am pretty sure, were rejected. I am well satisfied that the object of your proposed amendments, in part at least, was to reduce the price to actual settlers.

I distinctly recollect the zeal with which you urged your amendments, and the circumstance of your fainting at that time in the Senate Chamber. My recollection on this point is perhaps the more definite, since having been in the practice of medicine myself, I feared, when I saw you borne into the lobby, it was an apoplectic fit, which induced me instantly to repair to you and recommend bleeding, which was done, and I held the vessel that received the blood, and stood by you till your reason was so far restored that you were able by assistance to be removed.

What were the impressions of the Senate, in regard to the course you pursued on that occasion, I am unable to determine; but, for myself, I thought you were extremely tenacious of your views and zealous in supporting them—and this, I conclude, must have been the general feeling of the Senate.

A part of my library, and the journals of the Senate among the rest, being now in my office at Goffstown, where I formerly resided, I have not had an opportunity to have recourse to them, and of course have stated nothing except what was distinctly within my recollection—and this, I am sure, is perfectly correct.

I am, with great respect,
Your most obedient servant,
DAVID LAWRENCE MORRIL.

To Hon. Ninian Edwards.

HUNTSVILLE, *August* 23, 1825.

Dear Sir:

Yours, inclosing for my perusal two letters from Gov. Edwards, has been several days in my possession, and would have been answered sooner but for professional engagements, that claimed my attention during the session of court. I regret that my memory will not enable me to speak, now, as distinctly as I could have done at an earlier day, on the subject of his inquiries. I recollect that I argued a cause in the Supreme Court, about the time his nomination came to the Senate as Minister to Mexico, and perhaps was absent from the Senate on that account, at the time of his nomination, but of that I am not certain. The cause related to Africans, brought into this State, on the schooners "Constitution," "Louisa" and "Merino." The record of the Supreme Court will show the date of the argument, and the journal of the Senate the date of the nomination, should the fact be considered important.

I do not now recollect whether I visited him at the end of that week or not; it is highly probable that I did, as it was my custom to do so as often as my public duties would admit. The object of referring to that circumstance, I presume, must have been to fix the period of one or more of my visits to the Governor at his lodgings, pending his nomination; but memory does not connect the two transactions with sufficient certainty to throw any light upon the main point of inquiry. I recollect calling several times at the Governor's lodgings, while his nomination was pending, and also before it was made, and afterwards when it was confirmed. At one or more visits he occupied a room on the lower floor, at Mrs. Queen's; but, before his nomination was acted on, he removed to an upper room in the back building. I called several times, while he occupied the latter room, and recollect to have seen a gentleman there who was from West Point, as I understood, and was bound to Illinois, but cannot fix the precise date of the transaction; but I well recollect that the Governor was so unwell, at the time, as to be confined to his room as he alleged, and his appearance seemed to require it.

This was his condition for several days previous to the confirmation of his nomination. On account of his indisposition I called frequently, perhaps every time I happened in the neighborhood of his residence.

I recollect conversing with him on the subject of the postponement of the nomination, on account of its being stated that an absent Senator had, perhaps, objections that he would like to make, and inquired if it could be the "A. B." affair that founded the objection? to which he replied, that he could not say or conjecture the ground or nature of the objection, unless it should be the "A. B." affair or a newspaper controversey that had occurred in the West some years before—neither of which, he considered, ought to form any ground of objection.

I cannot say that the Governor was too sick to get out of his room and visit another gentleman in another apartment, at the time in question; but I should think it improbable, from his appearance, that he could travel far or gesticulate strongly, as he appeared to be considerably diseased with gout or rheumatism, and was under the action of medicine at several times when I called on him, shortly before his nomination was confirmed; but I cannot now fix the precise period of either visit. I recollect conversing with him on the subject of his being the author of the "A. B." letters, and he did not pretend to deny the fact to me. So far from it, he told me, upon one occasion, that he had prepared another document of considerable length, of a similar tenor, which he expected it would have been necessary to publish, but was glad that his political adversaries had not, by their conduct, made it necessary to do so. I requested him to let me peruse it, which he declined, alleging that if he remained unassailed, he wished to suppress it; and although he felt no want of confidence in me, he thought it most prudent to let the strife subside, and would, therefore, never show it to any one unless it became necessary in his own defense. The document alluded to, I presume, was pretty much embodied in his memorial to the House. I never had any conversation with Gen. Noble, on the subject of his nomination, further than passing a mutual statement that we should vote for the nomination; but no explanation of grounds was given on either side.

The foregoing contains as much as I can now say from memory. I accord it to Gov. Edwards, as an act of justice, which he may use in any manner that his prudence may dictate.

With great respect, etc.,

WILLIAM KELLY.

To Hon. Gabriel Moore.

City of Washington, *Dec.* 24, 1825.

Dear Sir:

I received your letter, some time since my arrival at this place, which you addressed to me at Frankfort, some time in the latter part of September, and which I should have answered earlier but from a desire to task my memory, which is a frail one, with the most anxious disposition to bring to my recollection the circumstances to which you allude, and in relation to which you again express a desire that I should make a statement.

Your former letter, addressed to me at Frankfort, during the summer, before the last, was received by me, my omission to answer which is ascribable to none of the causes which you suggest, but is ascribable in the first place to an impression entertained by me that the recollection of the circumstances alluded to was not impressed on my memory in such a manner as to enable me to give any statement with that precision and confidence in its correctness which the occasion seemed to call for; and because I saw it announced in a Washington paper, but a short time since the receipt of this letter, that you had left the city, and I had no certain means of knowing where a letter would find you.

Presuming from that time that the occasion had gone by which had produced the result, I thought nothing further of it, until the receipt of your recent letter; and have now to express to you my extreme regret that no effort at recollection, of which I am capable, enables me to state, with any certainty, what you may deem a circumstance material to your purpose; but of my finding you in bed when I made the call to which you allude—of my having made the call at the time and on the occasion to which you allude, I have a perfect recollection; that I found you, as well from your own statement as from any external appearance from which I could form an opinion, weak and seriously indisposed, and that you were in the apartment in the back buildings, to which you had recently removed from a chamber in the front of the building; that I stated to you, in the course of this visit, that an attack on your nomination as Minister to Mexico was meditated, and had been announced to the Senate—from what quarter I had no doubt; and my recollection enables me to speak of them with some confidence. But of the circumstance of your being *in bed* when the call was made and the conversation was had, although, from your statements and those of the highly respectable gentlemen to whom you refer, I cannot doubt, yet I have not been able to charge my memory.

In the supposition that this call and the conversation which followed were induced by feelings of friendly concern, and the communication from a sense of justice due you, from the discharge of which I deemed myself under no restraint, either of honor or morality, to forbear, is also true. And my delay or apparent reluctance in making this imperfect statement in reply to your request, I trust you may be assured, has proceeded from no other cause than the conscious inability which I felt, from defect of recollection, to make it with such fullness and precision as you might conclude you had a right to expect.

I am, with sincere regard,
Your friend and servant,
ISHAM TALBOT.

To NINIAN EDWARDS, Esq , Belleville, Illinois.

OAK HILL, *April* 27, 1826.

Dear Sir:

It is undoubtedly a painful thing to me to be brought before the public, in relation to any of those questions which were agitated with zeal and produced excitement between the contending parties, while I was in the Government; but your application is so just and reasonable that I think it incumbent on me to meet it by a fair statement of facts. With that view I have inclosed a letter for you, to our friend Mr. Wirt, and who will deliver it to you, if he sees no impropriety in so doing. I had communication with him on this subject, shortly after the affair occurred, and I wish him to compare this with what then passed, to see that it corresponds with the statement made while the impression on my mind was more recent.

When you see Gov. Edwards, assure him of my good wishes for his welfare and happiness.

With great respect and regard,
I am, dear sir, yours,
JAMES MONROE.

To DANIEL P. COOK.

OAK HILL, *April* 30, 1826.

Sir :

In reply to your letter of the 23d, requesting to be informed whether Gov. Edwards declared to me, before his nomination as Minister to Mexico, that he was not the author of the publications signed "A. B.," on which declaration, it is said, that his nomination was founded, I feel it due to candor to assure you, that he never made to me any such declaration, and that his nomination was not influenced in the slightest degree by any considerations except that the quarter of the Union in which he resided had claims to an appointment, and that he was believed to be as well qualified for the office as any other person in that quarter, who had been brought to the view of the Executive.

With great respect and esteem,

I am your obedient servant,

JAMES MONROE.

To HON. WILLIAM WIRT.

QUINCY, *August* 22, 1827.

Dear Sir :

Your frank and cordial letter of the 22d ulto. has been duly received. I am entirely satisfied with the assurance that you are neither personally nor politically unfriendly to me, and that the measures of the present Federal Administration have received your cordial support.

Your recommendation for the appointment of a sub-agent at Peoria will, in the event of a vacancy in that office, receive the deliberate consideration to which it is entitled, and a disposition altogether friendly to him as recommended by you; and your opinion in regard to any appointments of the General Government, in the State of Illinois, will always be acceptable to me, whenever you may incline to communicate it to me.

Accept my friendly and respectful salutations.

J. Q. ADAMS.

To NINIAN EDWARDS, *Governor of the State of Illinois*, Belleville.

NATCHEZ, *March* 26, 1828.

Dear Sir :

Your letter dated the 20th of March last was never received by me until lately. I did not return home from a journey through the Northern States until November, and was then much indisposed, and have continued so until lately. Your letter, among a vast number of others, was laid aside, and my health did not permit me to advert to it until lately. You cannot doubt my disposition to serve you, I trust; nor can I cease to consider it among my first duties while I recollect your former kindness and friendship towards me.

* * * * * * * * * * * * *

I had the pleasure of seeing your two daughters for a moment last summer, in Lexington. Mr. Cook was there in the last stage of consumption, and has since, I learn, fallen a victim to that disease. I had lived with him the winter before last, and had formed a high estimate of his talents, his virtues, and his social temper. He held, as you know, a distinguished place, for a man of his age, in the House of Representatives. During the last winter of his service he had been unusually laborious, which contributed, I have no doubt, to augment and hasten the ravages of his disease. He has, however, left a character behind him which ought in some measure to console his family and friends for his premature loss.

Be so kind as to present my respectful compliments to Mrs. Edwards; and believe me to be, as I really am,

Your friend and obedient servant,

THOS. B. REED.

To His Excellency NINIAN EDWARDS, Belleville, Illinois.

WASHINGTON CITY, *May* 8, 1830.

Dear Sir:

So soon as I received your letter I went to the War Department, and made application in favor of Dr. Todd's son; but, unfortunately, the only place due to your State had been filled by the appointment of the son of a Mrs. Prim. This I regretted very much, as I was prevented from repaying a debt of gratitude due to Dr. Todd and family. I hope, however, some occasion may present itself in which I can be serviceable to them. Nothing, I assure you, would give me more pleasure—of which I hope you will assure them.

You say you differ from me in opinion in relation to the public lands. You know the liberality of my feelings in regard to the rights of opinion. If others will only permit me to think for myself, I will never quarrel with them for the exercise of the same privilege.

I am gratified that you think favorably of my effort on Foot's resolution. You may take the following, as I believe, for certainties: 1st. Jackson will will be again run for the Presidency; 2d, his popularity is on the increase; 3d, his reëlection is as certain as his life, and he is in excellent health; 4th, his standing is of a peculiar character: his Ministers and his Congress may all become unpopular, and still his hold on the affections of the people not be weakened.

Your friend,

FELIX GRUNDY.

To His Excellency NINIAN EDWARDS, Belleville, Illinois.

PHILADELPHIA, *April* 4, 1832.

Dear Sir:

Your interesting and esteemed favor of the 20th of March was received this morning. I extremely regret that I have no recollection upon the subject of your *particular* inquiry, or it would give me infinite pleasure to make any statement within my power to serve you. I am detained at this place in the discharge of a public duty, and am very much engaged. Your political views and reflections are always interesting. For the last ten years I have not had *time* to indulge in such reflections with the most intimate friend, but I am often amused and interested and instructed by those of my friends; and I thank you, in this respect.

Truly and sincerely your friend,

R. M. JOHNSON.

To HON. NINIAN EDWARDS, Belleville, Illinois.

GREENVILLE, KENTUCKY, *May* 8, 1832.

Dear Sir:

Your letter has been received, but, owing to my absence from home, I have not been able to answer it until now.

I have but an indistinct recollection of your course, when in Kentucky, with regard to our public lands, as at that time I meddled but little in politics; but I have no doubt you were always friendly to the settlers south of Green River, as I do not recollect of ever hearing any complaints against you on that account, and I think I certainly would if you had been opposed to them.

With regard to your course in the Senate of the United States, my impression is that you and myself agreed on the subject of the public lands, although I was in the lower house and may be mistaken. I was in favor of reducing the price, but opposed to doing away the credit system—and finally voted against the bill, as it passed, believing the old system was better than the new.

My recollection is, that you were making a speech on the Missouri question, when you fainted in the Senate, and not on the public lands, although I was not present at the time. I recollect of seeing a complimentary note from Mr. Randolph, to you, on that occasion, in which he expressed great regret at your inability to finish your speech, which, from your commencement, promised to do you so much credit.

Although engaged in my official duties, I am not an inattentive observer of passing events—and really, sometimes, I am distressed to see how things are going on in the Union. I sometimes fear we will not stick together long, and one cause of this fear is, the kind of men that are selected by the people to fill the various public stations. It no longer appears to be a recommending quality, that a candidate for office should have intelligence or experience. The only inquiry is, is he a *whole-hog* Jackson or Clay man? and in this contest principles appear to be laid aside or forgotten. Shameful, indeed! Men seeking popular favor endeavor to ascertain what popular sentiment is, and then throw themselves into the current and float down with it, instead of forming their own opinions of what measures will advance the interest of the country, enlightening the public mind on them, and getting the people to go with them.

Dear sir, I really fear *Jacksonism* will ruin the country. I do think every public man ought honestly to approve what is right, and as honestly oppose what is wrong—and then I would expect to see a better state of things.

Your friend,

ALMY McLEAN.

To Hon. Ninian Edwards, Belleville, Illinois.

Frankfort, Kentucky, *May* 27, 1832.

Dear Sir:

Circumstances, not worth detailing, have prevented me from giving an earlier answer to your letter of the 16th of last month. In that letter you informed me that, at this late day, you are accused "of having opposed the reduction of the price of public lands, and the granting of pre-emptions to actual settlers," during the period that we served together in the Senate of the United States—you as a senator from Illinois, and I from Kentucky—and you request that I will state the part which you acted on those subjects.

During the short period that I have had the honor of serving with you in the Senate, I know that an attempt was made further to reduce the price of the public lands, and I remember well that you were a persevering and zealous advocate for reduction, and that you struggled obstinately and to the last against repeated votes of the Senate overruling your various propositions for reduction. I recollect, indeed, that your perseverance and zeal on the subject were thought, at the time, by some senators, to have been carried somewhat further than was altogether compatible with the decorum of the Senate.

I think that one of your propositions was for reducing the price of the public lands as low as thirty cents per acre, and your other propositions, successively moved, for intermediate sums between that and the price finally fixed by the Senate. I have not the journals before me, however, and cannot, therefore, undertake to speak positively as to these particulars. But as to your general course upon the occasion alluded to, I recollect it perfectly; and as far as my knowledge and humble testimony can go, great injustice is done you by the accusation that you opposed the reduction of the price of the public lands.

I remember nothing of the proceedings of the Senate in relation to the granting of pre-emptions to actual settlers, and consequently nothing of your course, or even of my own, on the subject.

Very respectfully yours,

J. J. CRITTENDEN.

To Ninian Edwards, Alton, Illinois.

Donaldsonville, Louisiana, *June* 8, 1832.

Dear Sir:

In consequence of an omission in the superscription of your letter of the 20th March, it has been forwarded from place to place, and accidentally reached my hands a few days ago. This explanation you will be pleased to accept as an apology for my apparent neglect in not answering it earlier. I well remember that during the second session of the XVth Congress, when Mr. Morrow of Ohio, Chairman of the Committee of Public Lands, reported to the Senate "a bill making further provision for the sale of public lands," the object of which was to abolish all credit, and sell for cash only, you made great efforts to amend the bill, so as to obtain a further reduction of the price than the bill contemplated, and to provide, also, for the actual settlers on public lands. I feel confident that not a single member of the Senate could have thought you opposed to either of those objects. On the contrary, I had the best reasons to believe that your standing with the Senate was somewhat impaired from an over-zeal you appeared to manifest on the occasion. The bill, as it passed the Senate, fixed the price of land, I think, at $1.50 per acre. It, however, failed in the House of Representatives. When introduced in the Senate, at the succeeding session, you renewed your efforts in favor of the actual settlers on public lands. Indeed, I do not hesitate in saying that I uniformly considered you in favor of reducing the price of public lands and in favor of providing for the actual settlers thereon. In attempting, myself, to effect these objects, in favor of the citizens of Louisiana, you always gave me your support. On one occasion, particularly, I recollect that at my request, and perhaps at the instance of my colleague and of the members from Mississippi, you exerted yourself in favor of pre-emption rights to the citizens of the districts of St. Helena and of Jackson court-house, the former of which is situated in Louisiana and the latter in the State of Mississippi.

I am, with great respect, sir,

Your friend and obedient servant,

H. JOHNSON.

To Gov. Ninian Edwards, Belleville, Illinois.

May 31, 1812.

Dear Sir:

Mr. Mackenzie, in his "History of the Fur Trade," is very exact, except as to the names of Rivers, etc., which I think he should have given in French, because, in Canada and in the North-west, they are generally called after the Canadians and in the French language, and in fact are so called by all voyagers.

On page 44, he speaks of "Algonquin nation." This is the name given to the Chippeways by the old French. They are now called Chippeways or Sauteaux.

On page 49, he says "Lake Superior, north side, coast-way, is 160 leagues." These are voyager leagues; I do not think it more than 130 leagues.

On page 58, "this corn." The voyagers call it "hulled corn."

In his description of the route from Montreal to Makina, he gives the names as called by the voyagers in French; but when he leaves Grand Portage to go to the north, he gives a number of names in English, many of which a voyager, who knows the route, would not know by that name. Thus:

On page 59, Partridge Portage should be Portage de Perdix.

On page 60, Elk Portage should be Portage de L'Orignal.

On page 61, Mountain Lake should be Lac de la Montagne.

On page 61, Rose Lake should be Lac a la Rose.

On page 62, Marten Portage should be Portage be la Marte.

On page 62, Pigeon River should be Riviere aux Pigeons.

On page 63, Cheval du Bois should be Cheval de Bois.

On page 64, Prairie Portage should be Portage de la Prairie.

On page 67, Chebois is here meant Chippeways.

On page 68, Beaver Dam should be La Chausé de Castor.

On page 68, Vermilion Lake should be Lac du Vermilion.

On page 74, Jacob's Fall should be La Chute a'Jacquaut.

On page 75, White River should be La Riviere Blanche.

On page 77, Assiniboin or Red River, is an error; Assiniboin River is a separate and distinct river, which comes from the south-west of Lake Winipic and empties itself into the Red River or River Rouge, which in turn comes from the east and empties into Lake Winipic 18 leagues from where the Assiniboin empties itself. It was on this river that I wintered, at a small creek called Riviere a la Souris.

On page 78, for Knestenaux say Christenau or Crees.

On page 80, for Swan River say Riviere au Cignes.

On page 82, for the Great Rapids of the Saskatchawine say Les Rapides de la Riviere du Pas.

On page 83, for Cedar Lake say Lac de Cedres.

On page 84, for Mud Lake say Lac aux Vases.

On page 85, for Sturgeon Lake say Lac Eturgeon.

On page 91, for Pine Island Lake say Lac de Lisle aux Pines.

On page 91, for Beaver Lake say Lac du Castor.

On page 83, for Missinissi River say La Riviere des Anglois.

On page 95, for Portage de Barcel say Portage des Barils.

On page 95, for Lake La Rouge say Lac Rouge.

On page 98, for Knee Lake say Lac aux Genou.

On page 99, for Croche Rapide say La Rapide Croche.

On page 104, for Lake Clear say Lac Claire.

On page 107, Athabasca called by the voyagers Arabasca.

On page 149, for Pimican the voyagers say Pimitigan; it is dried buffalo meat, pounded by the Indians and sold to the traders, who mix fifty pounds of it with forty pounds of tallow and sew it up in bags, made of the raw buffalo hides—a bag of which is allowed to each man for his provisions, on his journey from the north, in the spring, to Grand Portage. On their return, in the fall, from Grand Portage to Fort Pimitigan, they live on green and hulled corn. In going out of the north, it took me near five weeks, from my wintering ground on the Assiniboin River, to reach Grand Portage.

Yours, respectfully,

JOHN HAY.

To His Excellency Gov. EDWARDS.

RUSSELLVILLE, *March* 4, 1810.

Dear Governor:

My brother, Thomas Crittenden, is now here on his way to Kaskaskia, where he wishes to settle himself for the practice of the law. I wish to introduce him to your acquaintance. I think you will find him worthy of it, in every way. I have given him your character; I have told him of the noble generosity you have practiced towards me; I have told him, too, of the friendship and patronage with which you have honored me; I have inspired him with an eager ambition to obtain your good opinion and esteem. You will find him amiable in his temper. His heart is as generous as brave, and as friendly as ever was formed. If he can deserve and obtain your friendship and patronage, it will be to me a cause of the most delightful satisfaction, and will furnish another cause for all my gratitude.

Yours, with all gratitude and esteem,

JOHN J. CRITTENDEN.

To His Excellency NINIAN EDWARDS, Russellville.

P. S.—If you would be so good as to give my brother some letters of introduction, they would be of service to him at Kaskaskia, and he would be much obliged to you.—J. J. C.

ST. LOUIS, *Oct.* 27, 1818.

Dear Sir:

Our mutual friend, Gen. Bissell, wishes to command in this Department. Gen. Smith has retired; and if long and faithful services deserve any reward, it would be but just to gratify Gen. Bissell in this wish. Mr. Scott will speak with the Secretary of War, and your voice would doubtless have its weight if joined to his.

We shall wish you to give us all help in the advancement of our Territory.

Thine,

THOMAS H. BENTON.

To HON. NINIAN EDWARDS.

FRANKFORT, KENTUCKY, *Sept.* 10, 1816.

Dear Sir:

I perceive the sales of the United States lands in your Territory are about commencing. The migration to your Territory induces me to suppose there must be a rapid appreciation in the price of your prime lands within a few years. My desire of acquiring some portion of such lands, somewhere in your neighborhood, is again revived.

If good speculations should present themselves in any agreeable part of your Territory, either upon the Government terms or on advance of cash on hand not exceeding $3,000 or $4,000, will you be good enough to make the purchase for me, and draw on me for the amount, giving me a few weeks' previous notice of your intentions so to do? A line from you in answer, at an early day, would be desirable.

Please to present my best regards to your amiable partner; and believe me

Your sincere friend,

ISHAM TALBOT.

To His Excellency NINIAN EDWARDS, Kaskaskia, Illinois Territory.

P. S.—This will be handed you by Mr. Thomas Talbot, a resident of Missouri, a very agreeable young gentleman, whom I take the liberty of recommending to your polite attentions.—I. T.

WASHINGTON, *April* 13, 1818.

Dear Sir:

Mr. Edward Coles intending to pass through Illinois, probably to remain some time there, I take much pleasure in introducing him to your acquaintance and kind attention. I have long known and highly respected and esteemed him for his excellent qualities and good understanding. He was several years private secretary to the late President, and employed by him in a confidential mission to Russia, in which trust he discovered sound judgment, great industry and fidelity, and is generally beloved by those who know him best. Should he settle with you, you will find him a very useful acquisition, and I understand it is not an improbable event.

I hope that the arrangement made this winter will avail our country of your services in the proposed treaty with the Indians, in a manner satisfactory to yourself; for success, on just principles, is the object of my most ardent wishes.

With great respect and esteem,

I am, dear sir, very sincerely yours,

JAMES MONROE.

To GOV. EDWARDS, Illinois Territory.

April 12, 1822.

Mr. Blair's most kind respects to Gov. Edwards (of Illinois), and begs leave to present his best thanks for the speech (in pamphlet form) on the resolution proposing to give the old States lands for the purposes of education, etc.

At the same time, he cannot refrain from assuring Mr. E. that this *very able* speech has probably saved him from giving an erroneous vote. Mr. B. had thought it reasonable that the old States should participate in the benefit of the public lands equally with the new States, without considering that the school donations of land were made to the new States as a bonus for settling in a wilderness, etc. Mr. B. also begs leave to assure Mr. E. that in his opinion this speech is equally creditable to the head and to the heart. While it breathes the purest spirit of philanthropy and benevolence, it, in point of reasoning, " leaves no stone unturned."

SALISBURY, N. CAROLINA, *April* 21, 1822.

Dear Sir:

I received, a week ago, your much esteemed favor, and truly thank you for the pleasure its contents gave me. I could wish that your calculations as to Pennsylvania and other States north of Maryland were to be relied on, but I am well aware that all such calculations must necessarily be received with many grains of allowance. Let me, however, add, that my wishes accord with your own. You say that it is confidently calculated at Washington that Mr. Crawford will get all the votes of North Carolina. My opportunities during the past winter of forming a correct opinion upon this point were better than those of the calculators at Washington—and I took some pains to ascertain the general sentiment. I will give you my candid opinion. Whether Mr. Crawford will or will not command the vote of this State depends greatly upon who is his opponent. Against Mr. Adams, I believe North Carolina will be for him—and even then not without a contest. But if Mr. Calhoun is brought forward, you may rely upon it, Crawford's prospects in North Carolina become less flattering. I say it, without the hazard of contradiction, that Mr. Crawford's standing in North Carolina *has been*, *is still*, and *will continue*, in the decline. If he or his friends put down North Carolina as a certainty on his side, the chance is *at least equal* that he will be disappointed in the result. But, is Mr. Calhoun certainly a candidate? Is it distinctly understood at Washington that such is the fact? I have all along felt satisfied that Mr. Calhoun had no disposition to decline the use of his name if reasonable prospect of success presented itself; and I *know* that some of Mr. Crawford's friends looked at him in that light; but *as yet*, *here* it is not known that he is certainly a candidate. I see he is considered in that light in some of the Northern newspapers; and it is no doubt good policy that his support should begin from that quarter. I have received letters from several members, and have seen letters from members to other persons, in all of which Crawford and Adams, only, are spoken of as competitors. As soon as it is distinctly understood that Mr. Calhoun will run, rest assured, many who now say Crawford will change their object.

The scrape into which Crawford has gotten with your colleague is a good deal talked of, and it has its effect.

Should it come in the way, say to Mr. Calhoun, from me, that his prospects in North Carolina are *at least* equally good with the other gentlemen.

As to an opposition against Gen. Stokes, on the grounds you hint, rely upon it, it would operate to his advantage.

Dear sir, with great esteem, I am

Your obedient servant,

CHAS. FISHER.

TO HON. NINIAN EDWARDS, U. S. Senate, Washington City.

FAYETTEVILLE, *April* 27, 1822.

Sir:

I am on my way to the South, and have not had an opportunity of writing until to-night. I have seen and had a conversation with Gov. Branch on the subject of the Florida appointments, and, as we had anticipated, some letters of an inflammatory nature had been written to him; and some statements that the President had given positive assurances that the appointment of Governor should be given to North Carolina, and induced the delegation to believe that Branch should be that individual. Under such circumstances he expected the appointment; and finding it had been given to a man not residing in the State, he was induced to believe that something was behind the curtain more than had come to his knowledge; however, the only regret or disappointment he feels arises from an apprehension that his name has been in some way sported with, and, until some explanations from me, he felt disposed to attach the blame to the President; but I have in great degree succeeded in fixing the blame where it should be—and a good share of it rests—on the shoulders of *the chief prompter behind the curtain.* I took the liberty of stating to him that I did not believe the President had committed himself to the North Carolina delegation to the full extent of their representations to him—that there was a misunderstanding in relation to that *promise.* Branch will not accept the appointment of judge; but does not look upon it in the way the delegation would induce you to believe—as an insult—but will decline it in a becoming manner. Would you be willing to mention his name to the President for one of the missions to South America? I mention this to you without his knowledge, or even of mentioning it to him. He is not the devoted friend of Mr. Crawford as some would have you believe.

I spent two days at Halifax court, in Burton's district, where I met with a number of influential men, and I always introduced the subject of Presidential election; and although the people have not settled down upon any individual for that high office, I am glad to inform you that I have not met with a single man who was friendly to the election of Mr. Crawford, but all declare to me that they have not confidence in his talents, and they look upon him as an intriguing, disingenuous politician. They do not admire the political course of Mr. Clay; consequently will take the most prominent Southern man, which, I think, will be our friend Calhoun. I had a conversation with a member of the last Legislature on that subject, and he stated unequivocally that Mr. Calhoun could have had a Legislative nomination over Mr. Crawford, by a large vote.

I find in many instances the people have taken up erroneous opinions in relation to the disbursements of money by the War Department, particularly in the Indian Department. These impressions were formed from the debate on the bill appropriating $70,000 to cover the debts incurred in the last year, over and above the appropriation, for that Department, not recollecting that laws were in existence which made it obligatory upon that Department to disburse that sum; but with such explanations as I was able to give, they were perfectly satisfied; hence the necessity, on the part of Mr. Calhoun's friends, to make every effort to explain to the people the situation of these transactions.

I shall expect to hear from you before you leave the city. Do request Mr. Rogers to order my "Franklin Gazette" directed to the Agency. Gov. Branch has read your speech on the Maryland propositions, and says you have changed his opinion, and that your arguments are unanswerable. I wish you would send one to my father, Samuel Crowell, directed to Enfield, North Carolina. It is now bed-time. Good night.

I am, respectfully,

Your obedient servant,

JNO. CROWELL.

To Hon. Ninian Edwards, Washington City.

Great Crossing, *June* 26, 1822.

Dear Sir:

I have received your favor, and I sincerely thank you for your friendly sentiments and conduct towards me, and it is a principle of honor with me never to be outdone by friendly offices, if opportunity offers.

I have been very attentive to your reply to Benton as to the lead mines, and I have also noticed his remarks. I have anticipated your views on that subject, and besides two publications already, placing the thing in its true colors, I am prepared at all points if the least slur is made; but I assure you that, so far from injury, nothing has ever given a greater impulse to the popularity of Mr. Calhoun. He shall lose no popularity on our account.

I have received a letter from Col. John O'Fallan, requesting me to get Mr. Calhoun to let him and others have a lease, such as he had given to my friends. I have urged Mr. Calhoun to do this. It would destroy Col. Benton, or any man from Missouri, to oppose this leasing policy. If Mr. Calhoun would grant the leases to O'Fallan, it would take away the plea of favoritism; for no person had applied when he granted the leases to my friends. The policy pursued is very popular in this State; and men, women and children are interested in the success of my brother. I pledge you that I am ready at all points and in all ways to defend Mr. Calhoun's course in this business.

I have received many letters from St. Louis, from Peck, Strother, Wheeler, etc., etc., who say that my brother is popular there, and the policy of leasing the mines equally popular, and I am happy to find that you have turned your eye to this business. Col. Benton will gain neither credit nor advantage from his course in this business. He may have the right to accuse, but that does not take away the right of self-defense. Ficklin has your speech ready to publish if a paper in the State should publish Benton's, or should say a word of condemnation, without which, perhaps, we had better let the matter rest at present.

Sincerely your friend,

R. M. JOHNSON.

To Hon. Ninian Edwards, Edwardsville, Illinois.

TRENTON, NEW JERSEY, *March* 6, 1823.

My Dear Sir :

I was extremely gratified by the receipt of your letter—not because you had had a visit from your old friend, the gout, nor your new one, fever and ague. I would not wish my worst enemy either frequent or long-continued visits from either of them—much less would I rejoice at your being persecuted by them—but I was glad to hear from you and to know that neither of them alone, nor both united, could dispirit you, nor make you indifferent to passing events.

I had heard the rumor you mention about New York, but I do not dread the effort there; it will not, *for the present*, be successful. At least Thompson *can*, *if he will*, prevent it. It is too late to put any machinery in motion *here* to operate *there in time*. All that can be done is a *short* article or two in our leading papers, which I am told will appear immediately.

The symptoms in Virginia are very strong and will grow stronger. I know that State. It is misunderstood and misrepresented, and the friends of a certain man will find it so.

I look with some curiosity for "A. B." He is a troublesome fellow. I wish we could find him out.

I would write more, but am pressed for time.

Write frequently; I shall be pleased to hear often and freely.

Yours, etc., etc.,
SAMUEL L. SOUTHARD.

To HON. N. EDWARDS.

GEORGETOWN, *Saturday*, *Feb.* 21, 1824.

Dear Sir :

Owing to indisposition, I have not attended the sessions of the Senate until Monday. In the interval, I have heard of the nomination for the mission to Mexico. Intrigues and much personal intercourse are pursued upon this subject, in which you cannot be indifferent. Were I able to go abroad, I should, without delay, call upon you; this not being the case, I should be glad to see you whenever, and as soon as you may be able to call upon me.

With great respect,
I am, dear sir,
Your obedient and faithful servant,
RUFUS KING.

To HON. N. EDWARDS.

SENATE CHAMBER, *February* 29, 1824.

Dear Sir :

The nomination was read this morning, and, upon the suggestion of a member that an absent Senator was understood to be prepared to submit to the consideration of the Senate objections to the confirmation of the appointment to Mexico, and to afford an opportunity of this being done, I moved to postpone the nomination till to-morrow, when the absent Senator expects to be able to attend. It was intimated that it was desirable that some intimation of the nature of the objection should be given, in order that inquiries should be seasonably made by the friends of the candidate. Nothing particular was intimated, though it was understood that Col. Benton is the Senator who is to offer objections.

Yours, truly,

RUFUS KING.

To HON. NINIAN EDWARDS, of the United States Senate.

SENATE CHAMBER, *February* 25, 1824.

Dear Sir:

I am sorry to learn, by your note of this morning, that you are so much indisposed. I can be at no loss in forming the opinion that every delay will be attempted in the proceedings in the Senate. Mr. B. does not attend, the weather is unfavorable, and so nothing will be done to-day. I do not hear a whisper of the nature of the imputed charges. We must have a little patience, as too great urgency would be injurious; nothing that can be prudently done will be omitted. Were I not myself an invalid, I would call to see you.

Respectfully,

Your obedient servant,

RUFUS KING.

To HON. N. EDWARDS, of Illinois.

GEORGETOWN, *February* 29, 1824.

Dear Sir:

I have received your note of this morning, with the file of the "Washington Republican." This I may have an opportunity to examine, as Congress will adjourn early to-morrow until Monday or Tuesday afternoon, in consequence of the death of poor Ball.

I gave notice on Friday that I should call up the nomination of the Minister to Mexico to-morrow, but it will now go over to a future day. I have heard nothing further upon the subject of our last conversation. The mentioned objection may be persevered in, though I shall not be dissappointed if it shall be abandoned.

With esteem and respect,

I am, dear sir,

Your obedient servant,

RUFUS KING.

To HON. N. EDWARDS, of Illinois.

SENATE CHAMBER, *March* 4, 1824.

Dear Sir:

The nomination of the Envoy to Mexico was taken up this morning and confirmed—twenty-seven Senators rising in favor of it.

Yours faithfully,
RUFUS KING.

To HON. N. EDWARDS, of Illinois.

P. S.—There was no debate.—R. K.

SENATE CHAMBER, *March* 4, 1824.

General Jackson, with compliments to Gov. Edwards, congratulates him upon the ratification of his nomination—returns his thanks to him for the perusal of the extract of the letter inclosed, and returns it to him.

To HON. N. EDWARDS, of the Senate.

Tuesday, June 22, 1824.

Dear Sir:

I last evening received your letter of the 27th ult. Inclosed I send you two letters of Mr. Edwards to me, dated the 21st and 27th of February—the former being an answer to a note from me to him from the Senate, respecting his nomination—the latter, as I conjecture, the day after my visit to him, whom I found in his bed, in the back part of the house where he lodged. I have no other memorandum by which I may refresh my memory on the subject of his appointment to Mexico. According to my recollection, I am all but confident of this statement: the first motion that the Senate should name a day to consider the nomination of Mr. Edwards was made by myself. It was on this occasion that Mr. Eliot of Georgia informed the Senate that he had been desired to suggest to the Senate that important information respecting this appointment would be communicated by Mr. Benton of Missouri, who, by reason of ill health, could not now attend in his place. The matter, of course, was deferred without a question. I do not recollect that any previous observation or remark had been made to the Senate, respecting the appointment of Mr. Edwards, by Mr. Noble or any other person. Private conversations were doubtless had upon the subject. On a future day, I remember to have observed to the Senate that, while reasonable time should be allowed for the communication of charges that might affect the character of persons nominated to office, there was also something due to the members of our own body, by which we were bound to avoid those delays which would impair the reputation of the Senate; and as want of health prevented Mr. Benton from coming to the Senate, any charges in his possession might be sent to the Secretary, and in this way communicated to the Senate. No debate, at this or any other time, took place respecting Mr. Edwards' appointment. Mr. Benton made no communication, nor did he attend the Senate before the nomination was called up, and, without debate, the appointment of Mr. Edwards was confirmed.

With much respect and esteem,

I am, dear sir,

Your obedient servant,

RUFUS KING.

To DANIEL P. COOK.

P. S.—Please to offer my compliments to Mr. Edwards. Firmness and decorum avail much; it is plain to me that his reputation calls for both their aids in his actual condition—they can and will serve him.

FRANKFORT, KENTUCKY, *August* 2, 1824.

My Good Friend:

Yours of the 15th July has just come to hand.

When I arrived in Washington City in February last, you were at Mrs. Queen's, occupying the front room on the first floor. I visited you there several times whilst you were sick and confined to your room. You afterwards removed to the back part of the building, where I visited you also frequently. You were sick—most generally in bed—but sometimes got up. The time when you removed to the back-room of Mrs. Queen's, I cannot state. The morning after Judge Trimble arrived in Washington (that is, the first morning that I saw him), I went with him to visit you. You were then in the back-room, and had been there before that time. I recollect that whilst your nomination was pending in the Senate unacted upon, you were confined to your room in the back apartment. I had a conversation with Mr. King of the Senate, on the subject of an anonymous publication against you some twenty years ago, in Kentucky, which publication, I understood, was dug up from the grave and used or attempted to be used to your prejudice. I waited on you, at your own room, the same day and the next, and informed you of the conversation: found you sick and confined to your chamber. This was whilst your nomination was pending. Your note to me on the subject of the anonymous publication is not preserved; by that I could have ascertained the date. My memory cannot retain dates. I arrived in Washington early in February—you were sick and confined to your room when I arrived. I left the city in the latter part of March. I have no recollection to have seen you out of your apartment during my stay in the city. I visited you frequently, because of your sickness and because the presence and conversation of your acquaintances seemed to cheer your spirits.

Your friend,

GEORGE M. BIBB.

To HON. NINIAN EDWARDS, Shepardstown, Virginia.

NASHVILLE, *February* 20, 1825.

Dear Sir :

I returned home on last night and set out to a distant court in a few minutes. I shall, on next Friday week, leave this place for Edwardsville. I go on account of the late misfortune of Mr. Winchester. Among other reasons inducing me to visit your State, is the pleasure it will afford me to see and converse freely with you. I hope you will be in Edwardsville on the Saturday before the second Monday in March.

Your friend,
FELIX GRUNDY.

To HON. NINIAN EDWARDS, Belleville, Illinois.

OFFICIAL LETTERS TO NINIAN EDWARDS.

TREASURY DEPARTMENT, *Nov.* 25, 1809.

Sir :

Your several communications, respecting the Saline, have been laid before the President, and the following outlines adopted for the ensuing lease :

1. The quantity of salt to be made annually by the lessees, not to be less than 120,000 bushels, and as much more as you may think practicable and may be proposed by the lessees. And in order to insure the fulfillment of that condition, which was never complied with by the former lessees, a penalty of one bushel for each bushel falling short of the quantity agreed on, to be made a condition of the contract—securing the recovery of such penalty by a constant deposit of salt in the hands of the agent of the United States.

2. The maximum price of salt to be fixed at not less than eighty cents nor more than one dollar per bushel—leaving it between those two limits at your discretion and with such modifications as you may think proper.

3. A rent to be paid quarterly to the United States, in salt, equal to the difference between what is judged a fair price for the lessees to sell at, and the maximum price fixed by the lease ; but to be calculated only on 120,000 bushels a year, whether the quantity actually made exceeds or falls short of that number. Thus if seventy cents per bushel, the price now allowed to the lessees, be considered proper, and one dollar be fixed on the new lease as the maximum price, the rent should be 36,000 bushels, since this would leave to the lessees 84,000 bushels, which they would sell for eighty-four thousand dollars, a sum equal to the value of 120,000 bushels at seventy cents per bushel. It would, of course, be agreed that the salt paid to the United States should not be sold at a price less than that fixed by the lease, unless by common consent the price was lowered, in which case the rent would be diminished in the same proportion. Thus, if from the increased quantity made by the lessees, the market price should fall below a dollar, so as to render it necessary and

proper to reduce the price to eighty-four cents for instance, the rent would be diminished to 20,000 bushels, since this would leave to the lessees 100,000 bushels, which they would sell for eighty-four thousand dollars, the value of the 120,000 bushels at seventy cents per bushel. But it is left for you to determine whether the price of seventy cents allowed to the lessees be more than they ought to have.

You will easily perceive the principal object of this condition, as by making the rent fixed, whatever be the quantity of salt made, it will become a powerful inducement to the lessees to make at all events the quantity agreed on, and as much more as there will be demand for; an inducement which will be strengthened by the other condition, that we will diminish the rent if there be a fall in the price. But it is proper to observe that the Government contemplates the introduction of certain improvements, calculated to reduce the quantity of fuel to about one-third part of that now used, and through that and their means to perpetuate the benefit arising to that part of the country from a constant, certain and cheap supply of salt; and that it is, also, in order to provide funds for that object, that it is wished that the United States may receive a larger rent than heretofore. Although the mode here suggested appears, for the resons above stated, preferable to that adopted in the present lease, yet, if the next lessees should absolutely reject it, it is not intended to forbid, in that case, a lease on the same principles as the last, that is to say, with a reservation that the United States should receive the whole of the salt at the rate of seventy cents or any other less price which may be agreed on, and should sell it at such maximum price as they may think proper—in which case the rent would arise from the difference between the two prices. But I repeat that the conditions first stated under this head, are considered as much better calculated to obtain the great object in view—that of inducing the lessees to manufacture a quantity of salt equal to the demand.

4. It will be extremely important to introduce conditions calculated effectually to prevent the waste of timber and encourage the use of coal. But these, as they must depend upon a perfect knowledge of local circumstances, are left entirely to your discretion. I would only suggest, that a diminution of the rent might be allowed, in case coal should be used by the lessees.

5. There are several other conditions of less importance in the present lease, but to which you will of course attend. It is, amongst others, necessary that the new lessees should pay to the present ones the value of kettles, etc., which the United States are bound to pay for by the present lease; and the condition of such repayment by the United States, at the end of the next lease, must of course be continued. In relation to the advance of two thousand five hundred dollars heretofore made by the United States, it must, according to the lease, be repaid by the present lessees; but it does not seem necessary, in the present state of the works, to continue it for the next lease, whether this be taken by the present or other lessees. That, however, ought not to be made a *sine qua non*, if in your opinion there are other preponderating considerations in favor of it.

6. The preceding outlines are drawn as if the whole Saline was, as heretofore, to be let to one individual or company. On that subject, whether it should be let entire or divided, a decisive opinion has not been formed. On the one hand, a greater degree of competition may be created, and some grounds of complaint removed by a division. But it is believed, on the other hand, that the works can be carried on with more regularity and economy by a single company than by four separate ones. A division cannot well take place without rendering useless some of the existing buildings and causing an additional expense in the erection of others. For the purpose of effecting certain contemplated improvements, it would be necessary that the whole of the water should, as far as practicable, be brought to the same place; and, it is also apprehended, that in case of division, either it might become nominal by a positive or tacit agreement of the several lessees, or the competition might degenerate into unfair opposition, quarrels and a resort to means injurious to the works. Upon a full view of the subject, but apprehending that several other circumstances, known only on the spot, ought to be taken into consideration, the President has thought proper to leave that question to your discretion. If you should decide in favor of a division, the conditions must be the same for all; the aggregate of the quantity of salt made and of rent paid to the United States must be equal to what has been above stated; and it seems just that the present lessees should, if they think proper, have their choice on equal terms, of one of the lots into which the Saline may be divided. Whether divided or not, it must be an express condition that none of the lessees shall, directly or indirectly, be concerned with any other salt works.

7. One of the improvements contemplated by the Government being the erection of buildings now introduced in every saline of Continental Europe, and known by the name of "Buildings of Graduation," and as these must be erected on the premises let to the lessees, a condition must be inserted, that the United States shall be at liberty to erect on the premises the above mentioned buildings, and also, to make such other improvements not interfering with the works as they may think proper—leaving to subsequent private agreements the conditions on which the lessees should be permitted to use such buildings and other improvements, if they shall hereafter make application to that effect. The lessees will not be entitled to claim payment for any improvement made by them, unless it be of permanent nature, and shall have been previously authorized by the Government.

8. As the time approaches for making a new lease, I send an advertisement to the printers of Lexington, Frankfort, Louisville, Bardstown, Cincinnati, Nashville and Vincennes, a copy of which is inclosed and which you will be pleased to circulate, or, if necessary, to have printed in other places. In deciding between the several proposals which may be made, you will, however, be pleased to take into consideration, not only the nature of the offer, but also the character and capital of the parties, and generally all those circumstances which may insure a punctual compliance with the terms of the contract. Of the quantity of salt which may be made, and of the price at which it may be made, you must be a competent judge; and proposals, arising

from ignorance or an improper spirit of adventure, offering to make more salt or at cheaper rate than you know it to be practicable, ought at once to be rejected. Indisputable security must also be obtained in the same manner as heretofore. You will also be pleased to insert, as in the present lease, a reservation for the approbation of the President, and transmit for that purpose to this Department the writings, duly executed by the parties.

I have the honor to be,

Very respectfully, your Excellency's

Obedient servant,

ALBERT GALLATIN.

To Gov. N. Edwards, Kaskaskia, Illinois Territory.

Treasury Department, *March* 14, 1810.

Sir:

I had the honor to receive your letter of February 5th, inclosing the lease of the Saline to John Taylor, Charles Wilkins and Jas. Morrison, which was laid before the President of the United States, and has been by him approved and ratified. Of this, I will thank you to inform the lessees; and I can only add my entire satisfaction of the results.

Your letter of the 9th ulto. has been received, and I think that the mode which you propose for the disposal of the salt on hand is the best which can be adopted. I will thank you to direct Mr. White to pay the money on hand or which may be received in the Bank of Frankfort, to the credit of the Treasurer of the United States—keeping only as much as may be sufficient to pay his salary and to defray contingent expenses. He must take duplicate receipts of those payments in bank, and send one to this office. It will also be eligible, in taking the lessees' notes for the payment of the salt on hand, to make them payable also in Bank at Frankfort, and to have the amount, when thus paid, likewise passed to the credit of the Treasurer of the United States.

Be pleased also to recollect that the former lessees must repay the advance of ——— dollars, made to them by the Government, at the commencement of the lease.

I have the honor to be,

Respectfully, sir,

Your obedient servant,

ALBERT GALLATIN.

To Gov. N. Edwards, Kaskaskia, Illinois Territory.

Treasury Department, *June* 29, 1810.

Sir:

The lessees of the United States Saline having represented to me that, in consequence of the large supply of salt in the Western country, there is great difficulty in making sales, and having proposed that a reduction in the price should be made conformably to a provision in the lease, I have submitted the subject to the President, who has approved of a reduction of the price to the rate of seventy-five cents a bushel. This reduction is to take effect from the 1st of September next, after which day the salt of the United States, as well as that of the lessees, is to be sold at the Saline at seventy-five cents per bushel —of which circumstance you will please to apprise the agent.

A proportionable reduction in the rent being stipulated in the lease to take place whenever a reduction should be made, by mutual consent, in the price of the salt, I have annexed to the foot of this letter the calculations by which the ratio of reduction is ascertained. The result is, that the rent, from the 1st September next to the 1st March, 1811, will be at the rate of 6,333 bushels per annum, or 3,167 bushels for those six months; and for the two ensuing years 5,500 bushels a year. But this calculation being on the supposition that they will have reduced the consumption of fuel in the manner stipulated for in the lease, if they fail in that respect the rent will then be for the six months, from 1st of September to 1st March next, at the rate of 13,333 bushels per annum, or 6,660 bushels for those six months; and for the two succeeding years 12,500 bushels a year. The lease provides that the salt shall not be sold at a less price than eighty-seven and one-half cents, *unless that price shall be lessened by the consent of the lessees, etc.;* and although the application which the lessees have made for a reduction of the price may be considered as an expression of their consent, yet, for the sake of precision, it will be most advisable that an article should be executed, in which shall be expressly stated the reduction of the price to seventy-five cents, and the consequent reduction in the rent, in the way above stated.

I have referred the lessees to you for this purpose, and directed them to empower some person to execute an article of the foregoing tenor.

I have the honor to be, sir,
Your obedient servant,
ALBERT GALLATIN.

To Gov. N. Edwards, Kaskaskia, Illinois.

Treasury Department, *July* 5, 1810.

Sir:

I had the honor to receive, by this day's mail, your letter of 5th ult., with its inclosures. As the distance of Kaskaskia from the seat of government might produce delays prejudicial to the object in view, you will be pleased to consider yourself as fully authorized to take any measures and to make any arrangement which you will think most eligible for the disposal of the salt of the United States—whether proceeding from the purchases under the old lease or from the rent under the new. I had, however, understood the sale of the old salt to the new lessees to have been concluded, and, under that impression, transmitted the President's permission to lessen the price of salt. As this was done in order to promote the general object, and without regard to the loss of revenue arising therefrom, I cannot suppose the lessees will hesitate to comply with the agreement for the purchase of the old salt on the terms first proposed; and you are authorized to suspend the reduction of price until that is complied with.

I inclose an authenticated copy of the bond for the advance of money to the former lessees, which, on repayment thereof, you will be pleased to deliver to them, with a receipt in full annexed thereto. If the money be paid to you, you will deposit the amount to the credit of the Treasurer, in the Bank of Kentucky. But it will be more simple and probably more convenient that the former lessees should pay the money there, themselves, and transmit to you the cashier's receipt, which will be the evidence on which you will give your own receipt on the copy of the bond. In either case duplicate receipts from the cashier should be taken, one of which to be sent to this office.

I have the honor to be, sir,
Very respectfully,
Your obedient servant,
ALBERT GALLATIN.

To Gov. N. EDWARDS, Kaskaskia, Illinois.

TREASURY DEPARTMENT, *July* 11, 1810.

Sir:

I am honored with yours of the 22d ult.; and having already, by mine of 5th inst., stated that you were authorized to take any steps, for the sale of the salt, which you might think proper, I will only add that you are also requested to judge, in the manner most convenient to yourself, whether that reduction of fuel has taken place, which, according to the true intention of the lease, must produce the reduction in the rent from 30,000 to 24,000 bushels of salt.

I have the honor to be, respectfully, sir,
Your obedient servant,
ALBERT GALLATIN.

To Gov. NINIAN EDWARDS, Kaskaskia, Illinois.

WASHINGTON, *July* 16, 1810.

Sir:

Your friendly letter, of 23d June, is this moment received. I have done no act or given no opinion relative to the land claims in the Illinois Territory, but such as necessarily flowed from my official duties. Of such I must abide by the consequence—be it what it may. From the sound rule of *audi alteram partem* I never will depart; but it is true that the report of our officers is not calculated to produce favorable impressions for some of the land claimants. Having done nothing but officially, I would have no objection that all my communications to the land commissioners should be seen by all the claimants.

And, not knowing what use is made of my name, I cannot say whether it is done improperly or not.

With thanks for your friendly communication and friendly disposition,

I remain, with cordiality and respect,

Your obedient servant,

ALBERT GALLATIN.

To Gov. Edwards.

Treasury Department, *August* 1, 1810.

Sir :

I had the honor to receive your letters of 28th and 30th June. You are fully authorized to take all such measures, respecting the disposition of the old salt, either by arrangement with the lessees or otherwise, as you may think most eligible, losing sight neither of the public interest, in that respect, nor of the great object of encouraging the manufacture of the article. With a view to the last point, it will be best, if practicable, not to disagree with the lessees; but the decision is left entirely to your discretion.

Before any answer can be given, respecting the improvement of the navigation of the creek, the plan and estimate of expense must be submitted, by the lessees, to the President. The erection of a mill, at public expense, is inadmissible. Your suggestion, respecting the walls etc., to prevent the wells being overflowed, is approved, and the expense will be allowed, provided the work is made in a permanent manner.

I have the honor to be, respectfully, sir,

Your obedient servant,

ALBERT GALLATIN.

To Gov. N. Edwards, Kaskaskia, Illinois.

War Department, *March* 12, 1811.

Sir :

In making out the commision for the gentleman you were pleased to recommend for the office of Brigadier-General of the militia of the Illinois Territory, also in the letter addressed to him, inclosing the commission, an error was made in the first name: in the place of *Elias* Rector it should have been *William* Rector. If you will be so good as to have the commission returned to this Department, the mistake will be rectified.

I am, very respectfully, sir,

Your most obedient servant,

W. EUSTIS.

To Hon. Ninian Edwards.

WAR DEPARTMENT, *June* 26, 1811.

Sir:

I have the honor to acknowledge the receipt of your Excellency's letter of the 7th inst.

A reasonable compensation to an interpreter, whose services may be necessary in an intercourse with the Indians, as well as an indemnity for provisions issued to them on their necessary visits, including such presents as in the judgment of your Excellency it may be proper and expedient to make to them, will be allowed. These expenses will be regulated by your discretion and judgment, and may be provided for by bills drawn on the Department or by the transmission of money, as may appear to your Excellency to be most convenient. Moneys advanced for these purposes, will be accounted for to the accountant of the War Department, on such vouchers as the nature of the case will admit.

I have the honor to be,

Your Excellency's most obedient servant,

W. EUSTIS.

To Gov. NINIAN EDWARDS, Illinois Territory.

WAR DEPARTMENT, *June* 4, 1812.

Sir:

Your letters of May 6th and 12th have been received.

The militia which have been called out by your Excellency will be paid. Their accounts should be rendered as pointed out for the pay of the rangers, and transmitted to the paymaster of the army in this city.

The subalterns recommended for Capt. Whiteside's company, will be nominated for those appointments.

I remain, respectfully,

Your Excellency's obedient servant,

W. EUSTIS.

To Gov. NINIAN EDWARDS, Illinois Territory.

WAR DEPARTMENT, *July* 9, 1812.

Sir:

As emergencies may arise requiring an additional military force on the frontiers of the Indiana and Illinois Territories, the Governors of those Territories have been authorized to request of your Excellency, in the event of such emergency, detachments of militia from the State of Kentucky, and I am instructed by the President to request of your Excellency to furnish any detachments which may be required, which will be considered as a part of the quota detached, conformably to the law passed April 10th, 1812.

I have the honor to be, very respectfully,

Your Excellency's most obedient servant,

W. EUSTIS.

To Gov. CHARLES SCOTT, Kentucky.

TREASURY DEPARTMENT,
GENERAL LAND OFFICE, *May* 10, 1813

Sir :

Your letter of the 13th March last to the Secretary of the Treasury, communicating the understanding which has taken place between you and the lessees of the Wabash Saline, that they should continue to work it on the old terms, till the will of the President be known, has been received, and Mr. Gallatin having left the seat of government, in order to proceed on his mission to Russia, it has been handed to me. I have consulted the President on the subject, and he is pleased to direct that the temporary arrangement made by you should be continued till you can substitute one which had been suggested by Mr. Gallatin previous to the receipt of your letter—the nature of which you will understand from the inclosed copy of Mr. Gallatin's letter to me, dated 17th ulto.

I have the honor to be,
Very respectfully, sir,
Your obedient servant,
EDWARD TIFFIN, *Commissioner.*

To Gov. NINIAN EDWARDS, Kaskaskia, Illinois Territory.

TREASURY DEPARTMENT,
GENERAL LAND OFFICE, *Sept.* 8, 1813.

Sir :

Yours of the 17th ulto. has been received. In answer to which I can only call your attention (to the instructions given by the Secretary of the Treasury on the 25th August, 1809) to the late lease and my former communication. The present embarrassed state of the country on account of the Indian depredations, will inevitably leave much to the exercise of your sound discretion ; but, keeping the great leading objects of the Government in view, of which you are already well informed, relative to the Saline, and retaining a clause subjecting the terms to the approbation of the President of the United States, you cannot fail in discharging this trust satisfactorily.

In case the old lessees do not again take the works, I suppose the new ones ought to pay the value of the improvements.

With great respect,
I have the honor to be, sir,
Your obedient servant,
EDWARD TIFFIN.

To Gov. N. EDWARDS, at Russellville, Logan county, Kentucky.

TREASURY DEPARTMENT,
GENERAL LAND OFFICE, *Jan.* 10, 1814.

Sir:

Yours of the 8th and 9th of November have been received, and I lost no time in presenting the several subjects referred to before the President of the

United States; but, owing to the great press of national business, neither he nor the acting Secretary of the Treasury could, before this period, devote time to the consideration thereof. I am now instructed to inform you, that it will be best to let Pittway & Co. off from their proposals for leasing the Wabash Saline, and you are requested to issue advertisements in such papers as you suppose best calculated to give extensive information, that you will attend at such day at the Saline as you can conveniently and as soon as practicable, to receive proposals for leasing the works for three years, from and after such day as you may propose to make the lease—giving the present occupants notice that they may continue to work the Saline until the day so fixed upon, on the same conditions that they now have them—for it will be impossible to have the preparatory arrangements made before the 1st March, when their period expires. The Government expects that the present occupants, or any others who desire to take the works, may afford to give at least thirty thousand bushels of salt per annum—for you are authorized, in the lease to be given, to allow the persons who may take the Saline, to sell all the salt they may make, at one dollar and twenty-five cents per bushel, instead, as heretofore, at seventy-five cents. This will enable the people of that country to obtain salt cheaper than anywhere else in the Union, and will justify the Government in expecting, and the occupants of the Saline in giving, in future, thirty thousand bushels rent or an equivalent in money, at their option.

These instructions, with those heretofore given, will regulate you in making a future lease, still subject to the approbation of the President of the United States, who will doubtless approve of it, if made agreeably to your instructions.

With respect to the compensation you ask, for the expense, etc., of attending to this business, this subject is under consideration and the result you shall be duly informed of. I think, with you, that you ought to be paid.

With great respect,

I have the honor to be, sir,

Your obedient servant,

EDWARD TIFFIN.

To Gov. N. Edwards, Kaskaskia, Illinois Territory.

Treasury Department,
General Land Office, *April* 20, 1814.

Sir:

The President of the United States has approved the lease lately entered into by John Bates & Co. for the United States Saline near the Wabash, and I am instructed to request you to notify the lessees accordingly.

I am well pleased with the great attention you have paid to this business, and am of opinion that you ought to be compensated therefor, which opinion I have urged upon the Secretary of the Treasury. He is so entirely taken up with the important, pressing duties lately devolved upon him, that he cannot yet awhile devote time to the consideration of compensation, but soon will have more leisure. In the meantime, I think you might make out and forward an account—for no public moneys can be paid unless founded upon an account for services, etc. This account will then be attended to by me in your behalf, and of which I will apprize you. Your suggestion of leaving it to the discretion of the President is inadmissible, for it is too indelicate to trouble him with its consideration.

With great respect, I am,
Your obedient servant,
EDWARD TIFFIN.

To Gov. N. Edwards, Illinois Territory.

Washington, *June* 18, 1814.

Sir:

I have received yours and Mr. White's, relative to your remuneration for expenses while attending the United States interests at the Saline, both of which I have laid before the honorable the Secretary of the Treasury, and given my opinion that the charge ought to be allowed. He appeared to acquiesce, and I will inform you when I am apprised of the result.

With great respect, I am,
Your obedient servant,
EDWARD TIFFIN.

To Gov. N. Edwards, Sidney Grove, Illinois Territory.

Department of War, *Nov.* 23, 1814.

Sir:

I have had the honor to peruse your letter of the 18th October last, to the Hon. Mr. Stephenson, on the subject of supplies for the Kaskaskia Indians. I have to request your Excellency will supply these Indians with money and clothing to the amount of their annuity, if in your power to procure them in the Illinois Territory—for the payment of which your bills on this department will be duly honored.

I have the honor to be,
Respectfully, sir,
Your obedient servant,
JAMES MONROE.

To Gov. Ninian Edwards, Illinois Territory.

Treasury Department,
General Land Office, *Dec.* 12, 1814.

Sir:

Your favor of November 7th has been received. If the salt lick, which you state to have been discovered by Conrad Will and his associates, lies in the district of Shawneetown or Kaskaskia, you will be pleased to refer him to the register of the land office for the district in which the lick lies, to obtain a lease; if it is not in either district, you will be pleased to execute a lease, not exceeding three years, on such terms as you think just, subject to the approbation of the President of the United States. In my opinion the rent ought not to be less than the interest of the purchase money of the tract leased, with a clause to prevent waste of timber on the adjacent tracts.

I am, very respectfully, sir,

Your obedient servant,

J. MEIGS.

To Gov. NINIAN EDWARDS, Kaskaskia, Illinois Territory.

TREASURY DEPARTMENT, *July* 31, 1815.

Sir:

I have had the honor to receive your letter of the 15th ulto. It is cause of real regret to me that, in the recent correspondence between this Department and the agent at the Saline, the circumstance of your having been formally invested with the direction and superintendence of the Saline was not recollected. I beg you to be assured, however, that it was never contemplated to withdraw the confidence heretofore so justly placed in you, and that you will be pleased to consider yourself as possessing the entire direction of the Wabash Saline, any instructions to Mr. White from this office to the contrary notwithstanding.

With respect to the disposal of the salt already received and to be received from the lessees, for rent, I will only observe, that the mode, time and place of making the sales, are wholly committed to your discretion.

I have the honor to be,

Very respectfully, sir,

Your obedient servant,

A. J. DALLAS.

To Gov. NINIAN EDWARDS, Kaskaskia, Illinois Territory.

DEPARTMENT OF WAR, *Feb.* 28, 1817.

Sir:

As that part of the Illinois Territory west of the Illinois River will probably be settled with great rapidity, so soon as the soldiers' lands are brought into market, it will become desirable, in order to connect the settlements in the Territory, to procure a cession of the lands lying between those ceded by the Kaskaskia Indians, on the 13th of August, 1803, and the Illinois River, so as to include all the lands lying between the western boundary of that cession and the above mentioned river. I am, therefore, instructed by the President, to request that you would take measures to ascertain whether the Indians claiming that land, would be disposed to relinquish it. It is also desirable to know whether there are any conflicting Indian claims to the whole or any part of the above described tract of land.

So soon as you can ascertain the temper of the Indians on this subject, you will advise this Department; and should they be disposed to make a cession, you will be authorized to hold a treaty with them for that purpose.

I have the honor to be,

With great respect,

Your obedient servant,

GEO. GRAHAM

Acting Secretary of War.

To Gov. Ninian Edwards, Illinois Territory.

Treasury Department, *March* 1, 1817.

Sir:

You will, without delay, transmit to the Governor of the Illinois Territory an authority to lease, for the term of three years, the United States Saline, now occupied by John Bates. It is deemed expedient to leave it to the discretion of His Excellency to lease the whole premises to one individual or company, or to grant separate leases for distinct portions of that property. In this, as in every other case, the public interest will be promoted by competition, if there exists no particular reason against it. Of this Gov. Edwards will judge. In fixing the price of the salt, the practicability of selling it ought to have great influence.

As it is presumed, from the representations of Mr. Bates, the present lessee has but little if any salt on hand, a stipulation for the sale of that which remains unsold, in the hands of the Government, may be inserted in the new contract.

In valuing the improvements made by Mr. Bates, during the existence of the lease, it may be useful to value the improvements which he received upon entering the premises, distinguishing them from those which he made. I understand that it is customary on making a new line of pipes, to use the old pipes which are represented to be of cypress or gum, which are extremely durable. It will be desirable, also, to obtain from Gov. Edwards the practice, under that provision of the leases heretofore made, which relates to the remuneration of the lessee for his improvements. Has it been customary to repay him the amount which he paid, on entering, to the preceding lessee? The lease makes no provision for such repayment; but it is contended here, by some of the lessees, that such was the understanding of the parties, and the practice under the preceding leases.

I have the honor to be, etc.,

WILLIAM. H. CRAWFORD.

To Josiah Meigs, Esq., *Commissioner of the General Land Office.*

TREASURY DEPARTMENT, *March* 19, 1817.

Sir:

The lessees of the Saline, on the waters of the Ohio, who preceded Mr. Bates, in the order of time, allege that they have not received that compensation for the improvements which they made upon the premises, during the existence of their lease, to which they were entitled under it; and that they have received nothing for the improvements which were upon the premises antecedent to their occupancy of them, which were either made by them or their value advanced to those by whom they were made. They allege that your instructions excluded from the valuation which was set on foot, at the expiration of their lease, many improvements which are fairly comprehended by the letter and spirit of the lease; in consequence of which, one of the appraisers, as the agent or friend of the former lessees, declined the execution of the duty assigned him, and compromised the matter with Mr. Bates, by agreeing to accept a gross sum, without regard to the value of the improvements. It may be proper to observe, that the lease makes no provision for the repayment of any sum, which may be advanced by a lessee upon taking possession of the premises, for the improvements which have been made by those who have preceded him. This omission must have been the result of design or of accident. It may have been the intention of the Government to retain as permanent improvements, at the expiration of each successive lease, everything which had been put upon the premises during the existence of the antecedent and prior leases—considering the use of the property by the subsequent lessee, during the continuance of his lease, as a fair equivalent for the sum paid upon taking possession of the premises; or it may have been the result of a conclusion that such improvements would cease to be useful at the expiration of the second lease after they were made, or from the difficulty of distinguishing between the improvements made in successive leases, or from the constant changes in the value of those improvements. I understand that, in addition to the ordinary causes of change in the value of those improvements, the lessees are in the habit of breaking up one line of pipes and making another, using, however, the original pipes for the new line. In cases of this kind, it is manifest, that if the new line is considered an improvement for which the actual lessee is entitled to compensation, the Government will be subject to great injustice if the lessee is also entitled to receive back the amount paid by him for the line of pipes so changed during his lease. Notwithstanding the view here presented, it may have been the understanding of the parties that they were to receive, upon the expiration of their leases, the value of the improvements which they found upon the premises, and which were left by them in the same state of preservation and usefulness as they were received. It is true that the contracts in question have not been long enough in existence to establish anything like a special custom which, in a court of law or even of equity, would be permitted to control the rules of construction in relation to such contracts; but in a case of this kind the Government is willing that the legal construction of those leases should yield to the fair and explicit understanding of the lessees and the officer of the

Government charged with the execution of that duty, at the time the leases were made. Under this view of the subject, the lessees who preceded Mr. Bates are referred to you for a decision upon their claim for additional allowance. How far the person who acted as their agent, and entered into an agreement with Mr. Bates, by which a gross sum was paid for the improvements, ought to bind them, and how far their subsequent conduct has made his act their own, notwithstanding there may have been a defect of authority originally, is also referred to your decision. The evidence upon that point in the possession of this Department is very slight indeed. It is presumed that all the circumstances are known to you, and that if they are not, they can be easily obtained from Mr. Bates. It has, however, been intimated that some difficulty occurred in obtaining from Mr. Bates the amount agreed by him to be paid. If this intimation is well founded, the clearest evidence of their subsequent sanction of the arrangement can be obtained. If this compromise has placed the United States in a worse situation than if it had not been made, the censure ought to fall upon the lessees. The whole subject, however, is referred to your Excellency, with a request that you will do what is right and proper; and that if you feel any difficulty in deciding upon all or either of the points involved in it, you will favor me with your views upon it.

I have the honor to be,

Your Excellency's most obedient and humble servant,

WILLIAM H. CRAWFORD.

To Ninian Edwards, *Governor of Illinois Territory*, Kaskaskia.

Department of War, *March* 26, 1817.

Sir:

All the Indian Agents within the Illinois Territory, except the one at Green Bay, having been placed under your superintendence, as Governor of that Territory, you will take the necessary measures for causing the agents to make their reports and render their accounts, through you, to this Department. All bills (except for their own pay) drawn by them on this Department, must receive your sanction before they can be paid; and as all accounts in relation to Indian affairs are, in pursuance of a late law, to be settled at the Treasury, by the Fifth Auditor, it becomes necessary that the agents should, at the expiration of each quarter, draw for the expenses incurred during the quarter; the amount to be included, as far as practicable, in the same bill, accompanied by a letter of advice and a particular account of the expenditures, which expenditures should receive your approbation.

The state of the appropriation for the Indian Department requires the most strict and rigorous economy in the expenditures; those for rations and presents have very much exceeded the amount which the appropriations of the present year will admit, and will therefore require very considerable reductions. The regulations prescribed by this Department, on the 7th of May, 1816, in relation to the issues of rations, should be strictly adhered to; and you should cause a report of the amount of the issues of rations to Indians, at each post within the Territory, to be made to you; the whole amount of the expenditure for the Indian Department, within the Illinois Territory, including rations, presents, contingencies, salaries of agents, etc., must be limited to $25,000 per annum; and you will apportion this sum among the several agencies, including that for civilization, in such manner as you think proper.

Mr. McKenney will be instructed to forward to you six thousand dollars' worth of goods, to be assorted into three parcels of two thousand dollars each, as presents. He will also forward the amount of annuities payable to the Indians in the Illinois Territory. Those for the Sacs and Foxes will, for the present year, be sent to St. Louis, as it is uncertain in which of the Territories the greater part of these tribes reside. Gov. Clark and yourself will agree on the point where they are in future to be delivered, and advise this Department thereof.

The Agent for Civilization cannot be furnished, and will not require, for the present year, any other mechanics than a blacksmith and a wheelwright. The sum allowed to his agency must necessarily be limited by the amount placed at your disposal. The sum estimated by him for the construction of houses is totally inadmissible at present. Accommodations must be procured by the aid of the troops stationed at Peoria, and with such funds as you may be able to appropriate to that object out of those placed at your disposal.

The orders of this Department, dated October 21, 1816, requiring the agents to reside within their respective agencies, must be strictly enforced. It is observed that Mr. Forsyth, who was ordered to report to you, is still at St. Louis. If you have no occasion for his services within your Territory, you will advise Gov. Clark thereof, who will be instructed to employ him, if his services are required in the Missouri Territory; if not, to discharge him.

I have the honor to be,
With great respect, sir,
Your obedient servant,
GEORGE GRAHAM,
Acting Secretary of War.

To Gov. Ninian Edwards, Kaskaskia, Illinois Territory.

Department of War, *Nov.* 1, 1817.

Gentlemen:

I have the honor to inclose you a commission for the purpose of treating with the Illinois, the Kickapoos, the Pottawottamies and other tribes of Indians within the Illinois Territory. The object of this negotiation is to obtain a cession from the tribes who may have a claim to it, of all that tract of land which lies between the most northeastern point of boundary of the lands ceded by the Kaskaskias, in August, 1803, the Sangamo and the Illinois Rivers; and which tract of land completely divided the settled parts of the Illinois Territory from that part which lies between the Illinois and Mississippi Rivers, and which has been lately surveyed for the purpose of satisfying the Military land bounties, a circumstance which makes the acquisition of this tract of country peculiarly desirable.

If either of the tribes who have a claim to the land is desirous of exchanging their claim for lands on the west of the Mississippi, you are authorized to make the exchange; and your extensive local knowledge of the country will enable you to designate that part of it where it would be most desirable to locate the lands to be given as an equivalent. To other tribes, who may not wish to remove, you will allow such an annuity, for a fixed period, as you may deem an adequate compensation for the relinquishment of their respective claims. To enable you to give the usual presents on such occasions, you are authorized to draw on this Department for $6,000.

The contractor will furnish, on the requisition of either of you, the rations that may be necessary for the supply of the Indians while attending the treaty. Your compensation will be at the rate of eight dollars a day for the time *actually* engaged in treating with the Indians; and that of the secretary, whom you are authorized to appoint, will be at the rate of five dollars a day.

I have the honor to be,
With great respect,
Your obedient servant,
GEORGE GRAHAM,
Acting Secretary of War.

TO GOVS. WM. CLARK and NINIAN EDWARDS.

DEPARTMENT OF WAR, *Nov.* 1, 1817.

Sir:

Your letter of the 7th ult., recommending the appointment of B. Stephenson, Esq., as a Major-General of the militia of the Illinois Territory, has been received, and will be duly attended to, when the Senate is in session. You will receive, by this mail, a commission to treat with the Indians claiming the lands lying between those ceded by the Kaskaskias, in 1803, and the Illinois River.

As it is not only desirable but indispensably necessary that the boundary lines of all the lands ceded by the Indians should be established and well marked, the President has appointed Richard Graham, Indian agent, and ——— Phillips to act as Commissioners, for the purpose of running and marking, in conjunction with two chiefs to be appointed by the Indians, such boundary lines of the lands ceded by the Indians within the Illinois Territory as you may deem necessary. The lines will be run at the expense of the United States, and the two chiefs who may be designated to attend the commissioners will receive a compensation not less than that of the commissioners.

I would recommend that a contract be made with the principal surveyor, Mr. Rector, for running and marking the lines at a given sum per mile—the surveyors furnishing everything necessary for that purpose. As a specific appropriation will be asked for this object, I will thank you to advise this Department, at as early a period as convenient, what would be the probable expense of running and marking the lines, independent of the expense and compensation to the commissioners.

It is very desirable to have the boundary of that tract of land ceded by the treaty of August, 1816, and lying between the Illinois River and Lake Michigan, established, and a particular report made of the quality. If that tract of land was surveyed and settled, it would very much facilitate the migrations to the Illinois Territory from New England and the State of New York, by means of the lake navigation.

I have the honor to be,
With great respect,
Your obedient servant,
GEORGE GRAHAM,
Acting Sec'y War.

To Gov. N. Edwards, Kaskaskia, Illinois.

Office of Indian Trade,
Georgetown, *January* 17, 1818.

Sir:

I am honored with your communication, bearing date 10th ult., and exceedingly regret that interruptions should have retarded the more speedy arrival of the Indian annuities connected with your agency. I know how unfriendly such disappointments must be in their operation on the Indian mind; but the remedy does not lie in this Department. Orders are issued for those supplies and for the presents by the War Department, and as soon as this office receives them, or with as little delay thereafter as is possible, the orders are executed and the merchandize transported. It will, no doubt, comport with the facility of operation to have the St. Louis agency organized; although Mr. Kennerly, who acts as agent there, is a very attentive man, yet it is probable it might be more actively exercised. There is always difficulty in getting off the presents or the annuities together, or all at the same time; and that difficulty is not lessened much as they progress—the means of transportation being scarce, sometimes retards the progress of the goods. But no delay takes place after the orders are given, more than the time required for packing, unless, as it sometimes happens, wagons cannot be had.

I will use any additional exertions that I may be able to call up, to prevent a recurrence of similar delays in future; but should a depot be organized at St. Louis, the goods could arrive there no sooner—because I cannot anticipate the orders—and beyond that point, again, their movement would depend upon activity in the agent.

I will not forget to name to the Secretary of War your intimation for additional presents.

I am, with great respect, sir,
Your obedient servant,
THOMAS L. McKENNEY.

To Hon. Ninian Edwards.

OFFICE OF INDIAN TRADE,
GEORGETOWN, D. C., *May* 8, 1818.

Sir :

I have the honor herewith to inclose you several invoices of merchandize provided and transported to you, via Pittsburgh, pursuant to instructions received from the honorable the Secretary of War, bearing date March 5th, 1818.

First—Invoice made up of packages from No. 1 to No. 4, inclusive, amounting to $2,000, to be distributed by you, in presents, to the Indians at Kaskaskia.

Second—Invoice made up of packages from No. 1 to No. 12, inclusive, amounting, also, to $2,000, to be distributed by you, in presents, to the Indians at Prairie du Chien.

Third—Invoice made up of packages from No. 1 to No. 13, amounting, also, to $2,000, to be distributed by you, in presents, to the Indians at Peoria.

Fourth—Invoice made up of packages from No. 1 to No. 5, inclusive, amounting to $800, to be paid over to the Piankeshaws—it being in full their annuity due for the year 1818.

Fifth—Invoice made up of packages from No. 1 to No 6, inclusive, amounting to $1,000, to be paid over by you to the Ottaways, Chippeways, and Pottawottamies of St. Louis and south-western parts of Lake Michigan—it being in full for their annuity due them for the year 1818.

These goods are all progressing, and many of them, if not the whole, are by this time beyond Pittsburgh. The powder and tobacco will join them at Louisville, where I have provided them.

I sincerely hope these goods and their varieties will prove acceptable to the wants and the tastes of the Indians for whom they are intended. It will afford me pleasure to have this hope realized, by a letter from you, after they shall have undergone examination.

Be so good as to forward to me, as soon after the arrival of the merchandize as possible, receipted copies of the invoices, with a view to a speedy adjustment of my accounts on the books of the Treasury.

Only $500 were directed, by the War Department, to be provided for the Kaskaskias' annuity this year; for $400 of which you have drawn, which leaves $100 due—for which $100 you are authorized to draw on me, as Superintendent of Indian Trade.

I have the honor to be,
With great respect, sir,
Your obedient servant,
THOMAS L. McKENNEY.

To HON. NINIAN EDWARDS, Kaskaskia, Illinois.

DEPARTMENT OF WAR, *May* 16, 1818.

Sir :

It has been represented to this Department that the establishment of a blacksmith's shop, at Prairie du Chien, would be beneficial to the Indian Department.

If your Excellency should think it proper, you are authorized to employ a suitable smith, at reasonable terms, for one year. The experiment that will be made in that time will enable this Department to decide whether or not it be proper to continue the shop.

I have the honor to be,

Your Excellency's most obedient servant,

J. C. CALHOUN.

To HON. NINIAN EDWARDS, Kaskaskia, Illinois.

DEPARTMENT OF WAR, *May* 25, 1818.

Sir:

I inclose you a copy of a resolution of the House of Representatives, passed at their late session, by which you will perceive that it is contemplated to abolish the present system of Indian trade, and to leave it, under suitable regulations, open to individuals. What those regulations ought to be can be judged of, fully and correctly, by those only who have their knowledge from experience with the Indian character and affairs. I have, therefore, to request your Excellency to afford me your ideas on the subject of the resolution, as early as practicable, in order that I may avail myself of them, in reporting to the House, at their next session. It would afford me pleasure to have your ideas, also, on the relative merit of the present system as it is, or with the improvements of which it is susceptible, and the one proposed to be substituted.

I have the honor to be

Your obedient servant,

J. C. CALHOUN.

To GOV. EDWARDS, Kaskaskia, Illinois.

TREASURY DEPARTMENT, *March* 12, 1829.

Sir:

Your letter of the 9th ult., addressed to the Commissioner of the General Land Office, advising of your having drawn bills on account of the three per cent. fund, due to the State of Illinois, and requesting payment to be made at the Treasury, has been referred to me.

The act of Congress, of the 12th of December, 1820, entitled "An act for the payment to the State of Illinois, three per cent. of the net proceeds arising from the sales of public lands within the same," directs that "An annual account of the application of the money be transmitted to the Secretary of the Treasury, and, in default of such return being made, the Secretary of the Treasury is required to withhold the payment of any sums that may be then due or which may thereafter become due, until a return shall be made as herein required."

This provision of the act not having been complied with, on the part of the State of Illinois, and the act seeming to leave no discretion, I have been constrained to decline the payment of one of the bills mentioned in your letter—

which has this day been presented for payment; but the holder has, at the same time, been informed that the bill is for part of a sum now due to the State of Illinois, and that immediately upon the receipt of the return required by law, payment would be made.

I have the honor to be,
With great respect, sir,
Your obedient servant,
S. D. INGHAM.

To Gov. N. Edwards, Belleville, Illinois.

Treasury Department, *May* 13, 1829.

Sir:

Your Excellency's letter, of the 2d ult., was duly received; and, subsequently, that of your Excellency and the other Commissioners, dated on the 1st ult., inclosing an account of the disposition of the sums which have been paid to them for the encouragement of learning, within the State of Illinois, under the act of the 12th of December, 1820.

It would have afforded great satisfaction to the Department to have found, in that account and in the explanations presented in your Excellency's communications, a justification for the payment of the drafts of the Commissioners for the amount which has subsequently accrued. But the law must be the rule of action; and as the Department cannot consider the investment which the account shows to have been made of the moneys hitherto paid in purchasing the State debt as an application of those moneys, according to law, it deems itself prohibited by law from making any further payment until an account is presented, showing the application of the sums already paid to the purposes for which alone the law declares they shall be applied.

It is a cause of sincere regret to the Department that, with the strongest desire to regard as correct such a disposition of the funds in question as the authorities of the State of Illinois might have deemed proper, it has not found grounds to concur in the views which they have taken of the subject.

Anxious, as an occasion of so much delicacy and interest, that the State should not suffer by any error of judgment, on my part, I have submitted the whole subject to the notice of the President, who has been pleased to approve of the course which has been adopted.

I have the honor to be,
Very respectfully,
Your obedient servant,
ASBURY DICKENS.
Acting Sec'y Treasury.

To Gov. N. Edwards.

APPENDIX.—NOTES.

NOTE TO PAGES 7 AND 8.—The form of government established by the resolutions and ordinances of 1784 was in accordance with the principles of the patriots of our Revolution, as will be seen from the following extracts:

Resolutions offered by Mr. Jefferson at a meeting of the freeholders of Albemarle on the 26th July, 1774.

"*Resolved*, That the inhabitants of the several States of British America are subject to the laws which they adopted at their first settlement, and to such others as have been since made by their respective Legislatures, duly constituted and appointed with their own consent; that no other Legislature whatever can rightfully exercise authority over them."

"But that we do not point out to His Majesty the injustice of these acts, with intent to rest on that principle the cause of their nullity, but to show that experience confirms the propriety of those political principles which exempt us from the jurisdiction of the British Parliament. *The true ground on which we declare these acts void is that the British Parliament has no right to exercise authority over us*."—[*A Summary View of the Rights of British America, by Jefferson.*

"Can any one reason be assigned why 160,000 electors in Great Britain should give law to 4,000,000 in America; every individual of whom is equal to every individual of them, in virtue, in understanding and in bodily strength? Were this to be admitted, instead of being a free people, we should suddenly be found the slaves not of one, but of one hundred and sixty thousand tyrants."—*Randall's Life of Jefferson, pages* 95 *and ante.*

It was declared by the first Congress, in 1774, "that the foundation of English liberty, and of all free government, was the right of the people to participate in the legislative power; *and they were entitled to a free and exclusive power of legislation in all matters of internal* policy in their provincial Legislatures, where the right of legislation can alone be preserved, and that by emigration they have not forfeited, surrendered or lost any of those rights."

The Congress of the Colonies, in their plan for an accommodation with Great Britain, in 1775, "insisted on the repeal of the obnoxious acts, the *undisturbed exercise*, by the respective colonies, *of the powers of internal legislation*, and the free enjoyment of the rights of conscience; but conceded to Great Britain the power to regulate the trade of the whole empire." In the enumeration of their injuries, they said, "By one statute it is declared that Parliament can of right make laws to bind us in all cases whatsoever. What is to defend us against so unlimited a power? Not a single man of those who assume it is chosen by us."

"Rather than submit to the right of legislating for us assumed by the British Parliament," wrote Mr. Jefferson, from Monticello, in 1774, "I would lend my hand to sink the whole island in the ocean."

Recognizing the right of each Colony to regulate its internal policy, Benjamin Franklin submitted to the Congress of 1775, an outline for the confederacy of the Colonies, which provided "that each Colony was to retain and amend its own laws and constitution, according to its separate discretion, while the powers of the General Government were to include all questions of war, peace and alliance, commerce, cnrrency and the establishment of posts, the army, navy and Indian affairs, and the management of lands not yet ceded by the natives."

Virginia, in her Bill of Rights, in 1776, declared "that elections of members or representatives of the people ought to be free, and no one ought to be taxed or deprived of their property for public uses without their own consent or that of their representatives, nor *bound by any law to which they have not assented.*" And in the instruction of their delegates in Congress by the Colonies, nearly all of them insisted "that the power of forming government for, and the regulation of the internal concerns of each Colony be left to their respective Colonial Legislatures."

NOTE TO PAGE 147.—Among the letters referred to on page 147, for the purpose of showing the high estimation in which Gov. Edwards was held after his controversy with Mr. Crawford, I omitted to state that Gen. Jackson thus assured him on May 6th, 1829: "I now understand the state of parties well in Illinois, and am resolved to sustain your friends, and can with truth say, if your friends have not heretofore been noticed, it is because you have not written and notified me of your wishes." Very soon after this, Dr. B. F. Edwards, his brother, received the appointment of Receiver of the Land Office; the Rev. Samuel H. Thompson, who was the candidate for the office of Lieutenant-Governor on the same ticket with him in his canvass for Governor, that of Register of the Land Office, and the Hon. David J. Baker, who received the appointment from him of United States' Senator to fill the vacancy caused by the death of Senator McLean, was appointed United States' District Attorney, of whom Senator Kane, in a letter to Gov. Edwards, says, "Your appointee, Mr. Baker, has behaved with much prudence and like a man of good sense. I have become attached to him and will take some fit occasion to give him some substantial proof of my good opinion." Gen. Duff. Green also, in a letter to Gov. Edwards, dated September 6, 1826, says: "You will find Gen. Jackson your friend. I have seen and conversed with him, and I know that he thinks better of Mr. Cook than of any of the party who voted against him." The Hon. Nathaniel Pope, Judge, and Wm. H. Brown, Clerk of the United States' Court, Col. Thomas Mather, President of the State Bank, and the following persons who were appointed or elected to office during his administration: Alexander P. Field, Secretary of State; George Forquer, Attorney-General; E. C. Berry, Auditor; Hon. R. M. Young, Judge of the only Circuit Court—were his warmest personal and political friends, as was also Judge Breese, who, though at that time very young but very distinguished for his talents and learning, had held the offices of Postmaster, Secretary of State, State's Attorney, and District Attorney of the United States—all of which he filled with honor. In the continuation of my History, I will have it in my power to show that in the offices he has since held, no one could have discharged the duties imposed on him with greater ability and more usefulness than he has done; and that, as a Senator of the United States and as a Judge, both of the Circuit and Supreme Courts, he was not surpassed by any one who had filled either of those offices. The State owes him a debt of gratitude for many very important measures which he originated and which have resulted so beneficially in advancing it to its present prosperous condition. It is not true, as was stated in the January number of "The Western Monthly," that he was removed from the office of State's Attorney by Gov. Edwards. He was not reappointed because he had received the appointment of United States' District Attorney. I also know that in the year 1829, when it was supposed that there would be a vacancy in the Supreme Court of the State, Gov. Edwards intended to fill it by appointing him.

With the exception of the Black Hawk War, my present work closes with the administration of Gov. Edwards. I expect to resume it with the commencement of the administration of his successor, Gov. Reynolds, when I will speak of other prominent men (and among them Col. John Dement, who was, in 1830, elected Treasurer of the State) somewhat on the plan of the memoir I have given of the Hon. Daniel P. Cook.

POPULATION OF ILLINOIS.

In 1810, ... 12,282
In 1870, ... 2,529,410

ERRATA.

Page 4, for, above was adopted, read, above resolutions were adopted; page 101, for, Illinois question, read, Missouri question; page 103, for, which would have, read, and would have; page 120, for, have, read, has; page 147, for, scandles, read, scandals; page 148, for, expert, read, report; page 145, for, Lowne, read, Lourie; page 165, for, bills, read, wills; page 182, for, failure, read, future; page 184, for, Sheet, read, Street; page 199, for, o'er, read, ever; page 207, for, excited, read, exerted; page 213, for, forget, read, forgot; page 223, for, Yanctuni-form, read, Yancton uniform; page 226, for, pursuasion, read, persuasion; page 217, for Judges Pope, read, Judge Pope; page 291, for, Biswell, read, Bissell; page 425, for, batchelder, read, bachelor; page 429, for, seven, read, severe; page 451, for, do it, read, make it; page 236, for, fourta, read, fourth.

www.ingramcontent.com/pod-product-compliance
Lightning Source LLC
LaVergne TN
LVHW021242110826
845150LV00002B/389

9781425561017